Lavender Mansions

LAVENDER MANSIONS

40

Contemporary Lesbian and Gay Short Stories

edited by

IRENE ZAHAVA

WESTVIEW PRESS
Boulder • *San Francisco* • *Oxford*

Published in 1994 in the United States of America by Westview Press, Inc., 5500 Central Avenue, Boulder, Colorado 80301-2877, and in the United Kingdom by Westview Press, 36 Lonsdale Road, Summertown, Oxford OX2 7EW

Library of Congress Cataloging-in-Publication Data
Lavender mansions : 40 contemporary lesbian and gay short stories /
   edited by Irene Zahava.
     p.   cm.
   ISBN 0-8133-2030-5. — ISBN 0-8133-2031-3 (pbk.)
   1. Lesbians—United States—Fiction.   2. Gay men—United States—
Fiction.   3. American fiction—20th century.   4. Gays' writings,
American.   5. Short stories, American.   I. Zahava, Irene.
PS648.H57L38   1994
813'.01083520664—dc20
                                                                94-7858
                                                                    CIP

Printed and bound in the United States of America

 The paper used in this publication meets the requirements
of the American National Standard for Permanence of Paper
for Printed Library Materials Z39.48-1984.

10   9   8   7   6   5   4   3   2   1

Contents

Thematic Contents

Credits

VALERIE MINER

INTRODUCTION

The experience of reading *Lavender Mansions* is like that of getting a sublet in an apartment house where all the tenants are Lesbian or Gay. At first the other residents of Lavender Mansions may appear startlingly similar and, depending on your predisposition, this may make you comfortable, uncomfortable, or simply curious. As the days pass, differences emerge. Listen, for instance, to the music seeping from under the doorsills: Sweet Honey in the Rock, Bette Midler, the Kronos Quartet. You begin to distinguish who lives in the penthouse and who resides on the front step. You see older people chatting at the elevator and younger ones carrying their racing bikes down the back-porch stairs. You sit in the lobby on the mock leopardskin couch—pretending to wait for an absolutely crucial package—and you notice how the differently complexioned residents speak in a variety of accents and languages. You kick back and enjoy the fashion show: cross-dressing dykes, campy queens, joggers in sweat suits, executives in business suits. Even the ubiquitous red ribbons are individually knotted.

Before exploring Lavender Mansions, you may want to go down to the basement archives and read the rolls of former residents: Henry James, Herman Melville, James Baldwin, Hart Crane, Langston Hughes, Gertrude Stein, Willa Cather, Lorraine Hansberry, Djuna Barnes, Pat Parker. On a wall by the stairs you'll find a yellowed newspaper clipping about how when Allen Ginsberg's *Howl* first appeared, the San Francisco publisher was arrested for selling the book and the author was brought up on obscenity charges. Tacked next to it is a more recent article revealing that James Baldwin's *If Beale Street Could Talk* was removed from a St. Paul, Oregon, library in 1989 because of the book's "obscene language" and explicit representation of sexuality. And a letter posted beneath documents how May Sarton's work was expunged from an academic anthology not because it was sexually graphic but because she was known to be a Lesbian writer. Half the basement is filled with bookcases of well-thumbed novels and story collections. Although Lesbian and Gay literature is often censored in this country, and many homosexual writers have passed as straight, it is useful to remember that the forty stories in this book would not have been possible without the writing that preceded it: work that provides inspiration, provocation, permission to contemporary storytellers. We all owe a debt to those who lived in Lavender Mansions during the times of literary quarantine and frequent, random police raids.

This is a friendly place, so you can get acquainted with "the community" in any way you like. You may want to begin on the first floor, reading the stories in order. Editor Irene Zahava has located the fictions into eight open-ended themes, as if she were charting Lesbian and Gay existence from childhood through old age and death. Since everyone likes secrets, you may want to begin with the "Coming Out" stories. If you're having trouble at home, turn, perhaps, to the "Families" tales. You can ignore the editor's categories altogether and visit old friends first, reading stories by your favorite authors before making new acquaintances. You may decide to read the men's fictions first and then the women's. You may begin with the last story. There is no protocol here: These are narratives about breaking the rules. Read the anthology in whatever way makes you feel at home.

No matter what route you take, you'll find interesting coincidences and parallels in the stories. The sibling feelings between Lesbians and Gay men are explored by both Paul Monette and Rebecca Brown. As Jim says in Brown's "A Good Man," "You may like to think of us all as a bunch of unbalanced, volatile perverts, but every single screaming fairy prancing down this boulevard and every last one of you pissed-off old Amazons is my family. My kith and my kin and my kind." Meanwhile, Tommy in Monette's "Halfway Home" feels closer to his friend Mona than to his own biological family. "Mona's like my sister, she doesn't have to call first."

Both Jaime Manrique and Christopher Bram consider the way a legendary woman can act as catalyst for male intimacy. Christopher Bram's middle-aged government official wins favor with a younger man by agreeing to introduce him to the legendary Filipina: "'Let's go meet Imelda,' he said and grabbed Doug's arm. He led him across the room, wanting to get this over with as quickly as possible so he could be alone with the boy." And after Manrique's protagonist meets a famous film star, he observes, "In my short memory, I had thought running into Carmen Maura was the most fortuitous coincidence that could have happened before meeting my old friend."

The guilty pleasures of infidelity are discovered in stories by David Leavitt and Sandy Boucher. Andrew, in the last scene of Leavitt's "When You Grow to Adultery," finds himself tracing the name of a new lover on his partner's back. "'Jack Selden,' Andrew wrote next. 'I love Jack Selden.' His heart was racing. What if those messages, like invisible ink, suddenly erupted in full daylight for Allen to read? … Andrew gave himself up to this wild and villainous writing, the messages becoming longer and more incriminating even as Allen moved closer to sleep. …" Boucher's protagonist in "Humming" declares: "And I like the safety of marriage, the comforting routine, the coziness. My mother encouraged me to develop a practical attitude to life coupled with a vivid appetite for its pleasures. Jeanine cares about Ralph too: she does not want to hurt him."

Mapping the Neighborhood

It's interesting to revisit the original homes for these stories. Before coming to Lavender Mansions, many of these authors were first published by Gay, Lesbian, and feminist presses. Indeed, a number of these writers would not have been published at all if it were not for the welcome they found at alternative houses like Crossing, Seal, Firebrand, Naiad, and Alyson. Of course, authors have all sorts of reasons for publishing with particular presses: economic, aesthetic, political, whimsical. But some writers have more options in housing. If it often seems harder for Lesbians to publish with mainstream houses, that reflects the fact that American Lesbian fiction is notable for focusing on the social and philosophical implications of individual experience, dangerous stuff in a publishing scene hostile to the intersection of art and ideas. In the book industry, Lesbian fiction is also subject to the broader sexism that transcends sexuality.

I am excited to find all these stories collected by an academic press in a volume meant for classroom use. Given the inclination of conservative state textbook boards to ban alternative materials from schools, this anthology is not only a celebration of good writing but also an act of resistance. While the homosexual purges of Joseph McCarthy and Adolf Hitler may seem historical footnotes to some readers, it's not much of a memory stretch to recall the campaigns against gay rights in Colorado, Oregon, and other states. Last year in Oregon, two activists, a black Lesbian and a white Gay man, were murdered for their work against a homophobic law. Similar right-wing campaigns against the civil rights of homosexuals are currently being waged in nine states. In 1988, the British Parliament passed Section 28 of the Local Government Act, which forbids councils to "promote homosexuality." This has caused some officials to remove from public shelves literature that has homosexual references.

When I was teaching at the University of California at Berkeley in the 1980s, a nine-campus survey of the University of California system showed that 36 percent of the faculty refrained from doing research on Lesbian and Gay topics for fear of negative response from colleagues. As many as 41 percent decided against including such material in their courses. Therefore, writing and reading these stories is a frontline experience even for—perhaps especially for—those engaging Lesbian and Gay literature in the ostensible Demilitarized Zone of academic discourse.

Reading Outside the Classroom and Inside Out

For the general reader, *Lavender Mansions* can be a familiar bedside companion or a seductive initiation into a new literary territory. Students and teachers will find it useful in a variety of courses, including English, queer studies, gender studies, and women's studies. They may want to view some pieces in light of Sapphic modernism, Pacific naturalism, postmodern fragmentation. They may dwell on the construction of narrative in various forms: epistolary, diary, biomythography. These stories explore the joyful aspects of Lesbian and Gay life as well as the trials of dealing with homophobia in relation to other, interlocking forms of oppression such as racism, anti-Semitism, classism, and imperialism. Roey Thorpe dramatically names patriarchy as one of these oppressors in "Growing in Defiance":

> Two weeks later, I am almost asleep in a room I share with Tammy, one of my housemates, who is sleeping in her bed. Suddenly, a man is on top of me. It is Tammy's friend David, who is supposed to be sleeping on the couch downstairs. David is a born-again Christian, and as he tries to pull the covers off me he is saying that God wants me to experience a man, because homosexuality is a sin.

The diversity of Lesbian and Gay experiences is matched by a diversity in literary theme and aesthetic sensibility. In Lavender Mansions, people talk about otherness, invisibility, and multiple identity. They present themselves with lyricism, sober realism, and high campiness. In the end, this volume will be successful when the specialized reader *becomes* the general reader. *Lavender Mansions* shouldn't get filed away under the scholarly rubrics of sociology or cultural studies. Rather it should land on that shelf of meaningful books that we lend to friends, that we go back and re-read ourselves from time to time. I hope these stories will haunt you. As Eugenio Montale said, good literature is measured by the way it revisits us a week, a year later. The true test of writing is in that "second life of art."

Checking the Utilities

Just as an apartment building doesn't function if it isn't a haven of shelter and warmth—a place where doors open and close and the lights work—a book of good stories must metaphorically provide basic artistic needs such as evocative setting, acute characterization, authentic voice, and sensual description. Because of the way in which Americans publish books and organize classes, we tend to distinguish between modified literature (women's writing, Asian-American writing, Gay writing) and the real stuff (rarely named as white, heterosexual male writing). This is not a modified book, but rather a collection containing elegant, hilarious, profound stories, some of the best writing this country has to offer.

Splendid description of place is found in Judith McDaniel's "The Juliette Low Legacy," and Louie Crew's "Ben's Eyes." Here is Norman Wong's "Cultural Revolution":

> People scurried out of the ricksha's way. A thin sheet of dust hovered above the dirt road. Shops—groceries, bakeries, drug stores—occupied the first floor of the buildings. Above, families were crowded in two-room apartments; children hung out of windows, while their laundry blew lifelessly on the line, bleached shirts and trousers. The ricksha drove between the buildings, down an alleyway. Wooden stands sold local delicacies: wilted greens, hanging roasted ducks and dogs, and frogs in straw baskets, climbing on top of each other. An old woman sat on a stool, twisting a live chicken's neck.

I appreciate the inventive, idiosyncratic characterization in Ruthann Robson's "Kissing Doesn't Kill" and Richard McCann's "My Mother's Clothes: The School of Beauty and Shame." Jewelle L. Gomez imagines Billie in "Don't Explain":

> Once convinced, Billie became the show again, loud and commanding. She demanded her food be served at the bar and sent Mabel, who insisted on waiting on her personally, back to the kitchen fifteen times. Billie laughed at jokes that Letty could barely hear as she bustled back and forth between the abandoned kitchen and her own tables. The sound of that laugh from the bar penetrated her bones. She'd watched and listened, certain she saw something no one else did. When Billie had finished eating and gathered her entourage to get back on the road she left a tip, not just for Mabel but for each of the waitresses and the bartender. "Generous just like the 'business' girls," Letty was happy to note. She still had the two one dollar bills in an envelope at the back of her lingerie drawer.

Throughout the book is heard a concert of richly individual, everyday voices, such as in Douglas Sadownick's "Sacred Lips of the Bronx" and Terri de la Peña's "Mujeres Morenas." Listen to Becky Birtha's "In the Life":

> I never had time to paint that fence back then, neither. But it didn't matter none, cause Gracie had it all covered up with her flowers. She used to sit right here on this swing at night, when a little breeze be blowing, and say she could tell all the different flowers apart, just by they smell. The wind pick up a scent and Gracie say, "Smell that jasmine, Pearl?" Then a breeze come up from another direction, and she turn her head like somebody calling her and say, "Now that's my honey-suckle, now."

Lavender Mansions succeeds if you find yourself re-reading stories for the erotic texture of words, such as in William Haywood Henderson's "Myths": "Then, for a moment, the touch of flesh, the warm air drifting across us, the rhythm of breathing, my nose pressed into the hollow of his neck, light enough on his face above me that I knew it was Ray, knew suddenly the smell of him, knew he would settle into me, slowly, and we would laugh, and his voice and skin and his life would be close to me." Another sensuous coming together is offered by Donna Allegra in "Buddies": "I guide her around my center like a lullaby, kiss her forehead as earlier she'd reached out for me. I find her neck, her cheek. Her mouth is mine to open and I dip in, searching. I don't care who sees us. This is my dance and I don't let her pull away. I hold the woman I've asked, keeping her close."

Laughing and Crying

These forty stories raise real questions about how to relish life, where to be generous in love, when to be enraged by or serene about death, and how to expand our range of compassions for other human beings. It is wise to keep open the windows and doors onto homosexual life that these stories provide, for surely in the next large wave of censorship they will be slammed shut again and homosexual stories will return to literary quarantine.

But today out these windows, you hear a lot of laughter. Humor—especially irreverence—is a highly prized trait in Lavender Mansions. The wit of these writers results from years of eyeing the world from the margins. The critically intelligent, off-center comedy is often practiced here with subtle psychological nuance and elegant timing. Some of this humor is self-mocking, joking about internalized stereotyping, as in Jess Wells's "The Dress":

> So, I'm in the thrift store after work; I'm smudged up with ink and my back hurts from running a printing press all day. Shopping has been mildly successful: I've

found a wool sweater from Italy, a shirt for my lover and a 100% cotton bathrobe for myself. As I'm unloading my finds onto the counter for this dyke with a mustache and eye make-up to tally, I look up. There is this dress ... hanging there (my neck freezes in a tilted position) ... an incredible dress. ... Well, I'm glad it costs that much: I'm hardly going to spend 20 bucks on a dress.

Michael Schwartz uses wit to respond to external prejudices. "There's a slightly better chance that he'll scream, 'Faggots! They're gonna give my kids AIDS!' And then everyone will form a circle around us and stone us to death with Chicken McNuggets." And some of the humor is poignantly ironic, as in Lesléa Newman's "A Letter to Harvey Milk": "Dear Harvey: You couldn't let somebody else have such a great honor? Alright, alright, so you liked the boys, I wasn't wild about the idea. But I got used to it. I never said you wasn't welcome in my house, did I?"

If this is a book of laughter, it is also a book of mourning. An entire section is dedicated to people living with and dying from AIDS. Irene Zahava includes accounts told from the point of view of those infected with the disease ("Despair: August 1987," "Halfway Home," "Portland, Maine: An Essay," and "Running on Empty") as well as tales highlighting the experience of close friends of those with AIDS ("The Angel of Death on the Provincetown Ferry" and "A Good Man"). Sadly, several of the contributors to this anthology have recently died. George Stambolian and John Preston were casualties of AIDS, and Audre Lorde was lost to another epidemic, breast cancer. Not only were they fine storytellers in their own rights, but they were generous supporters of other people in the Lesbian and Gay writing scene.

I cannot conclude this tour of Lavender Mansions without thanking the architect/proprietor/superintendent. Irene Zahava reveals considerable skill and grace in her work of selecting and arranging these forty pieces. Anthologizing is a complex, arduous process involving hours and hours of reading. It requires acrobatic prowess in balancing stylistic, topical, and cultural representation. No doubt Zahava cultivated her choreographic talent during the twelve years she has operated a bookstore in upstate New York and while editing seventeen previous anthologies. Anything but an absentee landlord, Irene Zahava is passionate about her work and eager for reader response.

AUDRE LORDE

FROM

ZAMI: A NEW SPELLING OF MY NAME

WHEN I WAS AROUND the age of four or five, I would have given anything I had in the world except my mother, in order to have a friend or a little sister. She would be someone I could talk to and play with, someone close enough in age to me that I would not have to be afraid of her, nor she of me. We would share our secrets with each other.

Even though I had two older sisters, I grew up feeling like an only child, since they were quite close to each other in age, and quite far away from me. Actually, I grew up feeling like an only planet, or some isolated world in a hostile, or at best, unfriendly, firmament. The fact that I was clothed, sheltered, and fed better than many other children in Harlem in those Depression years was not a fact that impressed itself too often upon my child's consciousness.

Most of my childhood fantasies revolved around how I might acquire this little female person for my companion. I concentrated upon magical means, having gathered early on that my family had no intention of satisfying this particular need of mine. The Lorde family was not going to expand any more.

The idea of having children was a pretty scary one, anyway, full of secret indiscretions peeked at darkly through the corner of an eye, as my mother and my aunts did whenever they passed a woman on the street who had one of those big, pushed-out-in-front, blouses that always intrigued me so. I wondered what great wrong these women had done, that this big blouse was a badge of, obvious as the dunce cap I sometimes had to wear in the corner at school.

1

Adoption was also out of the question. You could get a kitten from the corner grocery-store man, but not a sister. Like ocean cruises and boarding schools and upper berths in trains, it was not for us. Rich people, like Mr. Rochester in the movie *Jane Eyre,* lonely in their great tree-lined estates, adopted children, but not us.

Being the youngest in a West Indian family had many privileges, but no rights. And since my mother was determined not to "spoil" me, even those privileges were largely illusory. I knew, therefore, that if my family were to acquire another little person voluntarily, that little person would most probably be a boy, and would most decidedly belong to my mother, and not to me.

I really believed, however, that my magical endeavors, done often enough, in the right way, and in the right places, letter-perfect and with a clean soul, would finally bring me a little sister. And I did mean little. I frequently imagined my little sister and I having fascinating conversations together while she sat cradled in the cupped palm of my hand. There she was, curled up and carefully shielded from the inquisitive eyes of the rest of the world, and my family in particular.

When I was three and a half and had gotten my first eyeglasses, I stopped tripping over my feet. But I still walked with my head down, all the time, counting the lines on the squares in the pavement of every street which I traveled, hanging onto the hand of my mother or one of my sisters. I had decided that if I could step on all the horizontal lines for one day, my little person would appear like a dream made real, waiting for me in my bed by the time I got home. But I always messed up, or skipped one, or someone pulled my arm at a crucial moment. And she never appeared.

Sometimes on Saturdays in winter, my mother made the three of us a little clay out of flour and water and Diamond Crystal Shaker Salt. I always fashioned tiny little figures out of my share of the mixture. I would beg or swipe a little vanilla extract from my mother's shelf in the kitchen, where she kept her wonderful spices and herbs and extracts, and mix that with the clay. Sometimes I dabbed the figures on either side of the head behind the ears as I had seen my mother do with her glycerine and rosewater when she got dressed to go out.

I loved the way the rich, dark brown vanilla scented the flour-clay; it reminded me of my mother's hands when she made peanut brittle and eggnog at holidays. But most of all, I loved the live color it would bring to the pasty-white clay.

I knew for sure that real live people came in many different shades of beige and brown and cream and reddish tan, but nobody alive ever came in that pasty-white shade of flour and salt and water, even if they were called white. So the vanilla was essential if my little person was to be real. But the coloring didn't help either. No matter how many intricate rituals and incantations and spells I performed, no matter how many Hail Marys and Our Fathers I said, no matter what I promised god in return, the vanilla-tinted clay would slowly shrivel up and harden, turn gradually brittle and sour, and then crumble into a grainy flour dust. No matter how hard I prayed or schemed, the figures would never come alive. They never turned around in the cupped palm of my hand, to smile up at me and say "Hi."

I found my first playmate when I was around four years old. It lasted for about ten minutes.

It was a high winter noontime. My mother had bundled me up in my thick one-piece woolen snowsuit and cap and bulky scarf. Once she had inserted me into all this arctic gear, pulled rubber galoshes up over my shoes and wrapped yet another thick scarf around the whole as if to keep the mass intact, she planted me out upon the stoop of the apartment building while she dressed herself hurriedly. Although my mother never liked to have me out of her sight for any period of time, she did this to keep me from catching my death of cold from becoming overheated and then going outdoors.

After many weighty warnings to me not to move from that spot, dire descriptions of what would happen to me if I did, and how I was to yell if any strangers spoke to me, my mother disappeared down the few feet of hallway back to our apartment to get her coat and hat, and to check all the windows of the house to make sure that they were locked.

I loved these few minutes of freedom, and treasured them secretly. They were the only times I ever got to be outside without my mother urging me along on my short stubby little legs that could never run fast enough to keep up with her purposeful strides. I sat quietly where she had put me on the slated top of the stone banisters of the stoop. My arms stuck out a little from my sides over the bulk of my clothing, my feet were heavy and awkward with sturdy shoes and galoshes, and my neck was stiffly encased in the woolen cap and wrapped scarf.

The sun shone with a winter milkiness onto the sidewalks across the street, and onto the few banks of dirty soot-covered snow that lined the sidewalks near the gutter's edge. I could see up to the corner of Lenox Avenue, about three houses away. At the corner near the building line, the Father Divine man ran his Peace Brother Peace shoe repair business from a ramshackled wooden kiosk heated by a small round stove. From the roof of the kiosk, a thin strand of smoke drifted upward. The smoke was the only sign of life and there was nobody on the street that I could see. I wished the street was warm and beautiful and busy, and that we were having cantaloupe for lunch instead of the hot homemade pea soup that was simmering on the back of the stove awaiting our return.

I had almost made a boat of newspaper just before I had to start being dressed to go out, and I wondered if my bits of newspaper would still be on the kitchen table when we got back, or was my mother even now sweeping them away into the garbage bag? Would I be able to rescue them before lunch or would there be nasty wet orange-peelings and coffee grounds all over them?

Suddenly I realized that there was a little creature standing on a step in the entryway of the main doors, looking at me with bright eyes and a big smile. It was a little girl. She was right away the most beautiful little girl I had ever seen alive in my life.

My lifelong dream of a doll-baby come to life had in fact come true. Here she stood before me now, smiling and pretty in an unbelievable wine-red velvet coat with a wide, wide skirt that flared out over dainty little lisle-stockinged legs. Her feet were clad in a pair of totally impractical, black patent-leather mary-jane shoes, whose silver buckles glinted merrily in the drab noon light.

Her reddish-brown hair was not braided in four plaits like mine, but framed her little pointy-chinned face, tight and curly. On her head sat a wine-colored velvet beret that matched her coat, and on the very top of that sat a big white fur pompom.

Even with decades of fashion between us now, and the dulling of time, it was the most beautiful outfit I had ever seen in my not quite five years of clothes-watching.

Her honey-brown skin had a ruddy glow that echoed the tones of her hair, and her eyes seemed to match both in a funny way that reminded me of my mother's eyes, the way, although light in themselves, they flashed alight in the sun.

I had no idea how old she was.

"What's your name? Mine's Toni."

The name called up a picture book I was just finished reading, and the image came out *boy*. But this delectable creature in front of me was most certainly a girl, and I wanted her for my very own—my very own what, I did not know—but for my very own self. I started to image in my head where I could keep her. Maybe I could tuck her up in the folds under my pillow, pet her during the night when everybody else was asleep, and I was fighting off nightmares of the devil riding me. Of course, I'd have to be careful that she didn't get squeezed into the cot in the morning, when my mother folded up my bed, covered it with an old piece of flowered cretonne bedspread and shoved the whole thing tidily into a corner behind the bedroom door. No, that certainly wouldn't work. My mother would most assuredly find her when, in my mother's way, she plumped up my pillows.

While I was trying to image a safe place to keep her by a rapid succession of pictures in my mind's eye, Toni had advanced towards me, and was now standing between my outspread snowsuited legs, her dark-bright fire-lit eyes on a level with my own. With my woolen mittens dangling down from cords which emerged from the cuffs at each of my wrists, I reached out my hand and lightly rubbed the soft velvet shoulders of her frock-coat up and down.

From around her neck hung a fluffy white fur muff that matched the white fur ball on the top of her hat. I touched her muff, too, and then raised my hand up to feel the fur pompom. The soft silky warmth of the fur made my fingers tingle in a way that the cold had not, and I pinched and fingered it until Toni finally shook her head free of my hand.

I began to finger the small shiny gold buttons on the front of her coat. I un-buttoned the first two of them at the top, just so I could button them back up again, pretending I was her mother.

"You cold?" I was looking at her pink and beige ears, now slowly turning rosy from the cold. From each delicate lobe hung a tiny gold loop.

"No," she said, moving even closer between my knees. "Let's play."

I stuck both of my hands into the holes of her furry muff, and she giggled delightedly as my cold fingers closed around her warm ones inside the quilted dark spaces of the fur. She pulled one hand out past mine and opened it in front of my face to reveal two peppermint lifesavers, sticky now from the heat of her palm. "Want one?"

I took one hand out of her muff, and never taking my eyes off her face, popped one of the striped candy rings into my mouth. My mouth was dry. I closed it around the candy and sucked, feeling the peppermint juice run down my throat, burning and sweet almost to the point of harshness. For years and years afterward, I always thought of peppermint lifesavers as the candy in Toni's muff.

She was beginning to get impatient. "Play with me, please?" Toni took a step backward, smiling, and I was terrified suddenly that she might disappear or run away, and the sunlight would surely vanish with her from 142nd Street. My mother had warned me not to move from that spot where she had planted me. But there was no question in my mind; I could not bear to lose Toni.

I reached out and pulled her back gently towards me, sitting her down crosswise upon my knees. She felt so light through the padding of my snowsuit that I thought she could blow away and I would not feel the difference between her being there and not being there.

I put my arms around her soft red velvet coat, and clasping my two hands together, I slowly rocked her back and forth the way I did with my sisters' big Coca-Cola doll that had eyes that opened and closed and that came down from the closest shelf every year around Christmas time. Our old cat Minnie the Moocher did not feel much lighter sitting on my lap.

She turned her face around to me with another one of her delighted laughs that sounded like the ice cubes in my father's nightly drink. I could feel the creeping warmth of her, slowly spreading all along the front of my body through the many layers of clothing, and as she turned her head to speak to me the damp warmth of her breath fogged up my spectacles a little in the crisp winter air.

I started to sweat inside my snow suit as I usually did, despite the cold. I wanted to take off her coat and see what she had on underneath it. I wanted to take off all of her clothes, and touch her live little brown body and make sure she was real. My heart was bursting with a love and happiness for which I had no words. I unbuttoned the top buttons of her coat again.

"No, don't do that! My grandma won't like it. You can rock me some more." She cuddled down again into my arms.

I put my arms back around her shoulders. Was she really a little girl or a doll come alive? There was only one way I knew for sure of telling. I turned her over and put her across my knees. The light seemed to change around us on the stoop. I looked over once at the doorway leading into the hall, half-afraid of who might be standing there.

I raised up the back of Toni's wine-red velvet coat, and the many folds of her full-skirted green eyelet dress underneath. I lifted up the petticoats under that, until I could see her white cotton knickers, each leg of which ended in an embroidered gathering right above the elastic garters that held up her stockings.

Beads of sweat were running down my chest to be caught at my waist by the tight band of my snowsuit. Ordinarily I hated sweating inside my snowsuit because it felt like roaches were crawling down the front of me.

Toni laughed again and said something that I could not hear. She squirmed around comfortably on my knees and turned her head, her sweet face looking sideways up into mine.

"Grandma forgot my leggings at my house."

I reached up under the welter of dress and petticoats and took hold of the waistband of her knickers. Was her bottom going to be real and warm or turn out to be hard rubber, molded into a little crease like the ultimately disappointing Coca-Cola doll?

My hands were shaking with excitement. I hesitated a moment too long. As I was about to pull down Toni's panties I heard the main door open and out of the front hallway hurried my mother, adjusting the brim of her hat as she stepped out onto the stoop.

I felt caught in the middle of an embarrassing and terrible act from which there could be no hiding. Frozen, I sat motionless as Toni, looking up and seeing my mother, slid nonchalantly off my lap, smoothing down her skirts as she did so.

My mother stepped over to the two of us. I flinched, expecting instant retribution at her capable hands. But evidently the enormity of my intentions had escaped my mother's notice. Perhaps she did not care that I was about to usurp that secret prerogative belonging only to mothers about to spank, or to nurses with thermometers.

Taking me by the elbow, my mother pulled me awkwardly to my feet.

I stood for a moment like a wool-encased snow-girl, my arms stuck out a little from my body and my legs spread slightly apart. Ignoring Toni, my mother started down the steps to the street. "Hurry now," she said, "you don't want to be late."

I looked back over my shoulder. The bright-eyed vision in the wine-red coat stood at the top of the stoop, and pulled one hand out of her white rabbit-fur muff.

"You want the other candy?" she called. I shook my head frantically. We were never supposed to take candy from anybody and certainly not strangers.

My mother urged me on down the steps. "Watch where you're stepping, now."

"Can you come out and play tomorrow?" Toni called after me.

Tomorrow. Tomorrow. Tomorrow. My mother was already one step below, and her firm hand on my elbow kept me from falling as I almost missed a step. Maybe tomorrow …

Once on the street pavement, my mother resumed hold of my hand and sailed forth determinedly. My short legs in their bulky wrappings and galoshes chugged along, trying to keep up with her. Even when she was not in a hurry, my mother walked with a long and purposeful stride, her toes always pointed slightly outward in a ladylike fashion.

"You can't tarry, now," she said. "You know it's almost noon." Tomorrow, tomorrow, tomorrow.

"What a shame, to let such a skinny little thing like that out in this weather with no snowsuit or a stitch of leggings on her legs. That's how among-you children catch your death of cold."

So I hadn't dreamed her. She had seen Toni too. (What kind of name anyway was that for a girl?) Maybe tomorrow …

"Can I have a red coat like hers, Mommy?"

My mother looked down at me as we stood waiting for the street light to change.

"How many times I tell you not to call me Mommy on the street?" The light changed, and we hurried forward.

I thought about my question very carefully as I scurried along, wanting to get it exactly right this time. Finally, I had it.

"Will you buy me a red coat, please, Mother?" I kept my eyes on the treacherous ground to avoid tripping over my galoshed feet, and the words must have been muffled or lost in the scarf around my neck. In any case, my mother hurried on in silence, apparently not hearing. Tomorrow tomorrow tomorrow.

We had our split-pea soup, and hurriedly retraced our steps back to my sisters' school. But that day, my mother and I did not return directly home. Crossing over to the other side of Lenox Avenue, we caught the Number 4 bus down to 125th Street, where we went marketing at Weissbecker's for the weekend chicken.

My heart sank into hopelessness as I stood waiting, kicking my feet in the sawdust that covered the market's floor. I should have known. I had wanted too much for her to be real. I had wanted to see her again too much for it to ever happen.

The market was too warm. My sweaty skin itched in places I couldn't possibly scratch. If we were marketing today, that meant tomorrow would turn out to be Saturday. My sisters did not go to school on Saturday, which meant we couldn't go pick them up for lunch, which meant I would spend all day in the house because my mother had to clean and cook and we were never allowed out alone to play on the stoop.

The weekend was an eternity past which I could not see.

The following Monday I waited again on the stoop. I sat by myself, bundled up as usual, and nobody came except my mother.

I don't know how long I looked for Toni every day at noontime, sitting on the stoop. Eventually, her image receded into that place from which all my dreams are made.

MY MOTHER'S CLOTHES:
THE SCHOOL OF BEAUTY
AND SHAME

*He is troubled by any image of himself, suffers when he is named. He finds the
perfection of a human relationship in this vacancy of the image: to abolish—in
oneself, between oneself and others—adjectives; a relationship which adjectivizes
is on the side of the image, on the side of domination, of death.*
—Roland Barthes, *Roland Barthes*

Lᴉᴋᴇ ᴇᴠᴇʀʏ ᴄᴏʀɴᴇʀ house in Carroll Knolls, the corner house on our block
was turned backward on its lot, a quirk introduced by the developer of the
subdivision, who, having run short of money, sought variety without additional expense. The turned-around houses, as we kids called them, were not
popular, perhaps because they seemed too public, their casement bedroom
windows cranking open onto sunstruck asphalt streets. In actuality, however, it
was the rest of the houses that were public, their picture windows offering di-
oramic glimpses of early-American sofas and Mediterranean-style pole lamps
whose mottled globes hung like iridescent melons from wrought-iron chains.
In order not to be seen walking across the living room to the kitchen in our pajamas, we had to close the venetian blinds. The corner house on our block was
secretive, as though it had turned its back on all of us, whether in superiority
or in shame, refusing to acknowledge even its own unkempt yard of yellowing
zoysia grass. After its initial occupants moved away, the corner house remained
vacant for months.

The spring I was in sixth grade, it was sold. When I came down the block from school, I saw a moving van parked at its curb. "Careful with that!" a woman was shouting at a mover as he unloaded a tiered end table from the truck. He stared at her in silence. The veneer had already been splintered from the table's edge, as though someone had nervously picked at it while watching TV. Then another mover walked from the truck carrying a child's bicycle, a wire basket bolted over its thick rear tire, brightly colored plastic streamers dangling from its handlebars.

The woman looked at me. "What have you got there? In your hand."

I was holding a scallop shell spray-painted gold, with imitation pearls glued along its edges. Mrs. Eidus, the art teacher who visited our class each Friday, had showed me how to make it.

"A hatpin tray," I said. "It's for my mother."

"It's real pretty." She glanced up the street as though trying to guess which house I belonged to. "I'm Mrs. Tyree," she said, "and I've got a boy about your age. His daddy's bringing him tonight in the new Plymouth. I bet you haven't sat in a new Plymouth."

"We have a Ford." I studied her housedress, tiny blue and purple flowers imprinted on thin cotton, a line of white buttons as large as Necco Wafers marching toward its basted hemline. She was the kind of mother my mother laughed at for cutting recipes out of *Woman's Day.* Staring from our picture window, my mother would sometimes watch the neighborhood mothers drag their folding chairs into a circle on someone's lawn. "There they go," she'd say, "a regular meeting of the Daughters of the Eastern Star!" "They're hardly even *women,*" she'd whisper to my father, "and their *clothes.*" She'd criticize their appearance—their loud nylon scarves tied beneath their chins, their disintegrating figures stuffed into pedal pushers—until my father, worried that my brother, Davis, and I could hear, although laughing himself, would beg her, "Stop it, Maria, please stop; it isn't funny." But she wouldn't stop, not ever. "Not even thirty and they look like they belong to the DAR! They wear their pearls inside their bosoms in case the rope should break!" She was the oldest mother on the block but she was the most glamorous, sitting alone on the front lawn in her sleek kick-pleated skirts and cashmere sweaters, reading her thick paperback novels, whose bindings had split. Her hair was lightly hennaed, so that when I saw her pillowcases piled atop the washer, they seemed dusted with powdery rouge. She had once lived in New York City.

After dinner, when it was dark, I joined the other children congregated beneath the streetlamp across from the turned-around house. Bucky Trueblood, an eighth-grader who had once twisted the stems off my brother's eyeglasses, was crouched in the center, describing his mother's naked body to us elementary school children gathered around him, our faces slightly upturned, as though searching for a distant constellation, or for the bats that Bucky said would fly into our hair. I sat at the edge, one half of my body within the circle of light, the other half lost to darkness. When Bucky described his mother's nipples, which he'd glimpsed when she bent to kiss him goodnight, everyone giggled; but when he described her genitals, which he'd seen by dropping his pencil on the floor and looking up her nightie while her feet were propped on a hassock as she watched TV, everyone huddled nervously together, as though listening to a ghost story that made them fear something dangerous in the nearby dark. "I don't believe you," someone said; "I'm telling you," Bucky said, *"that's what it looks like."*

I slowly moved outside the circle. Across the street a cream-colored Plymouth was parked at the curb. In a lighted bedroom window Mrs. Tyree was hanging café curtains. Behind the chain-link fence, within the low branches of a willow tree, the new child was standing in his yard. I could see his white T-shirt and the pale oval of his face, a face deprived of detail by darkness and distance. Behind him, at the open bedroom window, his mother slowly fiddled with a valance. Behind me the children sat spellbound beneath the light. Then Bucky jumped up and pointed in the new child's direction—"Hey, you, you want to hear something really *good?*"—and even before the others had a chance to spot him, he vanished as suddenly and completely as an imaginary playmate.

The next morning, as we waited at our bus stop, he loitered by the mailbox on the opposite corner, not crossing the street until the yellow school bus pulled up and flung open its door. Then he dashed aboard and sat down beside me. "I'm Denny," he said. Denny: a heavy, unbeautiful child, who, had his parents stayed in their native Kentucky, would have been a farm boy, but who in Carroll Knolls seemed to belong to no particular world at all, walking past the identical ranch houses in his overalls and Keds, his whitish-blond hair close-cropped all around except for the distinguishing, stigmatizing feature of a wave that crested perfectly just above his forehead, a wave that neither rose nor fell, a wave he trained with Hopalong Cassidy hair tonic, a wave he tended fussily, as though it were the only loveliness he allowed himself.

What in Carroll Knolls might have been described by someone not native to those parts—a visiting expert, say—as *beautiful,* capable of arousing terror and joy? The brick ramblers strung with multicolored Christmas lights? The occasional front-yard plaster Virgin entrapped within a chicken-wire grotto entwined with plastic roses? The spring Denny moved to Carroll Knolls, I begged my parents to take me to a nightclub, had begged so hard for months, in fact, that by summer they finally agreed to a Sunday matinee. Waiting in the back seat of our Country Squire, a red bow tie clipped to my collar, I watched our house float like a mirage behind the sprinkler's web of water. The front door opened, and a white dress fluttered within the mirage's ascending waves:

slipping on her sunglasses, my mother emerged onto the concrete stoop, adjusted her shoulder strap, and teetered across the wet grass in new spectator
shoes. Then my father stepped out and cut the sprinkler off. We drove—the
warm breeze inside the car sweetened by my mother's Shalimar—past ranch
houses tethered to yards by chain-link fences; past the Silver Spring Volunteer
Fire Department and Carroll Knolls Elementary School; past the Polar Bear
Soft-Serv stand, its white stucco siding shimmery with mirror shards; past a
bull-dozed red-clay field where a weathered billboard advertised IF YOU
LIVED HERE YOU'D BE HOME BY NOW, until we arrived at the border—a
line of cinder-block discount liquor stores, a traffic light—of Washington,
D.C. The light turned red. We stopped. The breeze died and the Shalimar fell
from the air. Exhaust fumes mixed with the smell of hot tar. A drunk man
stumbled into the crosswalk, followed by an old woman shielding herself from
the sun with an orange umbrella, and two teen-aged boys dribbling a basketball back and forth between them. My mother put down her sun visor. "Lock
your door," she said.

Then the light changed, releasing us into another country. The station
wagon sailed down boulevards of Chinese elms and flowering Bradford pears,
through hot, dense streets where black families sat on wooden chairs at curbs,
along old streetcar tracks that caused the tires to shimmy and the car to swerve,
onto Pennsylvania Avenue, past the White House, encircled by its fence of iron
spears, and down 14th Street, past the Treasury Building, until at last we
reached the Neptune Room, a cocktail lounge in the basement of a shabbily elegant hotel.

Inside, the Neptune Room's walls were painted with garish mermaids reclin-
ing seductively on underwater rocks, and human frogmen who stared longingly through their diving helmets' glass masks at a loveliness they could not
possess on dry earth. On stage, leaning against the baby grand piano, a *chan-
teuse* (as my mother called her) was singing of her grief, her wrists weighted
with rhinestone bracelets, a single blue spotlight making her seem like one
who lived, as did the mermaids, underwater.

I was transfixed. I clutched my Roy Rogers cocktail (the same as a Shirley
Temple, but without the cheerful, girlish grenadine) tight in my fist. In the
middle of "The Man I Love" I stood and struggled toward the stage.

I strayed into the spotlight's soft-blue underwater world. Close up, from
within the light, the singer was a boozy, plump peroxide blonde in a tight black
cocktail dress; but these indiscretions made her yet more lovely, for they
showed what she had lost, just as her songs seemed to carry her backward into
endless regret. When I got close to her, she extended one hand—red nails, a
huge glass ring—and seized one of mine.

"Why, what kind of little sailor have we got here?" she asked the audience.

I stared through the border of blue light and into the room, where I saw my parents gesturing, although whether they were telling me to step closer to her microphone or to step farther away, I could not tell. The whole club was staring.

"Maybe he knows a song!" a man shouted from the back.

"Sing with me," she whispered. "What can you sing?"

I wanted to lift her microphone from its stand and bow deeply from the waist, as Judy Garland did on her weekly TV show. But I could not. As she began to sing, I stood voiceless, pressed against the protection of her black dress; or, more accurately, I stood beside her, silently lip-synching to myself. I do not recall what she sang, although I do recall a quick, farcical ending in which she falsettoed, like Betty Boop, "Gimme a Little Kiss, Will Ya, Huh?" and brushed my forehead with pursed red lips.

That summer, humidity enveloping the landfill subdivision, Denny, "the new kid," stood on the boundaries, while we neighborhood boys played war, a game in which someone stood on Stanley Allen's front porch and machine-gunned the rest of us, who one by one clutched our bellies, coughed as if choking on blood, and rolled in exquisite death throes down the grassy hill. When Stanley's father came up the walk from work, he ducked imaginary bullets. "Hi, Dad," Stanley would call, rising from the dead to greet him. Then we began the game again: whoever died best in the last round got to kill in the next. Later, after dusk, we'd smear the wings of balsa planes with glue, ignite them, and send them flaming through the dark on kamikaze missions. Long after the streets were deserted, we children sprawled beneath the corner streetlamp, praying our mothers would not call us—*"Time to come in!"*—back to our oven-like houses; and then sometimes Bucky, hoping to scare the elementary school kids, would lead his solemn procession of junior high "hoods" down the block, their penises hanging from their unzipped trousers.

Denny and I began to play together, first in secret, then visiting each other's houses almost daily, and by the end of the summer I imagined him to be my best friend. Our friendship was sealed by our shared dread of junior high school. Davis, who had just finished seventh grade, brought back reports of corridors so long that one could get lost in them, of gangs who fought to control the lunchroom and the bathrooms. The only safe place seemed to be the Health Room, where a pretty nurse let you lie down on a cot behind a folding screen. Denny told me about a movie he'd seen in which the children, all girls, did not have to go to school at all but were taught at home by a beautiful governess, who, upon coming to their rooms each morning, threw open their shutters so that sunlight fell like bolts of satin across their beds, whispered their pet names while kissing them, and combed their long hair with a silver brush. "She never got mad," said Denny, beating his fingers up and down through the air as though striking a keyboard, "except once when some old man told the girls they could never play piano again."

With my father at work in the Pentagon and my mother off driving the two-tone Welcome Wagon Chevy to new subdivisions, Denny and I spent whole days in the gloom of my living room, the picture window's venetian blinds closed against an August sun so fierce that it bleached the design from the carpet. Dreaming of fabulous prizes—sets of matching Samsonite luggage, French Provincial bedroom suites, Corvettes, jet flights to Hawaii—we watched Jan Murray's *Treasure Hunt* and Bob Barker's *Truth or Consequences* (a name that seemed strangely threatening). We watched *The Loretta Young Show,* worshipping yet critiquing her elaborate gowns. When *The Early Show* came on, we watched old Bette Davis, Gene Tierney, and Joan Crawford movies—*Dark Victory, Leave Her to Heaven, A Woman's Face.* Hoping to become their pen pals, we wrote long letters to fading movie stars, who in turn sent us autographed photos we traded between ourselves. We searched the house for secrets, like contraceptives, Kotex, and my mother's hidden supply of Hershey bars. And finally, Denny and I, running to the front window every few minutes to make sure no one was coming unexpectedly up the sidewalk, inspected the secrets of my mother's dresser: her satin nightgowns and padded brassieres, folded atop pink drawer liners and scattered with loose sachet; her black mantilla, pressed inside a shroud of lilac tissue paper; her heart-shaped candy box, a flapper doll strapped to its lid with a ribbon, from which spilled galaxies of cocktail rings and cultured pearls. Small shrines to deeper intentions, private grottoes of yearning: her triangular cloisonné earrings, her brooch of enameled butterfly wings.

Because beauty's source was longing, it was infused with romantic sorrow; because beauty was defined as "feminine," and therefore as "other," it became hopelessly confused with my mother: Mother, who quickly sorted through new batches of photographs, throwing unflattering shots of herself directly into the fire before they could be seen. Mother, who dramatized herself, telling us and our playmates, "My name is Maria Dolores; in Spanish, that means 'Mother of Sorrows.'" Mother who had once wished to be a writer and who said, looking up briefly from whatever she was reading, "Books are my best friends." Mother, who read aloud from Whitman's *Leaves of Grass* and O'Neill's *Long Day's Journey Into Night* with a voice so grave I could not tell the difference between them. Mother, who lifted cut-glass vases and antique clocks from her obsessively dusted curio shelves to ask, "If this could talk, what story would it tell?"

And more, always more, for she was the only woman in our house, a "people-watcher," a "talker," a woman whose mysteries and moods seemed endless: Our Mother of the White Silk Gloves; Our Mother of the Veiled Hats; Our Mother of the Paper Lilacs; Our Mother of the Sighs and Heartaches; Our

Mother of the Gorgeous Gypsy Earrings; Our Mother of the Late Movies and the Cigarettes; Our Mother whom I adored and who, in adoring, I ran from, knowing it "wrong" for a son to wish to be like his mother; Our Mother who wished to influence us, passing the best of herself along, yet who held the fear common to that era, the fear that by loving a son too intensely she would render him unfit—"Momma's boy," "tied to apron strings"—and who therefore alternately drew us close and sent us away, believing a son needed "male influence" in large doses, that female influence was pernicious except as a final finishing, like manners; Our Mother of the Mixed Messages; Our Mother of Sudden Attentiveness; Our Mother of Sudden Distances; Our Mother of Anger; Our Mother of Apology. The simplest objects of her life, objects scattered accidentally about the house, became my shrines to beauty, my grottoes of romantic sorrow: her Revlon lipstick tubes, "Cherries in the Snow"; her Art Nouveau atomizers on the blue mirror top of her vanity; her pastel silk scarves knotted to a wire hanger in her closet; her white handkerchiefs blotted with red mouths. Voiceless objects; silences. The world halved with a cleaver: "masculine," "feminine." In these ways was the plainest ordinary love made complicated and grotesque. And in these ways was beauty, already confused with the "feminine," also confused with shame, for all these longings were secret, and to control me all my brother had to do was to threaten to expose that Denny and I were dressing ourselves in my mother's clothes.

Denny chose my mother's drabbest outfits, as though he were ruled by the deepest of modesties, or by his family's austere Methodism: a pink wraparound skirt from which the color had been laundered, its hem almost to his ankles; a sleeveless white cotton blouse with a Peter Pan collar; a small straw summer clutch. But he seemed to challenge his own primness, as though he dared it with his "effects": an undershirt worn over his head to approximate cascading hair; gummed holepunch reinforcements pasted to his fingernails so that this hands, palms up, might look like a woman's—flimsy crescent moons waxing above his fingertips.

He dressed slowly, hesitantly, but once dressed, he was a manic Proteus metamorphosizing into contradictory, half-realized forms, throwing his "long hair" back and balling it violently into a French twist; tapping his paper nails on the glass-topped vanity as though he were an important woman kept waiting at a cosmetics counter; stabbing his nails into the air as though he were an angry teacher assigning an hour of detention; touching his temple as though he were a shy schoolgirl tucking back a wisp of stray hair; resting his fingertips on the rim of his glass of Kool-Aid as though he were an actress seated over an ornamental cocktail—a Pink Lady, say, or a Silver Slipper. Sometimes, in an orgy of jerky movement, his gestures overtaking him with greater and greater force, a dynamo of theatricality unleashed, he would hurl himself across the

room like a mad girl having a fit, or like one possessed; or he would snatch the
chenille spread from my parents' bed and drape it over his head to fashion for
himself the long train of a bride. "Do you like it?" he'd ask anxiously, making
me his mirror. "Does it look *real?*" He wanted, as did I, to become something
he'd neither yet seen nor dreamed of, something he'd recognize the moment he
saw it: himself. Yet he was constantly confounded, for no matter how much he
adorned himself with scarves and jewelry, he could not understand that this
was himself, as was also and at the same time the boy in overalls and Keds. He
was split in two pieces—as who was not?—the blond wave cresting rigidly
above his close-cropped hair.

"He makes me nervous," I heard my father tell my mother one night as I lay
in bed. They were speaking about me. That morning I'd stood awkwardly on
the front lawn—"Maybe you should go help your father," my mother had
said—while he propped an extension ladder against the house, climbed up
through the power lines he separated with his bare hands, and staggered across
the pitched roof he was reshingling. When his hammer slid down the incline,
catching on the gutter, I screamed, "You're falling!" Startled, he almost fell.
    "He needs to spend more time with you," I heard my mother say.
    I couldn't sleep. Out in the distance a mother was calling her child home. A
screen door slammed. I heard cicadas, their chorus as steady and loud as the
hum of a power line. *He needs to spend more time with you.* Didn't she know?
Saturday mornings, when he stood in his rubber hip boots fishing off the shore
of Triadelphia Reservoir, I was afraid of the slimy bottom and could not wade
after him; for whatever reasons of his own—something as simple as shyness,
perhaps—he could not come to get me. I sat in the parking lot drinking Tru-
Ade and reading *Betty and Veronica,* wondering if Denny had walked alone to
Wheaton Plaza, where the weekend manager of Port-o'-Call allowed us to
Windex the illuminated glass shelves that held Lladro figurines, the porcelain
ballerina's hands so realistic one could see tiny life and heart lines etched into
her palms. *He needs to spend more time with you.* Was she planning to discon-
tinue the long summer afternoons that she and I spent together when there
were no new families for her to greet in her Welcome Wagon car? "I don't feel
like being alone today," she'd say, inviting me to sit on their chenille bedspread
and watch her model new clothes in her mirror. Behind her an oscillating fan
fluttered nylons and scarves she'd heaped, discarded, on a chair. "Should I
wear the red belt with this dress or the black one?" she'd ask, turning suddenly
toward me and cinching her waist with her hands.
    Afterward we would sit together at the rattan table on the screened-in
porch, holding cocktail napkins around sweaty glasses of iced Russian tea and
listening to big-band music on the Zenith.

"You look so pretty," I'd say. Sometimes she wore outfits I'd selected for her from her closet—pastel chiffon dresses, an apricot blouse with real mother-of-pearl buttons.

One afternoon she leaned over suddenly and shut off the radio. "You know you're going to leave me one day," she said. When I put my arms around her, smelling the dry carnation talc she wore in hot weather, she stood up and marched out of the room. When she returned, she was wearing Bermuda shorts and a plain cotton blouse. "Let's wait for your father on the stoop," she said.

Late that summer—the summer before he died—my father took me with him to Fort Benjamin Harrison, near Indianapolis, where, as a colonel in the U.S. Army Reserves, he did his annual tour of duty. On the propjet he drank bourbon and read newspapers while I made a souvenir packet for Denny: an airsickness bag, into which I placed the Chiclet given me by the stewardess to help pop my ears during take-off, and the laminated white card that showed the location of emergency exits. Fort Benjamin Harrison looked like Carroll Knolls: hundreds of acres of concrete and sun-scorched shrubbery inside a cyclone fence. Daytimes I waited for my father in the dining mess with the sons of other officers, drinking chocolate milk that came from a silver machine, and desultorily setting fires in ashtrays. When he came to collect me, I walked behind him—gold braid hung from his epaulets—while enlisted men saluted us and opened doors. At night, sitting in our BOQ room, he asked me questions about myself: "Are you looking forward to seventh grade?" "What do you think you'll want to be?" When these topics faltered—I stammered what I hoped were right answers—we watched TV, trying to pre-guess lines of dialogue on reruns of his favorites shows, *The Untouchables* and *Rawhide*. "That Della Street," he said as we watched *Perry Mason*, "is almost as pretty as your mother." On the last day, eager to make the trip memorable, he brought me a gift: a glassine envelope filled with punched IBM cards that told me my life story as his secretary had typed it into the office computer. Card One: *You live at 10406 Lillians Mill Court, Silver Spring, Maryland.* Card Two: *You are entering seventh grade.* Card Three: *Last year your teacher was Mrs. Dillard.* Card Four: *Your favorite color is blue.* Card Five: *You love the Kingston Trio.* Card Six: *You love basketball and football.* Card Seven: *Your favorite sport is swimming.*

Whose son did these cards describe? The address was correct, as was the teacher's name and the favorite color; and he'd remembered that one morning during breakfast I'd put a dime in the jukebox and played the Kingston Trio's song about "the man who never returned." But whose fiction was the rest? Had I, who played no sport other than kickball and Kitty-Kitty-Kick-the-Can, lied to him when he asked me about myself? Had he not heard from my mother the outcome of the previous summer's swim lessons? At the swim club a young man in black trunks had taught us, as we held hands, to dunk ourselves in wa-

ter, surface, and then go down. When he had told her to let go of me, I had
thrashed across the surface, violently afraid I'd sink. But perhaps I had not lied
to him; perhaps he merely did not wish to see. It was my job, I felt, to reassure
him that I was the son he imagined me to be, perhaps because the role of
reassurer gave me power. In any case, I thanked him for the computer cards. I
thanked him the way a father thanks a child for a well-intentioned gift he'll
never use—a set of handkerchiefs, say, on which the embroidered swirls con-
struct a monogram of no particular initial, and which thus might be used by
anyone.

As for me, when I dressed in my mother's clothes, I seldom moved at all: I
held myself rigid before the mirror. The kind of beauty I'd seen practiced in
movies and in fashion magazines was beauty attained by lacquered stasis,
beauty attained by fixed poses—"ladylike stillness," the stillness of manne-
quins, the stillness of the passive moon around which active meteors orbited
and burst. My costume was of the greatest solemnity: I dressed like the *chan-
teuse* in the Neptune Room, carefully shimmying my mother's black slip over
my head so as not to stain it with Brylcreem, draping her black mantilla over
my bare shoulders, clipping her rhinestone dangles to my ears. Had I at that
time already seen the movie in which French women who had fraternized with
German soldiers were made to shave their heads and walk through the streets,
jeered by their fellow villagers? And if so, did I imagine myself to be one of the
collaborators, or one of the villagers, taunting her from the curb? I ask because
no matter how elaborate my costume, I made no effort to camouflage my crew
cut or my male body.

How did I perceive myself in my mother's triple-mirrored vanity, its endless
repetitions? I saw myself as doubled—both an image and he who studied it. I
saw myself as beautiful, and guilty: the lipstick made my mouth seem the rip-
est rose, or a wound; the small rose on the black slip opened like my mother's
heart disclosed, or like the Sacred Heart of Mary, aflame and pierced by ar-
rows; the mantilla transformed me into a Mexican penitent or a Latin movie
star, like Dolores Del Rio. The mirror was a silvery stream: on the far side, in a
clearing, stood the woman who was icily immune from the boy's terror and
contempt; on the close side, in the bedroom, stood the boy who feared and yet
longed after her inviolability. (Perhaps, it occurs to me now, this doubleness is
the source of drag queens' vulnerable ferocity.) Sometimes, when I saw that
person in the mirror, I felt as though I had at last been lifted from that dull,
locked room with its mahogany bedroom suite and chalky blue walls. But
other times, particularly when I saw Denny and me together, so that his reality
shattered my fantasies, we seemed merely ludicrous and sadly comic, as
though we were dressed in the garments of another species, like dogs in human
clothes. I became aware of my spatulate hands, my scarred knees, my large feet;

I became aware of the drooping, unfilled bodice of my slip. Like Denny, I could neither dispense with images nor take their flexibility as pleasure, for the idea of self I had learned and was learning still was that one was constructed by one's images—*"When boys cross their legs, they cross one ankle atop the knee"*—so that one finally sought the protection of believing in one's own image and, in believing in it as reality, condemned oneself to its poverty.

(That locked room. My mother's vanity; my father's highboy. If Denny and I, still in our costumes, had left that bedroom, its floor strewn with my mother's shoes and handbags, and gone through the darkened living room, out onto the sunstruck porch, down the sidewalk, and up the street, how would we have carried ourselves? Would we have walked boldly, chattering extravagantly back and forth between ourselves, like drag queens, refusing to acknowledge the stares of contempt that are meant to halt them? Would we have walked humbly, with the calculated, impervious piety of the condemned walking barefoot to the public scaffold? Would we have walked simply, as deeply accustomed to the normalcy of our own strangeness as Siamese twins? Or would we have walked gravely, a solemn procession, like Bucky Trueblood's gang, their manhood hanging from their unzipped trousers?

(We were eleven years old. Why now, more than two decades later, do I wonder for the first time how we would have carried ourselves through a publicness we would have neither sought nor dared? I am six feet two inches tall; I weigh 198 pounds. Given my size, the question I am most often asked about my youth is "What football position did you play?" Overseas I am most commonly taken to be a German or a Swede. Right now, as I write this, I am wearing L. L. Bean khaki trousers, a LaCoste shirt, Weejuns: the anonymous American costume, although partaking of certain signs of class and education, and, most recently, partaking also of certain signs of sexual orientation, this costume having become the standard garb of the urban American gay man. Why do I tell you these things? Am I trying—not subtly—to inform us of my "maleness," to reassure us that I have "survived" without noticeable "complexes?" Or is this my urge, my constant urge, to complicate my portrait of myself to both of us, so that I might layer my selves like so many multicolored crinoline slips, each rustling as I walk? When the wind blows, lifting my skirt, I do not know which slip will be revealed.)

Sometimes, while Denny and I were dressing up, Davis would come home unexpectedly from the bowling alley, where he'd been hanging out since entering junior high. At the bowling alley he was courting the protection of Bucky's gang.

"Let me in!" he'd demand, banging fiercely on the bedroom door, behind which Denny and I were scurrying to wipe the makeup off our faces with Kleenex.

"We're not doing anything," I'd protest, buying time.

"Let me in this minute or I'll tell!"

Once in the room, Davis would police the wreckage we'd made, the emptied hatboxes, the scattered jewelry, the piled skirts and blouses. "You'd better clean this up right now," he'd warn. "You two make me *sick*."

Yet his scorn seemed modified by awe. When he helped us rehang the clothes in the closet and replace the jewelry in the candy box, a sullen accomplice destroying someone else's evidence, he sometimes handled the garments as though they were infused with something of himself, although at the precise moment when he seemed to find them loveliest, holding them close, he would cast them down.

After our dress-up sessions Denny would leave the house without good-byes. I was glad to see him go. We would not see each other for days, unless we met by accident; we never referred to what we'd done the last time we'd been together. We met like those who have murdered are said to meet, each tentatively and warily examining the other for signs of betrayal. But whom had we murdered? The boys who walked into that room? Or the women who briefly came to life within it? Perhaps this metaphor has outlived its meaning. Perhaps our shame derived not from our having killed but from our having created.

In early September, as Denny and I entered seventh grade, my father became ill. Over Labor Day weekend he was too tired to go fishing. On Monday his skin had vaguely yellowed; by Thursday he was severely jaundiced. On Friday he entered the hospital, his liver rapidly failing; Sunday he was dead. He died from acute hepatitis, possibly acquired while cleaning up after our sick dog, the doctor said. He was buried at Arlington National Cemetery, down the hill from the Tomb of the Unknown Soldier. After the twenty-one-gun salute, our mother pinned his colonel's insignia to our jacket lapels. I carried the flag from his coffin to the car. For two weeks I stayed home with my mother, helping her write thank-you notes on small white cards with black borders; one afternoon, as I was affixing postage to the square, plain envelopes, she looked at me across the dining room table. "You and Davis are all I have left," she said. She went into the kitchen and came back. "Tomorrow," she said, gathering up the note cards, "you'll have to go to school." Mornings I wandered the long corridors alone, separated from Denny by the fate of our last names, which had cast us into different homerooms and daily schedules. Lunchtimes we sat together in silence in the rear of the cafeteria. Afternoons, just before gym class, I went to the Health Room, where, lying on a cot, I'd imagine the Phys. Ed. coach calling my name from the class roll, and imagine my name, unclaimed, unanswered to, floating weightlessly away, like a balloon that one jumps to grab hold of but that is already out of reach. Then I'd hear the nurse dial the telephone. "He's sick again," she'd say. "Can you come pick him up?" At home I helped my mother empty my father's highboy. "No, we want to save that," she said when I folded his uniform into a huge brown bag that read GOODWILL IN-DUSTRIES; I wrapped it in a plastic dry-cleaner's bag and hung it in the hall closet.

After my father's death my relationship to my mother's things grew yet more complex, for as she retreated into her grief, she left behind only her mute objects as evidence of her life among us: objects that seemed as lonely and vulnerable as she was, objects that I longed to console, objects with which I longed to console myself—a tangled gold chain, thrown in frustration on the mantel; a wineglass, its rim stained with lipstick, left unwashed in the sink. Sometimes at night Davis and I heard her prop her pillow up against her bedroom wall, lean back heavily, and tune her radio to a call-in show: *"Nightcaps, what are you thinking at this late hour?"* Sunday evenings, in order to help her prepare for the next day's job hunt, I stood over her beneath the bare basement bulb, the same bulb that first illuminated my father's jaundice. I set her hair, slicking each wet strand with gel and rolling it, inventing gossip that seemed to draw us together, a beautician and his customer.

"You have such pretty hair," I'd say.

"At my age, don't you think I should cut it?" She was almost fifty.

"No, never."

That fall Denny and I were caught. One evening my mother noticed something out of place in her closet. (Perhaps now that she no longer shared it, she knew where every belt and scarf should have been.)

I was in my bedroom doing my French homework, dreaming of one day visiting Au Printemps, the store my teacher spoke of so excitedly as she played us the Edith Piaf records that she had brought back from France. In the mirror above my desk I saw my mother appear at my door.

"Get into the living room," she said. Her anger made her small, reflected body seem taut and dangerous.

In the living room Davis was watching TV with Uncle Joe, our father's brother, who sometimes came to take us fishing. Uncle Joe was lying in our father's La-Z-Boy recliner.

"There aren't going to be any secrets in this house," she said. "You've been in my closet. What were you doing there?"

"No, we weren't," I said. "We were watching TV all afternoon."

"*We?* Was Denny here with you? Don't you think I've heard about that? Were you and Denny going through my clothes? Were you wearing them?"

"No, Mom," I said.

"Don't lie!" She turned to Uncle Joe, who was staring at us. "Make him stop! He's lying to me!"

She slapped me. Although I was already taller than she, she slapped me over and over, slapped me across the room until I was backed against the TV. Davis was motionless, afraid. But Uncle Joe jumped up and stood between my mother and me, holding her until her rage turned to sobs. "I can't be both a mother and a father," she said to him. "I can't, I can't do it." I could not look at Uncle Joe, who, although he was protecting me, did not know I was lying.

She looked at me. "We'll discuss this later," she said. "Get out of my sight."

We never discussed it. Denny was outlawed. I believe, in fact, that it was I who suggested he never be allowed in our house again. I told my mother I hated him. I do not think I was lying when I said this. I truly hated him—hated him, I mean, for being me.

For two or three weeks Denny tried to speak with me at the bus stop, but whenever he approached, I busied myself with kids I barely knew. After a while Denny found a new best friend, Lee, a child despised by everyone, for Lee was "effeminate." His clothes were too fastidious; he often wore his cardigan over his shoulders, like an old woman feeling a chill. Sometimes, watching the street from our picture window, I'd see Lee walking toward Denny's house. "What a queer," I'd say to whoever might be listening. "He walks like a *girl*." Or sometimes, at the junior high school, I'd see him and Denny walking down the corridor, their shoulders pressed together as if they were telling each other secrets, or as if they were joined in mutual defense. Sometimes when I saw them, I turned quickly away, as though I'd forgotten something important in my locker. But when I felt brave enough to risk rejection, for I belonged to no group, I joined Bucky Trueblood's gang, sitting on the radiator in the main hall, and waited for Lee and Denny to pass us. As Lee and Denny got close, they stiffened and looked straight ahead.

"Faggots," I muttered.

I looked at Bucky, sitting in the middle of the radiator. As Lee and Denny passed, he leaned forward from the wall, accidentally disarranging the practiced severity of his clothes, his jeans puckering beneath his tooled belt, the breast pocket of his T-shirt drooping with the weight of a pack of Pall Malls. He whistled. Lee and Denny flinched. He whistled again. Then he leaned back, the hard lines of his body reasserting themselves, his left foot striking a steady beat on the tile floor with the silver V tap of his black loafer.

LOUIE CREW

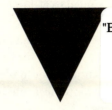

"Ben's Eyes." Lavender Mansions: 40 Contemporary Lesbian and Gay Stories. An Anthology edited by Irene Zahava. Boulder, Colorado: Westview Press, 1994. Pages 23-29.

BEN'S EYES

I LOVED GRANDMAMA'S. I loved the tin roof, the smell of the wood stove, the taste of the metal dipper, the tiny roof above the well, the tomatoes we picked and ate off the vine, the rope swing that hung on the tall hickory, but most of all Ben's eyes.

Long before six others and I integrated the high school in Stewartville, Georgia, or before I became the drum-major and broke the heart of the white football captain, back before I was a teenager, when we lived on an Air Force Base in Texas, I used to spend two months of every summer at Grandmama's house back in Clinton County, in South Georgia.

My older sister Hattie, 13, teased me before everyone as her "country kid-brother." She went to Georgia with me the first time, but didn't like the single room house, the bed she had to share with Grandmama, the goats in the yard, the weeding and the hoeing, collard greens every day of the week, no radio and the six mile walk, one-way, to the movies. She stood it for about three weeks and then cried until Grandmama let her return early to "Texas civilization and the twentieth century," as Hattie boasted to her girl friends at our large play-ground on the air base.

Ben was my older cousin, sixteen or seventeen, and he had gorgeous round, bedroom eyes, with long lashes like the kind women pay to have made up false. Ben's face was a richer black than mine, with not even a hint of tan. He had generous cheeks and a lean chin. His strong red lips could not conceal the slight smile he kept as I stared at him for minutes at a time, not just when we rested in the shade to guzzle water from the mason jar, but even while I rode with him on the rented single-seater, plowing Grandmama's field. I probably wasn't much help, but he made me feel that I was.

We watched for any rocks down the row. "Go get it, Cleveland," he would squeeze me, and I'd jump down, run ahead and put it in the big drum which we had hung on the back of the tractor for our collection. At the end of the row, we would add these to the border, built up for more than 50 years around this field. Yet and still this field continued to yield new chunks with each plowing.

"God makes them during the winter," Ben told me.

Ben had dropped out of school at 14, but anything he said convinced me, at least at the time that he said it. Most of the time he just sat silent, concentrating on the noisy tractor. Still short enough not to block his view, I braced myself on the narrow metal strip meant for his feet, and leaned against Ben's legs, just looking and looking and looking.

Ben was Grandmama's only help. Ben's mother, my aunt, and his father both had been killed in separate automobile wrecks, a week apart, when Ben was 13.

"Fancy. Mighty fancy," my mother used to tell me about them, "but a bit dangerous too."

Grandmama kept a picture of Ben's mama and daddy on the chifforobe near where she slept in the room. Ben's mama, my daddy's sister, a pleasantly fat woman with a broad, pretty face, sang the blues at backwoods clubs for black farmers all over South Georgia. His daddy, lean and less noticeable, more or less tagged along, or so I thought then from what Grandmama said whenever I asked about the picture.

Later, while at Stewartville High and no longer going to the farm for summers, I learned that Ben's daddy's accident had happened cause the Clinton County police had driven him off the road at high speed. They used the six cases of bonded whiskey in his trunk to prove that he was into "big crime."

Ben's sister and brother had already grown up and moved away when the two accidents happened. The sister worked as a hair-burner up in Macon, and the other brother worked for a packing house in Tallahassee.

Ben didn't talk about his people much, nor did he seem interested when Grandmama would answer my questions. While Grandmama and I cleaned up after supper, he usually sat over by the kerosene lamp looking at a *Jet* magazine, or studied his mustache with a pair of trimmers and a small hand mirror.

"You gonna break some gal's heart iffen you don't stop trying to be so pretty," Grandmama would tease him; "God done already give you sexy eyes. Why don't you leave well enough alone?"

Ben would laugh and continue to groom.

After we'd put away everything, sometimes we lolled around on the porch, or swang. In the top of the hickory, Ben had built a treehouse back when he had been my age, but I never got to see the inside of the treehouse. Long before I ever came to visit, Bessy Craddock, the girl who lived at the next house down the road, stepped on a weak limb, fell, and broke her arm. After that, Grandmama laid down the law: the hickory tree was only for swinging.

Sometimes I seem to convolute all evenings into one, so much did I enjoy our times in that swing, but I remember one particular evening as distinct, just for its sunset—dark reds and oranges, and then a streak of royal purple appeared just about as fast as Ben blinked his eyes. He sat on the seat and I sat in his lap, nose almost touching nose, my legs tight around his hips, his large hands clasping my ribs, my arms thrown loosely over his shoulders, as we swang higher and higher and higher. I did not grasp. I knew he held me.

Grandmama went to bed early, got up early. Sunrise. Sunset. That's what her "early" meant. "You young 'ens can do as you please, but if you want to live as long as I have, you'd better be payin' attention. Leastaways, don't disturb my rest with no kerosene lamp. Those folks' pictures in *Jet* seem a bit highfallutin' anyways ..." She would natter on until she gave us the cue: "Now I'll get into my night clothes."

Ben and I would dutifully step outside. When we came back in, we'd make our way in the dark to our own side of the room. Even without a moon, starlight sufficed. Each of us had a special chair to hang our clothes on. I slipped into some short pajamas Mama had made for me, but hot as Georgia stays at night in summer, Ben slept in his birthday suit.

Some nights, after we'd swung, Ben would not come to bed at once, but would go down the road to see Bessy and her brothers. One night a storm came up unexpectedly after he had left and I had gone to bed. It thundered and lightninged something terrible. Grandmama snored through it all, but I lay awake at least until well after midnight, listening to the rain batter our tin roof, looking at the green hands on Grandmama's wind-up alarm clock, wondering whether Ben was dry.

I awoke when I heard the tractor revving in the dark. He had stayed in the Craddock's barn until the lightning stopped, but had come back to put the tractor under the shed.

A few minutes later, the room deadly dark without even starlight, I felt cool air rush over me. He even sounded wet. I heard him sniffle as he closed the door. I heard him drip as he unlaced his shoes. I heard him peel off his socks. I heard a chair scrape the floor slightly as he tiptoed past it. I heard the zipper. I heard his buckle jiggle on the wooden floor. I heard him breathe and knew he must be arcing his t-shirt over his shoulders. It slapped the chair gently. I heard underwear ping his knees.

Then silence. An interminable silence. Even under the covers I shivered knowing he stood there wet, exposed, although I could see only his blackness shadow the slightly lighter darkness of the room.

I feared my eyes might glow in the dark like the hands on the clock, that he might know that I stared, so I slitted them. I held my breath to hear him breathing, slowly, evenly. A board squeaked slightly. I expected our bed to tilt to his weight, but still he stood there. It seemed an eternity.

When he did get in, he moved to me at once, not after he was asleep, as he usually did. His wet chest sent goosebumps down my back. His thick thighs seemed a bit drier at my hips. He sighed pleasantly through his nose as I warmed him. "Sleep well, my little heater; sleep well," he whispered softly.

I didn't love the outhouse. That's about the only place where I ever thought of Hattie and her "Texas civilization" during the entire summer. Hattie had made it worse, by telling me even before we went to Georgia that first time together, "Snakes lay down there in the holes just waiting to bite any ass black enough and delicious enough to sit there, particularly if they decides to sit there too long. And the spiders. You just look up to the ceiling. They be waitin' for you, country bumpkin!"

Mama had told me I should try not to use nasty public restrooms except for liquids, and to plan my days so I'd be near home when I had to go. So the first time that I went to Georgia, already warned by Hattie, I fixed my mind to see the outhouse as a public restroom. When I peeked at it and saw that it was a 2-seater, that cinched it. Besides, the shack stood separate from Grandmama's house. How much more public could you get? I decided to wait all summer until I got back to Texas before I would go again, except for liquids.

By the third day, I must have looked mighty ashen. After supper Grandmama asked, "Boy, you feelin' all right?"

"Yessum," I lied.

"You don't look it. Have you vomited or something?"

"Nome."

"Ben, you be out there with him all day on the tractor. Has this child seemed sick to you?"

"The boy probably just taking time to get used to eatin real food," Ben said, lost in *Jet*.

"You regular?" Grandmama asked.

Hattie snickered. "Have you gone down with the creepy, crawly snakes every day?" she asked. She had not yet thrown her screaming fit to escape.

"Hush your mouth, girl, or I'll creepy, crawly you," Grandmama said to Hattie. Ben laughed like he was on my side. I bowed my head.

"Answer me, boy," Grandmama said gently.

She finally got out of me that I had been too scared to go. Grandmama wouldn't hear a word of it when I explained that Mama had told me never to use a public restroom.

"Ben, you go down there with him and don't either of you come back until he's done a job, you hear?! Land's sake, all this Texas civilization will be the death of him for sure."

I thought I could not do it with someone else there. At least the restroom at school had partitions for those that dared to use them. Here Ben's thigh touched mine and I nearly choked on the cigar which he lit, "to scare away everything," he said. "Take your time, Cleveland."

It began to get dark fast. We left the door open for the clean air, and looked far down the field where we'd plowed all day long.

"I didn't know that you is circumcised," Ben said.

"What?"

"I didn't know that you is circumcised," he repeated.

"What's that?"

He reached over and touched the head. "That," he said.

"What's 'circumcised'? Ain't you?"

"Nope. See."

He held his up into the twilight. "Pull back the skin like this," he said. "Your's been cut that way by the doctor soon as you born."

I looked at his, then at mine. "Is that why yours hard and mine soft?" I asked.

"Soft?" he asked. I had not noticed the hard knot mine had made.

"Why the doctors do that to me?" I asked.

"Beats me," he said. "Must have something to do with Texas civilization."

I did my job easily now.

"Don't be 'fraid, Cleveland. Just tell me when you want me here witchya. Besides, see this stick." He leaned and reached just outside the door for an old broom handle he kept there. "You just take this pole and beat on the side before you ever come in here. That'll scare away anything that might harm you. Don't you listen to Hattie or everwho talks that way. Nobody can't make no sissie outa man like you."

I did not fear the outhouse anymore. Yet and still I waited most times until I knew he was going so I could go at the same time.

I liked being with Ben even better outdoors on the tractor, leaning against his lap, or in the swing, or taking a break in the shade at the far end of the field, or having him snuggle up after he thought I'd gone to sleep. One night while he was still out, I took my pajamas and hid them on the floor next to the wall under the bed, so Grandmama wouldn't see them and remember that I'd had them on.

One day right there on the tractor I took mine out and studied it. "Why the doctors do that to me?"

"They didn't hurt it none. It's as good as mine," Ben said.

I felt him grow stiff. I turned and tried to straddle him as in the swing.

"Just a minute, child, lessen we kill ourselves on this here machine." He idled it at the end of the row. Far at the other end clean white bedclothes whipped in the sun. In the shade I looked long into Ben's eyes before and after I inspected uncircumcision.

Before Daddy left the air force, we got stationed back in Georgia. When Grandmama fell sick, one of my aunts moved in to take care of her, cause Ben was away in the army. They did not have time or space for children then, and I was too busy with my paper route to laze away a summer in the country.

By the time I took home ec at Stewartville High, my sisters and brothers had gotten used to me, and were plenty proud when I brought home a national prize for one of my recipes. Besides, I led the parade and had the captain of the football team sneaking over to see me four nights a week.

After I graduated, I took up modeling in the North. I heard that Ben had married, not Bessy Craddock, but a jazz singer named Eula Hines, from Macon. My Mamma said Eula was as much a looker as Ben's mama had been, and that she and Ben lived just as dangerously as Ben's mama and daddy had.

So I had not seen Ben for about eighteen years when Grandmama died. I wanted to bring my lover with me, but he decided it wouldn't be right to make our lives upstage theirs, especially at a time of grief. Anyways, Mama and Daddy had already met him and liked him a lot. I can't believe he would have surprised the others. But I didn't insist, since probably he would have been bored. He didn't grow up in the South.

Neighbors and family came all over. They brought at least twenty kinds of deviled eggs, ten styles of fried chicken, and as many more of cornbread and collard greens, plus platter after platter of other good eatins. They laid it out on long picnic tables in the pecan grove between the church and the cemetery. Eula's band played gospel music all day inside, before the sermon and the burial in the late afternoon. Since the church was too small to hold all of us at once, we went to and fro, from feast to the funeral in shifts.

About one o'clock, Ben himself arrived. He had filled out lots more, but was still muscle, not fat. I recognized him first by his eyes.

"She was a good woman, Cleveland; a good woman. A real loss to the world."

All those outside came to greet him. Then Ben went in for some of the music. When he came out again, I eased to the same side of the food table so that I could strike up a conversation with at least a touch of privacy. I wanted to get off somewhere to ourselves, maybe alone in Grandmama's room, so I could tell him how much it meant to have learned about myself from someone who loved me, who was gentle, who taught me how to scare away the snakes. Before I met my lover, I discovered many people, women and men, who didn't seem to know that you can also love the person you hold through the night.

I never had heard "gay" when Ben and I were together. When I hit puberty, I needed the word to describe myself, but I never thought Ben was. I still think he is not. But I knew that he had loved me when we did those things together.

"You remember the outhouse?" I asked.

"Cleveland, you were one scared little boy, yes indeed!" he said, and moved on down the table to get some ribs.

"You remember the night you came back from Bessy Craddock's all dripping wet?"

"No. I can't say as I do. Which time?"

"You remember the swing and the tractor?"

"What about 'em?"

"You don't remember?"

"Cleveland, you've grown up a fine young man. I always said you'd go farther than most of us. You may have begun scrawny, but like the turtle and the rabbit, you passed us all!"

"You really don't remember, do you?"

"Hey, little brother, what happened a long time ago is not important. Don't go troubling yourself." He forked a deviled egg, nibbled it, and lifted his chin to catch some yolk.

"Man, it sure is good to see you!" He said it like he meant it.

With his eyes, he indicated that perhaps we ought to mingle with the others. I could not find a way to thank him.

WILLIAM HAYWOOD HENDERSON

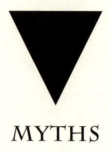

MYTHS

1

WHEN I WAS STILL a young boy, my mother moved us off the reservation to the edge of town, out where the only thing beyond us was dry buffalo grass full of tin cans and bedsprings and socks dried in stiff clumps. I walked out in the long, early morning shadows and looked across the fields to the line of mountains that ran toward our old place. Stickers poked through my soles—I never learned the magic that protects your soles if you're Indian. On open ground, I faced away from the sun and shifted my little hips. I did a snake dance on ten-foot legs.

The air was clean and empty. I could hear a car coming up the road from miles away, see the silver gleams across the brown flat fields and wonder who it might be. For a few months it had been a federal worker with a white shirt, yellowed mother-of-pearl buttons, and a tie so tacky he should have been hung by it, choked blue. He'd smell as if he'd just eaten a short stack of pancakes with an ice scream scoop of whipped butter and a lake of blueberry syrup. He'd say, "Morning," as if we hadn't figured that out yet. He'd say, "Just want to make sure you all are eating well and so forth."

Mother waited at the back door. She smelled like corn. Like beans. She would watch me approach, then back into shadow, and enter sunlight again at the kitchen table. She'd sit there, quiet, unmoved, as if her hair wouldn't go gray.

She painted her lips. I took the red, painted my own, and stood beside her in front of the mirror to make sure we looked alike. She said, "You're mine."

I said, "We could be the same person."

She laughed. "You think so? I think maybe you have a lot of your father in you. But you have me too. My color."

"And Father? Tell me again."

"Your father is a beautiful man."

"A beautiful man."

"With yellow hair."

"Yellow."

"And blue eyes."

"Blue."

"And he came from across the ocean."

"The ocean."

"And he loved your mother."

"Loved you."

"And I love my baby."

"Love me."

"And you'll be the best of your mother and the best of your father, so nothing can hurt you. Nothing in this world."

"Nothing."

Through dry mornings, we ate with the window open. A fly buzzed around the food or landed on the edge of the orange juice pitcher, if we had orange juice, and the warming breeze brought in shreds of cottonwood fluff, the only sound the song of a bird or a car from far down the road. The cars turned off the state route, took the curve fast past the yellow warning markers, and came straight and humming along the road as if there were nothing but morning and horizon ahead, nothing but sun always rising and hills like temples to be skirted.

For hours, I'd stand in the shade beside the house and listen for the whine of tires on the gray asphalt. In the next car would be a lady, maybe one of my mother's employers. She'd have feet that could take a shoe with a heel and eyebrows so perfect they'd seem painted. I drew pages full of eyebrows. She'd drift to a stop in front of the house, and the grass would bunch against the door. I'd lean in at the window from the passenger side and inhale the scent of her powder. She'd turn to me.

"Aren't you a beautiful boy," she'd say. "You come with me. You'll be mine."

2

People took our picture. Traffic flowed through town all summer, heading up into the mountains, over toward the national parks. The people wore plaid shorts. Mother and I had matching ponytails, a spot of turquoise on a wrist or finger. We held tightly to each other's hand as we were backed up against a storefront. A man ran his hand over my hair, shook my shoulder, and said, "Ain't you cute as the devil."

Mother decided to take me to church. "A good balance for what you are, what me and your father are." The night's cold moisture evaporated around us as we walked through the stark summer morning, down to the state route then straight toward the big square shadows of the buildings. Flies fought in the air over the trash bin beside the A & W. A truck passed, rumbling slowly, the only vehicle on the road this early, waiting to rev out into the vacant miles beyond town. I looked back. A few round clouds sat on the spine of the mountains. Cottonwoods shimmered along the river.

We sat at the back of the long, narrow room and pulled our shirts out from our damp skin. There was no clean light—our hands, laps, the necks of the family sitting in front of us, everything, was colored through pictures in the windows. A white man in a silver dress held his arms out toward the people, his fingers pulled into fists, and he spoke in a deep, tight voice, not letting a sound miss our ears.

"... the wicked bend their bow, they make ready their arrow upon the string, that they may privily shoot at the upright in heart."

In the building behind the church, I sat at the end of a table and listened to the woman with the gold cross and the stiff, copper hair tell us a story about fire raining in a plain and burning away cities and people and plants. I thought I smelled sage burning. If my mother were turned to salt, would she be a stack of the pink mineral blocks the ranchers put out for their herds? Maybe she would be white and pure.

The woman bent at my shoulder to hand me paper and crayons. She smelled of flowers and cigarettes. She said, "Do you know how to draw?"

"Of course."

"Okay. Let's see what you can draw to show us the story of Lot."

The other children hunched over their drawings. I tried to imagine what the men of the city wanted with Lot's two visitors. They wanted to know them— they wanted to know them enough to get struck blind. They didn't want Lot's daughters.

"What do we have here?" the woman said, taking my drawing. "Where did you learn this?"

I reached for the paper. She held it higher, glanced down at me. I pulled at her elbow, stood on my toes. She jerked out of my touch.

3

My grandmother's house on the reservation was a whitewashed square at the edge of a gully. Beyond the bare dirt that surrounded the house, prickly pear, sage, and short grass grew on clumps of their own refuse.

I'd sit by the back door and watch for Uncle Gordon. Granite spires rose around a fissure in the face of the mountains. I took a scrap of paper and drew petroglyphs for the walls of that high gate.

Copulating waterbugs. Strings of stars tangled. Figures frozen in dance, in flight.

My grandmother had dark teeth. She took me to where I would sleep during my visit, pulling me past walls hung with heavy blankets. Spirits watched me from the pottery designs and the bunches of herbs hanging from the ceiling. My room had no windows and smelled of tanned hides. I could reach out in the dark and stroke a deer's back or run my fingers through a bird's slick feathers. The animals waited with me. They heard what I heard, the sounds focused in the complete blackness.

It wasn't my language the adults spoke, the calm, slow expressions, Gran almost in a whisper, punctuated now and then by a clucking laugh or a light slap on her thigh, and Uncle Gordon talking as if he were about to cry, unable to say anything harsh. I imagined his lips moving. He would close his eyes as he spoke, as if his voice came from his sleep. The edges of his body—the shoulders solid, and his limbs loose and gangly and soft. His voice fell into the rhythm of footsteps.

He would follow the tracks of an antelope up through a stand of aspen, across rocky barren stretches, around the edge of a pond. When he finally approached the antelope, it watched his zigzag from cover to cover, and it stood its ground, waiting, curious. He stopped close and set his arrow, keeping eye contact. He said, "Please. I won't hurt you," just before he killed it.

Nothing moved in the house. I tried to sleep but the sound of my own breathing made me kick my legs, back and forth, beneath the blankets. The dead air against my face forced me down into my own warmth, away from the silence.

I imagined my uncle standing outside the house, the sun hazy on his arms, his long fingers, calves. He grew smaller out in the fast-moving shadows of clouds. I tried to keep him close to me so that I could see the rough skin on his elbows or his profile if he glanced to the side. Long strands of hair fell between his shoulder blades.

He walks toward me, and I wait in the shade beside the house, looking out into the glare where he moves. With the sun behind him I can't see his expression, just the mass of his body, so much larger than mine, like an idle space out in the rush of rising heat. He enters the shadow of the house, stands above me, and his face makes my breathing fast.

Our clothes lay in a heap among the roots of a tree. We slid down over the carpet of pine needles and entered the water. Steam rose around us. Uncle Gordon's prick submerged and floated out from his body.

We sat on the bottom, on the rusted, slick rocks, at the edge of the warm spring, only our faces out in the air. I rolled onto my side, a casual move. Uncle Gordon shifted into my embrace. We rarely talked, just fell to it. Now I was almost as tall as him, and I could hold him under water, throw his weight over.

We spread out on a slope of granite, crumbling black lichen, and water ran off us, pooled under us. The breeze traced along our exposed spines, our necks, between our legs. He flopped his hand onto my back and turned his face toward me. Bits of pebble and lichen clung to his cheek. With his eyes closed, he said, "You should live here. On the reservation. It's the only place."

"I'm not all Indian."

"Of course you are. Every bit I've touched is pure Indian, and I've touched every bit."

"I think about others sometimes. White boys."

"That's not right. You can think of me. You can think of other Indians. That's the only way. Look at what's happened to your mother."

"She's fine. She loved my father."

"Do you love him?"

"I love what I know of him."

"What do you know?"

"He's beautiful. He loved my mother. He was from across the ocean. He gave me my life."

"What life is that?"

"My *life*. My breathing."

"But he's not in you. I'm in you. Your mother's in you. Gran. We can give you the life of our people. You're berdache. You're magic here. That's the only way. With us."

"White boys."

"They're not for you."

"They were for my mother."

"Not for you."

4

Ray. I'd thought of offering him money to pose. I gave him a square of hard cornbread at lunch. He took it without looking up and ate it in three bites. I would have laid my hand out flat on his forehead and pushed his hair out of his face. I would have picked the crud from the corners of his eyes.

My friend Louise was big at a young age. Her breasts moved like dangerous waves inside her clothing. We sat in the fields out past my house and picked stickers from our socks. "All you do is take what you want," she said. "No one is going to put up a fight."

Louise was feeling ballsy. She picked me up in her Dart, red interior, Saturday night, and we headed out along the dark roads, the lights of town always off to the side, obscured, fenceposts flashing past in the headlights. We passed the dump road and pulled onto the shoulder. She shut off the engine, and we sat in darkness, listening to the car settle and pop, smelling the sage and the last of the exhaust fumes. "I can hardly stand it," she said, passing the Schnapps. "The air is so warm, it's like part of your skin. It's got me all tight. I've got to heat up or cool off, fast. I'm in trouble. Help me fix my lipstick."

I held the lighter while she looked at herself in her pocket mirror. Her lips took the greasy red. Then she reached over and placed a red dot on my upper lip, on my lower lip. A final swig of Schnapps.

We started out, across the ditch, through the lines of barbed wire, into the fields of short grass, the scattered humps of sage, the invisible cactus.

"You sure this is right?" I said.

"Never fails. Every Saturday night, all summer. You must know that. They'll all be stoked. I can't believe you haven't been out here before."

We walked in silence, came to the top of a broad, steady slope. The land dropped away in a shallow plain, the horizon a line of distant hills, flattened by the moonlight. At the center, a small flame burned.

As we continued, in step, our arms swinging and almost touching, the flame grew, became a bonfire of crackling dry sage. When we could just begin to see clearly the boys' faces, we knelt behind a low sage.

Bodies moved around the fire, stepped to the cooler, bent at the radio to increase the volume, bring up the bass. Ray, I was sure, in a stiff, off-balance swagger, passed across the fire. He held his arms over his head, his beer bottle glowed through with red from the flames, and then he spun around and shouted, howled, out into the darkness that the fire blinded them all against. His voice was familiar to me, but the howl, taken up now by the other boys, had an alien intensity, something they hadn't shown me, hadn't invited me into. I opened my mouth and tried to imagine the sound rising from my lungs, but all I felt was the dust and smoke blowing through my throat.

"This is it," Louise said, heaving herself up into a squatting position. "See that?" A boy had broken out of the circle of fire and wandered off to the left. "Good luck," she said, and she kissed me on the mouth quickly, stood up, and circled off, skirting the fire, in pursuit. The taste of liquor stung my lips. She faded, was lost, and then the close, huge noise of the bonfire faced me.

I felt heavy on the ground, unable to focus, as if her kiss had hammered my drunkenness straight between my eyes. Forcing myself up, grinding earth into my palms, I squatted there, watching. Another boy broke out and stumbled off to the right. On my feet, I moved quickly, without thought, pursuing, and the steps seemed natural. The moon opened the ground out before me, and I ran, long and wild strides, a hundred yards, and then I slowed, moved up, silently, to the boy, his legs spread in a rocky stance, far out from the music and the light. Another step and I reached around his waist from behind him, pulled his body against mine, ran my lips up his neck.

He arched back into my advance, his hands suddenly on me as he lurched around to face me, pulling my hair out from its ponytail, pulling me down to the ground with him, speaking in urgent commands, but I couldn't be sure of the voice, couldn't pull enough light from the surrounding darkness to recognize the features. He rolled on top of me, his weight and the liquor of his breath falling through me. Pain forced my voice out, but he continued.

Then, for a moment, the touch of flesh, the warm air drifting across us, the rhythm of breathing, my nose pressed into the hollow of his neck, light enough on his face above me that I knew it was Ray, knew suddenly the smell of him, knew he would settle into me slowly, and we would laugh, and his voice and his skin and his life would be close to me.

A sharp pain in my gut, his fist, my shirt yanked out, and the sound of voices. Not my own voice, not Ray's. He wouldn't stop, kept at me, his hard fists. His mouth was open, strange, an animal choking, eyes rolling into its head.

A burning branch, flashlights, approached with a whoop of voices. I fought to wedge myself out from beneath the weight, but my escape was cut off, my hands caught in his hands, legs tangled with his legs. They surrounded us. The light was full. His face, strong, sharp, pulled up from me, descended again. He shouted into me with the crowd's voices. The voices all aimed at me. And I heard nothing I recognized but the crackling of sage, the rich bones consumed by fire.

5

My uncle had always wanted me to live on the reservation with him, but we'd soured our luck. Things don't happen the way you want them.

Mother lets her fingers linger on her breast as she watches herself in the mirror. Her skin seems somehow altered. She closes the front of her cotton blouse—she won't look at herself anymore. She paints her lips, names the window, the door, in English, walks out onto the hot surface of the earth, steps up onto the gray asphalt as if it were a path, walks quickly to town. Inside the woman's house, Mother faces her employer with a strong smile, sets to her task, as if it is natural, as if she likes the scented cleaners, as if she appreciates the money, as if she has something to prove. She polishes white porcelain, tries to ignore her reflection looking up at her, as if it is confused with alien images, strange continents, as if she has betrayed her people, won't look up.

6

Uncle Gordon loved a boy who played on the green fields behind the school. He followed the kid out along the dirt roads. One day, he got courage and caught up with the kid and told him that he had money, that he had come up with a magical name for him, that he could cook and weave. The kid let him. Touch him. Once. Then the kid beat him. Maybe it was my fault. Gordon and me—we had no business being together, uncle and nephew. What could go right for him when we'd already gone wrong? The kid couldn't have known that Gordon was a prize.

Uncle Gordon died. He was in the hospital for a few days before he went. I brought Gran to see him. She rubbed the backs of his hands as they talked, their own language, never harsh. When he died, Gran loosened her braid and her hair came out in a wavy mass on her shoulders. She kept patting his hands. She cried when I drove her and the body back to her house. She cut her hair and ripped a sleeve from her dress, then laid them both at the foot of Uncle Gordon's bed. We dressed him in his Sunday suit, a dark brown cotton with wooden buttons, put his whitest shirt on him, and his red tie with the American flag clip. He seemed handsome, dressed as he was in the photo on his dresser, with me beside him in my mortarboard, high school graduation.

After a day of waiting—my mother wouldn't come onto the reservation—Gran and I took the dead body up the hill to a hole I'd dug. We got him down in there and Gran put her cut hair in his suit pockets before we closed him off. Then we piled on rocks and some thorny branches to keep the coyotes from digging.

Gran and I walked along the foothills to the hot spring and took a swim, rubbed each other's backs and arms with black dirt from the bottom, rinsed off and then dried in the breeze.

We sat at the grave each day and Gran cried. At night she burned some leaves in a clay pot. She only made a little food. No one came to visit. One morning, when she had finished crying, she brought me a bowl with thick red liquid in it and asked me to paint her. I spread the color on her face and hair. She sat out in the sun all day. Then she braided what was left of her hair.

7

A berdache would dress like he wasn't male and he wasn't female. A man would take a berdache as a wife as if it were something special.

A berdache was magic, the center of ceremonies, making rain, healing, spiritual power. To ensure a good crop or rain showers, take a berdache, at night preferably, and light a fire. Put the berdache in the center of a circle and bring out the warriors, start the drums, young warriors. They start dancing around the berdache, and then they screw the berdache to make the magic.

Not like I've ever made it rain or brought anyone luck.

Uncle Gordon and I wandered slowly down from the hot spring. I placed my arm around his shoulders, brushed my lips against his ear. Broken veins formed a delicate web on his nose. He laughed. Aluminum glinted along the creek.

DONNA ALLEGRA

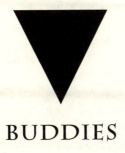

BUDDIES

Corey leaning against my locker—no pants to protect me now, just thighs glistening cold cream and the T-shirt damp from the shower. New wetness creeps in under my arms, dribbles between my breasts and throbs anew from the heart atop my thighs. I dodge her look and let a haze drift in to film my eyes.

"What for?"

She insists with questions. She means to say: I don't want you to go.

"I need to find something out. For me."

"You don't have to hang with them. Let's get something to eat and then go home—your place." Her smile—African sweet with a stop-off in Jamaica for mangoes and banana—knows honey catches more flies than vinegar.

"C'mon Boo. This is silly."

Almost persuaded, I remain stubborn. She's right. No need to seek answers in a bar when Life is handing me the next question. I'd like to pass on this dance. Corey blocking an exit frames the open door if I can find the courage to take on the step.

I consider wrestling across her to my clothes and circling around my nakedness. Nothing new to that play—and it'd prop me with a pose, contain my hands, mask what my eyes might tell before I'm ready with words. We're touchy-feely friends, not sissy-girl style, but buddy-type hands-on. I want to break the tension and shift us to another plane. Too much danger plays in this arena. The truth I hold captive must live for her too, but if Corey turns to salt, who can ever again slake my tears?

Other people manage to talk to each other, to deliberately weave out shared tapestries. How to make a change in our pattern? It'd be so simple to put out: I want you and if I can't have you, I'll find someone else—and it's going to be a woman.

I throw up a lie, still draped in a fear without textures I can touch and then reason through to undisguised acts.

"You my ace, right? But tonight I'm hanging with the girls—that is, if you let me get even halfway dressed."

She doesn't let up for any play. This ground is so shaky, I just don't know my way around. Usually she takes the bully stance when it's clear we're both agreed. I dug how she handled the dealings to make us always a pair. Our friends still say, "You can't have one without the other."

We don't speak about caring—it's just there, unmentionable. Like when I took that fall today. From street ball, I'm pretty much used to going for myself, but Corey's taught me there's also glory in sharing. I'd sent her the pass when my left foot unhinged a great show of team work. She threw the ball away, leaving her fastbreak lay-up, helped me down court and cradled me from the others. I couldn't forbid the tears, protesting to the high heavens against the injustice of another sprain. When I got up from nothing too much more than strained pride—I'd tripped over my own two feet—she kissed my forehead with everyone watching.

I want to hold her for real—not just on the occasion of accidents or horseplay. I want to touch from an upfront connection that's clearcut and not disguised, yet I hold back, afraid to speak words that ask plainly.

And now, she doesn't budge from her track—no sign that she scouts the path that'd let us both run free. I know my May-born bull, but something else shifts inside that she's not telling. I stay in hiding, too; tease with the truth, careful not to land too close.

"Hey, I always come back to you."

No reply: doubt marks the bad girl of Brooklyn. I search her eyes on this round, allowing space for her move. Two of my fingers trace her lips, a necklace line, then surprise me at the buttons on her shirt.

Her kiss surprises me much more. Life becomes right in small pieces that fit themselves together when I can't manage the moves. Clean tastes live in her mouth—they're fresh and warm as I explore the new land she's opened to me.

"BJ. This is just about you and me. I'm not that way, but I ..."

"Barbara Jean—you ready girl?"

I buckle against the interruption. We take it in and move apart carefully. Corey hands me the pants, has buttoned up when Sharon reaches our aisle. I still shudder inside.

"So what's the word, girly?"

"I'm, uh, not ..."

"We're coming. BJ has to finish dressing. How far away's this bar?"

"All right Corey! I was really hoping you'd break down and come. It's just through the park and down two blocks."

Walking through the park, the group of us fill the air with laughter and un-conquered spirit. Finals are over. May green looks like full-grown summer. I hang quiet by Corey; Sharon, Jess, and Kath argue about the game we lost to City.

"I don't care what you say, bitch. I was beautiful. My magnificent left hand worked wonders."

"I'm not saying you didn't look good, girlfriend. I'm saying we lost the game because so many of us had such good-looking moments. Posing all alone. Leaving the team behind. You know what I'm saying?"

I half-listen. They stop to light up some herb. I don't smoke, but Sharon al-ways passes to me. Corey motions for me to shotgun and while she holds the belt loops at my waist, I wonder what the others think about what we are to each other.

If anyone calls Sharon, Jess, or Kath gay, they'll shake your hand and say thank-you, just like if you point out they're Black. I'm not that bold. I've started talking about maybe being bi, but that's just a cover from people jump-ing too hard on my head.

They finish up the joint as we near the west edge of the park. Corey's leaning on my shoulder, counting stars. I nudge her to brace up for trouble heading our way: the hustler coming towards us looks totally off the wall. The other guys had just called out their wares and let us pass on through when no one was buying, but this fella isn't picking up on vibes. He's giving the once-over like we're supposed to drop everything and pay homage to him.

"Young ladies. Hold up a minute there, y'all. I got something for ya."

For such a puny-looking guy, he sure was bold about latching onto Corey's arm. In all fairness, I suppose, he couldn't know she wasn't a friendly type who'd welcome strange men she didn't invite onto her bodily parts. Corey's one of those baby-sweetfaced children, but she is still a strong-looking heifer. Muscles show up loud and clear when she wears a coat and flaming gold plums twinkled from her arms and shoulders under the T-shirt she wore now. The build alone would measure off most people's distance, and her mouth has killed a lot of bricks.

"Get the fuck off me before I kick your motherfucking teeth in, fool."

"Oh wow, you a big tough bionic woman—but you ain't no man yet, baby. Lookee here, y'all ..."

"You better chill out, dude."

"I got something right here to make you change up off that bull-dagger shit, momma."

I'm almost glad it turned out the dude could run. Corey laid him flat on his butt and I'd moved in behind to jump hard on his case. She suffers from a temperamental nature and I've often had to make up for slack in her tough tone, but my girl is swift behind feeling. As far as the guy was concerned, it wasn't him personally, so I really would've felt bad getting my shit off on his ass for all the dudes who felt they had the right to just impose themselves when they scope on a woman without a man. This one had instinctive good sense about high-tailing it out to the fountain right quick. He probably didn't even notice the bunch of us readying to get down.

"I'll say one thing for you Corey; with you around, nobody has to worry about being insulted."

"Yeah, with me and my temper, you will be respected. Or else dead."

Inside the bar, touches we'd ordinarily give lie stilled and left behind. No arm cradles my neck, no playful hand rests in my back pocket, no lap pulls me to sit down. She leans against a wall, her body cut off from me, no more to circle the fond and sweet trails of fire up my back now that we're in this place where women do touch openly and speak desire out loud. Struck suddenly shy, both of us have turned strangers to each other. Yet these women look like us, as if we'd all been dropped from trees of the same dense forest.

The fast records have played out and some women choose one another for the slow ones. I think how nice it'd be to hold her, to rock on Smokey's "Ooh, baby, baby." I want to so bad, what makes it so hard to ask? There's nothing I could lose: stepping on new land yields more ground for the two of us to cover.

"Dance?"

Her look begs off and would forbid, but I coax, then insist. She consents with a frown unsure and not far from shame, but she comes along. We didn't stop after Smokey, continue into the Stylistics' "La la means I love you."

I guide her around my center like a lullaby, kiss her forehead as earlier she'd reached out for me. I find her neck, her cheek. Her mouth is mine to open and I dip in, searching. I don't care who sees us. This is my dance and I don't let her pull away. I hold the woman I've asked, keeping her close. I hold to the one who's been in my corner, who goes where I lead, and yes, I've doubted, but now I know: who'll stand by me and stay.

CEREMONIES

I STOOD BEFORE HIM GRINNING, my undershorts and pants were down around my knees. I trembled and panted as he stroked me. After weeks of being coaxed and teased to come by, I had finally succumbed to George's suggestions. I had sneaked up to the store very early that morning, before it opened, after my mother left for work.

The sexual hunger that would eventually illuminate my eyes began then. I was a skinny little fourteen-year-old Black boy, growing up in a ghetto that had not yet suffered the fatal wounds and injuries caused by drugs and Black-on-Black crime.

My neighborhood, my immediate homespace, was an oasis of strivers. A majority of the families living on my block owned their homes. My sexual curiosity would have blossomed in any context, but in Southeast Washington, D.C., where I grew up, I had to carefully allow my petals to unfold. If I had revealed them too soon they would surely have been snatched away, brutalized, and scattered down alleys. I was already alert enough to know what happened to the flamboyant boys at the school who were called "sissies" and "faggots." I could not have endured then the violence and indignities they often suffered.

George was at least thirty years older than I, tall, and slightly muscular beneath his oversized work clothes which consisted of khakis, a cotton short-sleeved shirt, and a white apron. He wore black work boots similar to those of construction workers. Many of the boys in the neighborhood teased him viciously, but I hadn't understood before the morning he and I were together just what motivated them to be cruel and nasty by turn. At that time, I didn't know that George had initiated most of the boys I knew, and some of their older brothers, one by one, into the pleasures of homo sex.

Only months before my visit to him that April morning, I had roamed the parking lot of a nearby country bar—my adolescent desire drove me out there one night, and one night only—discreetly asking the predominately white patrons if they would let me suck their dicks for free. My request was never fulfilled because I believe the men were shocked that I would so boldly solicit them. I was lucky no one summoned the police to come for me. I was lucky I wasn't dragged off to some nearby wooded area and killed.

George was a white man. My initiation into homo sex was guided by the hands of a white man. The significance of this racial context was not lost on me, but it wasn't a concern strong enough to check my desire. For weeks George had whispered he wanted to suck my dick. Catching me alone in the store or responding to my request for a particular product, he would quickly serve me, seizing the opportunity to whisper in my ear. *And I was listening.*

Eventually I went to the store on pretense, requesting something I knew they wouldn't have, such as a specific brand of soap or floor wax, just so he would wait on me and whisper. If we had been caught when we finally began fucking, the law would have charged him with molesting and sodomizing me as a minor because of my age, but the law would not have believed that I wanted him to suck my dick. I wanted him to touch me. I wanted to fuck his ass. I, willingly, by the volition of my own desires, engaged in acts of sexual passion, somewhat clumsily, but nonetheless sure of my decision to do so.

When George liberated his equally swollen cock from his pants it sprang out engorged with blood and fire. The head of it was deep pink in color. I was startled to see that the hair surrounding it was as red as the hair on his head.

George again lowered himself to eye level with my cock and drew me into his mouth once more. It was hard to tell which of us was enjoying the cock sucking more. Suddenly, he pulled his mouth off my wet shaft, got up off his knees and hurried to the front of the store. He promptly returned with a short stack of grocery bags, newspapers, and a small jar of Vaseline.

"You're gonna fuck me." It wasn't a statement or a command from him, it was a fact neither of us could turn away from.

After spreading the newspaper and bags on the floor behind the deli counter to create a makeshift paper pallet, George opened the Vaseline, scooped out some with his index finger, and pushed it up into his asshole. He turned his back to me so I could see the pink entrance of his anus being penetrated by the steady in and out motion of his finger. My dick was so hard I thought it would break into a thousand pieces of stone around our feet. The lips of his asshole kissed and sucked his finger as he pushed it in and out, in and out. After thoroughly greasing his asshole, George then scooped out more Vaseline and smeared it all over my dick.

"Ahh! Ahh!" I sighed out in pleasure.

"Yeah, you're ready," he said approvingly, stroking me a few times more. Guided by George, who had now laid down upon the pallet and beckoned me to climb on, my cock, led by his hand, entered his ass in one smooth penetration. I didn't know at that moment that I would mount him all summer, night and day, and pour my adolescence into him. I would lie to get away from home and friends to be with him. I learned then that sneaking, ducking, and hiding were key components of a homo sex life simply because of the risk of exposure and the often devastating consequences.

I continued to visit George early in the morning before the store opened, fucking him at the back of the store behind the deli counter on bags and newspapers. I fucked him at his house at the end of his work day while his mongrel dog sat and watched us. From the spring through the late summer of 1971, George was the focus of my sexuality. He was the veracity of my sexual desire.

As it would turn out, I became his sole sex partner for that brief summer. I have often speculated that perhaps among all of the homeboys who passed through his hands, I was the one *wanting* to learn more. George knew this, and to the extent that he could exploit my youth for his pleasure, I allowed myself to be exploited and fondled and sucked, because I wanted this, too. I wanted him. I didn't come back to the store and tease him and curse him as did the other boys who had fucked him. I didn't demand money as some did. After their orgasms they resented him, but what they really resented was the recognition of their own *homo* sexual desire.

I kept silent about our activities. I would dare not say that we were in love. I wasn't sure I loved myself at fourteen, but I knew that my dick got hard for George. Never once did I give any thought to the possibility that I might be committing some sin I would be punished for in hell. Sin was the furthest thing from my consciousness. Hell was all around me in the ghetto of my adolescence.

My dick did not fall off in his mouth. I did not turn green from kissing him. I didn't burst into flames during our orgasms, nor did he. In fact, during orgasm, I often called out Jesus' name, which seemed appropriate for warding off such evil as I might have imagined we were committing. If anything, I was most concerned about being caught by my buddies or his co-workers. To this day I'm convinced the other fellas didn't know that I, too, was being initiated by George. Our group identity and rapport did not allow for this kind of discussion or candor to occur.

I regret that we were never able to talk about our visits to George. I regret, too, that we were not able to sexually explore one another in the same way that we allowed George to explore us. Ours was truly a fragile, stereotypical Black masculinity that would not recognize homo desire as anything but perverse and a deviation from the expected "role" of a man. The ridicule we risked incurring would have condemned us to forever prove our "manhood" or succumb to being the target of a hatred that was, at best, a result of hating *self* for desiring to sexually touch the flesh of another male.

At fourteen, I was astute enough to know my mouth should not reveal any desire that would further endanger me. There was no "older" brother at home to stand watch over my blossoming manhood. There was no father there, either. I was solely responsible for myself—the eldest sibling, the eldest son. Neither of those absences is an explanation for my sexual identity. Only nature knows the reason why.

During that same summer that George introduced me to homoeroticism, my public acceptance as "one of the boys" was severely challenged. The night is so clear to me. It was mid-August, sultry, humid, August, and the anticipation of returning to school was in the air. My buddies, Tommy, Tyrone, Leon, Peanut, and Kevin, we were all across the street from my house talking with some of the older boys—David, George, Doug, Wayne, Kenny, and Leon's brother, Crip.

My mother's bedroom was located at the front of our house and her windows faced out to the street. Her windows were open because there was no air conditioning in the house at that time. The night breeze was as much relief as we could hope for from the oppressive Washington summers.

Across the street from my house, on Douglas's and Kenny's front porch, we were talking about everything from sports to girls. It was the typical conversation of males in various stages of adolescence. We all shined in the streetlights that beat down on our variously muscular frames burnished by the summer sun. Our conversation rose and fell, exerting its brashness and bravado against the night, kicking around in our heads, drawing us into laughter and silence by turns, as we listened to stories of pussy conquests, petty scams, and recent ass kickings. The conversation was dominated by the older boys, who by turn tried to impact fragments of street warrior knowledge to us. We were sitting and standing, absorbing all this, relaxing our tough postures, allowing a communal trust to put us at ease and make us glib and attentive.

Crip was standing. I was sitting. It happened that from where I sat I could eye his crotch with a slight upward shift of my eyes. Well, one of the times that I peeked, Crip caught me. I would soon discover that I had cruised into very dangerous territory. Lulled by the conversation, I had allowed myself to become intoxicated on the blossoming masculinity surrounding me. I might as well have been shooting semen from wet dreams straight into my veins for the high I was on in this gathering of males.

Instantly, Crip jumped forward and got in my face. "I see you looking at my dick!" he hurled at me. I felt as though he had accused me of breaking into his house and violating his mother. Immediately, all conversation ceased and all eyes focused on me and Crip.

"Do you wanna suck my big, Black dick, muthafucka?" he demanded, clutching his crotch and moving up into my face. "Do you, nigga?"

Thank God my instincts told me to stand up. It was this defensive posture that perhaps saved me from an *absolute* humiliation, but my "No" was weak.

"Well, why are you looking at my dick? Is you a freak? You must wanna suck it. Are you a faggot? You can suck it, baby," he mockingly cooed, still clutching what was more than a handful of cock.

The fellas were laughing and slapping palms all around by this time. I was becoming visibly angry, but I had still uttered nothing more than a meek "No" to his challenge. I then remembered my mother's bedroom windows; they were open; she must have heard him.

The laughter began to die down. The sexual tension in the air was palpable enough to be slapped around. Crip's attitude changed for the worse.

"You shouldn't be lookin at a muthafucka's dick unless you plan to suck it," he sneered. It now seemed that all along he had been bellowing at me, so I was even more convinced my mother had heard him.

"Are you funny, nigga?" he asked, deadly serious, which elicited more raucous laughter from the fellas.

"No," I said, attempting to put more conviction in my voice. Crip was but an inch or two taller than me, and a pretty Black male. He carried beauty as agilely as some Black men carry footballs and basketballs and pride. I was surely attracted to him, but to even have hinted at that would have cost me more than the humiliation I endured that night.

So there we stood, me surrounded by gales of laughter punctuated by his booming voice, and all the time, in the back of my mind, I believe my mother was listening, in shock, hearing my humiliation. To her credit, if she overheard this she never confronted me with it.

Crip finally ended his tirade. The conversation resumed its boisterous, brash bravado. Shortly thereafter, I excused myself from the fellas, crossed the street, locked the door behind me, and cried myself to sleep in my bed. It would not be the last time I would cry myself to sleep because a male had inflicted me with emotional pain. It would not be the last time I would lock the door behind me and go to my bed alone, frightened of my sexuality and the desires I could not then speak of or name as clearly as I could articulate the dangers.

My sexual encounters with George ceased several weeks before summer vacation ended. In retrospect, I believe I stopped visiting him at the store and at his home as a direct result of the humiliation I suffered from Crip. I must have thought it would only be a matter of time before we would be discovered. Whatever my reasons, my refusal to engage in any more sex bewildered George. He continued to coax me to climb up on his back, but I could no longer be seduced. He enticed me with money but I refused that, too. When I was sent to the store by my mother, I would go two blocks out of the way to another convenience store just to avoid the longing I recognized in his eyes, a longing that was partially stoked by my mutual desire. I would later discover that such a longing inhabits the eyes of many homosexuals, particularly those who believe themselves to be unable to come out of the closet.

The school year resumed itself uneventfully. The only change, other than those occurring because of puberty, was the increasing burden of carrying a secret. I was learning to live with it safely hidden away, but for how long? It was surely dangerous knowledge. There was no one I could tell about my sexual adventures with George. There was no previous reference of intimacy to compare to sex. I continued nurturing my desire in the long nights of my adolescence, quietly masturbating in my bed as my younger brother slept above on the upper bunk.

Black male adolescent survival in a ghetto context made me realize the *necessity* of having a girlfriend, a female I could be seen walking home after school. It would be my luck to date girls who were "good," girls who were not going to experiment with sex beyond kissing and fondling, and even that was often only tolerated at a minimum if tolerated at all.

I was not the kind of male to force the issue of going all the way sexually. For me, it was enough to have a cover for my *true* desires, and that's what these girls were—covers. But I treated them with respect. They were girl *friends* more often than not.

I had the opportunity to have sex with one of the girls I dated. She agreed to skip school with me one day. We hid out at her house, our mutual motive: sex. After a long morning of petting and kissing the big moment arrived. We stumbled to her bedroom along an unfamiliar path that frightened and excited us. I was nervous because I expected her mother or father or one of her siblings to walk in and catch us.

In our adolescent nakedness we were beautiful, but if caught, we would have been seen as *being ugly.* We were sixteen and fifteen and ripe with curiosity and desire. Her skin was honey gold, smooth, so soft to my touch. Her breasts were full and sweet, the nipples brown and swollen by my tongue. Her hair was plaited in thick braids that coiled atop her head like snakes. We were both virgins. Nothing in our timid sex education had prepared us for walking into her bedroom to face our beautiful nakedness.

I believe we both felt we had to go through with the act because we had gone so far. In my mind, George appeared, but that was *different.* He had not instructed me about girls or young women. No one had. I kept hearing the older boys scat about breaking the cherry, but there was no cherry hanging between her legs when I looked. What was there was wet and warm to my fingers.

She laid so still on her bed. I knelt above her, fondling her breasts, kissing her, imagining these must be the things to do to seduce her. Neither of us spoke. As our breathing escalated I grabbed my cock and guided the head toward her vagina. She opened her legs to show me the mouth that was there, wet and waiting. Sunlight poured over us. Sweat bathed our bodies. We were straining ourselves to break rules we were taught not to break. We exerted ourselves against everything we were told not to do.

I pressed my head against the wet mouth. I pushed. She pulled away. I inched forward. Pushed. She pulled away again.

"Am I hurting you?" I asked nervously.

"Yes," she said softly.

"We don't have to do this," I assured her, saying this more for my comfort rather than her own. *I* didn't want to be doing this, after all.

"But I want to," she said. "I want to do this. It will make you—it will make *us* happy."

I rose up off her body. "Maybe this isn't the right time," I said. Looking down at her, I then realized how lovely she was and how little I knew of her. How little she *really* knew of me. I thought of George and a tingle stirred in my loins. I realized I didn't desire penetrating her. I was doing this for my reputation. I thought I needed to walk away with a bloody sheet to prove what—that I could break a hymen? I had no thought about consequences. There was no condom to prevent pregnancy, no pills being taken that I knew of. We were entangled in limbs we couldn't name, dry-throated, sweaty, pursuing different objectives in the afternoon bed we had stolen. My erection slowly fell. I lowered myself onto her again and kissed her lightly on the lips.

"We should probably get dressed," I encouraged her. "Someone might come home soon." That was the last and only time we were naked together. Not long after, we stopped seeing each other romantically.

A year later, she began dating an older boy around school. We saw each other less often, and then one day I saw her in a maternity blouse. I believe she finished school—I'm not sure—but by that time she wasn't my concern. I was seeing another "good girl," walking her home, holding her hand, pretending I was consumed by love—safe, by all appearances, from being identified as a faggot.

DOUGLAS SADOWNICK

SACRED LIPS
OF THE BRONX

THE YEAR I BEGAN escorting my grandmother to synagogue was the year I began dreaming of another boy's lips.

Even my parents noticed.

"It's not the Sabbath, Michael," my mother said, as I changed from a Patti Smith T-shirt to a double-breasted, aqua blue sports coat I had picked up at the Salvation Army. "What does a boy your age want with an old lady?"

My grandmother Frieda was said to be going through some kind of "breakdown" at the age of seventy-eight, so they all worried. Frieda had always been pious—and ignored. But when my grandfather Isaac died, she grew lax in following some of their more firmly cherished Jewish commandments. That's when she became the talk of our Bronx neighborhood.

If a butter dish touched a piece of roasted meat in the refrigerator, she didn't go overboard scouring the plate three times in scalding salt water. When the Day of Atonement came around during the first of the fall breezes, and she felt lightheaded from a morning of fasting, she helped herself to a piece of carrot boiled in onion broth. Then she downed a mug of buttermilk in three or four dense gulps. "God doesn't want me to die from hunger," she said, patting away a coating of creamy saliva from her old-lady's moustache. She used the corner of her white cotton tablecloth as if it were a napkin.

This behavior confused family members.

"I hated some of those customs," my father confessed to me one Saturday afternoon when he spied his mother-in-law waiting for a bus to Fordham Road on the holy Day of Rest. She was wearing her one fancy outfit: a black, gaberdine dress and shawl. "But it's a crime to see them *all* go."

There were other infractions. On the afternoons during which Frieda was growing more and more lonely and forgotten, she could be found chatting with six or seven black ladies in her cluttered living room. Thelma, Mildred, Lecretia—I knew their names. They were engaged in making Frieda into a Jehovah's Witness, and spread their *Watch-Tower* journals all over Frieda's 1940s coffee table like vacation brochures. My grandmother nodded over tea with them for hours, stringing them along about Jesus, just for the company. "Stupid *schwartzes*," she'd mutter the moment they'd leave.

And once, I spotted her frail form sitting off to the side in a local coffee shop, ordering a BLT in her thick Polish accent. "Holt da mayo, please," she said to a doll-faced, Italian waiter. I watched her for a half-hour from the L-shaped counter where you got your salt pretzels and malteds. When her lunch arrived, she peeled a slice of bacon from the triple-decker and regarded it as if it were a dollar bill she had discovered in her sandwich.

But, with all this, she never stopped going to synagogue. In fact, she began visiting the one-story, brown brick building as much as three times a day, usually after meals. Hung above the brass-lined doors, in reddish-gray clay, was the synagogue's official name: B'nai El. Once you stepped inside, the pine floors, brick walls, and dusty, stained-glass windows made you feel as if you had barged into an old lady's living room. Mostly everyone called this synagogue "the Jerome Avenue shul." You were supposed to feel at home here.

I remember entering the sanctuary with Frieda for the first time that year. There was a sudden brush with nostalgia. Four years before, I had been the shul's last Bar Mitzvah triumph. I sang; the Rabbi lifted the Torah scrolls; the crowd stood; Frieda and Isaac held hands. After that day, like most kids, I stopped attending services. What had happened? Now I was seventeen. The inescapable awkwardness of my bent posture, light olive skin, crooked nose, and fleshy cheeks had made me into an object of interest to those who were either lighter or darker than me. I had what guys from New Jersey or lower Manhattan called "a Bronx look." I didn't have to be in a room of half-blind Jews. But it was so tranquil inside, and I now felt a loyalty to that.

It was a below freezing day in January, and many streets were trapped under intricate layers of ice, slush, salt, and animal waste. (Frieda, who had refused to remain at home, took toddler steps. I held her by her tiny elbows wrapped in thick layers of wool.) I got a shock touching the brass knobs to the mahogany doors leading into the shul. I got another jolt once inside when I touched the metal bar holding the prayer shawls. "Such a pretty boy," the old congregants said when they saw me flinch. I heard whispers: "A *gootn yid*." "A good Jew." "God bless…" They beamed wide-eyed, like the well-dressed relations in *Rosemary's Baby*. As if pain was your sacred initiation here.

"Sit down, and pray to God, Mickey," my grandmother told me, her blood-shot gaze shifting from the smiles of her friends to the scene of screaming fire engines outside on a nearby Bronx street. "Before the whole world burns down."

Something was burning down.

You could smell the soot in the crisp air on the way to worship. The shul was located a block or two from Yankee Stadium, a few steps from the elevated IRT train on Jerome Avenue, the Lexington Avenue Line to be exact. It also was across the street from what was reputed to be one of the Bronx's finest network of basketball courts. That winter, only a lone crew of five or six Puerto Rican athletes dared challenge the bracing Bronx winds to shoot hoops. They burned newspapers, coffee cups, and milk cartons in New York City garbage cans to keep their hands warm.

"Hey, it's the chump ..."

"The one from high school ..."

"Hey, brain ... !"

I was the youngest person at the Jerome Avenue shul. At first I would find myself disdainful of the archaic Yiddish that hung in the air like Havana cigar smoke, Old Spice aftershave, and hair-nets. But Frieda had picked something up about me that no one else had. My high school life was crowded with year-book associates, theater rehearsals, and honor roll wannabes. My family was heaped high with aunts who spied on each other from nearby beauty parlors and uncles who owned Bronx automotive stores and talked business whenever you walked by. But it wasn't enough. "It's in your face," Frieda once said. "Come sit with me in the shul. It will ease you."

"Okay," I said.

I told myself that I would accompany her because it gave me an excuse to walk past those Puerto Rican b-ball players. Their improvised lay-ups, schizo dribbles, and psyched-out passes impressed even Frieda, who winced at them. On the first hint of a thaw, they removed their windbreakers and sweated hard. When I closed my eyes in the shul during the passages in which the old Rabbi muttered himself into a trance, I'd see their curvy backs and wild forearms spi-raling up and down in the air, and my breath would quicken, dart-like. "Mikey, you have so much feeling for God," Frieda would say, seeing this.

I had seen these guys even before Frieda began taking me to shul. Sometimes they killed time over at Jerome Avenue, near the stores underneath the El. They leaned against the green, iron-girded pillars that held up the tracks iced with pigeon shit. They had just moved to our neighborhood and didn't know anyone. My father would curse them out from our kitchen window: "Goddam spics" or "Go to goddam hell."

I'd sit in English class, answering a question about Shakespeare, and imag-ine myself having been raised with a tight, washboard stomach and thin, purple lips. I secretly took up smoking just to see how the thickened, yellow puffs would trail out of my lips when I licked them wet. I felt a little as if I were going crazy, like Frieda. I began talking to myself in the pidjin Spanish I picked up on the streets.

It got so bad that I'd leave chess club early and hang around the dilapidated Jerome Avenue newsstands waiting for the roving teenagers to show up so that I could act like I didn't know them. They always showed up, too. Their gold and black Giants T-shirts, damp from basketball sweat and Gatorade, sticking to their flat bodies. I'd page through the *Village Voice* and catch a glimpse of them talking and I'd feel lonely. It was a little like going to the movies by yourself. Here's one scene: Two of the more hyper guys run into a bodega and buy 7-Ups and exotic coconut drinks, before heading home, a mere stop or two from here. And another: I stare down at the asphalt, and then lift my head up fast, catching sight of an angled, quivering muscle on the back of a shirtless teenager—he's turning away from the wind to light a cigarette. Meanwhile, another boy—the quiet one—listens for the distant sound of an oncoming train.

Then: All five scamper up the forty or so stairs to the train platform, running into an open car door just as it's ready to shimmy close. They kick each other in the ass like Latino Harpos. Thump a basketball in front of a black lady's sleeping face. Scream out the train window. Collapse into graffiti-covered seats. They were bound for neighborhoods where they spoke only Spanish. Seeing them go, I'd feel lonely.

I picked up the quiet one's name: Hector.

"Hey, Hector! can't you play no basketball … ?"

"Hey, Hector! where'd you learn how to dribble, from your sister?"

"Hey, Hector! don't you eat, man … ?"

Hector was so thin. Sometimes I thought he was inhumanly two-dimensional. That one day he would turn to one side or the other and disappear off into the sky, like one of Frieda's secret demons. That he felt good about being empty inside, so that he could run around the basketball court and feel both feather-light and numb in case he made a mistake. He had green-veiny skin that was discolored in snowflake designs near his shoulders. You could see the beige polka dots trailing up from his biceps because he cut his T-shirts into shreds, making them into ragged tank tops. Maybe he liked showing off his disfigurement. Maybe he liked the way it was laid over his musculature like a doily. He was such an eccentric beauty, who knows? I couldn't keep my eyes off him.

"Whatcha looking at?" his pal, a heavy-set black Puerto Rican guy, once barked at me after their basketball game.

"I'm not looking at nobody."

"Shit …"

It must have been obvious. Hector turned around, slowly—ghosted. It was the first time I saw his entire face. It was ovalshaped, like a teaspoon, with a caffeine stain at his lips. He looked at me like I was a detraction from his full-time job, which was sweating and heading home. And being thin. He turned away.

The whole group of six knew a chump when they saw one and occasionally yelled. "Hey, whitey," or "Yo, faggot," or "Bitch," or "Kiss my pinga," when they saw one of us Jewish kids on the street. I always wanted to say something, but words stuck in my throat like they do in a dream. I felt terrible. I worried that Mrs. Minelli or Mr. McPhee, walking home from the butcher with brown paper bundles of chopped meat, had witnessed me being called a girl. "Move out the way, Sonny," I remember Mr. McPhee saying. To him, it was just noise. Goyim. Niggers. Kikes. Eyetalians. He hated us all. We all made noise.

Once, I ducked into a card and tobacco store when Hector caught me looking at him under the train tracks; a moment later, I saw him buying his mother an oversized birthday card. Another time, I stared at him when he was alone in front of a mailbox, and he looked right through me, blowing his nose in his fingers and then shaking the snot out on the street.

One afternoon after school, just as the late spring humidity came like a blast furnace to the Bronx, he and his friends saw me and yelled, "Hey you." My humiliation was a kind of jump start past my shyness, and I shouted back: "Hey you." A few Italian ladies, walking home from the fish market, stared at me like they had heard a terrible joke. The Puerto Ricans were laughing. "Hey you?" one of those guys said, his hysterics claiming something inside me, like a forceps or a fishing hook or a secret shot of my father's Seagram's Seven: "hey you! Hey You!! HEY YOU!!!" Hector just looked. Everyone's sweat was evaporating from his body; I thought I saw a mirage through the smoky city heat: Hector walking over to me—his thin arms and legs filling up my entire vision. But he was just standing still.

"Hey you!!! Hey you!!! Hey you!!!"

Eventually, a couple of friends from calculus class spotted me alone. They came over and yelled.

"Hey you, Puerto Ricans!!!"

"Hey you, Jews!!!"

One of the most irritating things you could do in the Bronx in those days was to call someone by his ethnic identity. It hurt, but not enough to cause a riot. It was at this very moment that Frieda appeared, as if from nowhere. I didn't see her approach, but I felt her warm, pulpy fingers on my hand.

"Hey ... you ..."

"Grandma!"

"You are becoming a hoodlum?"

I shook my head no, but her mind was already off somewhere. I took her hand, and we walked towards the synagogue. In the distance, I heard the guttural cries and the assorted Bronx accents: "Heee yyyyyoooo." I wanted to tell her something—that I was lonely, that those boys had called me names, but she shook her head. "Pray to God," she said. "You have the fire of the Evil One in your eyes."

So I went with her.

As a child I paid special attention to Frieda's tales of the Evil One. ("He is quiet like an angel," she'd whisper, "but swoops down at night—and gets you, and hits you on the face … !!!") The way she held me in her arms and kissed me!—I'll never forget that. It seemed to unhinge my mother, who made a point of calling Frieda into the kitchen: "Ma, help me with the brisket, will ya?" And as I grew older—eleven, twelve, thirteen—I went to synagogue with Frieda and Isaac and watched the old man weep during the mediational standing prayer. "Your grandpa is a good Jew," Philip, the Rabbi's son, said as I began preparations for my Bar Mitzvah. "The best." Like Frieda, the Rabbi was getting infirm and a little crazy, so Philip began taking over. And when I was rehearsing the ancient tunes, I made Philip cry with emotion. Philip: he was a revered basketball player on Sundays, a seminary student every other day. He'd teach me the singsong chants in cutoffs, smelling like the asphalt. The aloof Rabbi—a German refugee—seemed stirred by the progress I made in my renditions.

But one's parents saw it as a sign of imbalance to keep up such practices after the Bar Mitzvah was over. "Are you normal?" my mother asked me as I persisted in praying in synagogue on the Sabbath. "Normal kids play ball on the weekends." The Rabbi's son whispered in my ear, "Keep with it. It's in your blood." But it was not healthy. "There's no future in this," my mother said. "When you get married, then you can go and pray like an old man."

These were the days when the Bronx was changing, and the change was having a strange effect on all of us.

Frieda and Isaac moved here in 1946. It's where they raised a family of five boys, four girls, and twenty grandchildren. She spoke a Polish Yiddish and went to market on 167th Street, a full day's experience back then, considering how many Jewish stores (bookstores, dairy markets, religious books and clothing retailers, butchers, bakeries, pawn shops—never mind Frieda's and Isaac's tailor shop) you had to browse through. Now those places were either burnt up or selling food we weren't allowed to eat. That's where my parents, brothers, aunts, uncles, and cousins lived in fear and resentment. In five years, our neighborhood shifted from blue-collar Jewish, Italian, and Irish old-timers to poor Puerto Ricans and blacks. In our little courtyard you could hear the melodies: Zero Mostel from Mrs. Kaffel's kitchen, Machito from Mr. Candelario's. Barbara Streisand from me.

The competing sounds drove me crazy. In my dreams I would hear the mambo and see Hector's pencil-thin lips. He'd be dancing with his basketball in one hand and a Coca-Cola in the other. I would wake up in the middle of a hot summer night with an erection, unable to go back to sleep, the bed sheets soaked through. Murmuring "bitch," or "pinga," I'd relieve myself, thinking of Hector and the way the soda-pop made his lips shine like shellac.

One Saturday afternoon, the daydreams got very bad. I wished I could go to synagogue, but that was out of the question. My parents, seeing some profound but quiet change in me, had prohibited too many visits with Frieda. "She's a witch," my mother would say of her own mother. "I always suspected it, and now I know it." Playing baseball with friends was suicidal; I couldn't catch the ball. So I just turned on a metal fan in the bedroom I shared with my brother and read. But my mother played the Broadway recording of *Fiddler on the Roof* so many times that the album began to skip. Next door, a kid was blasting Santana's "You Got to Change Your Evil Ways." I ran out of the house—"I'll be back for dinner"—and reached Jerome Avenue. I took the subway down to Times Square, as I had many times that year.

I know now that the scenes in those theaters were no different from the shadows I saw in my head when I sat alone in synagogue and closed my eyes. Truth be told, I saw many of the same things in my mind's eye: men who smelled like my father's Chesterfields and whiskey; the reflection from a switchblade I once saw in the dark; the Puerto Rican kids who zoomed in on my nose like I was a long lost Mediterranean; the Italian boys who called out "Mamma" as they came on your sneakers; the cigarettes I was too fearful to inhale; the hours in the dark away from my father's golf games and my mother's voice—"Turn off the golf game!"; the heavyset men who hunted me down like I was a stupid, starved animal who didn't know how to say no (I did not know how to say no).

I had memories of hours spent sitting alone in a broken seat watching anal intercourse on the torn-up movie screen. These memories came easily to me as I sat on a velvet-covered bench in synagogue listening to the monotonous singsong of the Rabbi. Both places were stuffy, half-empty, and secretive. In the theater, I'd wash the crusts of dried cum off my jeans and stomach hairs; in the shul, I'd scrub the stink of saliva-heavy kisses off my cheek and forehead. Neither place had soap. In the theater, I'd sleep and recall being held by Frieda when both she and I were younger. In the shul, I'd dream too; Torah scrolls opening up, the words becoming big, human lips—both Philip's and Hector's. (They both said very sacrilegious things).

Now that I think of it, there are a hundred other similarities. A few years later, they would renovate the porn theater with neon lights and new carpets and make it feel like Saks Fifth Avenue, but it would get so popular with the punkers and AIDS activists that they shut it down right away. At about the same time, the city tore down Frieda's synagogue after the last refugee had died. There was an analogy of addictions, too. The hugs, kisses, grunts, and simple lifts of a skintight nylon T-shirt—never mind the leaden weight of skin and flesh in an Irish kid's corduroys—brought me closer and closer to the truth about my family and me. In a similar way, the pats on the head by Frieda's friends, the delicate crinkle of the yellowed pages in old prayer books, the scent of urine in the ladies' dresses, transported me to an invisible city where feeling close to God was your passport. Holding that passport in the rooms of my Bronx household was almost impossible.

At home, in my parents' bathroom, I read *Portnoy's Complaint* and thought "How odd." Sure, I knew I had to be very careful. I feared bumping into my mother or one of her sisters on my way out of the theater. I wore a Yankees cap over my face. It was all a tense experiment. But there was more, too. These secrets were buried in me like a stripper's sense of self-respect. I knew I wanted love. And a boy's lips. Things you couldn't find in Times Square or synagogue.

Frieda was becoming all love, which was why she was so dangerous to my parents and their world. "I wake up in the morning," she confided in me, "and see the Angel of Death. And Michael, he has your face." But she was not frightened. So I decided not to be, either. I kept a change of shul clothes at her house. I'd lie to my mother, running out of the house with a catcher's mitt or a hockey stick or a basketball or a bathing suit or a soccer ball, screaming: "Um, see ya. ..." But I was really bound for Frieda's house. We'd walk under the Jerome Avenue El to get to the shul, and see those basketball players.

"Hey, Hector," they yelled. "Here's your girlfriend walking by."

But, after a time, they stopped yelling. The sight of a young man helping an older woman conjured up something familial in them. They respected respect, it seemed.

"*Mira*, there's that *hombre* again."

"That old lady—she's a witch, man."

"No, man, that's his *abuela*!"

"Shalom," they screamed. "Shalomy."

Frieda would just smile, and hold my hand.

I began to know Frieda for real when I walked with her through the decaying Bronx streets to shul; the folds of flesh near her palm, so loosely wrinkled you could almost feel direct bone; the quiet sighs she took when she waited for the 168th Street light to turn green; the memories she entertained of her mother, now dead, whom she had left behind sixty years ago in Poland, and who taught her to listen to her own heart; the secret potions, amulets, and incantations she picked up from superstitious Poles and now resorted to more and more. Just like I began to know Hector and Hector's guys for real; their odd loneliness among each other as they traveled two miles from their ghettos to play at our more well-appointed basketball courts; the fear of the Jews and their holidays I saw in their eyes; the boredom that sometimes overtook them in the midst of an endless game.

Men cannot sit with women in Orthodox synagogues; so Frieda and I parted ways once we entered the little shul. The Rabbi was immobile and stick-thin, but his voice still shook the chandeliers. It blasted: "God, O Merciful One, Holy, Holy, Holy!" The old men who were already seated would gesture "come, sit down," and they'd wrestle each other to be the ones to show me the place in the prayer book. "Here." "No, here!" Frieda had many friends herself, but she preferred listening alone. From the laced, wrought-iron partition that kept the aging men from the aging women, I watched my old grandmother shake softly in her seat, her droopy eyes closed, her lipsticked lips mouthing the ancient words by heart.

It was on a fall Saturday afternoon—a year since I had been escorting Frieda to shul—that I understood why I thought so much of Hector here.

On cold afternoons, I'd see him. When the weather got warmer, I saw him. When I began going to shul with Frieda on Saturday mornings, and then on weekday evenings, I'd cross paths with him. That summer, I worked in a deli, cooking kosher franks on a grill full-time to make money for college. If I was energetic, I'd get up early and walk with Frieda to the morning service. I'd only linger in the hushed sanctuary for a few minutes; I needed coffee and some time to get ready for work. It would be very early—7 A.M. to be exact. (It wasn't uncommon to see the basketball courts start filling up by then. If you were an athlete during a New York City summer, you had to get up very early to get your practice in. By noon, you'd fry.) As my morning routine with Frieda became pattern, I'd see Hector on the Jerome Avenue streets at the crack of dawn, too.

Sometimes he'd be dribbling a lone basketball. Other times, he'd be paging through a *Playboy* or *Sports Illustrated* or *Redbook* magazine near the very newsstand I used to watch him from. As the weeks and then months passed, our eyes would meet, then bolt away. By the time the October breezes began turning the leaves on the city's oak and birch trees purple, orange, and red, we were on Bronx speaking terms.

"Yo."

"Yo."

I might have kept walking, but I slowed down, as if it occurred to me that it was finally time to buy a magazine. It was cool and dewy still, a morning breeze sending the smell of percolating coffee and toast from the greasy spoon across the street. I felt lonely and acutely hungry looking at Hector as his eyes trailed across words on a page. I could smell the scent of Dial soap from his body which seemed less sculpted than I had imagined from viewing him from afar. It was just a body, sharply carved and unpredictably pitched to one side or the other, depending on how his feet were planted on the concrete. I had looked at him so many times in so many different ways over the past year— sometimes in clandestine glimpses with Frieda; other times in defiant fast stares—that I had forgotten the difference between secrecy and reckless boldness. They both seemed the same, when it came to watching Hector.

When he turned to me, I saw his lips, framed by little flairs of peach-fuzz, quivering. Then he picked up another magazine.

"You a Jew boy?"

I stared at him.

"You go with your old grandmother to church?"

"It's not church …"

"Jew boy," he said, smiling.

"Puerto Rican." I said back.

He nodded, matter-of-factly.

"Right …" he said.

"… Right," I added.

He snorted. I opened my mouth, as if about to laugh (a Bronx gesture if there ever was one). "Yeah," I said. That seemed a little stupid, or even ill-mannered, but it came out of my mouth like a prayer and felt good. I said it again: "Yeah." It was a big step. I think I moved my hand, as if to acknowledge this. He held his small, brown fist to his side, like I'd better be careful. What was amazing? That we were talking. That he could both act dangerous and be dangerous, could act vulnerable and be vulnerable. These four directions played on his lips.

"Jew," he said, dispassionately. He gave me a look, as if to say: We have these lines.

"PR," I said.

I looked at his magazine: On the cover was a famous Puerto Rican pitcher.

He saw me looking.

"I got a subscription," he said. A few beats of silence. Then: "… a stack at home."

Cautious signals played on his eyes. My hands shook a little in the morning breeze.

Upstairs at his three-room apartment, two subway stops away, his mother looked a lot like mine. She balanced an unlit cigarette in her tight, cracked lips. She was a compact woman, with a youthful urgency and light brown, discolored skin, like Hector's. Hector and I sat at the orange and white Formica kitchen table, covered with peach-colored, plastic place mats. She served us espresso, and little cubes of sugar-iced yellow cake on a paper plate.

"He goes with his *abuela* to church," he told his mother, who nodded. Then she left the kitchen.

"Jew."

"PR."

We both drank our coffees.

In his room, a few minutes later. The plaster-cracked walls were covered with pictures of Jesus and Joe Namath and Roger Daltry and some Latin-looking keyboard player I didn't recognize. There were Catholic comic books, and neatly written homework assignments on white loose-leaf paper piled near eleventh grade textbooks, and ratty spiral notebooks. He showed me some drawings and then his homework, pieces of paper on which bold *A*'s and *B*'s had been inscribed in red ink. I was conscious of him watching me. There were more tours. I was conscious of Hector clicking his bedroom door with the help of his back. After some additional tours around stacks of *Sports Illustrated* and assorted seashells collected from "the clean beaches of Puerto Rico," he pushed me. By accident, I fell onto his linoleum floor, which smelled of Mr. Clean. By accident, he did too. He lay his thin, marionette arms casually over mine. It was more of a slow, motionless cascade than anything else. I was conscious of his fingertips searching for skin, like the feet of an upside down insect, scrambling for the ground.

"What did you call me?" he asked, making believe he was holding me down against my will, locking fingers into mine,

"What did you call me?" I asked back, making believe I was getting aggressive. He held my fingers too tightly.

And although I felt the breath from his scant mouth pressing on my neck, and though I heard the words, "I called you a Jew, Jew," I didn't dare let myself give in to him for fear that he would tell his friends. I stayed still, in one rigid place, my body unable to rest itself on the floor and take in this curious spot. Instead, I focused on the shock of a wish that was no longer just deferred, and the sense that Hector's incantory breath on my neck may have meant one thing to me and a different thing to him.

It was a new place, just as shul and the theater had once been new, and sensing this, I felt my neck release itself fully into the gravity of his small, little room. This is what it had all been for, hadn't it? We lay there for a few minutes. Some strands of black, oily hair rested in my face. It made my nose itch, but I didn't dare move to scratch. Nothing happened. The world of men had before been a mix of tactile boredom leading up to shattering appetites. Now: the smell of skin and a hint of mutual loneliness. Had all this been ordained by the forces of a Bronx in flux: the thud of a basketball, the cracked voice of a rabbi? I heard the thud in my head, and it hurt. It was a way of staying focused on the immediate problem: Now what? To my right I saw his bed frame and the dust balls beneath it. To my left was the bedroom door, against which his sneakered feet were jimmied.

I saw a look of wild despair in his eyes. "You like it?" he asked, his voice shaking, his eyes dark with shame.

"I don't know," I whispered, amazed to find myself unable to talk. The lips moved, but no words came out. I found myself uncontrollably—imperceptibly—caressing the skin in between his T-shirt and the black, leather belt holding up his shorts. I felt goose bumps trailing up and down his side, where my fingers were.

"What do you do in that church?" he asked me, speaking into my neck through sweaty tangles of black split ends.

"The same thing you do in yours."

"Nah," he said, starting to stir. He shifted his weight and pushed his face away from my neck in a jolting arc heading upwards. He propped his left elbow up on the floor and balanced the left side of his face on it. It was clumsy, but fast—like the way he dribbled a basketball. When he was done, his lips were positioned maybe a foot and a half from mine.

"What do you do in there?" he asked, staring.

I understood that he thought I carried magic amulets in my pocket, that I drummed up spells to make him follow me. He thought I was a demon, just as Frieda taught me to believe that he was one. "We pray for you PRs to go away."

He smacked my face.

"Well, we ain't going away."

The blow was not expected. My face stung in a million places, even though he had not hit me hard. His soft palm really just dusted the right side of my profile. I had never been slapped like that, a dusting. I would have wrested myself from his grasp, except that suddenly my hands had been freed. You learn things sometimes by learning and not thinking. Like a witch sensing her magic in old age. Or a rabbi closing his eyes and seeing the end of history. I smacked him back, mimicking the action of the palm touching his right profile, much in the way you pat a dog's back. He clenched his lips when I said: "We pray for you PRs to drop dead."

He smacked me again, saying nothing.

I hit him again—not too hard but hard enough. He made believe he lost balance and fell a little to his side. "Whew," he said, scratching an eye. When he regained his position, he made a scrambling motion with his bony legs that said with a certain unspoken insolence: move your legs. I did, making a "V" shape. I felt his crotch sink into mine.

"We want you Jews to drop dead," he said. This time he used a lighter touch, more of a brush than a smack.

"Then this place would really be a dump," I said, copying his style, but hitting the opposite side of his face, with a different hand. I had two hands free; he had only one.

His breath began to deepen. His eyes moved about in their sockets: little bloodshot marbles inset in Indian bones. "*Coño*," he said. The way he bit his lip, and allowed himself to slide into this new person now, made him seem superreal. As I had seen Frieda in the street after synagogue. I was aroused. I moved myself away from my sharp zipper, inserting a quick hand in my pants. I knew that he knew. He lifted his weight up and allowed his eyes to scan down to my crotch, seemingly blasé, the way he would look when a basketball circled around the hoop a dozen times before it eventually shook itself through.

Then he buried his face again in my neck so that I couldn't see his lips. His voice was muffled. He was afraid to say it: "faggot."

There had been moments in synagogue when I would feel tortured—out of place. Mr. Bluestein was incontinent. Mrs. Levine gave me the Evil Eye. At such times, a prayer would seize up on my lips, and I would find myself entertaining a strong impulse to murder Mrs. Levine or Mr. Bluestein. If I really went with the prayer to the next step—a repetition; a deep-throated tremor—a humble love of my people might flood over me. Strange, a simple prayer calling up a river like this.

"I hate the way you Jews pray."

"I hate the way you PRs ruin our neighborhoods."

And then: a blackout. His crotch swirling in place above mine like a flapping of wings—was it the Angel of Death? And then when the light came back, a bucking of youthful abandon. A few hidden muscles but no hidden moves. A curl in the torso, the necks ready to crack out of line. Pants stayed on; shirts shriveled upwards. A spinning by the lips, some saliva sputtering. Salty and strange tasting the sweat produced by despairing rapture. We lay, frozen.

When I heard Hector's father come home and lumber into the toilet, I left the house. (How did I know it was his father? The banging of doors, the drunken belching, the deep-throated cursing—that's how many Bronx fathers acted when they came home from work in those days.) My heart pounded numbly in my chest as I took the subway home.

When I got off the train, late for work, I spotted Frieda walking back from synagogue. Her shuffled gait looked more strained than ever. I felt ashamed to see her. She touched her fingers to my forehead and said, "God bless you." I walked her home. Her black leather shoes left a trail of marks on the concrete.

The next day, when I called on her to go to synagogue, she was dead, her little form curled up in the dirty cotton sheets.

I have tried to remember the scene in different ways over the years, but the only real memory I have is of holding her hand. Then dropping it, suddenly. It was cold and hard. Then a certain cloying shame. Could I not be more courageous with my grandmother? I was frightened to look out the window, for fear of seeing the Angel of Death flapping its huge black wings like a monster. For the first time in a year, I felt defenseless. I would have to call my mother, a thought that made me even more clenched and wary. She'd take over. "What were you doing over there?" she'd ask. I thought I should take my outfits and Frieda's stones and amulets—things she had shown me in secret—and toss them into the incinerator. But I was afraid to leave the body alone.

I walked towards the window and looked out. I still felt confused about what had happened with Hector, and now more confused by a thought that occurred to me as Frieda's body got colder and colder: For one year, I was a true Jew. I had lived as Frieda's people had lived for centuries in forests and slums, their darkened lives turning around and around because the passion of love kept them alive. Now it would all be a memory. The faculties of my heart were ebbing as Frieda's soul sailed up to the Master of the Universe. I had no will to pursue this course alone. It would take me ten years to remember what she had taught.

Outside, a million people populated our streets, and most of them were not white. Out from their mouths you could hear so many languages, even with the window closed: Spanish, Spanglish, Italian, blue-collar white ethnic English, Black English, Sicilian, Armenian, Greek, Creole, Pentecostal ravings. Buses lumbered by—destined for points further south of us. Mothers were calling after their kids. Jilted lovers sat on car hoods, waiting for dates, mouthing their own quiet prayers of brokenheartedness. Drunken husbands screamed at their wives in front of their children. It was a cloudy day.

I wanted to say a prayer over the body. Anything. Frieda's name. Or Hector's. It would have been something I would have done yesterday. Now I silenced myself. I looked at the filthy glass and saw a reflection of my face, the place where Hector had hit. In a minute, it'd be time to call my mother. For now, I looked out the window. I saw two different Bronxes: the scene outside Frieda's window and the spot on my face Hector had dusted with his hand. At one point, if I squinted hard, I could see both at once. Then all I could see was an image of myself squinting. I looked like a little, lost child.

LORRIE SPRECHER

SISTER SAFETY PIN

I.

"Why don't you try making it with other women instead of moping around all the time?" my roommate Patti said finally. We had been meditating to the Sex Pistols. I was depressed because my girlfriend had left me. Patti was anxious because she thought she was a lesbian but hadn't slept with a woman yet.

We sat on the couch with beer and tortilla chips. "My fantasy life is on hold," I said. "I'm too upset."

Patti muttered, "Oh give me a break, Melany." She threw a tortilla chip into my blue spiked hair and the rings on her leather bondage bracelet jingled.

"Fuck you," I said, exasperated. I pulled the chip out of my hair. "Since it's so easy, who do you fantasize about?"

"You," Patti said.

"Oh," I gasped.

"I mean," Patti said quickly, "you're the only lesbian I really know. So I have to think about you. It makes it easier somehow. I'm sorry if I startled you."

"That's OK," I said. "Let's talk about something else."

"OK by me," Patti said. "People are obsessed with sex anyway. We have so many other things to talk about. There's more to us besides the fact we're lesbians. Or trying to be lesbians."

"Right," I said. "Some people become lesbians and it takes over their lives. All they think about is sex. I mean, so what if we've been repressed all our lives. It doesn't mean we have to get obsessive."

I swung my feet into the chair to look at them. Patti read the label on her beer can as though she had to write a term paper on it. I cracked first. "So," I said, "Patti. Have you ever thought seriously about you and me having sex?"

"Sometimes," Patti admitted. "Have you?"

"Sort of," I sighed, "but not really. I've started to, but then I repressed it. I guess I'm good at that."

"I guess we all are," Patti said. "I guess, I guess. I wish I knew something."

"Do you think we should have sex?"

"Yes. No. I don't know. For myself, I'd say yes. It'd be my trial by fire. I could say afterwards I'm a real lesbian. That I've slept with a woman. Maybe then I'd feel more secure about trying to meet someone."

"Is that why you never talk to anyone at the bar except for me?" I gasped.

"I think," Patti nodded, "what if I talk to someone, and she expects me to know what I'm doing? To have done this before?"

"I never thought of you that way," I said. "This is a whole other side of you." Patti looked nervous. "It's kind of sweet."

"Is it?" Patti brightened.

"Don't do it on purpose," I said.

"Of course not. So what should we do?" Patti asked.

"Don't ask me. Should we have sex, yes or no? I know," I said suddenly, "we'll make a list." I rummaged around for a pen and some paper.

On one piece of paper we wrote all the reasons it would be a good idea for us to have sex. On another, all the reasons it would be a disaster. A third was for ambivalent responses which didn't fit on our either/or lists.

"Okay," Patti said, after we'd been at it for nearly an hour, "let's see what we've written so far."

"My throat feels dry," I said, and Patti got me another beer. "Thank you. Okay," I coughed, "on the 'Yes I think we should definitely have sex' list we have:

    a. P. wouldn't be a lesbo-virgin anymore

    b. M. wouldn't be so lonely

    c. it might help M.'s depression

    d. it might help P.'s anxiety

    e. P. would feel more secure about approaching other women

    f. even though we're not sure we feel sexual about each other, sleeping together is the only way to know

    g. if we did end up feeling sexual about each other it would be great

    h. we're best friends

    i. we're perfect for each other."

"What about on the 'No we shouldn't have sex' list?" Patti asked.

"On the 'No, we should not have sex under any circumstances' list we have written:

a. it could ruin our friendship
b. we feel too self-conscious
c. we would be embarrassed
d. we're not sure we could ever really think about each other in that way
e. we're best friends
f. P. still believes in vaginal orgasm
g. we are perfect together
h. P. still believes in vaginal orgasm
i. we have a really good relationship
j. we'd be too nervous to have good sex anyway.

I put in the vaginal orgasm stuff as a joke," I said, "to break the tension."

"Very funny," Patti said. "But you know biology is destiny. So let's just give it up."

"What?"

"For Christsake I'm kidding. Lighten up. What's on the ambivalence list?"

"Nothing," I admitted. "I was actually too ambivalent about any of our other responses to write anything down."

"Well," Patti said, "that's it then. We'll have to decide."

"Should we sleep on it?" I asked. "Bad choice of words."

"No, I'm too nervous with this hanging over my head."

"Okay, well then we'll just have to decide now. On the basis of information that we have. You go first," I said. "I'll listen."

"Let's take a vote," she said.

"That won't work," I said, "because I'll go along with anything you say. I'm too ambivalent."

She said, "Let's take a secret vote."

I said, "How secret is it going to be? If one of us says 'yes have sex,' and the other says 'no don't have sex,' someone's feelings will be hurt."

"We'll just have to decide it on the basis of the lists then. Objectively."

"I thought that's what we were doing," I said testily.

"That is what we're doing."

"I mean, I thought that's what we had been doing, before you made that remark."

"What remark?" Patti cried, pulling at her off-maroon hair.

"That remark about what we were supposed to be doing. I mean what we were going to do. Oh never mind," I snapped. "Let's walk to the market. We're out of beer."

We put on our coats and walked in silence. In the light of the market I looked at the side of Patti's face while I was pretending to compare prices of six-packs. I wanted everything. I didn't want to lose her. I didn't want to go to bed alone. I didn't want to take any risks.

"I don't know what I want," I said, suddenly close to tears next to a cardboard beer display of a waterfall and four draft horses.

"Generic beer's on sale," Patti said, picking up two six-packs of plain white cans with "Beer" in black letters. "Let's get that."

II.

"But let's not have sex," Patti lay on the floor. We finished the second six-pack of beer. "We're such good friends. It'll only screw it up."

"Do you mean let's not now or not ever?" I asked, sprawled beside her, my head on the carpet in a spot of knocked-over beer.

Patti hesitated a moment. "Not ever," she said finally, crushing her can and throwing it backwards over her head. "Let's never have sex."

"Thank God," I sighed. "Thank God, thank God," I reached for her arm and squeezed it. "I thought I was going to be called on to perform or something."

"I thought only men were into sex as performance," Patti teased, rolling on her side.

"Well, being the senior lesbian I would feel pressured," I said, sitting up.

"I don't mean to clip your wings," Patti said, "but I have as good an imagination as the next person in the sex department. Don't worry about me. If we ever have sex, I can take care of myself."

"But we're not going to," I said, "not ever. What a fucking relief."

III.

When fall semester ended, Patti got ready to go on vacation. I swung a bare foot over the arm of my chair, pretending to read. The front door was open and southern California sun combusted in our living room. Patti was in her bedroom packing. "Where are you going first?" I screamed over Iggy Pop singing "I Wanna Be Your Dog."

"Don't worry, I'll pay the rent," Patti screamed back. When I walked into her room she was trying to close a bright blue suitcase. "I'm going to San Jose, to spend Christmas with my family," she made a face, "then New York City." Patti had talked her parents into buying her a plane ticket to New York, where she could stay with cousins for a week, as a Christmas present.

"Don't mope too hard," Patti said, "and I'll bring you back something. They have great punk songs in the Village."

Patti's room was a work of art. The walls were covered with interviews and pictures of The Pretenders and The Clash. Her things were flung everywhere.

Neckties, safety-pins, buttons of punk groups, leather bracelets, studded belts, bondage trousers, hand-cuffs, chains and dog collars from pet stores.

On her full-length mirror there were 3-D Jesus postcards from a truck stop in Ohio and a page torn out of the Akron phone book listing all of the "Hyndes." Last summer before her band had broken up, Patti and Ray Ban, the drummer who modeled herself after Palmolive of The Slits, had hitchhiked all the way to Akron, Ohio on a pilgrimage to Chrissie Hynde's birthplace.

Sometimes when Patti was at school and I was not, I sat on her bed and read articles by people like Jane Suck and Lucy Toothpaste. Patti herself was a wealth of punk information. I knew the Clash had refused to lend Siouxsie their luminous pink equipment for a gig because she was wearing a swastika armband. I knew how Joe Strummer met Mick Jones and Paul Simonon in Ladbroke Grove. I knew Chrissie Hynde taught Johnny Rotten how to play guitar.

I said, "I'll miss you."

"Me too," Patti said. "I'll send you a postcard or something. And I'll see you sometime after New Year's. Now don't forget, I stuck my January's rent on the refrigerator."

Patti said I could have her car while she was gone, and I drove her to the station to catch a bus for San Jose. "Be good," she kissed me on both cheeks.

"Have fun in New York City. Be careful. Say hi to your parents," I hugged her, resting my chin on the shoulder of her leather jacket. She clasped me in her studded bracelets and chains.

"Take care," she said. I saw the silver earring in her right nostril flash, and Patti kissed me once briefly on the lips. She got on the bus and I waved. Then I stood alone in the bus exhaust, clutching Patti's car keys.

IV.

"So," Patti said, when she came back from New York City, "have you thought any more about us?" We were wearing our Jesus-crown-of-thorns T-shirts Patti brought back from a punk shop in the Village.

"What us?" I said. The "us" that kissed you right on the lips at the bus station you idiot, I told myself.

"I thought about it a lot when I was in New York," Patti said.

"Yes, I know. Your postcard was really sweet." I had gotten a sentimental but confused postcard from New York—Barbie driving a pink Ferrari in F.A.O. Schwartz—apologizing but not apologizing for "the kiss." "Patti," I sighed because I knew I had to say something, "listen, you've always kissed me. It's no big deal."

"I feel really tense," she said.

"But you always kiss me," I repeated. I felt frustrated, like throwing a really childish tantrum. "I like it. I mean, you didn't have to stop just because we've discussed—our sexual feelings."

"I don't know, I don't know," Patti said, wringing her hands. "It doesn't feel the same. I don't feel the same about it."

"Oh God," I said, "does it have to wreck our lives? Does it have to get in the way of us being us?"

"It. It, it, it. You can't even say it," Patti accused, brown eyes flashing. "I feel self-conscious about my body around you. I keep worrying if I brushed my teeth in the last five minutes. I keep thinking, sex. I can't behave like I naturally would under these circumstances."

"Let's get it out of the way then."

"What do you mean?" she asked.

"You know damn well what I mean," I said, "you're just making me say it."

Patti sulked, "Say what?"

"You know what. What is what. You say what," I screamed.

"I'm stressing, I'm stressing," Patti flung her hands over her ears, jumping up and down. "I just can't stand it anymore. I can't stand it. Can we get it over with? Can we please just simply get it over with?"

"All right," I said angrily. "We'll go to bed then."

"All right," Patti said. "Fine. Whose room do you want to use?"

"Oh. Well your room," I said, suddenly concerned. "I mean, your room would be fine. Whatever makes you feel more comfortable."

"Oh no," Patti said politely, "I couldn't do that. You should decide whose room."

"Whose bed is bigger?" I asked.

"You're so experienced," Patti said. "I never would have thought of that." We smiled at each other, then burst out laughing. Linking arms we went into my room.

I turned out the light. "Should I put a record on?" I asked.

"That would be nice," Patti said, lying down on my bed.

"'Germfree Adolescents'?" I asked, thinking X-ray Spex was a good choice because the lead singer was a woman.

"Perfect," Patti said. "Poly-styrene always makes me feel emotional."

"Is it dark enough, or too dark?"

"I can see you. But not too much," Patti added quickly. We took off our clothes. Patti reached a hand under the sheet and stroked my naked skin tentatively. I kissed her mouth. She touched my nipple lightly, then squeezed it.

"Yes it's real," I said.

"I feel really self-conscious," Patti said. She stopped her scientific exploration of the shape of my breasts. "Do you think getting drunk would help?"

"I think it will just make it take longer," I said. "I have to go to the bathroom." I slipped out of bed and moved away quickly. It was a relief to be my naked self in the bathroom. I peed, blew my nose, washed my hands and face.

"Are you all right?" Patti asked. I got into bed with her.

"Yes, fine thanks. I don't know if I can go through with this," I admitted.

"Me neither," Patti said. "But, well we're naked now. We might as well give it a chance."

"You're right," I rolled close to her. "Maybe we should stop talking." I kissed her. She grabbed my head and kissed me back, then ran her hand over my face. I pulled the sheet away from her body and kissed her breasts. Sex was possible between us. But we weren't sure what that meant.

"Every woman can be a lesbian," Patti said, when it was over, reciting a popular lesbian slogan from the seventies.

"All women are sisters," I reminded her, laughing. "Where does the women's movement leave us?"

"Up an incest creek without a paddle," Patti said. "No wonder we've been self-conscious about having sex."

"Sisterhood was powerful though," I said. "Should we try it again?"

"You mean go for the big 'O' while committing the big 'I'?" Patti asked. "Why not?"

"You're just relieved," I said, "because you're finally the big 'L.'"

"Oh I always knew I was a lesbian," Patti said.

"Then why didn't you 'come out'?"

"I decided to after I'd had my first orgasm with a woman," Patti said sensibly. "Well, the first couple," she laughed.

I opened my mouth but didn't say anything. I didn't know how to respond to a detail like that. I thought of a few unsatisfactory replies:

a. that's not what "come out" means, Patti

b. make sure you spell my name right

c. (politically-correct response #1) sex isn't just about orgasm, Patti—you're too goal-oriented

d. (politically-correct response #2) lesbianism isn't about sex, Patti—it's a whole emotional continuum based on egalitarianism and mutual affection

One side of the X-ray Spex album kept repeating itself and I got up to flip it over. I cut off Poly-styrene's impassioned plea, "I wanna be a frozen pea," and Patti said, "Speaking of which, I have to." She went into the bathroom. I watched her naked self cross my bedroom.

"Patti," I called over the sound of her peeing.

"I can't hear you," she yelled.

"Patti," I called again, "I'm talking."

"Jesus," Patti said, "just a minute. Jesus," she stalked across the room and climbed into bed. "One sexual encounter with you and I lose all my privacy. What is it that couldn't wait?"

"When are you going to 'come out'?"

"Well I don't know," Patti said. "Should I run into the street naked?"

"Don't be stupid."

"Should I rent a hall, throw a ball, buy a gown, go to town?"

"Don't be funny. Are you going to tell your parents?"

"Does this really bother you or something?" Patti frowned at me. "Like I'm not political enough? Hand me the phone."

"Oh Jesus, Patti, I didn't mean now. I was just asking."

"No, it bothers you. You think I'm still straight-identified or something, but I'll show you. Operator," she said, "I'd like to make a collect call to San Jose."

"Patti," I whispered, horrified, tugging on her arm, "you're calling your parents *collect* to tell them you're a lesbian? And you're naked, my God, put on some clothes before you talk to your parents." Frantically I threw a T-shirt at her head.

Patti waved me away and said, "Shush. Mom? Yeah, it's me, Patti. How are you? I'm fine."

I stuck my ear against the back of the receiver, trying to hear her mother's voice. "Mom, you know my roommate that I told you about? Yeah, Melany."

I felt proud and embarrassed, like a flag had been raised inside my stomach. It was nothing, I told imaginary reporters.

"Yeah," Patti said, "she wants to talk to you," and handed me the phone.

"No, Patti, no," I hissed, trying to knock the phone away. "Uh, hi. Patti's mom? This is Melany. How are you?"

Patti whispered in my free ear, "Tell her about the orgasms."

"I wanted to tell you how much I like your daughter. She's real—clean."

Patti snatched the phone back. "Bye, mom." She hung up and looked at me. "Chicken."

"She's your mother," I said. "Why should I tell her?"

"She already knows, you idiot," Patti laughed. "I told her over the vacation, what do you think?"

"Oh," I said, deflated.

"Thank you for saying that I'm clean, though. I think you're real clean too."

"Shut up, Patti," I said.

"I'm glad my 'first time' could be with someone whose room is a sanitary pad," Patti teased me. "But if you really want me to 'come out,' you should make love to me outside."

I pictured myself making love to Patti under the streetlight in front of our apartment, and said, "Bring enough money for the parking meter. Sisterhood takes a lot of quarters."

ROEY THORPE

GROWING IN DEFIANCE

Summer, 1981. I am eighteen. I have just spent the best summer of my life as a counselor at Girl Scout camp. The camp is located in Defiance, Ohio, a town that must surely have been named for the camp counselors who have passed through there. All I can say about why the summer was so great is that I have finally met women who feel like real friends. They have moved into a space inside me, very near my soul, that has always felt terrifyingly empty. All my life I have said (to myself, that is—all this occupies a vast unspoken territory in my mind) that no one really knows me, that there is something about me that no one understands or has ever touched. At the beginning of the summer my friend Julie said that if my personality was a color, it would be black, I am that mysterious. Now everything has changed. These women, these uniformed camp counselors with their woodsy nicknames and leather monkey-fists hanging tough around their sunburned necks, their tousled short hair and big grins, these women knocked away that empty feeling with their first slap on my shoulder and first race back to the tent. They have smoothed over that gaping, tatter-edged hole in my heart with their appreciation for gritty courage, of which I discover I have plenty.

Spring, 1982. I am in a car with Deb, a friend from camp. It is late at night and we are driving fast, but that is not the reason I am clutching the car door in desperation. My knuckles are numb and my wrist aches from gripping the door handle. Deb has just told me she is gay, and that she has become lovers with another woman from camp last summer. I am smiling and nodding. "Good for you," I say. I am terrified and I can't wait to get out of the car. Deb says she's glad I understand, that telling friends is hard. I crinkle my nose at her affectionately—a trick I learned from Liz, who's in my sorority. Liz is also gay, but thankfully I don't know that yet. It seems to me that Deb and I no longer have a destination—we're just going to hurtle on endlessly through the darkness with the word "gay" bouncing around in the air, ricocheting off the ripped upholstery of Deb's old Buick. Finally, Deb drops me off at home and I wave as I spring out of the car like a jack-in-the-box. We don't hug goodbye.

Later that night as I lay in bed, heart pounding in my ears, I think these words, slowly, deliberately: "Are you so scared because you think you might be gay, too?" "No," I tell myself firmly. And at the same time, a voice rises up from inside me, a voice I have not heard before. It hisses into my ear from inside: "Yes, you are gay. You want women, that's how you are different." I tremble until my teeth chatter in the cool night air, afraid of what I might be and of this voice I did not know lived inside me. If there was excitement to be had from the danger and the secrets, I did not yet feel it. I only felt frightened and once more, alone.

Summer, 1982. The first day of camp staff training week has finally arrived. I am delighted at the prospect of three months with these women I love so dearly, even though I now know that every one of them is a lesbian. Although my boyfriend, who some people call "faggot" but who I think is bisexual, could not be further from my thoughts, I say that I am straight. I say it repeatedly, to anyone who will listen. I do not know that my friends have made sizable bets about the short-term nature of this identity. They do not know that one of them is about to win big money.

I see her, hanging at the edge of this group of counselors, and I can't catch my breath. I am hugging my friends, trying to chat with them, but my eyes keep track of her movements, which are few, since she is shy. Her hair is bleached almost white from chlorine and sun, and she is tall and tanned. But what makes me stop dead are her eyes, brilliant blue and drooping at the corners, like her shoulders do when she lopes along with her hands in her pockets. I am captivated by her, and instantly, although we have not spoken to one another, I am in love. The intensity of this feeling will last for two years, my attraction to her fading gradually after that time, getting its last knocks as she marries a man to try to hide from a world that seems impossibly cruel. But that happens many years later, after we have, between us, lost our parents and many of our friends, and after men will have tried to rape each of us, and will have succeeded with one of us, who will then abort the child she conceived during the rape. This first moment, though, is as free as any I have ever experienced, and as she finally meets my gaze, which does not waver, I take my first step toward recognizing that frightening voice inside me as my own.

Fall, 1982. I am back at college, arriving early for the first day of marching band practice. Friends rush up to me, ask me about my summer. Ecstatic, I tell them I am in love. "Who is he?" they ask. "She," I blurt out. "It's a girl!" They are horrified and pull me into a practice room, closing the door firmly. "No," they say, "it can't be. And if it is, you must tell no one." Confused, I burst into tears. So much innocence has been lost in that moment. When I finally dry my eyes and rejoin the group, I tell people my summer was fine, nothing else.

Spring, 1983. The new semester arrives and with it comes the first women's studies class of my life. My college advisor insists on it even though it fulfills no requirements that I need. During our appointment I was belligerent and stubborn, and as I stormed out of his office he grabbed my arm and shoved a women's studies course list at me. Later, I see that this course will change my life and give me the focus for which I have always searched. I need something, because I have quit the music department, my grades are low, and my weekends are spent at a bar in Toledo called the Scaramouche, where I pick up a different woman each weekend night. I love the sex, but I'm also doing it because those nights are the only time I can sleep, safe in the strong arms of the oldest, toughest woman I can find. Every other night I toss and turn, afraid of the dreams I know I will have. In these dreams, as in life, I am president of my sorority, and, gavel in hand, I am bringing a chapter meeting to a close. But before I can do this, a woman shouts out, "The president is a queer!" One by one my sisters stand and remove their sorority pins and necklaces, drop them on the long table, and file out of the room, leaving me there, alone, a sorority of one.

Spring, 1984. I am going with my new friends from women's studies to hear Meg Christian. I have been a fan of her music since December, when I bought several of her albums and recorded them onto unlabeled cassettes so no one would know what I listen to on my walkman. I am excited because her songs make me think that maybe I can love women and still live. I have just gotten a job in the women's studies office and I have high hopes that his job will give me courage. I do not know I have been hired because the director can see very clearly what I am going through. I think no one can tell. Although I have quit the sorority, you would not know that to look at me. I am very perky, and have on a black cashmere sweater with a deep "V" in the back, tight jeans, and cowboy boots with three-inch heels. I am wearing a lot of makeup and my hair has been chemically straightened and sprayed into place. My friends walk ahead of me as we go into the concert, and I'm not sure if they are embarrassed by how I look or if I just can't keep up because of the heels. After the concert, we drive through McDonald's and, as soon as we get our food, we yell "Have a gay day!" at the drive-through window, and then peel out of the parking lot howling with laughter at our daring. The act is childish, but the rush of pleasure I get gives me a taste of how powerful visibility could be.

Two weeks later, I am almost asleep in a room I share with Tammy, one of my housemates, who is sleeping in her bed. Suddenly, a man is on top of me. It is Tammy's friend David, who is supposed to be sleeping on the couch downstairs. David is a born-again Christian, and as he tries to pull the covers off me he is saying that God wants me to experience a man, because homosexuality is a sin. How does he know about me? is my first thought, and my confusion gives him time to rip the bedspread back. I yell for help. I am screaming, but Tammy does not move. Suddenly I get it: she knows about this, she helped plan for me to be the victim of this missionary violence. But I am a camp counselor, I am strong and fast and he is a small man whose God cannot nearly match the rage I feel at this sin. I throw him to the floor and grab the pocketknife I keep by my bed. I open it and press it against his face, grabbing his long wild hair with one hand. I hold him there until his eyes roll with terror. When I let him go he runs out of the house and I fall back into bed, adrenalin surging through me. It has taken something this terrible for me to begin to understand: only by action, not by silence, will I save my own life.

Days later, I am eating lunch at a fast-food restaurant with a woman from a tiny rural town nearby. She has said she wants to discuss the Girl Scout troop I am leading there. She tells me that she wants me to promise that I won't take the troop on any overnight camping trips, which makes no sense to me since the girls in my troop are high school–aged. I don't get what she's saying until she pulls out a piece of paper and threatens that if I don't sign it, she'll tell the whole town I'm a homosexual. "Please don't do that," I beg, and then I hear my pleading tone of voice and stop short. In a split second I decide that I have had enough. I refuse to live my life like this, to act as though I share her filthy fantasy. I sit back and look her in the eye. In a voice that is much too loud and getting louder, I say, "Don't tell them I'm a homosexual. Tell them I'm a lesbian." I'm shouting now, "Tell them I'm a big fucking dyke and they'd better keep their women in the house when I'm in town," and then I'm standing up and throwing my giant Wendy's salad right onto her lap. Salad dressing spatters on her chest and chunks of bleu cheese and lettuce are moving slowly down her pantyhose. I stride out, hands in my pockets, head held high as everyone stares. I have just come out for real. Through my defiance I hear a voice, the one that I will come to trust, in my head, and this time it says, "At last, you are learning to be proud, and you are going to be fine."

Fall, 1984. I have found a community, or at least other women who want to create one. They asked me to live with them the night of the Meg Christian concert, and I told them I'd consider it even though I knew I wouldn't. But I have changed, and now we are living on the second floor of a big old house, all lesbians, and for the first time in years, my mind can rest easy. I don't worry about who knows I'm a lesbian and who doesn't. These women I live with are my comrades, and not only can I trust them to stand with me against whatever the world might dish out, I know they are strong enough and loving enough to defeat even the most terrifying enemy.

I know this because together we are doing just that: conquering the fear and self-hatred that lives inside our own heads. We are replacing old stereotypes of lesbian vampires and drooling crazy sicko queers with ancient goddesses and modern-day radical feminists. We learn how to give new meanings to old words, and we proudly proclaim ourselves dykes, hags, witches, and spinsters. We read and we talk and we tease each other mercilessly, and through this we push ourselves to think hard about the things we'd taken for truth. We make ourselves over, not with powder puffs and perfume, but with smoldering rage. We wield picket signs and pens and become a force to be reckoned with in our tiny rural town. We meet older women who are experienced feminists, and we forge friendships with them that we know will last. We learn from them, and from what we read, and from each other. We form reading groups, support groups, political action groups, and social groups. My favorite is the group that goes every night (or at least an outrageous number of nights) to the Big Boy restaurant to eat ice cream out of waffle cones. We sit on the curb under the Big Boy statue, the hair under our arms longer than that on our heads, and are dykey as we eat ice cream. We consider this a political act, and judging from the reaction of the people who spot us, we are correct.

We wish all women looked like us, and it's true, we're an attractive bunch, as would be any set of people who smile as much as we do. Although we are very angry women, we laugh harder and longer and more often than I have ever laughed in my life. We work and play together, and we sleep together, too, couples shifting frequently and seamlessly, then settling for a few months, only to change around again. There are rifts between us now and then, but they are the rough spots any family encounters. We are able to get through these times because we have all healed a great deal, and because we are committed to a vision of the future in which all women can live as we do, together and yet free.

All this feels so familiar to me. Although this community of women is far more self-aware than the camp counselors of that first summer, we are really not so different, nor is the strength that comes from learning to live in wild uncharted territory. Our vision of women's potential is our map, feminism is our compass, and I am packing enough friendship and defiance to last my whole life.

ARMISTEAD MAUPIN

LETTER TO MAMA

DEAR MAMA,

I'm sorry it's taken me so long to write. Every time I try to write to you and Papa I realize I'm not saying the things that are in my heart. That would be O.K., if I loved you any less than I do, but you are still my parents and I am still your child.

I have friends who think I'm foolish to write this letter. I hope they're wrong. I hope their doubts are based on parents who loved and trusted them less than mine do. I hope especially that you'll see this as an act of love on my part, a sign of my continuing need to share my life with you.

I wouldn't have written, I guess, if you hadn't told me about your involvement in the Save Our Children campaign. That, more than anything, made it clear that my responsibility was to tell you the truth, that your own child is homosexual, and that I never needed saving from anything except the cruel and ignorant piety of people like Anita Bryant.

I'm sorry, Mama. Not for what I am, but for how you must feel at this moment. I know what that feeling is, for I felt it for most of my life. Revulsion, shame, disbelief—rejection through fear of something I knew, even as a child, was as basic to my nature as the color of my eyes.

No, Mama, I wasn't "recruited." No seasoned homosexual ever served as my mentor. But you know what? I wish someone had. I wish someone older than me and wiser than the people in Orlando had taken me aside and said, "You're all right, kid. You can grow up to be a doctor or a teacher just like anyone else. You're not crazy or sick or evil. You can succeed and be happy and find peace with friends—all kinds of friends—who don't give a damn *who* you go to bed with. Most of all, though, you can love and be loved, without hating yourself for it."

But no one ever said that to me, Mama. I had to find it out on my own, with the help of the city that has become my home. I know this may be hard for you to believe, but San Francisco is full of men and women, both straight and gay, who don't consider sexuality in measuring the worth of another human being.

These aren't radicals or weirdos, Mama. They are shop clerks and bankers and little old ladies and people who nod and smile to you when you meet them on the bus. Their attitude is neither patronizing nor pitying. And their message is so simple: Yes, you are a person. Yes, I like you. Yes, it's all right for you to like me too.

I know what you must be thinking now. You're asking yourself: What did we do wrong? How did we let this happen? Which one of us made him that way?

I can't answer that, Mama. In the long run, I guess I really don't care. All I know is this: If you and Papa are responsible for the way I am, then I thank you with all my heart, for it's the light and the joy of my life.

I know I can't tell you what it is to be gay. But I can tell you what's it not.

It's not hiding behind words, Mama. Like family and decency and Christianity. It's not fearing your body, or the pleasures that God made for it. It's not judging your neighbor, except when he's crass or unkind.

Being gay has taught me tolerance, compassion and humility. It has shown me the limitless possibilities of living. It has given me people whose passion and kindness and sensitivity have provided a constant source of strength.

It has brought me into the family of man, Mama, and I like it here. I *like* it.

There's not much else I can say, except that I'm the same Michael you've always known. You just know me better now. I have never consciously done anything to hurt you. I never will.

Please don't feel you have to answer this right away. It's enough for me to know that I no longer have to lie to the people who taught me to value the truth.

Mary Ann sends her love.

Everything is fine at 28 Barbary Lane.

Your loving son,
MICHAEL

LEV RAPHAEL

SHOUTS OF JOY

Weeping may lodge with us at evening,
but in the morning there are shouts of joy.
—Psalm 30

Afterward, they would agree that Ken saw the woman first as she
stepped from somewhere to fill the empty seat at his left in the noisy Hillel dining room that Friday night. She was beautiful and still, a slim redhead with
bright bluish-green eyes, twenty-five, perhaps, dressed in rich dark colors—
plum, maroon. There was a fine gold pattern in her hair like the gleaming em-
broidery on a prayer-shawl bag, he later decided.

At the long table, where everyone waited for dinner, loud joking discussions
followed the blessing over the wine. The large room's baseboard heating could
only tease the Massachusetts November cold but could not displace it. The
woman sat, hands in her lap, smiling at the noise, the evening. When Ken told
her his name and his major, and asked if she was a graduate student, her "no"
made him look at her more closely. She seemed rested and very content, and
her heavy cowl-neck sweater, high leather boots, and wool skirt looked a shade
fuller and more luxurious than what people in their small college town generally wore.

"I'm Riva," she said. "I'm just here for dinner."

Hal and Amy, sitting directly opposite, introduced themselves.

Riva seemed so kind that Ken had an unexpected, frightening desire to tell
her he was gay, which he hadn't told anyone here, had hardly even told himself.
It had to be obvious, though. He never dated women and he could not stop

79

looking at men. Everyone at Hillel, the students who lived in the co-op up-stairs, those who like him came to all the Friday-night lectures and services, even Rabbi Keller, seemed to make a point of treating him casually. "We don't mind," their silence, their distance seemed to say, "but keep it to yourself." He sometimes felt like a drunken wedding guest at a reception with everyone screening him off by their politeness, muffling the explosion they feared he might make. And he was too uncertain and afraid to search out other gays, though he knew he could go to the Gay Council office at the Union Building, or to Rashid's, the local disco, for Wednesday's Gay Night, or even to the men's room in the basement of the Music Building.

Before, upstairs, at the service welcoming the Sabbath, he'd felt more lonely than usual. He wanted to share the service, to welcome the Sabbath bride not just with friends and acquaintances, but with a *man*—someone like Eric, Hillel's excellent cook. He loved watching Eric. A hotel-management major, Eric was short, tight-knit, with a mane of curly brown hair, and a broad, heart-shaped face, thick short mustache, and startlingly blue eyes that gave nothing away. He handled and served food with a formality that was sensuous, almost embarrassing—for Ken, anyway. And his stocky taut body seemed terribly confined by whatever clothes he wore. Tonight he had on a sexy thick deep blue turtleneck, which stretched across his hard and perfect chest.

What would his parents say if they knew that just fifteen minutes after prayer, Ken was sitting there hoping Eric would turn around and show the crack of his tight faded jeans, which were a kind of nudity under the long white chef's apron?

He looked away, to find Riva smiling at him, as if she had seen and under-stood everything. Eyes soft and sympathetic, she shrugged lightly, as if assur-ing him the future would be okay.

"Where are you from?" Ken asked as Eric wheeled the soup cart closer to their end of the table.

"The East."

"You must hate it here," Hal said from the opposite side of the table. "There's nothing to do, and it's so goyish." Tall, freckled, glaring, Hal was Ken's least favorite person at Hillel. He was from "Lawn Guyland," from one of the Five Towns, and was constantly complaining about how Amherst was nothing compared to New York—too quiet, too dull, too WASP. He always wore an enormous gold-plated Star of David, like some beacon sending off a distress signal.

"But the trees," Riva said. "The valley. The river. All so beautiful." Ken tried to place her accent—it sure wasn't Boston. She was right about Amherst; even though the UMass campus wasn't very attractive, crossing it, you kept catching rich glimpses of the green and gold Connecticut River Valley between build-ings.

Riva handed her bowl to Eric, who raised his eyebrows as if mocking Hal. The table was soon canopied by steam and the savor of lentil soup. "Besides," Riva continued, "where there are Jews is a Jewish place, no?"

Hal sneered and went at his soup.

His girlfriend, Amy, said, "I have friends in Boston."

"Yes." Riva nodded, which seemed strange to Ken, but Amy smiled as if the two women had just exchanged a confidence. Small, dark, shy, Amy had been dating Hal for a month, and next to him, her little light always seemed dimmer, almost extinguished. Ken hated how when he'd seen them walking together, Hal held his hand at the back of Amy's neck, as if steering her, or holding up a dead plucked chicken.

The huge aluminum salad bowl lurched closer, passed by eager, unsteady hands. Ken could hear Rabbi Keller at the other end of the table discussing Carter's recent triumph at Camp David.

"What do you do?" Amy asked, sipping her wine.

"I'm a violinist—"

"Then you must be with the chamber ensemble at the Arts Center tomorrow night. I *love* the violin."

Hal speared a radish. "Why are you *here?*"

"In a strange place," Riva said, "I wanted to be among Jews Friday night."

It was said with embarrassing simplicity, and Ken felt as if Riva was speaking the truth of his heart, or at least part of it. Amy studied Riva, smiling a bit oddly, and Hal just rolled his eyes. Meanwhile, the twenty others at the table did their imitations, argued politics, panned movies, talked about "Saturday Night Live"—the easiness and warmth that made Ken feel at home. He noticed a few people eyeing Riva.

"*This* nothing little place is what you want?" Hal began complaining about Rabbi Keller, who was new. His Orthodox background, Hal said, ruined their Conservative services. "I mean, if I wanted *Fiddler on the Roof* I'd see the damned movie, all right?"

Ken didn't listen. He *liked* how Rabbi Keller led services with quiet passion and authority. He liked being able to lose himself in the service it had taken him two years to fully understand and love. As the son of Reform Jews, the prayerbook's Hebrew rows had looked like impossible walls to him, unscalable, but now he was inside them and knew so many strange things: that he liked praying, that he believed in God, that he wanted to live a Jewish life, whatever that meant.

"We need more English," Hal was objecting.

"Hebrew's beautiful," Amy pressed.

"You can't read more than a *line!*"

"I'm learning." Flushed, Amy added. "It *sounds* beautiful."

"Why do you come here?" Riva asked Hal sharply, leaning forward. "Why come if you don't like anything?"

Hal just stared.

"*Why?* To feel superior? To laugh at people?"

Hal shook his head as the table quieted down.

"You think you know all about God, don't you? People like you keep God away."

Hal flung the wine in his glass at her, spattering Ken, too. People jumped up, knocking their chairs over. Amy shouted, "Stop it!" and in the sudden confusion, with knives and forks paralyzed or dropped and people standing, chattering, confused, asking what had happened, Riva was gone.

Amy stood up. "You are *disgusting*," she said, moving away from Hal.

Someone tapped Ken on the shoulder. It was Eric, handing him a washcloth to wipe his face. Eric said, "Why not help me clean up, later?"

In the kitchen after everyone else had gone home, when the cleaning was almost done, and all the co-op members were out or upstairs, they talked about Hal's mortified apology to Rabbi Keller, the small storm of gossip, with everyone wondering who Riva was, and people giving different descriptions of her voice, her hands, her hair.

"She sure got to Hal, like she knew just what would hit," Eric kept saying. "It's about time."

"I'd like to see her tomorrow, at the recital." Ken closed the dishwasher.

"You won't," Eric said, tying up a garbage bag. "She's not in the poster up in the hallway."

Ken felt relaxed, as if the wine had washed away his shyness, his longing, and he perched on the top of a step stool while Eric fixed them hot chocolate.

Eric handed him a steaming sweet mug.

Ken stirred his hot chocolate. "She didn't say she was *in* it. Maybe she's an understudy or something. No, that's dumb. Maybe she was sick when they took the picture. Or we just assumed—"

"—Maybe not."

"What do you know about her?"

Eric dried his hands. "I'm just guessing." The large kitchen, with its banks of cupboards, two massive aluminum-hooded stoves, suddenly seemed private and small.

"What do you know about her?"

"Wait." Eric went out to the hall closet and returned with his backpack. He fished inside for a paperback, searched for a page, and then handed the book over, open. "This is a book my sister sent me last month. I've been thinking about it ever since dinner. Look at the top on the right."

Ken read half-aloud: "Elijah wanders over the face of the earth in many and varied disguises ... bound by neither time nor space ... he acts as a celestial messenger. ... He brings consolation to the afflicted and chides the arrogant and proud."

Ken put the book down. "Oh come *on*," he said. "Passover's months away, and Elijah's a *man*."

"So are you," Eric said, moving closer to slip a hand over Ken's where it lay on the book of folktales. Then he grinned.

Ken suddenly felt as if he was soaring up in a World Trade Center elevator, alone, rocketing so fast that nothing would be left behind, not a trace of who he had been. The hard insistent beat of his pulse seemed to rock him back and forth like Orthodox men in prayer. He couldn't speak.

"We're done," Eric said, a little flushed. "We can go back to my apartment."

Eric lived in a large studio a few icy blocks from the Hillel building and close to the tiny downtown, at the top of a house with a view of the Emily Dickinson home, though you couldn't see it from Eric's place. The furniture, drapes, and wallpaper were splashed with a floral print of orange, gold, and green. "My sister's a decorator," Eric explained. "She wanted me to feel warm all winter." Two tall bookcases were stuffed with paperbacks on Jewish history, worship, and thought, Jewish fiction—a small library almost as rich and varied as the one at Hillel.

"Have you *read* all this stuff? Really?" As Ken stood scanning the shelves, afraid to turn around, Eric came up and started massaging his shoulders, slowly, with the easy authority of someone doing Japanese ideograms—it was exciting, tense, involved. Ken leaned back into the warmth, the pressure.

"Don't stop," he said, "or I'll think of some reason to leave."

"No you won't." Eric broke away and opened the couch bed as if he were a pirate revealing his treasure. And then he stripped. Ken had seen men like this at the campus gym, had sat next to them on locker-room benches, but they were always figures, not people, not anyone looking at him with open, inviting eyes. Eric stood like a wrestler, poised, tight, his tautly muscled body hairless, except at the base of his fat jutting cock. He was as beautiful as all those men Ken had gawked at in the weight room, or biking through town, arms and shoulders bulging with force, or jogging across campus with sweatpants tight across their firm asses and calves.

"Why would you want to leave?" Eric smiled. "Society? Your parents? The Torah?"

"All of that, especially the Torah."

Eric sat on the bed, legs wide. "Do you keep kosher? I didn't think so. Then why choose just one restriction to guide your life, to make you feel like dirt?"

"You've had this discussion before."

"So have you. Come here."

"I don't know what to do."

"You'll learn, you'll learn."

Eric slipped Ken out of his clothes so gently, he could have been a nurse. He pushed Ken back on the bed and moved on top of him, massaging him slowly with his whole body, kissing his mouth and eyes, his ears, stroking his hair, his sides, languidly rubbing his heavy penis up and down the length of Ken's, and across until Ken exploded from the pressure, the excitement, and the hungry, commanding look in Eric's eyes.

"You didn't turn off the lights," Ken murmured.

"There's time," Eric said, pushing a pillow under Ken's head and moving up to crouch across his chest, his cock throbbing like a slow metronome.

"I'm real close," Eric said, moving to Ken's mouth. And as Eric pushed Ken's mouth open, Ken felt his lips were as sensitive, as tingling as if he were high. He closed his eyes, licking and sucking with everything in his life somehow concentrated at that one spot. When Eric groaned and clutched the back of Ken's head, Ken didn't pull away, didn't cough or spit—he felt too peaceful and relaxed.

Eric got off and lay beside him, and Ken only knew that they had slept when he woke up near dawn, with Eric down between his legs, tongue tracing the curves of his balls.

Eric looked up, eyebrows twitching like Groucho Marx.

At services that morning, before the Torah was taken from the ark, Ken whispered, "Do you really think Riva was—?"

Eric shrugged. "It's some story, huh?"

And when the Torah was brought around, Ken was struck for the first time by the bold embroidered lions flanking the tablets of the law on the scroll's white velvet sheath. Their glass eyes were so very blue, like Eric's, like Riva's.

Ken reached his prayer book to touch the white velvet, and brought it back to his lips.

"It's a *great* story," Ken said to Eric as the Torah was borne away.

MUJERES MORENAS

She sleeps coiled beside me, como una gatita morena, her curly head snug against my shoulder. I like to reach over and feel her near me in the night. When I caress her bare shoulder, she stirs, but does not awaken. I watch her and smile.

Verónica alternates between sleeping soundly and platicando casi toda la noche. When she wants to talk, she wakes me con besitos and a whispered apology, but tonight she is too tired.

I'm wide awake, too wired to think about sleep. And so I leave the lamp on, rearrange my pillows and stretch out, feeling Verónica's steady breath on my arm.

My mind whirls with ideas about editing the video tape I shot today at La Celebración Latina Lesbiana. I'm still excited about spending hours there with Verónica and about fifty other Latina dykes. Scenes from the day's events flash through my memory, and I almost kiss her awake to brainstorm with her. But she sleeps peacefully. I stare at the beamed ceiling, imagining it to be a film screen, and replay the day.

Celebración

The wide corridor of the city college's administration building surges with brown-skinned women—young, old, butch, femme, and lots of in-betweens. Some are mujeres recently arrived from América Latina while others are U.S.-born Chicanas. The summer air sizzles with the lilting sounds of Spanish, Spanglish, and English.

Verónica and I join them. Mi morenita carries a leather binder under one arm while I balance my video camera on my shoulder. With her observant eyes and quiet demeanor, she offers more smiles than words. She seems to inhale the delicious aroma of the other Latinas, relishing their jovial spirits, their animated talk. She nudges me when she spots Felicia Montoya and Marti Villanueva, the event organizers.

"Orale, compañeras," I yell. Felicia and Marti look up just as I turn on the camera. They mug outrageously, and the four of us crack up.

The mujeres surrounding us share our laughter. The day begins with fun.

I glance at my sleeping lover. Like delicate feathers, her luxuriant eyelashes spread upon her high cheekbones. She lies so still. A few moments ago, she had been vibrant in my arms, rocking with me passionately. Mi morenita—does she dream of me? I find her always in my thoughts, en mis sueños.

At la Celebración, I'd buzzed from workshop to workshop, lugging my video equipment and worrying about Verónica being on her own. Yeah, I'm over-protective, but she's shy in crowds, especially when I know more women than she does—which is usually the case. And almost every mujer at la Celebración had been familiar—in one way or another.

Before I met Verónica, I used to make it my business to hang out with as many dykes as possible. Coming from Tejas, I ran wild when I got to Los Angeles and saw dykes everywhere. I'd built up quite a reputation, too. But, shy or not, she changed all that.

Over a year ago, la morenita lassoed mi corazón with su high-toned rap about my student film "Tortilleras." After the screening, I'd found out Verónica was a grad student, too, writing about Chicana lesbians. And, I fell in love with her—hard and fast like the first time. Pero sabes que? She gave me the cold shoulder. She was scared—tenía miedo of being hurt again. I wouldn't quit, though. And after a shaky start, we're living together and collaborating on a screenplay. Almost every day, I wonder if I'm dreaming.

To make sure I'm not, I gently touch her black hair. Its thick curls tickle my fingers and swirl between them. And I'm tempted to interrupt her dreams, if only for a little while. But she needs her sleep. With a sigh, I snuggle close and flash back on la Celebración.

Más Celebración

"I'm nervous, René. Lots of women here speak only Spanish. How can I read to them? They won't understand me." Verónica fidgets with her manuscript, dog-earing its corners. "Why didn't I think of that?"

I put my equipment aside and squeeze her con un abrazo fuerte. "English's your first language. You don't have to make apologies."

She stands back and shoots me a skeptical look. "That's easy for you to say. No wonder you made a silent film. Language isn't even an issue in 'Tortilleras.'"

"It won't be for you either." I love how she shares her anxiety with me. She needs my reassurance. And I give it, kissing her ear lobe right on the double women's symbol aretes I'd given her for her cumpleaños.

She pulls me closer when I do that. We're in a corner of the conference room, and I wish for privacy. I wrap my arms around her, anyhow. Most of las mujeres don't even notice.

I'm about to kiss her again when I spot Rosalinda strolling in, all femmed out in black tank top and leather mini. Her straight hair covers her shoulders like a cape of ravens' wings. It's been months since I've seen her. Rosalinda looks saucy—and sexy. She glares at me and I quickly turn away.

Verónica feels me flinch and her eyes question me.

"Rosalinda," I say.

"Behind me?"

"Si. Como araña, toda en negro."

"I saw her name in the program. She'll dance when the Cubanas play their timbales." Verónica touches my cheek. "Don't let her get to you, René. It's over, isn't it?"

I kiss the tips of her slender fingers. "Por que me preguntas? I love *you.*"

"I know." Her steady eyes meet mine. "But you did react when she came in."

"Just 'cause la esa's in my film and happens to be—"

"Your ex-lover," Verónica reminds me. "If you ignore her, René, it'll be obvious to everyone."

"The ones who know, anyway," I mumble.

Que mala suerte. Rosalinda's supposed to be in Albuquerque. I sure didn't count on meeting up with her here.

Verónica watches me. She's trying to size up my feelings. I keep hoping she doesn't ask any more questions. I flash a fast grin and back off, hoisting the camera to my shoulder.

With some relief, I notice Felicia Montoya elbowing her way towards us. She smiles and winks. She hasn't missed a thing.

"Verónica, I'm still looking for a podium for your reading. Want to come with me to check upstairs?"

Felicia's a long-time activist, with ties to both feminist and Chicana communities. I've done lots of video work for her, and now figure her plan is to take Verónica out of the line of fire.

"Sure, Felicia. I'm going to need something to hang onto when my knees start to shake." Verónica squeezes my shoulder. "Get back to work, Talamantes. And be careful."

I know she's not referring to my dropping the camera. As she leaves with Felicia, I blow her un besito. She looks edgy.

When she's gone, I survey the room and see no trace of Rosalinda. Hauling my stuff, I mosey over to Marti Villanueva and a group of Latinas setting up a slide projector. I aim the camera at them and zoom in on Marti. She faces me with a defiant stare and a butch stance, hands on thin hips, jean-clad legs apart.

"Ay, Martita. Que tough te mires."

"Estás celosa, René." Marti flicks me the finger and the other women razz us. Villanueva speaks in that low-down East L.A. sing-song and likes to clown around. She hands Toni Dorado the rest of the slides and comes toward me.

I glance at her over the camera. "So what do you think of the turnout?"

She shrugs. "There's got to be more Latina lesbians in town than this. I think lots of them're still scared to come out."

I put the camera on a low table and grab two Cokes from the cooler. "It's never easy. But the more celebraciónes you have, the more mujeres you'll attract." I pop open my can.

"You saw Rosalinda?" Marti takes the other Coke and digs her bony elbow into my ribs.

I nod and guzzle my Coke. "How could I miss her? Verónica says I shouldn't ignore her."

Marti grins again. "You were planning to?"

Villaneuva and I go back a ways. She was the first Chicana dyke I met when Mamá y yo settled in Venice. I'd pushed open the wooden gate on my way to buy tortillas and bumped into Marti rollerskating on the narrow sidewalk outside our house. I'd sent her sprawling.

Once I'd caught a glimpse of her loose-limbed body and her boy-cut hair, I knew I was face to face with the Lesbian Welcoming Committee of Venice, California. Marti'd sprung up, toda sonrisas, and wound up eating with Mamá y yo esa noche y muchas otras. Marti y yo somos como hermanas. But today I flip her a glare and pick up the camera.

She decides not to mess with me. "Rosalinda left to rehearse with the other dancers. Buena suerte, René." She salutes me with her coke as I leave the refreshment area.

In the hallway, I follow the sounds of recorded salsa music. Mujeres mill through the corridor on their way to workshops, and I flick on the camera. While I shoot, I explain the video's been commissioned by the organizers. I don't want anyone getting paranoid over my taping them. None of the mujeres do; they flirt with me and tease me.

Being with Latinas touches mi corazón. It isn't often that Verónica and I find ourselves surrounded by so many Latina lesbians. I enjoy the novelty of mingling with éstas mujeres morenas, hearing their bilingual joking, listening to them talk about being lesbians of color in a white and hostile world.

On my way to find Rosalinda, I smile and wave at many familiar faces, but don't pause to talk. I want to see her and get it over with. My stomach churns, and I wish she'd had the sense to stay away. But, why should she? Rosalinda's Latina tambien. She's here for the same reason Verónica and I are—to meet other Latina lesbians. At least, that's what I hope.

I peek into classrooms, looking for her. One is filled with gyrating dancers, but she isn't among them. In an empty classroom, she stands by a window and holds a compact mirror to her face. She meticulously applies lipstick la color de sangre.

"Is the camera on, René?"

"No." I stare at her from the doorway.

She snaps the compact, dumps the lipstick into her shoulder bag, and whirls around on her high heels. Rosalinda, for all her faults, definitely has grace.

"Remember when I wanted to dance desnuda in the film and we argued about it? You said those white robes would give the illusion of tortillas." With irony, she smiles, her lips a red slash. "I used to think you were gutless and I was so daring. But you knew what you wanted and made the film your way."

"It wouldn't have worked without your input, Rosalinda."

"You say that now." She tosses her long hair and her high heels click-click across the linoleum toward me. Her actions seem deliberately theatrical.

"Es la verdad." I set the camera on a nearby chair and slowly rotate my neck and shoulders. The camera is heavy and my right shoulder aches. Tension probably has something to do with it, too.

"And what's the truth about us?" She stops before me, her brown skin glowing against her black outfit. Mujeres morenas—why do they arouse me so?

I clear my throat. "I'm in love with Verónica."

"And I'm in love with you, pendeja."

I hold up my hands to ward off her bitter words. "Rosalinda, you and I were already apart when she came along."

Her eyes are like onyx. "You previewed the film while I was in Albuquerque. You didn't even wait for me to come back."

I try not to sound defensive. "I didn't know how long you'd be gone. When my advisor asked if I wanted 'Tortilleras' to be part of the Film Department's summer series, I took him up on it. I figured it was smart to get feedback early. That way, I could edit it again before fall."

Rosalinda's eyes remain stony. "Did you ever tell Verónica about me?"

I hope to sound cool. "She asked if we'd been involved. She guessed 'cause you got more close-ups than Beatríz."

"If Verónica's so smart, why's she sleeping with you?" Rosalinda crosses her arms and taps one foot on the chipped linoleum.

I make a move towards the camera. I've heard enough. The slide show is about to start, and I don't want to miss it. Toni Dorado, a Chicana librarian, had spent weeks researching historical Latina Americanas, and I had helped her photograph the slides.

"René, I'll pull out your greñas if you try to leave."

Since I value my scalp, I decide to stay a few minutes more. "Look, what do you want me to say? Things didn't work out between us. We fought a lot. Even so, I don't hate you, Rosalinda."

"But you love *her*. Y por que? She might as well be white—pura pocha."

I begin to seethe. "Verónica's Chicana and proud of it. Don't ever put her down. Entiendes?"

She recognizes my anger and tries another tactic. "You said you'd never live with a lover and leave your mother alone." She flicks a strand of her raven hair.

I sigh, wondering why I don't split. The Celebración's exuberant sisterhood seems fraudulent in view of Rosalinda's stinging words. I don't want to fight with her. I long to cherish mis hermanas lesbianas, ex-lovers or not. Rosalinda sure isn't making it easy.

I speak quietly. "Mama's not alone—she has a couple of viuda friends living with her. It all worked out."

"Except for us." She bends her head and I know she doesn't want me to see las lagrimas.

I reach over to touch her, but she edges away as if I'd slapped her.

"Lo siento, Rosalinda."

When she doesn't answer, I hesitate. Then I scoop up the camera and leave.

Leaning against the pillows, I close my eyes. Thinking about Rosalinda always exhausts me. We'd burned each other out with our passion and then parted coldly. She is so swift to accuse and unwilling to listen. With Verónica, I'm much happier. Sure, we have our share of problems, but her personality is calmer than mine. Verónica hates to bicker and prefers to talk things out. It's hard sometimes, but it sure makes sense. Rosalinda and I are both hotheads; no wonder we'd run out of steam.

After a few moments, I begin to doze. I feel Verónica cuddle closer, and awake to find her leaning across me. Resting on her elbow, she gazes at me with a drowsy smile. She nuzzles me, her body warm and inviting.

"Why's the lamp still on, chula?" In the dimness, her curly hair frames her face like a dark nimbus.

I yawn. "Did it wake you?"

"No, but your snoring did." With exaggeration, she rolls her eyes. "Every time you fall asleep on your back, you start in, René. What unusual noises— don't ever use them for a soundtrack—unless it's for a horror film."

I like her feisty answer. She loves to be romantic, but doesn't miss a chance to tease about my snoring. Most of the time I'm a good sport about it. Tonight, I grin across the pillows. "Te amo, Verónica."

"I love you, too, Talamantes." She lies on her tummy, one hand leisurely moving across my breasts. Her hands feel smooth, like fine velvet. "What were you doing before you started snoring?"

"Thinking about la Celebración. Wasn't it fun?"

"Once I'd finished my reading, I had a great time." Her index finger finds my left nipple and toys with it. The sudden sensation causes me to tingle from head to toe. I close my eyes and enjoy it. I hope she doesn't stop.

"What'd you think of my reading, René?" Her fingers continue fondling me, their pressure increasing. "I know you were taping, but did you get to hear any of it?"

"All of it." I open my eyes and lazily study her. Her hands do not pause, and she watches me intently, eager for feedback. She knows I'll be honest. "You paced yourself really well, and your delivery was right on target. Las mujeres were real jazzed. It didn't even matter that you read in English."

"De veras?" She beams with pleasure. "That's what I heard, too. I got lots of positive comments."

"Oh, yeah?" I enjoy her touch, the radiance in her eyes.

"Sure. I talked with lots of women while you were roaming around." She wraps one teasing leg around my torso and I feel singed from the heat of her body. "I was a little worried about coming across as brown on the outside and white on the inside, René. But I don't think that happened."

"Nunca, mi morenita." My hands bring her ever closer. I guide her over me and raise my head to kiss her chichis. They are small and soft, her nipples the color of bittersweet chocolate. In turn, I taste each one, and Verónica sighs, her eyes growing sultry.

"René—"

"No hables, querida." I savor the sweetness of her skin.

"I have to tell you something."

"Despues, corazón."

Verónica squirms in my arms, intensifying my desire. She laughs when she withdraws her breast from my mouth and the abrupt action sounds like a champagne cork popping.

"Como eres, Verónica!"

She wears an impish expression. "I just want to say one thing now." She pauses and suddenly her eyes mist. "I felt so proud when you introduced

Rosalinda as one of the dancers in 'Tortilleras,' right before you showed the film. She deserved that."

I look into her ojos oscuros and wind up smiling with her. "Do we have to discuss this ahorita?"

She smiles too, and shakes her head. "No, but I really think it made a difference."

"For her?"

"For both of you. You know that, René, whether you want to admit it or not." She gives my nose a playful tweak. "Sabes que? Estoy muy felíz."

I grin again, loving her, and how she knows me so well.

And Verónica leans forward and covers my mouth with hers. Her lips arouse me further and I cling to her: mujeres morenas—nuestras lenguas bailando con la musica de amor.

JEWELLE L. GOMEZ

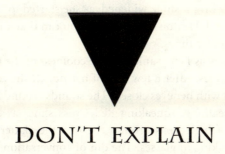

DON'T EXPLAIN

Boston 1959

Lᴇᴛᴛʏ ᴅᴇᴘᴏsɪᴛᴇᴅ the hot platters on the table, effortlessly. She slid one deep-fried chicken, a club-steak with boiled potatoes and a fried porgie platter down her thick arm as if removing beaded bracelets. Each plate landed with a solid clink on the shiny formica, in its appropriate place. The last barely settled before Letty turned back to the kitchen to get Bo John his lemonade and extra biscuits and then to put her feet up. Out of the corner of her eye she saw Tip come in the lounge. His huge shoulders, draped in sharkskin, barely cleared the narrow door frame.

"Damn! He's early tonight!" she thought but kept going. Tip was known for his generosity, that's how he'd gotten his nick-name. He always sat at Letty's station because they were both from Virginia, although neither had been back in years. Letty had come up to Boston in 1946 and been waiting tables in the 411 Lounge since '52. She liked the people: the pimps were limited but flashy; the musicians who hung around were unpredictable in their pursuit of a good time and the "business" girls were generous and always willing to embroider a wild story. After Letty's mother died there been no reason to go back to Burkeville.

Letty took her newspaper from the locker behind the kitchen and filled a large glass with the tart grapejuice punch for which the cook, Mabel, was famous.

"I'm going on break, Mabel. Delia's takin' my station."

She sat in the back booth nearest the kitchen beneath the large blackboard which displayed the menu. When Delia came out of the bathroom Letty hissed

93

to get her attention. The reddish-brown skin of Delia's face was shiny with a country freshness that always made Letty feel a little warm.

"What's up, Miss Letty?" Her voice was soft and saucy.

"Take my tables for twenty minutes. Tip just came in."

The girl's already bright smile widened, as she started to thank Letty.

"Go 'head, go 'head. He don't like to wait. You can thank me if he don't run you back and forth fifty times."

Delia hurried away as Letty sank into the coolness of the overstuffed booth and removed her shoes. After a few sips of her punch she rested her head on the back of the seat with her eyes closed. The sounds around her were as familiar as her own breathing: squeaking Red Cross shoes as Delia and Vinnie passed, the click of high heels around the bar, the clatter of dishes in the kitchen and ice clinking in glasses. The din of conversation rose, levelled and rose again over the juke box. Letty had not played her record in days but the words spun around in her head as if they were on the turntable:

> … *right or wrong don't matter*
> *when you're with me sweet*
> *Hush now, don't explain*
> *You're my joy and pain.*

Letty sipped her cool drink; sweat ran down her spine soaking into the nylon uniform. July weather promised to give no breaks and the fans were working over-time like everybody else.

She saw Delia cross to Tip's table again. In spite of the dyed red hair, no matter how you looked at her Delia was still a country girl: long and self-conscious, shy and bold because she didn't know any better. She'd moved up from Anniston with her cousin a year before and landed the job at the 411 immediately. She worked hard and sometimes Letty and she shared a cab going uptown after work, when Delia's cousin didn't pick them up in her green Pontiac.

Letty caught Tip eyeing Delia as she strode on long, tight-muscled legs back to the kitchen. "That lounge lizard!" Letty thought to herself. Letty had trained Delia: how to balance plates, how to make tips and how to keep the customer's hands on the table. She was certain Delia would have no problem putting Tip in his place. In the year she'd been working Delia hadn't gone out with any of the bar flies, though plenty had asked. Letty figured that Delia and her cousin must run with a different crowd. They talked to each other sporadically in the kitchen or during their break but Letty never felt that wire across her chest like Delia was going to ask her something she couldn't answer.

She closed her eyes again for the few remaining minutes. The song was back in her head and Letty had to squeeze her lips together to keep from humming aloud. She pushed her thoughts onto something else. But when she did she always stumbled upon Maxine. Letty opened her eyes. When she'd quit working at Salmagundi's and come to the 411 she'd promised herself never to think about any woman like that again. She didn't know why missing Billie so much brought it all back to her. She'd not thought of that time or those feelings for a while.

She heard Abe shout a greeting at Duke behind the bar as he surveyed his domain. That was Letty's signal. No matter whether it was her break or not she knew white people didn't like to see their employees sitting down, especially with their shoes off. By the time Abe was settled on his stool near the door, Letty was up, her glass in hand and on her way through the kitchen's squeaky swinging door.

"You finished your break already?" Delia asked.

"Abe just come in."

"Uh oh, let me git this steak out there to that man. Boy he sure is nosey!"

"Who, Tip?"

"Yeah, he ask me where I live, who I live with, where I come from like he supposed to know me!"

"Well just don't take nothing he say to heart and you'll be fine. And don't take no rides from him!"

"Yeah, he asked if he could take me home after I get off. I told him me and you had something to do."

Letty was silent as she sliced the fresh bread and stacked it on plates for the next orders.

"My cousin's coming by, so it ain't a lie, really. She can ride us."

"Yeah," Letty said as Delia giggled and turned away with her platter.

Vinnie burst through the door like she always did, looking breathless and bossy. "Abe up there, girl! You better get back on station. You got a customer."

Letty drained her glass with deliberation, wiped her hands on her thickly starched white apron and walked casually past Vinnie as if she'd never spoken. She heard Mabel's soft chuckle float behind her. She went over to Tip who was digging into the steak like his life depended on devouring it before the plate got dirty.

"Everything alright tonight?" Letty asked, her ample brown body towering over the table.

"Yeah, baby, everything alright. You ain't working' this side no more?"

"I was on break. My feet can't wait for your stomach, you know."

Tip laughed. "Break! What you need a break for, big and healthy as you is!"

"We all gets old, Tip. But the feet get old first, let me tell you that!"

"Not in my business, baby. Why you don't come on and work for me and you ain't got to worry 'bout your feet."

Letty sucked her teeth loudly, the exaggeration a part of the game they played over the years. "Man, I'm too old for that mess!"

"You ain't too old for me."

"Ain't nobody too old for you! Or too young neither, looks like."

"Where you and that gal goin' tonight?"

"To a funeral," Letty responded dryly.

"Aw woman get on away from my food!" The gold cap on his front tooth gleamed from behind his greasy lips when he laughed. Letty was pleased. Besides giving away money Tip liked to hurt people. It was better when he laughed.

The kitchen closed at 11:00 p.m. Delia and Letty slipped out of their uniforms in the tiny bathroom and were on their way out the door by 11:15. Delia looked even younger in her knife-pleated skirt and white cotton blouse. Letty did feel old tonight in her slacks and long-sleeved shirt. The movement of car headlights played across her face, which was set in exhaustion. The dark green car pulled up and they slipped in quietly, both anticipating tomorrow, Sunday, the last night of their work week.

Delia's cousin was a stocky woman who looked forty, Letty's age. She never spoke much. Not that she wasn't friendly. She always greeted Letty with a smile and laughed at Delia's stories about the customers. "Just close to the chest like me, that's all," Letty often thought. As they pulled up to the corner of Columbus Avenue and Cunard Street Letty opened the rear door. Delia turned to her and said, "I'm sorry you don't play your record on your break no more, Miss Letty. I know you don't want to, but I'm sorry just the same."

Delia's cousin looked back at them with a puzzled expression but said nothing. Letty slammed the car door shut and turned to climb the short flight of stairs to her apartment. Cunard Street was quiet outside her window and the guy upstairs wasn't blasting his record player for once. Still, Letty lay awake and restless in her single bed. The fan was pointed at the ceiling, bouncing warm air over her, rustling her sheer nightgown.

Inevitably the strains of Billie Holiday's songs brushed against her, much like the breeze that fanned around her. She felt silly when she thought about it, but the melodies gripped her like a solid presence. It was more than the music. Billie had been her hero. Letty saw Billie as big, like herself, with big hungers, and some secret that she couldn't tell anyone. Two weeks ago, when Letty heard that the Lady had died, sorrow enveloped her. A refuge had been closed that she could not consciously identify to herself or to anyone. It embarrassed her to think about. Like it did when she remembered Maxine.

When Letty first started working at the 411 she met Billie when she'd come into the club with several musicians on her way back from the Jazz Festival. There the audience, curious to see what a real, live junkie looked like, had sat back waiting for Billie to fall on her face. Instead she'd killed them dead with her liquid voice and rough urgency. Still, the young thin horn player kept having to reassure her: "Billie you were the show, the whole show!"

Once convinced, Billie became the show again, loud and commanding. She demanded her food be served at the bar and sent Mabel, who insisted on waiting on her personally, back to the kitchen fifteen times. Billie laughed at jokes that Letty could barely hear as she bustled back and forth between the abandoned kitchen and her own tables. The sound of that laugh from the bar penetrated her bones. She'd watched and listened, certain she saw something no one else did. When Billie had finished eating and gathered her entourage to get back on the road she left a tip, not just for Mabel but for each of the waitresses and the bartender. "Generous just like the 'business' girls," Letty was happy to note. She still had the two one dollar bills in an envelope at the back of her lingerie drawer.

After that, Letty felt even closer to Billie. She played one of the few Lady Day records on the juke box every night, during her break. Everyone at the 411 had learned not to bother her when her song came on. Letty realized, as she lay waiting for sleep, that she'd always felt that if she had been able to say or do something that night to make friends with Billie, it might all have been different. In half sleep the faces of Billie, Maxine and Delia blended in her mind. Letty slid her hand along the soft nylon of her gown to rest it between her full thighs. She pressed firmly, as if holding desire inside herself. Letty could have loved her enough to make it better. That was Letty's final thought as she dropped off to sleep.

Sunday nights at the 411 were generally mellow. Even the pimps and prostitutes used it as a day of rest. Letty came in early and had a drink at the bar and talked with the bartender before going to the back to change into her uniform. She saw Delia through the window as she stepped out of the green Pontiac, looking as if she'd just come from Concord Baptist Church. "Satin Doll" was on the juke box, wrapping the bar in cool nostalgia.

Abe let Mabel close the kitchen early on Sunday and Letty looked forward to getting done by 10:00 or 10:30, and maybe enjoying some of the evening. When her break time came Letty started for the juke box automatically. She hadn't played anything by Billie in two weeks; now, looking down at the inviting glare, she knew she still couldn't do it. She punched the buttons that would bring up Jackie Wilson's "Lonely Teardrops" and went to the back booth.

She'd almost dropped off to sleep when she heard Delia whisper her name. She opened her eyes and looked up into the girl's smiling face. Her head was haloed in tight, shiny curls.

"Miss Letty, won't you come home with me tonight?"

"What?"

"I'm sorry to bother you, but your break time almost up. I wanted to ask if you'd come over to the house tonight … after work. My cousin'll bring you back home after."

Letty didn't speak. Her puzzled look prompted Delia to start again.

"Sometime on Sunday my cousin's friends from work come over to play cards, listen to music, you know. Nothin' special, just some of the girls from the office building down on Winter Street where she work, cleaning. She, I mean we, thought you might want to come over tonight. Have a drink, play some cards. ..."

"I don't play cards much."

"Well not everybody play cards ... just talk ... sitting around talking. My cousin said you might like to for a change."

Letty wasn't sure she like the last part: "for a change," as if they had to entertain an old aunt.

"I really want you to come, Letty. They always her friends but none of them is my own friends. They alright, I don't mean nothin' against them, but it would be fun to have my own personal friend there, you know?"

Delia was a good girl. Those were the perfect words to describe her, Letty thought smiling. "Sure honey, I'd just as soon spend my time with you as lose my money with some fools."

They got off at 10:15 and Delia apologized that they had to take a cab uptown. Her cousin and her friends didn't work on Sunday so they were already at home. Afraid that the snag would give Letty an opportunity to back out Delia hadn't mentioned it until they were out of their uniforms and on the sidewalk. Letty almost declined, tempted to go home to the safe silence of her room. But she didn't. She stepped into the street and waved down a Red and White cab. All the way uptown Delia apologized that the evening wasn't a big deal and cautioned Letty not to expect much. "Just a few friends, hanging around, drinking and talking." She was jumpy and Letty tried to put her at ease. She had not expected her first visit would make Delia so anxious.

The apartment was located halfway up Blue Hill Avenue in an area where a few blacks had recently been permitted to rent. They entered a long, carpeted hallway and heard the sounds of laughter and music ringing from the rooms at the far end.

Once inside, with the door closed, Delia's personality took on another dimension. This was clearly her home and Letty could not believe she ever really needed an ally to back her up. Delia stepped out of her shoes at the door and walked to the back with her same, long-legged gait. They passed a closed door, which Letty assumed to be one of the bedrooms, then came to a kitchen ablaze with light. Food and bottles were strewn across the pink and gray formica-top table. A counter opened from the kitchen into the dining room, which was the center of activity. Around a large mahogany table sat five women in smoke-filled concentration, playing poker.

Delia's cousin looked up from her cards with the same slight smile as usual. Here it seemed welcoming, not guarded as it did in those brief moments in her car. She wore brown slacks and matching sweater. The pink, starched points of her shirt collar peeked out at the neck.

Delia crossed to her and kissed her cheek lightly. Letty looked around the table to see if she recognized anyone. The women all seemed familiar in the way that city neighbors can, but Letty was sure she hadn't met any of them before. Delia introduced her to each one: Karen, a short, round woman with West Indian bangles up to her pudgy elbow; Betty, who stared intently at her cards through thick eyeglasses encased in blue cat-eye frames; Irene, a big, dark woman with long black hair and a gold tooth in front. Beside her sat Myrtle who was wearing army fatigues and a gold Masonic ring on her pinky finger. She said hello in the softest voice Letty had ever heard. Hovering over her was Clara, a large red woman whose hair was bound tightly in a bun at the nape of her neck. She spoke with a delectable southern accent that drawled her "How're you doin'" into a full paragraph that was draped around an inquisitive smile.

Delia became ill-at-ease again as she pulled Letty by the arm toward the French doors behind the players. There was a small den with a desk, some books and a television set. Through the next set of glass doors was a livingroom. At the record player was an extremely tall, brown-skinned woman. She bent over the wooden cabinet searching for the next selection, oblivious to the rest of the gathering. Two women sat on the divan in deep conversation, which they punctuated with constrained giggles.

"Maryalice, Sheila, Dolores … this is Letty."

They looked up at her quickly, smiled, then went back to their pre-occupations: two to their gossip, the other returned to the record collection. Delia directed Letty back toward the foyer and the kitchen.

"Come on, let me get you a drink. You know, I don't even know what you drink!"

"Delia?" Her cousin's voice reached them over the counter, just as they stepped into the kitchen. "Bring a couple of beers back when you come, OK?"

"Sure, babe." Delia went to the refrigerator and pulled out two bottles. "Let me just take these in. I'll be right back."

"Go 'head, I can take care of myself in this department, girl." Letty surveyed the array of bottles on the table. Delia went to the dining room and Letty mixed a Scotch and soda. She poured slowly as the reality settled on her. These women were friends, perhaps lovers, like she and Maxine had been. The name she'd heard for women like these burst inside her head: bulldagger. Letty flinched, angry she had let it in, angry that it frightened her. "Ptuh!" Letty blew air through her teeth as if spitting the word back at the air.

She did know these women, Letty thought, as she stood at the counter smiling out at the poker game. They were oblivious to her, except for Terry. Letty remembered that was Delia's cousin's name. As Letty took her first sip, Terry called over to her. "We gonna be finished with this game in a minute Letty, then we can talk."

"Take your time," Letty said, then went out through the foyer door and around to the livingroom. She walked slowly on the carpet and adjusted her eyes to the light, which was a bit softer. The tall woman, Maryalice, had just put a record on the turntable and sat down on a love seat across from the other two women. Letty stood in the doorway a moment before the tune began:

> Hush now, don't explain
> Just say you'll remain
> I'm glad you're back
> Don't explain

Letty was stunned, but the song sounded different here, among these women. Billie sang just to them, here. The isolation and sadness seemed less inevitable with these women listening. Letty watched Maryalice sitting with her long legs stretched out tensely in front of her. She was wrapped in her own thoughts, her eyes closed. She appeared curiously disconnected, after what had clearly been a long search for this record. Letty watched her face as she swallowed several times. Then Letty moved to sit on the seat beside her. They listened to the music while the other two women spoke in low voices.

When the song was over Maryalice didn't move. Letty rose from the sofa and went to the record player. Delia stood tentatively in the doorway of the livingroom. Letty picked up the arm of the phonograph and replaced it at the beginning of the record. When she sat again beside Maryalice she noticed the drops of moisture on the other woman's lashes. Maryalice relaxed as Letty settled onto the seat beside her. They both listened to Billie together, for the first time.

NORMAN WONG

CULTURAL REVOLUTION

Michael felt too nauseated to look for the muffled laughter on the bus, more like an American school bus than a Greyhound. It rode slowly without shock absorbers to Xi'an from Macau, sixty miles past the Communist border. He brushed away his father's breath from his arm as he inched toward the window. Outside was a monotonous field of short rice plants, jutting out of a mirror of water. Occasionally there stood a half-naked Chinese farmer under an oversize straw hat.

"American school has taught him to forget all of his Chinese," Michael's father had said repeatedly to relatives in Hong Kong, with notes of shame and pride in his voice. When they arrived there two weeks before, Michael had found his relatives' accents difficult to understand; but he always understood his father, even though sometimes he pretended not to. And by the end of the first week he found himself deciphering his relatives' conversations, though he still could not readily contribute to them.

Father and son had spent eight days in Hong Kong with uncles, aunts, and countless cousins. Every meal was spent at a round table with a lazy-suzy, spinning Chinese delicacies around: dim sum, roast suckling pig, shark fin soup, sautéed frog legs. In large restaurants, noisy family parties were partitioned off in sections, each complete with a color TV and a Mah-Jongg set. The city's noise and its muggy heat, unlike Hawaii's drier heat, made Michael ill. A doctor gave him a prescription for antibiotics and told him to drink bottled water to clear out his system. Then they took a ferry to Macau, where they stayed with his grandmother. She lived in a second-floor apartment, cluttered with porcelain statuettes and smelling of incense, along with another old woman, her maid and companion, whom one of Michael's uncles had imported from the mainland.

On the bus to Xi'an, his father's home village, Michael complained about stomach cramps. His father answered, "If it's not one thing, it's another. It was a waste of money to bring you here in the first place." August was the only time that this trip to the homeland would have been possible. Michael was going off to college in two weeks, to the U.S. mainland. He could hardly wait. It was five thousand miles from Hawaii and his family to Chicago, white man's land. Michael again turned to the window, only to discover there a reflection of a white man's face staring at his reflection and laughing.

This was the real China. In high school Michael had learned about Sun Yat-sen, the Japanese invasion, and the Cultural Revolution. He had pieced these facts together with the few stories that he had milked from his father for an oral report in the eighth grade. Back then Michael had found these stories unsatisfying. He had written in his mind his own version of his father's life in China. When his father was just a baby, the Japanese had invaded his village. Michael remembered the story of his grandmother fleeing, fearless, with his infant father in her arms to hide in the rice fields. But on this trip he cared little for the real bits of his father's past which he discovered along the way. It was already too late; he wanted to be on his way to Chicago, writing his own future.

As his father led the way out of the bus, Michael turned around to look at the man in the front seat. He looked like an American college student, with short blond hair, white skin, a thick neck like a rugby player, a few strands of chest hair pushing up between his shirt's collar. His hand searched in his backpack, pulling a camera out of the pouch. He looked up at Michael.

The hotel was an ugly square building, six stories high, the tallest around. The lobby was decorated in fifties style, a green and white tile floor speckled with black dots, a simulated wood counter for a reception area, and a matching freestanding backboard. Off to one side of the lobby a pair of glass doors led to a restaurant where tables were covered with stained red cloth. Chinese men and women, uncomfortably dressed in black polyester trousers and wrinkled white shirts buttoned to their necks, lazily carried trays of water glasses and standard Chinese dishes.

After signing for their room, Michael's father insisted that they deposit their bags behind the counter and begin an immediate search for the old home. "I don't know if it's even still there. It's out by the rice fields. I can't believe it all looks the same as twenty-five years ago." Michael hated seeing his father so excited. The white man from the bus walked in the lobby, his backpack sealed, the camera heavy in his hands. He walked past Michael to the front desk. "We shouldn't just leave the bags behind the counter," Michael said. "They won't be safe."

He watched his father examining the receptionist behind the counter. She signed the white man into the guest book. Thick black-framed glasses accentuated the roundness of the young woman's face. The line of her bangs was uneven, and a noticeable strand of black hair stayed behind the lens of her glasses, though her own eyes were blind to it. She smiled with buckteeth. The white man showed her his American passport. "You go ahead, Dad," Michael said. "I want to go upstairs with the bags and lie down for just a little while. I'll catch up with you later. It must've been something I ate at dim sum this morning."

He and the white man rode the elevator together up to the same floor. Michael said how horrible the bus ride had been. They looked at each other once more before going to their separate rooms. Michael loved air-conditioning. He lay down on one of the two twin beds. He was glad that he and his father would be sleeping separately tonight. He rolled on the bed and then jumped up, giving it the appearance of being slept in. He then left the room and proceeded down the hallway, to the white man's room; the door was open a crack. He stepped in and closed it behind him.

"Quiet. We better not talk," the white man said. "Thin walls. My name's Alex." He moved closer. He was twice Michael's width, but the top of his head came to Michael's eyes. Michael was thin like a typical Cantonese man, like his father. But he had grown tall. "All that milk and white bread has made him so tall," his father had explained to the Hong Kong relatives.

His feet hit the footboard of the bed. "Damn," he called out. "This bed is too short."

"We should try to be a little quieter."

Michael liked the feel of Alex's thick flesh. They held each other tightly, and turned their bodies sideways. Alex ran his hand down Michael's knobby spine to the thin flesh of his buttocks and slowly patted him there, lulling him. When Michael was little, he had slept in the same bed with his father, while his sister had been in the other room with his mother. His father would pat him on the butt to sleep.

After sex, Alex began to doze off beside him. Michael avoided touching him by leaning to one side of the bed, almost falling off. He did not want to sleep here, but neither did he want to get up to look for his father. This trip to the homeland had already gone on for too long, in Michael's opinion. His feet knocked against the footboard again. "This is ridiculous."

Alex opened his eyes. "What, me?"

"No, the footboard."

Alex sat up in bed and massaged Michael's feet. "Is that better, baby?" Alex braced himself over Michael, pinning him down at the shoulders. Michael closed his eyes as Alex kissed him on his pressed lips and then on his neck, where he lingered wet and long.

"You're going to get me in trouble," Michael said. "Let me go."

"Too late."

Michael jumped out of bed and stood in front of the mirror on the wall. A red spot darkened on his neck.

"If I spoke Chinese to you, would you be able to understand me?" Alex asked.

"If you do, I'll ignore you like I do my father." He wanted to remind his pickup that they had met less than an hour ago and that he did not even find him that attractive. He had only looked at Alex on the bus because he was the first white man he had seen in a long time.

Michael did not say no when Alex asked to come along to look for his father. Alex would serve as a buffer between him and his father. Outside the hotel Alex immediately began to photograph everything around. "Everything is so simple," he said. "It's like the 1950s. A village, a country where time stood still. I bet this place is exactly the way your father remembers it." Michael stood by silently as Alex bargained with an old ricksha driver. His accent and diction were perfect. He asked the old man how far the rice fields were. The old man's legs were dark and wrinkled like beef jerky; lines divided his face. He laughed, showing a single rotten tooth, as Alex took his picture while he mounted the rusty bicycle.

"This white man knows how to speak Chinese," the old man shouted to another driver. The black hood overhead focused their view to the back of the driver and road ahead. The old man stood on the pedals, pushed downward, and started the bike in motion.

"I'm surprised that he's able to drive this thing," Michael said.

"I was in Beijing in the spring," Alex stated. "It's a wonderful place. Even more exciting than here. Canton and the South have been influenced and spoiled by Hong Kong."

Alex told Michael that he was studying in Hong Kong, where gay life was much more in the open. He made occasional trips to the mainland. Michael said that he was going to college in Chicago the following month. "The Midwest is culturally dead. It's white mall country," Alex said.

People scurried out of the ricksha's way. A thin sheet of dust hovered above the dirt road. Shops—groceries, bakeries, drug stores—occupied the first floor of the buildings. Above, families were crowded in two-room apartments; children hung out of windows, while their laundry blew lifelessly on the line, bleached shirts and trousers. The ricksha drove between the buildings, down an alleyway. Wooden stands sold local delicacies: wilted greens, hanging roasted ducks and dogs, and frogs in straw baskets, climbing on top of each other. An old woman sat on a stool, twisting a live chicken's neck.

"Did you meet anyone in Beijing?" Michael asked.

"Any gay men? Yes."

"That's pretty amazing. Chinese gay men. Chinese men gay in Beijing."

"And what about yourself?"

"I've been corrupted by America," Michael said. "You are the *bok gwei*, the white devil. First the man you corrupted in Beijing, and now me."

"I don't think I could've corrupted you any more."

"There weren't any gay men in China before the white man came along," Michael laughed. "Except perhaps the drag-queen opera singers. Every culture has their transvestites. But they were not real men; they were aberrations."

"You're being silly," Alex said. "Did you meet anyone in Hong Kong?"

"Are you serious? I've been with my father for the entire two weeks. We even had to sleep in the same bed at my grandmother's. It was such a small place. One of the bathrooms was just a dark room with a hole in the ground."

The ricksha drove out of the village and into a quieter countryside along the rice fields. Ahead was a small group of houses. Michael knocked Alex's hand off his lap. "We're almost there," he said. He began to wonder whether bringing Alex along was such a good idea. What if Alex told his father what had happened in the hotel room—but his father was too naive to understand, even if told. And besides, he was doing the white tourist a favor by bringing him along to visit a real Chinese home. "So tell me about the man you met in Beijing."

Alex again placed his hand on Michael's knee. "We met under the big Mao picture in Tiananmen Square, near the entrance of the Forbidden City. That's where you hang out if you want to pick up a local man. They're especially interested in white men. But they're very careful; it's a severe crime in China."

"Who did you meet?"

"He was a little older than me. Ming Tim. Very serious looking. Dark-skinned and lanky. I saw him. He saw me. We looked at each other for about fifteen minutes, and then as I walked away, he followed. After a while he joined me, and we continued walking without speaking. Then he told me that he had to leave. He had to pick up his *wife* at the factory. In China, they won't give you your own apartment unless you're married. The other alternative is to live with your parents for the rest of your life. As he walked, he said, 'I want to see you again. Tomorrow I'll meet you in front of your hotel.' Then he ran off around a corner."

"Did you spend your entire time in Beijing under the Mao picture?" Michael asked.

"No. Do you want to hear the rest of the story?"

"Yes, but hold off. Here's the old home. Now no gay stuff, or I'll drown you in the rice fields."

"Oh, that could be fun."

The ricksha slowed and stopped. On one side of the road stood a row of five brick houses, attached to each other, all alike, and on the other side, the rice fields. Up close, Michael could see that they were parallel rows of weedlike plants, rows and rows nestled in soft, dark mud; extending to the mountains beyond shrouded by clouds. A farmer stood in ankle-high water, his face hidden by his straw hat. He held up a plant to the sun. His skin, dark like leather, stretched over his protruding ribs.

"He's beautiful," Alex said.

"Rice queen," Michael scowled.

"I like the Chinese culture, and its men."

Out of the center house, Michael's father emerged, looking out of place in his polo shirt and belted trousers. "Nothing has changed," he said.

Michael and Alex walked towards him. "I used to live here," he said. "A few of the old neighbors are even still here."

Alex walked up to Michael's father. Michael froze. "Hello, I'm Alex. I'm staying at your hotel, where I met your son." Alex shook Michael's father's hand. "He told me that he was going to look for his father's old home. What a wonderful idea. I had to invite myself along. I'm a student at the University of Hong Kong. Modern Chinese history. Michael told me all about your visit back to the homeland. It's great that you can come back after all these years."

"Hello." Michael's father gave the stranger a lipless smile, and then walked directly over to his son. "Are you still sick? It took you a long time to get here. I was already planning to go back to the hotel. It's too hot. Is the hotel room air-conditioned? I'm feeling a little sick myself."

Michael was relieved by his father's cool reception of Alex, though he was disappointed that the only white man around did not pique his father's curiosity.

"They only have outhouses in back," his father continued. "The same ones that were here when I used to live here."

From behind his father, two old women emerged from the green doorway. Sticks, stones, weeds, and bricks littered the front yard.

"This isn't your son, is it?" said the younger of the two, pointing to the white man. Her hair was silver and uncombed, and she smiled a gold tooth. Beside her was a much older woman, hunched over like an insect. She looked only at the garbage on the ground. She was blind. Behind surviving white strands of hair, her hard white scalp was dotted with dark moles.

"No, this is my son. Michael, show your respect to Wu Tai Tai and her daughter, Mai Lee."

Michael held Mai Lee's hand. He could only feel bones. Her thin smile grew, and her eyes strained to open wider. He did not dare to shake the blind mother's hand.

"They lived next door when my mother and I lived here. Now they live here. The house is exactly the way that I remembered it. Nothing's changed."

Alex held his camera to the group. "I want a picture of this moment." The camera clicked. Michael turned and stared at him with contempt.

"Your son is tall," the old daughter said. She held her hand above her eyes to block the sun as she looked Michael up and down.

Inside, the old blind mother poured glasses of hot tea from an aluminum thermos and passed them to her daughter to hand to Michael and his father. Michael passed his glass to Alex. The men sat in large uncomfortable wooden chairs decorated with carvings of flowers on the arms and a Chinese character on the back. The door stood open, letting in a warm breeze and a view of the constant rice fields.

"Do you know what this means?" Alex whispered to Michael, pointing to the character on the chair.

Michael did not respond.

"Peaceful."

Michael turned away. The old woman spoke in heavy local accents. He strained his eyes to follow their conversation. His head began to ache.

"They're talking about you," Alex said. "Your father says you're going to college in Chicago. The old daughter said, 'Such a foreign, faraway-sounding place.'"

He began to regret the moment on the bus when he had given Alex that first look. He hated Alex for explaining the writing on the chair, for hiring the ricksha, for interpreting his father's conversation. He wanted to be away from all of this. But he did like the adventure of having sex in Communist China. He found Alex's preference for Chinese men odd because he himself had never been attracted to them. They would seem too much like his father: bony and without any body hair. He looked out at the farmer. He wanted to know the rest of Alex's pickup story. It seemed dangerous and perverse. If he could only get him alone again for a little while, he could hear the rest of the story and then tell him to leave.

"Not much has changed since you left," said the old daughter. "The old school is still there. If I remember correctly, you were such a bad boy, Mr. Lau. Crying all the way to school every day. A new house went up farther down the road, maybe ten years ago. America must be so exciting compared to all of this. All the furniture is still here. You didn't come back for anything? Did you?" Her eyes widened. "We haven't thrown anything out. It's all still here. We weren't sure whether or not you were coming back. Why would you want to? America sounds like a dream."

Hawaii is not America, Michael thought. Chicago, the mainland.

He looked out the door at the rice fields again. The Japanese had invaded this village—a long time ago, before the Mao picture on the wall, the color TV, before Peking was renamed Beijing. Slowly and patiently, the farmer examined his crop. His grandmother had been a brave woman. But could even the small body of a Chinese woman safely hide among those short plants, in all that water?

Michael was tired of listening to Chinese. "Let's look around." He led the way past the old mother.

"What a big boy," she said, looking at the wooden floor.

The ceiling of the adjacent room was two stories high, but still the room was dark. There were no windows, just an open doorway in the far corner, letting in some light. Against the left wall a wooden staircase led to a small platform and closed door. On the right, a bed neatly made up with white sheets and a red embroidered quilt. A sewing machine sat in the center of the room. Yards of olive green cloth unraveled from the tabletop onto the floor.

"I bet the real bedroom's upstairs," Alex surmised.

"Finish your story," Michael said. "I want to know what happened."

"You want me to tell you now? Here?"

"Yeah, while they're in the other room." Michael sat down on top of the bed.

"All right. Where was I? The next day Ming Tim was waiting for me outside my hotel. 'I've got it all figured out,' he said. 'My wife's spending the night at her mother's tonight. Forty miles away from here. I'll take her to the bus station and make sure she gets on the right bus. I'll meet you here again, tonight, at nine o'clock.' I agreed, and he hurried away again."

"This bed is hard as a rock." Michael moved his hand across the floral pattern of the quilt. "Sorry for interrupting. Go on."

"You sure you don't want to listen to them out there instead? I'll translate for you. You can hear my story later tonight—in my room. Your father and those two old women are talking about the real China. I want to know why the old mother is blind. She wasn't born that way, you know. The part of her face around her eyes seemed pushed in. But I can't really tell. She won't look up. I guess she doesn't have a reason to. They say that if you weren't born blind and become blind, you would always remember the last thing you saw."

"I don't care about her. Just tell me the rest of your story." Michael began to relish depriving Alex of a real Chinese conversation.

"All right. You're the Chinese emperor." Alex stood in between Michael's opened legs and began to stroke his hair.

"Stop it." Michael pushed him in the stomach. "Finish your story."

"At nine o'clock Ming Tim stood outside my hotel. His cap was pulled low over his face. He led me to a darkened alleyway and handed me a Mao jacket. I wore it over my own jacket. He pushed another cap on my head. The way I was dressed, I almost looked Chinese.

"At the mouth of the courtyard of an apartment complex, Ming Tim pulled me aside again. 'Look to the ground,' he said. 'Don't look up until you are inside my apartment. We'll be walking to the entrance now. There may be people around. When you see a light, put your sleeve over your mouth. Stoop over a little. If anyone sees you they'll think that you're a sick relative of my wife. Keep your eyes down. Don't look up.

" 'If you can't walk straight, watch my feet. Don't walk too close to me. And don't ever touch me. At least not until we are inside.' He laughed for the first time.

"First I saw the dirt courtyard floor for about a hundred yards, then I almost tripped up a short flight of stairs at the entrance of the building. Speckled tiles in the lobby. Fluorescent bulbs humming overhead. I kept looking for Ming's feet. We stopped at the beginning of a flight of stairs.

" 'Keep one hand on the wall, the other over you mouth,' he said. 'Let's go.' My Chinese was not as good back then. I was afraid that I had misunderstood him. I was sweating under all those clothes. He pushed me against the wall. 'Someone is coming.' "

Just then, Michael's father entered the room, the old daughter following behind.

Michael stood up from the bed. "What's upstairs, Dad?"

His father looked at him and then at the wrinkled quilt. "Don't lie on someone else's bed," he said in English. "Are you still sick?"

"No. What's upstairs?"

Alex took a picture of the sewing machine and the green cloth. The flash shocked the room to life. The old daughter jumped back.

"Don't do that anymore," Michael said.

"Upstairs is my mother's old bedroom, your grandmother's room."

"We don't ever go up there," Mai Lee said. "We sleep down here." She pointed to the bed.

Michael's father walked up the creaking stairs, followed by Michael and Alex.

"Take another picture, and I'll break your camera," Michael said.

Halfway up the stairs, his father turned to him. "I may have to use that outhouse after all. I don't think that I can wait until we get back to the hotel."

Michael rolled his eyes.

His father looked down at his neck. "What's that?"

Michael knew that he was referring to the hickey. He pulled up his collar. "It's nothing. I think it's a rash." He heard muffled laughter from behind.

"I hope you don't have to see another doctor. If it's not one thing, it's another."

As they continued up the stairs, Michael wondered if Alex would be joining them for dinner, further intruding on him and his father. If he did not have dinner with them, Alex would wander to the marketplace and sit by himself at a noodle stand. The soup would smell of freshly chopped scallions. A native farmer would sit with him, amazed by his Chinese, and talk to him, telling him about his family, life in China, the rice fields. Afterwards, they would walk around town, slowly veering off to the abandoned schoolyard for sex. Meanwhile, Michael and his father would have their dinner in the hotel restaurant. The food off the streets of China was too dangerous. In Macau, he and his father had ordered bowls of steamed mussels from a street vendor. He had vomited all night into a plastic bucket beside the bed. His father climbed over him out of bed and woke up the old maidservant who was sleeping on the rattan sofa in the living room. Querulously, he had ordered her to brew some roots. When she entered the bedroom, Michael saw that her blouse was half-unbuttoned; she had pulled it on before coming in. He could see the shadows of her jugular veins, as she set the bowl down beside the bed and picked up the bucket. She drained it out in the squat toilet, rinsed it in the kitchen sink, and brought it back to him.

"You're spoiling this entire trip," his father muttered from his side of the bed.

"Leave me alone." Michael held his breath and drank the bitter tea in one tasteless swallow.

"Here, put this on your chest," his father said to him.

"What is it?"

"Tiger balm."

"No." Michael felt his father's hand, spreading the greasy sweet ointment on his chest.

"You're so skinny."

"Just like you."

Michael looked past Alex on the stairway at the old daughter standing frozen below. She looked up at the three of them, each appearing less Chinese from top to bottom. The wood of the stairs squeaked painfully with the weight of human bodies for the first time in so many years. The old daughter clutched the railing; her foot mounted the first step and then stopped.

In the bedroom, a large bed, draped with a canopy of cobwebs and dusty silk sheets, sprawled out from the center. The mattress was full of rat holes. The engravings of the headboard told a tale of court life in ancient China. Facing the foot of the bed was a matching bureau, and on the wall above it, a white rectangle, lighter than the rest of the wall, where something used to hang, perhaps a mirror. Closed wooden shutters trapped a musty odor. They would open onto a panoramic view of the rice fields. Carved on the wood were more characters and floral scenes.

"I slept here with my mother after my father went off to work in the coal mines of South America," Michael's father said.

Michael remembered his father telling him that his grandfather had died in the mines there.

"Why haven't the old women come up here?" Alex said. "Do you believe them?"

"This is still my mother's house," Mr. Lau stated. "They only live here."

"Will she come back, your mother?"

"She told me she would never come back."

Again Michael wondered why his grandmother was so adamant about staying away. He stood at the doorway, ready to go back downstairs. He looked back in the bedroom to see Alex and his father read the writing on the shutters together. The perfect son-and-father team. Below, at the foot of the staircase, the old daughter was joined by her mother. The old daughter looked upwards, while her blind mother looked down at the steps. Maybe they were afraid that they would have to leave. His father would discover things missing, accuse them of theft. Michael surmised that the old daughter had sold the mirror which had originally hung on the wall above the bureau in order to buy the sewing machine—so that she would not need to leave her mother home alone all day. His father stood close to Alex, their fingers touching the shutters.

"I can't read this," Alex said. "It's faded away too much." He tried to pull them open.

Michael's father hit away his hands. "Don't. They've never been opened. My mother never opened them."

In the kitchen, the old daughter explained to Alex how the gas canister was hooked up to the stone stove. "We refill it once a month," she said. "I don't do much cooking. Only for my mother and me. We don't eat much." The old mother poured more glasses of hot tea. Michael sat on a stool in the kitchen, holding up Alex's camera, looking out the back door through the viewfinder. His father ventured to the outhouse with a few sheets of tissue in his hand. The chickens scurried out of his way. Once he was safely inside, under the thatched roof of the small stone closet, Michael snapped the picture.

"Come away from that wok," Michael called to Alex, "and tell me the end of your story. Tell me the juicy bits once you get inside Mao's apartment."

"Ming's. Now? In front of these two women?" Alex asked.

"They won't understand. Let these two old relics hear. Nothing else exciting happens here. Imagine living your entire life in this house, in this village. Tell me the end of your story before my father gets back from his reunion with the outhouse."

Alex took a glass of hot tea from the old mother's offering hands and pulled up a stool next to Michael. With wide eyes the old daughter stood over them, listening to the foreign words. "Once we were in the apartment, Ming locked the door. Then I heard another man's laughter. 'It's okay,' Ming said. Another

Chinese man was sitting in front of the TV. He was younger, my age. I don't re-member his name. I took off the Mao jacket and cap, and Ming and his friend took everything else off for me. They were so excited. They ran their hands through my chest hair, pulling it with their fingers. Then they cupped their small hands all over me, as if they were measuring me up: my hands, my chest, my nipples, my head.

"We took a shower together. It wasn't a regular shower, like what you're use to. It was a small square room, a single window way up high, a drain in the center of the white tiled floor. They sat on a bench across from me, huddled delicately, their fingers pointing as I poured warm buckets of water between my legs. We talked about the weather, America, China. They told me that they wanted to visit America. That nearly killed me, sitting there naked listening to them say that. We can visit them and see how they live, but they can't do the same—if they could even afford it in the first place, of course. And to think how dangerous it was to have me there.

"Later on, we did just about everything together, and then we fell asleep."

"What do you mean everything?" Michael asked.

"I'll show you later," Alex teased. "Let me finish my story. But sometime be-fore morning, someone pushed me out of bed and told me to get dressed quickly. When I reached for the Mao jacket, Ming held it down. He wouldn't let me have it. 'It's very late,' he said. 'No one will see you leaving.' Now I could clearly see the way that I had come in: the stairs, the cracks on the wall, the en-tire width of the entrance's tiled floor, and then the darkened courtyard. We walked maybe a hundred yards beyond the entrance way of the complex before he said, 'You go back alone now.' I reached out for him, but he had already turned around. There was no moon out. I strained my eyes to look for him. I felt so lonely that night, walking back to my hotel room."

"Here comes my father."

"Let's go back to the hotel now," said Michael's father as he stepped over the threshold. "The outhouse is disgusting. There are bugs all over the place, and the smell. Lucky that old woman's blind."

In the front yard, they shook hands with the two old women, and Michael's father handed them each several Hong Kong dollars. They humbly thanked him, shaking their heads from side to side, proclaiming, "No, no. This is too much." Through the viewfinder of the camera Michael looked at the rice fields. Still only one lonely farmer. He looked up from beneath his hat but was still too far away for Michael to see his face, to discover his age. He could have been eighteen or as old as his father.

"Go out there and pick up that farmer," Michael said to Alex. "You *bok gwei,* bringing your evil ways to China, ruining simple people's lives."

"Homosexuality is not exclusively a white thing."

"But you think you're our savior, don't you," Michael retorted. "We all want to sleep with you. Every Chinese man wants a white man. No? Because we ultimately want to be like you. The beauty of the imperialist."

"There are a billion people in China, and there are bound to be a few fags," Alex said, "like you."

"I don't want to be like you."

"Here, give me the camera and let me get a picture of you, of you and your father in front of the ancestral home."

"No."

"I told you my story, now give me my camera and get in the picture, *baby*."

"No." Michael pulled the camera away from Alex's reach. It fell onto the ground. The back flipped open.

"I don't believe you," Alex said. "You're a fuckin' baby."

"Shut up," Michael said. "It's been fun. I'll be seeing you around sometime."

Alex stared at him with annoyance. For a moment Michael feared that he would say something to his father and the two old women. But would they even understand? The three of them stood, smiling and nodding. His father fidgeted back and forth. He still had not gone to the bathroom. Alex bent down to pick up the camera. His father was having the perfect ending to his reunion. Alex began to walk alongside the field, a lonely tourist heading back to this hotel; he kept watch over the farmer in the field. Michael imagined Alex making love to the farmer, and then saw himself with the farmer. The farmer's body would be skinny like his own. With each movement their elbows, knees, bones would knock painfully together.

His father continued to pace the ground. "Hurry, hurry," Michael thought. He wondered if his father even suspected that his son had turned out so different from himself. His father had said to his mother, "If I don't take him to China now, he'll forget that he was ever Chinese." "Take him," his mother had added, "and find him a Chinese wife." His father should have never left China: Would he have turned out straight then? *I'm different from all your Chinese ways, Dad. I'm an aberration. This is your homeland. Not mine.*

"I'll always remember these rice fields," his father said to the old women. "It's so peaceful out here. What a green land of comfort. I remember the story my mother told me about how the rice fields saved our lives. How she ran out there when the Japanese came marching through. How she lay low in the mud with me wrapped in her arms."

The old blind mother looked up from the ground. Her eyes ached to open. "Is that what she told you?" she asked; her voice rose in the heat.

"No, Mother," the old daughter gasped. "Not now."

"You were in town that day, Mai Lee, when they came through. You did not see firsthand the horror they brought to us. You did not see what happened to these people here. *I* was standing in this field with your father that day, Mr. Lau."

"My father was in South America," he replied nervously. "You must be mistaken."

"I'll never forget," she continued. "Your father couldn't see that Japanese soldier approaching him from behind. When the soldier called over to him it was already too late. Your father started to run. You can't run in mud even if your life depends on it. And besides, where was he running to? The mountains? The soldier took aim. I jumped on that Jap's back and knocked him to the ground. He pushed me over, got up, and shot your father down."

"Enough!" the old daughter cried.

"My father was not here when the Japanese came. He died in the South American coal mines."

"Your mother was probably too angry and upset to bother to tell a little boy the truth." The old mother continued: "From the fields I could see all the brick houses. The killings, the rapes, the looting. But I could not hear a single cry for help. It's so quiet out there. You can see these houses from miles away.

"I saw your mother, looking down at me from her bedroom window, her face framed by the open shutters. She had witnessed the execution of her own husband. I was told that it was then that she ran off with you in her arms and hid in the outhouse. She stayed there in that darkened, stinking closet, until we found her there two days later. That outhouse saved your life."

"No," Michael's father said. He stood cold in his place.

"Believe me, Mr. Lau," the old mother pleaded. "He was shot down." She brought her hand to her face, the knocking of bones. "It was the last thing that I saw before the soldier bashed out my eyes with the handle of his rifle."

Michael reached out to steady his shaking father. He patted him on the shoulder, then on the back. His father moved away. He looked as if he wanted to vomit. He turned and walked off alone down the road.

Michael looked back at the mother and daughter, carefully framed in the green mouth of the door. Dollars stuck out of the open collars of their blouses, as if they were ancient prostitutes. Bricks and planks littered the ground. Slowly, his father's old home would crumble away. He turned down the road after him.

That evening they ate an early dinner in the hotel restaurant. "She's a crazy old woman. She doesn't know what she's talking about," his father said and then remained silent for the remainder of the meal. Lying in bed, Michael could not sleep; his feet knocked against the footboard. He turned to see the quiet face of his sleeping father. His father could only remember the past one way: the way it was told to him. This thought choked Michael. His father would never be able to accept his son's future as a gay man. Michael felt a pain in his stomach again. The air-conditioner hummed softly.

The next morning they passed over the dim sum breakfast downstairs and settled for packaged biscuits and boiled water. It was still early when they boarded the bus. They were heading back to Macau for a couple of days and then to Hong Kong; from there they would fly back to Hawaii. Michael would leave for Chicago soon after. His father dozed off beside him, their arms touching as the bus rocked on the dirt road. Michael was afraid that the rest of the trip would be as quiet as this.

He looked at his own reflection in the window and then outside. Beyond the fields, the sun was coming up over the peaks of the faraway mountains; the light slowly erased his reflection from the glass. The farmer in the field took off his straw hat. His face was gaunt, tired, resigned: an old man's face. The voices and the laughter on the bus melded into a single violent hum. Michael squinted his eyes. The farmer, upright and unmoving, began to sink. Michael ran toward him. His sneakers moved sluggishly in the mud. The glassy water took hold of the farmer's trousered legs, embraced his naked stomach and chest—the same color as the mud, and swallowed the bulging veins of his neck. The Chinese man's eyes turned into his head. Michael fell onto the rice field expanding out forever around him.

SHAY YOUNGBLOOD

MOTHERS KNOW

I WAS SCARED MAMA WOULD LOOK at me and know I was changed that first time Jesse came home with me. All my years of living with Mama I knew she'd see deeper than skin could cover. I was scared she would cut her eyes at Jesse and know she was a lesbian, take one swift look at me and know I was deep in love with her. After her knowing I could only pray she didn't have a stroke. But Mama hugged Jesse close like she was blood too.

When I was growing up, somewhere I learned early that women who liked other women were funny, or bull daggers. They looked, dressed and acted like men and were going against the nature of women to have babies. I also learned that it was supposed to be a white woman's disease, but that didn't make sense to me, because the only lesbian I ever knew when I was growing up was Tam and she was deep sun browned and I looked like her shadow.

They used to say Tam was funny. She didn't straighten her hair, wear dresses or take shit off nobody. I didn't notice nothing funny about Tam. She wore blue jeans and workshirts everyday to her job at the mill and sharp tailored pant suits on her days off. Those days she would brush back her short afro and go out driving in her white Mustang convertible. Mama would push me behind her as she and Aunt Tullie looked out the screen door toward Tam's apartment, shaking their heads and talking about Tam. They used to look down at me telling me to act like a lady or no man would want me. Remembering back then, I surely wasn't thinking about no man. As a matter of fact I was thinking about how much I wanted to be like Tam. She didn't let nobody tell her what to do and didn't care what folks said about her, even when they said it to her face.

When I looked in the mirror I didn't look funny, just felt real different from other girls. In high school I didn't go out with boys. Mama was proud that I was a good girl, not counting my thoughts. Mostly I was scared of having a baby I didn't want and scared of my feelings for other girls. Mama warned me to stay away from boys because they would ruin me and not get too close to girls because they either wanted your man, to know your business or they wanted to mess with you. "And once you get into that sinful habit with women, no man will want you," she would say. I still didn't want no man.

At the dinner table Mama fussed over both me and Jesse piling our plates high with collard greens, candied yams and corn bread, begging us to eat some dangerously delicious smelling fried pork chops, even though I said we didn't eat meat.

"Jesse will you make certain my other child eats? She ain't got sense god give a cow when it comes to nourishment. She'd eat grass and chew cud if nobody watched her. All she thinks about is books."

Jesse put her eyes on me and smiled when she answered Mama. "I'll make sure she eats ma'am. My greens aren't as good as yours, but nobody ever died from my cooking." Mama seemed satisfied that she had someone responsible to look after me. Jesse was older than me by more than 10 years and on top of that she had a respectable sprinkle of gray in her hair and Mama said a honest look in her eyes. Neither Mama or Aunt Tullie seemed to think our friendship or our decision to live together odd. They had gotten used to Jesse coming home with me on weekends and holidays. They asked her about my old habits and led her to agree with their memories.

"Do she still stay up all times of the night? Used to be she'd hide the lamp light by putting a towel under her door. That child be up reading 'til day break."

"Yes ma'am, she still insist on being up reading when other folks be sleeping."

When I was 14 I stayed up late one night looking out my bedroom window, watching the Saturday night crowd come and go. Just past midnight I saw Tam drive up in front of the apartments. She parked under the street light so I could see them clearly. Tam got out of the car and walked her left-handed strut around to the passenger side to open the door for her girlfriend Mickey. Mickey was so pretty she made my insides feel light. She was a Puerto Rican girl with deep dimples and dark laughing eyes. It seemed she was always showing those deep dimples and smiling at Tam, and throwing her long shiny dark hair over her bare shoulders. Mickey got out of the car and leaned back against it. She said something in Tam's ear that made them both laugh. It surprised me when Tam took Mickey's hand and said something that made her smile it seemed toward my window. They held hands as they walked to Tam's apartment like it was an everyday thing. In that moment of illumination under bright street lights I began to wonder what it would feel like to hold my best friend Connie's hand. Tam stopped just outside my window and kissed Mickey on the mouth before they went inside her apartment. After a while Tam's lights went out but I still imagined them kissing in the dark. That led to my wondering what it would be like to kiss Connie on the mouth in the dark and whisper secrets in her ear and make her laugh from loving her with my breath.

The discovery of a woman's mouth on mine came often after that, mostly in my day dreams but sometimes for real. I spent more time with Connie. Mama knew then that something was going on when Connie and I stayed locked up in my room for hours at a time doing our reading exercises. She would let me kiss her and hold her hand while she read out loud. I would watch her lips handle the words and feel them pressing against my ear. Mama was somewhere in the house thanking god that I hadn't started courting, boys that is. She never said a word about the affair.

My imagination hadn't prepared me for Jesse. The hot, wet touch of her tongue chasing mine or the way my heart hammered when her hands traced the curves along my face and neck. She saw things in a single cloud that made my eyes seem new when I looked. We saw things in each other that made being together feel as if we were under a spell. After two years the love still felt magic.

Mama knew something happened then. In the air I guess. She called me up the morning after and asked me if I was ever going to settle down since I was almost finished with college.

"If you're talking about marriage Mama, forget it, I'm much too independent for that kind of arrangement."

"Annie Lee's daughter wanted to be independent too. She run off to New York wid a woman. It hurt Annie Lee bad. Said she'd rather see the child pregnant out of wedlock than to see her shack up like that with another woman, without shame. It ain't natural," Mama said.

It was only my first day being an official newly initiated lesbian and I just wasn't ready to tell Mama about Jesse and me so I changed the subject and said a prayer my Mama never find out before I tell her.

Jesse said she'd never tell her very christian, very proper mother. When she was 16 her mother burst into her room with tears in her eyes and demanded to know if she was a lesbian. "The way she said lesbian, I knew I'd better say no. But she didn't give me time to answer before she went on about how she had found and read a letter my girlfriend Marie had written to me saying how much she loved me and what we did together. Mama talked about how perverts were sinners and she would have neither in her house. She read to me from the bible and made me swear on it not to see Marie again. Later I realized that she came to me knowing but couldn't face the fact that I was very butch and sexually active."

When dinner was over Aunt Tullie came over and promptly fell into endless conversations with Jesse. When we were leaving Aunt Tullie praised my selection in friends.

"You two take care of each other up there in the city. It's a mighty rough place and friends gotta stick together."

The following spring I had gotten up enough nerve to tell Mama about me and Jesse but before I could get a word in she had a piece of news for me. "You know they buried Mr. Harris Sunday before last. Folks was saying he was gay. Must have been 'cause the church was full of them. Even so, he always was nice to me, then too he paid his church dues more regular than most of the deacons." The words got stuck in my throat and I left them there that time.

Then Aunt Tullie died. I was home for the weekend so I was there to comfort Mama. Jesse drove 200 miles to be with me. She brought my black dress, cooked meals for dozens of people she didn't know and locked the door behind the last to leave. Even through her grief Mama saw.

"I'm glad that you two have each other. Sometimes I envy youth, but I had 47 years with someone I loved. A woman needs companionship." She smiled, looking at us far off like she was in another time.

After Mama had her gall bladder operation Jesse was the one to think of asking Mama to come stay with us till she got on her feet again. Finally convinced she wasn't putting us out, she came.

Mama stepped into our living room full of Jesse's plants and my books everywhere and she shook her head in approval.

"You girls got it looking like a home. I like this house, it's full of love. A house with growing things is full of love. It's a fine house, daughters," she said looking around the room.

"Both of you already old maids. Guess you two ain't never getting married, are you?" she asked not really expecting an answer.

"No Mama I guess not," I said, looking over at Jesse as we led her to our bedroom.

ENROLLMENT

Everyone says that my second cousin Monica's was the first mixed marriage in the family. Technically, this isn't true. Not if you count all the cousins in the previous generation—my first cousins—who married non-Italians. There was Angela, who married a Greek, and Denise, who married an Irishman, and Robert, who married a girl of indeterminate extraction. (My grandmother always referred to her as *l'inglese,* "the English-woman," a phrase that delivered more disdain than you might imagine). In the late fifties, my oldest cousin Johnny even became engaged to a Protestant, though apparently that doesn't count either, because she converted some months before the wedding. So what the family means, then, by mixed marriage is this: that Monica Scarpetto—the daughter of two nice Italian parents—married a Jew.

This was two years ago, and when Monica and David announced their engagement, though there were raised eyebrows and whispers about how they would raise the children, everyone was essentially happy for them. "Hey, Nicky, times change," my mother declared, as if I were the one who still needed convincing. And then she proceeded to tell me, for the umpteenth time, about the "antique days," when all a girl had to do was smoke to become a persona non grata with the family.

We'd all come to expect this marriage. Monica and David had been dating since college, and, by the time they graduated and were out in the work world—David as a financial analyst, Monica as a buyer for a large department store in Boston—he was showing up at all the major family gatherings. It didn't matter where we got together: at Monica's parents' or Aunt Carmella's, or my mother's. Whatever the occasion—Fourth of July, Thanksgiving, Christmas even—David would be there, well-dressed, well-mannered, and charming. He praised everyone's cooking, told appreciative stories of the summer he traveled in Europe—Italy was his favorite country, he said—and, but only when asked, gave sound, conservative advice about financial investment.

You could tell, Aunt Carmella said, summing up all the evidence, that David came from a good family, which, as she later explained in one of those tête-à-têtes that aunts in my family are always having with me, was as important to Jews as to Christians.

For our part, we learned to wish David "Happy Hanukkah" at Christmastime and "Happy Passover" at Easter. And when they announced their engagement, my father even congratulated them with a *Mazel tov*, chuckling at himself afterward the way one often does after using someone else's language for the first time.

If David's good upbringing—his *educazione*—made him eminently acceptable to the women in our family, what made him acceptable to the men was the fact that he was also a "regular guy." After dinner, he would join my uncles around the TV to watch football or basketball. And when the dining room table was finally cleared—dessert and coffee, nuts and fruit and confetti being an hour-long affair after the games—he would sit with the men for several rounds of cards and Sambuccas.

I was always the first to leave these parties. Even if it was Christmas. Even if it was my parents who were hosting. There we'd be, maybe fifteen or twenty of us—aunts, uncles, cousins—a kind of Italian Bob Cratchit and family, full of holiday *festevolezza*. I'd stay through the sweets and coffee and then, just before the card-playing got going, make my excuses: papers to correct (I taught school then) or other friends, perhaps old acquaintances from college, to whom I'd promised a drop-in call. After all, it was the holidays. None of this was a lie, though there were stronger, less explainable reasons why I really wasn't staying.

"Eh, Mr. Russo," my mother would call out to me, throwing up a hand, like a jilted soprano. In our family's personal mythology, Mr. Russo was another person from the antique days, a family acquaintance—a *cumpare*—who was forever having to be somewhere else. According to my mother, you could be enjoying a cup of coffee and a nice conversation with Mr. Russo when all of a sudden he'd put down his cup and announce that he had an appointment elsewhere. "He never stayed in one place for more than ten minutes," Aunt Carmella added.

Everyone who remembered Mr. Russo, called him a "curious" man. He might as well not have been Italian, I was led to believe, for all the regard he gave to the social customs of his own people. And now they were telling me—but jokingly, of course—that I was the new Mr. Russo. Aunt Carmella once even explained to David who Mr. Russo was and why it was such an apt name for me. She wanted him to understand everything about being a part of our family.

Mr. Russo was long dead and buried before I came on the scene in the mid-fifties. But in time I came to have my own speculations about his odd behavior. Speculations I shared only with my "roommate" Josh, the other—but unacknowledged—Jew in the family.

For Monica and David's wedding, my parents offered to buy me a new suit. "So that you make *'na bella figura,*" my mother told me over the phone one night. "You know *bella figura*—a good impression?"

This had been one of my grandmother's expressions. Since Nonna's death a few years back, my mother was more and more echoing her own mother's Old World idioms.

I told Mom that I knew *bella figura*. And that I hardly needed their money. At thirty-three, a math teacher turned computer programmer, I was doing fine.

"We just want to make sure you look great," Mom said. "We're proud of our son." She paused, then added, "And this time don't you dare do like Mr. Russo. You stay for the whole reception. I want several dances with you."

As it turned out, everyone—Jews and Christians alike—dressed to cut a good figure. And while I've never been the kind of guy who makes free with words like "stunning" and "ravishing," that's exactly how the women, especially the women in my family, looked. It was hard not to feel proud. A lot of my cousins and aunts, even the ones in their sixties and seventies, have aged well: "because of all the olive oil," my grandmother used to claim. And, though we're not a wealthy family—florists, dry cleaners, chefs being the family professions—still the women know how to dress. At Monica's wedding I felt caught up in all the enthusiasms they had for making *'na bella figura.* I wouldn't have pulled a Mr. Russo for anything. Not that day.

The ceremony took place, not in a church or temple, but in the ballroom of a swanky new hotel in Boston. Despite the little canopied pavilion under which Monica and David exchanged vows—Josh later taught me the name, *hupah*—the ceremony was an ecumenical affair. Monica and David had both a rabbi and a priest officiate. Apparently, it took quite a lot of doing before they were able to find two clergymen who would agree to such a service. The priest, Father Joe, was a silver-haired man in his middle fifties, the kind who had probably entered the seminary right out of college and who—I was guessing all this, trying to figure out what had brought him to this wedding—had probably, maybe during the Vietnam War, had an affair or a bout with alcoholism, or some crisis of faith, and come out of it a lot more relaxed about all the rules. In short, a guy who had come to see that love could make everything—rules, tradition, even family—irrelevant. The rabbi, too, it was reported, was sympathetic. He came from a liberal synagogue in one of the suburbs west of Boston. They were my heroes that day, even more so than Monica and David, who, I felt, didn't really know (not as well as I) what they were getting themselves into.

"Did they smash the wineglass? Did you dance the 'Havah Negilah'?" Josh asked me late that night when I crawled into bed. He'd had his back to me, but now he rolled over, letting me hold him in my arms.

"All of that," I told him, cuddling up close. "I wish you could've been there."

"Me too," he said.

"Eventually they'll figure out who you are," I told him. "I give them another six months. Wait till next year."

"Next year," he said, then chuckled. "Next year in Jerusalem."

It was a warm evening. We were both naked. I buried my nose in Josh's shoulder and breathed in deeply. We'd been together about a year, but I was feeling—all over again—something like that first rush of falling in love with him, the thrill of another's body, at once so alien and so familiar, being offered to me.

Last month, Monica and David had a baby, a little girl whom they named Danielle Louise (part David's family, Daniel being his grandfather; part Monica's, Louis—"Louie"—being her father's name).

"Save the twenty-fourth," my mother told me over the phone one evening in early October. "Monica's going to throw a party for the naming of the baby. She's sending you an invitation next week." In the family network, my mother is the clearing-house for invitations. "I don't think they're going to have her baptized," she went on. "Monica's calling it a Naming Party. It's like what the Jews do for baby boys, you know a *bar mitzvah*, except it's for a girl."

"Well, not quite," I said. "A bar mitzvah is for when the boy turns of age, like Confirmation. Josh's nephew just got bar mitzvahed."

In the two years since David and Monica's wedding, I had taken every opportunity possible of keeping Josh focused in my family's mind. I hadn't actually spelled it out for them, what kind of relationship we had, but I knew he had come together for them—in much the same way that objects begin to come together for an infant—as a distinguishable and significant "object" in their field of vision, as the person I was sharing more than just an apartment with, as the man, in fact, who had foreshadowed David and Monica's mixed marriage by almost a year. About six months after the wedding, we had taken a big step and invited my parents over for dinner. And when Uncle Rudolph died and Josh voluntarily attended the funeral, I think that clinched it.

"Well, whatever it's called, that's what they're doing," my mother said. "I think they're inviting Josh, too." In my mother's way of talking, "I think" means "I know." I tried to imagine what kinds of conversations had occurred to bring this invitation to pass. "I guess the rabbi will be there," my mother continued. "Remember the one who married them?"

"Sure," I said.

"But no Father Joe," she told me.

"Okay," I said, trying to sound as copacetic as a pear on a plate.

"What do you think?" she asked.

"About what?"

We were each waiting for the other to go first.

"I don't know ..." She sounded discouraged by my not taking up the ball, and I suddenly felt guilty, as if she'd asked for something and I'd refused. "I guess it would have been nice if the baby could have been baptized too, that's all."

"What about times changing?" I asked. "Isn't that what you said when they got married?"

"Oh, but you understand, don't you?" There was confusion and annoyance, and a tinge of panic in her voice.

"Let them do what they want," I told her.

"Nicky, it's not a question of letting them do what they want." Now she sounded just plain frustrated. "It's just that it looks like Monica's giving everything to David's family and nothing to ours."

"She's inviting all of us, isn't she?"

"Sometimes," my mother said—she was laughing, but I could tell she felt exasperated with me—"sometimes I just wish I'd had a daughter. She'd understand what I'm trying to say."

The Sunday of the naming, Josh and I took the Turnpike out to Monica and David's. The directions they sent us—a computer-generated map that David had printed up at work—were written as if the only places from which guests might come were the towns around Route 128 or Interstate 495, the circumferential highways that ringed the city. On this map, Boston existed only as an alternative directional marker—"To Boston"—somewhere off in the east, an undisclosed bull's-eye at the end of the sure, true arrow which was the Massachusetts Turnpike.

"Where *is* this place?" Josh joked as we passed the exit for Framingham.

"One of those M towns," I said. "Millis, Medfield, Middleborough, Marlborough. I don't know, they all sound alike to me."

We laughed. The suburbs were not our thing. Josh and I had been renting in the South End, the gay ghetto, for three years now. We had begun to ask realtors to show us property for sale, town-house condominiums as close to downtown as we could afford. Even Cambridge felt too rustic.

We got off at the next exit. The sky was overcast; gray and sooty-white like pigeons' feathers. And although it was just after noon, the sun, a dull glowing behind the cloud cover, sat low on the horizon. Sunday afternoons in winter we usually spent in one of three ways: curled up on the sofa reading the paper, giving or attending a brunch, or at the gym working out.

The directions took us through an old manufacturing town and then out beyond a sprawling high school. The road became country-ish, stone walls and large old maples flanking both sides. Maybe as recently as fifteen years ago this had all been farmland. On the hill to our right and through the leafless branches of the trees we could see the new development where Monica and David lived: one- and two-acre lots planted with large contemporary colonials.

"The next turn is ours," I told Josh. "Apple Creek Road."

He looked at me. "This isn't going to be one of those developments with names like Wisteria Way, is it?"

"Two hours," I reassured him. "I promise we'll stay just two hours."

"And then make like Mr. Russo, right?" he added, grinning.

David greeted us at the door and we stepped into the warm, tingly, humming world of the party. Handsomely dressed people, none of whom I recognized, were coming and going through the tiled entrance foyer, itself almost a room, decorated with furniture one might call "sharp"—all chrome, glass and marble. Descending the staircase from the second floor, where presumably they'd gone to leave coats and freshen up, were still other guests. Everyone seemed headed for the back of the house, from which I could hear the noise of the party in progress.

As we were unloading onto David our coats and gifts and congratulations, the doorbell rang again.

"Go on in," David told us. "I'll catch up with you guys later." He was beaming. I wondered if having a son could have made him any happier than he was at that moment.

The living room, a large, cathedral-ceilinged space with a white brick fireplace at one end, was packed. I didn't see anyone I recognized. What I had thought was to be a small family affair had turned into an enormous party. There were lots of young couples, and lots of children. It was the kind of party a couple of gay men would try to be anonymous in.

"I'm going to get a drink," Josh told me and headed off to the far end of the living room where a bar, complete with hired bartender—a young man in a crisp-fitting red vest—had been set up.

As if she'd tracked me on radar, my mother now appeared.

"You're here!" she said and gave me a kiss on the cheek.

"Mom, you look terrific," I told her before she could start in on the never seeing me bit. She did look great. Her hair, a strawberry blond that in the last few years has emerged as her color, was done up in soft, sweeping waves. She was wearing a new cocktail dress, a bold flowered print on silk, and gold jewelry. Though I knew she'd be sixty-eight in February, she could easily have passed for fifty. I hate the pretty boys at the gym, but when Mom dresses up she makes me realize that looking great often has more to do with generosity than vanity.

"Isn't this wonderful?" she gushed, as she absentmindedly fingered my sport coat. "Do you believe how much space they have?" She kept firing questions at me: had I been given a tour of the house? had I seen the new baby? "Look, over there." She pointed to the sofa where Aunt Carmella was cradling Danielle in her arms. "Isn't she adorable?"

In her exuberance, Mom seemed to have forgotten her dismay that this wasn't a baptism.

"Let me go over and say hello," I said, pulling her fingers off my jacket.

"Did Josh come?" she asked.

"Sure," I said. "He's here somewhere." I looked about casually, as if his whereabouts wasn't that big a deal: the same casualness I tried to affect whenever I pulled a Mr. Russo.

I gave Mom a so-long-for-now kiss and made my way over to Aunt Carmella, greeting people I knew, nodding and smiling at the others. Josh, I noticed, was chatting with the bartender.

"Eh, Nicky!" said Aunt Carmella when she saw me. She's my mother's sister, but the differences between them are amazing. Aunt Carmella's eighty-one, the oldest of my grandmother's eight children. She's got the heavy, doughy figure that Mom would have if she didn't watch her weight; and the bulbous Renzulli nose, a nose my mother had reshaped back in the fifties. "I haven't seen you in ages," Aunt Carmella scolded. "Where have you been?"

I never have a good answer to this question, not one that can do justice to both of us. As if she understood this, Aunt Carmella shifted her attention to the baby. "Look," she said.

I squatted down. Danielle's tiny face, smooth and pink, was folded up in sleep. "Isn't she adorable," I told her. It seemed ridiculous to be echoing my mother's very words, but I wanted to say the right thing. I wanted to do the right thing. I couldn't tell if I—but *who* was I to this new one? the second cousin once removed?—if I was allowed to touch Danielle, take her in my arms. Maybe that would have been too feminine, the kind of thing only men who say "stunning" and "ravishing" can get away with.

"You make a beautiful great-grandmother, Aunt Carmella." This time I used my own words.

In the past, such a statement would have been an occasion for Aunt Carmella to suggest that it was time I got married and started having family too. I had handed her the perfect opening. Instead she just blushed. "Three times a great-grandmother," she said.

Apparently, we were all learning to say our own words. Then Josh came over, a tall drink in his hand, looking like the Cheshire cat.

"Eh," said Aunt Carmella when she saw him.

I could tell that she recognized his face but couldn't quite come up with a name. That was okay; she had just done one wonderful thing. That was good enough for now.

"*Josh*," I said, loud and clear as a shofar, "I'll leave you and Aunt Carmella to visit awhile."

"Go get yourself a drink," he suggested, and gave me the Cheshire look again.

The young man in the red vest was standing, hands behind his back, waiting for business. When he saw me approaching, he immediately took a more formal stance. Then, just as quickly, his whole bearing relaxed. He smiled, and in an instant I knew what Josh's grin was all about.

"Hi," I said. He looked to be about twenty-six, twenty-seven—handsome, clean-cut, friendly looking—the kind of guy I see all the time at the gym, except without the attitude. "A brandy and soda."

"Sure," he said, giving me another friendly smile, and set about mixing my drink. He had brilliant blue eyes, the kind I've heard guys say are "to die for," except I'm a brown-eye man myself.

"It's quite a party, isn't it?" I asked. An innocuous enough question, but under the circumstances it had the ring of openers I used to use in the bars.

"Yes, it's a beautiful party," he said. He might have been agreeing with me out of a sense of professional duty—the customer is always right syndrome—though the way he said "beautiful" sounded too genuine for that.

When he finished making the drink, he held it out to me but didn't release it into my grasp until I'd looked up at him. Then he kept watching me as I took my first sip.

"Perfect," I said. There was an awkward pause. Our business now over, I was free to wander off. Instead, I took another sip. I was the only person standing at the bar: nobody else was looking for a drink. "I'm Nick," I said.

"Dennis." We shook hands. It felt daring—and thrilling—to be making this contact under the eyes of all my relatives.

"The baby's mother is my cousin," I told him, though as soon as I said this, I realized I was babbling, just as in the old, pre-Josh, days when I would try to keep alive whatever ember of a conversation I had managed to kindle at the bars.

But Dennis seemed happy to talk. And so we did, occasionally interrupted by other guests wanting drinks, which he mixed with a bartender's quick efficiency.

He told me that he came from a large Irish-Catholic family on the South Shore. Eight brothers and sisters.

"Nine kids," I acknowledged. "That beats anyone in my family, and we're Italian."

After we'd both chuckled over that one, he told me, "Usually on Sundays I'm at my mom's, unless of course I have to work a job like this. She does a big dinner for all of us who can come." He looked so happy telling me this.

"Every Sunday?" I asked. "Brother, would my mother love to have you for a son."

Someone came up to order a drink. While Dennis was mixing it, I tried to imagine spending every Sunday at my parents'. It was a tempting idea, all that family togetherness. And though I didn't think it could ever be more than a tempting idea, it made me want to know Dennis even more.

"So where do you live now?" I asked when he'd finished making the drink.

"Out this way," he said. "We moved here from the South End last year." He was handing me all the rest of the clues I needed.

"Funny we never ran into you," I said, handing him all the remaining clues he needed. "We've been in the South End for three years now."

Josh wandered over, taking casual mouthfuls of ice from his otherwise empty glass. From the way Dennis smiled at him, I could tell a couple of things: that they'd already introduced themselves, and that Dennis had already linked us.

"So," I said, "this is turning out to be quite an occasion." We all laughed. And then it was time—according to an announcement the rabbi was making—for the ceremony to begin. "We'll catch you later," I told Dennis. He nodded, and I winked.

Josh and I moved away from the bar, positioning ourselves with the other guests—there must have been sixty by now—to face the corner of the living room where the rabbi was standing. Monica and David had joined him, along with Monica's parents, and a couple whom I did not recognize.

Because we were toward the back, and therefore inconspicuous, Josh took the opportunity to whisper to me.

"Isn't Dennis cute?"

"Adorable," I mouthed, then whispered, "but I still go for dark-eyed Jews."

I took my eyes off him and looked out over the gathering. It was clear that most of the people here were not Jewish. Of David's family, only his parents and his brothers and their wives had come. Most of us were goyim—friends, neighbors, relatives of Monica. And yet, in the midst of this party, this innocent enough Sunday afternoon gathering, we were all about to stand witness to a religious ceremony with origins that went back five thousand years.

I brushed my hand against Josh's.

"In the traditional Jewish family," the rabbi began, "the birth of a male child is a cause for high celebration. In accordance with the covenant God made with Abraham, the ritual of circumcision—we call it the *berit milah*—is performed eight days after the baby is born to mark his enrollment as one of the Jewish nation."

It seemed strange to be holding a drink, like holding a drink in church. I glanced to my right where a large potted houseplant, a rubber tree of some sort, stood. On the Spanish moss that covered the base, I set my drink down.

"Good boy," Josh whispered to me.

"We in the reformed tradition," the rabbi went on, "think that the arrival of a girl should be attended with as much joy and celebration." A few people laughed.

He explained that, in addition to the baby, there were four people present who were most important in the ceremony: the godfather and godmother—he nodded to the couple I hadn't recognized—himself, the rabbi—again a few people laughed—and the prophet Elijah. "The empty chair here," and he gestured to a large easy chair, "is for Elijah."

Josh leaned over to me. "It's in case the baby is the Messiah. Elijah's present to announce the arrival of the Messiah."

"But this is a girl," I whispered back. "Girls don't get to be Messiah."

Neither Josh nor I are against religion—I go to Mass a few times a year; he does the high holy days—but right then I couldn't control the urge to enjoy with him that little irreverent conspiracy. I needed it against all the family stuff. Against this family embraced couple who, a generation ago, would have represented a greater blasphemy even than the sin—of Sodom! of Gomorrah!—which Josh and I performed weekly.

"Pay attention," Josh whispered.

Now David was reading from a book:

In accordance with Jewish tradition we present our daughter to enter into the Covenant of Abraham and to be part of the Jewish people. We praise You, O Lord our God, King of the Universe, who has permitted us to reach towards holiness through observance of Mitzvot and commanded us to bring our children into the Covenant of Abraham our father.

There was something both foreign and familiar about this prayer. There were phrases—"King of the Universe," for example—that seemed lifted right out of the words I remembered of the Mass; and others—"Covenant of Abraham," "Mitzvot"—that gave off an exotic perfume.

"'We are mindful that we have come through a time of uncertainty into strength and joy.'"

Monica was holding the baby, bouncing it slightly in her arms. I recognized it as a nervous gesture, a way of trying to calm herself. One hand went up to her eyes; she was wiping away tears.

A time of uncertainty, I thought. What was that for them, for her? Lots of possibilities occurred to me. Maybe my mother knew, or at least guessed, though I knew I would never dare ask.

Josh whispered, "At a briss we pray that the boy will one day get married, too."

"Typical Mediterranean fertility anxiety," I whispered back.

David was finishing with a prayer in Hebrew: "... *she-heh-chi-yanu v'ki-y'manu v'higi-anu lazman hazeh.*"

The rabbi then took up a crystal goblet into which had been poured ceremonial wine, blessed it, dipped his finger in the wine, and touched Danielle's lips. She cried out, and everyone laughed. The ceremony ended with the passing of the cup to Monica and David, their parents and the godparents.

"Don't we get to drink, too?" I asked Josh.

"What do you think this is," he said, "communion?"

What's left to tell is this:

After the ceremony everyone seemed more relaxed. The party got louder and friendlier, the caterers laid out quite a spread on the dining room table, Dennis was doing a brisk business at the bar.

I made myself a hefty sandwich and wandered about, happy to do some catching up with people, just as happy to blend in with the crowd. Once, out of the corner of my eye, I saw Josh checking out the prints and paintings Monica and David had hung on the walls; later I saw him talking to Dennis at the bar. I wanted to join them, but felt that where three were gathered eyebrows might be raised. And then Mom found me again, and our conversation turned to when I was coming home for a visit.

"Isn't this a visit?" I said.

"Nicky, we never see enough of you."

"How about Thanksgiving then?" I asked her. "It's only a month away."

"Well of course Thanksgiving." She sounded annoyed. Apparently, Thanksgiving didn't count. Visiting at Thanksgiving was a commandment.

"Who's doing Thanksgiving this year anyway?" I asked. "You, or Aunt Carmella?" I knew that the plans would already be under way.

"We're going to Aunt Carmella's." Then she added, cautiously, "Monica and David won't be there this year."

"Aha!" I said, jumping at the opportunity to tease her. "So I'm not the only Mr. Russo in the family!"

My father joined us. He, too, looks younger than his years: ruddy face and a head of thick, silvery hair that Mom loves to tousle. Whenever I think of Josh and me being together forty years, I think of my parents and how they still get a kick out of each other. I want that, too.

"Where've you been?" my father asked me.

"Dad, do you know how many people have asked me that today?" I said, laughing. I was enjoying all these opportunities to tease them.

"Well, just don't be such a stranger," he said. He was trying to be brave and feisty, like Mom, but I could tell he had really missed me.

"Do you think Josh would like to be invited?" Mom asked. She glanced quickly at my father.

I could still see Josh chatting it up with Dennis. The two of them looked like they were having a good time.

"Gee, maybe," I said. "I'll find out."

"And call once in a while," my father added.

"*Oy vey*," I said, raising my eyes heavenward. We all laughed.

Josh and I have friends who every year throw a big gay Thanksgiving party in the South End: fifteen, eighteen guys. We've been invited the last two years, and doubtless will be invited again this year, but again we'll decline. Josh will either come to Aunt Carmella's, a first, or he'll go to his folks' in New Jersey. We've often fantasized what it would be like to be with our "gay family" for just one of the holidays, and now, as my parents kissed me goodbye—the first time they'd ever left a party before me!—I thought about this again. I knew that even at that moment Dennis was being enrolled into our—Josh's and my—other family, and that one day we would invite him and his other half to dinner. And that that would lead to their meeting other friends of ours, and our meeting other friends of theirs. And so it would go, on and on, *in secula seculorum*, as some of us used to say. At the same time, I couldn't wait to tell Josh that Aunt Carmella was inviting him for Thanksgiving.

I started making my way over to the two of them, then noticed, on a coffee table in the middle of the living room, the crystal goblet from which the rabbi and all the parents had tasted of the wine. It was still half full—a rich ruby color—and seemed, for that richness, sadly abandoned. I picked it up, drank, then carried the rest to Josh and Dennis at the bar.

IN MY FATHER'S CAR

There, on the road ahead of us, a boy of sixteen is walking backward with confident strides, one arm extended, thumb erect. An Italian obviously, newly ripe and cocky, with flushed cheeks and limpid eyes. He is wearing one of those mesh jerseys that stops just below the chest, exposing a woolly stripe descending from his navel into his jeans. He bends his head as we pass, looks in, and smiles with a seductive mix of arrogance and pleading. A moment later he is in the rearview mirror, a torso locked neatly into hips, fierce buttocks pumping against denim on this hot August day.

What did he see? A man with glasses askew and a cloud of white hair slouched in the passenger seat. A gaunt driver with a black mustache who stared back at him hungrily. Two men together. Two old men.

"A hitchhiker," I say as though it mattered now, but my father remains silent. He is brooding over other images, thinking of no one's body but his own.

"Are you okay, Dad?"

"Sure, I'm okay. Why shouldn't I be okay?"

He is lying, of course. He would rather be driving himself, if he could. He would rather not be making this trip at all. And he considers it an insult to his manhood that he has to ride in the passenger seat, the woman's seat.

I am taking my father to the hospital where they are going to examine his heart and remove the catheter he has been wearing in his penis for over a month. Despite his impatience to rid himself of this humiliating tube, he almost called them this morning to cancel the appointment. "Doctors!" he muttered while I helped him into the car. I knew what he meant: Doctors are devils fooling innocent people just to make a fast buck. Doctors are idiots who couldn't fix a leaky faucet let alone a human being. What do doctors know about real people who work hard and don't take vacations every six weeks?

This is one of the few subjects on which my father and I agree, even though I am a doctor of sorts myself. This is how I remind myself that I am still, inescapably, his son.

My father thinks his troubles began when he started getting headaches threading needles in his tailor shop. Then a man sent back a jacket because the lapels were uneven. A woman complained noisily about a crooked hem. One day, while cutting open a seam with a razor, my father's hand slipped and deeply gashed a suede coat. My mother argued with him for months before he finally agreed to see a doctor who told him that the nerves in his eyes had begun to deteriorate, that one had already frayed to nothing.

"What are you telling me," my father shouted. "I can't work without my eyes. Work is my life."

"If you keep working, you won't have any eyes at all," the doctor said.

That night my father sat at the kitchen table with his head in his hands and refused like a child to eat his dinner.

"Quit while you're still the champ," I told him. "Look at Man O'War. Look at Muhammed Ali."

"Look at Garbo," my mother added, hoping to make him laugh.

My father clutched the edge of the table until the veins rose on his hands. "I was the best tailor in the world," he said. "There'll never be another like me. Never."

"Can't you go any faster?" he asks now despite the line of cars in front of us. He wants it to be over so he can return to his house, sit in his armchair, and watch his television. He must have a bet to make on a baseball game or maybe a horse race, and I am denying him a chance to win, reminding him perhaps, just by being here, of what he has already lost.

"Do you want us to have an accident so you can go to the hospital in an ambulance?"

He looks at me as though he were amazed I could imagine that scenario, then nods disdainfully at the traffic. "For Chrissake," he says, "why are these guys on the road? Don't they have work to do?"

He is an impatient man, my father, a stubborn man, and superstitious enough to drive one mad. He thinks that death has its own geography, its list of favored places where it congeals and waits: condominiums in Florida, funeral homes, and especially hospitals—go there and its bony hand will reach out for your throat. That is why he avoids attending the funerals of his friends. He is afraid he might catch death from the flowers or the embalming fluid, from the creaking chairs or the tears of wailing women. That is why he balks at the idea of a will and refuses even now to buy a cemetery plot.

"Please, Dad," I said to him a few months ago, "Lakeview is almost full. In another year or two there won't be any room left. Your parents are buried there, your sisters and your brother. All the Armenians are there and all your friends, Mr. Verelli, Mr. Syzmansky. Do you want to be put someplace in the suburbs with the WASPs?"

"Don't rush me," he said. "A man with a plot is a dead man." And when I told him I would buy it myself, if not for him then for my mother, he grabbed my arm. "Buy it and you'll kill me. Is that what you want, to kill your father?"

The truth is my father believes in miracles. He thinks he is never going to die. An afterlife of hymns and shining angels does not interest him. It is this life of flesh and corruption he intends to keep. People who think he is a religious man are mistaken. My father does not rely on faith. He has something better—overwhelming proof, irrefutable evidence that he will present point by point to anyone who asks:

At the age of ten, while bathing his father's horse in the sea, he swam out farther than usual and began to flounder. He went down once, twice, and then a third time. He said to himself, "I'm going to die," and saw his life pass before his eyes just as he had heard it would. But then, miraculously, his foot touched a smooth round stone, and pushing hard against it he burst up into the air gasping and happy to see the horse again.

At twelve he had a box kite he had made himself that was more beautiful and could fly higher than all the others. Some of his friends were jealous, and one day the meanest of them snatched the string from my father's hand and ran away. My father chased the boy along the shore, through the alleys of the city smelling of cumin, and finally onto a busy street directly in front of a Jewish undertaker's wagon with four horses. My father's body hit the center post and fell tumbling among the hooves and wheels, but somehow he got through with only a bruise on his chest that quickly healed. An undertaker's wagon!

Then it was the day Greek soldiers landed in Smyrna after the Great War to retake their ancient city from the Turks. A crowd was waiting at the harbor to greet them—Greeks and Armenians waving flags and cheering. My father was there too, next to the first line of soldiers, when a boy he had never seen before touched his hand gently and said, "Your mother wants you to go home and milk the goat." "What do you mean?" my father said. "You shouldn't make her angry." So my father gave the boy his flag and started to walk home when he heard a sudden volley of shots. Turkish patriots hiding among the roofs had fired on the crowd, killing several people. Despite the confusion my father struggled back to the place he had been and saw the boy's body on the ground, his eyes open to the sky. He was dead. He had died for him.

Finally, God spoke to my father. His spirit entered his seventeen-year-old body while he was walking home one day from the marketplace. It filled his chest with a dizzy heat, rose up and exploded from his mouth forcing my father to shout, "I want to go to America! I want to go to America!" People thought he was crazy. "Why do you want to leave?" they asked him. "The Greeks are here now, and everything's going to be fine—no more massacres, no more wars." Even my father doubted his sanity because he had never thought about America and knew nothing about the place. But his demands were so relentless his parents decided at last to send him across the Atlantic along with his brother Charles, and soon they also left to join their children after selling their house for a good price. The next year the Turks reoccupied the city, subjecting it to fire and vengeful slaughter. Those who survived lost everything.

"So I saved my family," my father says, "because God spoke to me, and He spoke because He loved me and because He knew I would hear him."

I have listened to these stories so often they have made a home for themselves in my mind. I see my father's head breaking through the waves and watch him as he bends almost lovingly over the pale face of the unknown boy. I repeat the horse's funny name—Muddy, and follow the magnificent kite as it soars above the Aegean. And if I asked my father now, in this car where he is slowly fading, he would tell those stories again, not to please me but to erect them once more into a fortress against death. He might even use them to ward off my doubts and questions because he knows that less fortunate people have told me other stories from those terrible years before the fall of Smyrna, and have filled my mind with other images—twisted bodies rotting along roadsides or half-swallowed by the desert, decapitated heads with gaping mouths impaled on spikes, skeletal women and children huddled in doorways silently screaming from hunger.

I was thirteen when I went to our city's murky library and found a forgotten book with photographs. One showed a mound of earth covered with the naked, freshly killed bodies of men all in their prime. Turkish soldiers were standing next to them led by a handsome officer who looked like George V or Nicholas II. And it struck me that the faces of these soldiers resembled those of their victims—the same mustaches, the same cropped beards. I had to remind myself that the languorously sprawled bodies were Armenians, uncircumcised Christians, until I realized they had probably been posed in this way—on their backs, their legs slightly spread—to draw attention to this difference. So I studied their nakedness, their white bodies against that black earth, until nausea and the ache of my erection forced me to close the book.

That night I asked my father why God had saved him and not the others.

"All those Armenians who were massacred," I said, "they must have prayed to God too. But God didn't hear them, or at least He didn't do anything to save them. And they didn't just die—they were starved to death and bludgeoned to death; they were drowned and burned alive, babies and children too, hundreds of thousands of them, all praying for nothing. Even those who killed them still say it never happened."

"I don't know about them," my father said. "God saved me. Be thankful for that."

"But that stone in the water, it was just there. Some people make it and some don't. It's just chance."

"Chance!" he shouted. "One time is chance, maybe two, four times, that's not chance, that's destiny. God knows everything that will happen."

"Then why does He *let* it happen?"

"That's God's business," he said. "Do you think you can know God's business? Now shut up or He'll hear you."

A rush of coolness enters the car. Dappled sunlight crosses my father's face and makes him rub his eyes. We are going along the vast park that was given to the city a century ago by a wealthy industrialist. His statue stands at the entrance, an elegant man in a frock coat defiled by graffiti and bird droppings. Not far from here there is an abandoned quarry filled with water where naked boys used to dive off the rocks to prove they were men. A fat boy in my sixth-grade class named Willie Korda told me about the place one afternoon when we were alone in the cloakroom. "They've got hair already," he whispered, "and you can see everything." He moved his hand across my fly and offered to take me there, but I found it myself. I crouched in a thicket of laurels and watched them leaping, their genitals catching the sun as they floated for an instant in the bright air. I imagined they were the young heroes in my comic books, Robin or Boy, their secrets revealed at last.

As soon as I got my license a few years later, I drove my father's car into the city and found a boy my age with curly black hair walking along a side street eating a candy bar. He had pulled up his T-shirt so that it hung from the back of his neck like a small white cape. I asked him directions to a nonexistent street then invited him for a ride. He wanted to drive the car for a while just to see how it felt, but I told him it belonged to my father. "Then let's cruise around for girls," he said, but I suggested something else. I took him down the tree-shrouded road that ends at the quarry, and he showed me what he had even before I could shut off the engine. "Sort of looks like a Coke bottle, don't it?" he said. When I sank down on him, I could hear his heart pounding and smell the chocolate on his breath.

Willie became a florist when he grew up and served for many years as the scoutmaster of our local troop. We would see him every Fourth of July proudly marching his boys down Main Street, banners flapping around his head. He married a shy woman as fat as himself but never had any children. And he never abandoned the habit of taking solitary walks in the park whose hidden paths he knew since childhood. One night a gang of teenagers trapped him in the bushes, tore away his clothes, and took turns beating his pink body with fists and chains until his heart gave out. In court they testified that Willie had made advances and had tried to molest them. His wife said that was impossible: Willie had been a loving husband, a leader in the community. She begged the jury to punish his murderers severely, but they won their case.

The quarry is surrounded now by a high metal fence posted with warning signs. Too many of those strong leaping boys split open their skulls on the jagged rocks below the surface.

"Do you remember the last time we rode this way, you in the passenger seat and me at the wheel?"

"I always drove my own car," my father says. "I never asked anyone for a favor."

"I was sixteen. You were teaching me how to drive. We used to go to the park on Sunday afternoons. You had the Chrysler then. Don't you remember the '51 Chrysler?"

"That was a beautiful car," he says. "They don't make cars like that anymore."

"Every time I made a mistake you'd pound the dash and yell, 'You never were any good, and you'll never be any good.' Do you remember?"

"What are you talking about? Why am I listening to you?"

"I went to a driving school. They told me I was the best student they ever had."

"So you learned, didn't you? And I sent you to college to get a good education—something I never had."

"You looked so sad the day you gave me the keys I thought you were going to cry. You asked me if I knew how hard you had to work just to earn enough for the down payment, if I understood the value of a dollar. Then you said, 'Driving a car is like having a gun in your hand, so when you're out there don't forget that the other guy's got a gun too, and the other guy can be a crazy idiot.'"

"That's right. There are idiots everywhere just waiting for another idiot to come along."

"At the end you rubbed your hand along the fender and said, 'She's a beauty. Take good care of her and remember I need her.'"

"I loved that car," he says. "I wish I still had her. This Mercury is a lemon."

My father's memories are not my memories. He thinks of the old country and recalls how sweet figs could taste in the morning when they were still cool and covered with dew. He always says, "There are no figs like Smyrna figs," and buys them whenever he finds them even though they are brown now and not green, dried and wrapped in cellophane.

He remembers the time he took all his savings, including the money my mother had hidden in a cookie jar for my sister's birth, and bought shares of Morman Motor Cars six weeks before the Crash because someone had told him it was a sure thing.

He relives the day a man came into his tailor shop who had fought in Vietnam. The man's right leg had been amputated below the knee at a field hospital in Pleiku. His left arm was paralyzed and had shrunk by a quarter. Shrapnel had twisted his spine. He asked my father if he could fix his new suit so he wouldn't look too ugly at his daughter's wedding. "I'll make you look like a king," my father said. He took out his tailor's chalk, lifted here, pulled there. "I'll be back in a couple of weeks," the man said when the measuring was finished. "What do you mean?" my father said. "Sit down. Have a Coca-Cola. It'll be ready in an hour." My father kept his word, and when the man put on the suit again he looked taller, straighter, even his shrunken arm seemed longer. "How can I thank you," he said. "Now I *am* a king." That night my father told everyone he had performed a miracle of his own because he had made a broken man whole again.

I see my father crouched at the kitchen table in our old house listening to race results on a radio station so garbled by static I imagine he is a spy picking up messages from the Germans or the Japanese whose secrets are encoded in the dollar figures for Win, Place, and Show.

I see him talking with others, making everyone laugh with his jokes, always the same, always successful. My father, the comedian, who still shows off his profile and says, "John Barrymore!" because someone once told him he looked like the actor, and because his name too is John. But in my mind he speaks to me only in monosyllables, commands or refusals, made harder by unsmiling eyes and cigarette smoke pouring from his mouth, yellowing his teeth, staining his fingers, and more present to me than his own body.

And I remember this scene at a church picnic when I was nine. The men are sitting outside in shirtsleeves admiring little Stevie Krikorian as he talks endlessly about his sacred Yankees while tapping his bat on his toe or punching his oversized mitt. He is their prince, the new generation in a new world, the pride of immigrants, practically a friend of Joe DiMaggio's and Yogi Berra's. "And what about your son, John," someone asks my father. "What does he like to do? Does he like ball too?" Their eyes turn to me, and I look to my father, but he only shrugs his shoulders.

I light a cigarette and blow the smoke out the window so it won't tempt him, but he catches the smell and savors it with flared nostrils. Then in a stern voice he believes is fatherly he says, "Don't inhale. It's not so bad if you don't inhale."

"What would be the point of it?" I ask him. "And how would I look smoking like that?"

"I'm giving you good advice," he says. "I'm speaking from experience."

"I know. The doctors had to scare you to death to make you stop so you wouldn't kill yourself."

He clenches his jaw and releases it with a hiss of breath. "So I made some mistakes," he says. "Does that mean you have to make the same mistakes? Is that some kind of law?"

The traffic light suddenly changes, forcing me to stop the car so abruptly it frightens an old Puerto Rican woman at the curb who is carrying brightly printed shopping bags filled with groceries. Although the light is now in her favor she still hesitates, uncertain of what I will do. She studies my face cautiously then sees my father—another person with white hair burdened by life and ungrateful children. Reassured, she grabs her bags more firmly, bows her head as though we were the lords of this place, and crosses the street with a heavy shuffle.

"She looks like Nene," I say, meaning my grandmother, my father's mother. "Nene used to come down to this neighborhood to buy bulgur wheat and halvah and those dried apricots pressed in sheets I liked so much."

"Oh, yeah," my father mutters, making me wonder if he remembers this street of small shops and sagging tenements that has taken on the appearance of a frontier town.

"Look over there," I say, pointing out the place to him. "That's where Assouni's market was where she shopped. And two doors away where it says *Comidas Latinas,* that used to be Angelo's Pizzeria. They made the best pizza in Connecticut."

I say nothing about the night the Syzmansky brothers barred the entrance to Angelo's, grabbed their crotches, and told me, "We don't want you in here, faggot." Jimmy the younger brother, pursued by all the girls, who liked to "fool around" with me in the basement of his house while we looked at dirty pictures. Mike the older brother, the star of our high school basketball team, who would call me on the phone sometimes, his voice trembling, and say, "No one's home. Why don't you walk over?" Both of them the lanky, blond, and smooth-skinned sons of my father's dearest friend.

I remain silent two blocks later as we pass a corner bar boarded up with plywood that once had a neon palm tree above its door and was called the Bermuda Lounge. At seventeen I hid in the darkness across the street and watched the men come and go—men with mascara and puffed-up hair who seemed to belong to another race, to have dropped from a doomed planet—until one of them discovered me with his blinking eyes and said, "Don't be afraid, sweetie. Come on in. No one's going to hurt you." My father will never know how I ran away that night and drove his beautiful car through the city telling myself, "I'm not like that. I'm not like them."

"They're gone now," I say, "the Lebanese, the Italians, all the people who used to live here."

"That's what it's all about," he says. "That's America. You make money and you move."

"Well, you made a little money, but you never got rich."

"Who says I wanted to be rich?"

"You wanted it all your life. That's why you played the horses with every dollar you could spare."

"So how many times did I win? Once or twice."

"And you spent years calculating the ups and downs of the Dow Jones so you could crack Wall Street. You filled stacks of notebooks with your figures. Einstein would have been impressed."

"It was just a way to pass the time, to occupy my mind. A man needs to occupy his mind."

"You could have passed the time talking to your family, but instead you dreamed of hitting the big one, finding the secret treasure. You wanted to be the Count of Monte Cristo."

My father's eyes open wider. His body seems to rise magically from the seat. He tilts back his head and proclaims, "*The Count of Monte Cristo!* What a story! Who makes movies like that today?"

"No one, Dad."

"It was the best. It still is and will always be."

"You're right, Dad."

He smiles at me with a rare look of pride. For this moment I am his ally, his pal walking arm in arm with him toward some glowing horizon. Then he lets his body sink again, his shoulders hunched, his eyes on the road.

The Count of Monte Cristo with Robert Donat—my father has seen the movie at least a dozen times, and I have watched it with him almost as often on the old Admiral in our living room. Of all the stories he has ever heard, this is the perfect one: Edmond Dantès, a handsome young sailor, is falsely accused of treason by three greedy men and condemned to the prison of Château d'If where for fifteen years he struggles with the old abbé Faria to dig a passage through the thick rock walls. Before dying the abbé reveals the secret of a fabulous hidden treasure, and Edmond finally escapes by placing his own body in the abbé's burial sack, which the guards then hurl into the sea. He finds the treasure with the help of pirates, becomes the Count of Monte Cristo, and thanks to the immense power of his wealth proceeds to destroy his enemies utterly, damning each one by name—Danglars, Mondego, De Villefort.

"It's a story about justice," my father always says, "and I believe in justice, and so does America. Look at Hoover, that bastard! He was robbing the people, taking the food out of our mouths until Roosevelt came along and kicked him out. And look at what the Japanese did at Pearl Harbor. America was just sitting there minding its own business, but we got back at them, didn't we? We smashed them. It's the same story."

It does no good to tell my father that Roosevelt probably knew of the attack in advance, or that Hoover never planned to steal the gold from Fort Knox. "What do you know?" he says. "Were you there? I was there." To make his point he has never bought a Hoover vacuum cleaner even though we have laughed and explained that it is not the same family. He doesn't want that accursed name in his house, especially on a vacuum cleaner that could suck the change out of our pockets and mow us down on the carpet. Hoover is the Evil One, the bloated capitalist in pin-striped pants. Roosevelt is the eternal friend of the working man, the Great Crippled Father.

One winter night I asked him why he never talked about the way the abbé becomes a father to Edmond while they're in prison:

"Remember that scene just before the old man dies? He says, 'I leave my mind behind in your possession. Use it for justice.' And later Edmond protects his enemy's only son, the young viscount de Mondego, who's afraid he'll become a coward like his father."

"That's the way it should be," my father said. "One generation helps the next."

"But you don't understand, Dad. The real fathers almost kill their children. It's the other fathers, the ones without children, who save and teach."

My father started to laugh. "If you're looking for a better father, don't waste your time," he said. "I'm the only one you're ever going to have."

"So that makes us even," I said, "because you'll never have another son. It'll all die with me—your name, your stories, everything."

"Is that what you're learning?" he scowled. "Did some man teach you to talk like that?"

Then, two years later, after watching the movie again, my father surprised me. He leaned forward in his armchair and confessed that his passion for *The Count of Monte Cristo* went beyond its associations with the Depression or the war.

"You see," he said, "I know what that story is all about because when I was young I was also falsely accused."

"Accused of what?" I asked him.

"You know, when people say you did something you didn't do, when they say you're something you're not?"

"But what was it? Did they say you stole something, that you lied?"

I waited for my father's answer, but it never came. He stared at the shifting images on the television screen until his expression, which had softened, became hard again. "Forget it," he said. "That's all in the past. I don't want to talk about it anymore."

For years I tried to lead my father back to this question without success, so for years I thought his refusal to speak meant that his "crime" was in some way sexual. Perhaps while playing with a friend in the shade of a fig tree one of my father's gestures had been misinterpreted by the boy himself or by a malicious observer. Perhaps a wandering merchant, plump and perfumed, had tried to seduce him with gaudy gifts and after being rebuffed had made accusations in order to defend himself. Whatever the cause, the results would have been the same: taunts and hateful names. I even imagined my father's story about the goatboy might be more dream than reality, that the boy was not unknown to my father but a beloved friend who had betrayed him, at once a savior because of my father's continuing love for him, yet someone to be punished by an imaginary death. And so my father's desire to come to America would not have been inspired by God but by his own desperate need to escape an unbearable situation and to save his family from further shame.

I wanted this interpretation to be true so I could tell my father I understood him in the hope that he would understand me. Hadn't I been taunted and maligned like him, called names on the street and in the halls of my high school? And like him wasn't I still dreaming of justice, or rather inventing impossible scenarios of revenge against my enemies in which I would threaten them with exquisite tortures only to forgive them with an outstretched hand? But I never spoke of these dreams to my father because I would have had to explain to him that some accusations can be true and still unjust. I would have been forced to confess that of all my enemies I considered him the greatest.

Just as my father had escaped to America, I went to Europe as a student and hitchhiked my way to Smyrna to see his birthplace with my own eyes.

"Did you find our house?" he asked eagerly when I came back. "Did you see the fig trees?"

"While I was looking for the house I met a Turkish boy who offered to guide me," I said. "His name was Genghis, and he had blond hair and blue eyes. I didn't know Turks could look like that. He was just fifteen so I bought him ice cream, but later he bought me tea to show he was grown up. We spoke German mostly because his father had worked in Munich. I told him my parents were born here and that they were Armenians. He didn't really know what that meant, I suppose because he was too young and because there were no Armenians left."

I thought my father would be bitter. Here was proof, once again, that the massacres would never be acknowledged by those who had committed them, but he said, "I'm glad you met that boy. Turks can be good people. They were our neighbors. We ate the same food and played the same games. Things didn't go wrong until the end."

I never told him the boy and I made love that night as easily as we had eaten ice cream while watching the boats rock in the harbor—so easily that I realized my father might have done the same without a thought in a culture so unlike my own. But I have not abandoned my theory because I am afraid if I do my father's secret will elude me forever. Whatever the injustice he suffered, it must have been very great to give him this enduring thirst for revenge, to make him want to be the best tailor in the world, to make him dream of finding at last a fabulous treasure, and to fill him at times with longing for a son better than I. Once he may have wished to stay young forever, handsome as a movie star, but now he knows his last chance for justice is to escape death, to become a wonder for succeeding generations—old certainly, blind perhaps, unable to move someday, but eternally alive.

The hospital is a new tower of steel and glass on a hill overlooking the city. All that remains of its old structure is a squat wing of faded brick where, according to my mother, I was born a healthy baby, just the right size and weight. I mention this fact to my father as we leave the car, but once again he has no mind for these matters. Now that we have arrived, his strategy is to get in and out as quickly as possible before some hovering creature has a chance to carry him off. Yet when we reach the entrance he stops and examines his reflection on the heavy glass doors. "When did I get so old?" he asks and repeats the question: "When did I get so old?" I don't think he would be surprised if a voice said to him: "John, remember the time you missed lunch so you could finish that wedding dress? Remember the day that truck cut you off on the highway and you cursed until your head ached? That was the day you got old. If you'd eaten your lunch, if you'd started out five minutes later or five minutes sooner, you'd still be young and strong."

As for me, the evidence is clear—I am beginning to look like my father. And now that he is dying, my metamorphosis has accelerated. He seems to be hurling his traits at me in a mad effort to guarantee their survival, or something in me is sucking them from him against my will. All I conceded to him before were my long legs and the line of my nose. The rest, or most of it, I credited to my mother. But now he has invaded every feature and has found a passage into my bones to give me the same slight stoop, the same forward thrust of the head. "Stand up straight," my mother would warn me. "Look at your father. He never learned to stand straight." For years I slept without a pillow on the firmest mattress I could find, I pressed my back against walls. What good did it do?

When we enter the lobby, my father sniffs the air to find what he expected—the sterile, chemical smell of death seeping from the pastel walls, rising from the hard gray carpet. He looks at a man shaking with palsy who is kissing the fingers of a nervous little girl with pink ribbons in her hair. He stares at the tumble of multicolored teddy bears in the gift shop window, their eyes black and bright, forever open. And as we stand waiting for the elevator, he studies the faces of the people around us to see if their fate is written there, to see if he is still the exception, the only one here by mistake.

The elevator arrives at last, and the crowd pushes us in, presses us back. The congestion is even greater when we reach the next floor. I maneuver my father into a bit of empty space, and as I try to regain my footing, my knee strikes something hard. "Excuse me," I say before realizing that I have hit the metal frame of a wheelchair. The man seated in it returns my smile, looks at my father, and smiles again. We have recognized each other instantly like compatriots in an alien land. He is young, no more than twenty-five, but his youth survives now only in the defiant curve of his dark lashes and in a milky tenderness on the side of his neck. The rest of him looks as though he had been exposed to a rapid succession of violent seasons, malarial heats and paralytic colds, wearing away the flesh, curing it down to the skull. I am tempted to touch his hand and ask his name, but we continue to stare at each other as I read our common language in his eyes: "I was handsome once," he is saying. "You would have wanted me. If you can choose, if that's possible, then choose to look someday like your father, not like me." A moment later an orderly forges a path for him out of the elevator. The wheelchair rattles then moves soundlessly down a long white corridor.

By the time we reach our floor my father is sweating despite the air-conditioning. I can smell the heat of his body, a hint of urine.

"Is that the only elevator they have in this hospital?" he asks. "Do they think we're sardines?"

"A lot of people are sick, Dad."

"Who's sick?"

"That guy in the wheelchair. He's dying, and he's just a kid."

"Okay, maybe him, but the rest of them have been fooled by the doctors. They've got to pay for this place, don't they?"

He continues to mutter complaints until we enter the doctor's office where we are greeted by a buxom nurse in an immaculately white uniform, her shoes like clouds at her feet.

"Well, here we are," she says with a wink. "Right on time."

"I'm always on time," my father answers. "A man should be on time."

"I'll tell that to Dr. Chin," she says, "but while we're waiting for him let's get you into a smock and do a few tests—a little blood, a little urine."

"I've got the tube on," my father says. "I've got the bag."

"The catheter. We'll take care of that. Don't worry, your son will be here waiting for you."

"I don't worry," my father says.

The nurse smiles at me as though we were the only grownups present. "Come along," she says, and my father plays his part—a child again, following his mother to the fearful first day of school.

From this height I can see almost the entire city stretching down to the Sound, and in the far distance the faint, reassuring silhouette of Long Island. This is still an industrial city of immense brick factories producing brass and corsets and handguns; a working-class city of innumerable taverns and churches: St. Augustine, Sts. Cyril and Methodius, and our own Church of the Holy Ascension, sold years ago to Black Baptists who have retained its octagonal cupola and trefoiled cross. I was an altar boy there. I sang in the choir about God's mercy.

When my father reached America he came to this city and got a job in a lace factory. He worked six days a week, ten hours a day, and every night went to Mr. Jacobian's shop and learned the tailor's trade. Then he made love for the first time with a woman thanks to his worldly cousin Harry who had connections. My mother revealed this to me one night after quarreling with my father. "He went to a prostitute before he married me, did you know that?" she said, crying. "That's why they made him get married, to save him from hell, to stop him from wasting his money." I asked my father later if it was true. "I was young," he said. "I didn't know English very well." I wanted to know what she looked like, the color of her hair, her age. Had he been afraid? Had she helped him? Was he trying to prove something to himself? My father glared down at me. "Men don't talk about those things," he said.

Well, I have become a man who does talk about those things, but not to my father, never to him. Even before he married his world was his neighborhood and his home where the women cooked for him and washed his clothes. But the day he gave me the keys to his car, this city became mine. The economic boom hadn't changed the landscape yet, and on summer nights the streets were filled with people, mostly boys like myself and young men with nothing to do. I would see them hanging out in front of drugstores, smoking lazily on park benches, hitchhiking without embarrassment. They would look at me as I passed. They wanted what I had, a car to kill time, and I wanted them.

A week after finding the boy with the candy bar, I saw two others fighting in a vacant lot, kicking and whipping each other with their belts. One was tall and stocky, the other wiry and quick. Both had crewcuts and were wearing identical red shirts with green collars. Finally, the big one fell clutching his belly, and the other stood over him slapping his belt against his thigh until he was sure it was finished. As he walked away I followed him in the car and asked if he needed any help.

"Help with what?"

"With anything you like."

He directed me to a street of decayed buildings and to an abandoned house with rusted balconies. We made our way over shards of glass until we reached the kitchen where the moonlight revealed a bare linoleum floor patterned in false mosaic. A cracked, blackened sink still hung from a wall.

"This used to be my house," he said. "I come here sometimes when I want to get away. It's peaceful. No one bothers you."

He drew me closer and put his arm around my shoulder. He had a bruise on his cheek and a streak of drying blood by his ear. I was surprised by his height, a full head shorter than mine.

"I need some relaxation. Would you like to be a buddy and give me some re-laxation?"

He took off his clothes and arranged them neatly on the floor, then stretched out on top of them, his small white buttocks slightly raised. I stood next to him unable to move.

"What's the matter?"

"I've never done that to anyone before."

"It's easy," he said. "Just use lots of spit."

He moaned when I entered him, but I came in a shudder after only a few seconds.

"I'm sorry," I said.

He looked back sorrowfully then buried his head deeper into his damp shirt. "You can't win them all," he sighed. "But will you do me a favor? Will you please just stay in there for a while?"

After that I hunted every night I could and found a mechanic with greasy tools in his pockets I was afraid would stain the seat, a sailor from Wisconsin who stripped but kept his cap on because I asked him to, a handsome deaf-mute who lived with his mother in a trailer camp and thanked me with signs. I found college students who sometimes felt guilty and workers' sons who never did—Poles, Slovaks, Greeks, and especially Italians with names like Sal, Tony, and Vinny. I caught boys in summer whose bodies tasted of sea salt, and boys who steamed up the car in winter so that I had to wipe the windows before going home. Boys fresh from dates whose lips were still red from kissing, and boys desperate to escape their lonely nights. Some who asked for money, no more than a dollar or two, and those who offered, incomprehensibly, to pay me. The ones who had to be reassured that I expected nothing in return, and the ones who reciprocated every act with a hunger that surprised me.

And on those nights when my father needed the car I would walk to the main road, stick out my thumb, and let myself be caught by others. Most were married men who, I imagined, had sons of their own—factory workers with lunch pails tossed on the back seat, businessmen stiff with dignity, nondescript men so timid their hands would shake at the wheel. I would sit through their game of innocence waiting for the opening line:

"There's this guy down at the plant ... You should see him in the showers."

"You're a good-looking kid. Do you have a girlfriend?"

"Boy, I'd like to do something tonight, anything."

At times I would have to encourage them, prompt them with a line of my own:

"I'm not going anywhere special. Just out for some excitement."

"I was just checking. I thought my fly was open."

When I spoke this way I would try to sound tougher, less intelligent than I really was. I would slouch in the seat, open my legs wider, and let them see what they longed to see, even turning my head away so they could look more easily. Whatever those men saw, I knew they wanted me, and that desire rushing beneath their words and glances made me feel as powerful as those slim-hipped street boys who so excited me.

It was after one of these hitchhiking adventures that my father offered the only sexual advice he ever gave me. He was sitting in the living room watching a baseball game on which he had confidently bet and would lose fifty dollars.

"How did you get home last night?"

"My ride didn't work out so I hitchhiked instead."

"I don't want you doing that."

"Why?"

An outfielder was staggering backward for a catch, but the falling ball was just beyond his reach.

"Damn it! He should've had that."

"Why shouldn't I hitchhike, Dad?"

He looked at me. The inning was over. "Because you can get into trouble."

"What kind of trouble."

"You're a young kid. People will take advantage of you."

"How?"

"Some men look for kids like you."

"What men?"

"Men. Bad men."

"Why?"

"What do you mean why?"

"Why are they looking for kids?"

"Never mind why. I'm just telling you not to do it. Do you understand? That's all."

Had my father listened more carefully he might have heard the irony in my voice and realized that more than a baseball game had been lost. I had gone through a rite of passage far more important than his giving me the keys to his Chrysler. I knew more than he did, not just about my life but about the world, and I thought he could no more comprehend me than he could transport himself onto that grassy field in Chicago where the winning team was celebrating its victory. Sitting there in his armchair he seemed to shrink away, to become as tiny as the figures on the television screen. I held the truth. I was the master. I could destroy him with a word.

What desires do I have now that friends I loved have died or are dying like the young man in the wheelchair, when others have been killed on the streets like Willie Korda by those who might have been their brothers or their sons? And what power do I have now that my father has armored himself with frailty and approaching death? Two years ago my mother made another revelation to me. We were drinking coffee in this hospital after a visit to my father who was recovering from a prostate operation. "Your father still comes to me at night," she said, "and it frightens me because he tries so hard. I told him, 'John, that's all right. Don't worry if you can't finish,' but he keeps trying and then he cries. 'What good is a man if he can't work anymore,' he says. 'What good is a man if he can't be a man.'"

Sometimes I wonder if my father's death will miraculously give me new life. Other times I imagine that he can still guide me, can teach me things the way the old abbé teaches Edmond Dantès in the dank prison of Château d'If. Like a good student I have questions for him that I have refined over the years. They have a place in my mind next to his stories about Smyrna. Here they are, the questions I will never ask:

If he had not escaped the old world in time, and if I had been born there, would we have been killed someday together? Would our naked bodies have been displayed together on a mound of earth or against a riddled wall?

Will we reveal our great secrets to each other before it is too late? Will we find a hidden treasure that will enable us to seek justice against his enemies and mine?

And will his God save and protect me too, even though He has failed to save so many others, and even though I have cursed him for forsaking them?

The nurse leads my father back to me. He looks weaker than before as though some nourishing fluid had been drained away, exhausted. His hair needs combing. He hasn't rebuttoned his shirt correctly.

"What did they do?"

"They took the tube out," he says. "They looked at this and that."

"How's your heart?"

"It's not my heart so much, it's my blood pressure. He gave me more pills. They always give you pills."

"What else did the doctor say?"

"He said I'm old."

"What does that mean?"

"Old. It means old. What else do you want it to mean?"

Once outside the sun presses down on us, almost blinds us as it glints fiercely off the windshields in the parking lot. My father raises a hand to his eyes and lurches toward the car. He attempts to open the door himself, forgetting that it is locked.

"Relax, Dad. We'll be home soon. You can take a nap and still have time to watch your game."

"I don't want to go home," he says. "What do I have to do at home? I want to see my tailor shop. Take me there."

"But, Dad, I don't even know if the building's still standing. They're tearing down that whole section of town for a shopping mall or something. They've blocked off most of the streets and ripped up the sidewalks. It's a mess, believe me."

"Did you hear what I said? This is my car. Take me or I'll drive there myself."

We go as far as we can and abandon the car two blocks from the site of my father's shop. The space in between is a jagged landscape strewn with slabs of broken concrete tilted at mad angles and rusted pipes jutting treacherously through the debris. Here and there remnants of softened macadam show treadmarks like the traces of prehistoric bones. We make our way together across this wasted land, sometimes side by side, sometimes with me a step ahead pointing out obstacles, suggesting footholds. My father wipes his brow and grunts in reply, determined to reach his goal. There are no workmen about, no sounds of machinery. Except for a haze of rising dust, the sky is cloudless. We are alone.

We come at last to the edge of a broad depression that was once an avenue. My father's shop is on the opposite side, its windows cracked, its door caked with mud, but still intact despite the demolition that has already devoured most of the structure housing it. The only way to reach it now without making a tortuous detour is to cross a makeshift bridge composed of narrow planks resting precariously on dented steel drums. I start to advise my father against following this route but he is already talking, telling me another story:

"There it is, my old shop. This is the old neighborhood. Emeric Verelli had a luncheonette next door to me. He served great blueplate specials—meat loaf, turkey, whatever you wanted. I used to eat there all the time. And across the street, right where we're standing, was Bill Syzmansky's tavern. In the summertime, when it got really hot and I was sweating over the pressing machine, he'd send one of his boys over with a cold bottle of beer. We were all friends, it was like a family with good times and bad times."

"I remember his boys. We went to school together."

"Do you know what it was like during the Depression? Roosevelt said, 'The only thing we have to fear is fear itself.' And he said it because people were afraid. I was afraid. Do you understand that? Every time I left the shop there'd be somebody outside trying to sell me an apple. 'Please, mister, buy an apple—just five cents, just two cents.' Old guys, young guys with kids at home looking for a piece of bread. Guys who used to be rich—bankers, big shots. It made no difference. Nobody had work."

"I know what fear is, Dad."

"But I wasn't afraid to work. I had to take care of your mother, your sister was a baby. I had my parents to support, my father was too old and sick to work. One day a man brought in some fabric, beautiful English worsted, and asked me to make him a suit. I was young then, still learning my trade. It took me three weeks to make that suit, and do you know what my profit was? A measly five dollars, and I was happy to have it."

"And now they're tearing the place down."

"So now they're tearing it down. John the tailor? Who was he? Maybe they'll build new shops for other people to work in, or just smash it all into a parking lot. What can I do about it? What can anyone do? But I want you to remember this—that shop put food on the table and clothes on our backs. We had a roof over our heads. Can you understand? It kept us alive."

My father does not expect an answer. He continues to stare at his old shop, caught in his memories, oblivious to everything else. Then, suddenly, his body stiffens, turns to stone. He has seen what I have already seen—a man with blond hair swept high on his head walking nimbly over the debris a hundred feet away. He is wearing large sunglasses with glittery ends, a flowing white shirt open to the waist, tight powder-blue pants that show off his fleshy rump and taper to a stop just above his ankles. His left arm is swinging in shallow arcs to balance his weight while his right hand remains firmly attached to the strap of his leather shoulder bag. He knows who he is—a queen of the old school preserved against all odds, an outrageous survivor, and now in this desolate arena almost an acrobat as he steps blithely onto the bridge without missing a beat and gives us a brief, regal nod.

My father has not moved, has hardly blinked his eyes. He is probably reviewing names to identify this creature in all the languages he knows—Armenian, Greek, Turkish, English. Or perhaps these words are too shameful for him. Perhaps the only thought he can permit himself is this: "He's one of those men, one of those bad men." And now my old anger returns fueled as always by the silences of the past. I want to say to my father, "Why stare at him when you can look at me, your son? Why search for names when I know all the names in even more languages than you do? Haven't you realized yet that I could die before you?"

"Oh!" my father shouts.

The man has slipped, has fallen with a bounce on his ample behind. His queenly legs rise and spread above him in the flawless sky. His arms become wings fluttering on either side of the narrow bridge. His bag drops from his shoulder and swings dizzily in the void.

"Oh, look!" my father says.

The man is up. He has lifted himself with a single agile leap. A quick brush to his buttocks, a quicker tuck to his hair, a final adjustment to his shoulder strap, and he is on his way again with undiminished energy—across the bridge, toward my father's doomed shop, and beyond to a place of his own, to a bar still open on a forgotten street where men laugh together under neon trees.

"Come on, Dad, let's go home," I say, anger lingering in my voice. "He may fall again, and then what will you do? You may have to go over there and help him, lift him up."

My father turns his tired face to me and lets me see the blue circles in his eyes. He puts his hand on my arm and leans his body against mine. He weighs me down yet seems about to fly away.

"Don't worry about him," he says. "He's still young like you and can take care of himself. But hold on to me, will you, so I don't fall too."

DOROTHY ALLISON

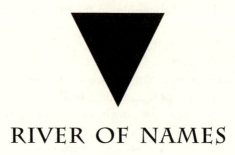

RIVER OF NAMES

A̲ᴛ ᴀ ᴘɪᴄɴɪᴄ at my aunt's farm, the only time the whole family ever gathered, my sister Billie and I chased chickens into the barn. Billie ran right through the open doors and out again, but I stopped, caught by a shadow moving over me. My cousin, Tommy, eight years old as I was, swung in the sunlight with his face as black as his shoes—the rope around his neck pulled up into the sunlit heights of the barn, fascinating, horrible. Wasn't he running ahead of us? Someone came up behind me. Someone began to scream. My mamma took my head in her hands and turned my eyes away.

Jesse and I have been lovers for a year now. She tells me stories about her childhood, about her father going off each day to the university, her mother who made all her dresses, her grandmother who always smelled of dill bread and vanilla. I listen with my mouth open, not believing but wanting, aching for the fairy tale she thinks is everyone's life.

"What did your grandmother smell like?"

I lie to her the way I always do, a lie stolen from a book. "Like lavender," stomach churning over the memory of sour sweat and snuff.

I realize I do not really know what lavender smells like, and I am for a moment afraid she will ask something else, some question that will betray me. But Jesse slides over to hug me, to press her face against my ear, to whisper, "How wonderful to be part of such a large family."

I hug her back and close my eyes. I cannot say a word.

I was born between the older cousins and the younger, born in a pause of babies and therefore outside, always watching. Once, way before Tommy died,

I was pushed out on the steps while everyone stood listening to my Cousin Barbara. Her screams went up and down in the back of the house. Cousin Cora brought buckets of bloody rags out to be burned. The other cousins all ran off to catch the sparks or poke the fire with dogwood sticks. I waited on the porch making up words to the shouts around me. I did not understand what was happening. Some of the older cousins obviously did, their strange expressions broken by stranger laughs. I had seen them helping her up the stairs while the thick blood ran down her legs. After a while the blood on the rags was thin, watery, almost pink. Cora threw them on the fire and stood motionless in the stinking smoke.

Randall went by and said there'd be a baby, a hatched egg to throw out with the rags, but there wasn't. I watched to see and there wasn't; nothing but the blood, thinning out desperately while the house slowed down and grew quiet, hours of cries growing soft and low, moaning under the smoke. My Aunt Raylene came out on the porch and almost fell on me, not seeing me, not seeing anything at all. She beat on the post until there were knuckle-sized dents in the peeling paint, beat on that post like it could feel, cursing it and herself and every child in the yard, singing up and down, "Goddamn, goddamn, that girl … no sense … goddamn!"

I've these pictures my mama gave me—stained sepia prints of bare dirt yards, plank porches, and step after step of children—cousins, uncles, aunts; mysteries. The mystery is how many no one remembers. I show them to Jesse, not saying who they are, and when she laughs at the broken teeth, torn overalls, the dirt, I set my teeth at what I do not want to remember and cannot forget.

We were so many we were without number and, like tadpoles, if there was one less from time to time, who counted? My maternal great-grandmother had eleven daughters, seven sons; my grandmother, six sons, five daughters. Each one made at least six. Some made nine. Six times six, eleven times nine. They went on like multiplication tables. They died and were not missed. I come of an enormous family and I cannot tell half their stories. Somehow it was always made to seem they killed themselves: car wrecks, shotguns, dusty ropes, screaming, falling out of windows, things inside them. I am the point of a pyramid, sliding back under the weight of the ones who came after, and it does not matter that I am the lesbian, the one who will not have children.

I tell the stories and it comes out funny. I drink bourbon and make myself drawl, tell all those old funny stories. Someone always seems to ask me, which one was that? I show the pictures and she says, "Wasn't she the one in the story about the bridge?" I put the pictures away, drink more, and someone always finds them, then says, "Goddamn! How many of you were there anyway?"

I don't answer.

Jesse used to say, "You've got such a fascination with violence. You've got so many terrible stories."

She said it with her smooth mouth, that chin nobody ever slapped, and I love that chin, but when Jesse spoke then, my hands shook and I wanted nothing so much as to tell her terrible stories.

So I made a list. I told her: that one went insane—got her little brother with a tire iron; the three of them slit their arms, not the wrists but the bigger veins up near the elbow; she, now *she* strangled the boy she was sleeping with and got sent away; that one drank lye and died laughing soundlessly. In one year I lost eight cousins. It was the year everybody ran away. Four disappeared and were never found. One fell in the river and was drowned. One was run down hitchhiking north. One was shot running through the woods, while Grace, the last one, tried to walk from Greenville to Greer for some reason nobody knew. She fell off the overpass a mile down from the Sears, Roebuck warehouse and lay there for hunger and heat and dying.

Later, sleeping, but not sleeping, I found that my hands were up under Jesse's chin. I rolled away, but I didn't cry. I almost never let myself cry.

Almost always, we were raped, my cousins and I. That was some kind of joke, too.

What's a South Carolina virgin?
'At's a ten-year-old can run fast.

It wasn't funny for me in my mama's bed with my stepfather, not for my cousin, Billie, in the attic with my uncle, nor for Lucille in the woods with another cousin, for Danny with four strangers in a parking lot, or for Pammie who made the papers. Cora read it out loud: "Repeatedly by persons unknown." They stayed unknown since Pammie never spoke again. Perforations, lacerations, contusions, and bruises. I heard all the words, big words, little words, words too terrible to understand. *DEAD BY AN ACT OF MAN*. With the prick still in them, the broom handle, the tree branch, the grease gun ... objects, things not to be believed ... whiskey bottles, can openers, grass shears, glass, metal, vegetables ... not to be believed, not to be believed.

Jesse says, "You've got a gift for words."

"Don't talk," I beg her, "don't talk." And this once, she just holds me, blessedly silent.

I dig out the pictures, stare into the faces. Which one was I? Survivors do hate themselves, I know, over the core of fierce self-love, never understanding, always asking, "Why me and not her, not him?" There is such mystery in it, and I have hated myself as much as I have loved others, hated the simple fact of my own survival. Having survived, am I supposed to say something, do something, be something?

I love my Cousin Butch. He had this big old head, pale thin hair, and enormous, watery eyes. All the cousins did, though Butch's head was the largest, his hair the palest. I was the dark-headed one. All the rest of the family seemed pale carbons of each other in shades of blond, though later on everybody's hair went brown or red and I didn't stand out so. Butch and I stood out then—I because I was so dark and fast, and he because of that big head and the crazy things he did. Butch used to climb on the back of my Uncle Lucius's truck, open the gas tank and hang his head over, breathe deeply, strangle, gag, vomit, and breathe again. It went so deep, it tingled your toes. I climbed up after him and tried it myself, but I was too young to hang on long, and I fell heavily to the ground, dizzy and giggling. Butch could hang on, put his hand down into the tank and pull up a cupped palm of gas, breathe deep and laugh. He would climb down roughly, swinging down from the door handle, laughing, staggering, and stinking of gasoline. Someone caught him at it. Someone threw a match. "I'll teach you."

Just like that, gone before you understand.

I wake up in the night screaming, "No, no, I won't!" Dirty water rises in the back of my throat, the liquid language of my own terror and rage. "Hold me. Hold me." Jesse rolls over on me; her hands grip my hipbones tightly.

"I love you. I love you. I'm here," she repeats.

I stare up into her dark eyes, puzzled, afraid. I draw a breath in deeply, smile my bland smile. "Did I fool you?" I laugh, rolling away from her. Jesse punches me playfully, and I catch her hand in the air.

"My love," she whispers, and cups her body against my hip, closes her eyes. I bring my hand up in front of my face and watch the knuckles, the nails as they tremble, tremble. I watch for a long time while she sleeps, warm and still against me.

James went blind. One of the uncles got him in the face with home-brewed alcohol.

Lucille climbed out the front window of Aunt Raylene's house and jumped. They said she jumped. No one said why.

My Uncle Matthew used to beat my Aunt Raylene. The twins, Mark and Luke, swore to stop him, pulled him out in the yard one time, throwing him between them like a loose bag of grain. Uncle Matthew screamed like a pig coming up for slaughter. I got both my sisters in the tool shed for safety, but I hung back to watch. Little Bo came running out of the house, off the porch, feet first into his daddy's arms. Uncle Matthew started swinging him like a scythe, going after the bigger boys, Bo's head thudding their shoulders, their hips. Afterward, Bo crawled around in the dirt, the blood running out of his ears and his tongue hanging out of his mouth, while Mark and Luke finally got their daddy down. It was a long time before I realized that they never told anybody else what happened to Bo.

Randall tried to teach Lucille and me to wrestle. "Put your hands up." His legs were wide apart, his torso bobbing up and down, his head moving constantly. Then his hand flashed at my face. I threw myself back into the dirt, lay still. He turned to Lucille, not noticing that I didn't get up. He punched at her, laughing. She wrapped her hands around her head, curled over so her knees were up against her throat.

"No, no," he yelled. "Move like her." He turned to me. "Move." He kicked at me. I rocked into a ball, froze.

"No, no!" He kicked me. I grunted, didn't move. He turned to Lucille. "You." Her teeth were chattering but she held herself still, wrapped up tighter than bacon slices.

"You move!" he shouted. Lucille just hugged her head tighter and started to sob.

"Son of a bitch," Randall grumbled, "you two will never be any good."

He walked away. Very slowly we stood up, embarrassed, looked at each other. We knew.

If you fight back, they kill you.

My sister was seven. She was screaming. My stepfather picked her up by her left arm, swung her forward and back. It gave. The arm went around loosely. She just kept screaming. I didn't know you could break it like that.

I was running up the hall. He was right behind me. "Mama! Mama!" His left hand—he was left-handed—closed around my throat, pushed me against the wall, and then he lifted me that way. I kicked, but I couldn't reach him. He was yelling, but there was so much noise in my ears I couldn't hear him.

"Please, Daddy. Please, Daddy. I'll do anything, I promise. Daddy, anything you want. Please, Daddy."

I couldn't have said that. I couldn't talk around that fist at my throat, couldn't breathe. I woke up when I hit the floor. I looked up at him.

"If I live long enough, I'll fucking kill you."

He picked me up by my throat again.

What's wrong with her?
Why's she always following you around?
Nobody really wanted answers.

A full bottle of vodka will kill you when you're nine and the bottle is a quart. It was a third cousin proved that. We learned what that and other things could do. Every year there was something new.

You're growing up.

My big girl.

There was codeine in the cabinet, paregoric for the baby's teeth, whiskey, beer, and wine in the house. Jeanne brought home MDA, PCP, acid; Randall, grass, speed, and mescaline. It all worked to dull things down, to pass the time.

Stealing was a way to pass the time. Things we needed, things we didn't, for the nerve of it, the anger, the need. *You're growing up,* we told each other. But sooner or later, we all got caught. Then it was, *When are you going to learn?*

Caught, nightmares happened. *Razorback desperate,* was the conclusion of the man down at the county farm where Mark and Luke were sent at fifteen. They both got their heads shaved, their earlobes sliced.

What's the matter, kid? Can't you take it?

Caught at sixteen, June was sent up to Jessup County Girls' Home where the baby was adopted out and she slashed her wrists on the bedsprings.

Lou got caught at seventeen and held in the station downtown, raped on the floor of the holding tank.

Are you a boy or are you a girl?

On your knees, kid, can you take it?

Caught at eighteen and sent to prison, Jack came back seven years later blank-faced, understanding nothing. He married a quiet girl from out of town, had three babies in four years. Then Jack came home one night from the textile mill, carrying one of those big handles off the high speed spindle machine. He used it to beat them all to death and went back to work in the morning.

Cousin Melvina married at fourteen, had three kids in two and a half years, and welfare took them all away. She ran off with a carnival mechanic, had three more babies before he left her for a motorcycle acrobat. Welfare took those, too. But the next baby was hydrocephalic, a little waterhead they left with her, and the three that followed, even the one she used to hate so—the one she had after she fell off the porch and couldn't remember whose child it was.

"How many children do you have?" I asked her.

"You mean the ones I have, or the ones I had? Four," she told me, "or eleven."

My aunt, the one I was named for, tried to take off for Oklahoma. That was after she'd lost the youngest girl and they told her Bo would never be "right." She packed up biscuits, cold chicken, and Coca-Cola, a lot of loose clothes, Cora and her new baby, Cy, and the four youngest girls. They set off from Greenville in the afternoon, hoping to make Oklahoma by the weekend, but they only got as far as Augusta. The bridge there went out under them.

"An Act of God," my uncle said.

My aunt and Cora crawled out down river, and two of the girls turned up in the weeds, screaming loud enough to be found in the dark. But one of the girls never came up out of that dark water, and Nancy, who had been holding Cy, was found still wrapped around the baby, in the water, under the car.

"An Act of God," my aunt said. "God's got one damn sick sense of humor."

My sister had her baby in a bad year. Before he was born we had talked about it. "Are you afraid?" I asked.

"He'll be fine," she'd replied, not understanding, speaking instead to the other fear. "Don't we have a tradition of bastards?"

He was fine, a classically ugly healthy little boy with that shock of white hair that marked so many of us. But afterward, it was that bad year with my sister down with pleurisy, then cystitis, and no work, no money, having to move back home with my cold-eyed stepfather. I would come home to see her, from the woman I could not admit I'd been with, and take my infinitely fragile nephew and hold him, rocking him, rocking myself.

One night I came home to screaming—the baby, my sister, no one else there. She was standing by the crib, bent over, screaming red-faced. "Shut up! Shut up!" With each word her fist slammed the mattress fanning the baby's ear.

"Don't!" I grabbed her, pulling her back, doing it as gently as I could so I wouldn't break the stitches from her operation. She had her other arm clamped across her abdomen and couldn't fight me at all. She just kept shrieking.

"That little bastard just screams and screams. That little bastard. I'll kill him."

Then the words seeped in and she looked at me while her son kept crying and kicking his feet. By his head the mattress still showed the impact of her fist.

"Oh no," she moaned, "I wasn't going to be like that. I always promised myself." She started to cry, holding her belly and sobbing. "We an't no different. We an't no different."

Jesse wraps her arm around my stomach, presses her belly into my back. I relax against her. "You sure you can't have children?" she asks. "I sure would like to see what your kids would turn out to be like."

I stiffen, say, "I can't have children. I've never wanted children."

"Still," she says, "you're so good with children, so gentle."

I think of all the times my hands have curled into fists, when I have just barely held on. I open my mouth, close it, can't speak. What could I say now? All the times I have not spoken before, all the things I just could not tell her, the shame, the self-hatred, the fear; all of that hangs between us now—a wall I cannot tear down.

I would like to turn around and talk to her, tell her ... "I've got a dust river in my head, a river of names endlessly repeating. That dirty water rises in me, all those children screaming out their lives in my memory, and I become someone else, someone I have tried so hard not to be."

But I don't say anything, and I know, as surely as I know I will never have a child, that by not speaking I am condemning us, that I cannot go on loving you and hating you for your fairy-tale life, for not asking about what you have no reason to imagine, for that soft-chinned innocence I love.

Jesse puts her hands behind my neck, smiles and says, "You tell the funniest stories."

I put my hands behind her back, feeling the ridges of my knuckles pulsing. "Yeah," I tell her. "But I lie."

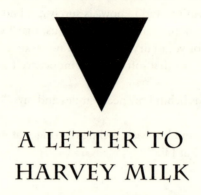

LESLÉA NEWMAN

A LETTER TO
HARVEY MILK

for Harvey Milk 1930–1978

I.

THE TEACHER SAYS we should write about our life, everything that happened today. So *nu*, what's there to tell? Why should today be different than any other day? May 5, 1986. I get up, I have myself a coffee, a little cottage cheese, half an English muffin. I get dressed. I straighten up the house a little, nobody should drop by and see I'm such a slob. I go down to the Senior Center and see what's doing. I play a little cards. I have some lunch, a bagel with cheese. I read a sign in the cafeteria, Writing Class 2:00. I think to myself, why not, something to pass the time. So at two o'clock I go in. The teacher says we should write about our life.

Listen, I want to say to this teacher, I.B. Singer I'm not. You think anybody cares what I did all day? Even my own children, may they live and be well, don't call. You think the whole world is waiting to see what Harry Weinberg had for breakfast?

The teacher is young and nice. She says everybody has something important to say. Yeah, sure, when you're young you believe things like that. She has short brown hair and big eyes, a nice figure, *zaftig* like my poor Fannie, may she rest in peace. She's wearing a Star of David around her neck, hanging from a purple string, that's nice. She gave us all notebooks and told us we're gonna write something every day, and if we want we can even write at home. Who'd a thunk it, me—Harry Weinberg, seventy-seven-years old—scribbling in a note-book like a schoolgirl. Why not, it passes the time.

So after the class I go to the store, I pick myself up a little orange juice, a few bagels, a nice piece of chicken, I shouldn't starve to death. I go up, I put on my slippers, I eat the chicken, I watch a little TV, I write in this notebook, I get ready for bed. *Nu,* for this somebody should give me a Pulitzer Prize?

II.

Today the teacher tells us something about herself. She's a Jew, this we know from the *Mogen David* she wears around her neck. She tells us she wants to col-lect stories from old Jewish people, to preserve our history. *Oy,* such stories that I could tell her, shouldn't be preserved by nobody. She tells us she's learn-ing Yiddish. For what, I wonder. I can't figure this teacher out. She's young, she's pretty, she shouldn't be with the old people so much. I wonder is she mar-ried. She doesn't wear a ring. Her grandparents won't tell her stories, she says, and she's worried that the Jews her age won't know nothing about the culture, about life in the *shtetls.* Believe me, life in the *shtetl* is nothing worth knowing about. Hunger and more hunger. Better off we're here in America, the past is past.

Then she gives us our homework, the homework we write in the class, it's a little *meshugeh,* but alright. She wants us to write a letter to somebody from our past, somebody who's no longer with us. She reads us a letter a child wrote to Abraham Lincoln, like an example. Right away I see everybody's getting nervous. So I raise my hand. "Teacher," I say, "you can tell me maybe how to address such a letter? There's a few things I've wanted to ask my wife for a long time." Everybody laughs. Then they start to write.

I sit for a few minutes, thinking about Fannie, thinking about my sister Frieda, my mother, my father, may they all rest in peace. But it's the strangest thing, the one I really want to write to is Harvey.

Dear Harvey:

You had to get yourself killed for being a *faygeleh?* You couldn't let somebody else have such a great honor? Alright, alright, so you like the boys, I wasn't wild about the idea. But I got used to it. I never said you wasn't welcome in my house, did I?

Nu, Harvey, you couldn't leave well enough alone? You had your own camera store, your own business, what's bad? You couldn't keep still about the boys, you weren't satisfied until the whole world knew? Harvey Milk, with the big ears and the big ideas, had to go make himself something, a big politician. I know, I know, I said, "Harvey, make something of yourself, don't be an old *shmegeggie* like me, Harry the butcher." So now I'm eating my words, and they stick like a chicken bone in my old throat.

It's a rotten world, Harvey, and rottener still without you in it. You know what happened to that *momzer,* Dan White? They let him out of jail, and he goes and kills himself so nobody else should have the pleasure. Now you know me, Harvey, I'm not a violent man. But this was too much, even for me. In the old country, I saw things you shouldn't know from, things you couldn't imagine one person could do to another. But here in America, a man climbs through the window, kills the Mayor of San Francisco, kills Harvey Milk, and a couple years later he's walking around on the street? This I never thought I'd see in my whole life. But from a country that kills the Rosenbergs, I should expect something different?

Harvey, you should be glad you weren't around for the trial. I read about it in the papers. The lawyer, that son of a bitch, said Dan White ate too many Twinkies the night before he killed you, so his brain wasn't working right. Twinkies, *nu,* I ask you. My kids ate Twinkies when they were little, did they grow up to be murderers, God forbid? And now, do they take the Twinkies down from the shelf, somebody else shouldn't go a little crazy, climb through a window, and shoot somebody? No, they leave them right there next to the cupcakes and the donuts, to torture me every time I go to the store to pick up a few things, I shouldn't starve to death.

Harvey, I think I'm losing my mind. You know what I do every week? Every week I go to the store, I buy a bag of jellybeans for you, you should have something to *nosh* on, I remember what a sweet tooth you have. I put them in a jar on the table, in case you should come in with another crazy petition for me to sign. Sometimes I think you're gonna just walk through my door and tell me it was another *meshugeh* publicity stunt.

Harvey, now I'm gonna tell you something. The night you died the whole city of San Francisco cried for you. Thirty thousand people marched in the street, I saw it on TV. Me, I didn't go down. I'm an old man, I don't walk so good, they said there might be riots. But no, there were no riots. Just people walking in the street, quiet, each one with a candle, until the street looked like the sky all lit up with a million stars. Old people, young people, Black people, white people, Chinese people. You name it, they were there. I remember thinking, Harvey must be so proud, and then remembered you were dead and such a lump rose in my throat, like a grapefruit it was, and then the tears ran down my face like rain. Can you imagine, Harvey, an old man like me, sitting alone in his apartment, crying and carrying on like a baby? But it's the God's truth. Never did I carry on so in all my life.

And then all of a sudden I got mad. I yelled at the people on TV: for getting shot you made him into such a hero? You couldn't march for him when he was alive, he couldn't *shep* a little *naches*?

But *nu,* what good does getting mad do, it only makes my pressure go up. So I took myself a pill, calmed myself down.

Then they made speeches for you, Harvey. The same people who called you a *shmuck* when you were alive, now you were dead, they were calling you a *mensh.*

You were a *mensh,* Harvey, a *mensh* with a heart of gold. You were too good for this rotten world. They just weren't ready for you.

> Oy Harveleh, alav ha-sholom,
> Harry

III.

Today the teacher asks me to stay for a minute after class. *Oy,* what did I do wrong now, I wonder. Maybe she didn't like my letter to Harvey? Who knows?

After the class she comes and sits down next to me. She's wearing purple pants and a white T-shirt. "*Feh,*" I can just hear Fannie say. "God forbid she should wear a skirt? Show off her figure a little? The girls today dressing like boys and the boys dressing like girls—this I don't understand."

"Mr. Weinberg," the teacher says.

"Call me Harry," I says.

"O.K., Harry," she says. "I really liked the letter you wrote to Harvey Milk. It was terrific, really. It meant a lot to me. It even made me cry."

I can't even believe my own ears. My letter to Harvey Milk made the teacher cry?"

"You see, Harry," she says, "I'm gay, too. And there aren't many Jewish people your age that are so open-minded. At least that I know. So your letter gave me lots of hope. In fact, I was wondering if you'd consider publishing it."

Publishing my letter? Again I could hardly believe my own ears. Who would want to read a letter from Harry Weinberg to Harvey Milk? No, I tell her. I'm too old for fame and glory. I like the writing class, it passes the time. But what I write is my own business. The teacher looks sad for a moment, like a cloud passes over her eyes. Then she says, "Tell me about Harvey Milk. How did you meet him? What was he like?" *Nu,* Harvey, you were a pain in the ass when you were alive, you're still a pain in the ass now that you're dead. Everybody wants to hear about Harvey.

So I tell her. I tell her how I came into the camera shop one day with a roll of film from when I went to visit the grandchildren. How we started talking, and I said, "Milk, that's not such a common name. Are you related to the Milks in Woodmere?" And so we found out we were practically neighbors forty years ago, when the children were young, before we moved out here. Gracie was almost the same age as Harvey, a couple years older, maybe, but they went to different schools. Still, Harvey leans across the counter and gives me such a hug, like I'm his own father.

I tell her more about Harvey, how he didn't believe there was a good *kosher* butcher in San Francisco, how he came to my store just to see. But all the time

I'm talking I'm thinking to myself, no, it can't be true. Such a gorgeous girl like this goes with the girls, not with the boys? Such a *shanda*. Didn't God in His wisdom make a girl a girl and a boy a boy—boom they should meet, boom they should get married, boom they should have babies, and that's the way it is? Harvey I loved like my own son, but this I never could understand. And *nu*, why was the teacher telling me this, it's my business who she sleeps with? She has some sadness in her eyes, this teacher. Believe me I've known such sadness in my life, I can recognize it a hundred miles away. Maybe she's lonely. Maybe after class one day I'll take her out for a coffee, we'll talk a little bit, I'll find out.

IV.

It's 3:00 in the morning, I can't sleep. So *nu*, here I am with this crazy note-book. Who am I kidding, maybe I think I'm Yitzhak Peretz? What would the children think, to see their old father sitting up in his bathrobe with a cup of tea, scribbling in his notebook? *Oy, meyn kinder,* they should only live and be well and call their old father once in a while.

Fannie used to keep up with them. She could be such a *nudge,* my Fannie. "What's the matter, you're too good to call your old mother once in while?" she'd yell into the phone. Then there'd be a pause. "Busy-shmusy," she'd yell even louder. "Was I too busy to change your diapers? Was I too busy to put food into your mouth?" *Oy,* I haven't got the strength, but Fannie could she yell and carry on.

You know sometimes, in the middle of the night, I'll reach across the bed for Fannie's hand. Without even thinking, like my hand got a mind of its own, it creeps across the bed, looking for Fannie's hand. After all this time, fourteen years she's been dead, but still, a man gets used to a few things. Forty-two years, the body doesn't forget. And my little *Faigl* had such hands, little *hentelehs,* tiny like a child's. But strong. Strong from kneading *challah,* from scrubbing clothes, from rubbing the children's backs to put them to sleep. My Fannie, she was so ashamed from those hands. After thirty-five years of mar-riage when finally, I could afford to buy her a diamond ring, she said no. She said it was too late already, she'd be ashamed. A girl needs nice hands to show off a diamond, her hands were already ruined, better yet buy a new stove.

Ruined? *Feh.* To me her hands were beautiful. Small, with veins running through them like rivers, and cracks in the skin like the desert. A hundred times I've kicked myself for not buying Fannie that ring.

V.

Today in the writing class the teacher read my notebook. Then she says I should make a poem about Fannie. "A poem," I says to her "now Shakespeare you want I should be?" She says I have a good eye for detail. I says to her, "Excuse me Teacher, you live with a woman for forty-two years, you start to notice a few things."

She helps me. We do it together, we write a poem called "Fannie's Hands":

> *Fannie's hands are two little birds*
> *that fly into her lap.*
> *Her veins are like rivers.*
> *Her skin is cracked like the desert.*
> *Her strong little hands*
> *baked challah, scrubbed clothes,*
> *rubbed the children's backs.*
> *Her strong little hands*
> *and my big clumsy hands*
> *fit together in the night*
> *like a jigsaw puzzle*
> *made in Heaven, by God.*

So *nu*, who says you can't teach an old dog new tricks? I read it to the class and such a fuss they made. "A regular Romeo," one of them says. "If only my husband, may he live and be well, would write such a poem for me," says another. I wish Fannie was still alive, I could read it to her. Even the teacher was happy, I could tell, but still, there was a ring of sadness around her eyes.

After the class I waited till everybody left, they shouldn't get the wrong idea, and I asked the teacher would she like to go get a coffee. "*Nu*, it's enough writing already," I said. "Come, lets have a little treat."

So we take a walk, it's a nice day. We find a diner, nothing fancy, but clean and quiet. I try to buy her a piece of cake, a sandwich maybe, but no, all she wants is coffee.

So we sit and talk a little. She wants to know about my childhood in the old country, she wants to know about the boat ride to America, she wants to know did my parents speak Yiddish to me when I was growing up. "Harry," she says to me, "when I hear old people talking Yiddish, it's like a love letter blowing in the wind. I try to run after them, and sometimes I catch a phrase that makes me cry or a word that makes me laugh. Even if I don't understand, it always touches my heart."

Oy, this teacher has some strange ideas. "Why do you want to speak Jewish?" I ask her. "Here in America, everybody speaks English. You don't need it. What's done is done, what's past is past. You shouldn't go with the old people so much. You should go out, make friends, have a good time. You got some troubles you want to talk about? Maybe I shouldn't pry," I say, "but you shouldn't look so sad, a young girl like you. When you're old you got plenty to be sad. You shouldn't think about the old days so much, let the dead rest in peace. What's done is done."

I took a swallow of my coffee, to calm down my nerves. I was getting a little too excited.

"Harry, listen to me," the teacher says. "I'm thirty years old and no one in my family will talk to me because I'm gay. It's all Harvey Milk's fault. He made such an impression on me. You know, when he died, what he said, 'If a bullet enters my brain, let that bullet destroy every closet door.' So when he died, I came out to everyone—the people at work, my parents. I felt it was my duty, so the Dan Whites of the world wouldn't be able to get away with it. I mean, if every single gay person came out—just think of it!—everyone would see they had a gay friend or a gay brother or a gay cousin or a gay teacher. Then they couldn't say things like 'Those gays should be shot.' Because they'd be saying you should shoot my neighbor or my sister or my daughter's best friend."

I never saw the teacher get so excited before. Maybe a politician she should be. She reminded me a little bit of Harvey.

"So *nu,* what's the problem?" I ask.

"The problem is my parents," she says with a sigh, and such a sigh I never heard from a young person before. "My parents haven't spoken to me since I told them I was gay. 'How could you do this to us?' they said. I wasn't doing anything to them. I tried to explain I couldn't help being gay, like I couldn't help being a Jew, but that they didn't want to hear. So I haven't spoken to them in eight years."

"Eight years, *Gottenyu,*" I say to her. This I never heard in my whole life. A father and a mother cut off their own daughter like that. Better they should cut off their own hand. I thought about Gracie, a perfect daughter she's not, but your child is your child. When she married the *Goy,* Fannie threatened to put her head in the oven, but she got over it. Not to see your own daughter for eight years, and such a smart, gorgeous girl, such a good teacher, what a *shanda.*

So what can I do, I ask. Does she want me to talk to them, a letter maybe I could write. Does she want I should adopt her, the hell with them, I make a little joke. She smiles. "Just talking to you makes me feel better," she says. So *nu,* now I'm Harry the social worker. She says that's why she wants the old people's stories so much, she doesn't know nothing from her own family history. She wants to know about her own people, maybe write a book. But it's hard to get the people to talk to her, she says, she doesn't understand.

"Listen, Teacher," I tell her. "These old people have stories you shouldn't know from. What's there to tell? Hunger and more hunger. Suffering and more suffering. I buried my sister over twenty years ago, my mother, my father—all dead. You think I don't think about them every day? Right here I keep them," I say, pointing to my heart. "I try to forget them, I should live in peace, the dead are gone. Talking about them won't bring them back. You want stories, go talk to somebody else. I ain't got no stories."

I sat down then. I didn't even know I was standing up, I got so excited. Everybody in the diner was looking at me, a crazy man shouting at a young girl.

Oy, and now the teacher was crying. "I'm sorry," I says to her. "You want another coffee?"

"No thanks, Harry," she says. "I'm sorry, too."

"Forget it. We can just pretend it never happened," I say, and then we go.

VI.

All this crazy writing has shaken me up inside a little bit. Yesterday I was walking home from the diner, I thought I saw Harvey walking in front of me. No, it can't be, I says to myself, and my heart started to pound so, I got afraid I shouldn't drop dead in the street from a heart attack. But then the man turned around and it wasn't Harvey. It didn't even look like him at all.

I got myself upstairs and took myself a pill, I could feel my pressure was going up. All this talk about the past—Fannie, Harvey, Frieda, my mother, my father—what good does it do? This teacher and her crazy ideas. Did I ever ask my mother, my father, what their childhood was like? What nonsense. Better I shouldn't know.

So today is Saturday, no writing class, but still I'm writing in this crazy notebook. I ask myself, Harry, what can I do to make you feel a little better? And I answer myself, make me a nice chicken soup.

You think an old man like me can't make chicken soup? Let me tell you, on all the holidays it was Harry that made the soup. Every *Pesach* it was Harry skimming the *shmaltz* from the top of the pot, it was Harry making the *kreplach*. I ask you, where is it written that a man shouldn't know from chicken soup?

So I take myself down to the store, I buy myself a nice chicken, some carrots, some celery, some parsley—onions I already got, parsnips I can do without. I'm afraid I shouldn't have a heart attack *shlepping* all that food up the steps, but thank God, I make it alright.

I put up the pot with water, throw everything in one-two-three, and soon the whole house smells from chicken soup.

I remember the time Harvey came to visit and there I was with my apron on, skimming the *shmaltz* from the soup. Did he kid me about that! The only way I could get him to keep still was to invite him to dinner. "Listen, Harvey," I says to him. "Whether you're a man or a woman, it doesn't matter. You gotta learn to cook. When you're old, nobody cares. Nobody will do for you. You gotta learn to do for yourself."

"I won't live past fifty, Har," he says, smearing a piece of rye bread with *shmaltz*.

"Nobody wants to grow old, believe me I know," I says to him. "But listen, it's not so terrible. What's the alternative? Nobody wants to die young, either." I take off my apron and sit down with him.

"No, I mean it Harry," he says to me with his mouth full. "I won't make it to fifty. I've always known it. I'm a politician. A gay politician. Someone's gonna take a pot shot at me. It's a risk you gotta take."

The way he said it, I tell you, a chill ran down my back like I never felt before. He was forty-seven at the time, just a year before he died.

VII.

Today after the writing class, the teacher tells us she's going away for two days. Everyone makes a big fuss, the class they like so much already. She tells us she's sorry, something came up she has to do. She says we can come have class without her, the room will be open, we can read to each other what we write in our notebooks. Someone asks her what we should write about.

"Write me a letter," she says. "Write a story called 'What I Never Told Anyone'."

So, after everyone leaves, I ask her does she want to go out, have a coffee, but she says no, she has to go home and pack.

I tell her wherever she's going she should have a good time.

"Thanks, Harry," she says. "You'll be here when I get back?"

"Sure," I tell her. "I like this crazy writing. It passes the time."

She swings a big black bookbag onto her shoulder, a regular Hercules this teacher is, and she smiles at me. "I gotta run, Harry. Have a good week." She turns and walks away and something on her bookbag catches my eye. A big shiny pin that spells out her name all fancy-shmancy in rhinestones: Barbara. And under that, right away I see sewn on her bookbag an upside down pink triangle.

I stop in my tracks, stunned. No it can't be, I says to myself. Maybe it's just a design? Maybe she doesn't know from this? My heart is beating fast now, I know I should go home, take myself a pill, my pressure, I can feel it going up.

But I just stand there. And then I get mad. What, she thinks maybe I'm blind as well as old, I can't see what's right in front of my nose? Or maybe we don't remember such things? What right does she have to walk in here with that, that thing on her bag, to remind us of what we been through? Haven't we seen enough?

Stories she wants. She wants we should cut our hearts open and give her stories so she could write a book. Well, alright, now I'll tell her a story.

This is what I never told anyone. One day, maybe seven, eight years ago—no, maybe longer, I think Harvey was still alive—one day Izzie comes knocking on my door. I open the door and there's Izzie, standing there, his face white as a sheet. I bring him inside, I make him a coffee. "Izzie, what is it," I says to him. "Something happened to the children, to the grandchildren, God forbid?"

He sits down, he doesn't drink his coffee. He looks through me like I'm not even there. Then he says, "Harry, I'm walking down the street, you know I had a little lunch at the Center, and then I come outside, I see a young man, maybe twenty-five, a good-looking guy, walking toward me. He's wearing black pants, a white shirt, and on his shirt he's got a pink triangle."

"So," I says. "A pink triangle, a purple triangle, they wear all kinds of crazy things these days."

"*Heshel,*" he tells me, "don't you understand? The gays are wearing pink triangles just like the war, just like the camps."

No, this I can't believe. Why would they do a thing like that? But if Izzie says it, it must be true. Who would make up such a thing?

"He looked a little bit like *Yussl,*" Izzie says, and then he begins to cry, and such a cry like I never heard. Like a baby he was, with the tears streaming down his cheeks and his shoulders shaking with great big sobs. Such moans and groans I never heard from a grown man in all my life. I thought maybe he was gonna have a heart attack the way he was carrying on. I didn't know what to do. I was afraid the neighbors would hear, they shouldn't call the police, such sounds he was making. Fifty-eight years old he was, but he looked like a little boy sitting there, sniffling. And who was *Yussl*? Thirty years we'd been friends, and I never heard from *Yussl.*

So finally, I put my arms around him, and I held him, I didn't know what else to do. His body was shaking so, I thought his bones would crack from knocking against each other. Soon his body got quiet, but then all of a sudden his mouth got noisy.

"Listen, *Heshel,* I got to tell you something, something I never told anybody in my whole life. I was young in the camps, nineteen, maybe twenty when they took us away." The words poured from his mouth like a flood. "*Yussl* was my best friend in the camps. Already I saw my mother, my father, my Hanna marched off to the ovens. *Yussl* was the only one I had to hold on to.

"One morning, during the selection, they pointed me to the right, *Yussl* to the left. I went a little crazy, I ran after him. 'No, he stays with me, they made a mistake,' I said, and I grabbed him by the hand and dragged him back in line. Why the guard didn't kill us right then, I couldn't tell you. Nothing made sense in that place.

"*Yussl* and I slept together on a wooden bench. That night I couldn't sleep. It happened pretty often in that place. I would close my eyes and see such things that would make me scream in the night, and for that I could get shot. I don't know what was worse, asleep or awake. All I saw was suffering.

"On this night, *Yussl* was awake, too. He didn't move a muscle, but I could tell. Finally he said my name, just a whisper, but something broke in me and I began to cry. He put his arms around me and we cried together, such a close call we had.

"And then he began to kiss me. 'You saved my life,' he whispered, and he kissed my eyes, my cheeks, my lips. And Harry, I kissed him back. Harry, I never told nobody this before. I, we … we, you know, that was such a place that hell, I couldn't help it. The warmth of his body was just too much for me and Hannah was dead already and we would soon be dead too, probably, so what did it matter?"

He looked up at me then, the tears streaming from his eyes. "It's O.K., Izzie," I said. "Maybe I would have done the same."

"There's more, Harry," he says, and I got him a tissue, he should blow his nose. What more could there be?

"This went on for a couple of months maybe, just every once in a while when we couldn't sleep. He'd whisper my name and I'd answer with his, and then we'd, you know, we'd touch each other. We were very, very quiet, but who knows, maybe some other boys in the barracks were doing the same.

"To this day I don't know how it happened, but somehow someone found out. One day *Yussl* didn't come back to the barracks at night. I went almost crazy, you can imagine, all the things that went through my mind, the things they might have done to him, those lousy Nazis. I looked everywhere, I asked everyone, three days he was gone. And then on the third day, they lined us up after supper and there they had *Yussl*. I almost collapsed on the ground when I saw him. They had him on his knees with his hands tied behind his back. His face was swollen so, you couldn't even see his eyes. His clothes were stained with blood. And on his uniform they had sewn a pink triangle, big, twice the size of our yellow stars.

"*Oy,* did they beat him but good. 'Who's your friend?' they yelled at him. 'Tell us and we'll let you live.' But no, he wouldn't tell. He knew they were lying, he knew they'd kill us both. They asked him again and again, 'Who's your friend? Tell us which one he is.' And every time he said no, they'd crack him with a whip until the blood ran from him like a river. Such a sight he was, like I've never seen. How he remained conscious I'll never know.

"Everything inside me was broken after that. I wanted to run to his side, but I didn't dare, so afraid I was. At one point he looked at me, right in the eye, as though he was saying, *Izzie, save yourself. Me, I'm finished, but you, you got a chance to live through this and tell the world our story.*

"Right after he looked at me, he collapsed, and they shot him, Harry, right there in front of us. Even after he was dead they kicked him in the head a little bit. They left his body out there for two days, as a warning to us. They whipped us all that night, and from then on we had to sleep with all the lights on and with our hands on top of the blankets. Anyone caught with their hands under the blankets would be shot.

"He died for me, Harry, they killed him for that, was it such a terrible thing? *Oy,* I haven't thought about *Yussl* for twenty-five years maybe, but when I saw that kid on the street today, it was too much." And then he started crying again, and he clung to me like a child.

So what could I do? I was afraid he shouldn't have a heart attack, maybe he was having a nervous breakdown, maybe I should get the doctor. *Vay iss mir,* I never saw anybody so upset in my whole life. And such a story, *Gottenyu.*

"Izzie, come lie down," I says and I took him by the hand to the bed. I laid him down, I took off his shoes, and still he was crying. So what could I do? I lay down with him, I held him tight. I told him he was safe, he was in America. I don't know what else I said, I don't think he heard me, still he kept crying.

I stroked his head, I held him tight. "Izzie, it's alright," I said. "Izzie, Izzie, *Izzaleh.*" I said his name over and over, like a lullaby, until his crying got quiet. He said my name once softly, *Heshel,* or maybe he said *Yussl,* I don't remember, but thank God he finally fell asleep. I tried to get up from the bed, but Izzie held onto me tight. So what could I do? Izzie was my friend for thirty years, for him I would do anything. So I held him all night long, and he slept like a baby.

And this is what I never told nobody, not even Harvey. That there in that bed, where Fannie and I slept together for forty-five years, me and Izzie spent the night. Me, I didn't sleep a wink, such a lump in my throat I had, like the night Harvey died.

Izzie passed on a couple months after that. I saw him a few more times, and he seemed different somehow. How, I couldn't say. We never talked about that night. But now that he had told someone his deepest secret, he was ready to go, he could die in peace. Maybe now that I told, I can die in peace, too?

VIII.

Dear Teacher:

You said write what you never told nobody, and write you a letter. I always did all my homework, such a student I was. So *nu,* I got to tell you something. I can't write in this notebook no more, I can't come no more to the class. I don't want you should take offense, you're a good teacher and a nice girl. But me, I'm an old man, I don't sleep so good at night, these stories are like a knife in my heart. Harvey, Fannie, Izzie, *Yussl,* my father, my mother, let them all rest in peace. The dead are gone. Better to live for today. What good does remembering do, it doesn't bring back the dead. Let them rest in peace.

But Teacher, I want you should have my notebook. It doesn't have nice stories in it, no love letters, no happy endings for a nice girl like you. A bestseller it ain't, I guarantee. Maybe you'll put it in a book someday, the world shouldn't forget.

Meanwhile, good luck to you, Teacher. May you live and be well and not get shot in the head like poor Harvey, may he rest in peace. Maybe someday we'll go out, have a coffee again, who knows? But me, I'm too old for this crazy writing. I remember too much, the pen is like a knife twisting in my heart.

One more thing, Teacher. Between parents and children, it's not so easy. Believe me, I know. Don't give up on them. One father, one mother, it's all you got. If you were my *tochter,* I'd be proud of you.

Harry

FRUITSTAND II:
HONEYDEW MOON

You know that song about the moon hitting your eye like a big pizza pie—how that's amore? Well, that's what the moon was like on our honeymoon, only it wasn't a pizza pie, it was a honeydew. A fat juicy honeydew, perfect, like I sometimes get for my fruitstand, almost white, but with the tiniest bit of yellow in it to remind you about the sun that grew it, hanging loud in that night sky, looking like it would fall right into our laps. And if it did, it'd pop right open, split clean in half: half for her, half for me. We'd roll back on the cool night grass on the edge of that sand cliff like we were the only people in the world, lay back for a while on the edge of our lives together, and we'd be sucking sugar from that honeydew moon.

Now what got me started on that? Right, you want to take your girl away for the weekend. You should, you definitely should. New York might be the greatest city in the world, and Queens the greatest borough in the city, but fresh air and the ocean are something you remember all your life, am I right, Beanpole? Okay, okay, I'll tell you the whole story of my honeymoon, but first, look, it's late already, we got to start cleaning up. Hand me the broom. You start weeding out the fruit that's too manhandled to sell full price like I showed you. Here, ouch—stooping's not as easy as it was back when we took our honeymoon, Kathy and me—here's a crate to put the bad stuff in.

Yeah, those berries are too far gone to save. Would you look at this light? I swear, if they made syrup out of gold this is what it'd look like, the way the sunrays look coming in these little windows in the late afternoon. Did you ever see anything so pretty? Gold-syrup. That's why I like to keep the windows so clean, it makes everything look prettier, more open, with all the little panes clear as air for the gold-syrup to pour through the fruit. My dad had this all closed in, all wood, but I put in plenty of windows, maybe from that taste of open air markets I got on our honeymoon. I wanted something that looked more like the country, more like where fruit deserves to be sold. Not food factories like the supermarkets.

You said you're thinking about Atlantic City? I wouldn't. I mean, I hear the beach is okay down there, but it's too crowded. No place to get away from it all. Am I right? How about the Cape? Or out on the Island? No. I hear they got a lot of good restaurants on the Cape, and you need them. Never mind you want to do *that* with your girl all weekend. You take her to some of those good restaurants and feed yourself. Skinny as a rail. I don't know how you lift these crates, except you have to if you want to keep your job. Little dykes like you are a dime a dozen, Beanpole. You get some weight on your bones or you'll keel over someday and I'll sweep you out with the old straw.

Yeah, me and Kathy went to Long Island for our honeymoon. Way out near Montauk, the Hamptons. What do you mean? Of course they let us in, there's working people out there too. Who do you think makes life so easy for the rich people? We stayed with friends—but stop asking questions, I'm not telling you another story until we get this place cleaned up. Look—look how the light's shining on those red apples, like they're going to catch on fire any minute. What a sight.

I'll tell you what, why don't you come over tonight, Beanpole. Come have supper with us and I'll tell you the story of the honeymoon—maybe Kathy will fill in what I leave out—and we'll feed you. No, don't worry, we eat so little meat we're practically vegetarians too. No, I'll make you something nice, and fattening, right out of this store, what do you think of that?

Okay, Beanpole, how does this dinner look to you? Has Kathy been chewing your ear off while I fixed supper? Oh, the picture albums, did she bore you with those already? No, we didn't have a camera on our honeymoon. They weren't as easy to come by back then. Now I have two. Wait, let me get the Polaroid, take your picture with Kathy here and the fruit salad. I'll call it Fattening the Beanpole. You don't like me calling you that? Too bad. Let the kids call you whatever cool nicknames you think up, you're the Beanpole to me. There, it's starting to develop already. The salad came out better than you! See, I made strawberries in gold-syrup—or the closest I could get with the sun already down—they're soaked in honey instead of sugar water. The rest here is chunks of watermelon, cantaloupe, some pieces of fresh coconut, pineapple rings, banana slices. And here in the middle, I cheated, this isn't from my store, some sherbet. Now that ought to fatten you up a little. Let's eat before it melts!

So she wants to hear all about our honeymoon, Kath, you want to help me tell it? That's a long story to tell all by myself, you just butt in when I leave something out. Wish we had some May wine with this. Kathy makes good May wine, learned how from Monica, one of the women we stayed with on our honeymoon. She died real soon after Johnnie did, her lover. They had a good long life, though, don't you worry, Beanpole. Am I right, Kath? They didn't die till their eighties. That made them, what sixty-something when we stayed there.

This wasn't long after my folks died and left me with the fruitstand. It was harder to find little baby butches like you back then, so I had to close the stand for a week. But I never took a vacation before. Figured I deserved it. And Kathy was determined on a honeymoon. Said she was tired of falling in love and breaking up in a month or a year. She had this idea that when she found the girl she wanted to spend her life with, if we did some of the things straight people do to tie the knot, maybe ours would have a chance of staying tied longer than most gay people. You know, since the religions won't bless us or anything, she thought up other ways to make what we were promising each other more important so we'd take it serious when things got rough.

You bet it worked. This year will be our twenty-fifth anniversary! Good, I'm glad you're impressed. Some of these little dykes today think it's not such a hot idea to stay together, to have a rock in your life you can lean on. As far as I'm concerned, except for my stand and my girl, life wouldn't be worth living. I couldn't enjoy it and I'd probably be drinking myself to death. It's rough out there. Didn't you find that out yet? Wait, you'll see what I mean.

Me, I wanted to really do it right and go to Niagara Falls. But Kath was right, as usual. Hey! What are you giving me a dirty look about, can't I pinch my girl?

Maybe Long Island wasn't the perfect honeymoon spot, but at least we weren't stuck in the middle of thousands of straight people showing off how straight they can be and staring at us because we weren't like them. Besides, we had a lot of time alone there at first.

See, Monica and Johnnie lived right on the beach. How can I explain it to you? In the old days, queers didn't have it so easy as now. For some reason the world hated us even more. Johnnie had a really bad time of it, so she had to do things different.

You ever hear about women who dressed like men, pretended they were men? No, it's not disgusting. Sometimes that was the only way you could be queer and get along. Our friend Johnnie did it when she couldn't get a job any other way. The story she told, through Monica, was that between looking so much like a man—she was almost as tall as me, but I guess you'd call her burly, and she had these real rough features. She'd be called ugly if she dressed like a girl, but in the kinds of clothes she wore she was just mean looking. Had a scar on her chin that healed all red and ugly because she didn't have the money for a doctor. She hated doctors, anyway, from listening to their comments when she had to strip to get examined. Professional? No, there's something about a woman who looks like a man that makes even doctors get nasty. On top of all that she had a beard. Really, she had to shave. Dressed as a woman she'd shave every day to hide it, but pretending she was a man, she didn't have to worry about it.

Oh, and the worst thing for her—she was mute. Could hear, but didn't talk. So she couldn't explain herself. You see why she had a hard time? Yes, she really was a woman. It was only the world said she wasn't. Monica told us the older Johnnie got, the gladder she was to be a woman. Acting like a man she saw a lot of the stuff men do that women wouldn't usually see. She hated them. Wanted to start a woman's army and someday take over the world.

But meantime, she had to earn a living. She kind of fell into gardening. She was from a city, some place upstate, so she grew up without knowing much about growing things. Still, when she was looking for any kind of work at all, getting knocked around by the men who found out she was a woman, laughed at by the women who found out she wasn't a man, Johnnie heard about a job as a gardener. It didn't pay much, but it didn't need any talking neither and the guy let her use his garage to sleep in till she made some money.

He was the only man I ever saw her smiling about. He thought she was a mute boy, and Johnnie let him as he took a liking to her. She learned everything he had to teach that summer and would have worked with him forever except it turned out he was gay. He was married, see, and toward the end of the summer Johnnie began to figure out why he went downtown one night a week. When he started coming on to her on his night out she knew she'd better take off before he found out he really did love a woman.

So she hit the road again, spent a bad winter cleaning johns, whatever she could find to do, and ended up on Long Island, washing dishes in this mansion. It was spring, and having no one she could be friends with, Johnnie used to wander around the grounds a lot taking care of them out of love. Her luck changed again when the gardener quit. The rich people who lived in the mansion had noticed her work and gave her the job. To make sure she would stay, they let her have an unused cottage on the beach. She wouldn't make a salary off-season, but she wouldn't have rent either. All around the cottage she grew her own garden, and she learned from the cook at the house how to preserve the fruits and vegetables the rich people didn't want. This was the second happy season of her life. She had a job, a home, and so far nobody bothered the strange mute gardener who lived all by himself in the cottage on the beach.

Hey, Beanpole, eat up, your sherbet's melting. No, you didn't have enough. What's the matter? The story's upsetting you? Hey, this is the way it was, count your blessings.

Anyways, to make a long story short, here's Johnnie living on the beach in back of this mansion, happy as a peach pit about to grow a tree, when she starts to get real lonely. She remembers the few friends she's had in her life, and being young and healthy, remembers in particular this girl back home who used to walk with her in the woods. And kiss her.

Then, on a trip to town, she notices the new girl at the hardware store. They always had a man before, but all the sons were off fighting the war, so the daughter got the job. It was a welcome change for Johnnie since the sons never had the patience to listen to what she needed. Instead of dreading going into town once a month, she began to go weekly. There was something about this girl.

Next thing Johnnie knows, she's sitting outside her cottage one night after dinner, watching the birds fish, when the girl comes walking up the beach. She's in pants, like Johnnie, and that was unusual then. Johnnie pulls her other chair out of the cabin and they sit together awhile, the girl chattering enough for the two of them and making Johnnie laugh. The next night the girl comes back and Johnnie pulls the chair out again. By the third week Johnnie's bought another chair at the junkshop in town, and she's suffering. She's wondering if this girl is like the one back home. By the flush on her cheeks when she looks Johnnie's way she might be. But of course Johnnie knows she hasn't got a chance with a girl who thinks she's a man. Except there's the pants, which the girl wears every night, like she might be trying to tell Johnnie something.

One day the girl shows up early, when Johnnie's still washing her dishes inside. Wandering around the cabin she picks up an old picture of Johnnie as a young girl, holding her mother's hand. Johnnie figures it's now or never and points first to the little girl in the picture, then to herself. The girl from town smiles, put the picture down carefully and walks over to Johnnie. Without saying a word she reaches up to put her arms around Johnnie's neck and presses herself to her. "I know," the girl says, kissing Johnnie. The girl's name was Monica.

Will you look at this table? Picked clean. Looks like Beanpole could do with a good feeding once in a while, am I right, Kathy? Let's clear it off and put up coffee. You want tea? Herb tea? No, we don't have any of that stuff. What's the matter with you, Beanpole, you got to be different? Yeah, I heard caffeine's bad for you, but I got to have my fix. Wait, I know what we'll do. How about tea made from fresh mint leaves? Think that'll work? I'll try it too. Sit, sit. This kitchen's not big enough for the three of us to work in. And yes, I'm getting to the story of the honeymoon. You had to know the whole story.

No, Monica's folks weren't upset. Johnnie and her ran off to New York City and came back saying they'd gotten married. Nobody even asked to see the certificate. I guess Monica's folks might have been disappointed she didn't marry a man with money and looks, instead of a mute gardener, but Monica was so happy. She said she suspected her mother envied her, living such a simple life right on the water, instead of having five sons and an ambitious husband to take care of.

They never did find out Johnnie was a girl, or bother the young couple much. Monica kept working at the hardware store till the war was over. Then, because she still needed money when the brothers who were left came home and took her job, she began housekeeping for the rich couple. They were pretty nice, for rich people, and years later, when Johnnie and Monica were getting too old to work like they had, they gave them a small pension and told them the cottage was theirs for life. What more could they ask?

Give me the dishtowel, Kath, I'll dry. Your coffee's almost ready. I don't know, Beanpole, this tea's pretty weak stuff, no wonder it's so good for you.

How we got to honeymoon out there, Kathy met Johnnie and Monica through some friends of hers. It seems Monica was not exactly innocent when she put her arms around Johnnie that night. She'd known a couple of women like her from the school where she went. Those women knew a couple more and on like that till there was a little circle of them, and that's how Kathy met them. Johnnie and Monica never had parties or anything because of being afraid Johnnie would be found out, but once in a while some of their friends would visit them, quietly. They loved Kath, of course, how could they resist her? And she had a standing invitation to bring a friend and stay in the unused cabin down the beach.

Umm. Mint-water. I think I'll start a company. Sell mint-water and gold-syrup. Mix them and bottle Henny's Golden Mint-Syrup. Healthy, refreshing, dull as an unripe watermelon. You don't think it'll catch on?

By this time, when she met me, Kathy was visiting the old folks a couple times a year, and she hadn't seen them for months, so that's where we decided to honeymoon. Besides, I guess you kind of thought of them as your own people by then, am I right, Kath? Wanted them to approve of me or something. Goodness knows I was nervous enough to need their approval to marry you. I closed up the stand that Saturday night and we drove out there, pulling in real late. We didn't want to wake them, so we slept in the old panel truck I hauled the fruit in. I kept a couple of old blankets in the back and Kathy brought pillows, so we were all set.

Yes, that's where we spent our first honeymoon night, locked in the dark old truck, lying on the ridged metal floor, covered by smells like cantaloupe rind, strawberry juice, lemons and limes and bananas, all gone a little musty, like in a dream. I called it my cornucopia. Kathy was my new treat and I had a feast. Oh, stop blushing, Kath, I didn't mean *that*. Besides, Beanpole knows the facts of life.

In the morning I met two of the finest human beings on earth. I though Kathy was a magician to have found those two. Monica was this little grandmother type in a faded bib apron with flour up to her elbows and hairpins sticking out of her grey hair. Johnnie was still pretty burly, but bent from gardening so many years. She had a kind of rough way about her like some people get when they have had a hard time being understood, but once you caught on to how she talked, with her hands, with Monica's help, with scraps of paper and a shaky, old-fashioned handwriting, she was just as shy and gentle as could be. Birds would pick crumbs off her big palm, am I right, Kath?

The grounds around their cottage, even with the sandy soil and the salt water, were like a picture book. She had flowering vines trailing all up and around their porch, rose trellises, fruit trees. You could see why the rich people were letting her live out her life in that cottage: she'd planted so much of herself in it.

And the way they were together! Their eyes still shone when they looked at each other. They were so patient and appreciative you would have thought they were the ones on a honeymoon. I mean, who ever thought of two old ladies like that loving each other? All of a sudden I could see me and Kathy twenty, fifty years down the road. Being gay had always meant being young, fooling around, going out. Now I was looking at the happiest people I ever met and they didn't fit any of that. We had a future!

That week, what a week it was. The pretty little cottage we stayed in was all open to the wind and sun. It was painted white outside, but inside was rough wood that smelled just cut under the sunlight. One whole side of the beach ran into the monastery next door, so we had that whole stretch all to ourselves and we would get up in the morning and run along the water's edge as far as our breath lasted, holding hands and hugging. There were little sand-cliffs above the beach with short trees and tall grasses on top of them and we'd lie there making love carefully, always alert, because we would've killed ourselves if we gave Johnnie away like that.

They didn't have a car, so we made a big shopping trip into town to save them the bus ride. Johnnie put on a tie and Monica her best hat and dress. It was a small shady town, after all that white beach, and we carried their packages as they visited every store. Here and there along the road were produce stands. I had to stop at all of them. That's where I got some of the ideas for my place: the straw on the floor, all the light coming in, the bushel baskets I use. Little tricks like that make people feel they're in the country, think my fruit is fresher. Even the supermarkets are catching on now, prettying things up.

In the town I saw for myself what Johnnie had gained by playing a man. I guess I was like you, because even though I like her a lot, it really bothered me: the shaving, the haircut, men's clothes even down to the boxer shorts Monica hung on the line. It seemed perverted. And I suspected Johnnie liked playing a man, Monica didn't really want a woman. But when I saw everybody Johnnie

met on the street stop and say hello to her, smiling and passing the time of day
…

I mean, twenty-five years ago Kathy and me were still being careful not to be
seen together on the street too much, afraid people would put two and two together and stop shopping at the fruitstand. And here was little old Monica
leaning on her lover's arm like she'd been doing for years, wearing a matching
wedding band, and doing this in a small, stuffy rich town.

So don't put Johnnie down, Beanpole. If she had looked like you they might
have killed her, wouldn't have given her work for sure. Her life, even if somehow she stayed, wouldn't have been as full as it was. What choice did she have,
anyway, being queer and looking the way she did? You compromised then.
Even now, maybe you're not afraid, Beanpole, with your marches and your
bookstores, but I am sometimes. There may even be some Johnnies left.

But that day, the four of us were happy as bananas grinning an a tree: us two
on our honeymoon, even if we couldn't act like it in town, those two enjoying
the fruit of their long years of hard work and caution.

We got back to the cottage exhausted, and sat around talking. You'd think
me and Kathy would have wanted to get off by ourselves for a while, but we
knew we had a whole lifetime to do that and every minute with those old people was too precious to waste. They gave our honeymoon something nobody
who goes to Niagara Falls will ever get. We even talked about setting up a farmers' market and lunch counter out there—Kathy was waitressing back then too.
Now and then Johnnie's eyes would brighten and she'd put in her two cents,
her hands going a mile a minute in her own kind of sign language, and Monica
trying to keep up with her.

After a while when the ideas were flying fast and it really seemed like me and
Kathy might move out of the city, this big silver car pulled up in the driveway.
Monica threw her hands up. "It never rains, but it pours," she said like she
knew it was trouble. She hadn't mentioned any problems to us, but we felt
their fear. While Johnnie sat tight and tense the lawyer talked at Monica. I had
trouble following, he talked so smooth and polite and slimy. He said he represented the monastery.

What Monica hadn't wanted to worry us with, was that the rich people from
the estate died, and their kids sold everything to the monastery next door. Now
Monica and Johnnie, they said they signed the papers when the rich people
gave them the cottage, papers saying the house was theirs to live in all their
lives, rent free. But they never got copies of the papers, the church people
claimed there never *were* any such papers, and the lawyer was there to tell them
they had to leave.

Me and Kathy sat there speechless while the lawyer said he'd be back with
the final papers ordering them out. The brothers had offered to put them in a
senior citizen project, but Johnnie's pension didn't include rent because she'd

gotten the cottage. They wouldn't be able to pay rent and they wouldn't be able to grow their own food to stretch the money they had if they moved. Until this afternoon, they hadn't been too worried. One of the things pretending to be straight had done for them was to make their church respect them like the townspeople did. They figured ministers were just too ignorant to look past what the world thought and see their love was a good thing. They'd been praying up a storm, sure they'd be saved in the end. It was beginning to look to them like their religion wasn't all they thought.

Didn't they have a lawyer, we asked? No, they said, they didn't want to make a scene with the church. Besides, lawyer talk was over their heads, they weren't the kind to hire lawyers. How would they pay him? And what if, somehow, in all this, Johnnie got found out?

Kathy and me spent the rest of the day trying to figure something out with them. "That's okay, girls," Monica told us, "all we ever had was each other. And the good will of the people on the hill." Nothing we came up with worked, or suited them. The threat of the monastery was over us all night, like evil. After the lies and the pretending, the hard work and the fear, it could wipe out all Johnnie and Monica had. They might just as well have been themselves from the start as go through all they had to prove they deserved a decent life.

By the next day, when the damn lawyer came again, I was mad as hell.

"What's the matter with the Brothers?" I shouted at him as he tried to get out of his slimy silver car. Somebody had to speak up for these women. "Are they afraid of the real world? Let *them* come down here and throw the old people out." Monica and Johnnie watched me, Monica frightened, Johnnie's sensitive eyes worried.

"Why can't your so-called Christians let these old people stay? What do they need the damn cottages for?" I asked. He claimed they'd love to let them stay, but their insurance made it impossible.

"What you mean," Kathy says, "is you don't want to spend the money insuring two old people who have always lived on the water and now might all of a sudden fall in?" Even Monica laughed.

Silverslime didn't like our tone at all. He finished getting out of the car and pulled himself up. He was prepared to make them one final offer, he said.

"We're listening," I answered.

He wanted to move them up to the caretaker cottage on the monastery grounds. If they were employees, and not as close to the water, the problem would be solved. The old people looked interested, but not at all happy. Seeing that, I couldn't help myself, I risked everything because I knew they were right and even if their church wasn't on their side in the crunch, somebody had to be. Besides, except for the sin of being queer, they lived a godlier life than anyone I knew. Their world was full of peace and love and kindness and even, with the little they had, charity. The god of flowers and fruit and sea and sun had claimed this little piece of land for them and big old Henny was suddenly their appointed priestess. I couldn't help it.

"No, they're not going to settle for changing their whole lives this late, mister. Johnnie paid for this place with all the years of his labor. It's not much reward. You know how little pension he gets. But he and Monica feel they own something here. You can keep them from selling it, from passing it on, but it just isn't right to pull it out from under them. I own my own business back in the city and I know a bit more about your games, unfortunately, than they do. They've got me in their corner now. So get yourself and your papers back in that car and get out of here. Their lawyer will contact you."

Old Silverslime huffed up, looked like he was either going to give me a speech or have a heart attack, and I didn't much care which, but at the last minute he slid back into the slimemobile and roared off.

Maybe I was being hasty, and getting involved where I didn't belong. Maybe I was bluffing a little to prove to these people that I'd be a good mate for their adopted daughter. Maybe it was just my sense of fair play that was offended.

And what did I have to offer them if we lost? My parents' old apartment where Kathy and I already lived? Damn it, I wanted that home for them. For all those years they'd had to swallow their pride and their own natural ways, for all the things they did without to get what they had, for all the queers who had to live half-lives to get any peace at all, I wanted that home.

So our honeymoon took a different turn. We didn't run along the beach that day, or make love that night. We waited and thought, and I'm sure the old people prayed. I wanted to call my lawyer, but Monica said she'd call the one in town, the old one the rich people had used. I said I'd pay him and she accepted gratefully, despite Johnnie's gruff shake no. But she kept putting off calling, like she was still waiting for that church to fix things up.

When two of the Brothers from the monastery came to the front door that night, just as Johnnie was building a fire in the fireplace, I wondered if the old peoples' faith was paying off. How could they order such frail old people out of their home, now that they saw them in person? But an hour later they were gone, whining at not getting their way.

"Faggots," Kathy decided, and we all laughed out loud except Johnnie, whose eyes laughed for her.

In the morning we found a formal letter in the mailbox. In two days the sheriff would begin eviction.

Kathy persuaded Monica to call the lawyer immediately. I paced around outside watching to see if any busybody sheriff dared stick his nose into our business. Kathy called me in. Another setback. The old lawyer had died. His daughter had taken over his practice. Great, a woman, she'd care. But Monica and Johnnie were old-fashioned. They were dead-set against using a "lady lawyer."

Things were at a standstill again. Hell, I decided, I'd gotten them that far against their obstinate wills. I picked up the phone and dialed the lady lawyer's number. Once she heard who was involved she got very interested. The rich people's daughter had been her best childhood friend, and she remembered how happy she'd been that the old couple got their home. She would check her father's files.

We sat down to a cold supper of homegrown vegetables and cold sliced meat, each with the thought this might be the last dinner on the beach, these the last homegrown vegetables ever. Would it kill Monica and Johnnie to move up to the monastery, I wondered, take on some light tasks? It would be better than wandering around Queens, living a new life among strangers.

After the old ones went to bed we sat staring, Kathy and me, long into the night on the front porch of their cottage. Near midnight we were startled— there was a sound in the cabin. It was like a child's cry, or the whimpering of a hurt animal. Kathy put her hand on my arm.

"Johnnie, are you crying?" we heard then. The bedroom was right behind the porch and its window suddenly threw light out the side of the house. Their small sounds carried to us over the sounds of the water.

"I don't want to leave this place," said a sad, raspy, high voice. I felt the blood fall out of my face. It was Johnnie talking.

"Something will happen," Monica comforted her. "And if we do have to move to the city with the kids, why then you can be yourself for these last years. No one will know us. No one cares anymore about the way we are."

"Maybe we *have* been wrong to live like this, though. Maybe we *are* being punished. If only I could use my voice." She cried again. We could barely make out her next words. "I'm so ashamed, Henny having to do this for me. If anyone has to fight for our home it should be me."

"Johnnie." Monica sounded as if she was whispering a prayer. "Don't you forget, whatever happens, we still have each other."

We could hear Johnnie sigh as she turned over on the bed. There was a smile in the little voice. "That's most important, I know," she answered her lover.

Kathy and I stared at each other in the dark. The voices went on for a while, Johnnie's breathy, unused. It gave me the chills because it was so female in a body I didn't think of that way, and because we never guessed she did have a voice. We waited about an hour after the voices had faded away and then very carefully snuck off the porch and over to the cottage. We were still too stunned to talk, but held each other while we cried over Johnnie's girlish sobs, her few rusty words. By the time we went to sleep, I'd realized completely how terrible it had been for Johnnie, how she'd given up her voice so it wouldn't hurt so much to live in her body. I was bowled over thinking how awfully, awfully strong she'd had to be all those years, how she'd stayed as true to herself as she could, and kept loving women, living the whole time like a tomato plant without a stake, holding herself up by sheer will. And now, if she lost everything she'd earned by giving up her voice ...

By eight o'clock that morning I was at the lady lawyer's office. When she showed up I insisted on helping in some way. The sheriff might come at any-time, I told her.

She was a pretty lady, very straight, and looked at me like I was a beetle about to attack her rose garden. "No need," she said, waving a folder at me. I followed her upstairs as she explained. "I found this in Dad's personal files at home with a few closed cases that never made it to the office files." Once in the office she handed me a sheet of paper. It was a notarized statement giving Johnnie and Monica the cottage. I was so happy *I* almost prayed in thanks.

Then the lawyer pulled out two more copies of the same sheet. "He was sick at the end," she said, "and never made it back to the office. If he had, these would have been mailed out."

She thanked me for calling her, both for the old couple and her father's rep-utation. Then she offered to deliver a copy to the monastery lawyer. She thought the Brothers might still fight it, since the cottage wasn't mentioned in the sale of the property to them, but felt something could be worked out.

Before she knew what hit her, I grabbed her and gave her an enormous hug. I'd swear she was almost smiling despite herself when I ran off to show Monica and Johnnie that beautiful piece of paper. They cried with joy, Monica loudly, Johnnie silently, though Kathy and I listened hard for a familiar whimper. Kathy treated me like the conquering hero when, later that day, the lady lawyer called to say our problems were over.

Out of respect for their father's wishes, out of a sense of responsibility be-cause her father's office had been at fault, the children of the rich people and the lady lawyer would make a donation to the monastery. But it could only be used to pay the insurance on the beach cottage.

Hey, Kathy, will you look at the grin on Beanpole's face. What's the matter, you were worried? With friends like me and Kathy, you needed to worry?

Our honeymoon? Oh sure, we got back in the mood, what with all the cele-brating we did that night. But we were so exhausted from being scared and from fighting we collapsed the last two days.

I kept hoping Johnnie would thank us by breaking her silence, but she never did in words. It was okay, she didn't need to. They gave us so much. Just being themselves, staying together, going through what they did. It was like having parents to look up to. We wanted to live like them, to be decent as they were in spite of what they went through. And we wanted to stay together forever, like they had, because we could see how happy they were.

Yeah, Beanpole, like me and Kath are now. Like maybe you're going to be someday.

Don't get me all misty about it, though. I see you two looking for the tissues. Here, it's late anyway. Take these pastries and get home to your girlfriend. But don't stay up so late looking for honeymoon dew you can't keep your eyes open at work tomorrow!

What's honeymoon dew? Look at Kathy winking at me over there. It's just something we discovered on our honeymoon. You'll figure it out.

RICHARD HALL

COUNTRY PEOPLE

I HAD MISGIVINGS the minute I walked in. The classroom was too small, the desks were for kids, and the blackboard was on rollers. When the first students turned up, my worries increased. I knew that adult education courses tend to attract the odd and the lonely, but this bunch looked more displaced than most. Taking the enrollment slip from a large, sad woman in her midforties, I wondered if my job was just to keep them occupied till they found what they were missing.

The woman's name was Emilia Quinn. She was wrapped in yards of yellow fabric like a sari. Her dark hair was in a tangle, but her eyes were beautiful. She gave me a wounded smile and took a seat by the window.

It had started with Ray Stonington last month, August. Ray had been in one of his mild, helpful moods, which should have warned me. We were sitting in his dining room, the candles illuminating the pine table, the Dutch corner cabinet, the spinning wheel in the corner. The dinner had been superb, as elegant as this eighteenth-century tavern in the Hudson Valley which Ray had converted to a residence.

He had spoken too casually: "They're looking for someone to teach a night course in literature for adults." Ray named the college, one of those two-year affairs that Governor Rockefeller had sown around the state—an institution without the distinction of Vassar or the sectarian rigor of Marist or the blue-jeans cheerfulness of Bard. "Why don't you ring up the dean? He's a friend of mine."

I shook my head. I was through with all that. Twenty years in the New York City public-school system was enough. "Why do you think I moved up here?"

"This won't be anything like New York, Michael. One night a week, no knives, no drugs, sweet country people." I looked skeptical, and he continued. "It'll help with the shop."

Ray was manipulating me, but I fell for it. Since retiring from teaching, I had been living out a lifelong fantasy—running an antique store. The hardest part of selling antiques is finding the damned things. Suddenly I could imagine the students inviting me over to look at Grandpa's sea chest, at Great-aunt Laetitia's sewing dummy. I gave a reckless laugh.

"The only course I'd consider teaching would be a gay-lit course. That's what I couldn't do in the city."

Ray had given me another mild look and changed the subject.

A young man with fluffy sideburns under a blue Civil War cap handed me the class chit. The rest of his outfit was also vaguely military, though I spotted the edge of a beaded vest. He looked at me with wide brown eyes, unsmiling. *This* country person didn't look so sweet, though he gave off a sexy glow. His name was Cornelius Graef.

Yes, I'd proposed the course as a lark, an after-dinner joke, but a few days later Ray had called back. "I talked to John Sterling at school. Would you write up a proposal for a gay-lit course? He'd like to get it approved—on a non-credit basis."

I hung up the phone quite stunned. I'd meant it when I said I wanted to get away from all that—not only from teaching but from the old preoccupations. Too much despair, too many deaths. Besides, a new literature was being born, post-AIDS, coming from the generation after me. Did I really have anything to say about it?

Daniel Boone was standing in front of me. Where did these people get their clothes? Maybe I should expand the antique-clothing department in my shop. ("Care to see something in a designer deerslayer, sir?")

Daniel Boone's name was Nicolas Hillebrant. He was seriously handsome, powerfully built. "Question, sir." Greenish eyes played over me, calmly judging.

"Have a seat, Nicolas, we'll have questions later."

He didn't stir. He was beyond taking orders from teachers. "I have no money for books. I hope they won't be required."

"We'll discuss that in a few minutes, if you don't mind."

Nicolas turned at last, looking disgusted, and sat down next to Cornelius. They were friends apparently. I felt an old vulnerability stab at me—if I wasn't careful I'd give them too much attention, work for their approval, even flirt with them. My palms started to sweat. There were unexpected pitfalls in teaching a gay class.

The rest of the students straggled in. There were two more women—Millie Herkimer and Teage Dane—looking butch and paired, in short hair, work shirts, slacks. There was Israel Solomon, an elderly man with a pouter-pigeon figure and clouds of cottony hair. He took the front seat eagerly—a red-hot, as we used to say in grade school. The remaining two—William Astbury and Bradford Gower—were pale youths, no more than twenty, both afflicted with shyness. They slunk, more or less, to the back seats.

I waited for more latecomers. Eight pairs of eyes studied me. Not friendly, not unfriendly, just waiting. Maybe the sweetness would come later, I thought.

I began the introduction as planned. Michael Littman, formerly of New York, now of Livingston. Please call me Michael. I had never given a course like this. I owned the Den of Antiquity on Route 22. We would explore together. I would need their help. We would be reading and discussing selections from several thousand years of gay and lesbian literature.

I paused for questions. Nicolas Hillebrant spoke up. "I have no money to buy books, Michael. Neither does he." He jerked his head at Cornelius. A few others murmured in agreement.

"I'll either circulate my own books, borrow extra copies, or make Xeroxes. You won't have to buy anything."

A little relaxation—legs spread forward, sighs released, glances exchanged. It had been a problem for everyone. "Let's talk about the material," I began. "Also what periods interest you—classical, medieval, nineteenth-century, modern." I paused. "I'd like to make the course as democratic as possible."

Cornelius Graef spoke up. "Did any of them write about war, comrades-in-war, that stuff?"

I mentioned Whitman and the Civil War diaries, *Billy Budd,* then worked back to *Amis and Amile* and the Theban Band. Cornelius's face lit up. "You're gonna give us all them?" He smiled at Nicolas. *They're lovers,* I thought.

Millie Herkimer, the older of the two butch women, asked if there were stories about women living in the countryside. At first I could think only of May Sarton, then recalled *Patience and Sarah.* I sketched the tale, and her eyes glittered.

Gradually everyone spoke up. Their interests varied. The Bible, Oscar Wilde, Sappho, South Sea natives. The women liked poetry; the men wanted true stories. Only Israel Solomon was interested in political essays.

At last, when we had more or less settled on the shape of the course, which would meet once a week for twelve weeks, I asked them why they had signed up. Their reasons tended to be vague. Indeed, many of their comments were bewildering.

"People around here won't talk." Emilia Quinn shifted her bulk in the ridiculous child's seat. "Pretend they didn't hear you and clam up if they do."

William Astbury in the back spoke up. "We hear things've changed, but you 'd never know it in the valley. They keep us in the dark."

I wondered who was keeping whom in the dark, but I said nothing. Millie Herkimer took her girlfriend's hand. "We want to borrow some of that pride."

We broke up early. Israel Solomon walked me out to my car, informing me that he hadn't sat in a classroom for forty years, had run the apothecary shop in Livingston all his life, and was now retired. The shop, he said, had been founded by his grandfather. Israel had modernized the place but finally sold out to August Hardwick, the present owner.

He hesitated, shuffled, leaned into the car after I got in. He wanted to tell me something else but couldn't quite manage. Well, there'd be plenty of time. I'd probably hear everyone's story before we were done.

As I drove off I saw them all standing in a knot by the road in front of the building. When I waved, eight hands shot up. A surge of hope and, yes, sweetness barreled across the space. A ball formed in my throat. There were pitfalls, but there were pleasures, too.

During the following week, I looked up every time my shop bell jangled, hoping it would be a student, but no one showed. In fact, the bell rarely rang. My one sale consisted of a pine blanket chest, the milk-based paint still intact, which brought $135 from a New York dealer.

Only one event reminded me of my class—near Putnamville I saw a sign pointing to the Herkimer School. Ray Stonington informed me it was a home for problem kids—part reform school, part psychiatric hostel. No doubt a member of Millie's family was involved in some way.

The following Tuesday six Bibles were produced on my instructions—most of them small, old, and giving off musty smells. We started on Genesis 19, which most of them knew. After we got through with the fire and brimstone, I started on some of the new theories. The sin of Sodom might be inhospitality to strangers. "That we may know them" could be interpreted in many ways. The dogma of several thousand years was being questioned nowadays.

They hardly stirred as I spoke, their eyes wide. When I finished, Israel raised his hand. "They taught us that if a man lieth with another man as with a woman, that's an abomination."

Cornelius sputtered. "That's just a slander."

"There are no Sodomites," Nicolas chimed in. "There never were."

"We need new words then," Teage Dane said.

"Let's call ourselves squinchies and frimsters." It was Bradford Gower in the back row. Everyone hooted.

By the time the discussion ended, we were one awareness, one crew aboard the good ship *Revision*. The notion of unlocking minds had lured me into teaching twenty years before, but I had never released excitement like this.

After class, everybody bustled into the hall with me, still throwing out ideas. Emilia Quinn took my arm—her eyes fiery, her hair damp across her forehead.

"You should have come up here a long time ago, Michael. Everything would have been different."

"A lot of things had to happen first."

"Well, thank God they did." She squeezed my arm.

I left them, as before, in a knot in front of the building. I wondered if they would walk home. More likely a van would pick them up. Livingston was loaded with vans.

As I drove home I speculated about their living arrangements. The class chits hadn't listed home addresses and we hadn't given any personal histories yet. A new thought struck me. Could there be a commune tucked in the hills around here, something left over from the sixties? That would explain the costumes, the occasional swap of odd decorations. It would also explain their ignorance. I pictured them reading *Godey's Ladies Book* and Mark Twain by kerosene lamp—an oddly gratifying image.

My thoughts moved on to the Herkimer School. Millie said her father's sister, her aunt Millicent, had started it as a seminary for young ladies. Millie didn't seem surprised when I told her about its conversion to a home for juveniles—her family had sold it years ago. She only smiled when I informed her I was going to take some of the school's antique fixtures on consignment. She said they should fetch a good price.

Now, turning into my own driveway, I was filled with contentment. I recalled my old habits, lying awake in the New York night, converting the screech of fire engines and ambulances into something more harmonious—the rattle of coaches, the echoes of post horns. Those fantasies always produced sleep. Now they were all around me—in my shop, the countryside, the classroom.

I unlocked the front door. I had just four rooms on one floor, not fully furnished yet, but I was more settled than I had ever been on Thirteenth Street. For a moment, coming in, I had the crazy notion that some of the original air from 1819 had been trapped under the floorboards and I was actually inside the last century. Then I laughed, fixed myself a drink, and flicked on the TV.

Nobody had bothered to read the *Symposium* clear through, despite the trouble I had gone to in Xeroxing it. In fact, nobody even brought a copy to class. When I asked why, they got fascinated with the dust on the floor and molding on the walls. At last Emilia Quinn spoke up. "We like to hear you preach, Michael."

"She means lecture." Nicolas laughed. "You do really fine at that."

I started on responsibility, the contract between student and teacher, then decided to can it. If they didn't want to read I'd preach. They must have seen the surrender in my face, because they settled back, grinning.

By the time I got into my favorite passage, everyone was paying close attention. "For they love not boys, but intelligent beings," I read from the Jowett translation, "whose reason is beginning to be developed, much about the time at which their beards begin to grow. And in choosing young men to be their companions, they mean to be faithful to them and pass their whole life in company with them, not to take them in their inexperience and deceive them. … And observe that open loves are held to be more honorable than secret ones, and how great is the encouragement which all the world gives to the lover."

A pause. The words, so simple and so radical, did their work. I could feel a chunk of the twentieth century breaking off and dissolving.

"That's very interesting, yessir." Israel Solomon was mashed down, quivering, in his seat. He half turned around. "Some of you remember David. David Whitmore." He looked up at me again, breathing hard. "He was just that, my companion for life. But he didn't realize it." A strange sound came from his chest. "I'm not sure I did either."

I put down the Plato. Here it was.

Israel and David had been classmates in Albany, both studying pharmacology. Then they had worked together in the drugstore founded by the first Mr. Solomon. But in a long lifetime Israel hadn't told his friend how he felt. "There was once," he said, "when David was sick—meningitis, very common in those days—when I almost did tell him. I thought it was my last chance. But his wife came in, and I lost my nerve." Israel studied his hands for a moment. "If I'd known about Plato, I could have quoted him. It would have made everything, well, respectable."

He closed down. Heavy, unsaid things washed around the room. I let the silence lengthen. Wasn't this why we'd come together—to know our history, to make sure it didn't happen again?

At last Emilia spoke softly. "It's never too late to mend things, Israel."

He didn't reply. There was a scuffling of feet. Time to move on, I thought. Nothing can be changed, only corrected in the mind.

Israel came up after class and finished the story. David Whitmore hadn't died of meningitis but of a fall two years later while climbing Overlook Mountain. "So I had a second chance," he concluded, "but I didn't have the nerve then either. I sold the pharmacy. I didn't want to work if David wasn't there."

I patted him lightly, resisting the urge to hug him. There's nothing wrong with hugging, but it can't undo a lifetime of secrecy. "Try reading the Xerox," I said as I got into my car. "It'll help." He looked pleased and dubious at the same time. How could Plato help, really?

The drive to the Herkimer School took me through the center of my town. Downtown Livingston is only a few blocks long, but it offers all your basic services. I was interested in some extra-strength Tylenol. Last night had not been one of my better nights—due more to financial worries than to Israel's history, however. The drugstore—now the Hardwick Rexall—had been established in 1912, according to the script on the window. I stepped back to check out the brick building. I wasn't surprised to see a familiar name stamped on the iron plate just under the eave. *Solomon.* And below it, 1868.

A middle-aged man in a pharmacist's jacket sold me the pills. "Mr. Hardwick?" I asked.

"That's me, John Hardwick."

I introduced myself. He had heard about the Den of Antiquity. He was glad to make my acquaintance. I started to tell him that I knew Israel Solomon, grandson of the Solomon upstairs, then checked myself. Hardwick might ask how we met. It wasn't my job to yank Israel out of his hometown closet. I thanked him for the Tylenol and left, with a final glance at the plaque up top.

The Herkimer School was a rambling building in the Dutch style. Now it showed signs of abuse—torn screens, tar-paper patches, dying shrubs. It was as mismanaged as the lives of the boys within, I thought. The manager, an Irishman named Scully, with a varicosed face and a slight limp, turned me over to the caretaker. As we descended to the basement of the main building it occurred to me that my antique hunting always took me to places where people no longer lived.

The gem of the collection was a pewter chandelier, eight-branched, in good condition. I put the date at 1780–1790. There were also some light fixtures—tulips of amber glass, three to a stem, with rotted wiring, and an imitation Tiffany table lamp. Not a bad haul, I thought as we lugged the stuff upstairs.

I was waiting for the manager to reappear to sign the consignment papers, when I noticed the founder's plaque to one side of the front door. *The Herkimer Institute for Young Ladies,* read the florid script—an incongruous touch, considering the male adolescent snarls coming from upstairs. The first name on the plaque was faint, oxidized, but I managed to make it out— *Millicent Herkimer, Headmistress.* I pictured her as a tall maiden with a spine like a ruler and an immutable sense of right and wrong. Nothing like her confused niece. My eye ran down the names of the original faculty—each introduced with a cursive *Miss*—but I was interrupted by Mr. Scully. We chatted about the fixtures, my job being to keep his expectations low. Most people who consign antiques think they'll make a killing.

Again that night I had trouble getting to sleep, but not because of financial worry. I had convinced myself by bedtime that it was unrealistic to expect a shop to turn a profit the first year. Something else was tugging at a corner of my mind. Finally it let go of me, and I drifted off.

The class began to go more smoothly, even though their reading was patchy. I had the impression that one of the women—Emilia or Millie—read the text and did summaries for the others. We progressed from the Greek poets to the medieval ones, from Michelangelo to Shakespeare to Byron and Edward Carpenter. We managed Emily Dickinson, Radclyffe Hall, Djuna Barnes, and Gertrude Stein.

It was hard to catch them at their goofing off. At least one member of the class was always up on the homework. Sometimes I caught references to materials not under discussion, which made me wonder if their reading was wider than they let on.

But one night, when it was apparent that only Teage Dane had read the Willa Cather story and that everybody was taking cues from her, I recalled my commune theory. "Do you all live together or something?"

Cornelius, usually so guileless-looking, coughed and turned away. Nicolas filled in. "We've known each other a long time."

"It's not a commune, is it?"

Emilia stared at me hard. "How did you know?"

I tried not to sound pleased. "It wasn't hard. The clothes, the way you always leave together, somebody does the coaching for the next class. Where is it?"

"Just off Sisleytown Road," she replied.

I paused, expecting an invitation to visit. A slight unease swept through the room. "What do you grow?" I asked finally.

William Astbury piped up. "Timothy, sorghum, alfalfa, bluegrass." He laughed briefly. "Plus a lot of weeds."

"You sell it to the dairy farms around here?"

He nodded. "Or they pasture right on our land, though it's against the by-laws."

Well, that explained it. It might explain some other things too—their insularity, their timidity. "Don't you miss traveling, seeing the cities?"

Millie Herkimer replied in a reproving voice. "Americans are one thing today and another thing tomorrow. We prefer a settled life in one place."

Who was I to blame them? Hadn't I taken refuge in the past, which was a community of sorts? The room was quiet. They were waiting, slightly embarrassed. I got the clear message that their urge to include me in their lives had been neutralized by something else. Were they growing a secret cash crop on that land of theirs? They wouldn't be the first around here. Well, I might or might not find out eventually.

In the meantime, "Paul's Case" by Willa Cather was waiting. They took a dim view of Paul's suicide, once they heard about it.

Little by little, as the weeks went by, their stories came out. I kicked things off with my own. I told them about teaching in New York, my increasingly desperate search for a lover until, ten years before, when I was thirty-three, I'd met Tom Ritenour at a bar in Greenwich Village. They listened as I told about setting up house, our five years of fidelity, the difficult "open relationship" that followed, Tom's illness and death.

After this had been absorbed, Millie had a comment. "Maybe if you'd lived in the country, you would have been more content with each other." She glanced at her friend Teage. "Not so many temptations."

"Maybe so," I agreed. It was a moot point, and it didn't matter anymore.

Emilia Quinn weighed in next. She had lived with her mother. They took in summer guests—city people mostly. "So you see, Michael," she scolded, "we weren't as isolated as you like to think." She had a lover, a woman neighbor who managed her own farm and raised her children alone. But it had been difficult—not only the fear of gossip but the presence of the children and the elder Mrs. Quinn. At last her lover's farm had failed, the furnishings auctioned off, the place repossessed, and the woman herself committed to the state hospital at Wingdale.

"Our difficulty," Emilia said finally, brushing the tangle of dark hair from her eyes, "was fear. They were all lined up against us. We didn't know there had been others before, just like us."

I got a bright idea. "Why don't you bring your friend to class next week? If she can get a day release?" Emilia looked shocked. "She might learn something, feel better about herself."

Emilia took a deep breath. "It's too late for that, Michael." There was so much death in her voice I let the matter drop. Everyone else chimed in to cover my stupidity.

It was the week we were doing *Maurice,* near the end of the course, that Nicolas, looking mischievous, produced a photo. He waved it around. "Recognize him?" I had no trouble. It was a sepia print, mounted on cardboard, of Cornelius Graef. Cornelius, a bewildered eighteen, was posed in a fake Civil War uniform, with a fake musket in his hand. I turned the photo over: "W. A. Reed, Artistic Photographer, Copying a Specialty, Negatives Preserved."

Nicolas let out a teasing chuckle. "We took it in Rensselaer one afternoon. There's a photographer who lets you strike old poses."

I gave the photo back. Nicolas kissed the bewildered young face. "I think he's embarrassed," he said.

Cornelius sank down in the seat, pulling the cap—maybe the same one—over his face.

"Try to think of Plato," Israel remarked. "An open love is more honorable than a secret one."

"Shove off, Israel."

"If Plato is beyond your grasp," Israel went on, "try to think about Edward Carpenter and George Merrill. Or Gertrude Stein and Alice Toklas. Or Maurice and ... what's his name."

Millie Herkimer clucked. "Cornelius, you were always a bad sport."

"Yeah?" The cap came off. "Why don't you tell your happy story, Millie?"

Millie flushed and turned away. But everyone was waiting.

"I was a teacher until a few years ago," she began.

"Like your aunt Millicent," I added.

She nodded. "A family weakness. But at school I met another teacher who forced me to face certain things." She reached over and touched Teage's hand. "I wasn't made for marriage, children, all that. It was my antagonism toward the opposite sex." She smiled apologetically. "Toward some of them anyway. We ... this other teacher and I ... wrote several letters. The letters were discovered; we were both discharged." She paused. "So here we are, trying to understand what happened."

"The heterosexual dictatorship," Bradford Gower remarked. He had become quite fond of that phrase.

"Also the male dictatorship," Millie amended. "They often go together."

Nobody disputed that.

We broke early that evening. *Maurice,* for all its Edwardian passion, had paled beside the pain in the classroom.

When the final session rolled around, we were deep in December. The fields were rusty, the trees like frozen bolts of lightning. We had all pulled closer, huddling around the lives we discussed, drawing warmth from old passions. I hoped I had given them more than literature, though—courage maybe, or freedom. I asked for comments, suggestions, evaluations. But for some reason the old reserve was back tonight. The course had been "interesting," "informative." My suggestion that we all repair to the Maverick Inn for a last drink was met with an embarrassed shuffle. Finally, irritated, I asked point-blank what they'd gotten out of the course.

Bradford Gower broke he silence. "Now I won't be ashamed if people call me names." A nod from William Astbury. "We won't run away."

Emilia spoke next. "You've given us ammunition, Michael."

"Pride too, I hope."

Cornelius started to speak. I could feel the words forming, wild things under the moon, but he beat them back. Pride wasn't in his vocabulary—at least not yet—but he had tried.

When the class ended, each student filed forward to shake my hand. Teage Dane kissed my cheek, then pressed a few strawflowers in my hand—dry and lavender. I laughed and thanked her.

Outside they huddled against the cold, knotted up as usual, as I struggled with my ignition. I let the engine warm up as we traded a last long look. I was full of sadness. We would never be a group again, never merge into a whole, examining prejudice, hunting justice. We might run into each other at fairs or auctions, but we'd never be a family again. It was the nature of every enter-prise, I reminded myself, and might stand for the impermanence of all human connection. Still, as I drove off with a final wave, I felt a lash of the old rage. Why must all meetings end in parting? This was another, muted version of Tom's death. *Goodbye,* I thought, is the saddest word in the language.

I was due at Ray Stonington's for dinner the next night—a small celebration to mark the end of the course, he'd said. I was grateful. Even if the students had vetoed the idea of a party, Ray had come through. I really didn't want to be alone, not even inside my favorite year, 1819.

I drove carefully into Ray's driveway—he'd just put in more bluestone. Maybe, I thought, heading up the walk, I'd give the course again. Do it better next time—different selections, sharper commentary. But, luckily, I spotted this as a fantasy, a bad habit from the old days. Courses often got worse instead of better. And these students, for all their quirkiness, had given all they had to give. I had no complaints.

Ray had other guests: a young stage designer visiting for the week; the real-estate agent who had sold Ray his house; an assertive middle-aged woman named Jane Snow, who was helping Ray plan a garden of eighteenth-century produce—not an appetizing idea, I thought, unless you liked gourds.

We talked a little about my course. Ray had filled them in before I arrived. "You were right," I said to Ray at one point. "They were sweet country people. But it was harder to get to know them than I thought."

"That's often the way." Ray removed his glasses and rubbed one eye. "But once you know each other, it's for life."

I laughed. "I hope so."

It was a typical evening at Ray's—good food, good company, and everybody had to wear a lady's hat to dinner. "That's a Lily Daché,"Ray said approvingly when I chose a snappy little number in black velvet with eye veil. "It would have cost you a fortune in 1940."

We were still at table, lingering over coffee, when Ray passed around his lat-est treasure, found in a box of miscellanea purchased at auction. It was a photo of his own house, before the north wing had been added. "I can date it quite easily," he said. "About 1895. They'd already cleared the land for the new wing."

It was sepia, with a familiar border. Something stirred in me and I turned it over. "W. A. Reed, Artistic Photographer, Copying a Specialty ..." and the street address in Rensselaer.

I let out a whoop. "One of my students just had his picture taken there."

Ray looked disapproving. "Somebody's pulling your leg, Michael. That placed closed fifty years ago. There's a Burger King there now."

The next instant a shudder went through me, and the knowledge uncoiled from the place it had been waiting. *Teage Dane's name was on the founder's plaque at the Herkimer Institute.* I had seen but not seen. Everything else fell into place. Israel Solomon had sold his store to the Hardwick family in 1912, the year his friend David died. The farm woman at the state hospital couldn't visit our class because she was no longer there. Cornelius Graef had been snapped in a studio by a photographer who mounted his pictures in the style of the day.

I tried to pay attention after that, but it was difficult. My head was buzzing, and my palms were wet. I left as soon as I could, apologizing for my behavior. "That's okay, Michael," Ray said at the door. "We know you teachers are hopeless when you lose your precious students."

I drove the little car as fast as it would go. A half-moon was climbing as I parked on the shoulder of Sisleytown Road. Luckily, the stones faced west. I'd be able to read them.

It took me a while, but finally I came to the last row. I had collected them all, every one. "Okay," I said aloud, the wind whipping my voice, "why didn't you tell me?"

I walked back to Cornelius's grave, then ran my hand over the granite marker, touching the dates. All except Emilia and Israel had died young. Why? Suddenly I knew—and also why they had disapproved so harshly of Willa Cather's Paul.

Snow began to drift down. *They died of the plague,* I thought, *and the plague was ignorance.* Maybe that was the worst of all, because it brings darkness to a living soul.

Snow settled inside my collar. I hunched down, into myself, as far as I could go.

But they had overcome it, because all plagues end sooner or later. There's no telling how or when, but they end.

It was too cold to stay out now. I turned and walked back to the car. The moon shone through the brightness, illuminating the stones. I got in, started the engine, and drove home, thinking about the course I would give next time.

MICHAEL SCHWARTZ

PUBLIC DISPLAY

STEPHEN TOOK ANOTHER BITE of his Quarter Pounder (with cheese), and let images from the McDonald's commercials gambol through his mind: boy meeting girl, grandparents spoiling grandkids, the nuclear family eating nuclear food, images all shiny-bright and squeaky with normality. Stephen was happy, lapped in the warm waters of irony. My God, he thought, it's wonderful how easy it is to be subversive when you're gay. Just do something that all the normal people do—like eat at McDonald's, or make love—but do it with a man. You feel like you're undermining society.

Stephen looked across the table at John, who was scowling at his Filet-O'-Fish sandwich. They were both more or less vegetarian (John more, Stephen less), and the fish was marginally less objectionable than the other non-beef entree, the Chicken McNuggets. Poor John, Stephen thought. But that's what he gets for treating this as food, instead of a socio-politico-esthetic field trip. Still, he was grateful that John would occasionally relax his standards and indulge him in these ironic excursions. "You know I can't help myself," Stephen would explain.

"I know, you've told me," John would answer. "You're from New Jersey."

"Right. It's like a vampire, when he has to carry some of his native soil in his coffin, so he can sleep on it. Every so often, I have to touch trash, or I die."

John abandoned his sandwich, and focused instead on the conversation. It had actually been running for days, because he was trying to solve a problem at work. "I just have to tell my boss that I can't agree to a schedule that I know is impossible."

"Are you going to get blamed for making the project late?"

"No," John answered. "Everybody knows that Jim is going to be a month late with his part, and that gives me more than enough time to finish."

"So why doesn't Jim make a more realistic schedule?" Stephen already knew the answer, from previous conversations, but he also knew his role in this exchange. He was to ask the questions that would help John figure out what he had to do.

"Because," John said, exasperated, "because they all have this macho attitude, this refusal to admit any weaknesses, and that means we all have to promise what we can't deliver, and we can't even question what anyone else—"

He stopped, and they both turned to look at a nearby table, where a man and two boys were sitting. Then they looked back at each other.

"It was him, right?" John asked.

"Yes," Stephen answered, disgusted. "Why do they have to do this?"

"Was he talking about us?"

"I don't think so. I'm pretty sure he used the singular—'that goddamn faggot.' If he meant us, he'd probably say 'those goddamn faggots.' Or maybe 'them there goddamn faggots.'"

John was intent on trying to hear. "Is he still saying it?"

Stephen looked at them again. The man was in his midthirties, about their own age. He wore a tight white polo shirt—his leisure clothes for this Saturday outing—and had a powerful build, which was obviously acquired on the job, not in the gym. He was balding, and his face was apoplectically red, as if always ready to explode. His two sons, both around ten, were thin and blond. They sat quietly, as if cowed by the anger in their father's voice, even though it wasn't directed against them.

"No," Stephen answered, after listening for a while. "The thing about the faggot was just a one-shot deal. Now he's complaining about the unions … or maybe it's the Japanese … whatever it is, he's against it."

John was visibly shaken. "This has never happened to me before."

"You've never heard anybody say 'faggot'?"

"Of course, but they usually yell it at you from a car, and then they speed away, like they know they're doing something wrong."

"Right. Then you give them the finger, and you hope they see it in the rearview mirror, and then you hope they don't turn around and come back and kill you."

"But this guy …" John looked at him again. "He's not running. He's just sitting there. He thinks he can just say it, and nobody will do anything about it."

"He's a straight white male. Nobody's told him yet that he doesn't own the world. It's probably because he does own it."

"Stephen, he can't get away with this."

"Oh, but he can. The Supreme Court said so: five-to-four decision."

"We've got to confront him."

"John ..."

"What could happen? If we go over to him, and say, 'Excuse me'—"

"'Excuse me'?" Stephen echoed. "*That*'ll have him quaking in his boots."

"Okay," John laughed. "We'll work on the wording later." The laugh snapped John out of his initial shock, as Stephen had hoped. "But if we tell him that we're gay, and that what he said is offensive, what would he do?"

"Well," Stephen said, studying the man, "there's a chance—a slight chance—he'd say," Stephen dropped a half-octave, "'Gentlemen, I'd like to thank you for showing me the error of my ways. I'll never make a homophobic comment again. And, by the way, I want to thank you in particular for humiliating me in front of my sons.'"

"A chance. You think so?"

"I said 'a slight chance.' There's a slightly better chance that he'll scream, 'Faggots! They're gonna give my kids AIDS!' And then everyone will form a circle around us and stone us to death with Chicken McNuggets."

"Well," John mused, "martyrdom has always had its appeal."

"Actually," Stephen said, "what would probably happen is that you'd initiate a dialogue, and he'd start talking about how it's a free country and he has the right to say anything he wants, and how the family is threatened and do we want to wind up like the Roman Empire, and how God would have created Adam and Bruce, *et cetera*. And you'd be rational while he was being stupid. And he'd get annoyed, and you'd stay patient, and I'd get morose, and I'd probably have to kill both of you right there, just to get away."

John pretended to ponder. "I see. Well, if that's the worst, then I don't see any problem." Stephen flared his eyebrows at John, who quickly said, "Just joking! But seriously ..."

Stephen interrupted. "I am serious."

"I know," John said. "But seriously. I know you think we can't do anything to educate him. But those kids—we can't let them think it's all right to call somebody a faggot."

"Oh," Stephen said, "they probably saw that after-school special. You know, the one about the quiet, sensitive boy in class, and how you're not supposed to make fun of him, even if he does throw like a girl."

"That's not enough. They have to see it in real life, too. Stephen, we can't just sit here. We've got to do something."

Stephen knew John would say this. John had said it before.

These were in fact the first words that Stephen had ever heard John say. It was at a party, one of those early-evening parties where the point is moderate drinking and immoderate conversation. Stephen was walking toward the kitchen, the party around him a pleasant hum of amusing comments and amused laughter, when he became aware of a voice, distinct, cutting through the noise, saying, "But we've got to do something!" The speaker's urgency and earnestness were so out of place that Stephen was instantly alert to them.

Stephen saw the speaker, who was still addressing his audience of four listeners. Stephen didn't know him, but he knew he would. It wasn't just the prominent nose, the strong chin, the hairline beginning to recede over the temples—those physical traits that Stephen found so devastating. It had more to do with the way the man leaned forward into his explanation, his eyes alive with boyish enthusiasm and adult intelligence, his brow furrowed in concentration and concern. It was also the fact that, intent on his argument, the man had no idea that his audience was totally bored.

The man's lack of awareness made him seem absurd, vulnerable, and, to Stephen, heroic and beautiful. He wanted to rescue him, to protect him, to listen to him as he deserved to be listened to, to put his arms around him and fuck him and hold him all night long. He knew they'd sleep together that night: his desire was too precise to be wrong.

So Stephen joined the group, and picked up half the conversation, which was about the imminent demise of yet another gay rights bill. Stephen addressed the political issues, but with a wit and irony that wrapped themselves snugly around the other man's earnestness. The previously bored audience became attentive again, not so much to the political subject as to the sexual dynamic that was blossoming between the two speakers.

Stephen had been right. He charmed the pants off John that night—literally. What he hadn't foreseen was that, more than three years later, they'd still be together.

People who knew them declared the match inevitable, in retrospect, because they were both so serious about politics. And these people were right, up to a point. For both of them, growing up had been equal parts Mickey Mouse and Martin Luther King, the Fabulous Four and the Chicago Seven, Gloria Gaynor and Gloria Steinem—civil rights, antiwar, feminism. And, for both, these movements had served as rehearsals, preparations, for the central political action of their lives, which was also the most personal: accepting themselves as gay, and affirming that their life was worth living, and was worth protecting. For both, to be gay was to be political, because they saw the enormous power wielded by people who at best pitied them and at worst would be happy to see them dead. They took politics seriously—the way you would take a boulder seriously if it was perched on a cliff above your house.

But there were differences within this similarity; in the early seventies, Stephen had lost faith in public demonstrations—that article of belief so central to the creed of the sixties. In high school and college, he had marched against the war. He felt his single strength multiplied to infinity by the crowd of demonstrators; he saw himself as part of a force for historical change. But, when the war was over, and he watched the television footage of the last American helicopters leaving Saigon, he had a terrible realization: the protesters hadn't ended the war. Nixon and Kissinger had, when it suited their purposes to do so. Stephen never forgave them that. In that moment, the sixties ended for Stephen, and the old Phil Ochs anthem took on a new meaning: "I ain't a-marchin' anymore."

Stephen remained political, but with a severely reduced sense of what an individual, or even a group of individuals, could accomplish when up against the mass of idiocy that democracy had endowed with power. His new creed was simple: you get involved in local politics, because you can have some impact. You vote Democratic in national elections, because you have no other choice. You give money to the ACLU, because court decisions matter. You maintain a supple sense of irony, because you're going to need it. And you live your life righteously, because anything else is death. Stephen made sure that everyone he touched directly—friends, colleagues, family, doctors, the clerks in the local convenience store—that they all knew he was gay, so that, if they had to vote on gay issues, they could picture an individual, rather than the child molester in drag pictured in homophobic propaganda. From an accumulation of these small actions, social change would come. Eventually. Maybe.

But he had no more illusions about educating the masses through public demonstrations and the like. To be educated, the masses needed to be capable of rational thought; and too many Republican administrations had proved that the masses would rather die than think. Instead of thought, they had tropisms, amoeboid movements prompted by primitive appetites and fears far beneath the reach of reason.

So these public demonstrations, these symbolic actions, these marches, rallies, and civil disobediences—they were worthless, and worse than worthless. They encouraged the participants to believe they were accomplishing something, when in fact they were doing nothing except making themselves feel good, which the current phrase-makers tried to ennoble by calling it "empowerment." It wasn't power; it was an opiate, no more. Better, Stephen maintained, to know that you can do nothing than to believe that your pathetic symbolic actions were accomplishing something. Better despair than delusion. Stephen didn't march, and he felt contempt for anyone who did.

John marched. He went to noontime rallies and all-night vigils; pro-union, anti-FDA, anti-antiabortion. He had been to every major Washington march since the massive antiwar demonstration in 1969. He had been arrested three times: nuclear power twice, and most recently at the Supreme Court. John marched because of the civil rights protests of the sixties. They had moved him, and educated him, and changed his life. Because he had been educated, he was generous enough to believe that others could be educated, too.

John's belief had a special fervor when it came to gay and lesbian issues, where standing up and being counted took on a literal meaning. Our invisibility, he argued, is our greatest enemy, and we must let the public know how many of us there really are. If tens or even hundreds of thousands of gays and lesbians poured into the streets, publicly demanding our rights, how, he reasoned, could we possibly be denied?

From the beginning, Stephen knew that John believed in the power of public demonstrations. Their first conversation was a debate on whether the many rallies for the gay rights bill were having any influence on public opinion. John said yes. Stephen said no. From that simple opposition, they launched into a sparring courtship. Each elaborated his views with wit and verve, spinning out more and more ingenious arguments, employing ever more hyperbolic rhetoric, drunk with words and ideas and desire, each trying to tease the other into yielding, each laughing at the other's stubbornness.

That night and afterwards, the charge between them transformed any differences into part of their erotic dance, elements in the interplay of irony and earnestness that formed their mutual attraction. When the topic of marching came up, it was a contact point that was guaranteed to generate sparks. John would call Stephen a cynic, and Stephen would call John a sentimentalist, and the unresolved dispute would add a texture of tension to the way their bodies came together.

Then, one night a few months after they met, John asked Stephen where they should rendezvous the next day for the Gay Pride March.

Stephen was incredulous. "I don't march, John, you know that."

John laughed. "Oh, but, Stephen, couldn't you just come along? Think of it as taking a walk with me—and a couple thousand of my homosexual friends. It'll be cozy."

"You haven't been listening to me!"

"I know you say you don't march. But you were just being ironic, right? You weren't serious, were you?"

Stephen mustered all the earnestness that he was capable of. "I'm always serious. Irony is my way of being serious. I thought you understood that."

They were both silent, aware that something had changed between them. Until now, their conversation had been a joyous discovery of commonalities and complementaries. Some differences had of course turned up. John had been disappointed that Stephen didn't like *Hiroshima, Mon Amour;* Stephen had been appalled that John did. But those differences seemed peripheral— matters of taste, unlike this one, which came from deep within. It marked the first real limitation on what had, up to this point, seemed limitless.

Stephen looked at John—that nose and chin, those eyes, that hairline—who was sitting next to him, but who now seemed so separate. There is nothing, he thought, so alien as another human being. The difference between them suddenly felt like distance and, for the moment, the distance seemed unbridgeable. From that moment, his desire for John seemed pathetic, a doomed at-

tempt to negate the distance. Bodies, beliefs, ideas—they're all barriers, not
bridges: they mark a boundary that you can't go beyond; they keep you apart,
even as you seem to be coming together.

Of course, the moment passed, and the common ground they had established outweighed the differences. Adjustments were made. The next day, John
went to the Gay Pride March alone. His friends wondered at Stephen's absence
and worried about a possible breach in this new and promising romance. But
John just shrugged: "That's how Stephen is." There it was—a fact to be accepted.

Once, about a year later, they did try to domesticate the difference by turning it into an advantage. John was going to a Washington march, and they decided Stephen should go along. While John was marching, Stephen could go to
the National Gallery. It didn't work. The separation during the day exaggerated
the awareness of the difference between them. When they met for dinner that
night, their talk trailed off into embarrassed silences, the kind that occurs at
the reunion of two people who used to be friends. Since then, John would tell
Stephen that he was going off to a march or protest, and Stephen would tell
John to have a good time.

Stephen still believed that anyone who marched was a contemptible, self-de-
luded fool: major premise. He knew that John marched: minor premise.
Ergo—but Stephen never finished the syllogism. For John's sake, Stephen ac-
ceded to a logical inconsistency in his inner world. There was too much of
value between them, and a little disregard for the laws of logic seemed a small
price to pay. Besides, this willed lapse in logic was probably what other people
meant when they talked about love.

Anyway, the issue of public demonstrations came up only infrequently. It
was certainly less visible than the standard relationship issues, like which holidays had to be spent with whose parents, and whether watching reruns of
"Donna Reed" constituted sociological research. They didn't need to talk
about demonstrations—except on occasions like this current one at
McDonald's, when John felt that they had to "do something."

"Look," Stephen said, still trying to steer John away from a confrontation he
knew would be pointless, at best. "It's too late to do anything now. There's a
statute of limitations on responding to insults like this. You can't say, 'Sir,
about that remark you made fifteen minutes ago'—"

"But, Stephen, if he's going to learn anything—"

"Exactly. It's like training your dog. If your dog shits on the rug, you've got
to rub his nose in it right away. If you wait, he doesn't see the connection. It's
the same with bigots. Except they're harder to train, because they're not as
bright as dogs."

John frowned, deep in thought. Then he decided. "Well, we just have to
make him say it again."

"What do you mean?" Stephen asked, apprehensively.

"We've got to provoke him into calling us 'faggots.'"

"I'm not sure it counts if we provoke him. It's entrapment, like a vice cop standing in a men's room pretending to be an available homosexual."

"Right." John agreed, warming to the argument. "It's time *we* tried that. And, besides, we're not pretending."

Stephen felt the discussion slipping out of his control. "But what do you want us to do?"

"Well," John answered, not quite sure, "we've got do something that's … you know, obviously gay."

"Like what?" Stephen demanded. "Hold a brunch? Start a fashion trend? How about my Bette Davis imitation?" Stephen patted the side of his head. "I'd love to kiss ya, but I just washed my hair."

"That's it!" John cried.

"No, please, my Bette Davis is awful. How about my Jeanne Kirkpatrick?"

"No, I mean we could kiss."

Stephen was thunderstruck. "At McDonald's!" Even in his most subversive fantasies, he had never imagined this ultimate act of revolution.

"Sure," John insisted. He waved his hand, indicating the people around them. "They're doing it. We can, too."

"John. Look around. Nobody's kissing. It's McDonald's, for Christ's sake. Even straights have their limits."

"Okay," John conceded. "But they could kiss, if they wanted to, so they don't. We can't, so we have to."

Stephen felt outmaneuvered. This was exactly the kind of logic he understood. He shifted ground. "John," he said, a hint of mock pleading in his voice, "you're asking me to commit a PDA."

John was stumped. "Politically—Dysfunctional—Anachronism?"

"Public Display of Affection. In high school, senior year, we took a class trip to Washington. The principal lectured us on how we were representing our school, so we shouldn't commit any PDAs. Of course, I wasn't about to commit any. The only PDA I wanted to commit was on Jeff Samuels, and Michelle Czernak would have scratched my eyes out."

"The thing is," John said, "that they eventually get to commit their what-do-you-call-its, their PDAs. We don't. Our whole life is like high school, with everybody saying, 'Don't commit PDAs.'"

Stephen was silent, so John continued. "We've been together, what, three years?"

"Three and a half."

"And in all that time, have we ever committed a PDA?"

Stephen thought for a moment, then smiled. "Well there was that time on the night flight from California."

"That was not intended to be public! We were just lucky that the flight steward turned out to be … uh …"

"Simpatico?" Stephen suggested.

"Yes." John smiled, and blushed at the memory. "My God, you're evil. The things you make me do! And you know that's not what I mean. I mean a time when we're affectionate in public, when other people, straights, strangers can see … you know, what we mean to each other."

Stephen threw his hands into the air. "I'm a WASP. We don't do PDAs. Even married WASPs just shake hands with each other. I think we procreate through our palms."

John motioned Stephen to be quiet. "No, there was that time last year when I had to go home for my uncle's funeral, and you drove me to the airport. You kissed me, right on the lips, at the security gate. You were so sweet. I was so surprised. It got me through the whole dismal weekend."

Stephen sank into glumness. "I was afraid you'd bring that up. Okay. I surrender. You're right."

"What do you mean?" John asked, perplexed.

Stephen sighed deeply, hung his head, and confessed. "All the way to the airport I was brooding about it, before I did it. I felt I had to do it, so I rehearsed it in my mind, over and over." He spoke with surprising bitterness. "It was totally preplanned. I kiss my grandmother with more passion."

John hesitated, then put his hand on Stephen's arm. "Don't be so hard on yourself. It's not easy."

Stephen looked up at John. "It never ends, does it? You keep finding new ways that they've fucked you up. And you keep fighting to unfuck it. Okay. Let's kiss. But this isn't only for that guy's benefit. I'm asserting my right to be publicly tacky, just like Jeff Samuels and Michelle Czernak."

"That's my boy!" John said.

They sat there, frozen.

Stephen moaned, "Why do I feel like an adolescent on his first date?"

"Okay," John said, giving himself a pep talk. "I've organized rallies with hundreds of people. I can organize this."

"Oh, great," Stephen muttered.

"Stephen! You agreed."

"Okay, it's your scene. So what do you want—a quick peck?"

"No," John answered, considering carefully. "It has to be a good long kiss. We need to make sure he sees it."

"Do you want sound effects? A nice, wet smack at the end?"

"No. Too adolescent. We want to project an image of maturity."

Stephen smiled slyly. "Can I slip you some tongue?"

"Absolutely not!" John reprimanded. "We want to be affectionate, not lewd. This is an assertion of our right to love. It's just a spontaneous expression of our affection for each other."

"This is about as spontaneous as brain surgery. I feel like a panda in a zoo, about to be mated. Maybe we should call the press in before—"

"Oh, no!" John was looking at the next table. Stephen looked, too. The man and his sons were leaving, preempting the little performance that was being so carefully prepared just for them.

They sat silent for a while. John was obviously disappointed at having missed his chance to make a public statement. Then he rallied himself. "Oh, well. At least we're ready for the next time. We'll know what to do when it happens again."

Stephen looked at John—his die-hard marcher, his brave little demonstrator, whose sixties gleam was still shining bright, even as the nineties were darkening around them. In his enthusiasm for public encounters, John seemed as absurd as the first time Stephen had seen him, over three years ago, at the party—as absurd, and as beautiful. He knew he'd never convince John that his marching was pointless. And he was not sure that he wanted to convince him. There would be this part of John that was forever beyond his reach.

Desire, Plato tells us, can be only for what we do not possess, because, since desire is the desire to possess, once we possess something, we can no longer desire it. By that definition, and by so many others, what Stephen felt for John at this moment was desire.

Stephen leaned across the table, and said, in a hoarse whisper, "Let's kiss anyway."

"What?" John was surprised, a little startled by Stephen's tone.

"You're so hot when you're being political."

John lowered his head, and blushed profoundly. "I still can't tell when you're being serious."

"I keep telling you. I'm always serious. Just kiss me. You'll see."

So they did, and John did see. So did everyone else. Most of them didn't like it, but that didn't matter. Because this was a private moment, that just happened to be occurring in a public place.

KISSING DOESN'T KILL

"Kɪss me," Cecile commands. She is standing against the bedroom door in her underpants and a ripped undershirt. The Saturday morning sun—which slants at its unique Saturday angle—pierces the cracks in the bamboo window shade and refracts off the pink wall. I can hear Cecile's soft breathing. I can hear seven-year-old Colby's snorts of sleep in the next room. I can hear my own heart.

"Not unless you come back to bed," I reply.

"What's the matter, don't you like standing-up sex?"

"Cecile, don't be gross."

"What's gross about it?" Cecile asks, laughing.

"My knees," I laugh back. "My knees would be totally gross if we did that."

"Totally gross?" Cecile echoes.

"Hey, I teach teenagers. What can I say?"

"You can say you remember when your knees were stronger and how you used to lean against me."

"You and the wall," I correct.

"You used to throw me to the floor with passion."

"Until I hit my head on the chair leg and saw stars for weeks."

"You used to see stars all the time."

If I didn't know Cecile so long and so deep, I'd think she was complaining. She isn't. She's tracing our romance. Soon she will slide next to me with her coffee cup and mine, and ask me if I remember the first time we ever made love. What we remember is not the first time, but the accumulation of memories of the first time. We reinscribe it in our memories with our words. Then we will relive it, not as reenactment, but as reinvention. With Cecile, every time is different.

This morning's love is intense. The mouth, the tongue, the body, blur and re-blur. I am chalky, pastel. I am crying. Sobbing, really.

Cecile is the one who should be crying, not me. I should be comforting her, holding her, allowing her to think about Estela. Estela, a Chilean artist whose work Cecile was close to placing with a new feminist art gallery downtown. Estela, dead. Visiting her mother and sister in Santiago. Everyone suspects the government, although which one is uncertain.

I only met Estela once. At dinner. She sat next to Colby and talked with him. So many adults ignore him, but she talked with him about the colors of clothes splashed around the table. Her fingers had a stubby beauty as they pointed. They crossed and recrossed as she and Colby compared the numerous shades of purple. They laughed. Her fingers could laugh.

The death of that laughter could make me cry for weeks.

But our weeks are not for crying; they are for work. For Cecile, there is the work of representing lesbian artists from South America. For Colby, there is the work of trying to survive in a New York public elementary school and maybe even learn something that nourishes love instead of narrowness. For me, there is the work of trying to survive in a New York public high school and maybe even teach something that encourages the risk of expansiveness instead of hate.

I'm teaching philosophy to high school students in a special pilot program. Eight classes of twenty students each, each class twice a week. I am really a teacher now, something I never thought I'd survive to do. Teaching kids who are a lot like I was. And a lot like I wasn't.

At least once every other week, and sometimes twice, a student will make an appointment to see me about "something really important." Her fourteen-fifteen-sixteen-year-old face is shining, womanly, but she looks more like Colby than Cecile. She glows with innocence, but she is also cynical, slick, and yes, sexy. The same way I was at fourteen-fifteen-sixteen. In fact, every one of these creatures I call young women remind me of myself: no matter that I wasn't Asian or Black, that I didn't streak my hair purple or wear bracelets from Guatemala, that I wouldn't talk to a teacher unless I had to, never mind sit in her office and tell her I was in love with her. The more sophisticated students talk about strong attractions and feelings that can't be denied and something that isn't just a crush.

I thank them for sharing their feelings. I am not at all grateful.

The bolder (and less sophisticated) students ask about my feelings for them. They want me to say that I love them. I would never say this. Not because I don't love them, but because the them that I love is the me that I was. I love them only as mirrors that would allow me to love myself like I never did. And because the them that I love is ephemeral. I love them only as girls who might grow to love themselves as women.

And because I don't love them, not really. Not as individuals. Sure, teaching is a lot like being in love, but with no one in particular. And for me, love is Cecile. I don't tell them I have been loving the same woman since they were in the third grade.

Because I want to take them seriously. Because I want to tell them that they are worth loving. I don't tell them about transference or role models or the difficulties of coming out. I don't tell them to find a nice girl their own age or even suggest that they direct their attentions to their best friends, Claudia and Ernestine, who were in my office confessing love just last week. I want to take them seriously.

I say thank you and nothing else.

To anyone.

Not even to Cecile.

Especially not to Yvette, a co-teacher who comments on the line of girls that sometimes snakes by my office door.

"I'm role-modeling," I joke to Yvette.

"More like making all the girls at this school into lesbians," Yvette grumbles. Maybe she is just jealous that she doesn't have a line of girls, or even an office with a door. The office is part of the pilot program's perks, but I'm not sure it's worth it.

Yvette doesn't wear the crooked smile of envy. She is not smiling. I turn away and look back at her. She still is not smiling.

I close the door to my office. I am more innocent than any of my students. Despite the violence that has been my life, I never really expect people to be mean. Grumpy, yes, but not humorlessly mean. I should walk back to Yvette. I should tell her that I am not making anybody into anything, tell her these girls are as much lesbians as I was at their age. Don't tell her about current debates about sexual identity formation. Tell her I don't know why she hates me. Accuse her of being closeted or latent.

But I am not that innocent.

And she isn't the only one. And she isn't even among my private suspects for what comes to be known as the poster-burning incident. It's my poster, given to me by an admiring student. KISSING DOESN'T KILL: GREED AND INDIFFERENCE DO. By the Gran Fury Collective. Political art marking AIDS as a political crisis. Interracial and intersexed. Appearing on public buses in New York. And appearing in a public school library hallway outside my office. My favorite part is the women's hairstyles.

It's the women who are burned off. KILL THE QUEERS is black magic-markered across the remains, including the kissing couple of a black man and white woman. There are different sorts of accuracy.

The students in philosophy want to talk about the poster burning. I've scheduled us to talk about Foucault. Sometimes I think that they see philosophy as current events, or their feelings, or just gossip. Sometimes I wonder if I've gone overboard with my message that philosophy is accessible. Sometimes I want to know if they're as unfocused in their other classes, but I'm vulnerable in my pilot project and can't/won't/don't ask other teachers.

So, I try to make connections, try to surface assumptions. There is not a complete contradiction between rambling discussions and disciplined inquiries. And I try to cover the material, for the school administration cares less about discussion or discipline than measurable achievements. After this pilot program, the students should be able to name the names of philosophy: to know who Plato is and when he lived, to be able to correctly identify postmodernism from four reductive multiple choices. To score better on the statewide Regents exam.

"Let's think about what Foucault might have said about the destruction of the poster," I say. "He died of AIDS." I add some poignant gossip.

My students do not succumb to my attempt. This is my favorite class of twenty: they are bright, articulate, culturally and politically mixed, and usually respectful. Sometimes they even do the assigned reading. But today they want to talk about me.

The student is white. Female. Sincere. Apparently heterosexual. She has never been in my office swearing undying love. She asks me, in front of the class, whether I feel threatened.

She wants me to bleed. To slash my flesh and bleed so that she can inspect my blood to see if it is really red.

I am vulnerable.

Ridiculous. She is sixteen, at most. I am one of the few out lesbians she knows. Maybe the only one. Certainly the only one teaching at this school. And it was my poster.

So, I answer her—her and the other nineteen teenagers in the classroom—being careful not to look at any one person in particular, especially not Claudia or Ernestine. I clothe my answer in the purples of untaught history, talk about lesbians burned as witches, or as criminals, or both. I clothe my answer in the purples of my own history, talk about being cornered by boys yelling dyke and throwing sharp rocks. I even manage to mention Foucault.

"You must feel really vulnerable," the white sincere young woman says.

She doesn't see how tough I am to have survived.

"We are all vulnerable," I say, trying to imagine how this young woman could not walk down the same streets near the high school as I do. "If we are lesbians or gay men, we are stalked on the street for being queer. If we are women, we are attacked on the streets and in our houses for being female. If we are African-American or Spanish or Asian, we are attacked for being not-white-enough. If we think we belong only in certain places at certain times and with our own kind, then we are vulnerable. And all of us are vulnerable."

I think my speech has all the right shades of pathos and passion. Maybe it can be a segue into Foucault's theory of power in the next class.

None of my students compliment me on my comments. No one comes that week to confess love, or even strong attraction. The hall outside my office feels strangely silent. I write the principal a memo about the incident in which I suggest/demand an investigation. I am very careful to straddle the slash between suggest and demand. I give copies to all my fellow teachers. The principal never replies. None of the other teachers talk to me about it except Yvette, who smiles as she says, "You've caused a lot of trouble, haven't you?"

When the war starts, it is another thing not to talk about. Yvette wears a flag pin on her daily dress. Soon, it nests in a yellow bow. The other teachers are like mirrors. Someone official orders yellow ribbons tied to the fence around the school. I start carrying Cecile's pocket knife, slashing the strips of cloth, watching them float toward the piles of garbage that fertilize the fence. I see Yvette watch me and my knife. She stands against the fence smoking a cigarette, those cancerous substitutes for kisses. The students want to talk about the war in class. They have relatives "over there in the Gulf." Brothers. Uncles. A few aunts and sisters. Lots of cousins. I lecture on Foucault. "This will be on the test," I say. *Support our troops,* the students say with buttons on their jackets.

Colby's button says, *War is not good for children and other living things.* A child in school rips it off his backpack and then spits on him. "He's just a jerk," Colby says. But he doesn't wear any more buttons.

Cecile threatens to kill the kid that spit on Colby.

"That will solve everything," I say.

We listen to the radio. It is our TV substitute. It is sufficient to provoke.

"What are you, a fuckin' third-grader?" I yell back at some general in some press conference.

"What's wrong with third-graders?" Colby wants to know.

"Wasn't that kid who spit on you in third grade?"

"No, he's a fourth-grader," Colby corrects.

"Well," I calm a bit, "I guess I'm just trying to say that these men should be acting like grownups rather than kids."

"Kids don't have bombs," Colby corrects again.

"Finish your breakfast, get ready for school, and come kiss me good-bye."

The ones with bombs drop them on Iraq at night.

Somewhere in Iraq there are two lesbians, holding onto each other in the darkness. Kissing. Kissing. Kissing as if their lives depend on it.

Cecile tells me to stop imagining things. "Besides," she says, "lesbians aren't allowed over there."

"Cecile," I yell at her louder than I did at the general, "what are you talking about? Have you forgotten Estela? Do you think they allow lesbians in Chile? Goddamn it, Cecile, you think they allow lesbians over here? In New York?"

"Look," Cecile says, "I just don't want to think about it." She turns the radio station.

To my favorite station instead of hers, like an apology. Yet the (post)-modern rock I usually find so soothing (the jarring chords cannot compete with its failure to remind me of the songs before Cecile) is being interrupted by news bulletins and commentaries on news bulletins.

And they are saying *We,* as in, *We are bombing Iraq.*

It's more than enough to make me long for the songs before Cecile. *It ain't me babe.* Where's Bob Dylan when we need him? Joan Baez? Hell, where's Buffy Saint-Marie?

And they are saying that they've made arrangements with a chain of florists to provide all the station listeners with yellow ribbons for our houses and cars.

I spin the radio dial, searching for what is now called classic rock. They're playing Rod Stewart.

We scatter numbers across the FM-band. Then the war ends.

They/we won.

It was tidy, and Americans are happy. It was expensive but hardly anyone talks on the radio about that. The country is in a recession. People continue to die of AIDS. New York City is laying off teachers.

The forsythia are in bloom, but they are yellow.

"Cecile," I say, "I'm losing my job."

"Kiss me," she says.

"Cecile," I say, "I'm being fired. There are other teachers hired the same time as me, but they're staying."

"Kiss me," she says.

"Cecile," I say, "you don't understand. I'm losing my job. We can't live on your salary. And I don't want Colby to grow up in this stupid country."

"You're right," Cecile says. "Let's move to Australia."

"That won't solve anything," I say. But I've always wanted to drive across that continent. Now might be the time to do it. "Besides," I add, "I don't know where we'll get the money."

Cecile laughs.

"Kiss me," I say.

Our laugh is so deep and so long that I know I will never kill or be killed. And maybe I will never die.

And maybe we will go to Australia.

HUMMING

How glad I am that she doesn't look like any of my three daughters. In the last years especially, in which I have pursued a meditation practice and the study of the great, elegant texts of Buddhism, often I have felt that time does not exist, or that all of it exists in this very moment, or that the space of a lifetime is no bigger than a drop of dew trembling on a petal of a flower, and as evanescent. Given this perspective, what can our relative ages matter?

Still, if Jeanine were to remind me of one of my daughters, I'd be uncomfortable. After all, I do inhabit the time-limited world of conditions. One condition being my aging body, wracked these days with the storms of menopause. Another being the old shingle house in which Ralph and I live. Rotting at its foundation and threatening to slide down the steep lawn in back, still it sits with shabby charm in the Berkeley hills. The house speaks to some people of a gracious, leisurely decade when trees were more numerous than houses up on the hill; as my presence must awake in some people a nostalgia for the late forties, early fifties, when young people were supposedly more innocent and trusting in life than they are today. I am not, myself, interested in that time of my youth, or in the years of mothering that came after.

I am really only interested in this particular moment in the big shadowy bedroom with its view of the distant Golden Gate Bridge red above the shining water. In this quiet afternoon now and then I hear the cooing of the doves who live under the eaves. A soft gray sound, from somewhere far away, it enters my mind as I look at the black curls lying flat, like a baby lamb's, wet with our sweat and a sweeter, thicker juice. Wisps of curl feather down her thighs a few inches, lie softly up against the undercurve of her belly. This bower of dark hair, thin enough that the skin is visible underneath, damp and warm, welcomes me. I lick each curl, moving to where the hair grows more thickly, the odor deepens. Odor of salty wetness that opens caves in my mind, rich odor of deep-sea secrets, of sun-warmed olives, the sunshine transmuted to a thick golden liquid in which I lie suspended. Jeanine's odor.

I stroke the tender skin of the inside of her thighs, my fingers converging at the rosy lips visible under the hair, brushing lightly over them. Her voice comes, a soft ohhhh of anticipation. I lift my head to look up at her, see her brown eyes watching me with that same intent look that takes over her face when she leans to my breast, takes my nipple in her mouth and examines it gently with her tongue, nurtures it with her lips. Such concentration, such passionate attention. My own cunt has begun to throb, my body going hot and seeming to swell, heightening my skin's sensitivity.

While the fingers of my right hand play in her hair, moving lightly over her vulva, with my left I reach to take her small, callused hand. I kiss her fingers, linger in her palm, suck her thumb, moving my tongue around it in slow revolvings. Ahhhh, she says, lifting her pelvis, offering herself. I let my breast lie against the open lips, feeling their wet warmth on my skin, my tightening nipple. Jeanine shudders, says my name, and I lower my face to brush her thigh, move carefully upward until I am kissing her outer lips. She has begun to move her pelvis in smooth, subtle circles, each coming toward me a gesture of desire, each drawing away an invitation to follow her. I do now. Slightly spreading her lips with my fingers, I place my wet mouth between them, greeting her tight bud of a clitoris, slipping my tongue down to probe the opening of her vagina, moving up again to suck. Jeanine makes a low crooning sound that vibrates through her body into my mouth. Slipping my arms under her lifted thighs, I reach up to cup her breasts, tease the hard pink nipples as my mouth answers hungrily each thrusting, seeking movement of her desire.

These same breasts I gently cradle half an hour later as we sit in the deep hot water of the bathtub. When I invited her into the tub she asked, "When is Ralph coming home?" "Not until seven, I think." Her eyebrows knotted. "You *think!*" But she got in with me, lifting short, muscular legs over the side of the tub, lowering her small ass into the water so that she now sits facing me. I soap her breasts, long breasts with nipples pointing down, while she tells me that when she loses weight her breasts hang like empty bags on her chest. I can't imagine it, they are so full now, overflowing my hands with their slippery weight. She touches mine, and murmurs into my hair, "Your breasts comfort me." Hummmm," I say, small sound of acknowledgment, of satisfaction.

It is only in these stolen afternoons that we are able to be together. I have been married for thirty years, to three different men. Some women find marriage restricting: I find it liberating, even marriage to a man like Ralph, who runs a metaphysical bookstore and cares more about meditating than making money. He does support me. And I like the safety of marriage, the comforting routine, the coziness. My mother encouraged me to develop a practical attitude to life coupled with a vivid appetite for its pleasures. Jeanine cares about Ralph too: she does not want to hurt him. She carries her love for me like a secret treasure, folded and wrapped, close to her heart. Her desire sends flames up through her body, lighting her eyes. Sometimes those eyes catch me unawares, as when, leaning over Ralph to pour his coffee, I glance up to where she sits on the window seat, the newspaper held before her. She is not reading: her eyes are watching my movements with an attention so focused it startles me. She looks into me, and without moving an inch I feel myself falling toward her, plummeting with her down, down, deep inside to the place we visit together, the place where stillness lies, holding us.

Now, in the bathtub, we have leaned our heads into each other's shoulder; the steam rising from the water wets our faces. I don't know whether it's my rampaging hormones or the heat of the bath that causes the sweat to streak my forehead. As my hands move under the water to stroke her sides, cup her buttocks, Jeanine turns her head to nuzzle my neck. I smile, remembering my first sight of her, how impossible it would have been for me then to imagine this joy that floods through me at the touch her lips on my throat. She was a thirtyish woman in dirty blue overalls whose black hair hung limp and straight to just below the ears. She was digging with a shovel in our front yard. I liked watching her work, her arms pushing and lifting, her back bent, then straight. Then I noticed her eyes, which are the color of old mahogany, the flash of interest that lit them when she looked at me. I noticed her mouth, with its full pouting lower lip. On the second day, she had washed her hair to shiny softness and wore clean overalls; she sat on the porch talking to me, smiling an invitation, before she started work. On the third day I began to help her.

Jeanine and I have often giggled, since, about her having been our gardener, remembering *Lady Chatterly's Lover*. Actually we are far from the classic master-servant model of dime-store romances, for she is only taking a break from the media jobs that have supported her very well during the past five years: now she luxuriates in physical exertion, the relative simplicity of her job as a gardener. If anyone comes from humble beginnings it would be I, daughter of a widowed mother who supported my sister and me by working as a cashier in movie theaters. Marriage was my way out of the crowded, threadbare apartment where we all slept in the same bed because there was only one; it was my ladder up and out of worry and want. I climbed it gladly.

I am feeling the flat, strong muscles of her upper back and shoulder, kneading them, smoothing them as Jeanine murmurs in appreciation, when suddenly she stiffens, sending a little tidal wave of hot water across my belly. Her head snaps back, her eyes widening.

"Was that a car in the drive!?"

I listen, hearing nothing.

Jeanine rises from the tub, her body streaming, and lunges for the window that faces on the driveway. "Oh, god, it's *Ralph!*"

The flat sound of a car door slamming rises from the driveway.

She comes back to stand next to the tub, her body arranged in odd, stiff angles of panic.

"What should I *do!*" she asks, her eyes on me pleadingly.

I sit in the hot water, surrounded by steam, and the nervousness erupts from me in a low giggle.

She is convulsed for a few moments too, and then she asks again, "But what should I *do?*" spreading her hands in a helpless gesture.

"Put on your clothes," I sputter "Quick!" For I can hear the sound of Ralph's opening the door downstairs, his footsteps in the living room.

She's pulling on little gray socks, they look so ridiculous, then her corduroy pants, her red shirt, over her wet body.

"He's in the kitchen now," I hiss. "Go down and talk to him."

"Oh, shit, my underpants!"

"I'll hide them."

She rubs the steamy mirror to clear it, looks at her red, moist face, her tangled hair.

I am still giggling.

Halfway out the door, Jeanine turns to me, fixing me with a fierce look.

"I *hate* this!"

Then I see only the smooth white-painted wood of the door.

In a few minutes I hear voices in the kitchen, Ralph and Jeanine carrying on a conversation. He has probably offered her a drink of freshly Osterized carrot juice; she has probably asked him about a book, something mildly exotic and hard to find, like *Initiates and Initiations in Tibet,* by Alexandra David-Neel. This bibliographic communication will make a safe cover for Jeanine's suspiciously flushed appearance, for when queried about esoteric volumes Ralph loses all connection with the world about him and goes off into his mind like an ancient labyrinthine library where one title leads him to the next in contented quest for the most worm-eaten, mildew-encrusted tome ever unearthed. He cares little for the content of these books, or for their physical beings; it is the search that brings color to his cheeks.

In my steamy hideaway, I let myself go, slipping down into the still-hot water, giving myself to the shudders of mirth that contort me. Downstairs, the voices go on, or Ralph's voice, that is. I can imagine his rapt face, the excited lift of his chin. And Jeanine looking at him with big, relieved eyes.

I do not see her again until the next Sunday. Ralph and I have come to the chanting session at the Clear Light Institute, of which he is a director. I had almost decided to stay home because I was suffering the weakness and heat that accompany my periods now. I've heard other women describe hot flashes, but this is different, not a flash but a constant deep radiating heat that leaves me sweaty and lethargic. I'd been in bed all afternoon, reading, when Ralph came to ask me if I wanted to go with him. On reflection, I decided the chanting and meditating might be just the thing to cool my raging blood.

"If women had written the Buddhist canon," I told Ralph as we drove across Berkeley, "there would be special meditations for menopause."

Ralph pondered this, and then began to tell me about the *Therigatha*, a volume of poems written by the first Buddhist nuns. "They were contemporaries of Buddha. They wrote in Pali, the ancient language. It's quite a volume … stories of monastic life, songs of their moments of enlightenment. …" He went on for the next ten minutes, telling me of the various translations, the whereabouts of the original and how it was found. This recital was so thoughtfully given, with such erudition and sensitivity, that I was filled with my fondness for Ralph, and reached to rub him gently on his arm.

The meditation room of the Clear Light Institute is hung with sumptuous Tibetan paintings on silk scrolls: blue-faced demons dance before spread fans of orange flames, green-skinned goddesses wave multiple arms. The panels of the walls are painted deep red and that clear flat blue that the Tibetans love. Gold leaf climbs the pillars. Perhaps thirty people sit on pillows, eyes closed, mouths open to sing the sacred syllables, these sounds which vibrate in the belly, in the throat, connecting one up to the great sound that is always echoing in the universe. Sometimes I really do feel that merging of sound, when the chant sings me, rather than I sing it, but tonight I'm restless, impatient with the slow droning, enduring my heat and dizziness. Maybe it was a mistake to come. I consider sneaking upstairs to sit in the lobby or on the porch.

Then Jeanine arrives. I *feel* her enter. It's a sensation like a cool hand slid up my back, signal to wake up. Opening my eyes I see that she has just slipped through the door, her embarrassment at being so late obvious in the stiff way she holds her shoulders. She wears a purple, loose top and jeans; her small feet are bare. A slim gold chain encircles one sun-bronzed ankle.

Does she know I'm here? My heart pounds. It takes all my strength not to call to her, not to lift my hand. Then I realize she has settled herself on a pillow to my right, facing me. Her attention falls over me like a cloak. I feel faint with excitement, knowing she has taken that seat to watch me.

The chant stops now, the last long syllable drawn out into the room by a few deep male voices, loud under the steady higher voices of the other men and the women. And then there is silence, a silence in which the chanting still exists, in which it has built a many-layered sensitivity. I can feel my body still vibrating as I settle myself for the half-hour silent meditation that always follows the chanting.

To ease the stiffness in my crossed legs, I shift position slightly, and then I place my right hand on my knee. A simple action, and simple to describe, but the significance of it is staggering. As I begin to move my hand toward my knee, I become aware that all her attention is focused upon it. There are an excruciating few moments of held breath as my arm moves, bringing my palm-down hand closer to the round promontory of my knee. Jeanine's watching with every cell of her body hangs upon me as if I lift her with my arm and move her through space. My arm is heavy, weighted with its mission, as it traverses the distance and pauses, my hand hovering just an inch above my knee. Then, with a sound not uttered, like the fluttering ahhhh of surrender, I let my fingers sink to touch the cloth of my skirt, my palm settles gently over the curve of my kneecap. It is as if the air has thickened to solidity. There is nothing in the room now but that hand resting upon that knee. It is enormous, utterly deserving of the passion Jeanine offers it. It is magically alight, pearly with the glow of its mysterious presence. The gilded pillars, the faces of demons and people, fall back before its mystic power.

I open my eyes slightly, to see from their corners the figure of Jeanine clenched forward, her mouth slack in dazzlement. I feel how tenderly my hand lies upon my knee, like a cloud of morning mist upon the top of a hill, poised there without weight, holding us both in a condition of grace.

After the chanting, we meet in the lobby. Ralph has gone off for a meeting with the directors, having touched me on the elbow and assured me he will not be long. This gentle patting of one another's arms seems to have developed into a rite between us, expressing the affection and shared inertia that bind us to each other. Jeanine is studiously not looking at me from the other side of the room, where she talks with one of the young male meditation teachers. So it is my turn to watch her. I like how she responds, even to this young man who is being a little too proprietary with the insistent tilt of his body toward her, his gaze intent upon her mouth. Jeanine hums with a steady enthusiasm when she is with people. He may imagine that her looking full into his eyes is designed to encourage his attentions, but it is only how she looks into everyone she meets. Her hair is sleek and glistening tonight, in that little Dutch-boy haircut that I find so humorous sometimes. The purple of her shirt sets off the brown skin of her throat.

Just now her eyes meet mine, and I find myself grinning in sheer pleasure. Jeanine excuses herself from the young man: she is suddenly before me.

Still smiling, I want to give her myself, my difficult day, my weakness.

As she reaches to hug me, I feel how sticky my skin is, how my body trembles inside.

"I'm sorry. I've been sweating so much. I must smell."

Holding me, she has lowered her head to my shoulder, her cheek against the thin damp cotton of my dress. "I *love* how you smell."

The words come to me as if from her arms, her collarbones, her thighs; and something is pushed aside in me.

"Ah, why are you crying?" Jeanine cups my cheek, wipes the tears with her thumb.

"Come with me," she whispers. "I want to hold you."

I hesitate, glancing around at the people in the lobby, who are chanting quietly in small groups, seemingly oblivious to us.

"I know just the place," Jeanine mutters as she leads me toward the stairway to the basement.

We descend narrow, winding steps to a corridor into which several doors open. At the end of the hall, Jeanine pushes aside a heavy curtain to lead me into a tiny dark room like a cave, lit only by small candles on an altar. This is the room set aside for individual meditation. Jeanine pulls the curtain tight at the door and fastens it, then turns to touch my wrist with cool, reassuring fingers. "You know when the curtain's pulled," she whispers, "no one would dare come in."

I look around, my eyes slowly adjusting to the dimness of this familiar room. It is perhaps ten feet square, with one meditation pillow placed near the door, the altar opposite. Rugs and tapestries cover its walls, muffling the sound of the prayer wheel that turns in the corner. The wheel is a tall wide cylinder wrapped in green paper, with a flounce of vibrant red. It hums in its turning, a sound steadily insistent in the room, spinning its assembled prayers out into the universe.

Jeanine folds me into its throbbing as she takes me in her arms. She holds me gently for a time, her chest rising as she breathes deeply.

This room is as dark, as enclosed, as a womb. Jeanine begins to sing with the prayer wheel, the tone like the pulsing of blood in our veins. She rocks me, comforting my body, smoothing my burning skin. Her smell merges now with the odor of incense that permeates the room. Slowly she moves her head back to seek my lips, and I taste her smooth moistness, mint, a slight reminder of the tea she drank after the chanting. Her lips move now, seeking me, her tongue asking questions of my mouth, and my answer is a quickness of breathing that shakes my chest. She teases, probes, tantalizes my own tongue to follow her movements; and I feel a tingling in my clitoris. Abruptly I want her closer and closer to me. I want to enfold her completely, draw her inside me.

The prayer wheel sings of sunshine, bright mountain air, a many-windowed monastery clinging to a cliff as Jeanine invites me to lie down on the layered rugs. "Here?!" I whisper. "How *can we?*" Her brown eyes smile at me, brilliant with desire. "No one will come … not with the curtain drawn. They'll think we're meditating."

I glance around, uncertain. The Buddha sits with closed eyes on the altar, minding his own business. The silks spread under him are the color of the soft inner tissues of the body; they glow richly red and rose in the candlelight. One large scroll painting hangs on the wall. It depicts a female deity dancing. She is nude except for a rope of jewels that snakes down between her breasts and laces across her thighs Her body is silvery, her face golden. Her eyebrows sweep up like birds above wrathful eyes. Her headdress depicts a pig carved of gold and encrusted with jewels.

But Jeanine is touching me, coaxing me, drawing me down until I look up to see the dark ceiling covered with paintings so old their colors have muddied. Now we lie breast to breast, and the heat of my body that has been so unwelcome all day intensifies. "Yes," Jeanine murmurs against my throat. "Oh, yes, love …" Her hands have lifted my loose dress to move beneath the cloth, cupping my breasts, her thumbs fluttering against my hardening nipples. She kisses me, her tongue moving deep in my mouth, and I feel myself opening to her, giving in to the heat of my body until it becomes a steady surge, powerful as an ocean wave. Jeanine rides the wave, swimming closer and closer to my center. Her hips move against mine, the firm mound of her pubic bone thrusting ever so subtly, tantalizing me with its pressure.

Then she pulls away a little, and I see that she has caught my heat, her cheeks flushed darkly, her eyes wildly shining. "We've got to take off your dress," she murmurs, "or it'll get all wrinkled and damp."

I glance at the curtained door. "But how can we …?"

"Yes, it'll be better …" To convince me, she lifts her purple shirt. For a moment her arms are held high, her torso lifted, and my body trembles with pleasure at the sight of her breasts, long and full, the nipples pink tight berries. She is stripping off the blue jeans, throwing them to the side. The ankle bracelet is a fragile gold line on her nude body.

"I'll help you." She lifts the dress higher, works it up over my head. And I am nude too, the air touching my skin.

Slowly she lowers herself to lie full length upon me, one leg between my thighs, and her pelvis seems to sink into mine. I am so without resistance. I feel her heart pumping in quick rhythm against my chest.

She begins to kiss my shoulder, and moves down my arm until her mouth finds the inside of my elbow. Her tongue licks the tender skin, her lips kiss wetly. My whole arm vibrates with pleasure, and I can feel my cunt opening under the weight and warmth of her body. She moves to my wrist now, her tongue examining every millimeter of sensitive skin, until she leaves it to kiss my palm, lingering.

Deftly, she lifts herself and moves down to smooth my thighs. She leans to kiss, her cheek brushing my pubic hair, beginning a hot throbbing in my cunt. She moves down to my knee, her mouth encircling my kneecap, tongue tracing its contour. Then she sucks the muscle just below the kneecap, sending flutters of energy up inside my thigh to my vagina. She moves down again, briefly stroking my calves, and arrives at my feet, which she holds in comforting hands. She kisses my instep, and then sucks, as I begin to moan.

I have opened my eyes to find the image of the deity dancing on the wall above me. Her breasts flicker in the dim light. An arm, a foot, are raised. She tilts toward the next step, establishing a rhythm that travels from her silvery body to mine. Moving, I join her in it, my hips circling now, slowly, subtly, my breasts lifting, hands braced against the rug.

Jeanine comes up to lie upon me, her mouth seeking my breast. I close my eyes as she kisses, teases, lifts and cradles, and I see the body of the silver woman moving in her passionate dance. I recognize those breasts, those neat narrow hips, the thickness of dark pubic curls. Opening my eyes, I see her face bent to my breast, the black hair falling forward, her look of intense concentration. Her lips close on my nipple and she sucks, tentatively at first, tenderly. Our movements happen together now, our hips and thighs undulating. Letting my head fall back, I close my eyes, giving in to this dance as Jeanine sucks more hungrily, her teeth closing with tantalizing care upon my hard, straining nipple. I thrust my breast into her mouth and she takes it, sucking in as much as will fill her mouth.

Her hand has moved down between my legs, seeking in my vagina, so wet and open. She slips her fingers into me, moving them inside, and the heel of her hand slowly rubs my tight clitoris. My clitoris is a nipple now, wanting to be sucked.

My hands grip Jeanine's back, kneading her shoulders, pressing her to me. We are slippery with sweat where we touch. My mouth is hungry to taste her.

Jeanine lifts up, turns, leaving my breast to cradle my hips, lifting her leg across me. Just before she lowers herself onto me, I look up into the dark expanse of hair between her thighs, reach to spread the small silkily pink lips of her vagina. On the wall above the moons of her buttocks, leaps the silver-bodied woman in ecstatic movement.

Then she is upon me, her mouth closing over my cunt, her breasts pressing into my belly, the weight of her hips on my shoulders, and, at last, the hot, soft opening of her vagina for my mouth to suck and stroke. Jeanine moans, moves in quick instinctive shudders as she settles on me. I receive the weight and feel of her whole body; it opens me more. My face is lost in her cunt. We have become one being, our movement taking us in an ancient joyous pattern. There is no inside or outside. There is only this movement, yet I know I grip Jeanine's buttocks, stroke her back, press her even closer inside me. Within the storm of desire are the subtle movements of the dance in our bodies, moving deep inside us, taking us to the moment of dissolution.

Jeanine hums into my vagina, the vibrations lifting my body as I hear the pulse of the prayer wheel loud in the room. We are nothing but sound now, carried out beyond the limits of our minds, as our movement becomes an uncontrollable undulation. I know only the pungent hot softness of her cunt, my face plunged into it to suck and suck. Her own sucking sends waves up through me. The urgency peaks, and there is a moment of wanting so intense it feels like pain. I thrust against her and her mouth presses on me, hard now, she'll stay with me, she'll come with me, I suck and suck.

The moment breaks. I turn my head to muffle my cries against the soft flesh of her thigh. Long high ragged sounds are torn from me. I feel her groan of completion vibrating into my cunt, as my hips jerk, my fingers twitch against her back.

And then we are free, floating outside our contours in emptiness. A stillness, a perfect stasis opens beneath us.

Peace.

I let my arms fall from her body as I lie beneath her. She has rested her cheek against my thigh, absolutely still.

Turning my head I open my eyes to see the dancing goddess once again. She has returned into her fixity, one bangled foot eternally raised. But I see that the expression of her open mouth, which I had interpreted as a fierce snarl, is instead a smile of such rending sweetness that it draws from me a long quavering sigh.

"Yes, love," Jeanine answers me. "Oh, yes, my darling," her breath hot against the inside of my thigh.

We hold each other for a long time before we are able to sit up. And then it is a while before she lifts the dress to slip it over my head, stopping to kiss me, our mouths slippery, wet with the heavy odor of our bodies. Then I watch the purple blouse eclipse her breasts, the jeans slip up over her thighs. We stand touching each other gently, hands on each other's waist, and I sink into those dark eyes, so open now, carrying me deep. The sound of the prayer wheel is a steady throb, reminding us of the eternity we have just left. As we lift the curtain to go out, I glance back at the woman whose body flashes in her dance, whose golden face beams at me.

When we stand outside the room, smoothing our clothes, we have entered another reality. A lighted corridor, blue-paneled, stretches away to the stairs. Closed doors flank us. Jeanine and I look at each other with wide open, sated eyes.

We wander off separately, I to find Ralph, who waits for me on the porch.

"You disappeared," he says, without reproach.

"Feeling better?" he asks as he helps me into the car. And as he gets in the other side he fixes me with a concerned gaze. "You look ... hmmm ... more relaxed ..."

I can only nod, mutely gazing at his long serious face.

We drive beneath old trees, heavily black and looming in the dark. High above is the pale crescent of moon. The night seems ancient beyond believing.

MEETING
IMELDA MARCOS

THREE WEEKS AFTER his return to the States and the dank chill of Washington in winter, Jim Goodall drove down to Virginia Beach for his nephew's wedding. The occasion only deepened his low spirits. He was forty-five years old and useless in the world. Marcos had seized power by declaring martial law and Kissinger supported the ruse, despite everything Jim and a few others had reported from Manila. Robbie dropped out of college and married a nice girl who worked in a Fotomat, despite Jim's years of hoping for something original from the boy.

At the reception at the Ramada Inn, his sister's family exiled Jim in his perfect Hong Kong-tailored tux to a small table with his niece, Meg, her new boyfriend from William and Mary, and a wet-eyed old woman in a beige wig whom nobody seemed to know. The rest of the family shared the big table up front with the raucous new in-laws. Jim had learned over the years one can't improvise a personal life through someone else's family, but it hurt to be reminded again how superfluous he was.

"Poor old Robbie," Meg scoffed. "So proud and smug up there. Like marriage was the Nobel prize. Well, even dork brothers deserve to be happy."

She sounded more good-humored than nasty about it, a witty twist to her mouth. Meg seemed to be at an age where she saw through everyone, and wanted people to know. Jim wondered if she saw through him. He had to remind himself repeatedly she was nineteen now, because he couldn't look at her baby-fat cheeks or large brown eyes without seeing his niece at fifteen, ten or seven, as if she would always be the little tomboy who admired him without reason, who disappeared a half hour before he ended each visit because goodbyes embarrassed her. Today she wore a velvety blue dress with a high womanly collar, but her long straight hair and lack of lipstick suggested a girl in jeans and a sweater.

"You feeling okay, Jim?" She'd been dropping the "uncle" all day, as if toying with who they were to each other.

"I always cry at weddings," Jim teased.

"If they really were in love," said Meg, "they would've eloped. This is like they need to act it out in front of people to tell themselves it's real."

"Bad faith," said the boyfriend, nibbling at a wingette. "This must seem rather comical, sir. After embassy parties, dinners with dictators."

"Not at all," Jim replied. "This is family."

The boyfriend, Doug, was terribly polite and respectful, but phrases constantly popped out, which suggested he thought Jim was the enemy. His dull blond hair tied back in a ponytail, anemic sideburns and faint stars of acne on his pale face, he looked like the kind of cocky student who'd consider anyone with the Establishment the enemy. His mouth kept closing in a placid, lipless smile.

"Doug read your piece in *Foreign Affairs*," said Meg. "Before he knew we were related. Doug reads almost everything."

Doug smiled at Jim. "I'm just curious. Power fascinates me. Corruption, too."

There were the usual rituals after the cake, but Meg didn't join the girls jumping for the bouquet, and neither Jim nor Doug got up for the bride's garter. Dancing followed and Meg and Doug sat that out too, but Jim went over and asked his sister for a dance.

"It's almost over," Ann groaned through her grin while Jim gingerly steered her around the floor. Looking lively and inexhaustible from across the room, she appeared shell-shocked up close, her grin a weary baring of teeth. "You're welcomed to come back to the house afterwards. But Rick and I are just going to collapse."

"I should go back to the motel and collapse myself, thank you."

"Might be best all around." Ann sounded relieved. "You been having a good chat with your niece?"

"She's becoming quite the woman," Jim said automatically.

"Still waters run deep. I don't know what to make of this Doug. Two of a kind, eggheads both of them. You were like that at their age. What do you make of him?"

"He seems nice enough. Well-spoken. Polite."

"Too polite," said Ann. "I wish he didn't remind me of Eddie Haskell."

The music changed and Jim and Ann stepped off to the side to make their goodbyes. Ann patted Jim's stomach, a new gesture. His brother-in-law's stomach bulged badly in his rented tux and Jim wondered if Ann missed the presence of a flat male stomach in her household.

"But you had a nice time? Did it make you feel sorry you never got married?"

"A little," Jim lied. He loved his sister and needed to humor her. He kissed her goodbye on the cheek, thanked her for inviting him and returned to the table to say good night to Meg.

"We were leaving too," said Meg. "In fact, Doug and I were wondering if you'd like company. It's going to be a regular marriage morgue back at the house."

Jim had thought he wanted to be alone, but he liked the idea. Ann was concerned about Meg; maybe she needed his advice. He invited them back to his motel, warning them he was in no shape to do anything except sit and talk. On their way out, Jim noticed Robbie dancing and laughing with his bride and long-haired buddies, having too good a time to notice old Uncle Jim's departure.

His motel was down at the oceanfront, ten miles away. Meg rode with Jim, Doug following in his yellow Volkswagen bug.

It was cold in Jim's car and Meg kicked off her shoes to sit on her nyloned feet.

"Good to see you again, Meg-wump. Been what? Almost four years. And now you're in college. I can hardly believe it. Where have all the flowers gone?" Jim used to know how to talk to his niece, but tonight he heard himself babbling.

"God I hate family," said Meg. "Oh, not you, Jim. You were smart to go off on your own. My nuclear family. There's times I'd like to nuke *them*."

Meg claimed Robbie's wedding had given her parents marriage fever. All through Christmas break she'd been feeling everyone thought she should be the one dropping out to make grandchildren, that money for a college education was wasted on a girl. Jim enjoyed being an ear for her unhappiness; it made him feel tender.

"They don't think that," Jim assured her. "Your mother finished college."

"And look what she did with it," Meg muttered. "What do you think of Doug?"

"Doug? Well-spoken. Polite." Jim decided he should return Meg's trust with honesty. "I just met him, but he seems bland to me. Unformed. Young."

"Really?" Meg sounded intrigued by his disapproval, not hurt. "You know, he really wanted to meet you."

Jim hesitated, then snorted. "The family eccentric? The black sheep?"

"*I'm* the black sheep," Meg insisted. "But seriously. Doug was curious about you. He's interested in foreign policy and life overseas. I kind of used you as bait to get him down here for the wedding."

He wouldn't visit without bait? What kind of boyfriend was that? Jim looked in the rearview mirror and saw the yellow Volkswagen puttering close behind them. A streetlight swept overhead and there was a glimpse of Doug at the wheel, pale and vague, his mouth lightly sealed in that catlike smile. "I take it *you* like him."

"Oh, yeah." Meg had roped some hair around her fingers; she gave it a tug. "I think I'm in love with him. Or something."

Ocean boiled and snored in the darkness out beyond the empty parking lot of Jim's motel. As they stepped inside, Jim found himself irritably conscious of Doug. Ponytail whisking from side to side, the boy walked with Meg with his hands in the pockets of his bulky army jacket, showing more interest in the layout of the motel than in Meg or her uncle. The boy wasn't unattractive, yet there was nothing lovably solid about him. He seemed self-effacing, yet something about him suggested he smugly believed he would never be invisiible.

"What did you guys want to do?" Jim asked in his room. "Watch television? Talk about the weather? I'm afraid there's nothing I can offer you to drink."

Meg and Doug said they'd drunk too much already. They sat together on the bed.

Jim opened the curtains. The ocean was barely visible through the reflection in the sliding glass door, rows of silent white breakers floating through the image of a motel room. Jim watched himself there while he undid his bow tie and shook off his black jacket. His red hair was thinning, his face still burned from Manila. Jim never tanned, only burned, peeled, then burned again. He expected Meg and Doug to hold hands, but they didn't. This generation must express love—"Or something"—differently.

They talked. Actually, Doug and Jim did most of the talking, Jim seated in a chair at the vanity table, Doug at the foot of the bed. Meg sat beside Doug, leaning back on her elbows, calmly watching the men.

"But you were mainly in Manila, Mr. Goodall? Never Vietnam?"

"Oh, made a few inspection tours of the embassy in Saigon when I was with INR. Odd city. More like an American service town than anything Asian, until recently. You hardly know there's a war going on until you get out in the countryside." But Jim couldn't talk about that. "No, Manila, Singapore for six months, Bangkok. A year in Finland to keep me from going native."

"Do you think the Paris Peace Accords are close to getting signed or did Kissinger say that just to get Nixon reelected?"

"They'll get signed. Soon." Which was what made Kissinger and the rest so blindly confident about their decisions. Jim couldn't discuss that either.

"Doug and I are going up for the Inauguration next week," said Meg.

"You don't say. Seats in the President's box?" Jim teased.

Meg frowned.

"There's a protest rally," Doug explained. "A kind of anti-Inauguration on the Mall. They're expecting hundreds of thousands."

"I see." Jim hadn't pictured his niece taking part in any of the demonstrations and rallies he read about overseas. He wondered if this were Doug's doing.

"Do you disapprove, Uncle Jim?" Meg used his title mockingly.

"Not at all. I came to the conclusion years ago this war was a mistake. To protest now is to flog a dead horse, I feel, what with the talks in Paris. But no, if you believe in this rally, you should go. Just be careful."

Meg's mouth remained budded in an angry pout. What other response had she wanted from him? She suddenly locked eyes with him and said, "Uncle Jim? Do you smoke grass?"

He blinked, but refused to be intimidated. "Why? Do you have some?"

"As a matter of fact—"

She grabbed at Doug's army jacket heaped on the bed behind her. Doug smiled sheepishly at Jim and nervously watched Meg, who took a cigarette pack from one of his pockets. She dug into the pack with two tiny fingers and brought out a tightly rolled joint.

"What're you doing, Meg-wump? You out to shock poor Uncle Jim?"

"Not shock. Share. I always thought you were someone I'd like to get high with." She placed the joint in her mouth and lit it, smiling at him.

Doug glanced around the room, pretending not to be there.

She passed the joint to Jim, who sniffed at it, tasted it, then took a deep toke. He didn't understand what game she was playing, but he played along, flicking ash like a connoisseur and saying, "Harsh. We get better over there." He passed the joint to Doug.

The tips of Doug's fumbly fingers were very cold and soft.

They passed the joint around, Meg watching Jim, pleased with him, intrigued. Her calm brown eyes disturbed him, as if someone else scrutinized Jim from the back of her head. He tried winking at Meg to break the stare. Not looking at what he was doing, his hand stumbled around Doug's hand, until Doug had to grip Jim's fingers to take the joint. Touch lingered like a mild electric shock in his knuckles.

"That's enough," said Jim the next time the joint came to him. He wetted his fingertips and snuffed the thing out. "You two have to drive back."

He stood up to crack the sliding glass door. An icy jet of salt air reminded him where he was. Everything he associated with this burned muddy smell was on the other side of the world. He wasn't stoned; he was remembering.

Sitting on the bed, Meg held Doug and grinned into his armpit. Doug looked only uncomfortable, indifferent, vague. He gave another sheepish smile to Jim, as if he were more concerned with what Jim thought than with what Meg was feeling.

Jim suddenly understood. Meg loved a boy who didn't love back. And the first reason Jim could imagine for any man not to love his niece was that the man must be just like Jim. A feeling of indignation came over him, and protectiveness.

He returned to his chair. With a note of reprimand in his voice, he told Doug, "I love my niece."

"A terrific person," said Doug, parking his hand on her shoulder.

"Guys," Meg groaned. "Can't we talk about something else?"

Jim finished his challenge. "And I'd hate to see her hurt in any way."

Doug looked blank.

Meg looked annoyed. "Why're you getting so sanctimonious, Jim? Just grass. You smoked some yourself."

Jim loved the girl and wanted to protect her. But just as one had to be careful saving a small country from itself, one had to be doubly prudent with a niece.

"I'm not a dope-a-holic," Meg insisted. "I thought it'd be fun to get high with you. And I wanted you to see I'm not naive little Meg-wump anymore."

"I wasn't referring to the grass," said Jim. "I meant only …" He looked into Doug's eyes. He smiled apologetically at Meg. "Just showing my concern for your future. In a clumsy, uncle-ish manner."

Meg laughed at him. "Are you stoned? I'm not stoned. Doug, are you? We didn't smoke enough to stone a hamster. Did we? No. We're *not* stoned."

Doug was boyish without being pretty, pale and thin without grace or effeminacy. Jim knew appearances meant nothing, but he looked for something to support his suspicion. The boy's eyes were a washed-out blue, his eyelashes long and colorless.

"We should be heading back," Doug told Meg.

Jim needed to know. He had a responsibility to Meg to learn the truth and protect her with it. She didn't know men the way Jim did. "When you came up for this rally," he asked, "were you coming up for the day or did you plan to spend some time in D.C.?"

They were planning to spend the entire weekend, staying with Doug's family across the river in Fairfax. Jim should've guessed Doug was from inside the Beltway; he had that suburban Washington knowingness about politics, unlike the cynical indifference of people down here, such as Jim's brother-in-law. Perhaps Doug's sociable ambiguity was merely the result of growing up among bureaucrats.

"Did you want to come with us to the rally?" Meg asked.

"That's an idea. Or another possibility: I've been invited to a round of parties the night before the Inauguration. All Democrat, of course, but lots of bigwigs. Would the two of you be interested in that?"

Doug looked interested. Meg asked, "Would we have to dress up?"

"What you wore today would be fine. It would give you a chance to see your uncle's world firsthand, Meg." It would give Jim a chance to study Doug. "And Mrs. Marcos is coming to town. I could introduce you to her."

Imelda Marcos was not quite a household name in 1973, but Doug knew who she was. His eyes lit up and he told Meg, "Imelda herself! Wouldn't that be wild? Can't you just hear Harry and Jane when we tell them we met Imelda?"

Meg was already tempted and Doug's excitement convinced her completely. Everything was arranged. Still on semester break, Meg was riding up to Fairfax on Friday afternoon to join Doug. They'd come into town that night, meet Jim at his apartment near Dupont Circle and he'd take them on a tour of parties inside the very government they'd be protesting the next day. The duplicity was part of the night's appeal. Meg became more excited. Doug became hesitant for a moment, perhaps wondering why a grown man wanted to share an important evening with two college kids. Jim wondered himself.

Doug gave Jim a firm handshake at the door—"Been a pleasure, sir. We'll look forward to next week"—and Meg kissed Jim on the cheek, importantly, almost gratefully. They went down the hall with their arms around each other's waist, Doug holding on to Meg very, very tightly.

Jim closed the door, sat on his bed and said aloud, "What in blazes are you doing, Goodall?" Now that Meg's boyfriend was out of sight, he could find no reason for suspecting him. It was like a temporary insanity brought on by the wedding, anxiety over his return to Washington, and the fact he could no longer fly out to Bangkok for a weekend whenever he felt like it. He didn't think he felt like it now, but after a lifetime of celibacy followed by the past three years of controlled indulgence, Jim understood his libido well enough to know sexual frustration was in there somewhere. Not that he was sexually attracted to Doug. The boy was too unformed, bookish and familiar, too American. Jim seemed sexually attracted to the idea of protecting Meg, even though she might not need to be protected. He should forget the whole thing.

Driving back to D.C. the next day, through the dreary grayness of Virginia in January, Jim thought more about Doug and Meg and found his sexual interest gone. All that remained were the abstract questions, the problem-solving aspects. If this Doug were homosexual, what then? Did he tell Meg? Did he confront Doug and persuade him to break off with his niece? Knowing the truth was just the beginning. Jim was relieved the entire business existed only in his unhappy imagination. He went to the State Department gym as soon as he got back, worked off his tensions in a good game of racquetball with a divorced bureau chief and felt much better.

The week passed slowly. Jim was walking the corridors since his return from Manila, in limbo between assignments. He had so little to do he was pleased when one of Imelda's Blue Ladies, her entourage of hired friends, called to ask for help in getting into the Inaugural Ball. Jim had a few last-minute regrets about the task of chaperoning a niece through a night of stuffy parties, but decided it'd be good to have someone with whom he could share the jokes and comments he usually had to keep to himself.

Friday arrived and he picked up the tux he'd had cleaned and pressed after the wedding. Cleaners all over the city were swamped with evening clothes that week. Jim preferred the simpler life of his studio apartment here to the complicated households he had to keep overseas, yet there were nights like tonight when he missed having a couple of servants to launder his clothes or shine his shoes. He sat on a stool in his underwear and polished his shoes himself, then washed his hands and finished getting dressed.

The doorman buzzed to say there was a Mr. Brattle to see him. It took Jim a moment to remember Brattle was Doug's last name. "Send them up, Zack."

A minute later Jim opened the door. Doug stood in the hall, wearing the same navy blazer, wide necktie and ratty army jacket he had worn at the wedding. He was alone. "Hello, Mr. Goodall."

"Where's Meg?" said Jim.

"Ah, Meg. Well, sir. Meg's running late and"—Doug explained how Meg's ride from Virginia Beach left later than scheduled and she wouldn't get to Doug's house until after midnight—"she said we were to go ahead without her and I'll see her tonight when I get home. Oh, and I'm supposed to arrange for us to meet somewhere tomorrow, at the rally or parade, whichever makes you more comfortable."

Doug spoke quickly, smiling his placid smile, arrogantly looking Jim in the eye. He had both hands in the pockets of his army jacket.

"Dammit, is that the only coat you own?" Jim barked.

"What?" Smile and arrogance disappeared; the boy looked frightened. "I'm sorry. I didn't think—"

"Here." Jim went to his closet and grabbed the tweed overcoat he bought twenty years ago when he thought he'd be in Europe. "Out of style, but they'll think you're a damn terrorist in that thing," he said, trying to sound more friendly. "Come along. We're cabbing it tonight."

Jim hurried them downstairs and out into the cold. He remained angry with Doug, not for the coat but for coming without Meg. He didn't know what to say to Doug, how to talk to him. Meg was their only bond. Doug, too, seemed lost without her. His self-assurance was gone and his tone changed wildly. "I'll try not to embarrass you," he said in a small pathetic voice during the cab ride to the Cosmos Club. "The powers that be," he smugly declared, looking out at the large wainscotted room full of important people in expensive clothes. "Drinking champagne out of plastic goblets."

Not until they were at the first party did Jim realize what people might assume about him and this boy. Everyone knew Goodall was a bachelor. He considered introducing Doug as his nephew, until he remembered "nephew" was also a euphemism. Then Jim noticed other young people in the room, a scattering of males and females, some dressed as elegant miniatures of the adults, others looking as shabbily collegiate as Doug. The boy did not stand out. If only he would mingle on his own and stop following Jim like a nervous puppy.

"The bar's over there, Doug. That's the buffet table if you're hungry. You'll have to excuse me, I have business to discuss."

Actually, Jim had nothing to do tonight except make appearances at three different parties. To escape Doug, he let himself be trapped in a conversation with Mrs. Weed, wife of a former ambassador to Burma. She wore an odd metal collar that went up to her chin with what looked like a bit of tractor tread hanging below. Jim didn't know her well enough to ask if this were fashion or a neck injury. Listening to stories about Mr. Weed's hunting trip in Kenya, Jim glanced past the cogwheel earrings and watched Doug down drinks at the bar.

The next party was in a hotel ballroom. They spent more time checking and unchecking coats than they did among the guests, union people and the few Congressmen the unions still elected. The backslapping was loud and incessant.

"Fascinating. Very fascinating," said Doug while they waited in line outside for the doorman to find them a cab. Doug's cheeks and ears were pink, his thin lips relaxed in that meaningless smile again. "Like wandering in and out of scenes from *War and Peace*."

"With disposable cups," Jim reminded him. But he found Doug less irritating now, almost pleasant to be with. He had had a few drinks himself. "I'm glad to hear you're enjoying this. It's still a pity Meg couldn't join us."

"Yeah, well, Meg's great and all that. But there's times she can be a drag, always needing to be the center of attention. This is more fun without her."

And Jim was annoyed with Doug all over again. "That's a strange way for a man to talk about the woman he loves."

Doug shrugged inside the enormous overcoat and smiled at Jim. "I guess I'm not a conventionally passionate person."

Which was similar to the excuses Jim had given himself in college and law school before he understood his real reason for not looking for a wife. At least he'd been considerate enough not to mislead anyone before coming into knowledge. Doug seemed less considerate than Jim had been, more selfish.

"Hey, Jim," said Doug as they climbed into a cab. "You promised me Imelda Marcos."

Alcohol made the boy terribly forward. "Maybe the next stop," said Jim. "If we're not too late."

The last party was in a posh residential neighborhood off Wisconsin Avenue. A fleet of matching limos parked up and down the tree-lined street announced Imelda and her court were still inside the enormous Tudor house surrounded by boxwood. Jim immediately saw her from the entrance hall. She sat in a wing-backed chair, which had been moved to the center of the living room, circled by laughing men and women. Her olive-skinned hand with its gold bracelets gracefully twisted and turned like a charmed cobra while she spoke.

"Is that a boyfriend behind her?" Doug asked much too loudly.

Jim whispered, "No. Just Jack Valenti. A family friend."

"We going to talk to her?"

"In a minute." Jim assumed Imelda was doing the entire circuit, Democrats tonight, Republicans tomorrow. He hoped she might leave before he had a chance to approach her. She made him oddly nervous tonight, perhaps because he no longer had the armor of an official role to play with her. He motioned Doug toward the grand piano, where a sulky pianist played jazz variations on the Philippine national anthem.

"But she *will* talk to you," said Doug. "Even if you're her husband's enemy?"

Jim grimaced. "Not enemy," he whispered. "Critic. A foreign service officer can't afford to be anyone's enemy. Besides, she can't imagine they have enemies. Only misunderstandings, which she thinks she can sweet talk you out of." She had tried it a few times with Jim, on a lewdly narrow loveseat. His colleagues came away from this treatment nervous wrecks, but not Jim. You can't sexually intimidate someone whose compass points elsewhere. Yet it was all a game that affected nothing.

Thinking about Imelda, Jim found himself staring at Doug. He had to confront the boy about Meg. He would not be as ineffectual here as he had been over there.

"Let's go meet Imelda," he said and grabbed Doug's arm. He led him across the room, wanting to get this over with as quickly as possible so he could be alone with the boy.

"*Jeem.* How nice to see you again."

A gracious winner, Imelda was her sweet, genially corrupt self tonight. She looked up at him with perfectly stenciled eyebrows and smile, still Miss Manila of 1953 and incapable of showing an honest emotion. Her face was on too tight.

"We were *so* sorry when they took you from us," she said poutily. "Washington must've needed you *so* badly." No trace of sarcasm came through. She offered him a handful of bright red beetles, her enameled fingernails.

Her touch shamed Jim with memories of failure and helplessness. "I have someone who'd like to meet you, Madam President. Douglas Brattle, a friend of my niece."

"*Imelda Marcos!* Madam President, I mean. This is such an honor!" Doug bowed when he took her hand, looking ready to kiss it. He was as fulsome and fawning as Imelda herself.

"Douglas? That is our favorite American name in my country. I didn't know Jim had a niece. That's good. Family is important to us too."

Jim stood by while Imelda flirted and Doug gushed. The boy was so slippery. If Jim confronted him about his sexuality in words, Doug would deny it, just as Imelda had denied artful accusations about her husband's ruthlessness and her brother's greed. Words were good only for diplomatic courtesy and lies.

"We won't take up any more of your time, Madam President. I trust you'll enjoy the weekend festivities." Jim set his hand on Doug's knobby shoulder to lead him away—and suddenly knew what he had to do to protect Meg.

"Thank you so much, Jim. And it was a pleasure meeting *you*, young man."

Doug grinned goodbyes and final compliments and Jim had to push him toward the door, resisting an urge to grab his ponytail and drag him out. His hand pressed against the bone and muscle beneath the boy's clothes.

"The dragon lady herself," Doug clucked while they pulled on their coats. "This year's model, anyway. What a weird, seductive woman."

"Only with those who want to be seduced." Jim had never seduced anyone in his life. Even in legal arrangements, he simply presented the facts and stood back, making no attempt to charm or bully his way through. Did he actually intend to seduce Doug? He was irritated enough to feel ruthless for the sake of his niece. Without knowing how far he should take it, Jim looked for a way to begin.

They took a cab that had dropped off two laughing Navy officers and their dates. Jim gave directions to the driver, then turned to Doug and said, "You've had an awful lot to drink. Are you sober enough to drive home?"

"Am I?" Doug touched his cheeks and forehead, grinning. "I'm so excited right now, I don't know what I feel."

"I'll fix some coffee when we get back to my place. I don't want to have to worry about you on the road." Jim spoke brusquely, harshly. "If worse comes to worse, I suppose you *could* sleep over."

"Oh? Oh," said Doug. "No. I'll be okay," and he went off on Imelda again, asking if it were true she sang "Hello Dolly" at the White House for LBJ.

When they arrived at Jim's building, Doug swayed when he got out of the cab. "Damn. Maybe I did drink too much."

"I thought so," Jim scolded. "Well, come on up and I'll make coffee. You have to get your coat and give me mine back, anyway."

"Right," said Doug and he followed Jim inside. "Maybe I should call the house and see if Meg's there yet," he announced in the elevator.

Upstairs, Jim put the kettle on and took off his tux while Doug called home. The apartment felt much too warm. Jim tried to plan his next move. In the Patpong in Bangkok, just being on the right street said it all. A middle-aged American wearing sunglasses in bars, Jim knew he looked like either a secret agent or a blind man. The "gift" of crisp baht notes afterward made it as natural as buying dinner. Jim felt like an awkward teenager in more personal, informal transactions.

"Uh-huh. Uh-huh. You don't have to wait up for her, Mom. Can't Barney? You're not excited I met someone famous? No, she's Argentina, Imelda's the Philippines. It's like meeting Mrs. Adolf Hitler! A few drinks, yeah. Champagne, some bourbon. A little, but—" Doug glanced over at Jim, who stood half behind the open door of his closet. The boy sounded more drunk on the phone than he had in the cab. "Sure. But what about my guest? No, we're riding in tomorrow with Harry and Jane."

Jim kept his trousers on but hung up everything else. He tucked his shoes into their pocket of the shoe bag on the inside of the door. His undershirt fit snugly over his shoulders and flat stomach. When he came out from behind the door, Doug was off the phone and looking thoughtful on the sofa.

"Meg's still not there?" Jim asked.

"No. But the people she's riding with live on Old South Time. They do everything a couple of hours late. Uh, my mother thinks I'm drunk and wants me to ask if I can spend the night." Doug rolled his eyes over his mother.

"I said you could." That the boy's mother *wanted* him here put a different light on what Jim intended. But Jim was doing this for his family, not Doug's. "You won't be needing coffee then." Jim stepped into the kitchen to turn off the boiling water. "Would you like a nightcap?" he called out.

"Sure. Why not?"

Jim never drank alone, so his kitchen cabinet was full of bottles of liquor given as presents over the years. He filled two tumblers with Dutch herb-flavored gin, which should be enough to keep Doug loose without making him pass out. He wanted to seduce the boy, not rape him.

"Here's a new experience for you," he said, gave Doug a tumbler and told him what it was. He sat on the sofa beside Doug. It wasn't a loveseat, but sitting a foot from the boy should suggest something.

"Different," said Doug after taking a sip.

Jim leaned in closer, setting his arm on the back of the sofa. He was at a loss as to what to say or do next. He was no Imelda Marcos.

Doug smiled at Jim and took another sip. His ponytail flopped over his shoulder and Doug gripped it with one hand while he held the tumbler with the other.

"Your hair," said Jim, seeing a subject. "I thought only fire-breathing radicals wore their hair long."

"I'm radical," said Doug. "In my fashion." He stroked his ponytail. "I just like the way it feels."

"Do you wear it loose or tied up when you go to bed?"

"Tied up. Or it gets all tangled. Will I be sleeping out here on the sofa?"

Jim narrowed his eyes at Doug. "There is no in and out here. It's a studio apartment. And *this*"—he patted the back of the sofa—"is a sofa bed."

Doug looked over the square-armed, salmon-plaid sofa, then at the rest of the neat, spartan apartment. "This is all you can afford?"

"It's all I need when I'm in the States." Jim was confused by the boy's calm, his failure to be disturbed by Jim leaning over him, his easy acceptance of the fact they'd be sleeping together. Attempting a suggestive gaze, Jim lowered his voice and said, "Maybe we should be going to bed?"

"Okay." Doug calmly finished his gin, stood up and began to undress.

Jim wondered again if he'd misread Doug. The boy took off his blazer and unknotted his tie as matter-of-factly as someone who thought only of sleep. Jim stacked the sofa cushions and set them in their corner. He gripped the handles and unfolded the bed across the room. He presented the fact of a bed, and even that failed to make an impression.

"Right out," said Doug and he went into the bathroom and closed the door.

Jim hung up his trousers and removed his socks and garters. A man in garters was too absurd to seduce anyone. The whole situation was absurd and Jim didn't think there was going to be a seduction. Maybe the boy wasn't homosexual after all. Or maybe he was, but so indifferent to old men Jim didn't register as a sexual possibility. Jim looked down at himself, his undershirt tucked into his blue silk boxer shorts, his arms covered with copper hair and the seams of dried skin left by all his burnings and peelings. Jim felt too old to be playing this game. Waiting for Doug to finish in the bathroom, he turned off all the lights except the reading lamp beside the bed.

The toilet flushed and Doug came out, yawning. His shirt and undershirt were in one hand, his pale chest ribbed and hairless. He saw Jim standing importantly beside the bed. He padded around to the other side, tossed his things on a chair and stood there, shyly looking down at his belt buckle.

"You know," he said, "I've never been to bed with a man."

The sudden acknowledgment of sex startled Jim. His first reaction was to turn it against the boy. "Is that a disclaimer, Doug, or a proposition?"

Doug looked at Jim, his mouth pulled straight, his eyes nervous and apologetic. "I just wanted to know what was going on here."

"You tell me." Jim pulled his undershirt over his head. If Doug could be bare-chested, so could Jim. They seemed to be daring each other to declare himself; Jim refused to declare himself further than Doug had. Mystery was power.

Doug frowned, then shrugged the matter aside and unbuckled his belt. "I'm zonked," he said, stepped out of his trousers and draped them over the chair. His white briefs hung across his hips like a loose bandage. He stood flicking the waistband with his thumbs, looking down at the bed, not looking at Jim. His thighs were pebbled with goosebumps. He pulled off the briefs and slid under the blankets.

Jim pulled off his shorts as he turned off the light. Climbing into the dark, he wondered if Doug meant to trick him into making a fool of himself. Or if the boy intended to submit passively to the old man out of fear and good manners. Or if Doug always slept nude and was simply declaring his innocence.

You think too much, Jim told himself two seconds later.

They were instantly all over each other. Hands, legs and mouth, Doug turned into a different person, his kissing all tongue and teeth, his long bare length wildly three-dimensional. The world was usually so flat and remote.

"Ah! Never held another guy's dick. Hold mine. Oh, yeah."

Unafraid of seeming depraved or corny, Doug was in a hurry to touch and try everything, even scooting down to try that, timidly at first, then ineptly, his breath and long hair tickling. Jim was accustomed to more Buddhist lovemaking, leisurely and proficient, and a different set of smells. Doug smelled strongly of baby shampoo and faintly like butter. Jim palmed the small bottom in one hand while the boy eagerly humped himself against Jim's groin. Even his finish felt new and Western, a grimace followed by groans, a sharp cry and the tossing back of his head. The face was so close Jim needed his reading glasses.

He fell on Jim's chest, rolled off and lay on his back, rib cage heaving.

The blankets were thrown on the floor and Jim's eyes had adjusted to the dark. He wanted to finish too, then the strangeness of it all began to catch up with him. This was different from his friendly, professional encounters, dreams of sex where he went to bed with nations not individuals. This was someone Jim knew in the real world, specific and familiar. It felt like incest even without the involvement of a niece. Jim was remembering he had intended to do this for Meg.

Doug lay there with one hand over his eyes, gasping like a landed fish. "I'm sorry," he said in a hurt voice. "I feel awful all of a sudden."

Jim was uncertain how to respond to that; it sounded as excessive as Doug's finish. "You seemed to enjoy yourself," he said dryly.

"I guess." He lifted his hand and smiled weakly at Jim. "So. You are gay, aren't you?"

"Like you," said Jim, although he found that word too slangy, too coy.

"I don't know," Doug sighed. "I feel so bad I must be straight."

"After sex all animals are sad." Jim spoke from experience.

Doug took a deep breath and worriedly asked, "There, uh, something you want me to do for you?"

"Be honest with Meg."

Doug lay still a moment. "I meant so you could have an orgasm."

"I know what you meant." Jim was afraid of what he'd feel after sex. And he wanted to use his failure to finish as proof to himself that he had really done this for Meg. He wasn't convinced.

"If you're sure you don't want anything, is there something I can wipe off with?"

Jim went to the bathroom to get a towel. He remembered other conversations after sex, all the cheerful questions about American music, appliances and farm animals. This was going to be more intimate and unpleasant.

Jim sat at the foot of the bed. Doug shyly rolled away while he used the towel.

"What's Meg told you about me?" he asked Jim.

"Very little. That you're smart. Book smart anyway. And that she's in love with you."

"Yeah. Well." He reached down for his briefs, then decided he didn't need them. His ponytail had come undone and he used both hands to draw his weeping willow of hair behind his shoulders as he sat against the sofa part of the bed. "She's told me lots about you. How you're the one interesting person in her family. How I shouldn't be misled by the way you sometimes talk like a used car salesman. How you took her to *Lawrence of Arabia* when she was ten years old and she caught you crying in a couple of scenes." Doug drew his knees up to his chest. "She thinks you might be gay, you know."

Jim froze. He didn't want to believe anyone in the family knew, not even Meg. "A common assumption about a bachelor uncle," he muttered. "A cliché, in fact." Yet something in him was thrilled Meg guessed at him correctly.

"But you are gay," said Doug.

"Does she suspect you are?"

"She knows men fascinate me in a way women don't. Intellectually, sometimes emotionally. Maybe I'm just horny and curious. I don't know. But Meg gets threatened and angry about that. She's kind of a feminist, about herself. She doesn't particularly like other women."

Jim listened with half an ear, wondering why he should feel pleased Meg knew about him. He felt less alone in the world, which was frightening.

"Meg's very perceptive about other people. But she was only half right about you." Doug smiled. "She thinks you're gay, but so moral and repressed you probably don't even know it."

Hearing how he looked in Meg's eyes finished changing her in Jim's. She was an intelligent, emotional adult, capable of understanding what had happened here, capable of judging him. The rules had changed since he was their age, but not that much. The idea of Meg hating him gave her a solidity and importance she had never had before.

"I sure proved her wrong on that one," Doug crowed. "Oh, she doesn't look down on you for being innocent. She might even envy you. Despite everything she says, Meg has very mixed feelings about sex."

"You've slept with her?"

"Oh, yeah, several—" Doug stopped, remembering who Jim was. Then he laughed and shook his head. "This is too weird. It's not like you and I have anything to hide from each other," he said, lowering his knees and uncovering himself. "We have sex. Not very often. I feel funny not feeling about her the way she feels about me."

He was so blithe about it, his guilt or depression completely gone. Yet Jim couldn't feel indignant for Meg's sake. The angry protectiveness that had brought this about was numbed by his awareness of Meg and confusion about himself.

"You don't have to worry about Meg," Doug insisted. "She's on the pill. But see? I can have sex with women. I must be pansexual."

Jim stood up and went to the kitchen. He turned on the light and was blinded. When he could see again, he opened the refrigerator and saw only beer and Gatorade.

"You're in good shape for someone my father's age," Doug called out.

Jim had forgotten he was still naked. Annoyed, he looked out and saw Doug sprawled on the bed, a very white, scrawny boy, hair peeking from his crotch and armpits like mattress ticking. He insolently sat there, too shameless to cover up, talking to Jim as an equal. What was it about this nebulous cipher that put him in bed with both an intelligent girl and her blundering uncle?

Jim left the kitchen light on when he returned with a bottle of Gatorade.

"Thank you." Doug swigged from the bottle and passed it back to Jim. "Does anyone in the State Department know about you?"

"Why?" Jim said flatly. "You won't tell on me if I don't tell on you?"

"No." Doug looked surprised. "I assumed we weren't going to tell anyone."

"Not even Meg?"

Doug made a face, puffed his cheeks full of air and blew the air from a corner of his mouth. "Damn. I've blanked that out all evening," he said indifferently.

"I intend to tell her," said Jim. Did he?

Doug looked at him skeptically, worriedly. "The thing is," he said, "Meg might figure it out just reading my face tomorrow. Especially since she didn't want me coming into town without her."

"You said she did."

"It was more like, 'Go ahead, see if I care.' She said she was afraid you'd like me more than you liked her. But she was running late and I really wanted to meet Imelda Marcos." Doug was grinning sheepishly. "And maybe I was curious about what would happen without her."

Of course. The boy had come here to be seduced. Even Meg had sensed that possibility. All the time Jim felt this was something *he* did, he'd been just a gear in a machine of other people's experiments and accidents. It was as bad as his career in the foreign service, only this time his own body had been one of the chief conspirators. He wasn't a hero, he wasn't even a good villain. He regretted not having finished his sex. He could not feel any more guilty or helpless.

The telephone rang.

It was almost one o'clock. Jim and Doug looked at each other.

The second ring sounded more accusing than the first. Doug gritted his teeth, miming fear, mocking it. Jim was genuinely afraid. His guilty voice would give them away. He wanted it to be his voice, not Doug's. He stood up and walked toward the telephone.

"Dreams of virtue breed monsters," Meg said—in a letter from graduate school several years later. Long after Jim freely resigned from the State Department, after Meg had forgotten Doug and forgiven Jim, she periodically needed to pick apart that night in an effort to make herself a full participant in it. "Your old monsters fascinate me. 'Curious George' did it out of sexual selfishness. You, on the other hand, did it not for sex, and not (as you once proposed) out of a confused need to get closer to your niece by hurting me. I now suspect you did it as an act of revenge against my family, who never needed you the way you wanted to be needed. I don't hold it against you. Blood is thicker than water, spilled blood thicker still."

J U D I T H   M C D A N I E L

THE JULIETTE LOW
LEGACY

W HEN I LOOKED AROUND, the two women were wrestling on the floor in front of the fireplace, wrestling with serious intention, but not with anger. The woman whose back was toward me was slowly losing her pants as her body strained and bent over. I watched with fascination as her pants slid down over her large, solidly built ass, revealing dimples on either side of her crevice.

The women sitting at the table with me seemed not to notice, and I wanted them to notice. "They're wrestling," I said, nodding toward the two on the cement floor in front of the fireplace. The three women at my table glanced over quickly, then drew their eyes back, but they had lost the focus of their conversation.

"*That* tends to happen here sometimes," said Gwen, the woman sitting directly across from me. I wanted to ask her what she meant by *that,* make her say it out loud, here in this all-woman setting that seemed so safe to these married women. But when I caught her gaze, she frowned, and I knew I shouldn't ask. Not if I wanted to keep knowing her better. And I did.

Gwen shifted uneasily and turned to the woman perched sideways on the bench next to her. "Do you want to go out with one of the canoe trips this summer?"

"If I can, but not a long one or I won't be able to do the first aid program for the main camp." The woman's words came out in a rush, as though she might not say them if she slowed to think. "I think I'll be able to stay the whole week this year—sleep over and all. My sister and I are swapping kids for a week. She'll take my girls …"

I let their voices drift away from me as I turned back to watch the two women wrestling on the floor. It was after midnight and the smoke from the fireplace had drifted into the old Girl Scout camp winter lodge and collected at the top of the stairs to the sleeping loft. Most of the women had gone to bed, but several of the wrestlers' friends were watching, giving quiet encouragement. It was not a rowdy match. They were breast to breast now, legs entwined, arms glued together, waving slowly in the air as the heavier woman tried to pin her friend's shoulders to the floor. They should be kissing, I realized, as I watched the nearly silent pantomime.

Maxine had come over to our group earlier in the evening. I liked her warm smile, butch cut, and diesel-dyke build.

"Max," Gwen had greeted her. "I'm glad you could make it. Any trouble getting away?"

"Naw. I took the kids to Barry's mother and he's off ice fishing with the boys. You know I wouldn't miss this weekend. It's the social event of the year."

We all laughed. I looked with surprise at Maxine's ring finger when she mentioned her husband. Sure enough, it was there. The wedding band was there for almost all of them. Two married ladies, I thought wryly, as I watched the woman-to-woman body contact on the floor in front of the fireplace. It puzzled me. It was what I sensed in Gwen—this desire that moved toward women, but stopped just within the safety zone.

When most of the women had finally wandered off to bed, Gwen and I propped our backs against the wall and stretched our legs out the whole bench length. This way we could see the entire room, be sure no one could hear our conversation, and talk openly without having to look closely at one another's eyes. At least I hoped we could talk openly. We had been talking in hints, raised eyebrows, silent question, and innuendo for several months now. I was curious, but my patience for Gwen's elaborate ritual of self-revelation had about run out. I wanted an ally in this world, someone who would know who I was and not run scared from it. Being known was my hedge against insanity in the insane world I lived in. At times the charade of being "normal" seemed to turn on me, threatened to engulf me unless I could whip out a safety line that would reattach me to my own reality. It wasn't a lot I asked, I thought, my eyes wandering back to the two women wrestling. I just want someone who will acknowledge with me what this is really all about.

Gwen sat quietly across from me. The flesh on her face was heavier than on her trim athletic body. It was the only part of her that looked forty-three. Her left hand, slowly turning the wine glass in the center of the table, was firm and muscular. Nice hands, I smiled to myself, noting that her wedding band was small and unobtrusive.

"You look depressed, Gwen. Isn't the weekend going well?"

"Oh, yes," Gwen roused herself briefly to enthusiasm. "It's an excellent turn-out. The council should be pleased. We've never had this many leaders who would do winter camping training before." Her voice slid back down into the lower registers of boredom or depression.

"So what's wrong?"

"I'll tell you after I've had another glass of wine."

"Tell me now or I'm going to bed."

And the story came out. Mary, the woman I had led a troop with for two years. Gwen. Other women from our area at an adult Girl Scout training session, learning a new scouting ceremony from another country. Standing in a circle. Told to turn and embrace the woman standing next. Mary, embarrassed, awkward, hugging Gwen, muttering, "This is ridiculous. They'll think all Girl Scouts are lesbians."

I was silent when she came to the punch line. This is it, I told myself. I could hardly complain about her reticence if I couldn't say something now. I was scared.

"Yeah, well," I cleared my throat. Lie. Truth. Or silence. "Well, lots are." I paused again and looked away. The wrestlers were sitting quietly on a bench in front of the fireplace, talking, bodies touching from shoulder to ankle. "I am."

"I know," she said, turning forward on the bench and peering at me intently. "I mean, I had figured."

"You had?" I took a gulp from my Coke bottle. Why was I surprised? I'd been dropping hints for three months.

"I always think of it when two women live together." Gwen seemed quiet, calm. She was looking at me curiously now.

"You do?" I took a deep breath. This was ridiculous. I'd expected her to be o.k. about it, so why was my voice shaking? Talk normal, I told myself, just talk normal.

"Does Mary know?" Mary. That was the fear. We'd worked together for two years and never exchanged a single item of personal information. Mary loves the outdoors like I do, but I'd always known—at some level—how wary she was of unpremeditated human involvements. And her husband taught in my high school.

Gwen was silent for a moment, thinking about Mary. "I doubt it. I doubt if it would occur to her."

I nodded, calming. There, that hadn't been so hard.

"I thought you'd never tell me." Gwen was peering at me again. I looked away. "I tried to let you know. ..." Her voice trailed off as though she didn't want to make the accusation.

"Gwen, for god's sake, your husband is on Jessica's school board. She's an elementary school teacher. I can hardly go around proclaiming it from the roof tops." I was angry, let my relief spurt out in anger. Gwen looked as though I had missed the point.

"Sure," she said. "Sure. I know."

The sun came up slowly the next morning, pushing against the resistance of a night that was below zero. I woke at seven and peered outside my sleeping bag. In the dim half-light several women were dressing, moving around. I sat up, pulled my warmed-up long underwear out of the bottom of the sleeping bag, took off my sleeping sweatshirt, and started to dress for an outside day. The latrine seat was covered with ice crystals when I lifted the lid. I squatted gingerly over the dark hole.

"Minus thirty degrees wind chill factor," said a short red-haired woman cheerfully as I came into the kitchen. "Glad I didn't have to sleep in a tent last night."

"Me, too," I agreed, wondering whether I had met her last night or if she had just arrived. "It will be cold out on the ice today, for sure."

We were scheduled for a training session on hypothermia, then a chance to learn how to ice fish out on the lake our lodge overlooked. Northern pike and lake trout, we were promised, and Gwen had brought the potatoes for fish chowder.

More women came in during breakfast, women who had not been able to spend the night, red-cheeked from the morning cold, boisterous about leaving their families for this single day of adult training. I wondered how many of these leaders had ever thought of taking their troops winter camping, how many came for themselves, the day away from home with friends.

"I had to find two baby-sitters," one woman complained loudly as she took off her heavy snowmobile boots. "One for the kids and one for my husband." She continued against the laughter. "Really, he won't cook his own lunch."

"Get him to eat out, Lorraine."

"Are you kidding? Who can afford that?"

"Well, we're catching dinner today," Gwen said briskly. "Stop undressing, Lorraine. Let's get out and get started."

I slid down the embankment to the lake and started across the ice, my skates slapping awkwardly against my shoulder. The lake was frozen deep, but still freezing from underneath. As the freezing water expanded into ice, the lake crust pressed against its own resistance, cracking, shifting, a chorus of moans and sharp grunts as our weight moved across the smooth surface.

"Indians used to say it was the lake talking," Gwen reassured one nervous woman. "It's frozen o.k. Really." She handed me the ice auger. "Dig a hole. Let's see how thick the ice is."

I leaned over the tall drill and turned the handle. As the bit caught against the ice, shavings started to mound around the handle. I pressed down and the muscles in my left arm strained as I pushed the auger into the ice. When it went through, Gwen said, "Now pull it out and slosh the water around to clear your hole." We could see that the ice was over a foot deep.

I learned the language of the ice fishers. Auger. Sounder. Line. Minnow-bait. Tip ups. I found the spot on the minnow's back under the dorsal fin and inserted the fish hook. The minnow sank when I threw it down the ice hole, swam down and down to get to the warmer water, pulling my line with it. I leaned over the eight-inch-wide hole and watched the slim silver body spiral gracefully down through the ice into darker waters, apparently oblivious to the hook and line attaching it to this surface world. When it had played out the line to my marking knot, I hooked the knot over a little flag. If a larger fish took the bait, it would pull the line free and my flag would "tip up," telling me I had a fish.

Gusts of wind scudded across the ice. We set fifteen holes, rushed to one when the flag went up and pulled out a pile of weeds the minnow had gotten tangled in.

"Raise the level of the bait," Gwen told Mary. "It's best to be just above the weeds. No tangles that way." She grinned at me when I raised an eyebrow to question her innuendo. "Walk me over to the other side of the lake and we'll set up the group that's just coming out."

We walked away from the voices until the only sound was the wind. "How long have you and Jessica been together?" she asked.

"Oh, about five years." I looked over to see what her face was saying, but it was silent behind the sunglasses.

"There was no one living like you that I knew when I was younger," she said.

"Me neither," I agreed, then paused. "I mean, I guess there were, but not in my nice suburb," I didn't know how much else I wanted to say. I hadn't talked to anyone but Jessica about the two women who worked the maintenance crew when I was a freshman in college, how I laughed at them like the other kids, not understanding the discomfort in my gut, the fear. And I did not know Gwen well enough to talk about why I hadn't been able to understand my connection to those women—those protections that seem so obvious in retrospect—how I'd wanted so badly as a child to fit in, to find approval for who I was. "Some women know it without seeing it first, I guess, but I just never thought of it until I met Jessica."

"I knew it from the first," she said.

I was silent. Afraid to interrupt, afraid I would not know what to say.

"But no one was doing it. I didn't know how I would live. It was the fifties. So I got married. The kids. The youngest is ten, so I figure I've got another seven years to serve. Then I don't know what, but it will be something else." She was crying behind her sunglasses, but I could not put my arm around her, here in the bright glare of the sun on ice.

"Did you ever have a woman lover?"

She nodded. In a low voice. "Now."

I turned at the sound of steel blades coming up behind us.

"Hey, watch my tip up for me, will you?" Mary called out to me. "I'm going to get a skating lesson so we can teach the girls to skate backward next time."

"Sure," I hollered, "but anything I catch is mine."

Gwen nodded and I turned abruptly back across the ice, not sorry to have this moment to myself. I walked from ice hole to ice hole, checking the minnows and resetting the flags, trying to understand what I had just heard. What did it mean, I wondered, to have a husband and a woman lover? I could not imagine it. But I had no children, was never married, and needed to ask no one's permission to love Jessica. Not that it had been easy, even then. I always heard the voices that said, you do what? oh, god, how disgusting. And when my sister finally met Jessica, she told me she was disappointed. "She's nice. We'd hoped she'd sort of look like a truck driver, so you'd get over this woman thing in a hurry."

I was feeling lonely and cold when the red-haired woman I'd met in the kitchen at breakfast trotted over from the other side of the lake.

"Let's jog from hole to hole," she suggested. "It's the only way we'll keep warm today."

"Do you fish often?" I'd noticed she had brought her own tip ups and set each reel with finesse.

"My husband and I fish all winter down on Lake George. We put them in the freezer and eat fish year round. It's a great budget helper." She laughed, half embarrassed at the admission.

"It must be," I agreed.

"Where did you and your husband buy your house?" she asked, turning toward the next hole.

"Me?" I asked, flabbergasted. "I'm not married."

"Oh." Silence. "I'm sorry. I heard you talking about renovating a house last night. Didn't you say we?"

"Yes." I smiled. Here goes. "I live with a woman. We bought the house together. It's out in Paulet, just before the Vermont border."

She was silent for a minute as we checked the next reel for freeze up. "Are you girls teachers?"

"Yes," I said, laughing inside. "Yes, in fact, we are." And she turned comfortably back to the minnow bucket.

"They don't pay teachers much," she said, freeing the line of lake weed and sending the minnow back down. I wondered if the bottom of the lake seemed familiar to this small fish raised in a stainless steel tank for bait, or whether it found itself a stranger swimming back into what should have been its natural habitat.

She brushed a strand of hair back and tucked it under her ski cap, then looked directly at me and smiled. "It must be hard to live alone on what they pay."

"Yes," I said. "It must be." Loneliness settled back down across my shoulders as we moved across the ice, trying to catch sight of each of the flags, shielding our eyes against the sun's glare.

At noon we left the reels set and headed back to the lodge for lunch. I put on my skates and let the wind push me across the ice, dodging the small drifts of snow that had accumulated.

The lodge was crowded. More women had arrived and were cooking lunch outside over fires. Inside, I took off my boots, put on dry socks, and went for some hot coffee. In one corner I saw Max, sitting with a woman I hadn't met. Curly dark hair framed the newcomer's face, a face that seemed to have crumbled or melted slightly. The mouth slid down, her cheeks were slack beneath her gray eyes. It was not an expression I could define, and my eyes drifted back to the two, deep in conversation, apparently isolated in this crowded room. Women just coming in from the lake waved and greeted the newcomer, then moved away.

"Who's that?" I asked Mary as she sat down on the bench next to me. Then I wondered whether I should have asked, remembering Gwen's story about Mary from last night.

"E.J." Her voice was matter-of-fact. "She's here from Hartford. She ran the waterfront program at the camp here for nearly ten summers." She dismissed my inquiry with a wave toward her dessert plate. "Try the dessert," she urged. "I know you don't like chocolate, but Gwen says our girls will love the chocolate fondue with marshmallows. I'm going for more." I made a face of pure disgust at her departing back.

Sitting in silence, I ate my soup and watched the movement of women around me as they wove in and out of tables and conversations. Across the room was E.J. My eyes went back again and again to her face. Her eyes met no one's. She sat at Max's side staring straight ahead, spoke without turning toward the heavyset comfortable woman sitting next to her.

"I thought I could wait." Gwen's voice was small, whispering in my ear. I had not felt her sit down beside me.

"When I met HER something in me said, uh, oh. We were always together. Whenever I needed another driver to take my troop somewhere, she would go. We camped together. Bicycled somewhere for the day. It never mattered what we did, we had fun together."

I nodded, but did not look at her. I was beginning to understand this mode of communication.

"I'd known her about six months. I had a camp reunion party and she came. My husband was out of town. The kids were farmed out. I was supposed to leave the next morning at six to take the troop to a conference downstate. She was driving the other car." Her voice dropped even further.

This must be it, I thought, looking around nervously to see whether anyone was watching us as I had watched Max and her friend.

"When they all left, she brought in her sleeping bag. She asked me where I wanted her to sleep. Oh, god, can you imagine?"

I couldn't, but nodded my head astutely, eyes fixed on the soup bowl.

"I said I wanted her to sleep with me. *With me,* I said. I couldn't believe I'd said it. Neither did she, but she never gave me a chance to take it back."

There was silence. I turned to look at her profile, impressed now, willing her to go on.

She would not look at me. "Neither of us had ever done it—made love to a woman—before. I thought, this is going to be a mess. How are we going to figure this out? But it wasn't. It was simple." She paused again. "It was the most natural thing I had ever done in my life."

I realized she had finished speaking. "What will you do?" I asked in hushed tones, not moving my lips, "Live together?"

"Oh, no." Her voice was shocked and she sat up straight at the table. "On, no. I couldn't do that. I mean, there's nothing to do. I have the children. And him." She gestured vaguely, including the whole room.

"But what about your lover?" I pursued. "What does she want?"

"I don't know." Gwen looked puzzled. "We'll just have to go on as we are. She understands."

"Oh." I thought about that as I scraped the last bit of soup from the bottom of my bowl. Gwen was silent beside me. Could I have asked the same of Jessica? I thought not, but then neither of us had children, neither was committed to an earlier promise. Still, I remembered my first erotic realization, the knowledge I had possessed in that first moment of being with a woman, that nothing, nothing would ever be the same for me. I wondered why it had seemed so obvious to me, so inevitable, so exhilarating.

The room was beginning to stir around me as women prepared for the afternoon's activities. "Do you think it will make a difference?" I asked. "Loving her?"

"It can't," she said, her voice rising from behind me. "I won't let it. I can't afford to."

Gwen directed the afternoon activities and I listened with half an ear. When it was time for me to leave, I asked her to walk me to the car. I had fabricated a late afternoon dentist appointment that would free me in time to be at my own home for dinner. These women fought free of their homes for this single day. I had to fight to create my home, to move toward it rather than away from it, and I had known weeks before I registered for this event that I would want to leave before it was over.

"Tell me about E.J.," I said as we climbed the hill to the parking lot.

"Oh," she said dully, "she's in bad shape."

"I could tell. Why?"

"She was with the woman who ran this camp. They met here. Were together every summer. Lived together, too, for a while, I think."

"Lovers?"

"I was sure they were. Her girlfriend got married last spring. It's the first time E.J.'s been up to camp since."

I remembered her face, the fragile mouth, the eyes that wouldn't meet mine.

"It's real hard for her," Gwen continued. "They all know it's hard."

"But all of this is unspoken?" It seemed cruel. Suddenly I was tired and the wind chill seemed more noticeable.

"Of course. No one can talk about it. There's not support for that." She paused. "I'm sorry you're not staying for dinner. We got enough fish for the chowder."

I looked into her eyes, trying to understand what was not being said. If the message was there, I could not read it. I was angry and sad and did not know what else to say.

Gwen shrugged. "Well, have a nice dinner at home tonight." I tried to lean forward to embrace her and say good-bye, but I could not move against the re- sistance in the cold air between us.

"Good night," I said. "See you." And I watched her back as she turned and walked back down the path toward the lake.

BARBARA WILSON

IS THIS ENOUGH
FOR YOU?

Two women, almost strangers, are walking through a large college campus at night. It is October, but mild; there's a warm, southerly wind, though they are far north. The leaves are dry and abundant; they skitter in the slight breeze; they crackle underfoot.

The women don't know where they are. They have never been here before.

One of the women, Ellen McDougal, is giving a paper tomorrow. It's on lesbian literature in the United States before 1968. She's been writing a book about it, about Gale Wilhelm, Ann Bannon, Dorothy Baker, Jane Rule. Her paper is called "When Desire Had No Name." She comes from a northern California town where she teaches English and Women's Studies at a small college and where the fog comes in winter and summer to muffle the spaces between the redwoods.

The woman walking with Ellen is Nan Hazlett, a librarian from a large Midwestern city. She was a radical leftist once, now she spends her free time going to meetings for various urban causes. She lives in the inner city and has a stake in its survival. She is in charge of the women's collection at the University library. She's younger than Ellen by about six years, but neither of them are really young. They are middle-aged feminists who have led somewhat complicated lives, who have been actively committed to the lesbian-feminist movement for many years, who have been lucky enough to have increasingly meaningful professional lives, who have had some periods of despair and many of happiness, who have had therapy, who have run away and come back, who have started over. Several times.

They both have lovers at home.

At first they didn't know that about each other. Now they do. They walk, not touching, around and around the enormous campus, filled with commodious brick buildings from the twenties and tall towers from the sixties. There are lamps at intervals along the path, and then the women can see each other quite clearly. At other times they're almost in darkness—the leaves swirl around them and they have to trust their feet.

Nan has been in a relationship with Marina for two years. Marina is a potter and a day-care worker. She is fat, even-tempered, good with kids, good with her hands. She and Nan thought carefully before they became involved. They were both on the rebound from unhappy affairs; they wanted to move slowly. So they aren't living together and they don't see each other every night. They're happy together and believe that this relationship is one that can last. For this time they have built on the firm foundation of friendship, not desire. They respect each other, they like each other, they love each other. They are honest with each other.

They have made certain promises.

Ellen has been involved with Cora for five years and they have been in the process of breaking up for the last two. Sometimes it's Ellen who wants to break up, sometimes it's Cora. Both of them, at bottom, know that this relationship is no longer possible for them, that it has no future. But when it comes time to actually pronounce the words that will set them free of each other, the future seems less important than the past. Both Cora and Ellen have an investment in continuing. Back at the beginning when they were in love, they bought a house, furniture, a camper, a washer and dryer, a computer, an endless number of things. They both love their house, and their garden. They have two cats and an elderly dog. Most people they know consider them a successful couple, both professional women (Cora is a lawyer), both intellectually stimulating, both fun to be with. The friends who know their problems with each other assure them that it's just a stage: "If you started over with somebody else you'd just have to work out some of the same problems."

Nobody wants them to break up.

Nan and Marina have been faithful to each other; Ellen and Cora have not. Cora had a fling with an old lover one vacation; she came close to leaving Ellen, but instead, for various reasons, the affair brought them closer together. The old lover re-left Cora and Cora realized how much Ellen meant to her. Ellen has, for the last year, been sleeping infrequently with a colleague at work. This woman is married and has two children under the age of ten. Even though Ellen knows Cora would be very upset if she found out, Ellen doesn't think it really causes the relationship any harm. Maybe it even helps it.

Nan and Marina have an unwritten contract with each other to be monogamous. It was Nan who first brought up the subject of her previous "weakness"; she felt that her last relationship had been undermined by a series of flirtations and attractions. There was a time when Nan had believed in and had practiced a mild form of promiscuity, but that time is, she has been grateful to realize, over for good. She no longer wants an open relationship and believes herself a more mature person for having decided that. She loves Marina and the calm, secure life they have together. Nan hasn't been attracted to another woman since she met Marina; she thinks of that fact often, with wonder and with joy.

"It's getting late," Ellen says to Nan.

"Yes," says Nan.

They keep walking.

Ellen and Nan began to talk, at first casually and then with more interest, two days ago at lunch. There was a group around them at first; gradually the group fell away, went on to the next seminar. Ellen and Nan stayed talking for another hour. They talked about books they'd read mostly, the books they'd discovered. Nan has very pronounced tastes: "Oh, that's a terrible novel," she says. "Idiotic." She likes foreign writers best: Yourcenar, Lispector, Marie-Claire Blais. Ellen likes popular fiction, genre writing, and writers who identify as lesbian. "What good does it do to know that Yourcenar was a lesbian if she didn't write or speak about it?"

They laughed, they contradicted each other, but suddenly, in a flurry of warm embarrassment, they felt they had to part. Ellen stood for a moment looking after Nan. A friend passing by saw her, saw Nan's back, said, "Conference crush?"

"Oh, god, no," said Ellen. "Never."

She was opposed to such things, in the first place, on principle and in the second place because she was here to exchange ideas. The atmosphere was too hectic for romance at a conference. She knew—she'd been to dozens of them.

Nevertheless Ellen lay awake that night and thought about Nan. She lay there in her narrow college bed listening to her roommate breathe, and from time to time she put her hands on her upper thighs and pressed lightly, as if to feel a body lying on top of her.

Nan's face was becoming beautiful in her mind.

Nan slept soundly. She thought it had been a wonderful first day and she'd been quite busy.

The next day Nan and Ellen happened to go to the same seminar together. As if it were the most natural thing in the world Nan came over and took the chair next to Ellen, and began to tease her about being in a seminar about French feminist writers.

"I just came to see you," Ellen joked back, then caught her breath, because it was true. Don't be a fool, she told herself violently, then softened, because Nan was smiling at her.

"That's why I came too."

Nan didn't think anything of it. She was so secure in her affection for Marina that she didn't even notice that she had begun to flirt with Ellen, had begun to look at her with different, meaning-filled eyes.

Ellen now thought that Nan was one of the most attractive women she'd ever met. She couldn't understand how she'd fallen so far so fast. You're a fool, she told herself as the seminar leader droned on about Cixous. But at the same time a delicious heat began to envelop her. It was emanating from Nan's Levi-clad leg which was exactly two inches away, parallel to Ellen's black denim leg. At the same moment Ellen became conscious of Nan's neck. Not much was visible, and Ellen certainly couldn't turn her head to stare, but somehow, out of the corner of her eye Ellen started to know a little patch of skin showing above Nan's collar. I would like to kiss this woman's neck, she thought. She imagined pulling Nan's collar down slightly and running the tip of her tongue lightly along the skin, murmuring, Nan, darling, Nan ...

Are you insane? She snapped herself back. You don't have crushes, you don't get crushes on women you meet at conferences. What the fuck is wrong with you? You're too old for this.

Nan was feeling a certain tension too, though she interpreted it as high spirits. Mischievously she whispered to Ellen, "Isn't this woman incredibly boring?"

Ellen choked back a laugh and suddenly a terrible joy overwhelmed her. *Now* she knew who Nan reminded her of. It was Stacy Collins—from sixth grade. They'd passed notes to each other all day, walked each other home at night and happily reunited every morning. Ellen remembered how she'd wait for Stacy on their corner the last two blocks before the school and how when she first saw Stacy approaching she'd pretend to be elaborately indifferent, but the closer Stacy got the more unbearable it would become to pretend not to look at her, and Ellen could never hold out, she sprinted towards Stacy and Stacy ran towards her and just before they met, they stopped and started laughing, breaking off the feeling that if they hadn't stopped running they could have run *right* into each other, like a double ghost image becoming whole. This sudden, visceral memory heartened Ellen, and she thought, Nothing can be wrong with this woman, nothing can go wrong with this woman if she reminds me of my childhood.

Nan's silliness was turning restless. She picked up a pen and began to write notes to Ellen: questions about what writers she liked, and then mini-reviews. She didn't ask herself why she was unable to pay attention to the discussion or why her foot tapped constantly or why she found herself trying to be amusing just so she could see Ellen's swift, bright smile. She simply wrote faster and faster, almost snatching the pad out of Ellen's hands to read what she'd written, and to respond to it. Nan was hungry for ideas, that's why she'd come to the conference. She didn't know why but she and Marina didn't seem to ... but this infinitesimally disloyal thought never finished itself in her brain.

The seminar was over and Nan and Ellen skulked out, a little ashamed of having been "bad students" (one of the presenters had given them a sour look, Nan recalled), and a little exhilarated. Then they were facing each other in the hall.

"Well, good-bye," said Ellen, and quickly walked off.

This time it was Nan who remained standing, staring after Ellen. The first little glimmer of the danger she was in made itself known to her. But that's impossible, Nan said to herself in genuine bewilderment: You can't possibly have a crush when you're truly in love with someone else.

She spent the rest of the day avoiding Ellen, but it was as if a virus had taken hold and was spreading rapidly through her system. With something like horror Nan recognized each and every one of the symptoms: her heart was beating quickly, much faster than usual; her stomach felt fluttery; her appetite vanished. The more she tried to say to herself, You're imagining things—your heart is *not* beating more quickly, your stomach is not *fluttering*—the stronger and more violent the symptoms became. They were frightening symptoms because she'd had them before, and they had prompted her, had impelled her, to do rash sweet things that caused a great deal of trouble for her in her life.

Nan evaded Ellen successfully all afternoon and instead of eating in the cafeteria that evening she went off campus to a pizza parlor with two old friends. Once away from the conference surroundings she began to feel more like herself. Her friends asked her about Marina and she talked with great pleasure and pride about the life they had together, how happy they'd been, how this was something they both thought would last. The tension she felt began to dissipate and by the end of the meal she had rationalized her earlier emotions almost completely. Falling in love with people, having crushes and infatuations, was an old pattern. It was finished. She might still have some of those old feelings from time to time; that was all right. The important thing to realize was that she didn't have to act on those impulses. To act was to destroy. Knowing the consequences freed her from the compulsion to act.

Nan was so relieved to have discovered self-control somewhere in her psychological make-up that she felt the urge to call up Marina immediately and say, I was tempted, but I overcame temptation! On further reflection she decided this sounded absurd and might even cause Marina some distress. No, she'd tell Marina when she got home, when she was holding Marina in her arms. They'd have a good laugh over it and maybe Marina would say that the same thing happened to her sometimes.

Nan retired early to bed with a book of feminist literary-criticism. From time to time an image of Ellen's large gray eyes and her half sweet, half ironic, always quick smile flashed in front of her eyes. Nan let it flash. Repressing Ellen's face only led to butterflies in her stomach, made her feel as if she were doing something wrong. And she wasn't doing anything wrong! She wasn't going to do anything wrong either.

In her own room Ellen sat disconsolately at her small student desk attempting to write a letter to Cora, a letter that would end their relationship once and for all. Crumpled paper lay around her, she had written six pages and it felt as if she hadn't even begun. She wanted to take all the blame on herself, on her own suspect motives for beginning the relationship in the first place, but every sentence seemed to end in recriminations against Cora. *I wanted a sensible person, a kind person, I wanted a person who wouldn't shake me up, a person who I could live with peacefully into old age,* she wrote, and mentally finished, You're smug, you're dull, all your cases are boring and so are you!

Oh god. There must be some way through this. Dimly, dimly Ellen recalled how happy Cora made her at the start of their relationship. It wasn't a grand passion, Ellen told her friends. We're friends first, lovers second. But the sex had been steady and generous and had lasted on past the second, the third, on into the fourth year. They had thought themselves well-suited, not just sexually, but in other ways as well: values, politics, friends.

It was a mystery then why Ellen wanted so desperately now to get away from Cora. It couldn't be because of Nan, that was nonsense. Nan was a stranger, they'd hardly talked, Nan lived in the Midwest, how could they possibly work out a living arrangement? Maybe Nan had a lover, yes, she almost certainly had a lover. And that wasn't how Ellen wanted to end things with Cora either, not by going off with another woman. That was insulting, that was criminal, Cora would never forgive her and it would make everything worse about the house and furniture, the camper, the dog. The only way to do it was to do it decently and honorably, and then in a few months, when Cora had gotten over it, then Ellen and Nan could …

You are absolutely insane, Ellen told herself, and beat her head with her fists. She hadn't seen Nan all day and Nan hadn't been in the cafeteria that evening, though Ellen's eyes had darted anxiously around all through the dinner she couldn't eat. Obviously, if a woman is attracted to you she doesn't just disappear. Ellen stood up, pushed the curtains aside and looked out the window on to the campus. There were women walking in small groups and couples across the square outside the dorm. Was Nan out there among them? Should Ellen go out and look for her? Maybe she could find out from someone what room Nan was in, she could go to her room, they wouldn't even speak, Ellen would push her down on the bed, tear open her shirt and begin kissing her neck, her collar bones, her breasts. And Nan would say ...

Ellen found herself sucking on the tender piece of flesh between her thumb and forefinger, exactly as she had the night of her first dance at fourteen, when Bob Peck had unaccountably walked her home without kissing her, leaving her to lie in bed with a confused sweet inexpressible desire. She wasn't supposed to be wanting to be kissed. She was supposed to say no if he asked.

"Aargh!" Ellen said, wrenching her hand from her mouth and beginning her letter all over again.

Dear Cora,

I'm sure this will not come as a complete surprise to you ...

Ellen had decided to be absolutely cool and distant when she saw Nan (if she saw Nan, maybe she'd gone home early, that could explain everything) the next morning at breakfast, but instead her face split into a wide, pure smile.

"Hello!" they both said, and started to talk about the conference and what workshops they'd gone to and were going to.

This can't be wrong, thought Ellen. Not to feel such a ... liking ... for her.

I can feel attracted and not do anything, thought Nan stalwartly, and she said, "Well, see you later," and they got up from the table.

"What about," Ellen rushed in, "dinner tonight?"

"Oh," said Nan, staring down at her feet. "I've got kind of a meeting ... actually ..."

"Oh fine," said Ellen hastily, thinking, The conference is ending tomorrow, I can hardly wait to get out of here.

They stood staring at each other, feeling foolish, crazy, naked.

"Well, bye!" Ellen said finally, brightly, and fled.

Later in the day Nan caught up with her. "I was thinking ... maybe we could get together after my dinner, just for coffee or a drink ..."

"Well," said Ellen, who had spent much of the day not attending workshops or seminars but wandering this strange city's streets, coming to the decision that she wouldn't approach Nan again, that in fact, given the opportunity, she would spurn her. "All right."

It is now two a.m. and the two women are still walking around the campus. Every once in a while they get close to their dormitory, but then they shy away and continue this restless pacing. They have only stopped a few times; they're afraid to stop any more.

They should know more about each other than they do; after all, they've been together nearly five hours. They could have exchanged more information, discussed ideas and books—why for instance, when they love lesbian literature, aren't they talking about that? But conversation, in the known sense of the term, stopped somewhere around ten thirty in the cafe where they were both leaning forward into the candlelight, and suddenly Nan said, "I have a lover," and Ellen said, "So do I," and Nan said, with more anguish than joy, "I'm very attracted to you," and Ellen, longingly, said, "Yes."

They talked enough to get the basic facts straight. That Ellen had been unfaithful and was willing to be again. That Nan could not, *would* not. What was there to say after that? They left the cafe and started walking because, even though their minds are filled with cliches and their veins with heavy cream, they still believe that somehow they can say something meaningful about this attraction, make it comprehensible, safe, friendly, unthreatening. In each of their minds runs the refrain, I don't understand why this is happening to me now. They want to deny the importance of whatever it is, and at the same time revel in it, acknowledge it. Instead they are silent.

The first time they stopped was just after leaving the cafe, just inside the dark protective boundaries of the forested campus. Ellen stopped first, said nothing, simply held out her arms to Nan. Then for an instance it was terribly sweet, an enormous relief. They clung together. But nothing was solved, it was worse. Still, Ellen's lips moved of their own volition to Nan's neck. She had been waiting to kiss that neck such a long time. What a delicious smell of soap, what a very very fine gold chain. Ellen curled the chain on her tongue and pulled at it. Vast violent shudders went through Nan's body. "Are you cold?" Ellen whispered.

"No," said Nan. It was desire. And beads of perspiration stood out on her upper lip. Ellen tasted them when they kissed.

They got lost in that kiss. Ellen wanted to say, I've never felt like this. But how could that be? She was forty-five, she'd had many lovers. At the moment she couldn't remember any of them.

She said, "I want to sleep with you." Of course she had forgotten that she had a roommate.

"I want to, too," said Nan, into her hair. Then she stepped back. "But will I?" She began to talk rather wildly about Marina and their promises, and how she couldn't betray her. And then she groaned as she realized she was already betraying Marina, Marina whom she truly loved. How could she be doing this to Marina?

"No, no," she said, but her hands couldn't leave Ellen's face and hair. "I can't, do you understand?"

"No," said Ellen. "Yes, I understand."

"I don't want to hurt you," said Nan desperately. "I realized I've already started. But I can't go on. We must stop ..." She stroked Ellen's face. "Is this enough for you?"

"Of course it's not enough," Ellen said. She tried to pull herself together. "At the same time, maybe it is enough. Just to have met you. To know you're alive. I don't know. I don't know."

That's when they began to walk.

Ellen is remembering something her mother used to say to her when she was a child: "I want to eat you up." She would be hugging Ellen when she said it, pressing her closer and closer, while Ellen giggled. But once or twice Ellen got a little afraid, almost as if her mother really could swallow her up whole just from love. When Ellen was older she pushed her mother away. "Oh Mom, let go!" But once she had said it to Stacy Collins: "I want to eat you up!" She didn't know what she meant by that, but she meant it. She couldn't get enough of Stacy; she wanted to run right into Stacy, become part of Stacy, or have Stacy become part of her. It didn't matter. Stacy had laughed when Ellen said it; she hadn't really understood. The following year Stacy and her family had moved away, and Ellen had never seen her again.

Enough. What could that mean between her and Nan? When they stop walking their bodies flow together like streams meeting to form a river. Their bodies persist, even though their voices say no, in trying to get to know each other, like two dogs their owners are attempting to pry apart.

Would it be enough to kiss Nan for an hour? For two hours? For two days? Would it be enough to lie down naked with her, to caress her, to bring her and be brought to climax? How many caresses, how many climaxes, how many days, weeks, months, years would be enough? Or does she only want to get to know Nan, to be her friend, to look at her and to love her? Does sex have to be involved? How much would be enough? How little would suffice?

Nan knows that she has betrayed Marina and her despair is so great that it threatens to overwhelm all reason. The more she kisses Ellen the more she wants to kiss Ellen. Desire becomes need, despair begets greater and greater rashness. What does it matter if she kisses Ellen's lips, neck, breasts, thighs? What does it matter if she and Ellen stand behind one of the sighing trees and slip fingers into wet underwear, what does it matter if they go to a motel, if they go away to another country? Or if they do nothing, say good-bye and part? The damage has been done. The first betrayal will lead to others. To Marina it will not matter whether Nan kissed Ellen or not, whether they made love or not.

The impossibility of her situation suddenly causes Nan's knees to buckle. They find a bench, talk quietly, attempt to talk themselves out of this madness. The desire has become a heavy thing; they've gone past the tingle into the ache, past the ache into the dead weight of longing. Ellen's cunt is so hard and burdensome it feels like a black bowling ball pressing in on her intestines. They kiss, and even as Ellen longs for the kissing never to end, her nerves shiver and snap like icy little twigs in a bitter wind. She begins to cry.

Nan is furious with herself. She's hurt this woman, this woman she would want never to hurt. She's hurt so many women in her life, the list is endless, it won't end unless she stops herself.

"Ellen, Ellen," she murmurs. "Darling, please, honey, we've got to go. We've got to say good-night."

Ellen nods numbly, stands up obediently. Something is ending that was never begun. Something is dying that shouldn't have been so alive.

They stand close to each other. Absurdly Nan takes Ellen's hand, as if she wants to shake it. They laugh, and for an instant nothing is tragic, everything is funny, spirited, right. Again Ellen has that unexpected, charmed sense of re-connecting with her childhood, with the child she once was.

"Maybe I'll see you next year," says Nan.

"Who knows what will happen?" says Ellen, with some of her former light-ness, even flirtatiousness. By next year she will no longer be with Cora, she knows at least that much. And she steps back from Nan, turns and begins to walk away.

"Ellen!" Nan calls after her, frantic. Then she doesn't know what to say. She would like to apologize, but that's absurd. Do you apologize to a woman you've almost fallen in love with for the love? Or for the almost?

"Yes?"

"You understand, don't you? If it weren't for Marina ..."

"I know."

They're apart now, and that steadies them, not to smell each other, not to touch each other. They're both moving away.

Then Ellen stops. Turns.

If this were thirty-five years ago, in her old neighborhood, if this were Stacy not going away but coming to meet her, Ellen wouldn't hesitate. She would run towards her, faster than she'd ever run before, right into Stacy, right into Stacy's blood and muscle and heart, at peace finally with desire and love.

But it's not Stacy. It's Nan, a woman she hardly knows, rapidly becoming a total stranger again, walking away without, more than once or twice, looking back.

DAVID LEAVITT

WHEN YOU GROW
TO ADULTERY

Aɴᴅʀᴇᴡ ᴡᴀs ɪɴ ʟᴏᴠᴇ with Jack Selden, so all Jack's little habits, his particular ways of doing things, seemed marvelous to him: the way Jack put his face under the shower, after shampooing his hair, and shook his head like a big dog escaped from a bath; the way he slept on his back, his arms crossed in the shape of a butterfly over his face, fists on his eyes; his fondness for muffins and Danish and sweet rolls—what he called, at first just out of habit and then *because* it made Andrew laugh, "baked goods." Jack made love with efficient fervor, his face serious, almost businesslike. Not that he was without affection, but everything about him had an edge; his very touch had an edge, there was the possibility of pain lurking behind every caress. It seemed to Andrew that Jack's touches, more than any he'd known before, were full of meaning—they sought to express, not just to please or explore—and this gesturing made him want to gesture back, to enter into a kind of tactile dialogue. They'd known each other only a month, but already it felt to Andrew as if their fingers had told each other novels.

Andrew had gone through most of his life not being touched by anyone, never being touched at all. These days, his body under the almost constant scrutiny of two distinct pairs of hands, seemed to him perverse punishment, as if he had had a wish granted and was now suffering the consequences of having stated the wish too vaguely. He actually envisioned, sometimes, the fairy godmother shrugging her shoulders and saying, "You get what you ask for." Whereas most of his life he had been alone, unloved, now he had two lovers— Jack for just over a month, and Allen for close to three years. There was no

cause and effect, he insisted, but had to admit things with Allen had been getting ragged around the edges for some time. Jack and Allen knew about each
other and had agreed to endure, for the sake of the undecided Andrew, a tenu-
ous and open-ended period of transition, during which Andrew himself spent
so much of his time on the subway, riding between the two apartments of his
two lovers, that it began to seem to him as if rapid transit was the true and final
home of the desired. Sometimes he wanted nothing more than to crawl into
the narrow bed of his childhood and revel in the glorious, sad solitude of no
one—not even his mother—needing or loving him. Hadn't the hope of future
great loves been enough to curl up against? It seemed so now. His skin felt soft,
toneless, like the skin of a plum poked by too many housewifely hands, feeling
for the proper ripeness; he was covered with fingerprints.

This morning he had woken up with Jack—a relief. One of the many small
tensions of the situation was that each morning, when he woke up, there was a
split second of panic as he sought to reorient himself and figure out where he
was, who he was with. It was better with Jack, because Jack was new love and
demanded little of him; with Allen, lately, there'd been thrashing, heavy
breathing, a voice whispering in his ear, "Tell me one thing. Did you promise
Jack we wouldn't have sex? I have to know."

"No, I didn't."

"Thank God, thank God. Maybe now I can go back to sleep."

There was a smell of coffee. Already showered and dressed for work (he was
an architect at a spiffy firm), Jack walked over to the bed smiling, and kissed
Andrew, who felt rumpled and sour and unhappy. Jack's mouth carried the
sweet taste of coffee, his face was smooth and newly shaven and still slightly
wet. "Good morning," he said.

"Good morning."

"I love you," Jack Selden said.

Immediately Allen appeared, in a posture of crucifixion against the bedroom wall. "My God," he said, "you're killing me, you know that? You're killing
me."

It was Rosh Hashanah, and Allen had taken the train out the night before to
his parents' house in New Jersey. Andrew was supposed to join him that afternoon. He looked up now at Jack, smiled, then closed his eyes. His brow broke
into wrinkles. "Oh God," he said to Jack, putting his arms around his neck,
pulling him closer, so that Jack almost spilled his coffee. "Now I have to face
Allen's family."

Jack kissed Andrew on the forehead before pulling gingerly from his embrace. "I still can't believe Allen told them," he said, sipping more coffee from a
mug that said WORLD'S GREATEST ARCHITECT. Jack had a mostly per-
functory relationship with his own family—hence the mug, a gift from his
mother.

"Yes," Andrew said. "But Sophie's hard to keep secrets from. She sees him, and she knows something's wrong, and she doesn't give in until he's told her."

"Listen, I'm sure if he told you she's not going to say anything, she's not going to say anything. Anyway, it'll be fun, Andrew. You've told me a million times how much you enjoy big family gatherings."

"Easy for you to say. You get to go to your nice clean office and work all day and sleep late tomorrow and go out for brunch." Suddenly Andrew sat up in bed. "I don't think I can take this anymore, this running back and forth between you and him." He looked up at Jack shyly. "Can't I stay with you? In your pocket?"

Jack smiled. Whenever he and his last boyfriend, Ralph, had something difficult to face—the licensing exam, or a doctor's appointment—they would say to each other, "Don't worry, I'll be there with you. I'll be in your pocket." Jack had told Andrew, who had in turn appropriated the metaphor, but Jack didn't seem to mind. He smiled down at Andrew—he was sitting on the edge of the bed now, smelling very clean, like hair tonic—and brushed his hand over Andrew's forehead. Then he reached down to the breast pocket of his own shirt, undid the little button there, pulled it open, made a plucking gesture over Andrew's face, as if he were pulling off a loose eyelash, and, bringing his hand back, rubbed his fingers together over the open pocket, dropping something in.

"You're there," he said. "You're in my pocket."

"All day?" Andrew asked.

"All day." Jack smiled again. And Andrew, looking up at him, said, "I love you," astonished even as he said the words at how dangerously he was teetering on the brink of villainy.

Unlike Jack, who had a job, Andrew was floating through a strange, shapeless period in his life. After several years at Berkeley, doing art history, he had transferred to Columbia, and was now confronting the last third of a dissertation on Tiepolo's ceilings. There was always for him a period before starting some enormous and absorbing project during which the avoidance of that project became his life's goal. He had a good grant and nowhere to go during the day except around the cluttered West Side apartment he shared with Allen, so he spent most of his time sweeping dust and paper scraps into little piles— anything to avoid the computer. Allen, whom he had met at Berkeley, had gotten an assistant professorship at Columbia the year before—hence Andrew's transfer, to be with him. He was taking this, his third semester, off to write a book. Andrew had stupidly imagined such a semester of shared writing would be a gift, a time they could enjoy together, but instead their quiet afternoons were turning out one after the other to be cramped and full of annoyance, and fights too ugly and trivial for either of them to believe they'd happened afterwards—shoes left on the floor, phone messages forgotten, introductions not tendered at parties: these were the usual crimes. Allen told Andrew he was typing too fast, it was keeping him from writing; Andrew stormed out. Somewhere in the course of that hazy afternoon when he was never going back he met Jack, who was spending the day having a reunion with his old college roommate, another art-history graduate student named Tony Melendez. The three of them chatted on the steps of Butler, then went to Tom's Diner for coffee. A dirty booth, Andrew across from Jack, Tony next to Jack, doing most of the talking. Jack talking too, sometimes; he smiled a lot at Andrew.

When one person's body touches another person's body, chemicals under the skin break down and recombine, setting off an electric spark which leaps, neuron to neuron, to the brain. It was all a question of potassium and calcium when, that afternoon at Tom's, Jack's foot ended right up against Andrew's. Soon the accidental pressure became a matter of will, of choice. Chemistry, his mother had said, in a rare moment of advisory nostalgia. Oh, your father, that first date we didn't have a thing to talk about, but the chemistry!

At home that evening, puttering around while Allen agonized over his book, Andrew felt claustrophobic. He wanted to call Jack. Everything that had seemed wonderful about his relationship with Allen—shared knowledge, shared ideologies, shared loves—fell away to nothing, desiccated by the forceful reactions of the afternoon. How could he have imagined this relationship would work for all his life? he wondered. Somehow they had forgotten, or pushed aside, the possibilities (the likelihoods) of competitiveness, disagreement, embarrassment, disapproval, not to mention just plain boredom. He called Jack; he told Allen he was going to the library. The affair caught, and as it got going Andrew's temper flared, he had at his fingertips numberless wrongs Allen had perpetrated which made his fucking Jack all right. He snapped at Allen, walked out of rooms at the slightest provocation, made several indiscreet phone calls, until Allen finally asked what was going on. Then came the long weekend of hair-tearing and threats and pleas, followed by the period of indecision they were now enduring, a period during which they didn't fight at all, because whenever Andrew felt a fight coming on he threatened to leave, and whenever Allen felt a fight coming on he backed off, became soothing and loving, to make sure Andrew wouldn't leave. Andrew didn't want to leave Allen, he said, but he also didn't want to give up Jack. Such a period of transition suited him shamefully; finally, after all those years, he was drowning in it.

In skeptical or self-critical moments, Andrew perceived his life as a series of abandonments. This is what he was thinking about as he rode the train from Hoboken out toward Allen's parents' house that afternoon: how he had abandoned his family, fleeing California for the East Coast, willfully severing his ties to his parents; then, one after another, how he had had best friends, and either fought with them or became disgusted with them, or they with him, or else just drifted off without writing or calling until the gap was too big to dare crossing. There were many people he had said he could spend his life with, yet he hadn't spent his life with any of them, he saw now. Nathan and Celia, for instance, who it had seemed to him in college would be his best friends for all time—when was the last time he'd seen them? Five, six months now? Berkeley had severed Andrew from that ineradicable threesome of his youth, and now that he was in New York again it seemed too much had happened for them to fill each other in on, and in the course of it all happening their perceptions and opinions had changed, they were no longer in perfect synch, they weren't able to understand each other as gloriously as they once had because, of course, their lives had diverged, they did not have endless common experience to chew over, and on which to hone shared attitudes. After those first few disastrous dinners, in which arguments had punctuated the dull yawn of nothing to be said, he had given up calling them, except once he had seen Nathan at the museum, where they stood in front of a Tiepolo and Nathan challenged Andrew to explain why it was any good—a familiar, annoying, Nathan-ish challenge, a good try, but by then it was too late. All of this was guilt-inspiring enough, but what made Andrew feel even guiltier was that Nathan and Celia still saw each other, went to parties together, lived in the clutch of the same old dynamic, and presumably the same glorious synchronicity of opinion. They were going on ten years with each other even without him, and Andrew felt humbled, immature. Why couldn't he keep relationships up that long? As for leaving Allen for Jack—wouldn't it amount to the same thing? In three years, would he leave Jack as well?

Perhaps it was just his nature. After all, he had lived for the entire first twenty-two and most of the next six years of his life virtually alone, surviving by instinct, internal resources. This was not uncommon among gay men he knew; some reach out into the sexual world at the brink of puberty, like those babies who, tossed in a swimming pool, gracefully stay afloat; but others—himself among them—become so transfixed by the preposterousness of their own bodies, and particularly the idea of their coming together with other bodies, that they end up trapped in a contemplation of sex that, as it grows more tortured and analytic, rules out action altogether. Such men must be coaxed by others into action, like the rusty Tin Man in Oz, but as Andrew knew, willing and desirable coaxers were few and far between. For him sexual awakening had come too late, too long after adolescence, when the habits of the adult body were no longer new but had become settled and hard to break out of. Chronically alone, Andrew had cultivated, in those years, a degree of self-containment which kept him alive, but was nonetheless not self-reliance, for it was based on weakness, and had at its heart the need and longing for another to take him in. He remembered, at sixteen, lying in his room, his hands exploring his own body, settling on his hip, just above the pelvis, and thinking, No other hand has touched me here, not since infancy, not since my mother. Not one hand. And this memory had gone on for six more years. Had that been the ruin of him? he wondered now. Doomed by necessity to become self-contained, was he also doomed never to be able to love someone else, always to retreat from intimacy into the cozy, familiar playroom of his old, lonely self?

Outside the train window, the mysterious transformations of late afternoon were beginning. It was as if the sun were backing off in horror at what it had seen, or given light to. The train Andrew was on had bench seats that reversed direction at a push, and remembering how impressed by that he had been the first time Allen had taken him on this train, he grew nervous: suddenly he remembered Allen, remembered he was on his way to a man who considered his life to be in Andrew's hands. Already he recognized the litany of town names as the conductor announced them: one after another, and then they were there. By the crossing gate Allen sat in his father's BMW, waiting.

He smiled and waved as he stepped off the train. Allen didn't move. He waved again as he ran toward the car, waved through the window. "Hi," he said cheerily, getting in and kissing Allen lightly on the mouth. Allen pulled the car out of the parking lot and onto the road.

"What's wrong?" (A foolish question, yet somehow the moment demanded it.)

"This is the very worst for me," he said. "Your coming back. It's worse than your leaving."

"Why?"

"Because you always look so happy. Then you fall into a stupor, you fall asleep, or you want to go to the movies and sleep there. Jack gets all the best of you, I get you lying next to me snoring." He was on the verge, as he had been so many times in these last weeks, of saying inevitable things, and Andrew could sense him biting back, like someone fighting the impulse to vomit. Andrew cleared his throat. A familiar, dull ache somewhere in his bowels was starting up again, as if a well-trusted anesthesia were wearing off. It felt to him these days, being with Allen, as if a two-bladed knife lay gouged deep into both of them, welding them together, and reminded anew of its presence, Andrew turned futilely to the car window, the way you might turn from the obituary page to the comics upon recognizing an unexpected and familiar face among the portraits of the dead. Of course, soon enough, you have to turn back.

Andrew closed his eyes. Allen breathed. "Let's not have a fight," Andrew said quietly, surprised to be on the verge of tears. But Allen was stony, and said nothing more.

As they pulled into the driveway the garage doors slowly opened, like primeval jaws or welcoming arms; Sophie, Allen's mother, must have heard the car pulling up, and pushed the little button in the kitchen. A chilly dusk light was descending on the driveway, calling up in Andrew some primeval nostalgia for suburban twilight, and all the thousands of days which had come to an end here, children surprised by the swift descent of night, their mothers' voices calling them home, the prickly coolness of their arms as they dropped their balls and ran back into the warm lights of houses. It had been that sort of childhood Allen had lived here, after all, a childhood of street games, Kickball and Capture the Flag, though Allen was always the one the others laughed at, picked last, kicked. A dog barked distantly, and in the bright kitchen window above the garage Andrew saw Sophie rubbing her hands with a white dish towel. She was not smiling, and seemed to be struggling to compose herself into whatever kind of studied normalness the imminent arrival of friends and relatives demanded. Clearly she did not know anyone could see her, for in a moment she turned slightly toward the window, and seeing the car idle in the driveway, its lights still on, started, then smiled and waved.

A festive, potent smell of roasting meats came out the porch door. "Hello, Andrew," Sophie said as they walked into the kitchen, her voice somehow hearty yet tentative, and she kissed him jauntily on the cheek, bringing close for one unbearable second a smell of face powder, perfume and chicken stock he almost could not resist falling into. For Jack's sake he held his own. Of all the things he feared losing along with Allen, this family was the one he thought about most. How he longed to steep forever in this brisket smell, this warmth of carpeting and mahogany and voices chattering in the hall! But Allen, glumly, said, "Let's go upstairs," and gestured to the room they always shared, his room. Even that a miracle, Andrew reflected, as they trundled up the stairs: that first time Andrew had visited and was worrying where he'd sleep, Sophie had declared, "I never ask what goes on upstairs. Everyone sleeps where they want; as far as I'm concerned, it's a mystery." It seemed a different moral code applied where her homosexual son was concerned than the one that had been used routinely with Allen's brothers and sister; in their cases, the sleeping arrangements for visiting boyfriends or girlfriends had to be carefully orchestrated, the girls doubling up with Allen's sister, the boys with Allen himself—a situation Allen had always found both sexy and intolerable, he had told Andrew, the beautiful college boys lying next to him in his double bed for the requisite hour or so, then sneaking off to have sex with his sister, Barrie. Well, all that was long past—Barrie was now married and had two children of her own—and what both Allen and Andrew felt grateful for here was family: it was a rare thing for a gay man to have it, much less to be able to share it with his lover. Their parents had not yet met each other, but a visit was planned for May, and remembering this, Andrew gasped slightly as the prospect arose before him—yet another lazily arranged inevitability to be dealt with, and with it the little residual parcel of guilt and nostalgia and dread, packed up like the giblets of a supermarket chicken. His half of the knife twisted a little, causing

Allen's to respond in kind, and Allen looked at Andrew suspiciously. "What is it?" he asked. Andrew shook his head. "Nothing, really." He didn't want to talk about it. Allen shrugged regretfully; clearly he sensed that whatever was on Andrew's mind was bad enough not to be messed with.

"Well," Allen said, as they walked into his room, "here we are," and threw himself onto the bed. Andrew followed cautiously. The room had changed hands and functions many times over the years—first it had been Allen's sister's room, then his brother's, then his, then a guest room, then a computer room, then a room for visiting grandchildren. It had a peculiar, muddled feel to it, the accretions of each half-vain effort at redecoration only partially covering over the leavings of the last occupant. There was archaeology, a sense of layers upon layers. On the walnut dresser, which had belonged to Allen's grandmother, a baseball trophy shared space with a Strawberry Shortcake doll whose hair had been cut off, a two-headed troll and a box of floppy disks. Odd-sized clothes suggesting the worst of several generations of children's fashions filled the drawers and the closets, and the walls were covered with portraits of distant aunts, framed awards Allen had won in high school and college, pictures of Barrie with her horse. The bed, retired here from the master bedroom downstairs, had been Sophie's and her husband Lou's for twenty years. The springs were shot; Allen lay in it more than on it, and after a few seconds of observation Andrew joined him. Immediately their hands found each other, they were embracing, kissing, Andrew was crying. "I love you," he said quietly.

"Then come back to me," Allen said.

"It's not that simple."

"Why?"

Andrew pulled away. "You know all the reasons."

"Tell me."

The door opened with a tentative squeak. Some old instinctual fear made both of them jump to opposite sides of the bed. Melissa, Allen's five-year-old niece, stood in the doorway, her hand in her mouth, her knees twisted one around the other. She was wearing a plaid party dress, white tights and black patent-leather Mary Janes.

"Hello," she said quietly.

"Melly! Hello, honey!" Allen said, bounding up from the bed and taking her in his arms. "What a pretty girl you are! Are you all dressed up for Rosh Hashanah?" He kissed her, and she nodded, opening her tiny mouth into a wide smile clearly not offered easily, a smile which seemed somehow precious, it was so carefully given. "Look at my earrings," she said. "They're hearts."

"They're beautiful," Allen said. "Remember who bought them for you?"

"Uncle Andrew," Melissa said, and looked at him, and Andrew remembered the earrings he had given her just six months before, for her birthday, as if she were his own niece.

"Look who's here, honey," he said, putting Melissa down. "Uncle Andrew's here now!"

"I know," Melissa said. "Grandma told me."

"Hi, Melissa," Andrew said, sitting up on the bed. "I'm so happy to see you! What a big girl you are! Come give me a hug!"

Immediately she landed on him, her arms circling as much of him as they could, her smiling mouth open over his face. This surprised Andrew; on previous visits Melissa had viewed him with a combination of disdain and the sort of amusement one feels at watching a trained animal perform; only the last time he'd been to the house, in August, for Sophie's birthday, had she shown him anything like affection. And it was true that she'd asked to speak to him on the phone every time she was visiting and Allen called. Still, nothing prepared Andrew for what he saw in her eyes just now, as she gazed down at him with a loyalty so pure it was impossible to misinterpret.

"I love you," she said, and instantly he knew it was true, and possibly true for the first time in her life.

"I love you too, honey," he said. "I love you very much."

She sighed, and her head sank back into his chest, and she breathed softly, protected. What was love for a child, after all, if not protection? A quiet descended on the room as Andrew lay there, the little girl heavy in his arms, while Allen stood above them in the shrinking light, watching, it seemed, for any inkling of change in Andrew's face. Downstairs were dinner smells and dinner sounds, and Sophie's voice beckoning them to come, but somehow none of them could bring themselves to break the eggshell membrane that had formed over the moment. Then Melissa pulled herself up, and Andrew realized his leg was asleep, and Allen, shaken by whatever he had or hadn't seen, switched on the light. The new, artificial brightness was surprisingly unbearable to Andrew; he had to squint against it.

"We really ought to be going down now," Allen said, holding his hand out to Andrew, who took it gratefully, surprised only by the force with which Allen hoisted him from the bed.

Chairs and plastic glasses and Hugga Bunch plates had to be rearranged so Melissa could sit next to Andrew at dinner. This position, as it turned out, was not without its disadvantages; he was consistently occupied with cutting up carrots and meat. The conversation was familiar and soothing; someone had lost a lot of money in the stock market, someone else was building a garish house. Allen's sister sang the praises of a new health club, and Allen's father defended a cousin's decision to open a crematorium for pets. All through dinner Melissa stared up at Andrew, her face lit from within with love, and Allen stared across at Andrew, his face twisted and furrowed with love, and somewhere miles away, presumably, Jack sat at his drafting table, breaking into a smile for the sake of love. So much love! It had to be a joke, a fraud! Someone—his mother—must have been paying them! Wait a minute, he wanted to say to all three of them, this is me, Andrew, this is me who has never been loved, who has always been too nervous and panicked and eager for love for anyone to want actually to love him! You are making a mistake! You are mixing me up with someone else! And if they did love him—well, wouldn't they all wake up soon, and recognize that they were under an enchantment? Knowledge kills infatuation, he knew, the same way the sudden, perplexing recognition that you are dreaming can wake you from a dream. He almost wanted that to happen. But sadly—or happily, or perhaps just frustratingly—there appeared to be no enchantment here, no bribery. These three lovers were real and entrenched. His disappearance from any one of them was liable to cause pain.

Even with Melissa! Just an hour later—screaming as her mother carried her to the bathtub, screaming as her mother put her in her bed—no one could ignore who she was calling for, though the various aunts and cousins were clearly surprised. Finally Barrie emerged from the room Melissa shared with her on visits, shaking her head and lighting a cigarette. "She says she won't go to sleep unless you tuck her in," Barrie told Andrew. "So would you mind? I'm sorry, but I've had a long day, I can't hack this crying shit anymore."

"You don't have to, Andrew," Sophie said. "She has to learn to go to sleep."

"But I don't mind," Andrew said. "Really, I don't."

"Well, thanks then."

Sophie led him into the darkened room where Melissa lay, rumpled-looking, in Cabbage Patch pajamas and sheets, her face puffy and her eyes red from crying, then backed out on tiptoe, closing the door three quarters. Immediately upon seeing him Melissa offered another of her rare and costly smiles.

"Hi," Andrew said.

"Hi."

"Are you all right?"

"Uh-huh."

"You want me to sing you a bedtime song?"

"Uh-huh."

"Okay." He brushed her hair away from her forehead, and began singing a version of a song his own father had sung to him:

Oh go to sleep my Melly-o
And you will grow and grow and grow

> *And grow and grow right up to be*
> *A great big ugly man like me ...*

Melissa laughed. "But I'm a girl," she said.

"I told you, honey, this is a song my daddy sang to me."

"Go on."

> *And you will go to Timbuktu*
> *And you'll see elephants in the zoo.*
> *And you will go to outer space*
> *And you will go to many a place.*
> *Oh think of all the things you'll see*
> *When you grow to adultery.*

This last line, of course, caught him. It had always been a family joke, a mock pun. Had his father known something he hadn't?

"That's a funny song," said Melissa, who was, of course, too young to know what adultery meant anyway.

"I'm glad you liked it, but since I've sung it now, you have to go to sleep. Deal?"

She smiled again. Her hand, stretched out to her side, rested lightly now at that very point on his hip he had once imagined no one would ever touch. Now her tiny handprints joined the larger ones which seemed to him tonight to be permanently stamped there, like tattoos.

Though he'd left the light on, Allen was already tightly encased between the sheets by the time Andrew came to bed. He lay facing rigidly outward, and Andrew, climbing in next to him, observed the spray of nervous pimples fanning out over his shoulders. He brushed his fingers over the bumpy, reddened terrain, and Allen jumped spasmodically. Andrew took his hand away.

"Don't," Allen said.

"All right, I won't, I'm sorry."

"No, no. Don't *stop* touching me. Please, I need you to touch me. You never touch me anymore."

Andrew put his hand back. "Don't," he said. "Stop. Don't. Stop. Don't stop, don't stop, don't stop."

"Thank you," Allen said. "Thank you."

"Switch off the light."

"You don't know," Allen said, "how much I've missed your hands."

"Allen, I've been touching you plenty," Andrew said.

"No, you haven't. You really haven't."

"This really is a stupid topic for an argument," Andrew said, not wanting to let on the sensation he was just now feeling, of a spear run through him, the whole length of his body. He reached over Allen's head and switched off the light. "Just relax," he said, and settled himself into a more comfortable position against the pillow. "I won't stop touching you."

"Thank you," Allen whispered.

In the dark things broke apart, becoming more bearable. His hand traveled the mysterious widths of Allen's back, and as it did so its movements slowly began to seem as if they were being controlled by some force outside Andrew's body, like the pointer on a ouija board. He had the curious sensation of his hand detaching from his arm, first the whole hand, at the wrist, and then the fingers, which, as they started to run up and down Allen's back in a scratch, sparked a small moan; this too seemed disembodied, as if it were being issued not from Allen's mouth but from some impossible corner or depth of the room's darkened atmosphere. Allen's back relaxed somewhat, his breathing slowed, and Andrew, with his index finger, scratched out the initials "J.S." My God, what was he doing? For a moment he lifted his hand, then thrust it back, ordering his fingers into a frenzy of randomness, like someone covering up an incriminating word with a mass of scribbling. But Allen didn't seem to notice, and breathed even more slowly. Andrew held his breath. What was possessing him he couldn't name, but cautiously he wrote "Jack" on Allen's back, elongating the letters for the sake of disguise, and Allen sighed and shifted. "Jack Selden," Andrew wrote next. "I love Jack Selden." His heart was racing. What if those messages, like invisible ink, suddenly erupted in full daylight for Allen to read? Well, of course that wouldn't happen, and closing his eyes, Andrew gave himself up to this wild and villainous writing, the messages becoming longer and more incriminating even as Allen moved closer to sleep, letting out, in his stupor, only occasional noises of pleasure and gratitude.

VALERIE MINER

TRESPASSING

EXHAUSTED FROM four hours of traffic, Kate and Josie almost missed seeing the two doe and their fawn drinking at the pond. The women waited in the car, cautious lest the noise of opening doors disturb the animals. The deer lingered another five minutes and then stepped off gracefully into the wings of sequoias. Last sun settled on the golden hills. Night noises pulsed: Frogs. Crickets. Mallards. Wind whispered across dry grass. Jays barked from the top of the hill. As the sky grew roses, Kate and Josie watched Jupiter blaze over the Eastern mountains.

They unloaded the Chevy quickly and sloppily, eager for the comfort of the compact wooden cabin they had built with their friends over five summers.

Josie opened the gas line outside the house. Kate lit a fire, reflecting on the joys of collective ownership when the rest of the collective was absent. She could hardly believe it—two whole days away from Meredith High School; forty-eight hours of privacy and peace.

Suddenly starving, they decided to eat right away. Afterward they would sit in front of the fire and read to each other. Kate chopped salad while Josie made pasta and whistled. The sky got redder and then, abruptly, the cabin was dark. With heavy reluctance, Kate walked around and lit the lanterns.

"Oh," Kate said.

Josie turned and caught a flick of brown before her, like an insect crashing on a windshield.

"Damn bats," Kate shook her head and picked up the broom.

"Bats!" Josie screamed. "I thought Iris got rid of those gruesome things last month."

"Must still be some holes in the sun porch," Kate shook her head.

A dark object dropped beside Josie, like a small turd falling, from the eaves. It disappeared. She fretted the wooden spoon through the pasta, watching another tiny brown mass cut its fall in mid-air and swoop across the room. It was too much. "Bats!"

Josie ran outside. She felt safer in the dark.

Kate stayed in the house, sweeping bats out of the windows and back door.

Staring up at the stars, so benign in their distance, Josie considered vast differences between Kate and herself. Rational, taciturn Kate was probably calculating the increasing velocity of wing movement as the bats ignited to wakefulness. Josie, herself, still cringed at Grandma's tales about bats nesting in little girls' hair. And raised as she was in a willful family where intentionality was more important than action, where danger didn't exist if one closed one's imagination to it, Josie was given to the substitution of "good thoughts." Let's see, she forced herself to concentrate on a pleasant memory: how she and Kate met. It was a miracle if you thought about it; *who* would have expected romance at the school xerox machine? But there was Kate copying quark diagrams for her Physics students while Josie waited to xerox a new translation of "La Cigale et La Fourmi." If Kate hadn't run out of toner, they might never have become acquainted.

"All clear," Kate called. There was no disdain in her voice for she had always envied Josie's ability to show fear. She should tell Josie this.

Josie craned her neck and stared at the sky. "Glorious night," she called back. "Wanna see?"

Ducking out the front door, Kate ran through the pungent pennyroyal to her friend. Josie took her hand. Together they stood quietly until they could hear the frogs and the crickets once more.

They slept late and spent the next morning eating eggs and fried potatoes and rye toast. Josie noticed some wasps dancing around the table, so they cleaned up and went outside to lie on the warm deck.

Later they spent an hour fitting molding around the edges of the sun porch's glass door, sealing the house seams against nocturnal trespassers.

At noon the women drove five miles to town for forgotten country necessities—ice, water and flashlight batteries. Josie secretly checked the grocery shelves for bat killer, but she didn't find any and she knew Kate wouldn't approve. As they drove back to the land, Josie tried to renew her enthusiasm for the weekend. She stopped in front of the cabin. Kate, now completely restored by country air, bounded into the house with the grocery bag.

Josie moved the Chevy into the shade of an oak tree which was being gradually occupied by Spanish moss. As she locked up the car, she saw a fat man with a rifle, waddling out of the forest. He wore a yellow cap, a striped T-shirt and bluejeans.

A giant bumblebee, she thought. Then she warned herself to get serious. The land was clearly posted, "No Trespassing. No Hunting." A shiver ran along her collarbone. They were half-a-mile from the highway here. It could be weeks before anyone investigated.

Josie decided to be friendly and waved.

"Hello there," he was winded, hustling to meet her.

Josie closed her eyes and hoped Kate would stay in the house until it was all over.

"I got lost," he said, nodding his whole body. "How do you get back to the highway?"

"That direction," Josie tried to calm herself. "Up the road there."

He looked her over. "You got any water? A glass of water? I've been walking for hours."

Biblical tales filled her head. The Woman at the Well. The Wedding at Cana. The Good Samaritan. "Sure," she said as noncommittally as possible. "I'll be right back."

"Who's that?" Kate greeted her.

Josie tried to be calm. "Water man. I mean, a lost man who needs water." She watched Kate's jaw stiffen. "Now let me handle it. He just wants a glass of water and then he'll be on his way." Josie poured water from a plastic jug into an old jam jar they used for drinking.

"Water, my foot, what is he doing on the land? It's posted 'No Trespassing,' for godsake."

"Listen, Kate, he was hunting and. ..."

Kate took the glass and poured half the water back into the jug. "Don't *spoil* him. He may return."

She stalked out to the man, who was leaning on their car, his gun on the ground. Josie stood at the door, watching.

"Thanks, Mam," he reached for the water.

"No shooting on this land," Kate said as she released the glass.

"Sorry, Mam. I was hunting up there on the North Ridge and I hit a buck. But he got away. I followed, to make sure I got him good. Then I got lost and I guess I wound up here."

"Guess so," Kate said. She held her hand against her leg to stop it from shaking.

"I'll be off your land soon's I finish the water," he promised.

"That's right," she kept her voice even.

"But I'll need to be coming back to get the buck. See, I finally did get him. But since I was lost, I couldn't drag him all over tarnation."

"We don't want a dead buck on the land," Kate conceded. "When're you coming?"

"Tomorrow morning?" he asked. "About 8:00?"

"Fine, and no guns," she said.

"No Mam, no guns."

"Right then," she held her hand out for the jam jar. "Road's that way."

"Yes, Mam."

Kate watched him climb the hill and walked back to the house, shaking her head. Josie reached to hug her, but Kate pulled away. "God damned hunter." She was on the verge of tears.

"How about some coffee or lunch?"

"Naw, are you nuts, after all we ate this morning? No, I think I'll just go for a walk. See if I can find the buck. If there *is* a buck."

Josie nodded. "Want company?" She wasn't keen on viewing a dead animal, but she didn't care to admit being afraid to stay in the house alone, not after her melodramatic performance with the bats last night.

"Sure," Kate was grateful. "Let's go."

Josie locked the ice chest and dropped the jam jar in the brown paper garbage bag on the way out.

It was hotter now, about 85 degrees. The pennyroyal smelled mintier than last night. The day was dry and still—bleached grass, golden hills scumbled against teal sky. A turkey vulture glided above the oak grove. As they walked around the pond, they could hear frogs scholop into the water. Kate stopped to inspect the eucalyptus trees they had planted in the spring. Four out of five still alive, not bad. Further along, a salamander skittered across their path. Josie felt cool even before she entered the woods. In a way, she hoped they wouldn't find the buck. But if there was no buck, who knows what the bumblebee man really wanted?

The woods were thick with madrone and manzanita and poison oak. It was always a balance on the land, Kate thought, pleasure and danger.

Josie wished she had worn sneakers instead of sandals. But Kate didn't seem to be bothered about her feet as she marched ahead. Right, Josie reminded herself, this wasn't a ramble. They continued in silence for half-an-hour.

"'Round here, I guess," called Kate, who was now several yards ahead. "See the way the branches have broken. Yes, here. Oh, my god, it's still alive. God damned hunter."

They stared at the huge animal, its left front leg broken in a fall, panting and sweating, blind fear in its wide eyes.

"I told Myla we should keep a gun at the house." Kate cried, "What are we going to do?"

Josie didn't think about it. She probably wouldn't have been able to lift the boulder if she had thought about it. But she heard herself shouting to Kate, "stand back," and watched herself drop the big rock on the buck's head. They heard a gurgling and saw a muscle ripple along the animal's belly. Then nothing. There was nothing alive under the boulder.

Josie stared at the four bullet wounds scattered up the right side of the buck. The animal's blood was a dark, cinnamon color. She noticed sweat along the hip joints.

Kate walked over to her quietly and took her hand. "Good, brave," she stuttered. "That was good, Josie."

"Yeah, it seemed the right thing."

Kate hugged Josie and gently drew her away from the dead buck and the broken bush.

They walked straight out to the trail. Neither one seemed to want to stay in the woods for their customary ramble. Kate watched her friend closely, waiting for the explosion. This silence was so uncharacteristic of Josie. Soon, soon, she would erupt with anger and aggravation and guilt and a long examination of what she had done in the woods. For her own part, Kate could only think of one word. Brave.

"Let's go swimming," Josie said, trying to focus on the trail. "It'll cool us off."

The two women stripped on the makeshift dock and lay in the sun beside one another. Kate was slim, her legs long and shapely. She didn't think much about this body which had always served her well. She never felt too thin or too plump. Josie, in contrast, fretted about her zaftig breasts and hips. Her skin was pinker than Kate's, a faint pink. Kate curled up beside Josie, her legs across Josie's legs, her head on Josie's shoulder.

Josie closed her eyes and told herself it was over. They were all right. She had never killed anything before and she felt terribly sad. Of course, the animal had been dying. It was a humane act. Still, her chest ached with a funny hollowness.

"What's that?" Kate sat up.

They listened, Josie flat and Kate leaning forward from her waist.

The noise came again.

A loud whirrr.

Like an engine.

Whirrr.

"Quail," Kate relaxed back on her elbow. "Come on, let's wash off the feeling of that creepy guy."

She lowered herself into the water from the wooden ladder, surprised as Josie jumped in.

"Freezing," Josie laughed, swimming around her friend and noticing how Kate's blond curls sprang back the minute she lifted her head from the water. "Freezing!"

"You'll warm up," Kate said, herself breathless from the cold.

"You're always telling me to stop daydreaming, to stay in the present. The present is freezing." Josie giggled and splashed her friend.

Kate laughed. She ducked under the water, swimming deep enough to catch Josie's feet, which were treading earnestly.

"Hey, watch it." But Josie called too late. Now she was below the surface, tangled in Kate's legs and the long roots of silky grass. It was green down here and very cold.

They dried out on the sunny dock and dressed before starting toward the house. Often they walked naked across the land, especially after swimming when they didn't want to wear sweaty clothes. Today that didn't feel safe.

Back at the cabin, the afternoon grew long and restless. Both women felt fidgety. Kate put aside her equations and washed all the windows in the house. Josie couldn't concentrate on her translation, so she worked up lesson plans for the following week.

About five o'clock, she glanced at Kate, stretching recklessly to the skylight from the top of a ladder.

"Careful up there."

"Sure, hon."

"What did we bring for dinner?" Josie's mind was blank.

"That beef chili you made last week. And rye bread."

"Why don't we go out?" Josie paced in front of the wood stove. God, she wished Kate would be careful on that ladder.

"Out. But the whole point of being here, oops," she tipped precariously and then straightened. "Hey, just let me get one more lick in here and we can talk. There." She started down the steps. "But the whole point of being in the country is to retreat together in solitary bliss. And what's wrong with your chili? I thought this batch was perfect."

Josie shrugged and looked out the big bay window across the grass. She told herself to watch the horses ambling along the ridge or the hawk hovering over the pond. Instead she was caught by a line of lint Kate had left in the middle of the frame. "I don't know. Not in the mood. Guess I'd like vegetarian tonight." Her eyes stung.

Kate stood behind her; still Josie could sense her nodding.

"Why not," Kate said. "Be nice to take a ride this time of evening."

Edna's Cafe was practically empty. But then—Kate checked her watch—it *was* only 5:30. Edna waved menus from behind the counter. Josie and Kate said yes.

"Coffee, girls?" Edna carried the menus under her arm, pot of coffee in one hand and mugs in the other.

"Thanks," Josie said.

"Not just yet," Kate smiled. Edna reminded her of Aunt Bella who worked in a coffee shop back East.

While Kate studied the menu, Josie excused herself to the restroom.

Kate breathed easier when Josie returned to the table looking relaxed. She felt a great surge of affection as her companion intently appraised the menu.

"I think I'll have the chef's salad with Jack cheese," Josie decided.

"Sounds good," Kate nodded. She was relieved to see Josie looking happy. "Two chef salads, with Jack cheese," she called over to Edna.

They talked about plans for the following summer when they could spend four consecutive weeks on the land.

"You two girls sisters?" Edna served the enormous salads.

"No," laughed Kate. "Why?"

"Don't know. You kinda look alike. 'Course when I stare straight at you like this, there's not much resemblance. I don't know. And you always order the same thing."

"In that case, I'll have tea," Kate laughed again. "With lemon."

They ate silently, self-conscious of being the only ones in the restaurant. Kate could hardly get down the lettuce. She'd feel better after she made the phone call. She wouldn't tell Josie, who would get nervous. But it was responsible to report the intruder to the sheriff. "Excuse me. Now I've got to use the bathroom," she said to Josie. "Don't let Edna take my salad."

"I'll guard it with my life," Josie grinned.

The sheriff's number was posted beneath the fire station number. She dialed and heard a funny, moist sound, as if the man were eating or maybe clicking in his dentures. She concentrated on the sturdy plastic of the phone.

"Hello," he said finally.

She began to report the incident.

"Listen, you're the second lady to call me about this in twenty minutes. Like I told the other one, there's nothing I can do unless the man is actually trespassing on your land. Since you've invited him back tomorrow, he ain't exactly trespassing."

"We didn't exactly invite him."

"OK, if it makes you feel easier, I said I'll swing by about 8 a.m. That's when the other lady said he'd be coming."

"Thank you sir."

"Sir," she shook her head as she walked back to the table. She hadn't said "sir" in fifteen years.

Josie had finished her salad and was doodling on a paper napkin. Definitely signs of good mood. Kate sat down and stared at her until she looked up. "So I hear you have a date with the law tomorrow morning."

Josie smiled. "Hope you don't think I'm stepping out on you."

By the time Kate finished her salad, the cafe was getting crowded.

"Refills?" Edna approached with a pot of coffee and a pot of hot water.

"No thanks, just the check," Josie said.

"Guess you girls didn't mind my asking if you was sisters?"

"No, no, not at all," they spoke in unison.

It was a warm, richly scented evening and they drove home with the top down. Jupiter came out early again. Josie thought how much she preferred Jupiter to the cold North Star.

They were both worn out as they collapsed on the couch together. Their feet on the fruit crate coffee table, they watched pink gain the horizon. It was almost pitch dark when Josie reached up to light the lanterns.

She hesitated a moment, remembering last night, and then proceeded. Light, voila, the room was filled with sharp corners and shiny surfaces. Kate picked up her book, but Josie drew it away, cuddling closer.

"Here?" Kate was surprised by her own resistance. After all, they were alone, five miles from town.

"Where then?" Josie tried to sound like Lauren Bacall.

Kate sighed with a breath that moved her whole body, a body, she noticed, which was becoming increasingly sensitive to the body next to her. "Mmmmm," she kissed Josie on her neck, sweet with late summer sweat.

When Josie opened her eyes, she thought she saw something. No, they had sealed off the sun porch this morning. She kissed Kate on the lips and was startled by a whisssh over her friend's head. "Bats," she said evenly, pulling Kate lower on the couch.

"Don't worry," Kate said. "I'll get rid of him."

Worry, Josie cringed. She wasn't worried; she was hysterical. Calm down, she told herself. Think about the invasion of Poland. This was her mother's approach to anxiety—distract yourself by thinking about people with *real* problems. Worry is a perversion of imagination.

Kate opened the windows and set forth again with the broom, but the bat wouldn't leave. Eventually it spiraled upstairs into the large sleeping loft. Kate shook her head and closed up the house against further intrusion. She shrugged and returned to the couch, where Josie was sitting up, considerably more collected than the previous night.

"It'll be OK," Kate said. "It'll just go to sleep. You know they're not really Transylvanian leeches. They're harmless little herbivores. And rather inept."

Herbivores. Josie thought about eating salad for absolution after she murdered the buck.

Kate reached over and brushed her lover's breast, but Josie pulled away. "Not now, sweetie. I can't just now."

Kate nodded. She picked up her book. Josie fiddled with a crossword puzzle. About 10 o'clock, Kate yawned, "Bed?"

"OK," Josie was determined to be brave. "I'll go up first."

"Sure," Kate regarded her closely. "You light the candle up there. I'll get the lantern down here."

They settled comfortably in the double nylon sleeping bag. Kate blew out the light;. She reached over to rub Josie's back in hopes something more might develop. Suddenly she heard a whissh, whissh, whissh.

"Looks like our friend is back," Kate tried to keep her voice light.

"Just a harmless little herbivore," Josie rolled to her side of the bed, putting a pillow over her head.

That night Josie dreamt that she had become Mayor of Lincoln, Nebraska.

Kate slept fitfully, hardly dreaming, and waking with the first sun.

She lay and watched Josie breathing evenly, blowing the edges of her black hair, her body ripe and luscious in the soft light. If she woke up early enough, they could make love before Mr. Creepo arrived. And the sheriff. Had they made a mistake in phoning the sheriff?

The loft grew lighter. Kate lay on her back with her head on her palms, wondering where the bat had nested, about the reliability of her research assistant, whether she would go home for Christmas this year. Then she heard the noise.

Her entire body stiffened. No mistaking the sound of a car crawling down the gravel road toward their cabin. She checked her watch. 7 a.m. Shit. The sheriff wouldn't arrive until their bodies were cold. Maybe Josie would be safer if she just stayed in the house; maybe she wouldn't wake her. Yes, Kate pulled out of the sleeping bag. She was grabbed by the nightgown.

"Not so quick, brown fox," Josie said sleepily. "How about a cuddle?"

She was adorable in the morning, thought Kate, completely "dérangé" as Josie, herself, would admit, before two cups of coffee.

The noise outside grew closer and Kate tightened.

"Don't you even want to hear how I got elected Mayor of Lincoln. ..."

"Not now," Kate couldn't stem the panic in her own voice.

Josie sat up. "What is it?" Then she heard the truck's motor dying.

"I'll just go check in with him," Kate said nonchalantly. "You wait here and I'll come back to snuggle." She pulled on her clothes.

"No you don't, Joan of Arc." Josie stood up and tucked her nightshirt into a pair of jeans.

The two walked downstairs together.

The fat man was approaching the house empty-handed. His friend, also bulky and middle-aged, stayed behind, leaning against the red pick-up truck.

Kate called out to him when he was three yards from the house. "Back again."

"Sorry to bother you, Mam. As you can see we didn't bring no guns. We'll just get that deer and then git offa yer property as soon's we can."

His friend shuffled and looked at his feet.

"OK," Kate said gruffly. "We don't want dead animals on the land. By the way, we finished him off for you yesterday."

The man opened his mouth in surprise. His friend moved forward, tugging him back. They closed up the truck and headed into the woods.

Josie watched until they were out of sight. Kate went inside to make coffee.

Half-an-hour later, as they sat down to breakfast, another vehicle crunched down the hill. Josie looked out at the black and white sedan. "Our hero, the sheriff."

They walked over to greet the sheriff, a solid man, who looked them over carefully.

"You the girls who called me yesterday?"

"Yes, we did," Josie smiled.

"Yes," Kate nodded, the "sir" gone as quickly as it had come. She didn't like his expression.

"Only ladies listed on the deed to this land, I see. Looked it up last night. All schoolteachers. Some kind of commune? Something religious?"

"Just friends." Kate stepped back.

"Edna says she thought you was sisters." He squinted against the bright sun. "One sort or another."

"Just friends." Kate's voice was more distant.

"Soooo," the sheriff held his ground. "You want to run through the nature of that problem again?"

As Kate talked with the sheriff, Josie inspected the hunters' pick-up truck. The bumper sticker read, "I live in a cave and one good fuck is all I crave." Inside dice hung from the rearview mirror. On the seat were a parka and two empty cans of Dr. Pepper. The dashboard was plastered with several irridescent signs. The sun glared so that she could read only one. "Gas, Ass or Grass—No one rides for free."

The sheriff noticed her and observed, "Leon's truck. Just as I figured. Leon Bates, a local man. He's, well, he's strayed off the hunting trail before."

"Isn't there something you can do about him?" Josie felt the heat rising to her face. "He might have killed one of us. On our property. With a gun."

"Today," the sheriff's voice was cool, "today your friend tells me, that he has no gun. That in fact, you said he could come back here to get his buck. That right?"

Josie closed her eyes, feeling naive for imagining this man might protect them. Now bureaucracy seemed the only recourse. "Right. Can't we make some kind of complaint about what he did yesterday?"

"Sure can," the sheriff nodded. "If that's what you want."

"What do you mean?" Kate's back tightened.

"You're weekend folks, right?" He lit a cigarette.

"We work in the city, if that's what you mean," Kate spoke carefully, "and don't live here year around."

"None of my business what you all have going on here. None of Leon's business either. But if you file a complaint and we take it to court, well, he's bound to do some investigating and. ..."

"There's nothing illegal about our land group," Josie snapped.

"Miss, Miss, I never said anything about legal, illegal, but you know there are natural pests the law can't control. And it's better maybe not to get them roused."

Kate and Josie exchanged glances. "Well, perhaps we'll check with Loretta; her sister's a lawyer. We'll get back to you."

"Yes, Mam," he grew more serious. "That about all for today, Mam? I mean you said they didn't bring no guns with them. You feel safe enough on your own?"

"Yes," Josie said. "We're safe enough on our own."

"Then if you'll excuse me, it's almost 8:00 and services start early around here," he stamped out his cigarette and softened. "Church is always open to outsiders and weekend people, by the way. Just three miles down, on the road by the gas station."

"I know where it is," Josie said. "Good-bye, Sheriff."

They watched him roll up the hill, then returned to the house for breakfast. They were both too furious to talk. Kate hardly touched her food, watching out the window for the trespassers.

About 10 o'clock, she saw two pregnant-looking men pulling a buck through the dust by its antlers. Her first thought was how powerful those antlers must be. She tightened and Josie looked up from her book. "At last."

It took the men ten minutes to reach the truck. They were huffing and sweating and Josie had to resist the urge to bring them a pitcher of water. She followed Kate out on the front porch.

Leon Bates glowered at them, as if weighing the value of wasting breath for talk. He and his friend heaved the buck into the truck. On the second try, they made it.

Leon's friend wiped his hands on his jeans, waiting with an expression of excruciating embarrassment.

Leon straightened up, drew a breath and shouted. "That'll do it."

"Good," called Kate.

"Gotta ask one question," Leon leaned forward on his right leg. "What'd you have to go and bust his head for? Ruined a perfect trophy. Just look at the antlers. Would of been perfect."

"Come on, Leon," his friend called.

Kate stood firmly, hands on her hips. Josie tried to hold back the tears, but she couldn't and pivoted toward the cabin.

"The road's that way." Kate pointed. "Only goes in one direction."

Kate stamped into the house. "Damn them. Damn them!" she screamed.

"Hey, now." Josie reached up to her shoulders and pulled Kate toward her. "Hey now, relax love."

"Don't tell me to relax. This man comes on our land, shoots living things, threatens us. And you tell me to relax." She banged her hand on the table.

Josie inhaled heavily and pulled Kate a little closer. "They've gone now." She looked over Kate's shoulder and out the back window, which gleamed in the mid-morning sun. "See, they're over the hill."

"Out of sight, that's what you think, you fool," Kate tried to draw apart.

Josie held tight, hoping to melt the contortions from her friend's face.

Kate pushed her away. Josie lost balance, hitting her head against a pane of glass in the sun porch door.

The glass cracked, sending a high-pitched rip through the room.

Josie ducked forward, her eyes tightly shut, just in time to avoid most of the showering glass fragments.

Drenched in sweat, Kate shook her and shouted, "Josie, Josie, are you all right? Oh, my god, Josie, are you all right?"

"We'll never keep out the bats this way," Josie laughed nervously, on the verge.

"Josie, I didn't mean it." Tears welled in Kate's eyes. "I love you, Josie, are you all right?"

Josie nodded. They held each other, shivering.

Josie stepped forward, "OK, yes, but I feel a little like Tinkerbell. Scattering all this glitter."

"Tinkerbell!" Kate laughed and cried and choked. The room seemed to be closing in on them. Hot, tight, airless. She could feel herself listing.

"But you, hey," Josie frowned, "Let's go upstairs and have *you* lie down."

They sat on the bed, holding hands and staring out at the land. The day was hot, even dryer than yesterday and the golden grass shimmered against the shadowy backdrop of the woods.

"We really should go down and clean up the glass, put a board over the shattered pane." Kate whispered.

"Yeah, if we don't head home soon, traffic's gonna be impossible."

Kate rested her head on Josie's breast. She smelled the musk from the black feathers beneath her arms. Her hand went to the soft nest at the bottom of Josie's generous belly. Josie slipped off her clothes. Kate followed. They sank down on the bed, swimming together again, sucked into the cool sleeping bag.

"Home," Josie murmured.

"Hmmmm?" Kate inhaled the scents of Josie's sweat and sex. Forcing herself to be alert, she pulled back. Was her friend delirious? Maybe she had a concussion.

"Home," Josie kissed her with a passion so conscious as to take away both Kate's concern and her breath.

"Yes," Kate moved her fingers lower, separating the labia, swirling the honey thicker. "Yes."

Josie crawled on top of Kate, licking her shoulders, her breasts; burying her nose in her navel; kissing her thighs. Then she was distracted by a slow fizzzz, as if their airmattress were deflating.

Josie looked up. Two wasps hovered over them, bobbing and weaving and then lifting themselves abruptly out of vision. Maybe if she just continued Kate wouldn't notice. But it was too late.

"They always come out in the middle of the day," Kate said drearily. "For food. For their nests."

Josie shook her head, staring at the unsteady, fragile creatures.

"What the hell," Kate shrugged, inching away from Josie.

"What the hell," Josie whispered seductively. They returned to the pleasures between them. When they finished making love, Josie curled around Kate. She explained how she had been elected Mayor of Lincoln, Nebraska.

The wasps wove over and around the two women. Even as they fell asleep.

JAIME MANRIQUE

THE DAY
CARMEN MAURA
KISSED ME

I WAS ON MY WAY to the Algonquin Hotel to have a drink with my friend Luis whom I hadn't seen in several years. It was 4 p.m. in mid-June, and looking up the vertical canyons of midtown Manhattan, I saw a lead-colored, spooky mist engulfing the tops of the skyscrapers, threatening rain. As I passed Sardi's, my eyes snapped a group composition made of three men, TV cameras, and a woman. Living as I do in Times Square, I've become used to TV crews filming in the neighborhood around the clock. But the reason I slowed down my pace was that there were no curious people hanging around this particular TV crew. The four people were not students, either—they were people my age. I noticed, too, they spoke in Spanish, from Spain. Then, to my utter astonishment, I saw her: *la divina* Carmen Maura, as my friends and I called her. Almodóvar's superstar diva was taping a program with these men outside Sardi's. It's not like I'm not used to seeing movie stars in the flesh. O'Donnell's Bar, downstairs from where I live, rents frequently as a movie set. Just last week, coming home, I ran into Al Pacino filming in the cavernous watering hole. You could say I'm starstruck, though; and I'm the first to admit it was my love of the movies that lured me to America. But after ten years on Eighth Avenue and 43rd Street, I'm a jaded dude.

Carmen Maura, however, was something else. She was my favorite contemporary actress. I looked forward to her roles with the avidity of someone whose unadventurous life needs the vicarious thrills of the movies in order to feel fully alive. I adored her as Tina, the transsexual stage actress in *Law of Desire*. But what immortalized her in my pantheon of the divine was that moment in *Women on the Verge* when, putting on a perfectly straight Buster Keaton–face, she orders the girl with the Cubist profile to serve spiked gazpacho to everyone in her living room. After I saw the movie, I fantasized carrying with me a thermos of gazpacho to offer a cup to (and put out of circulation) all the boring and obnoxious people I encountered in my humdrum routines.

Carmen stood on the sidewalk, under the restaurant's awning, speaking into a microphone, while the cameraman framed her face and Sardi's sign above her head.

Riveted, I stood to the side of the men and diagonally from the star, forming a triangle. For a moment, I fantasized I was directing the shoot. What's more, I felt jealous and resentful of the technicians working with Carmen. To me, they seemed common, unglamorous, undeserving of existing within range of the star's aura. I stayed there, soaking in her presence, thinking of my friends' reactions when I shared the news with them. Momentarily there was a break in the shooting and, getting brazen, I felt compelled to talk to her. The fact that I was dressed up to meet Luis at the Algonquin helped my confidence. I was wearing what I call my golf shoes, a white jacket, a green Hawaiian shirt and a white baseball cap that says "Florida" and shows two macaws kissing. Therefore, it was unlikely that Carmen would mistake me for a street bum.

As I took two tentative steps in her direction, I removed my sunglasses so that Carmen could read all the emotions painted on my face. I smiled. Carmen's eyes were so huge, and liquid and fiery, that the rest of the world ceased to exist. For an instant, I felt I existed alone in her tunnel vision. I saw her tense up, and an expression of bewilderment, unlike any I had seen her affect in the movies, showed in her face. Carmen exchanged looks with her men, who became very alert, ready to defend their star from any danger or awkwardness.

"Carmen," I popped, in Spanish. "I love your movies. You've given me so much happiness and I want to thank you for it."

The star's full-toothed smile took me aback. Her men smiled too, and went back to loading their camera or whatever they were doing.

"We're taping a show for Spanish television," Carmen said. She was wearing a short white skirt, and a turquoise silk blouse and red pumps, and her Lulu hair was just like in *Women on the Verge*, except a bit longer. Her lips and fingernails were painted an intense red, and her face was very powdered. Extremely fine blonde fuzz added a feline touch to her long, sleek cheeks. "This is where *Women on the Verge* received an award," she was saying as I landed back on earth.

A momentary silence ensued, and we stood face to face, inches away from each other. Her poise and her ease and her friendliness were totally disarming, but suddenly I couldn't help feeling anxious. I decided to finish the encounter before I did something silly or made her yawn. It seemed ridiculous to ask her for an autograph so, as a goodbye, I babbled, "You're the greatest actress in the contemporary cinema." That somehow wasn't enough, did not convey the depth of my emotions. So I added, "You're the most sublime creature that ever walked the face of the earth."

Any reserve she may have had left, melted. Diamond beams flashed in her coal-black eyes, which were like huge pearls into which I could read volumes.

"*Ala!*" she exclaimed, which is an expression that means everything and nothing. Before I realized what was happening, Carmen glided toward me, grabbed my chin and kissed me on the cheek, to the left of my lips.

I bowed, Japanese style (Heaven knows why!) and sprinted down the street. At the corner of Broadway and 44th, I turned around and saw that Carmen and her men had resumed their taping. My heart wanted to burst through my chest. I was out of breath, almost hyperventilating. I felt strangely elated. Aware of the imbecilic smile I must have painted on my face, I put on my sunglasses. Although the DON'T WALK sign was on, I crossed the street. A speeding taxi missed me by half an inch, but I didn't care—at that moment I would have sat smiling on the electric chair. Standing at the island in the middle of Broadway and Seventh Avenue, I had to stop for a moment to recollect where I was going and why.

"Wait 'till Luis hears about this," I thought.

My friend Luis is a filmmaker and a movie nut; it was our love of the movies that had brought us together. He had been educated in the States, where he graduated in filmmaking at UCLA. We had met in Bogota, in the early '70s. I made my living at that time reviewing movies and lecturing about the history of the cinema at the Colombian Cinematheque. Luis, who was wealthy and didn't have to work, published a film magazine and made documentaries. We were leftists (although we both despised the Moscow-oriented Stalinist Colombian left), smoked a lot of Santa Marta Gold, ate pounds of mushrooms, and it wasn't unusual for us to see three and four movies a day. We were the angry young men of the Colombian cinema; we had declared war on the older generation of Colombian filmmakers, whom we considered utterly mediocre and bourgeois. I'm speaking, in other words, of my youth. Later I moved to Europe and even later to New York, where I now make a living as a college professor. Nowadays I'm haunted by the Argentinean refrain: "In their youth they throw bombs; in their forties, they become firefighters." Luis, on the other hand, had remained in Colombia where he continued making documentaries and feature films that were distributed in Latin America but had never been released in the States. Slowly, we had drifted apart. He never called me anymore when he was in New York. But this morning, when I had heard his voice, the years in between had been obliterated in one blow and I had joyously accepted his invitation to meet for drinks at the Algonquin like we used to do in the old times when we dressed in jackets and ties so we could have a few drinks while we watched the film critics, movie directors and stars that we idolized and who frequented the place at that time.

It began to sprinkle heavily when I was about a couple of hundred yards from the hotel's awning. I broke into a fast sprint in order not to mess up my jacket and shoes.

The last time I had been in the Algonquin had been to meet Luis. I felt like I was walking into a scene of the past. Maybe the crimson carpet was new, but the rest of the place was dark and quaintly plush, as I remembered it. I told the waiter I was meeting a friend for drinks. There were a few people in the vast room. I scanned the faces looking for Luis. The times had changed, indeed: I saw a couple of kids in shorts and T-shirts drinking beer and munching peanuts. But I couldn't find Luis. I was about to ask for a table when a woman waved at me. I waved back as a polite reflex. When she smiled, I recognized her: it was Luis, I mean Luisa, as he was called in drag. I forgot to mention that even though Luis is heterosexual and has lived with a girlfriend for a long time, he is a militant drag artist.

Blushing, I said to the waiter, "That's my party."

Luisa offered me her hand, which I judged it would be inappropriate to shake, so I bowed, kissing the long fingers which reminded me of porcelain pencils.

"You look like a Florida tourist in Disneyland," Luisa said in English, the language in which we communicated in the States. In this regard we were like the nineteenth-century Russians who spoke French among themselves.

"Guess who I just met," I said, taking the other chair.

"Let me guess. You have stars in your eyes—the ghost of D. W. Griffith."

"You're as close as from here to the moon," I said, noticing the waiter standing between us. We both ordered Classic Cokes and this, too, was a sign of how much we and the times had changed. I told him.

"Was Almodóvar with her?" Luisa asked, reaching for a peanut.

Of course neither Luis nor Luisa would have been thrilled by my encounter. I remembered they both worshipped film directors; whereas for me, the star was everything. I felt disappointed. In my short memory, I had thought running into Carmen Maura was the most fortuitous coincidence that could have happened before meeting my old friend.

I shook my head, fully exasperated. "She was taping a program with some guys for Spanish television." I desperately wanted to change the subject. Luisa chewed the peanut interminably. There was nothing effeminate about Luis when he was in drag. I can easily spot transvestites because of their theatricality and ultrafeminine gestures. But Luisa behaved like Luis: reserved, parsimonious in gesture, and with exquisite aristocratic elegance. She wore brown alligator boots, a long banana-colored skirt, a wide black snake belt around the small waist, and a long-sleeved blouse that closed at the neck with an eighteenth-century school of Quito silver brooch. The chestnut mane of hair was long and flowed all the way to her fake bust. It helped that Luis was extremely skinny and that his features were delicate and that he had a marvelously rosy complexion. His jade-colored eyes, framed by profuse pale lashes, were utterly beguiling. Luisa could have been mistaken for a structuralist pre-Columbian expert, or an Amazonian anthropologist, or a lady photojournalist who photographed ancient cities in Yemen or some place like that. It took me a few seconds to remember the dynamics of our friendship: Luis and Luisa were the passive ones, the listeners who laughed at my jokes. I was their court jester.

Obviously I had gotten out of the Carmen Maura incident all the mileage I was going to get. I was rescued from my predicament by the waiter who set the Cokes down, asked us whether we wanted anything else, and left mortified with our drinking habits.

Instead of asking about our friends in common back in Colombia, I began with the most generalized question I could think of, "So what's the gossip?"

"I can't go back to Colombia," Luisa said with a twinge of sadness in her voice. She sipped her Coke to give me time to digest the news. "I had to get out of there in a hurry. I was in the middle of shooting a movie. Can you imagine the timing of these people!" Luisa reached for her big straw pocketbook and pulled out a small wooden box. It looked like one of those boxes where guava wedges wrapped in banana leaves are packed for export, except that it was painted black. She set the box between our glasses.

"It's a box for *bocadillos*. Is it for me?" I asked.

"No, it's for me. But open it," she prodded me.

Suddenly the box looked creepy, weirding me out. "What is it? A bomb?"

Luisa teased my curiosity cruelly, with her characteristic gothic humor. "You're not even warm. Just open it."

"No, you open it," I said, thinking she was about to play one of her nasty jokes on me.

"Okay," Luisa acquiesced, removing the top of the box.

Inside the box there was a crudely made replica of Luisa. Now I got it: it was supposed to be a small coffin, and something like dried ketchup was generously splashed over the little doll.

"That's real blood," Luisa said pointing at the red stuff.

"What the fuck is that supposed to mean?" I asked, horrified.

"Have you become such a gringo that you don't know what's going on in Colombia?" Luis wanted to know.

"I read the papers," I said, shrugging. "I know paramilitary groups are killing prominent members of the opposition. Furthermore," I continued with my recitation to show Luisa I was still a Colombian through and through, "I know they're killing left-wing sympathizers and outspoken liberals. I keep in touch," I said, as if to absolve myself of all guilt. And yet, it just blew my mind to even think that Luisa might have become a leftist. If we had resisted the temptation back in the early '70s when the pressure had been intense, I refused to accept that twenty years later Luisa had finally succumbed to Marxism-Leninism. On the other hand, I had heard of people in Colombia who had become socialists just out of exasperation with the telephone company.

"First they call you. And they say something like, 'We saw your wife yesterday in the supermarket.' Or, 'we know at what time your little son comes home from school.' That's the first warning. Then they send you a blank telegram. And finally, you receive this little coffin, which means you have 48 hours to get the hell out before they pop you," she explained.

I felt nauseous. "Do you mind?" I asked, taking the top of the box and covering it. Next I gulped down half of my Coke. I looked around: Kathleen Turner was now seated at the table nearest to us. She was accompanied by an equally famous journalist. In the past, we would have been dizzy at the proximity of these luminaries; we would have sat there eyeing them, imagining their conversation, reviewing what we knew about them.

"But why did they send this ... thing to you? Have you become a member of the Party?"

"I hope never to sink that low," Luisa smirked.

"Then why?"

"Those creeps are our moral majority. They hate communists, liberals, nonconformists and homosexuals."

"But you're not gay."

"Of course not. But you tell them that. You try to explain to them that I dress in drag because of ... artistic necessity. Just like Duchamps did. And Chaplin."

"I hear Muammar Qaddafi loves to dress in drag," I said, realizing immediately how inappropriate my remark was.

Luisa smiled. "He must do it for religious reasons, or something like that."

"So what are you going to do?"

"I'm going to Spain for a while. I'll look up Carmen Maura and say hello for you when I'm in Madrid," he teased me. "Sylvia will meet me there in a few weeks," he added, referring to his longtime girlfriend. "She had to stay behind to wrap up my affairs. Then we'll wait a year or two until the situation blows over. I don't think I could live permanently abroad. Colombia is home for me."

Becoming defensive, I said, "But you can't blame me for not living there. It sounds like I would have been one of their first targets, don't you think? I'd rather be a homeless artist than a dead hero."

Luisa sighed before she took a long sip. "Tell me about you. Are you happy? What have you been up to all these years?"

"You'll have to wait until I write my autobiography," I joked. Becoming serious, I thought: How could I make her understand my present life? A life so different, so far removed from all that stuff? She probably could see for herself that New York had become a third world capital, like Bogota; and America a class society, like Colombia. But how could I explain my new interests nowadays: bodybuilding, a vegetarian diet, abstinence from sex, nicotine and most mood-altering substances? How could I explain that my current friends were not into revolution, not into changing the world, but into bioenergetics, rebirthing, Zen, Buddhism, healing groups, Quaker meetings, *Santeria,* witchcraft studies, neo-paganism and other New Age phenomena?

We did go on to lighter subjects as we consumed a few Classic Cokes. We gossiped about old acquaintances and friends in common, the Colombian film industry, the despised enemies of the past, and our favorite new movies. We agreed to meet for a farewell movie before Luisa left for Europe.

It was past six o'clock when we left the Algonquin, which by then was abuzz with all kinds of artistic and quasi-artistic people talking deals.

It had stopped raining, and the rain had washed away the layers of dust and papers that had accumulated since the last summer shower. The oppressive mist had lifted, too, and the worst of the dreaded rush hour was over so that although Manhattan was alive with the promise of night's splendors, the atmosphere felt almost relaxed. Or maybe it was just my mood.

At the corner of Avenue of the Americas, we hailed a cab. I kissed Luisa on both cheeks, closed her door and waved goodbye as her taxi disappeared in the uptown direction. I felt rejuvenated. It cheered me to realize that the affection for my friend was intact and that we'd probably go on meeting for many more years. I meandered across town, enjoying the nippy air, and the pinkish glow of the bald sky over the metropolis. The sun must have hovered someplace over the Hudson, but night seemed to be pushing not far behind it. The lighted buildings and billboards blazed like a high-tech aurora borealis. As I passed Sardi's, I noticed its emerald green sign, and the mailbox next to which I had stood watching Carmen, and the lamppost next to it, which now projected a circular beam of red-gold light under which I bathed, basking. I was about to continue on my way when, looking across the street, I spotted Carmen and her men still shooting their program. I stood still, becoming aware of the street separating us and the cars streaming by, and the slick Manhattanites, and the pristine tourists hanging in front of the theaters that lined 44th Street. And none of these people were interested in *my* Carmen. It was as if on the screen she had been created for all people, all over the world, but in the streets of Manhattan she was only visible to my eyes. I also knew that the magic of the moment when we first met was past; that it would have been inappropriate to interrupt her now or to say hello, or to remind her that just a couple of hours ago she had kissed me. As if to snap the picture forever, I closed my eyes upon the scene and then I started walking toward home, without once looking back.

I crossed Eighth Avenue. As I passed in front of Paradise Alley, the porno palace next door to O'Donnell's Bar, the score or so of crack addicts hanging out in front of my place of residence were no longer hideous to me. This evening I accepted them as the evil spirits necessary in all fairy tales. Pity arose in my heart for them. In their dead angry eyes, I read their hopelessness and suddenly they seemed as doomed and tragic as the people who were being wiped out back home. The man and the woman smoking crack in front of my door moved reluctantly as I opened the door and leaped over the puddle of piss that the rain had not washed away. Taking the steps of the stairs two at a time, I felt happy and sad in the same breath. It was a new sensation, this happy/sad feeling I experienced. It was sadness for all that was sad in this wide mysterious world we tread upon; and it was the unreasonable happiness produced by the tinsel gleam of the glamorous dreams that had brought me to America and for which I had had to wait for many years before brief, heart-breaking in their fleetingness they became real.

THE DRESS

So, I'm in the thrift store after work; I'm smudged up with ink and my back hurts from running a printing press all day. Shopping has been mildly successful: I've found a wool sweater from Italy, a shirt for my lover and a 100% cotton bathrobe for myself. As I'm unloading my finds onto the counter for this dyke with a mustache and eye make-up to tally, I look up. There is this dress ... hanging there (my neck freezes in a tilted position) ... an incredible dress.

"Woa," I say to the dyke, who has seen my mouth open and is grinning while she looks at my tags. "So ... how much is the dress?"

"Twenty-one fifty," she says, "It's a steal, believe me."

I look back at the bathrobe. Well, I'm glad it costs that much: I'm hardly going to spend 20 bucks on a dress.

But I can't take my eyes off it.

It's black. It's a work of art. It's a strapless, knee-length gown with a skirt like a pyramid, layers and layers of black shiny stuff (I don't know what you call it: I know cotton and I know flannel). Anyway, black and then another layer of black and then gauze and net. Sewn onto the layers, in no kind of pattern, are these gorgeous hot pink poppies made of satin; little ones and big ones glowing in different intensities through the layers—not gaudy, mind you, "just a suggestion," as my mother would say. And then over the top of all of it and up the tight bodice to the breasts, is this black lace.

It's probably too small, I think, and besides, my hundred percent cotton bathrobe and such are all bagged up in front of me. It's time to go.

But instead, I say, "Here, will you keep these a minute?" and push the bag back, "I have to try on that dress."

Well, just then another worker takes the dress down for an older woman who is obviously buying it for someone else and there's a whole crowd of people standing around her because I'm telling you, it's a work of art, this dress. She's holding it up and women are fingering the layers and admiring the stitching. She's definitely decided to buy it.

Suddenly, I'm tapping her on the shoulder.

"May I try it on?"

"Certainly, dear, go right ahead," she says, giving me a motherly once-over.

Now, let me tell you very clearly that I am a dyke. I am not a gay lady or a homosexual woman, I am a fucking man-hating dyke. I do not look straight. I don't wear nice girl make-up or sweet-little suits or passable shoes. I am a fucking spikey-dyke. And this noisy dress, rustling even while it's cradled in my arms, is like a foreign object, like nothing I've ever touched before. I strip off my tank-top and my sweat pants and fuzzy crew socks and high-top Adidas. It probably won't fit, I think.

I slip it onto my naked body. I zip it up the back, very, very slowly. It's going to catch somewhere, this dress isn't really for me, I'm thinking.

It zips. To the top. And it's incredible, because that slinky material is lying in folds across my ass and I can feel the air rushing up to my cunt. There are these stays in the bodice that touch my ribs like fingers and I can feel the air coming down around my breasts, my breasts that touch against the sides of this lacy thing, pull away and then touch it again. I turn a circle and the layers fan out and slide across my ass: it feels like the tease of lifting the sheets up and laying them down again. What a dress. The top of me feels totally naked, even though I know it's not and my cunt feels buried beneath this black lace, ass feeling a fabric that only it knows about. My cunt, in the middle of 17 Reasons Why Thrift Store, is getting totally juiced out.

Oh Goddess, I'm thinking, I could wear it to a Sleaze Dance, with fingerless black gloves and big ol' chains, nasty, nasty make-up and spike heels. I could surprise my lover with it. I would drop her off at the door, tell her it was bad luck to see my costume first or some such excuse and she would complain and ask questions and try to have things her way as usual but I would insist.

Then, about a half hour later, when I was sure she had made the rounds and was standing with a beer and two or three friends, I would come in. Not, repeat, NOT, like a helpless femme-bot. Like a bad-ass, no-games, knows-her-mind-and-will-tell-you-too, femme. First, I would just stand there, and let her wonder. Maybe I would just stand there altogether, and let her come to me. Or maybe, while all the heads were turning (because of the dress, now, I'm not fooling myself) I would stride across the dance floor in a bee-line for that green-eyed woman I love, so that everyone would see who the one in that black dress was going to fuck tonight; everyone would see her frozen in her tracks, exposed, just like me. Standing in the thrift store dressing room, I can see her squirming. It's making by blood sing.

Now, I am one of those lesbians, who, unfortunately, was not born a lesbian; I didn't know at age five that I was queer. I spent (totally regrettable) years as a heterosexual and it made me very uncomfortable with any amount of beauty I might have. I pull the dressing room curtain tighter around the door. Goddess, don't let anyone see me. As a straight girl, I was not beautiful, I was "intelligent." I didn't look hot, I looked "serious." Lace was out of the question—femmes are belittled, thought to be weak, stupid, and forget it, honey, that isn't me. This is a dress I wouldn't even have thought of wearing when I was straight.

But now it's safe. My lover isn't going to think me incompetent if I dress a little femme-y, I think, fingering the strange layers hanging off my waist. Now it's possible to embrace ... well, more of my ... beauty. And this dress is the hidden side of me. I know this in the dressing room from the flush on my face. The dress's erotic power doesn't feel anything like the terrible memories I have of wearing skirts in the straight world. The air coming up my legs doesn't tell me that I'm exposed and unprotected in a world of men, but that in my safe world of sex with women I choose at this moment to make myself vulnerable to my lover.

I don't remember taking the dress off: the next thing I know, I'm climbing back into my sweat pants and begging the woman, is she sure she wants to buy it? She is, and does.

Then I'm striding across Valencia St. towards the gym to lift weights and practice my boxing. Only as a lesbian, I think: one minute covered in lace and nearly coming in a dressing room, the next minute charging down the street towards the punching bag.

On a folding chair in the women's locker room, staring at the tips of my high-tops and trying to calm my shaking hands, I'm amazed at how much I want this dress. I'm kicking myself for not insisting on buying it. I suppose if I hadn't been so struck with the dress's effect on me I would have argued with the woman or beat her to the cash register. Or maybe I was thinking, "this is so powerful, take it away from me, I don't want to deal with it." Or maybe, "this thing is so beautiful, I don't deserve it." Like a first kiss, no dress will ever be quite the same as this one. My hands are not a-quiver, or trembling even, I am out-and-out shaking with the way I felt in that dress. Naked. Powerful. Vulnerable. In fact, so vulnerable that I think perhaps the scenario would not be me, striding across the floor like a tough femme-top, but me, so raw, that I would arrive at this imaginary dance at my lover's side and hold onto her arm, both of us aroused by my exhibition.

I move into the gym to the big bag. I think about all that black lace. As I cover my knuckles, entwine my fingers with the wide Everlast fighters wraps, take a stance, pull one fist to my face, the other ready for the punch, I just shake my head and think, "Oooh, that dress."

SUSANNA J. STURGIS

DEER OUT OF SEASON

From the air the island lies like a sleeping dragon: its back humped in a roughly triangular shape, tail curled up to the east, head stretched out to the west. From the air the dragon's green hide is lavishly scarred with brown, scored with gray and white. The pattern on its haunch is the airport's dovetailed runways, the long east-west line across its belly the Edgartown–West Tisbury road. Cars move along this and the other lines like dragon mites.

From the sky the mainland seems a quick step away, but the ferries take almost forty-five minutes to cross Vineyard Sound, stitching the same path over and over again. Islanders mutter incessantly about the boats, about the cost of getting a car off-island, the difficulty of securing reservations from May through October, and the consequent long waits in the standby line. They complain when howling northeasters force cancellation of one trip after another, and when, every other decade or so, Vineyard Haven harbor ices up and no boats can get through. Ask, though, if they would prefer a bridge and the fire in their eyes will scorch your hide.

Like the ferry lanes, most of the island's roads are invisible from the air; so too are its houses. Likewise the lives within them, a visitor might suggest, and with good reason. But few events, no matter how clandestine, go totally unremarked. At least one person living on a less-traveled dirt road will notice, say, the old green Volvo station wagon that appears one afternoon outside a neighbor's house. Maybe the observer will mention as much to a relative or a co-worker; maybe not.

Consider one Saturday morning in mid-October. In Oak Bluffs Kevin Swanson, a high school junior, sits in his bedroom, cleaning a shotgun he has

298

never used. Once his grandfather's, it was passed to Kevin on October 8, for his sixteenth birthday. Years ago, Kevin's grandfather taught him to shoot a .22 and walk quiet in the woods; now, barely 60, he battles emphysema in the hospital's long-term care unit. Because Kevin has a brother and sister, both several years younger, ammunition is kept locked in his father's closet, but Kevin is entrusted with one of the two keys. He is counting the days till deer week begins on November 30th.

In the same hour on the same Saturday, Katherine Ferrelli drives her beige Trooper up to her front door. Her hair, loosely caught in a beaded barrette, glows silver in a brief splash of sunlight. A computer consultant by profession, Katherine also provides emergency shelter and court advocacy for battered women. Her front-seat passenger, a dark-haired woman in paint-flecked denims, an Irish fisherman's sweater, and dark glasses, doesn't move. "Here we are," Katherine says. Less restrained, the woman's two younger children—a girl of 11, a boy almost 9—pile out the back.

Also in the same hour, in an Edgartown neighborhood whose existence is unsuspected by tourists, where the pitted dirt roads turn marshy in the rain, Giles Kelliher towels his curly brown hair. He is 31 and has lived on the Vineyard for less than a year. Though he didn't get home from the restaurant until three, the morning light in his kitchen won't wait while he sleeps in. As coffee brews, he pulls his easel in from the hall and takes watercolors and brushes from the drawer next to the flatware. If the phone rings, he will let the machine answer it.

Later the same day, as the eastern horizon is darkening blue and the westering sun pauses on the top of the pines, a white van drives slowly through a West Tisbury subdivision. "SWANSON PAINTING," say the block letters on both sides, "INTERIOR & EXTERIOR." The driver notes the old Volvo wagon parked beside the newly shingled Cape but sees no lights, no unusual activity in the house, so he speeds up again. Where next? Pick up a pizza and a six-pack on the way home, he decides; then he'll know what to do.

Two days later, in the last hour of Columbus Day, Jay Soares drives westward along the long road that traverses the sleeping dragon's underbelly. Though his job often takes him out on island roads at all hours, he is not working now. He is utterly sober but exuberant enough to be driving 15 miles per hour over the speed limit. Why not? The road is deserted, and he has driven it since he first got his license. As always, his seat belt is secured. The minute hand on the dashboard clock snaps to 11:16.

The blast hits his car from the right. Gunfire he knows, from his years in Springfield, then in Worcester, and longer ago from the Army Reserve. The steering wheel fights his hands like a rubber-mouthed horse, pulling for the shallow shoulder and, beyond, the scrubby oak and the line of pines. Don't brake in a skid, he remembers his dad saying, over and over; is he skidding? A tree throws him back with a terrible jolt, the rear end of the Volvo pivots, bouncing, to the left.

Improbably, the engine still labors, with an ominous metallic rasp, trying to propel the car through the tree. Hand shaking, Jay switches the ignition off. The right headlight is out; he turns the other one off. The clock, unreadable in the dark, says 11:17.

In the abrupt silence, terror shoots through him, leaving a weirdly elated aftertaste. Can I get out? he wonders. Are they waiting? Have they run? Where the fuck am I? It's safer away from the gas tank, he decides, if they start shooting again. Outside the car his left ankle buckles on the uneven ground and he falls headlong. He hears the rip and thrum of an accelerating motor, then silence. As he rises carefully to his feet, light sweeps far above his head. The airport, he realizes with relief; close.

As he limps along the roadside, he is inventing a story, in case anyone asks, to explain why he was driving home from Edgartown to West Tisbury at 11:15 Columbus Day night. Sitting with a client, of course; emergencies are common in his line of work, and no one will ask him to break confidence. He thinks about Wayne, his brother-in-law, a quick-tempered man whose drinking has grown worse in recent years. Relations between them are so strained that he has joked more than once, *If they ever find my body at the bottom of a dumpster, get thee hence and arrest my brother-in-law!*

On Thursday the *Martha's Vineyard Times* editorializes sternly about what many people keep calling "the accident." "In Serbia, Somalia, Boston," it says, "acts of violence are so common that many go unreported. When it happens here, we are shocked. We can talk of nothing else."

Don't be fooled. The island is not immune to hatred and fear, or to the violence they so often beget. Every day the ferries ply Vineyard Sound, bringing people to the island, taking them away. Underwater cables supply the island with electricity and long-distance telephone service. The water surrounding the island is at best a permeable membrane.

The newspaper's lead headline shouts "Midnight Gun Blast Shocks Island" in 48-point type which is about as emphatic as *Times* heads ever get. In one photo the two Edgartown police officers study a station wagon whose right front end seems to have fused with a slender pine. In the other, Jay Soares, Youth Center director, speaks into a microphone at last summer's gala dinner dance, the center's biggest annual fundraiser.

Shannon Merrick bought the paper at the A&P across the street and has stuffed it, unread, into the canvas sack that lies beside her. She is sitting cross-legged on the shallow beach between the Steamship Authority dock and the Black Dog Tavern, dunking bite-size pieces of cookie into her coffee and waiting for her old friend Addy Ruth, who is due on the 3:30 boat. When Addy called on Sunday night—"Hey, I really need to get out of Dodge for a while. Could I come visit?"—Shannon immediately extended an invitation, though it's been most of a decade since they were close. Addy had just been laid off her job as a computer tech when her life partner of five years split for Brooklyn with a Deep Ecology activist (male).

When Shannon stopped by the nearby bakery, several regulars were talking about Monday night: "The paper says they still don't have any real leads" and "Do you believe he actually walked away?" and "What do you bet it was one of the cops?" Unwilling to be drawn into the conversation, she accepted her change, poured cream into her coffee, and slipped out the screen door without making eye contact with anyone.

Shannon knows the story from Jay himself, who has been her friend since he returned to the island more than three years ago. His most recent update, at 8:30 this morning, was that on Wednesday afternoon the police found two spent shotgun shells about 100 yards north of the tree into which his wagon had crashed. Unfortunately, these weren't distinctive enough to be useful.

As the incoming ferry, the *MV Uncatena,* rounds the long stone breakwater, Shanon slips her sandals back on and wanders toward the dock. The balding gent who waves, heavy leather carryall stooping his shoulder, is her dentist. She flips her squashed coffee cup into the trash barrel from about 15 feet out. Someone applauds.

Sliding into her slip, the ferry churns the placid blue water into a green frenzy. Addy Ruth is the short-haired brunette in blue jeans and brown suede jacket who is scanning the crowd from the top deck, a blue nylon knapsack at her feet. Shannon waves; Addy waves back, then turns and disappears down the stairs to the freight deck.

Shannon has live on Martha's Vineyard long enough—an astonishing nine years—to mistrust her memories of the decade of feminist activism that came before. Addy shares the same past, knew the same people, held the same convictions. Whatever distance the intervening years have imposed, that remains a bond between them.

When Shannon moved to the Vineyard in 1983, Addy predicted that after a year or two in the hinterlands, her sister-in-arms would be back on the front lines. But, guided by the island's ways, Shannon clerked in shops and waited tables and spent one winter scalloping with a short-term lover; gradually she built up a circle of friends and, more recently, a freelance graphics business. As the years passed, she was less and less inclined to return to the city, as Addy continually pressured her to do. Since the obvious alternative was an ugly fight, they drifted apart.

In the early 1990s, Shannon still occasionally wonders if Addy is right. Have the last nine years of her life been a cop-out? The more distraught Addy is about losing her job and her girlfriend, the more likely it is she will raise the question. For Addy Ruth, veteran organizer, getting up on her political high horse is one of the essential stages of grieving.

So Shannon is ready for a little shadow-boxing. She is as involved in her new community as she was in the old, though activism looks rather different in a semi-rural, semi-small-town setting. She can defend her choices if she has to. In any case, she remembers enough of city pace and city pressure to know that Addy needs a break.

Addy, once settled into the small second bedroom (from which Shannon's computer and office equipment have been temporarily removed), wants to walk on a beach and watch the sunset. But the glorious light on Lambert's Cove goes mostly unnoticed by both women as one listens to the other's tale of hope and betrayal, as convoluted and as bland, thinks Shannon, as a plate of undressed linguini. Each new player is introduced with something like "oh, you must remember her, she was lovers with Georgia, then they broke up and she and her new girlfriend started the first AIDS support group for women in Somerville."

Shannon likes that part; it reminds here of how island stories are knitted, with the back sides more intricately textured than the fronts. Gossip, she thinks, is like water to a drooping cyclamen, and the best part about Addy's tale is that she is unlikely to encounter any of the principals in the foreseeable future. If Addy can be believed—and to Shannon's ears her story does not seem especially self-serving—her newest ex was dogmatic, manipulative, and probably addicted to prescription tranquilizers.

Later, after stir-fry and several bottles of Dos Equis beer, Shannon retires to her computer while Addy browses through the newspapers and magazines spread out on the coffee table. Not fifteen minutes pass before Addy stands in Shannon's door, shaking today's *Times*. "This guy," she wants to know, "Jay Soares, the one who was run off the road, where did he come from? I could swear I know his name from somewhere."

Shannon forces her attention to stay focused on her Macintosh screen, wondering one more time if she is cutting the projected outlay for color separations a little too close. On a hunch she ups it by $300. When she tallies the numbers, she grins. The total looks right, feels right; when she prints it out, she knows it will even smell right. Maybe the Hill-Nakamura Foundation will actually buy it. "Excuse me," she says, "what were you asking?"

"This Jay Soares," Addy answers. She pronounces his name correctly: "Swarez," not "Sores." "His name's familiar. Where's he from?"

"He grew up in Oak Bluffs." Shannon sends the revised estimate to the laser printer and starts her cover letter. Addy doesn't go away. "He moved back to the island a few years ago to become director of the Youth Center. Now he lives in West Tisbury."

"Did he used to live around Boston?"

"I don't think so," Shannon replies. She then suggests that Addy take some ice cream out of the freezer and put the kettle on for tea, while she finishes her letter.

Ten minutes later, the kettle shrieking behind her like an untended baby, Addy is ensconced in an overstuffed chair, telephone clamped between her ear and left shoulder, scribbling notes on the back of Shannon's phone bill. For Shannon, the scene is straight out of the mid-1970s, when you couldn't leave Addy alone for two minutes without her getting on the phone to make or check arrangements for whatever meeting, demonstration, or concert was coming up. She realizes abruptly that Addy, once the Butt Queen of the women's community, has given up smoking.

Making up a tray—two mugs of Lemon Zinger tea, two dishes of ice cream, a squeeze bottle of honey—in the kitchen, Shannon listens to Addy's *Yeah* and *I'm here* and *What was that number again?* and *Is she reliable?* and wonders to whom she is speaking.

When Shannon returns to the living room, Addy is studying with pursed lips the notes she has scrawled on the back of the phone bill. "Don't worry," she says. "I'll reimburse you for the long-distance calls. So how much do you know about this Jay Soares?"

Shannon nudges magazines, newspapers, and clothing catalogs to one side to make room for the tray, whose burden she deftly distributes while considering her answer. "Why do you ask?" she counters, dribbling some honey into her tea.

"In May of '86," says the private investigator, "he was accused of molesting an eight-year-old girl. Did you know that?"

"Yes, actually, I did," Shannon answers. "I was on the search committee that hired him for the Youth Center job. He helped get the girl out of a god-awful abusive home, and it was her father who made the accusation. He had less than no evidence, his daughter said he was lying, and the so-called charge went nowhere. Jay brought it up at the first interview as something we should be aware of. We checked it out, thoroughly. I don't know who your source is …"

"I know people in Worcester."

"You might suggest that they track down the rest of the story before they scatter any more bits of it about." By breathing slow and steady, Shannon curbs her urge to throttle her guest. That's Addy, she reminds herself, and Addy out of both job and girlfriend is going to prove her usefulness somehow. "Jay's a good man, and he's done a hell of a good job so far," she adds mildly.

A little over three years ago, in July 1989, when Jay Soares accepted the Youth Center job, his old friends shook their heads. The center, they thought, was a vicious shoal that reached out of the sea to wreck careers. Some even swore, with some evidence, that it was a hangout for adolescent drug dealers. Best let it die, they said, and something else arise to take its place. .

Shannon was inclined to agree. As a cofounder of Safe, Strong, and Free, a program that teaches elementary school kids to recognize and resist "unwanted touch," she had been continually irritated by a series of Youth Center directors who wouldn't cooperate with anyone they couldn't control. Each time the director's office became vacant, the center's governing board would bestir itself to choose a replacement, then when that was done they would go back to sleep. Finally they found themselves stuck with a world-class alcoholic, who, after floundering in office for most of a year, led police on an impressive care chase through four of the island's six towns. Not only did his blood alcohol level test out at a spectacular 1.6, he also had two almost equally intoxicated female high school students in the car with him.

Half the board took that cue to resign, and for several weeks the center was a hot topic for coffee shop conversations and letters to the editor. Even the state Department of Youth Services took an interest. When he put in an application, Jay Soares—who not only had the right degrees and references, but was born and schooled on the island—shone like the golden knight born to win the kingdom. Why did such a paragon want to risk his career for a $12,000 cut in pay? Most assumed it had to do with his father, whose chronic respiratory illness had finally forced his retirement from the Oak Bluffs highway department. And who wanted to keep battling those mean urban streets if he could find a good job on the island?

Three years later, Jay Soares, going on 42, had lived up to advance billing. He had acquired a mortgage and, said the grapevine, was getting serious about a divorced high school classmate. It looked as if Jay was settling in.

Friday morning, Shannon makes coffee and raisin toast and tries to figure a tactful way to get Addy out of the house. Sloshing coffee into a West Tisbury Centennial mug, Addy obliges by asking if she can borrow Calamity Jane, Shannon's Corolla, to run into town; she's short on Tampax, she says.

Five minutes after Addy's departure, Shannon calls Jay, who—banged head and sprained ankle be damned—is at work, and explains what Addy is up to. "It never rains, et cetera," he says with a laugh, which actually sounds genuine.

"Listen, dear," Shannon rushes to get the question out, before tact overcomes her, "I don't want to be nosy, but has anyone asked what you were doing in Edgartown at that hour on a Monday night?"

After a long silence, Jay laughs abruptly. "Good thing you aren't working for the papers or the police. It was ... social," he says. "Any guess what your friend will do next?"

Shannon is surprised by his evasion. "Buckle up, honey," she advises. "We may be in for a bumpy ride. Addy just lost her job, then the love of her life left town. She'd rather die than admit she's hurting, so she's shifting into what we used to call her 'missionary position'—convert 'em even if it kills 'em."

Jay is interrupted before he can respond. When he calls back, the jangling phone startles Shannon out of a computer trance. More than an hour has passed; Addy doesn't seem to be back. How long does it take to buy Tampax?

Jay explains. "Well, it has certainly not been a quiet morning in Lake Wobegone," he begins, "and my old friend Ben from the Edgartown police is due any minute. Guess what? Leslie just called from the *Times* and said that a woman—fortyish, five-sixish, athletic-looking brunette?"

"Bingo."

"This woman came in, wanted to talk with a reporter, was directed to our friend, and said that the paper might want to know that blah blah blah. Leslie was very cordial."

"Good thing she got Leslie and not Carl Bernstein, Sr."

"Leslie thinks so too," Jay says drily. "She said she wouldn't have encouraged the woman if she hadn't been, quote, 'just my type.' I'm supposed to ask you if she's single."

"Leslie is incorrigible," Shannon can't help grinning over the phone. "The answer is yes. I'll see what I can do to head Addy off, or to set the two of them on a collision course. So what are you going to do?"

"If the phone stops ringing and cops stop showing up," Jay answers, "I'm calling my old boss to alert him, just in case anyone decides to call. Will I see you at Carol and Marion's tonight?"

"Yes," Shannon replies, delighted that Jay—whose social life generally revolves around Youth Center fund-raising activities—will be there too.

A little after noon, driving up to Gay Head on the first leg of their afternoon tour, Shannon glances in the side-view mirror and remarks, "So I hear you checked out the newspaper office this morning."

Obviously disconcerted, Addy asks, "Who said that?"

"For speed and comprehensive coverage," Shannon says, shielding her eyes against the sun just ahead, "the women's community grapevine has nothing on the Vineyard's."

"I thought ..." Addy begins.

"I understand," Shannon heads off the argument. "Listen, I know it would be simpler if we could take every charge of rape and child sexual abuse at face value, but we can't and you know it as well as I do. Those charges in Worcester were as bogus as those charges ever get, believe me. No one's going to benefit from dragging them up again—except maybe a couple of guys who carry a grudge against Jay for helping their families get help."

Addy watches the road rush by in silence. Shannon hopes she's been listening.

Carol and Marion are rare in Shannon's circle; rather than stop at "We should get together for dinner," they actually extend invitations and set dates and times. With Shannon's help, they drew up the guest list with Addy in mind, hoping that, should the visitor decide to remain on the Vineyard for a couple of weeks, she would have a few new acquaintances to do things with.

As she makes introductions in the living room, Shannon watches Jay mime a bucking steering wheel for Carol, who was en route to the table with the main course. In mock exasperation, Marion sweeps the burden from her partner's hands and carries it into the dining room.

"This is Addy Ruth, my buddy from my feminist politico days," Shannon tells Leslie. "Addy, Leslie Benaron, star reporter ..." She adds, with lifted eyebrows, "I gather you've already met?"

Addy is flustered enough to stumble through "Ah, I guess we have." Leslie winks.

Shannon introduces Addy to Jay and smiles to herself when Addy opens with "I read about what happened—are there any clues?" Addy has decided that she and Jay are on the same side.

As the guests move toward the dining room, Katherine Ferrelli arrives, the formality of her tailored suit tempered by the daring flounce of the flowered silk scarf around her neck. "My God," Leslie says, "you must have been to America."

"Just Hyannis," Katherine replies, hanging her jacket on the coat rack in the hall. "The plane was late again."

"And I thought it was something I said," Jay grins, calling Katherine's attention to the vacant chair on his right. Shannon notes the rough scrape that reddens Jay's left cheek before it disappears into his neatly trimmed beard.

"Your French braid is so elegant," Shannon says. She has for years lusted after Katherine's hair, whose color reminds her of a full moon high in the sky. "Did you do it yourself?"

"Actually not," the new arrival confesses. "I have a house guest with nimble fingers and more patience than I."

Giles Kelliher pauses in mid-step en route to his place. "Heavens," he says, with an exaggerated bat of his eyelashes, "if Leslie said such a thing, I'd suspect a new romance."

"You're very wicked, Giles," says Shannon.

"Heavens yourself," Katherine retorts. "My guest is all of eleven years old. Besides, Mitch and I are doing quite well." As Giles continues on his way, laughing, Katherine adds, "God knows why—nobody else is."

"*I'm* doing fine," Giles says, also to Shannon, patting the empty chair next to him. "See? I saved you a seat."

Shannon sits. "So what's new with you?" she asks Giles. "I don't think I've seen you in a month." As she watches, Addy interrupts her animated conversation with Leslie to help herself from the big wooden salad bowl.

"Did I tell you I'm going to show at the Field Gallery next summer?" Giles fairly bubbles. At parties he crackles with enough energy to run a marathon; painting, he can be as still as a contemplative monk.

"Excellent," Shannon responds.

He replaces her empty plate with one bearing a generous square of spanakopita. In a hushed voice he adds, "Plus there's this *man*."

Between passing the plates and wondering whether Addy will go home with Leslie, Shannon almost misses the news. "Do tell," she says. "Anyone I know?"

"Can't say yet. He's *really* in the closet."

"No fair!" So Shannon makes a series of guesses, each more improbable than the last: a notorious right-to-lifer, the lawyer who has campaigned against Representative Gerry Studds every year since 1978, the teacher who accused the local AIDS Alliance of promoting homosexuality. "Okay, be that way," she concedes. "Just not a word to Sherlock Holmes over there. My old buddy Addy Ruth is cruising for a cause."

"I could swear she's cruising Leslie," Giles counters after a moment's observation. "Or vice versa. Bet you a white chocolate crème brulée that they go home together."

When Shannon leaves the party, midnight has come and gone and she owes Giles a crème brulée.

Pausing only to flick the outside lights off, Leslie pulls Addy through the dark kitchen and up the uncarpeted stairs. "If you need to pee," she stage-whispers, "that's the bathroom."

Addy whispers back, "Is there anyone else home?"

"Nah, my roommate has a boyfriend and she's never here," Leslie replies in a normal voice that booms in the stillness. "She doesn't want her parents to know. Can you believe it? In 1992?"

The sudden overhead light is blinding; laughing, Leslie apologizes. After lighting the two squat candles on the bureau, she turns the overhead light off, shrugs out of her corduroy jacket, then takes hold of Addy's belt buckle. "Jeez," she mutters, "you don't have a stomach. Do you work out or what?"

Addy hears herself giggle and is mortified. "I study aikido."

Leslie unbuckles the belt and draws it out of its loops, wrapping it around her left hand. Then she unzips Addy's jeans. As Addy's belly goes cold with anticipation, Leslie murmurs, "Do you do this sort of thing often?"

Her fingers squeeze the other's bare nipples; the other gasps.

"How much do you trust me?" Leslie whispers.

A leather-wrapped hand circles Addy's neck, a hand on her stomach pushes her back to the bed. Very slowly her belly, hips, and thighs are exposed to the night air, then unrelenting fingers find her cunt, which has grown hot and wet as a sauna.

Not till sunlight and the smell of coffee wake her up does Addy remember to think about HIV status or safe sex. Not that she really thinks she's in jeopardy, but she hates to believe that she could be that, well ... carried away.

Later that same Saturday morning, around 10:00, two lovers do not meet at Cedar Tree Neck. One is five minutes early; the other has lost his nerve. At the latter's house forty-five minutes later the telephone rings and rings.

Not much later, Kevin Swanson stops once again outside his younger brother Brian's room. He who will gladly stand still in a cold, clammy forest for hours hates the foggy silence that has settled on his once-warm house. Now, for the first time since Saturday, he opens the door and looks in. In the corner, above the neatly made bed, a poster pterodactyl spreads its wings. On the floor there are no dirty socks, no crayons, no matchbox cars.

Even in their deepest hush, he thinks, the woods are alive with motion and noise: leaves rustle here, squirrels chitter there. This house is D-E-A-D dead. His father didn't even bother to come home last night.

He continues past his sister Judy's room to the end of the hall, where his own door stands open. He gazes at his grandfather's shotgun, mounted on the wall. His finger traces the dark walnut curves of the gun rack and finds them perfectly smooth. He is pleased with his handiwork.

He takes the gun down and sits on the bed with stock in right hand, barrel across his lap. The gun—*his* gun—has not been cleaned since Wednesday morning, before school, when the faint whiff of powder told him that someone had been using it. It is not loaded now. For three days he has forced the thought to the back of his mind.

The telephone rings and rings and rings. Head and ankle throbbing, Jay Soares fears that his own life is coming back to destroy him. Why didn't he turn the answering machine back on? Why doesn't the phone just leave him alone? He sits up slowly on the couch and reaches over for the receiver.

"Uncle Jay? Are you feeling OK? I just talked to Mom—can you give me a ride to the Ferrellis'?"

Like a magnet passing over scattered iron filings, the call pulls all his thoughts in one direction. "I'll be right over," he says. "You're at home?"

"Yeah. I just want to get out of here for a while."

Physician, heal thyself, Jay thinks as he carefully works his swollen left foot into an old oxford. The right goes in easily. He glances at the hall mirror as he shrugs on his russet-brown corduroy jacket. His hair could stand a trim, he thinks. The best thing about beards is not having to worry about five-o'clock shadow.

Clothes worn two days in a row always feel half a size too big, Addy Ruth reflects as she tries the front door to Shannon's house and, with no small relief, finds it open. Her right hand closes around the laden key chain in her coat pocket. Doesn't anyone lock doors around here?

Calamity Jane is nowhere in sight, thank god. Shannon has left a note on the guest bedroom door: "So what's new? Back suppertime at the latest. Raid fridge and cupboards at will. Do feel free to make other plans." Shannon's signature hasn't changed a bit in ten years: a bold S with a straight line flying out to the right, signifying the next six letters of her name.

Addy wrinkles her nose. She was half-hoping that Shannon had plans for later, giving her a reason not to see Leslie again. Leslie plans to come by after the meeting she had to cover, a town planning board hearing at which fireworks were predicted.

Fireworks, Addy thinks; tell me about fireworks. Sleeping with strangers is stupid.

The smell of marijuana smoked two or three hours ago is being slowly vanquished by brewing coffee and baking blueberry muffins. "The munchies are the best part of smoking dope," Giles says over the sound of running water, loud enough for Shannon to hear.

By the kitchen window Shannon watches as a white Swanson Painting van pulls into the driveway of the cottage next door, which seems to be closed for the winter. Jay's useless brother-in-law, Shannon thinks, wondering if he's lost. The van backs out and drives away, the ladders on its roof rack rattling loudly with every rut in the road. She turns her attention back to Giles's work in progress. It's his new boyfriend, of course, or, she gathers from the distraught phone call that brought her here, ex-boyfriend. Giles hasn't painted in oils since he was an undergraduate; "Working in oils is scary," he says, "it's so slow and permanent."

This one is both softer and more solid than his watercolor portraits; it feels androgynous to Shannon, though the taper of shoulder to hip is certainly male, as is the beard, though that could be shadow, the way the face is turned. Man and bedclothes seem jarringly suspended, held in place by head and feet, which are braced against the edges of the canvas. The ceiling above and the dark floor below seem out of reach.

"Shannon," Giles is saying in the silence, "you're a good friend; promise you'll shoot me if I get mixed up with another closet case?"

"Sure," Shannon replies, still gazing at the painting, "if you promise to tell me about it before you break up. Why did you do this up and down like that?"

"I don't know." Giles leans back against the sink but doesn't move. "It felt right."

"It reminds me of a tarot card, half-reversed," Shannon muses. "Maybe an unhung hanged man?"

"Or a well-hung unhinged man?"

"Oh, please!" Shannon grimaces at Giles over her left shoulder.

Giles turns to the counter and pours coffee into two matching ceramic mugs, whose shimmering glaze suggests the aurora borealis. "Half-and-half?"

"Lots, no sugar."

After passing carton, butter dish, and a jar of strawberry jam to Shannon, he addresses the sparsely stocked interior of the junior-size refrigerator. "Why am I so pissed anyway?" he wonders aloud. "It was doomed from the start, the stuff of tragedy. Romeo and Julian."

Shannon recalls her favorite college English professor, waxing persuasive on how *Romeo and Juliet* was really a comedy.

Giles closes the refrigerator and turns to the oven. The kitchen is so narrow that when fridge and oven are open at the same time, hot blast and cold collide above the brick-red linoleum. "I wouldn't be in his shoes for anything, that's for sure. He has too much to lose."

Shannon's shoulders tense and relax as she stares out the window. *It was social,* she remembers, and the reflexive change of subject. She thinks she gets it: "Jay?"

"Keep it to yourself, will you?" Giles says with the wryest, slightest of smiles.

Driving his father's Dakota pickup—six years old, barely 35,000 miles—over the drawbridge between Oak Bluffs and Vineyard Haven, Jay glances over at Kevin. Ever since he got into the truck, the youth has been staring out the window in silence. The ferry *Islander* is gliding into the harbor. "What's on your mind, man?" Jay asks.

"Not much," Kevin replies. They both know he means the opposite. "Listen, Uncle Jay," he continues almost at once, "if a guy at work told you something that made you think that maybe someone had committed a crime, what would you do?"

"Depends on what kind of crime it was, and on whether anyone might be in immediate danger."

Gas storage tanks obscure the boy's view of the harbor; the truck rattles over the tracks of the shipyard's marine railway. Jay threads through the Five Corners traffic and heads up State Road. For the next mile or so, he and his passenger reflect separately, in silence.

As the road curves down past the Tashmoo overlook, Kevin says, "You know Grandpa gave me his deer rifle?"

"I know he wanted you to have it," Jay responds.

"I take good care of it—I clean it after every target practice, and sometimes when I haven't even fired it. I always unload it when I put it away, so even if the kids decide to fool with it …"

Though Jay no longer hunts, he remembers his first gun. "I know how it is," he says.

"Wednesday morning I saw someone had used it besides me, and they hadn't cleaned it after."

The hair starts to prickle on the back of Jay's neck. "When did you clean it last?" he asks.

"Late Monday morning," Kevin says out the window. "That was a holiday; we didn't have school."

Between Monday morning and Wednesday morning was Monday night, when an unidentified shotgun in the hands of person unknown had sent Jay's car spinning off the road and into a tree.

"My dad really hates you, Uncle Jay," Kevin blurts out. "He thinks it's your fault …"

"… that your mother decided to leave?"

"Yeah."

"Is he right?"

Kevin snorts in disgust. "You think I never heard him beating up on her?" Angry words ricochet front and back, side to side in the cab of the truck. "Dad gets crazy when he drinks, and in the last couple of years he's been drinking a lot."

None of this surprises Jay. *If they ever find my body at the bottom of a dumpster, get thee hence and arrest my brother-in-law!* But Monday night? He wants to attribute his "accident" to chance, to some sniper, however unlikely, taking random potshots at cars on the Edgartown–West Tisbury road. Anyone gunning for him in particular must have had reason to suspect that he would be passing that way at that hour.

Jay's chest goes hollow; his mouth tastes of bile.

She hasn't been alone for an hour, but Addy is prowling the house. Though the sun is warm on the deck, she can't sit still for long; she flips through back issues of *Ms.,* a glossy quilters' magazine, even the public television program guide, but nothing catches her fancy. She searches Shannon's shelves for basic information about HIV and AIDS, without success.

Addy Ruth doesn't wait easily. Her thoughts float to the surface like macaroni in a bubbling pot: Could Leslie be HIV positive? What does Shannon think of her? Were they ever lovers? If not, why not? If so, why not still? How is her worthless ex doing in New York? Does Leslie sleep with every new woman on the island? Does she sleep with men? Why didn't I think about AIDS?

From collarbone to pelvis, Addy's insides radiate cold. When she last slept with a man, she was a sophomore in college; she has cruised through the first decade of the epidemic with no partners at risk. Her knowledge of the disease is so porous. She thumbs through magazines without registering much until Shannon stamps in, ranting about closet cases, society, and the sexually confused. Addy asks if there's AIDS on Martha's Vineyard.

"Yeah, some," Shannon answers, momentarily perplexed by the question. "Mostly, but not entirely, among heterosexual ex-intravenous drug users." Then she understands and grins. "Oh, hell, don't worry about Leslie; she hasn't slept with anyone in a high-risk category since 1975."

Early Sunday morning, the sky is bleak, the southeasterly wind not at all playful. Gunfire brings Jay out of sleep to immediate attention.

The gun goes off again. Nothing shatters, nothing explodes. In the front yard, Wayne Swanson is shouting: "Where's my son, you double-faced prick? You've been trying to turn my family against me since the day you came back with all your city ways, and I'm not putting up with it any more. You're going to tell me where they are!" The shotgun booms again; again nothing breaks.

Jay can already hear the sirens; he prays that no one will be injured.

"I know where you are," his brother-in-law is roaring. "I'll always know where you are."

Early the next Friday afternoon at the Vineyard Haven post office, Shannon turns from her box with the usual clutch of catalogs, fund-raising letters, and a couple of bills. Sorting his own mail on the table is Jay Soares, who is on Shannon's shit list for not returning her phone calls. He looks so sheepish that she starts to relent.

"Well," Shanon says, "I suppose you've been busy, talking to all the reporters and all."

He shrugs.

"I hear they sent Wayne off-island for psychiatric evaluation."

"Yeah."

"I guess you're all talked out, huh?" Shannon almost grins. "Addy and Leslie left yesterday morning for a long weekend in P-town."

"That's a pretty big commitment for Leslie," Jay ventures.

Shannon glares at him. "You should talk," she says.

Jay glances toward the door. "You've talked with … ?"

"I have," Shannon replies. "How is he doing, I hear you ask? Well, he's smoking too much dope, but he's painting. Wild stuff, in the most garish oils he can find. You need to settle with him, you know."

"Maybe when things settle down," Jay says, wavering.

"Maybe before then," Shannon counters firmly. "Do you think Wayne knows?"

Slowly Jay slides a supermarket circular off the counter and into the waste basket. Then he shakes his head. "Wayne's always been a both-barrels-in-your-face kind of guy," he says. "If he had a clue, we would have heard it last Sunday."

Shannon agrees. She recalls the white van outside Giles's house last Saturday and thinks, *He was close, though. He was pretty damn close.* Feeling a little more conciliatory, she asks, "So, are you going to Katherine's Halloween party?"

"Sure," Jay says, his voice thickening, with an expression Shannon can't read. "I'm coming dressed as a deer."

He's hardly limping at all, she notices, as he strides toward the door.

DAVID B. FEINBERG

DESPAIR:
AUGUST 1987

MY ANXIETY LEVEL WAS HIGH, and it was time to do something about it. I had reached a particular level of anxiety that corresponded to the resonant frequency of my brain; one more day in this state and it would explode. I needed to either elevate it to a frequency that only dogs hear or decrease it to a reasonable level so I could focus my anxiety on things like nuclear war, famine, torture in Third World countries, Beirut, Afghanistan, Lebanon, the West Bank, crack, the homeless, and my relationship with my mother. In short, it was time to take the Test.

I decided to take the Test after I discovered by reading articles in *The New York Times* that two former sexual partners of mine had AIDS. The first article dealt with AIDS in the workplace. "Why look! There's Morgan," I said to myself, coughing up breakfast and several unrelated meals from the past two weeks. The second was a human-interest story about AZT in action. "Gee, I didn't know Lloyd was on AZT these days," I commented from a supine position on the floor, having just fainted.

I decided to take the Test after reading an article in *The New York Times* in which the New York City health commissioner said that all those with the virus were doomed. The prevailing figures I had been reading stated that approximately fifteen percent of those exposed to the virus come down with AIDS within five years of infection. I figured I could wait it out: If I stayed well for five years, I'd be home free. I neglected to consider that at that time the epidemic had been tracked for only five years, and that the estimates stopped at

five years simply because there were no further data. Now it turned out that after seven years' incubation of the virus, the incidence rose sharply.

I decided to take the Test after reading seventeen well-meaning liberal heterosexual columns in seventeen well-meaning liberal heterosexual periodicals
where seventeen well-meaning liberal heterosexual people described how they
each underwent their own personal well-meaning liberal heterosexual hell by
taking the Test: their fear and trepidation, their casual doubts and anxieties,
along with their awkward self-reassurances that it would be extremely unlikely
to get a positive antibody result, although they may have had more than three
sexual experiences with more than two partners in the past seventeen years,
and it's conceivable that one of the partners was a hemophiliac bisexual who
did intravenous drugs in between weekly blood transfusions, and it's conceivable that they were inoculated with a tetanus vaccine using a needle that had
just been used on a hemophiliac bisexual who did intravenous drugs in between weekly blood transfusions when they were twelve and stepped on a rusty
nail at Camp Mohonka in the Catskills, and it's conceivable that their mother
could actually be Haitian and there could have been a mix-up at the hospital or
the midwife's, and it's conceivable that the blood transfusion from the heart-
lung-kidney-and-thyroid transplant by Dr. Christian Barnard had contained
some tainted blood from a hemophiliac bisexual who did intravenous drugs in
between weekly blood donations. I mean, I appreciated the first article where a
well-meaning liberal heterosexual columnist described the trials and tribula-
tions of taking the Test; and even five articles of well-meaning liberal heterosexual columnists would have been within the bounds of propriety and taste;
but *seventeen* of those abominable articles just made me want to scream. I had
it up to here with well-meaning liberal heterosexual ass-holes so far removed
from the crisis that they could be living on Jupiter. You see, these well-meaning
liberal heterosexual columns all ended exactly the same way, with the results
sheepishly revealed in the final sentence, almost casually, nonchalantly: Oh, by
the way, I was negative. What was this, I thought, some fucking dating service?

I decided to take the Test even though I had not had the mean amount of
one thousand five hundred and twenty-three sexual partners in the past ten
years that the papers reported from the initial group of AIDS patients (I was
rather shy for my age), even though I had not undergone what was coyly referred to in the press as traumatic sex (although in some sense all sex is traumatic) in certain downtown clubs in the presence of a large audience, even
though I had never been considered what was coyly referred to in the company
of my friends as a slut (which is undeniably a relative term).

I decided to take the Test even though it wasn't necessarily the politically
correct thing to do, and certain radical gay columnists in certain radical gay
periodicals were predicting the most unbelievable repercussions: mandatory
testing for HIV antibodies; discrimination in insurance, housing, and employ-

ment of those who tested positive; closing the borders to aliens who tested positive and at the same time other countries closing their borders to Americans who tested positive; internment camps for those who tested positive. As time passed, a significant portion of the above alarmist predictions became realities.

I decided to take the Test even though the local gay paper insisted, virulently, that HTLV-III was *not* the cause (although the virus had been renamed HIV two years earlier by an international committee in an effort to solve a dispute about who had discovered the virus first, an American scientist who discovered the virus in 1984 or a French scientist who discovered the virus in 1983), and the local gay paper was backing the African Swine Fever Virus Theory or the Tertiary Syphilis Theory or the Chronic Epstein-Barr Virus Theory or the Cytomegalovirus Theory or the Track Lighting and Industrial Gray Carpeting and Quiche Theory or the Immune-System Overload Theory or the Amyl and Butyl Nitrite Theory or a variation of Legionnaire's Disease Theory in which some contaminant got into the air-conditioning system of the Saint discotheque, or perhaps a new noise virus at a certain frequency had gotten into the sound system, or the Government Germ-Warfare Theory, where some experimental poisonous gas had leaked, not to be confused with the Government Genocide Theory, where the government deliberately distributed contaminated K-Y lubricant at homosexual gatherings and contaminated needles at shooting galleries, or the Airborne Mosquito Theory or the Toilet-Seat Theory or the No Gag-Response Theory, where male homosexuals as a consequence swallow vast quantities of as-yet unidentified toxins. The local gay paper offered a new and improved conspiracy theory each and every month, and I suppose it was *just my problem* that I couldn't keep up with all of these new trends and fashions in disease consciousness; I mean, I guess I was being pigheaded and stupid to accept a parsimonious explanation that had been offered by our admittedly mendacious government, and maybe I was just too irritable and lazy not to make a concerted effort to keep track of each new crackpot theory (based on a somewhat-justifiable paranoia) that more or less ignored all scientific research to date and was generally so incredibly stupid that were the theory to be rated on the Stanford-Binet test of general intelligence, I doubt it would be able to tie its own shoelaces unassisted or balance a checkbook or cross the street without being run over by a Mack truck.

I decided to take the Test because I was from a rational background, and I decided that it wouldn't kill me to know, even though a friend who had AIDS told me that if I found out I was positive, this would create additional stress, which would in turn weaken my immune system, thus allowing the virus to replicate, a sort of Heisenberg effect where the knowledge of a situation affects that situation, so in fact it *could* kill me, a little faster than otherwise, and what would the benefits be of finding out if I were positive because there wasn't a cure, and why would it help to know my status if it wouldn't change my behav-

ior because I would continue having safe sex and getting enough rest and eating right and exercising and taking Geritol either way? I told him that if I
turned out positive, I would brood and contemplate suicide and lose perspective and quit my job and go to Italy and finally learn how to deal with my
mother and stop transferring money to my Individual Retirement Account
and move it into an insurance policy and only renew magazines by the year
and would insist on being paid in a lump sum if I won a lottery as opposed to a
twenty-year payment scheme because I would probably be dead in twenty
years and the tax benefits would be outweighed by the worldwide cruise
through whatever countries still allowed HIV-positives to travel, and maybe I
would take one of those fancy new placebos that everyone is talking about, like
active lipids or naltrexone or dextran sulfate or wheat-grass juice, or maybe I
would see a nutritionist and stop eating sugar and become macrobiotic and
then die a lot faster from not eating enough protein, or maybe I would start
meditating, or maybe I would finally achieve a sense of spirituality and meaning in my life as it neared the end and drop this worn cloak of cynicism for
crystals or Gurdjieff or reincarnation or God or free parking, or maybe I would
start writing like Anthony Burgess, who, when misdiagnosed with a brain tu-
mor, wrote four novels in a year, or maybe I would have some mystical cosmic
revelation because I was ready for it, or maybe I would join a bowling league,
or maybe I would just give up. I mean, I operated under the basic premise that
ignorance is *not* bliss, and why should I stick my head in the sand when I
should perfectly well be able to stick the gun in my mouth instead? And then,
of course, there was the extremely slim chance that I was, in fact, HIV-antibody
negative. Maybe—who knows?—I could actually relax for a few minutes. I
mean, Rome wasn't built in a day.

I decided to take the Test because although I generally don't believe in pre-
destination as opposed to free will, from a logical standpoint we are all born
with certain finite constraints: None of us is immortal; hence, none of us has
an unlimited number of heartbeats left. Women are born with a finite number
of ova, ready to plop down the fallopian tubes at the rate of one every four
weeks, from puberty to menopause; similarly, we are each born with a finite
number or orgasms to experience, cigarettes to smoke, and lovers to betray.
Knowing whether I tested positive or negative could help me determine more
precisely what those numbers were. I was just moderately curious to find out
what would be a reasonable number of cocktails, nightmares, Lean Cuisines,
boyfriends, vacations, apartments, breaths, jobs, and bowel movements to expect in this lifetime. Perhaps if I knew I had only a few sexual encounters left, I
would avoid intercourse in order to stretch things out.

I decided to take the Test because I had reached the point where I believed
that it was a fundamentally irrational act *not* to take the HIV-antibody test,
and after all, I *did* graduate from Northeastern University several aeons ago,

majoring in mathematics and minoring in philosophy, and consequently I still felt a responsibility to behave rationally.

So, nervous like when I was seventeen and in college and still a virgin and went to a drugstore and spent hours studying depilatories and decongestants and diuretics before finally asking the kindly pharmacist for condoms in a cracked voice, I picked up the phone and dialed the city AIDS hotline and made an appointment to take the test at the earliest available time slot, six weeks later. Like a secret agent, I was identified by a numeric code only.

During the next six weeks I did the usual things: made a will, sold my co-op, changed my job, upped my insurance, reconciled with my family, worked out at the gym seven times a day, had sixteen failed romances, volunteered as an astronaut at NASA so I could experience the relativistic effects of traveling at high speeds (time contracts when approaching the speed of light, thus the six weeks' wait would seem less interminable).

The six weeks' wait was an eternity.

That morning ("There's still time to chicken out," said my friend Dennis) I woke up early and took the bus. I had scheduled my appointment for 8:30, when the clinic opened, so I could take the test, vomit, and then casually waltz into work fashionably late, as usual.

There was no time for breakfast; I didn't want to be late. I took the bus down Ninth Avenue. I had to stand until Forty-second Street. I couldn't concentrate on the *Times*. The bus let me off right in front of the Chelsea clinic. I hadn't been there since 1980 to get treated for a venereal disease.

Outside, several homeless people were sleeping on benches. A man swept debris from the concrete with a broom. The clinic was next to an elementary school, with a jungle gym outside. It was 8:15. The building was closed.

I circled the block. On the sidewalk several sexually responsible individuals had thoughtfully left their used condoms. I recalled the first time I ever set foot in a gay bar, back when I was nineteen, in Pasadena, California. I had circled the street seventy-two times before gathering enough courage to enter. I was shy; I wasn't ready to make a life-style commitment at that point in time, and I thought entering a gay bar would be an irrevocable step. I mean, they'd all assume I was a homosexual.

I had a quick bite to eat at an awful deli on Tenth, surrounded by the harsh accents of the outer boroughs: the snide voices, the know-it-alls, the wise-crackers. "How could they joke at a time like this?" I wondered. I returned to the clinic, ten minutes late for my 8:30 appointment. Two people were already in front of me. I was given a brief and informative booklet to read. Why did the print fade the harder I tried to concentrate? The woman at the desk asked for my number and then asked me to make up a new one, tossing the first away. I signed a release form by copying a statement instead of signing; with no signature, I remained anonymous. Then I had a brief counseling session with a therapist, a woman with dark hair cut butch, a warm and sympathetic lesbian.

"How do you think you were exposed?" she asked.

"I may have forgotten to use a condom five or six thousand times back in 1982, before there were rules and regulations to follow."

"Why are you taking the test? What will this knowledge do for you?"

"I thought"—I thought that this was a test, and the right answer would be judicious and thoughtful and beneficial to humanity—"that I might be able to help further the cause of science and medical research by becoming an experimental subject should I test positive."

"I wouldn't if I were you," she counseled. "They have double-blind experiments. For all you know, you could be eating sugar pills. And what's worse, you may be on some toxic drug. Suppose you're in a study and they find out another more promising drug. You can't switch." Then she told me about stress reduction and homemade AL 721 and macrobiotic diets.

"That's a bit drastic for me. I mean, should I give up meat just to live another six months?" There was this trade-off between sex and life, between red meat and a few more years. Why should I have to be making these choices?

"For the next two weeks, I want you to act as if you have already tested positive," she advised. "Prepare yourself." Did she know something that I didn't know? Why couldn't I enjoy my last few possibly blissful weeks relatively stress-free (although by this time my anxiety meter-reading was off the scale)? I made an appointment for two weeks later to get my results.

A Pakistani medical assistant looked up from his textbook and put on two pairs of red plastic gloves. "Give me your arm," he instructed. Carefully, he stuck me with the needle and filled a test tube with my blood, then wrapped the gloves around the sample for safety. I wondered how he could do this all day. How could he stand it?

That night I found out that Gordon had died in the afternoon. My first reaction was "See what you get for taking the test?" Although I eventually convinced myself there was no cause-and-effect relationship between the two events, still, I felt it was not a good sign.

"You can always take it and not bother getting the results," said Dennis. "You can back out at any time."

The next day I called Richard in California.

"If it turns out I'm positive, I'm going to take the next plane out of here and get a cab to your apartment and knock on your door, and you'll answer, and I'll say, 'Thanks,' and pull out my pearl-handled revolver from my purse and shoot you dead."

"Come on, Benjamin, I didn't necessarily infect you. It could be any one of thousands."

"I know it was you. Who else fucked me with such relish and regularity? Who else do I know who had lymphadenopathy in 1982? Besides, it's easier for me to deal with when I can pinpoint the blame on someone else."

"You should be here in San Francisco. There are so many twelve-step and self-help groups out here, we even have groups for people who are waiting to find out whether they tested positive or negative."

"Two-week groups?"

"That's right."

"If only they came out with safe-sex regulations two months earlier, I'd still be alive."

"You *are* alive, Benjamin."

"You know what I mean." Was it better to have loved and gotten infected than never to have loved at all? Was I even capable of love? Who knew?

Instead of San Francisco I went to Provincetown, the only gay mecca to which I hadn't yet made a pilgrimage (I had already been to Key West and West Hollywood). I had another disastrous safe-sex romance, and then I got too much sun and not enough sleep, because there was sand in my weekend lover's bed, and being the Jewish American Princess that I am, it felt just like a pea; the pullout mattress hadn't been turned since the War Between the States, so I tossed and turned and created my own force field of anxiety, and my face decided to punish me with a minor outbreak of herpes, which, in turn, got infected with impetigo, which, in turn, increased my level of anxiety, so the herpes got worse and worse, and by the time it had reached its nadir I looked more or less like Jeff Goldblum in the remake of *The Fly*, and this was not during the first half-hour of the picture; this was *serious* skin disorder. So I went to my doctor, who had fled the city that January because of burnout from the AIDS crisis, and saw his cruel replacement, a cold and inefficient reptile who misdiagnosed me with shingles, a disease that typically affects only half of the face, whereas my face was a *complete* disaster area. And then this lizard had the tact to tell me that I should definitely take the HIV-antibody test because shingles was one of those opportunistic infections that tends to strike people with lowered immunities, and he said that he felt there was a ninety percent chance that I would be positive. At which point I told my own personal nominee for Mr. Compassion and Tact of 1987 that I had already taken the test and as a matter of fact was expecting my results the following day.

I went back to the clinic for my results, looking like the Creature from the Black Lagoon. Guess what? Unlike the seventeen well-meaning liberal heterosexual columnists in the seventeen well-meaning liberal heterosexual periodicals, I turned out to be positive. Hold the presses! This had to be front-page news. If I wrote a column, I'd make *The Guinness Book of World Records* and the covers of *Time, Esquire,* and *Women's Wear Daily* as the first columnist to turn out positive in the history of civilization and parlay this into immediate financial gain, a guest spot on *Hollywood Squares,* a bit part in *Miami Vice.* Then I realized I would be dead before the residuals came because my life expectancy wasn't quite so long as it was even a week ago; there I was thinking like an actuary. I decided it was time to get a television set, something I had been struggling successfully against acquiring for the past ten years, along with a VCR, so when my apartment was converted into a sanatorium, I'd be able to amuse myself. Although I didn't go whole-hog: Cable would have to wait.

And oddly enough I fell into this deep funk.

I had a friend who was nice and supportive, and after I took the test and got the results, he got really mad at me because I was depressed because what did I expect? and didn't I realize the likelihood of being positive? and what difference did it make anyway? and I told him it was the doom, the absolute doom, that got to me, and he said didn't you know that before, you imbecile? and I said this is the sort of thing you can't really figure out what your reaction will be until you do it, and I tried to explain to him about the Heisenberg principle, but he had math anxiety in a bad way, so he stuffed his fingers into his ears and said I don't want to listen. And of course a couple of months later he took the test anyway, on the advice of his doctor, who told him that if he had high blood pressure, wouldn't he want to know if he was at risk of a heart attack, even if it was only a ten percent chance? And he was negative. And another friend who had moved to Japan three years ago to evade the AIDS crisis and the Reagan administration and also because something snapped in his brain when he turned thirty and he—with no prior warning—became a deeply depraved rice queen who had to move nine thousand miles just to get laid; well, he took the test and was negative too. And then another friend who had according to conservative estimates sucked every Negro penis in the tri-state area in such venues as subway tearooms, trucks, changing rooms, and in the back seats of cars; well, he took the test, and he was negative too. And part of me, since misery loves company, wanted just one close friend to be positive too, but the sensible part of me, the part that still has occasional communication with my cerebral cortex, said, "Thank God they're negative," using the expletive for effect, since thank god my experience had not changed me so profoundly that I was no longer an atheist.

So this is what I do: I go on with my life. I go to ACT UP meetings, never saying a word, and end up more stressed-out than I was before; I go to demonstrations and scream myself hoarse and then visit my new primary health-care practitioner who, unlike the lizard, gives me hugs and prescribes medication for my sore throat and my various and sundry female disorders; I get my T-cell

count taken every three months; I go to a few Body Positive meetings and at-
tend a group rap-session that is headed by a psychopath and shortly thereafter
drop out because once again my stress-level has tripled; and I want to end the
AIDS crisis and stop the government logjam of red tape and paperwork, and
there should be some sort of cure in the near future, and the only thing is
whether I will still be alive to use it; and I'm wary of the macrobiotic diets and
crystals and lipids and other untested and unverified treatments, but at the
same time I'm afraid to do absolutely nothing—maybe I'm paralyzed by inertia and fear, I don't know—and I don't want to take AZT when the T-cell count
drops below 200 because it's highly toxic, but at the same time I know it can't
be all bad because some more insane people at the local gay paper want to sue
all doctors for malpractice for prescribing it. And I take acyclovir for my herpes twice daily to prevent recurrences because herpes is particularly bad for
the immune system, and I'm avoiding the sun: This summer I'm going to be an
alabaster nymph, a pale creature of the night. And sex: What about sex? When
I see a guy I've been flirting with for the past four years, what do I say? What
are the rules? Should this be broadcast? Are there any tactful ways of telling the
relatives? How can I have sex with someone without telling? Does it matter if
the sex is absolutely safe? What do I say when I meet someone new: Would you
like to have sex with someone who may or may not have a fatal disease?

And now I never sleep through the night; I always wake up at three or four,
tense, filled with anxiety. Like Dorothy in *The Wizard of Oz,* I sit, watching
helplessly as my T-cell count drops every three months, the sands of time running out.

Once I awoke from a wet dream, swimming in a sea of infected sperm; I
leapt out of bed to wipe it all up quickly (how does one stem the tide, the
flow?). And one day I was sitting at a coffee shop, and my nose began to bleed
spontaneously. I hadn't had a nosebleed in years. The blood dripped bright red
onto the plate, onto the napkin. All I could think of was infection and disease.
All I could think of was the virus that was coursing through my blood. I blotted it out with the napkin and sat there ashamed, frightened, in despair.

PAUL MONETTE

HALFWAY HOME

MY BROTHER USED TO TELL ME I was the Devil. This would be while he was torturing me—not beating me up exactly, since he didn't want to hurt his knuckles and maybe miss a game. But he'd pounce and drag me to the floor and pin my shoulders with his knees. Then he'd snap his fingers against my nose, or drool spit in my face while I bucked and jerked my head, or singe my hair with matches. He was ten, I was seven. Already he had enormous strength. I never thought of Brian as a kid. He'd loom above me with that flame-red Irish hair, his blue eyes dancing wickedly, and he was brute and cruel as any man. There are boys in Ireland now throwing pipe bombs and torching cars. That was Brian, a terrorist before his time. And I was his mortal enemy.

"Is Tommy gonna cry now?" he'd taunt me, rubbing those knuckles across my scalp. "You big fuckin' baby."

And I would, I'd cry, not from pain but sorrow. I'd blubber and bite my lip till Brian would release me in disgust, full of immense disdain because I couldn't take it. He'd lumber away and grab his glove, off to find one of his buddies from Saint Augustine's, tough like him. I'd stare in the mirror above the dresser in the room we shared, still gasping the sobs away, hating my sallow skin and my blue-black crewcut.

That's why I was so diabolical to him, because I didn't look anything like Brian or Dad, both of them fair and freckled, lobster-red in the summer sun, big in the shoulders like stevedores. I got all the Italian blood instead from Mom's side, so that I was the only Sicilian in a mick neighborhood. Hell, it seemed the whole county was Irish, from Hartford all the way to New Haven. And the Irish hated everybody, but especially wops. So I never stood a chance, lean and olive and alien as I was. But the reason I cried had nothing to do with my differences, not then. It was because I wasn't good enough to play with my big brother. This boy who never ceased to make me suffer, beating me down and plucking my wings like a hapless fly, and all I ever seemed to feel was that I'd failed him.

I haven't thought about any of that in twenty years. Well, nine anyway: since the day my father was buried in the blue-collar graveyard behind Saint Augustine's. Brian and I had our last words then, raw and rabid, finishing one another off. He was twenty-eight, I was twenty-five, though in fact we hadn't really spoken for at least ten years before that. As soon as Brian understood I was queer—and I swear he knew it before I did—he iced me out for good. No more roughhouse, no more nugies and body checks. I didn't exist anymore. By then of course Brian had become a delirious high-school hero, the darling of the Brothers as he glided from season to effortless season, football and hockey and baseball. Me, I was so screwed up I missed being tormented by him. I played no games myself.

It doesn't matter anymore. I sit out here on this terrace, three thousand miles from the past, and stare down the bluff to the weed-choked ocean, and the last thing I think of is Chester, Connecticut. Once a day, toward sunset, I walk down the blasted wooden stairs jerry-built into the fold of the cliff, eighty steps to the beach below. At the bottom I sit at the lip of the shallow cave that opens behind the steps, the winter tide churning before me, the foam almost reaching my toes.

I brood about all the missed chances, the failures of nerve, but I never go back as far as being a kid. I put all that behind me when I came out, Brian and Dad and their conspiracy of silence. I never look in the mirror if I can help it. My real life stretches from coming out to here, fifteen years. *That's* what I'm greedy for more of. Sometimes out of nowhere perfect strangers will ask: "You got any brothers and sisters?" No, I say, I was an only child. I never had any time for that family porn, even when I had all the time in the world.

Which I don't have now. I know it as clear as anything when I turn and climb the eighty steps up. I take it very slow, gripping the rotting banister as I puff my way. This is my daily encounter with what I've lost in stamina. The neuropathy in my left leg throbs with every step. I wheeze and gulp for air. But I also love the challenge, climbing the mountain because it's there, proving every day that the nightmare hasn't won yet.

The cliff cascades with ice plant, a blanket of gaudy crimson that nearly blinds in the setting sun. The gray terns wheel above me, cheering me on. I feel like I'm claiming a desert island, the first man ever to scale this height. As I reach the top, where a row of century cactus guards the bluff with a hundred swords, I can look back and see a quarter mile down Trancas Beach, empty and all mine, the rotting sandstone cliffs clean as the end of the world.

Not that the Baldwins own all of it. But the beach house on the bluff sits in the middle of five acres, shaded by old trees, shaggy eucalyptus and sycamores eight feet thick, which makes it feel like it's been there forever, no neighbors in sight on either side. To the north is a pop singer's compound, a great white whale of a house that's visible from the coast road, all its new-planted trees still puny and struggling for purchase. To the south an aerospace mogul has gussied himself a Norman pile complete with drawbridge and watchtower, which the surfers in the Trancas Wash call Camelot.

The Baldwin place is like none of these—a lazy overgrown bungalow with red-tile roof, balconies off the bedrooms and a drizzling Moorish fountain in the courtyard. Built in 1912, when the Baldwins *did* own as far as the eye can see, twenty-two miles of coastline all the way south through Malibu to the edge of Santa Monica. Till the thirties this was the only house on the water, with a bare dirt road that snaked up into the mountains where the big ranch house stood, seat of the vast Spanish land grant. Gray remembers his Baldwin aunts saying the only way to the beach house was half a day's ride on horseback from the ranch.

That's how it feels to me still after two months here, remote and inaccessible. I've only had to leave twice, to go see my doctor in Hollywood, about an hour away—who had the gall to tell me I was fine, without a trace of irony. "He's right," insisted Gray, who drove me there and back, "you look terrific." I'll say this much: considering I'm on Medi-Cal, living on six hundred bucks a month disability, I'm doing very well to be in a house in a eucalyptus grove, with a view that seems to go all the way to Hawaii. No hit record, no Pentagon kickbacks, and I live like a fucking rock star. You get very used to being lord of all you survey.

But even here reality intrudes. Yesterday was full of portents, now I see that. I didn't go down to the beach till almost five, because I woke up late from my nap. The sun was already dancing on the ocean when I started, and gone below by the time I reached the sand. Immediately it's colder, even with the gold and purple rockets trailing in the afterglow. I saw right away there was junk in the mouth of the cave, beer cans and an empty bag of chips. I was furious. I snatched up the litter, grumbling at the trespass. The property line goes to mid-tide. In theory nobody ought to walk on my three hundred yards of beach at all.

I started back up the stairs sour as a Republican. No one had ever violated my grotto before. Maybe a sign was in order: No Loitering. This Means You. Then, at about step 60 I got this terrible stab in my heart—doubled me over. I dropped the trash and sagged against the crimson ice. Oh shit, I was going to die of a heart attack. Even in that bone-zero panic I could feel a sort of black laughter welling up inside. Leave it to Tom Shaheen not to die of AIDS, after all the drama and street theater.

It passed as quick as it came but left me heaving, clammy with cold sweat. For a minute I was scared to breathe too deep, and kept kneading my chest in some fruitless amateur version of CPR. But no, the pain was gone. If anything there was a queer feeling of utter emptiness at the center of the chest, the way you feel when someone walks out on you.

I took the last twenty steps most gingerly. It was folly to think my little coronary event wasn't AIDS-related. I was probably heading for a massive stroke, the virus in my spinal column swirling like eels in a sunken ship, and I'd end up mute and paralyzed. Generally I don't waste a minute, especially out here in Trancas, figuring how short my time is. I've been at this thing for a year and a half, three if you count all the fevers and rashes. I operate on the casual assumption that I've still got a couple of years, give or take a galloping lymphoma. Day to day I'm not a dying man, honestly.

But I reached the top pretty winded and shaken, gazing down the bluff with a melancholy dread that things could change any minute. I've given up everything else but this, I thought, don't let me lose this too, my desert island. I couldn't have said exactly whom I was addressing, some local god of the bluff. Not big-G God. I've been on His hit list now for a long time. If He's really out there, I'm douched.

Then I saw Mona. She lay on one of the white chaises, her back to me and the view, smoking a cigarette. From the top of the beach stairs it's maybe twenty paces across the lawn to the terrace. I flinched and tried to think if I could sneak around her, but no way. Mona's like my sister, she doesn't have to call first. But after my *crise de coeur* I wanted to collapse. And Mona doesn't indulge me like Gray. She wants me *up*. For a renegade dyke committed to anarchy, in fact, she is remarkably Donna Reed in her dealings with me, cutting the crusts off sandwiches.

I started across the lawn, emitting a tentative whimper. Mona turned in startled delight. "Pumpkin! I've just come from the workshop!" She leaped off the chaise and darted toward me. Her tortoise-rim glasses covered half her face, her platinum hair beveled and moussed. "They were appalling, all of them," she said, reaching a hand with black-painted nails and scratching the hair on my chest. "Dumb little standup routines, clubfoot dances, thrift-shop chic. The usual. But oh, there was this girl from Torrance, squeaky clean—"

She stopped and peered more closely at my face. "*Cara mia,* are you all right? You're looking more than usual like the French leftenant's woman."

"I just had a heart attack."

"Come on, I'll make you hot chocolate." See? Very Mom-is-it-lunch-yet. "I brought you a tin of shortbread. Twenty-two bucks at Nieman's. Now this *girl.* Rosy as a cheerleader, practically carrying pompoms. I was wet all day."

She steered me across the terra-cotta terrace, through the peeling colonnade and into the musty cool of the house. I tried on a pouting scowl, but Mona was off, full of raptures about her little bimbette from Torrance. In the kitchen I sat at the zinc-top table, a palimpsest of dents and scratches, while Mona free-floated about, putting the milk to boil.

The workshop she speaks of is Introduction to Performance, a grab-bag of mime and movement and "auto-exploration," thirty dollars for three Saturday sessions, a veritable magnet for the egregiously untalented, who will probably never perform beyond their bathroom mirrors. But it keeps the wolf from the door of AGORA—our feisty open space in Venice that we reclaimed from a ballpoint pen factory, famous throughout the netherworld of Performance, with its own FBI file to boot. Except "our" is not exactly right. It's Mona's. I am no longer an impresario.

"Someone was looking for you today," says Mona, mixing the cocoa.

"A rabid fan, perhaps."

"Some guy. Looked like he sold insurance. He came by during the break—said nobody'd seen you around your apartment since Christmas."

"Probably sent to cancel my disability. I've been getting these 'Aren't you dead yet' letters from Sacramento."

We took the tray of chocolate and biscuits into the parlor. Through the arched gallery windows the sunset had turned to dusty rose. Mona went to the woodbox, knelt and laid a fire, more butch than I. I cozied up in an afghan as old as the shedding velvet that covered the swayback sofa. No one has bothered to upgrade anything at the beach house, not for decades. When Gray dies this last piece of the Baldwin vastness will be disposed of, and then some starlet can swath it in white upholstery, so it looks like everyone else's house. Meanwhile the tattiness and furred edges are just my cup of tea.

Once the fire is crackling, Mona snuggles in under the afghan with me. "You know," she says conspiratorially, "we don't have anything set for tomorrow night. Queen Isabella canceled—the piece isn't ready. If you just did forty-five minutes, you'd save our ass." I begin to shake my head slowly, as if I have a slight crick in my neck. "Oh, Tommy, why not," says Mona, more pettish now. "It'd do you good. You're stronger than you realize."

I turn and give her a withering look. Mona is of the persuasion, diametrically opposed to the *Aren't you dead yet* theory, that I am not really *sick* sick, and thus should push my limits. "My life on the stage is like a dream to me now," I reply in a dusky Garbo voice. "I have put away childish things."

"People still call and ask, 'When are you having Miss Jesus?' I swear, we could fill the place three months running."

Mona sighs. She knows I am not convinceable. Not that I'm unsympathetic. I understand the longing for a break-through gig that sets the whole town buzzing. In the first two years of AGORA, before I retired, Miss Jesus was a sensation whenever I did it. Bomb threats would pour in, and church groups from Pacoima would picket back and forth in the parking lot, practically speaking in tongues. Mona and I were devastated to only have ninety-nine seats, with ten standees additional permitted by the fire laws; because at the height of the outrage we could have packed two-fifty in.

I lay my head on her shoulder and offer her the plate of shortbread. She shakes her head no thanks. We sit there slumped against each other, watching the fire, not needing to talk. I love the smoky elusiveness of Mona's perfume, a scent she swears is the very same Dietrich wears, a beauty tip passed in whispers through the shadowy dyke underground. She seems more pensive than I today, unusual for her, an action girl. I think she's about to ask me something about my illness, like how do I stand it, but then she says, "Do you ever think about your brother?"

I shoot her the most baleful look I can summon. "In a word, no."

"But don't you ever wonder? He's prob'ly got kids—" She waves her hands in a circular motion, flailing with possibilities. "I mean he could be *dead,* and you wouldn't even know."

If anything I grow more icily impassive. "I believe I'm the one who's passing away around here."

"Don't be defensive. I just wondered."

"Mona, how is it you are the only person in the world who knows this person exists, and yet you forget the punchline. He *loathes* me. I make his skin crawl. I have not imagined these things. He said them, over and over for years, knuckles white with passion. Get it?"

She pulls her head slightly in under the afghan, rather like a blond turtle. Cautiously she observes, "People change."

I scramble out of my side of the blanket. Kneeling almost on top of her, I push my face close and hiss. "Girl, what's your problem today? I did not request an Ann Landers consultation. I *hope* he's dead, frankly, may he rot in hell. And I hope his orphan children are begging with bowls in the street—"

"Sorry I brought it up."

"Well, it's a little late for that now, isn't it?"

I'm actually feeling rather juiced, more energy than I've had in days. Mona knows I'm not going to actually pummel her. I'm a total wimp, abuse-wise. She may even think it's good for me to blow off steam. I am speechless though as I pant with rage, my head reeling with images of Brian. Midfield, running for daylight. Serving Mass with Father Donegan. Riding away laughing in his first new car, surrounded by his mick buddies, leaving me in the driveway eating their exhaust. Not even the really painful stuff, the punishment and the hatred, and still I want to let out a primal scream, as if I know I have to die before all of this is really put to rest.

Then we hear a knocking on the screen door in the kitchen. And the really strange thing is this: suddenly Mona looks terrified. She blanched a bit as I railed at her, wincing as I rose above her in high dudgeon. But now when I clamber off the sofa to go and answer, her face is ashen, the hand on my arm beseeching, as if I am about to let a monster in. I *know* who it is, and zap Mona with a perplexed frown—what's *she* on—as I amble into the kitchen. "Coming!"

Gray stands resolutely on the back stoop, a bag of groceries in either arm, which was why he couldn't let himself in. The beach house is never locked, unlike the compounds on either side, which have laser rays and aerial surveillance. "Did I say I needed anything?" I ask as I bang the door wide.

"Just a few staples," he says, trooping by me to set the bags on the zinc table, then turns and searches my face. "How you feeling?"

Earnest Gray, in drab and rumpled Brooks Brothers mufti, his wispy vanishing hair making him look much older than fifty-one. But then WASPs on the high end age in an absentminded fashion, like the old shoes they never throw away. In addition Gray has been effectively retired his whole life. He is also the least vain man I have ever known.

"I had heart failure coming up from the beach, but otherwise I'm dandy. How much was all this?" I grab my jacket from behind the door to pull out my wallet, but Gray, who is already unloading muffins and ginger ale, waves vaguely, as if money is something vulgar that gentlemen don't discuss. "Come *on*, Gray, you can't keep buying me groceries."

And I wave twenty dollars by his shoulder, but he has that maddening WASP habit of pretending things aren't happening. "I thought I'd barbecue tonight," he says with boyish enthusiasm, and I lay the twenty on the table, in no-man's-land.

The irony is, Gray doesn't have a lot to spare, despite being the last of one of the nine families that owned California. There's a trust of course, and coupons to clip, and the beach house is his for life, as well as the gardener's cottage on the ranch where he's lived for twenty-five years. But none of this amounts to very much actual cash, because the old man poured almost everything into his wacko foundation. With all those connections no one ever expected Gray to grow up to be a loser, unable to make his own harvest in the fields of money. In fact, he's spent most of his life giving away his share, as a sort of patron saint of the avant-garde.

"That one he injected looks smaller to me," observes Gray, slapping a couple of steaks on the counter. He's talking about the eggplant-purple lesion on my right cheek, the size of a nickel. This is the only visible sign of my leprous state, and on my last visit the doctor gave it a direct hit of chemo. It doesn't look any different to me. Gray is the only one who ever mentions my lesion. Everyone else steps around it, like a turd on the carpet. "And look, we'll make some guacamole," he says, triumphantly producing three dented avocados.

Then Mona is standing in the doorway, giving a hopeless impersonation of demure. Gray spots her and instantly wilts. "Oh, I'm sorry," he murmurs fret-

fully, unable to meet our eyes, gazing with dismay at all the groceries he's un-
packed, as if he's come to the wrong place.

"Listen, I was just leaving, you guys go ahead," declares Mona magnani-
mously.

"Don't be silly, there's plenty," I say, perversely enjoying their twin discomfort. They don't exactly dislike each other, but they're like in-laws from different marriages, unrelated except by bad shit. "*You* make the margaritas," I command Mona with a bony finger. And because I am the sick boy, what can they
do? Guilt has gotten more dinners on the table than hunger ever dreamed of.
Mona goes right to the liquor cabinet, and Gray is already peeling the avocados. Like a veritable matchmaker I decide to give them some time alone and
run up to my room for a sweater.

First thing I do, I check my cheek in the mirror. Maybe he's right, one edge is
somewhat lighter, but nothing to write home about. It's not like I could cruise
a boy at the Malibu Safeway. I move to shut the balcony doors, catching a
glimpse of the gibbous moon as it flings its pearls on the water. Then I grab my
red-checked crewneck from the dresser and shrug it on.

Even though I only brought a single duffel bag with me here when I came
just after New Year's, right away this place felt more like home than my own
place ever did. My bleak one-bedroom in West Hollywood, with a view out
over four dumpsters, looks like a garage sale driven indoors by rain. Nothing
nice or comfortable, not a nesting person's space by any stretch. Whereas here I
have a lovely overstuffed chaise across from the bed, swathed in a faded Arca-
dian chintz, and a blue-painted wicker table by the window with shelves underneath for books. The ancient curtains are swagged and fringed and look
like they would crumble at the touch. If it sounds a bit Miss Havisham, don't
forget the sea breeze blowing through clean as sunlight every day.

Above the mahogany bed is a poster of Miss Jesus. The cross is propped
against the wall at AGORA, and I'm leaning against it in full drag, pulling up
my caftan to show a little leg. The expression on my face can only be called
abandoned. My crown of thorns is cocked at a rakish angle. In the lower right-
hand corner, in Gothic script, it says "Oh Mary!"

This is only the third time I've managed to put Mona and Gray together, and
I find myself excited by the prospect of spending an evening, just us three. The
two of them have come to be my most immediate family, somewhat by elimi-
nation, my friends all having died, but I couldn't have chosen better. I realize I
want them to know each other as well as I know them, for when it gets bad.
When I'm curled in a ball and can't play anymore, sucking on the respirator,
and then of course when it's over. They'll be good for each other, so opposite in
every way.

I've forgiven Mona already for bringing up Brian. It clearly won't happen
again, she's not *that* dumb. The memory overload has passed, and once again

my brother has faded into the septic murk of the past. What surprises me is this: as I trot down the spiral stair and hear my two friends laughing in the kitchen, I am so happy that some part of my heart kicks in and takes back the curse. *I hope you're not dead and your kids are great.* That's all. Goodbye. Fini.

Gray is regaling Mona with the tale of his three Baldwin aunts—Cora, Nonny and Foo. Mona is riveted. These three estimable ladies, maiden sisters of Gray's grandfather, the old rancher tycoon himself, had the beach house built for themselves and resided here every summer for sixty years. I who have heard this all before never tire of the least detail.

We bear the steaks and our margaritas out the kitchen door to the side terrace, where Gray lights the gas barbecue. At the other end of the arbor we can hear the fountain playing. The moon is all the light we need. It's too cold to actually eat outside, but for now there's something delicious being together around the fire, knocking down tequila and imagining the aunts.

"They used to put on plays and musicales, right here," says Gray, gesturing down the arbor, then to the gentle slope of lawn beside it. "We'd all sit out there. I don't remember the plays, except Foo wrote them. They were very peculiar."

"And none of these women ever married?" Mona stares over the rim of her drink into the shadows of the arbor, willfully trying to conjure them. "Were they ugly?"

"Oh, no, they were all very striking. Wonderful masses of hair, even when they were old ladies. And they wore these flowing gowns like Greek statues."

"They sound like Isadora Duncan," I say.

"They sound like dykes," Mona declares emphatically, then turns to Gray. "Weren't they?"

I feel this sudden protective urge toward Gray, as he lays the steaks sizzling on the grill. He has barely ever admitted to me that he's gay himself. There's not a whole lot to admit, I gather. He seems to carry on his rounded shoulders centuries of repression. But now he shrugs easily as he slathers on the barbecue sauce. "You'd have to ask them," he declares. "I never really gave it a thought. Something tells me they never really did either."

Mona is very quiet, but the answer seems to satisfy her. I have a bit of a brood myself, thinking how much the history of my tribe lies behind veils of ambiguity. Ever since I've been at the beach I've had this romantic longing, wishing I'd lived here during the aunts' heyday. But now I wonder, were they happy? Or were they trapped, making the best of it, away from the rigid straightness of the ranch? They seem more real to me tonight than half the people I know in L.A., who can't take my illness and talk to me funny, as if I'm a ghost.

"Isn't it curious, Tom," Mona says softly. "They ran a little art space, just like us."

Gray laughs. "Not quite. You guys are much more over the edge." He says this proudly. "Their stuff was more like a *school* play. Historical pageants, that kind of thing."

He bends and studies the meat, poking it with a finger. And yet, amateur though the aunts may have been, they were obviously the core influence on this, their oddball nephew. Gray Baldwin was subsidizing beat poets and jazz players in Venice—hundred here, hundred there, covering rents and bad habits—when he was still in high school. If you were way out enough, dancing barefoot on broken glass, painting the sand by Venice pier, Gray was your biggest fan. All the while, of course, he was having a sort of extended breakdown, growing more and more dysfunctional, estranged from the Baldwin throne. And no one pretends that Gray put his money on names that lasted or broke through to greatness. Marginal they stayed, like Gray himself.

"Still," Mona says puckishly, "I wish I'd had women like that around. In my house the drift was very home ec."

"I don't want to overcook it," Gray murmurs gravely, "but I can't really see."

"I'll go get the flashlight," pipes in Mona, darting for the kitchen.

"And I'll set the table." I hurry in after her. We are both laughing, at nothing really. Not drunk at all, just glad to be here together. Mona doesn't have to say she finally gets Gray Baldwin; I know it already. She grabs the flashlight from the shelf above the stove, while I fetch plates and three not-too-bent forks. We will have to share the steak knife. Minimal, everything's minimal here, that's the way the beach house works. Mona is lurching toward the screen door, I am making for the dining room, when suddenly she turns. "I love you, Tom," she says, blinking behind her tortoise rims, half blushing at the overdose of sentiment.

"Yeah," I reply laconically, but she knows what I mean.

In the dining room I set us up at the big round pedestal table, the base of which is thick as the mast of a schooner. In the center of the table is a bowl of white-flecked red camellias, three full blooms floating in water. These I picked days ago from the bushes behind the garage. They last a week in water, which is why I like them. Most cut flowers are dead by morning, just like all my friends. I move to the sideboard and pull a drawer. Laid inside are heaps of mismatched napkins, from damask to burlap. I take out three that are vaguely the same shade of green, and caper around the table, setting them under the forks.

Through the window from the courtyard Gray and Mona call in unison: "It's ready!"

"Great!" I bellow back at them, tucking the last napkin, and then I look up—

And Brian is there.

For a second I think I have died. He's standing in the archway into the parlor, the dwindling firelight flickering over him. He can't be real, and for the moment neither am I. But he is more stunned than I am. He gapes at me, and his mouth quivers speechless. He wears a dark suit and tie as if he's going to a funeral. Still it's more like a dream—I *want* it to be a dream. Somehow I've summoned him up by too much invoking his name.

Then he says, "Tommy, I should've called. But I didn't know how."

The beach house has no phone. Brian is apologizing. I'm very slow, like I'm still dreaming. Finally I say, "Mom died?"

"No, she's the same."

But then why has he come, and *how?* Nobody knows I'm here. Merrily through the kitchen the others come parading in, Gray with the steaks on a platter, Mona bearing the salad. They stop laughing as soon as they see the pair of us standing frozen. I turn helplessly to make the introductions, and suddenly I understand. Gray is completely bewildered, but Mona gives a brief shy nod in Brian's direction. It's Mona who's betrayed me! All that bullshit about the stranger at the theater, the *faux*-innocent speculations about my long-lost brother. Without being tortured even a little she gave out full particulars of my whereabouts.

"Gray Baldwin, this is my brother Brian," I say with chill formality. And as Gray steps forward to shake his hand I add with acid tongue, not looking at Mona, "I gather you know Ms. Aronson."

"I was out on business, Tommy," Brian says. His face is thicker and slightly doughy, the dazzle gone. "I just decided to wing it and come say hello. But then I couldn't find you, and then—" He makes a fruitless gesture, vaguely in Mona's direction. "—I couldn't leave till I saw you."

I am so unbelievably calm, considering. "Well, you've seen me," I retort, giving no quarter.

Gray's super WASP manners can't stand it. "We're just about to eat. Will you join us?"

"No no, I ate already, you go ahead."

There's a general fluster of embarrassment, everyone clucking apologetically. Gray and Mona hurry to take their seats. Gray beckons insistently to Brian, indicating that he should sit, even if he's not eating. I stand stonily, and Brian makes no move. Gray and Mona are serving the dinner so fast it's like Keystone Kops, a blur of slapstick. Finally, because even I don't have it in me to just say get out, I relent and nod curtly to Brian, and he follows my lead and sits. Instantly a plate of sliced steak and salad is plunked in front of me. Gray and Mona are already eating, as fast as they can, smiling gelidly at my brother.

I stare across at Brian. "So. What've *you* been doing the last nine years?"

He doesn't know if the question is real, or just a caustic put-down. Neither do I. "Oh, same old grind," he replies, studying his hands. His hair is still like fire. "I got married," he adds almost sheepishly.

I say nothing. Mona, downing the dregs of her margarita, gives it another go. "And he has a son. Seven, right?" She beams encouragement.

"Right, Daniel," Brian responds, and then shifts the weight of his big shoulders forward, almost yearning across the table toward me. "What about you, huh? She showed me around the theater. That's great."

"I've got AIDS."

Brian looks down. "Yeah, she said."

I turn to Mona. "I don't know why we're bothering. I believe you've covered the major points."

"Tom, give it a break." It's Gray, who never makes the slightest ripple of protest, so it must be bad. "Eat," he says.

And so I do. Anything to stop this racing panic of rage. I cut my meat into little pieces, tasting the char on my tongue like the ashes of all I've lost. I listen with genuine curiosity to the surreal conversation they have without me. As it's Brian's first trip to L.A., they speak of the weather, the smog, how it all looks like a movie set. I am already looking anxiously at Gray's and Mona's plates, realizing they are nearly done, and they aren't about to stick around for ice cream.

Brian is telling about his own house, on a marshy shore in Connecticut, 1710 and picture-perfect. Again I hear the old chatter from Gray, the aunts and the ranch and the musicales, twenty-two miles of ocean free as Eden. But now it isn't charming anymore. I feel threatened and helpless, not wanting Brian to know so much. It's as if my desert island is being stolen, right in front of my nose.

But the story fascinates Brian, who explains that he works for a builder, same job he's had for fifteen years. "Tommy knows him," he says, glancing a small remark in my direction, but nobody really looks at me. We are all just getting through this. Nevertheless, the last thing I will do is acknowledge Jerry Curran, the pigfuck who rode shotgun through my brother's arrogant youth.

Mona lays her fork and knife side by side on her empty plate. I give her a pleading look as she announces she has to leave for the theater. When Gray takes the cue, siding the dishes, drawling that he'll be heading back to the ranch, Brian looks as desperate as I do. Either of them might have stayed, I realize, if I hadn't been acting so truculent and glacial. Clearly I have bought this meeting one on one with Brian with my own special horde of bitter pennies.

I have no choice but to follow Mona and Gray through the kitchen and out to the yard, chattering as if nothing's wrong. What's so unusual, after all? A guy's brother drops by to surprise him. It's the most natural thing in the world that they'd want to be alone. I lean my elbows on the windowsill of Mona's Toyota as she starts the car. She turns and plants a kiss on my nose. "God, he must've been beautiful," she sighs. "Now take it easy, okay? Fratricide is very hard to clean up."

"Don't worry, this is going to be short and sweet."

"And remember, I need forty-five minutes tomorrow night."

I laugh heartily, pulling back as she swings the car around. I haven't performed in fifteen months, since the week the first lesion appeared on my arm. I move to the pickup as it pulls out of the garage. I shove my hands in my pockets and grin at Gray in the truck. We never touch goodbye or any other time. "Thanks for dinner."

"I'll be down Monday to fix that screen," he says. "Remind me to check the fuses." Endlessly polite, Gray wouldn't dream of saying too much about my brother. Family is something you talk about from three generations back.

"I thought I'd run away far enough that no one would ever find me."

Gray chuckles. "Foo always said we never should've let 'em build that coast road."

"I'm with Foo," I declare, waving as he drives away, crunching over the gravel. At the end of the drive he doesn't turn and follow Mona down the infamous Highway 1, but shoots across all three lanes and heads straight up the mountain road through the moonlit chaparral. I turn and head back to the torments of Chester, Connecticut.

Brian is standing in the parlor by the fire. He's taken off his jacket and loosened his tie, and he's paging through an old scrapbook, yellowing photos of picnics out on the bluff, aunts in costume, miles of open space. "This is quite a place," he says cheerfully. "You rent it by the month?"

"It's free," I reply flatly. "Was there something specific you wanted?"

He closes the album and sets it down, wearily shaking his head. Just in that second, sullen and heavy, he reminds me of my father. "Tommy, we shouldn't be strangers. We never should've let all this time go by."

"Really? I was for giving it a couple of millennia—you know, like they do for toxic waste." He turns to me full-face, his arms beginning to reach toward me, and I have this flash that he's going to drag me down. I scuttle back a pace and hurl my next volley. "I believe where we left it was that I caused Dad's stroke because I was queer. Jerry Curran and Father whatsis were holding you back, remember? So you wouldn't kill the little fag. Am I forgetting the nice part?"

I can see the zing of pain across his furrowed brow. It excites me that I've made my brother wince—a first. "So I was wrong," says Brian, weirdly meek and powerless. He also seems to have a set speech he needs to get through. "I treated you terrible. I hated my own brother, just because he was gay. I don't want it to be that way anymore."

If it's meant to disarm me, it succeeds. Suddenly I feel drained and almost weepy, but not for Brian's sake. I step past him and slump down heavily on the sofa, the afghan curling instinctively over my legs. The whole drama of coming out—the wrongheaded yammer, the hard acceptance—seems quaint and irrelevant now. Perhaps I prefer my brother to stay a pig, because it's simpler. And even though he's not the Greek god he used to be, fleshier now and slightly ruined, I feel *more* sick and frail in his presence. Not just because of AIDS, but like I'm the nerd from before too. "You can't understand," I say, almost a whisper. "All my friends have died."

There is a long silence before he speaks again. He sits on the arm of a battered easy chair, and I feel how uncomfortable he is in this room. The dowdiness unnerves him. Our sainted mother kept her house tidy enough for brain surgery. But it's more than that: he can't stand not being on his own turf. He's always been a neighborhood tough, the same as Jerry Curran, their territory staked, pissing the borders like a dog.

"I didn't have any idea," says Brian, "that all this was happening. I'd read about it and push it out of my mind. Nobody we know—" He stops, thinking he's said the wrong thing. But I don't care. His ignorance is oddly comforting, proving I don't have to like him. "It just hasn't touched our world. Is there anything I can do?"

"Sure," I say. "Find a cure. And then we'll sprinkle it all over Bob Manihan's grave, and Ronnie's and Bruce's and Tim's, and we'll all be as good as new."

Protracted silence again. This could go on all night, at this rate. I see him stealing little looks at me, fixed no doubt on the purple on my cheek. I wonder how sick I look otherwise, compared to a decade ago. In between I had some years when I felt pretty sexy. Pumped my tits regular, rode my bike with my shirt off, and connected up with a run of men as dazzling as any on Brian's team. Now I feel pained, almost cheated, that he can't know what I was like, that I had it all for a while. Not that I was so beautiful, or anybody's hero, but a man after my own kind.

Then I hate myself for caring what he thinks. The whole idea of talking about myself seems like a kind of special pleading. "So tell me, what're they like? Daniel and—I don't even know her name."

"Susan." Visibly he relaxes. Home turf. "Oh, they're terrific. Best thing could've happened to me."

And he's off on a staggering round of clichés, as if none of the rest of this lurching conversation had ever happened. Susan teaches special ed, and Daniel plays peewee hockey. A pair of golden retrievers and a summer place in the Berkshires. Somewhere in there the crusts are cut off bread. Brian is hypnotized by the sound of his own voice, pouring it out like an aria, morning in America. He makes it all sound like the fifties, a decade I only caught the tail end of, but even at three years old I wanted to poop all over it.

"We go see her on Sundays," Brian says, and I realize he's talking about my mother. "She's pretty bad. Barely knows who I am. But she seems to like seeing Daniel."

Within a year of Dad's death she was in a fog, and two years later she'd shrill into the phone: "*Who?* I don't have a son. I don't have any children at all." Somehow she remembered only her miscarriages, before Brian and me. I never called again.

"At least she's still in her own house," declares Brian with passionate Irish pride. This is the kicker, that our zombie mother gets to wander through her lace-curtain rooms, frail as a Belleek cup, instead of being a veggie in a nursing home. Nothing in Brian's voice betrays that he's bitter about having to shoulder this burden himself, or pay for the daily nurse/companion.

Then he segues into a peroration about his business, and here I really tune out. I remember the great drama that erupted when Brian graduated Fordham, deciding not to go after the glittering prizes of Wall Street, opting instead to throw in his lot with Jerry Curran. The only time I ever recall my father faltering in his worship of Brian, who had to woo the old man shamelessly to convince him Curran Construction would make him rich. Which it did, but more than anything else it let him stay on his own turf, so he and Jerry could strut and raise hell, till life and high school were one and the same.

"I don't know, maybe we got too big too fast," observes my brother with a labored sigh. And I realize things aren't perfect at Curran Construction, but haven't been following what he's said, so I haven't a clue what's wrong. Last I heard they were pouring an interstate and building twin towers in Hartford. Brian stares at the blue-red coals in the fireplace, lost in a troubled reverie. This alone is startling enough. In the twenty-five years I knew him before the breach, I never saw him stop to think. He was always in motion, always grinning, as wave after wave of cheering greeted his every turn.

"The stress must be pretty intense," I remark, lame as a radio shrink. "Sounds like you need a break."

"Yeah, I need somethin'." The brooding is still in his voice, but I can hear him shutting down. It's not that he won't discuss it any further with me, but that he doesn't want anymore commerce with his feelings. This is a peculiar phenomenon of straight males—the shutdown valve—which I used to think was the exclusive province of the Irish. Now I know it crosses all cultures, instinctive as the need to carry weapons. Brian turns back to me with a smile, as if he's never felt anything at all, and reaches over and slaps my knee. This is his idea of a kiss.

"You still a good Catholic?"

He laughs easily. "Sure, I guess so. We go to Mass on Sunday. Don't ask me when I made my last confession."

There's a Bing Crosby twinkle in his eye. I feel the old urge to desecrate, to flash my dick in church. "According to them I'm evil, you know. That's the last doctrine, from God's mouth to the Pope's ear. 'Intrinsic evil.'" I spit this last phrase out like it's poison.

Brian writhes slightly on the chair arm. He wedges his hands between his thighs, clamping his knees together. "That doesn't mean gay *people*," he retorts. "That's just about … acts."

A regular moral theologian, my brother. "Oh, fabulous. You can be gay, but you can't have a dick. Pardon me while I piss out my asshole."

"Tommy, you know what the church is about. Sex is for making babies." He grimaces and rolls his eyes, as if to bond us against the folly and the hypocrisy. "Nobody takes that seriously. Including half the priests."

"Excuse me," I hiss back at him, scrambling out of the afghan. "Maybe you guys get to wink at the priest while you fuck your brains out." He doesn't like my language, not one bit. "But they're still beating up fags in Chester, because Her Holiness says it's cool."

"Hey, ease up. It's not *my* doctrine."

"And sixty percent of the priests are fags anyway!" I'm wild. I have no idea where that statistic came from. It's like I've been waiting for a little doctrinal debate for years. "They *hate* us for being out. They liked it the old way, where you get to be special friends with the altar boys, and maybe you cop a feel off little Jimmy Murphy after Mass—"

"For someone who doesn't believe, you sure get yourself worked up."

"Don't give me that smug shit." I can feel his coldness, the backing off, though he doesn't move from the arm of the chair. "I bet you get all kinds of points for coming to visit a dead man. Corporal act of mercy—you should get a big fuckin' discount in Purgatory."

I'm pacing in front of him, panting with fury, and he sits there and takes it. But there's no satisfaction. I feel impotent and ridiculous—feel as if Brian has *won*. All I can do is wound him and push him away. I stagger against the mantel, my forehead pressed to the great splintered slab of wood that's anchored in the stone.

"Dad went to Mass every Sunday too," I declare with a wither of irony. "And you know what? He was still a scumbag drunk who hit me for nothing at all. He used to hit me for *reading*. And when I finally told him I was gay, he told me I made him want to puke." Then a very small pause. "Isn't that where you learned it?" Nothing, no answer. He's still as a rock. "So you'll forgive me if I keep my distance from all good Catholics."

Brian stands and reaches for his jacket, thrown over the back of the sofa. "I thought we could heal it up between us. I was wrong. I don't want to upset you like this. You've got enough to deal with." He shrugs into the jacket and turns to me. There is oddly no shyness between us, and nobody looks away. Perhaps this is the proof we are brothers. "Look, if there's anything …"

He lets it hang, and I shake my head. "You can't help me."

He nods, and we move together. Through the dining room and kitchen, then out to the yard, shoulder to shoulder across the grass. The silence between us doesn't feel strained, and is even rather soothing. We are ending it before it comes to blows. This is so sensible, we are practically acting like WASPs. The faint spoor of a skunk feathers the night air, and the moon is still bright, casting ice shadows across the gravel drive. We reach the boatlike rental car, nosed in between two Monterey cypresses. I wish my brother no harm and hope he knows it, but I say nothing. We both feel it's better this way.

Brian opens the door and half-turns again. His mouth works to speak, another set speech perhaps, but all that comes out is "Take care."

I stand with my hands in my pockets as he fishes the keys. We will never see each other again. No drunken promises to visit, no embrace to pass on to my nephew, no jokes. This is a surgical procedure, the final separation. And then the key turns in the ignition, and there's a clunk. Brian tries it again, this time pumping the gas. Nothing.

It is so ludicrously a symbol of the deadness between us, I want to laugh out loud. But it's so clearly not funny, the useless click of the key as he tries it over and over, because now my brother is stuck here. I know this a second before he does. In fact I can see the bloom of shock in his face as he remembers there's no phone. It's nine o'clock on a Saturday night, and the nearest pay phone is two miles south at the Chevron station, which closes at six, country hours. I have no car and no jumper cables. Our mogul neighbors with Uzi guard dogs are not the sort you bother for a cup of sugar.

Brian looks at me, dazed and slightly foolish, like a man who can't get it up. He seems to understand instinctively that he's trapped. "Fuckin' piece o' junk," he grumbles, so raw you can almost hear the brogue of Gramp Shaheen.

"You'll have to walk down to the Chevron in the morning. When's your flight?"

"Noon."

"Oh, you'll be fine. Don't worry, there's lots of room." My own voice amazes me, so solicitous and chummy. I open the door like a bloody valet. You'd think the bile and snarling never happened. But this is different, a matter of hospitality, like laying down the guns on Christmas Eve. Brian grabs his briefcase from the backseat, and we head back to the house. The skunk is nearer, or at least sending out a stronger warning. The silence between us is comfortable. We both appear to agree that this part can be handled in purely practical terms, no frills and no demands.

In the house I douse the downstairs lights, and Brian follows me up the spiral stair. "This is where I sleep," I say, pointing into Foo's room. Then we cross behind the stairwell, and I throw open the door opposite. "Cora's room," I inform him as we enter, by way of historical orientation.

In fact, this is where Gray stays when he spends the night, though he's never done that during my two months, so assiduous not to intrude. I snap the light on the bedside table, bathing the room in peach through the old silk shade. This room's not so tatty, though, its green wicker furniture crisp as Maine. Brian nods approval, soberly indifferent, even when I open the balcony door at the foot of the bed, the beckoning shine of the moonlit sea.

"We share a bathroom," I explain, pushing through yet another door. Even as I flick the light I wish I'd had a minute to tidy up. It's pretty gritty. There's prescription bottles all over the sink and counter, like Neely O'Hara in *Valley of the Dolls*. Funky towels on the floor and underwear strewn haphazardly. The plumbing hasn't been scoured in ages, and green blooms around the fixtures.

"Beautiful tile," Brian says gamely, as I snatch up shorts and toss them into my room.

"Look, you don't have to go right to bed. Maybe you want a drink or something." I'm rattling on as I scoop the prescriptions and push them to the far end of the counter. I open the cupboard above the tub, and *Eureka!* There's one clean towel. I present it to Brian. "I think there's vodka in the freezer. Whatever you like. It's just that I get real tired."

"Sure, sure, you go to bed. I'll be fine." There's a crease of worry between his eyes as he studies my face. "I'll just do a little work and then turn in myself."

"I bet you were supposed to call Susan."

"No, that's okay. They know I'll be home tomorrow. I'll be fine."

As he repeats this ringing assertion of life, he lifts his free hand in an awkward wave and backs out of the bathroom. Gently he closes the door. I who will not be fine turn and blink in the mirror above the sink, which I usually avoid like a nun. All I can see is the lesion on my cheek. My sickness is palpable, and indeed I'm completely exhausted. I splash my face with water, then use the hand towel to scrub at the smegma on the sink. It's hopeless.

I stand at the toilet and pull out my dick—oh useless tool, unloaded gun— and dribble a bit of piss, not a proper stream. The virus does something in the bladder to tamp the flow, or else there's lesions there as well.

I leave the light on for Brian and close my own door. I don't even bother to turn on the lamp as I shrug the crewneck and kick off my jeans. I duck into the bed and under the covers, the old down comforter that's shredding at the seams and spilling feathers like a wounded duck. Moonlight streams in, blue-gray on the furniture.

And I lie there, I who sleep like the dormouse now, nodding off into naps two or three times a day, ten hours solid at night. I stare at the ceiling, and the rage comes back. My father with the strap, my useless mother whimpering, "Don't hit his head." Brian on the field swamped by fans at the end of the game. Laughing with his girlfriend, horsing around with his buddies. My memory is split-screen, the Dickensian squalor of my woeful youth against the shine of Brian. No slight or misery is too small for me to dredge up. I am the princess and the pea of this condition.

I don't know how long it goes on. At one point I realize I'm clutching the other pillow as if I'm strangling someone, and my teeth are grinding like millstones. Then I hear Brian and freeze. The water goes on in the sink, right through the wall behind my head. I can hear him scrubbing his face—can *see* it. Because it's as if the fifteen years have vanished since we shared a room in Chester. I in my scrawny body have finished brushing my teeth, and Brian the god, a towel at his waist from the shower, steps up to the sink to shave. At sixteen he's got hair on his chest. His stomach is taut, the muscles cut like a washboard. I am so in awe of him that I have to force myself not to look, for fear of the dark incestuous longing that licks at my crotch like the flames of hell.

The water goes off. There's a shuffle of feet on the tile, and then I hear him pissing. But with him it's a geyser, a long and steady stream that drums the bowl like a gust of tropical rain. I am spellbound by the sound of it. I can feel the exact shape of my brother's dick—heavy and thick with a flared head—more clearly than my own. The pissing is brutally sensual, beyond erotic, and I'm not especially into kink. The stream abates to spurt, gunshots in the water. Then Brian flushes. The bar of light under the door goes out, and there's silence.

Still I stare at the ceiling, but now the rage is replaced by an ache, just like the empty throb that followed my little heart attack. Not that I want my brother anymore—not his body anyway. At least my own carnal journey has brought me that far, slaking the old doomed hunger. I used to jerk off sniffing his underwear, the uniforms he'd peel off after practice. But even with the incest gone, a darker yearning wells up in me, undiminished by years. I still want to *be* him. He's what a man is, not Tommy. From seven to seventeen I walked around with a sob in my throat, the original crybaby, mourning for what I would never become. And now it's come back like a time warp. I'm still wearing the glove I can't catch with, a Wilson fielder. I'm flinching in the middle of a scrimmage, terrified someone will pass me the ball.

This goes on for maybe half an hour, a sort of anxious misery, leaving me wired and desolate. I'm sick, I need my sleep. Eventually the rage comes back around like a boomerang, because it's also Brian's fault. I get up and grope into the bathroom, flicking the light, my ashen squinting face looking dead and buried. Fishing among my prescriptions I palm a Xanax and down it. Neely O'Hara again. I turn off the light and take a silent step to Brian's door, cocking my ear. I don't even know what I'm doing. *Go back to bed,* I order myself, but that is the voice I have always ignored, the one that used to tell me not to pull my pud or stare at boys.

By inches I open the door into the darkness beyond, barely breathing, craning to hear. And there it is: the deep rolling surf of my brother's breathing, a soft whistle at the end. He sleeps a hundred fathoms deep, he always has. Please, I slept in the twin bed next to him for seventeen years. I step inside and stand there a moment to orient myself. The moonshine is strong, though it throws deep shadows on the clutter of wicker, crazy expressionist angles.

Brian in the bed is lit up clear, the white of the sheets like a luminous ground. He's turned on his side and facing me, one arm under the pillow that cradles his head. Bare to the waist, the top sheet drawn up only to his hips, so I can see the waistband of his briefs. He doesn't even bother with a blanket, for the Irish side is very cold-blooded. Unlike me, who's always shivered in the California nights, shrouded in quilts and comforters.

Yet the cold doesn't bother me now, even in just my underpants, as I move to the wicker armchair by the bed. Though I sit carefully, perching on the edge, still it creaks and rasps under my weight. I scan Brian's face for any stir, but he sleeps right through. Now I am only three feet from him, so close I could reach out and touch him.

But I just watch. His red hair is silver in the moonlight. The arm that's crooked under his head has a bicep as round as a melon. The other arm rests on his side, and now that he's bare I see that his chest and stomach are still in shape, if not so finely chiseled as when he was young. All evening I've been trying to find him battered and soft, but it's not true. He's beautiful still, and even the puffiness in his face has soothed in sleep. If anything, the greater bulk and mass the years have wrought have only made him more of a warrior, king instead of a prince.

Am I still in a rage? Yes, livid. The last thing I need is this mocking reminder that life goes on for straights, mellowing and ripening into an ever richer manhood. In the glint of the moon Brian's skin fairly radiates with health. The bristling hair on his belly is thick with hormones. He'll be fifty, sixty, seventy, and still be winning trophies. And I'll be dead, dead, dead. Of course I know I can't blame my illness on Brian, but I can still hate him for being so alive. And the deep, deep irrelevance of his shiny life, with the peewee games and the goldens, I can hate that too. The white-bread sitcom cutesiness and the lies of the Nazi church.

I'm leaning forward with gritted teeth, my face contorted with nastiness. I'm like a bad witch, rotten with curses, casting a spell even I can't see to the end of. And maybe Brian picks up the vibes, because at last he stirs. A soft murmur flutters his lips, and he rolls from his side onto his back. His hands are on the pillow on either side of his head, so he lies defenseless. You could plunge a dagger into his heart.

Except I have shifted position now too, the roller coaster of my feelings bringing me up from down. Perhaps it's the Xanax starting to work. But suddenly it's like I'm guarding him, watching over the last of my clan, the only one whose luck has held. Oh, I still want him out of there. Back to his sweet vanilla life, every trace of him expunged, all the torrent of stinging memories he has brought in his glittering train. I wish to be left to die in peace. I don't need a brother—it's far too late in the game. But I stand watch anyway, keeping him free of harm as he sleeps, from curses and daggers.

Tears are pouring down my face, silent and futile, without any reason. Crybaby. Finally I think I will sleep. I stand, creaking the chair again, and I'm superconscious of every broken thing in my body. My six lesions, my old man's bladder, my nerve-warped knee. I wrap my arms about myself, huddling in my smallness. I take a last long look at Brian, and on impulse I lean above him, hover over his face and brush my lips against his cheek, just where my own cheek bears the mark.

I've never kissed my brother before. He doesn't flinch, he doesn't notice. Then I turn and stumble back to my room, pleading the gods to be rid of him.

VIRGINIA WITT

THE ANGEL OF DEATH ON
THE PROVINCETOWN FERRY

ELAINE, THE INQUISITIVE ONE, noticed him first: a thin, elflike man squatting by the pier, reading a book. Unlike the rest of the crowd waiting to board the ferry to Provincetown on an unusually hot Boston day, the frail little man was covered from head to toe. A broad-brimmed Panama hat hid most of his face, followed by a khaki suit, and finally tan socks and handsome brown leather shoes. The shoes were so loose on his slender feet that they instantly conjured up the image of the much larger, stronger man he must have been before he met the illness that had left him with one, surely no more than two, months to live.

Elaine nudged Amanda, and for a moment, the two young women looked at the thin man with mingled curiosity and pity. Following their gaze, Larry glanced at him too, but with very different emotions. He felt, all over again, the cold sweat that had swept over him the week before, in the drab little waiting room of a clinic, while awaiting the results of a certain important test. And they had been negative. They had been negative.

As Larry absently watched the thin little man, something in the tilt of the man's head, the exact angle of his hat brim, reminded him ... Larry brushed his muscular forearm, frosted with golden hair, across his face. He walked over to the chain fence that separated them from the blue water, where the ferry sat waiting for them.

"When will they let us on this damn boat?" he said under his breath.

A few minutes later, two ramps were lowered from the ferry's top deck, and the crowd began to push its way aboard.

The thin man got up, or, rather, unfolded, for he turned out to actually be very tall. He watched the crowd of vacationers surge forward, standing with his hand on his hip as the harbor breeze tugged at his loose clothing. Clearly, he no longer saw the point of rushing. Amanda watched him, almost as if she expected him to say something to her, while her friends struggled, laughing, with their elaborate mess of beach chairs, tennis rackets, and suitcases. But the thin man simply drifted off, holding his hat carefully at a slight angle, like one who has long been in the habit of unconscious arrogance.

A long boat ride stretched ahead of the vacationers, a perfect time to begin a suntan or finish a novel. While the two women went below to buy a sandwich, Larry spread out his beach towel on the crowded top deck. The wide-open space quickly took on a party atmosphere as young men unrolled towels and blankets and stretched their near-naked bodies in the sun, talking and laughing and playing music on their transistor radios. Larry carefully applied suntan oil on his golden-haired chest, arms, and legs, attracting a few interested glances from the men around him. He put on his tape player headphones, lay down, and was soon fast asleep.

He woke up sweating; it had become intolerably hot. Now fully midday, the sun and sky and water had reached a scorching brightness. Larry sat up and murmured to the two women who were stretched out next to him that he was going to go below for a soda.

"Honey, would you put more lotion on my back?" Elaine asked. Larry obliged her, rubbing it gently into her olive skin, pursing his lips in an oddly maternal expression. He ended with a tickle under her arms.

"Would you like the same?" he asked Amanda, whose pale skin was already turning pink.

"No, thanks," she murmured into her towel.

Elaine had known and adored him for years, but his charm had yet to capture Amanda, her new girlfriend. Larry was not overly concerned. He pulled on a fresh shirt and fished in his bag for a pack of cigarettes.

Down below, out of the sun, it was much more comfortable. A five-piece band was playing a very slow, lilting show tune, and several elderly women on a group tour were stepping about to the music. On his way past, Larry paused long enough to take one of them on a spin around the improvised dance floor. She smiled at him shyly, delighted, and her blue-haired friends all clapped.

Farther down the deck, Larry found a nice quiet spot at the railing, from which he could see the first faint outline of land, like a dark edge forming on the horizon. He lit a cigarette and, sucking the smoke in deeply, raked his hands through the tangles that the wind had made in his blond hair. Thinking of Elaine's and Amanda's prone and shiny bodies stretched out upstairs, he smiled.

Just then, he felt something as light as a dead leaf settle on his arm. He turned, startled. The thin man they had seen on the dock stood close, touching him. Looking up, Larry saw deeply into a face from which the flesh had fallen away, leaving only a slight flicker of life in eyes that must have once been irresistibly handsome. The look brought back, unavoidably now, a lover of a long-ago summer, a Broadway dancer named Paul Adair. Surely this man, standing so near that Larry could hear each labored breath, could not be Paul. Larry was overcome by a sudden terror that the ghostly man was going to embrace him, for their silent exchange of glances had the nakedness of two people who have just pulled away from a kiss.

"Pardon me." A quiet voice issued from the man's unmoving lips. "May I trouble you for a light?"

"I'm sorry, I haven't got one," Larry said quickly, reflexively taking a step back and causing the man's slender hand to slip from his arm. Then, realizing that his cigarette made his lie obvious, Larry turned scarlet.

"I see." The shadowed eyes under the hat brim registered first pain and then, very faintly, amusement. "Larry, wasn't it? I suppose you're thinking that I've changed, Larry." The thin lips curved. "You haven't." He coughed, covering his mouth with a silk handkerchief. Then he soundlessly slid away. When Larry looked around again, the apparition had disappeared. After a moment, Larry felt a burning sensation at the tips of his fingers—his cigarette.

"Shit," Larry said. He tossed the cigarette into the sea.

Half an hour later, when the boat's horn sounded, Larry had not moved. All around him, people were gathering their belongings and hurrying to the top deck. Again he felt a hand on his arm, but this time the touch was charged with energy. He turned to find Elaine's pretty face, already brown, grinning at him. Her teeth looked very white.

"Boy-watching again?" she teased. "We'd better get our asses in gear, pumpkin, or we'll have to wait an hour to get off this boat."

Provincetown looked slightly unreal, like a tinted photograph of a toy village, in the unflinching sun. Walking down the pier leading into the town, the girls pointed at gray-shingled houses and sailboats.

"Look at the windsurfer," Elaine shouted. "There I go!"

"Just don't get yourself killed," Larry said, a bit absentmindedly. He was keeping an eye on a familiar Panama hat well ahead of them in the crowd yet clearly visible above the heads of the other tourists. When Larry's group reached the center of town, they would turn left, toward the west end. Just then, it seemed the most important thing in the world to Larry that the Panama hat not turn left as well. It was a long, hot walk to the end of the pier, even hotter when carrying, as Larry was, two suitcases as well as Elaine's golf clubs. The perspiration was dripping into his eyes. He watched with gradually increasing relief as the Panama hat slowly drifted over to the right side of the pier, turned right on the main street, and vanished.

At the lodgings, Larry took charge and got them settled in quickly. He had made all the arrangements, "Uncle Larry," as Elaine jokingly said. They were in a sunny little apartment overhanging the harbor. On the tiny balcony, pink geraniums planted in tubs tumbled about in the breeze.

"Even the bed's decent," said Amanda, flinging herself down.

"Larry, you're wonderful," Elaine said.

But Larry was already in his room, carefully unpacking his outfits for the week's vacation: seven casual shirts, three t-shirts, four pairs of good shorts, two pairs of cutoffs, two pairs of casual slacks, two bathing suits. He stripped off his soiled clothes quickly and dressed without his usual care. On his way out, he looked in on the girls. They were curled up together on the bed, already asleep. A peculiar look crossed Larry's face. Soundlessly, he let himself out of the apartment.

As the cocktail hour approached, people flooded out of their lodgings into the street. Most of the men moving toward and past and around Larry were young and brown and healthy, and many were also very handsome. Larry, as a good-looking man walking alone in the street, attracted some interested glances. He ducked into Sharkey's, one of his favorite bars in town, a tiny underground cafe done up in turquoise and pink. As usual, the lesbians were crowded around the bar. Larry chose a table in the back and ordered his favorite drink, a milk shake flavored with Kahlua. He felt an odd uneasiness, a sense of somehow being out of place, but reminded himself that he always felt that way at the beginning of a vacation.

Two dark men, perhaps ten years younger than Larry, watched him from a nearby table. They looked vaguely familiar—maybe he had met them at a party last summer? Finally, one of them, a stocky boy in a fishnet tank top, walked over.

"Weren't you on the Boston boat?"

"Today? Yes," said Larry.

"Want to join us?"

"Sure." After Larry sat down and introduced himself (using his first name only; he'd been at this longer than they had), he reached for a cigarette. But his fingertips still stung from the cigarette burn. Larry took another sip of his drink and smiled at the boys. "Your first season? My ninth, believe it or not. Maybe I could point you in the right direction."

"What about that club across the street?"

"That's strictly for the girls. But you must try the Flute, just two blocks down. Gorgeous decor, lovely view …"

"But where's the action?" the boy in the fishnet top wanted to know. "We're only here three days."

Larry's eyelids flickered briefly—a sign of disdain, had his companions known it—and then he smiled. "Try the Dominion, on the east end. Some leather, lots of fabulous boys."

"Keep on talking," the boy said, gesturing to the waiter.

"This round is on me," Larry said smoothly. "When you go to the beach, feel free to take your suit off, but watch out—rangers do patrol on horseback. Someone will warn you. One time years ago I fell asleep in the nude. I woke up with a man I'd never seen before shaking me and shouting, 'Ranger, ranger!' I thought: these New England boys are *very* forward."

Everyone laughed.

"Maybe we'll bump into you at the beach tomorrow," the stocky one said, "with or without your suit."

Larry smirked, showing his dimples. "Which would you prefer?"

"I'd prefer tonight," the boy countered boldly, but then he glanced nervously at his friend. "Why not?" he added, looking openly at Larry's well-muscled arms and chest. "You don't look sick to me." Seeing a slight change in Larry's expression, the boy quickly added, "You can't be too careful nowadays."

There was an unexpectedly long silence. Larry looked away, not at anybody in Sharkey's, but at some abstract and distant point. "But you can," he said softly. "You can be too careful." He got up awkwardly, dropped some money on the table, and pushed his chair into place. "Tired ... traveling ... sorry ... bump into you again," he muttered.

After he left, the two boys agreed that the "blond beauty" must have tested positive.

That night, when the girls asked him to join them for dinner, Larry excused himself, saying that he was tired. He went to bed at ten o'clock, but he did not sleep. Again and again he relived his encounter with his dying friend, rewriting the exchange to make his part less shameful, inventing long conversations in which Paul told him about his suffering while he, Larry, listened and gave comfort.

He heard, dimly, as if from a great distance, the girls returning, moving stealthily so as not to wake him. But their presence did not comfort him. Larry felt that Paul alone held up the mirror in which he must look at himself forever.

The very next day, Larry's strange search began. Walking down the beach, his eyes combed the crowds of sunbathers for a frail and slender form, but all he found was an endless parade of bronzed and muscular men. Often, they returned his gaze as if expecting something more, but he looked past them, frowned, and kept on walking. The same happened in the bar that night: Larry fell into conversations easily but dropped out in midsentence, looking around every time the door opened and a new group of men walked in.

Each succeeding day was very much like the first one, only they slipped by faster and faster. Larry became increasingly restless, unable to remain still or to break away from his secret search. He even called the local hospital to ask if there was a patient named Adair. He walked up and down the main street, seeing little of the people or goods on display, but soothed by being in motion.

On the last day of his vacation, Larry was walking in the most crowded part of town when he saw something that made his heart jump. Three blocks up the street, where the crowd was thinner, a nun was pushing an invalid in a wheelchair. The thin figure was wrapped in shawls and almost blocked from view by the nun's black cape. But Larry caught a glimpse of a Panama hat.

His heart pounding, he pushed his way though the crowd. Young men walking hand in hand and families strolling five abreast cheerfully ignored his attempts to get past them. The wheelchair disappeared around a corner. Freeing himself from the crowd, Larry dashed around the corner and ran up the hill after the nun's flapping black cape.

"Please—please let me help you," he panted. The nun stopped and stared at him. Then the figure in the wheelchair turned. Under the wide hat brim was the plump, pouting face of an old lady, carefully rouged and lipsticked. Frowning, she tapped her cane on the sidewalk.

"We're in a hurry to get home," the nun said. "We appreciate your kindness, sir."

"I'm sorry," Larry said. "I'm really very sorry." He stepped back into the street without looking, and just missed being hit by a cyclist.

"What the fuck do you think you're doing!" the cyclist yelled.

On the ferry that afternoon, Larry stood in the stern and watched the town's gray shoreline slip away until there was nothing left to watch.

"We've lost sight of land!" a little girl cried out.

Larry felt the tears rise up from the deepest part of his insides, rolling up and through him and shaking his whole frame. He became aware, not by sight but somehow through his pores, of Elaine's warm presence beside him. He grabbed her and clung to her and wept like a child, forgetting, for the moment, everything but his need for comfort.

Elaine just held him quietly, not yet asking any questions, but deeply touched—and surprised. In ten years of friendship, she had never once seen Larry cry.

JOHN PRESTON

PORTLAND, MAINE:
AN ESSAY

(The following selection is an autobiographical essay, not a work of fiction.)

I GOT MY DRIVER'S LICENSE IN 1961, when I was sixteen. The great activity that year was taking long trips in the family car. The periphery of my courage and my parents' patience was Portland, Maine, a hundred miles and change from our home in Massachusetts.

It wasn't a very exciting place to go. Back then Portland was a city that had been down so long no one could imagine it would ever make it back up again. Portland had been a major seaport when sailing ships ruled the sea, and its proximity to Maine's great forests created a shipbuilding industry. It got a reprieve in the days of the steamship because it was the closest warm-water port to Montreal. When the St. Lawrence River froze, much of Canada's commerce moved through Portland's waterfront. The hectic activity during those three or four months of the year made the longshoremen and chandlers rich and prosperous.

During the Depression, the Canadian government built a new railroad from Montreal to the Maritime Provinces as a matter of national defense and national pride. Just as the shoe and textile industries around Maine were beginning to go broke, the economic lifeline was cut by the new rail route to Halifax. World War II brought a reprieve, but when it was over, Portland sank into a slump that lasted for decades.

I used to drive the station wagon down to the empty wharves and cruise around the abandoned warehouses. Congress Street, the main street of the city, was lined with styleless shops centered around an antiquated department store. Ugly plastic façades covered most of the commercial buildings in town that were still used, vain attempts to make the structures appear up-to-date. Portland seemed, really, just a place to pass through. It was where you got the ferries to the resort islands of Casco Bay, perhaps where you changed buses to go farther north to Bar Harbor and the other seaside resorts. Portland, itself, was a destination only for traveling salesmen and teenagers who had no place better to go.

So it was a shock when I was sitting in my apartment in Manhattan's East Village in 1979, trying to think of a place to move, that Portland came up on the top of the list. I had never considered living there, not once that I can remember.

I was looking for someplace to go to because I was tired of the cities. I had gone to college in Chicago, then, in quick succession, had lived in Minneapolis, Philadelphia, New York, Los Angeles, San Francisco, and now, again, New York. I had spent so much time in Denver, Houston, and Washington that I sometimes forgot I'd never actually lived in any one of them and put them on the list of places I had. Now I was in my mid-thirties and I had become a writer. It was time to change.

Having this vocation was as unexpected as thinking about moving to Portland. I had been a magazine editor and a public speaker, but I hadn't thought of myself as a writer until I had moved this second time to New York. I had begun by pushing out some erotic fiction, thinking it wasn't important—probably the reason I was able to do it in the first place—and I discovered that it was all being published. More than that, it was well received. I was quickly being asked for essays and reviews, even being encouraged to write a book. I could earn my living at this, I realized. This could become my life.

If I were going to be a writer, though, I needed to live somewhere else. The cities had become a distraction, they were no longer a stimulation. The pace and expense of New York was too much pressure. The struggle to survive economically and to block out the noise and turbulence of the streets was too much of a diversion from my work.

I also wanted to move back to New England. When I'd first left Massachusetts for college, I discovered myself returning as often as possible, at least once a year, to Provincetown. I had told myself that I was doing it because it was the capital of my new gay life, but I came to realize that I was going back to Provincetown in an attempt to return home. No matter how much of a gay center it might be, Provincetown was still a Yankee village. The sights, the sounds, the streets all made sense to me when I visited there. The resort was a lifeline that kept me precariously in touch with my roots.

Of course I considered Provincetown as a place I might go, but the idea of living there year round didn't appeal. I knew how deserted and isolated it is in the off-season. The crowds of people who swarm through the streets and decorate the beaches don't persist in the winter months on Cape Cod. They are home working to save the money for their return the next summer, or they'd gone to Florida or California on an annual migration.

I wasn't willing to spend the better part of the year alone. I didn't want to give up all the positive aspects of a city, just the oppressive ones. That meant that Boston also was out of the picture. It would have satisfied my desires to live in New England again, but there seemed little reason to trade the hassles of New York for those of Boston, a city almost as pressured and just as expensive as Manhattan.

I sat down in my apartment and wrote out the things that my new home should have. It should be something of a city. Though as small as possible, it should still have some kind of cultural life—theaters, decent movie houses, good restaurants. I wasn't at all ready to give up my gay life. I wanted a place with at least a few bars and perhaps an organization or two that could allow easy access to a social life and support system.

Those were very important considerations. The visible gay communities back then were limited to the few resorts like Provincetown and Key West and Fire Island and certain neighborhoods like Greenwich Village and West Hollywood. We had just finished establishing those places as our own and we didn't really know if we could exist outside them.

There were noises of other locales where a gay man could find some safety and community. Certainly university cities Madison and Boulder had something to offer, but I wasn't so sure that the new gay life in smaller cities like Portland was really viable. Above all, I didn't want to move to a hometown where I had to hide. I wasn't willing to go back into the closet just to enjoy life in New England. I had developed very strong opinions about myself and community and they didn't include that kind of payoff.

But as I went through the points on my list and considered other places, none of them made as much sense as Portland. Portsmouth, New Hampshire, was too much of a tourist community and too close to Boston, it would be like living in a suburb. Providence, Rhode Island, wasn't an attractive option. New London, Connecticut, and Burlington, Vermont, were too small.

There was another detail that had to be thought about. The idea of leaving New York wasn't without its risks. My contacts with the publishing world seemed frail. I wasn't sure I could maintain them if I didn't visit them often. I wanted someplace that gave me quick access to both Boston and Manhattan. No matter how little I wanted to reside in those places, I wanted to be able to get to them easily. Portland had regular airline service to New York, and not just prop commuter planes; it had jets that would get me to LaGuardia in less than an hour. It was also only a two-hour drive to Boston.

I made a visit to Portland that Thanksgiving. All those years of economic hardship had one positive outcome: It hadn't been worth anyone's effort to tear down all the old buildings and replace them with characterless modern structures. By the time Portland's economy began to resurrect itself—and it had just happened recently—attitudes about urban development had altered. A grand railroad station was gone and there was a glaring Holiday Inn at the center of the city, but those were aberrations. Restoring and preserving the older buildings was the new goal. The plastic façades had been torn down and what was exposed was handsome architecture from the mid-nineteenth century. Most of Portland had burned to the ground as a result of an industrial accident in 1866. The core of the city had been reconstructed quickly and left the place with a unity of red brick and gray granite stone.

The waterfront was one of the centers of renovation. Where I had seen deserted warehouses twenty years earlier, there were now handsome office buildings and new restaurants. The pavements had been redone, asphalt was replaced with cobblestone streets and brick sidewalks. The area even had a name, The Old Port, to attract tourists and businessmen.

Gay life was much better than I'd remembered. There used to be a bar on Cumberland Avenue with a dance floor in the rear. Whenever a policeman or an unknown visitor came into the front, the bartender would press a silent button that would make the lights in the back room flicker, a warning for all the same-sex couples to stop touching one another and sit down, so they wouldn't be arrested. Now there were more bars, much less circumspect. I found a Maine gay newspaper stacked in the entrance to one of the pubs. It wasn't sophisticated, but it gave some hope that there was real political and cultural gay life in the city.

I moved to Portland that December. Most of my memories of the first few months are wonderful. I was happy to be in New England again, and Portland proved to be the archetypical Yankee city in many ways. Even the early winter snowfalls seemed romantic. I was at home.

Many of the first impressions of living in Maine were surprisingly erotic. I discovered that I loved, most of all, the voices of the men. When I'd gone to college my accent had been the cause of cruel ridicule. I sounded as exotic as a Kennedy to my new schoolmates, but not nearly so sophisticated. My words had the weight of the country about them, and they knew it. I was humiliated by their jokes and retreated to my room, where I spent my freshman year learning how to talk in a way they wouldn't make fun of. I succeeded, and my social life and sense of comfort increased dramatically in my sophomore year.

I always knew that I had lost something important, though. I would always make a connection between changing my way of speaking with hiding my way of being. To have given up my accent for the sake of social peace was the same, in some profound way, as hiding my sexuality had been during those college years.

Now I was surrounded by the sounds of New England men, all of them speaking in just the way I had. The sounds of their voices were alluring. It was, somehow, a mingling of my open sexuality and my return to the region. I would find any way possible to keep the men talking, their heads on a pillow beside mine, or standing in a bar while we seduced one another, or dancing together on the open floors of the new bars.

New England men provided another erotic element, one that I thought was hilarious. Being gay in Portland doesn't have much to do with the media image of gay life. For one thing, most of the men I know here are working class. There's none of the ostentatious wealth that gay men are supposed to have. Most social occasions with other gay men in Portland consist of cheap restaurants or potluck suppers in someone's home. During all the years I had lived in the big cities, the emerging gay cultures had developed certain styles of dress whose purpose was frankly sexual. The carefully cultivated images of construction workers or motorcyclists or seamen were all affectations of office managers, lawyers, and editors. I was surprised that few of those likenesses were obvious in Portland bars. At first I took it as a sign of backwardness that none of the gay men here dressed in the fads of Greenwich Village or Castro Street. Then I got to know more of the men and I discovered the reason.

The men I would meet in the bars in Portland really *were* construction workers. They drove motorcycles because they were cheap transportation, not because they were stylish. They worked on the waterfront because the pay was good, not because it was sexy. When they went out at night, none of them wanted to draw attention to their working-class jobs. They dressed in sharply creased chinos and crew-neck sweaters because they didn't want to be reminded of what they did during the day.

I became known as the one who would ask others to come over to his apartment right from work, so he could see them in their uniforms. A few began to understand what I was after and I remember, with great pleasure, the first time Mike gave me his hard hat, not one worn to a disco for appearance's sake, but the one he wore while he was a linesman for Central Maine Power Company. Then there was the day when Brian, who worked on the wharves, showed up wearing his hip boots, his yellow slicker hat, and layers of thermal underwear. He was embarrassed to be seen in that outfit. I could only tell him that he would make a fortune if he could package it and sell it in the Village. I had worried that my sexual fantasies wouldn't be possible in a small place like Portland; instead I discovered them being lived daily by all the men with whom I came in contact.

I didn't like a lot of other things about being gay in Portland those first few years. My concern about my connections with publishing led me to make sure that a post office box was my first purchase when I moved. The clerks began to eye me curiously as they handed over the packages from gay newspapers and magazines. Religious tracts were left conspicuously on their counters, sometimes I thought they were brought out especially for me, when they'd seen me coming into the station. I hated the hoops they made me jump through, and silently prepared to complain to the federal authorities if the local clerks dared step any further out of line.

Having been such a public figure in other, larger cities, I didn't think twice when asked to speak on gay views for newspapers and television. It was unheard of back then for local gay men to do that, even gay liberationists would speak on camera only if their faces would be shown in silhouette. Most of the guys I had been meeting were excited by my activism, which was very low-key so far as I was concerned. A few of them worked at L. L. Bean, one of the largest employers in the state, and they started to use their employee discounts to let me buy myself better clothes, so I would look more like a spokesman they'd admire.

Others were much less pleased. It came as a shock to be asked not to acknowledge a couple of acquaintances when we met on the street. They were frightened that my notoriety would wear off on them.

I was even more angered by the way the writing community dealt with me. My being gay overwhelmed whatever common interests we might have held. It was years before another writer in Maine would approach me or invite me to take part in community activities, even though the fact that I was working with large publishing houses was quickly well publicized. One of my goals when I moved to Portland was to write books. I accomplished that in the first year. When *Franny, the Queen of Provincetown* was published, *The Maine Sunday Telegram* sent a writer to interview me. He seemed uncomfortable and finally blurted out a question he'd obviously been holding inside for quite a while: How could I write a gay book that wasn't pornographic? What was the reason for a gay book if it weren't explicitly sexual? It didn't surprise me when the paper canceled the interview and when the review, written by this same man, was the most scathing gotten by that otherwise well-received sweet book.

Probably the most enraging incident occurred when the manager of the large state-of-the-art photocopying shop in town took me aside and told me that she no longer wanted my business. She was sure that my work, erotic or not, was something she wanted nothing to do with, and she let me know she *hoped* it was illegal as well. It didn't really help when I learned, years later, that the (numerous) gay employees had been illegally copying all my material and passing it around to their friends. They weren't about to defend me to their employer, but they were happy to have access to the stories and articles I was writing.

The tension from all these events built up. I had to move twice in the first year or so I was in town for utterly routine reasons. I had always admired the stolid line of Georgian buildings that lined one block in the center of the city. It was called "The Park Street Row" and held for me all the elegance and grandeur of Boston's Beacon Hill, whose architecture these structures mirrored. The last time I had to move, there were apartments for rent in a newly renovated building in the middle of the Row. I was one of the first people to show up on the first day they were being shown. Hugh, the landlord, led me to a flat on the second floor, the parlor floor in the days when this had been a Victorian mansion. The tall ceilings were lined with hand-painted cornices and the living room was crowned by a grand plaster of paris rosette. The apartment was perfect, with two large rooms for living and sleeping and a third small one, the perfect home office. I wanted to live here desperately, but I was bruised. I discovered myself bursting out to Hugh, "But you have to understand that I'm gay. I'm angry I even have to mention it. It's none of your business. But I don't want it to become an issue in the future." I would *never* had to have told a landlord in New York or San Francisco that I was gay. They could have assumed it, but here in a small city, I had been forced into being defensive.

Hugh looked at me and said quietly, "You're right. It's none of my business. And I couldn't care less."

I moved in the next week and I still live here. In fact, I've lived in this apartment for ten years, longer than I'd ever even lived in a city before in my entire adult life.

Life in Portland became almost all good. The annoyances seemed to disappear. Dale McCormick began her campaign to establish a gay and lesbian political organization and hundreds of people came out of the closet to join her statewide movement. Gay men and lesbians in Maine were no longer silhouettes on the screen, they had more and more faces of real neighbors, and the Maine Lesbian and Gay Coalition became one of the most successful organizations in the country.

I had my personal victories as well. The rest of the media didn't feel as constrained as the Sunday paper. Over the next few years, as I began to publish more, they took me on as a local figure, and I was profiled on the front page of the daily newspaper. When I won awards, the local television stations gave my trophies major play. When a friend visited from New York once, a bag boy at the supermarket made me eternally happy when he asked, in front of my guest, "Aren't you that famous writer?" To be known in one's supermarket is the final accolade a community can give.

I made some money by writing some mass market pulp adventure novels that had a certain pseudonymous success. There was a new crew at the post office, men my age with my own background, who loved them. I even ended up dedicating one of the series to "The Men of Station A." The world might have thought they were Cold War warriors, but my dedicatees were actually my postmen. While their predecessors had been guarded about any mention of where my mail came from, the new guys watched the return addresses and complimented me whenever one was Avon or Dell or St. Martin's.

They even got over my sexuality. Once a soft-core heterosexual porn magazine was mailed to me. I couldn't imagine how it had come to be addressed to me, but it was. There weren't another customers in the place and when the clerk handed it over the counter, he yelled to the other postal workers, "Hey, look what Preston got! I knew it all the time. He's just faking that gay stuff. There must be money in it!" The rest of them laughed and made jokes about the way the world had changed. Everyone used to hide his homosexuality, they said, but now, here I was, cashing in on the new trend.

One of the few sumptuous social highlights of my year isn't even gay; it's an annual Christmas party that Hugh and his wife, Linda, give. Some years it's only been for the tenants, sometimes the list is made up of their business contacts or other homeowners on Park Street Row. Through sheer attrition, I'm the lodger who's been here the longest; whoever else is invited, I'm always on the list. Their apartment, on the fifth floor, is the most modern in the building. It's a stylish loft with windows that show a panoramic view of the harbor and Casco Bay. I dress up and climb the stairs right on time, anxious to see what Hugh, a gourmand, has cooked this holiday season.

I always stay the whole time, I'm not one of those who come in for a quick social nod and leave. By the end of the party, Hugh and I have usually had more than a fair share to drink. (Actually, while most people are satisfied with a glass of wine, Hugh usually has a bit of Scotch tucked away for the two of us.) A couple years ago, after we were both pleasantly blushed with holiday cheer, Hugh saw me to the door when the party was over. He asked me, "John, we hear all about this AIDS stuff. We're so concerned. You're okay, aren't you?" I looked at him blankly, I couldn't find any words, I couldn't lie to him.

"Oh, god, why did I ask?"

I had kept my diagnosis a secret. I had watched the spread of the epidemic for years before I learned that I was infected myself. I had thought, quite frankly, that my move to Portland might have saved me. Sure, there had been trips back to New York, to Boston, to California, but I had learned the new rules of the sexual game early and there hadn't been many times in Maine when I thought I could have been infected.

But I had been. I had just learned a few months before Hugh asked the question. I had thought that the news would be easy for me to accept. I was trained as an educator and had been one of the people who had founded the first AIDS organizations in Maine. I was aware, conscious of what was happening, certainly I should have been able to deal with this. But I hadn't been able, not at all. I didn't know who to tell, I couldn't figure out what I would ask for. I was certain I'd find nothing but trouble when the news spread.

However I thought I should have handled the situation, I also knew very well how viciously so many people were treated when the news of their diagnosis had been spread. I had seen them abandoned by their lovers, kicked out of their apartments, scorned by their families. I might have information about the virus that I could use, but I didn't know what was going to happen to people when they found out.

Hugh was embarrassed by his question. He came to my apartment the next day and apologized for having intruded into my privacy, but I was glad he'd asked. I knew I couldn't sit alone in my apartment and take everything on myself forever. It was time to take some risks, time to test the waters. I had to find out what my supports were going to be.

The next year was tough. There were many choked conversations on the phone with friends and relatives and many awkward revelations over lunch or drinks. When I finally spoke to my brother, the person in my family with whom I had the strongest relationship, he asked what he should do with the information. I told him it was his. I didn't want to control it anymore. If it was appropriate and comfortable for him to tell others, he should. If not, he shouldn't feel an obligation. He did tell the other members of our family and they came to visit me, one by one, uncomfortably, but honestly.

When things got hardest, Hugh was one of the people I called. We went to lunch once when I phoned him in a panic. It was a day when I felt utterly out of control of my life. Over a decent meal and a glass of wine he sat there and listened and talked about his own aging. We were just a couple of guys sitting around talking about our mortality that afternoon. He and Linda began to ask questions about my therapies, what doctors was I seeing in Boston? Asking about my well-being wasn't something we saw as an intrusion anymore.

They were part of my healing, not my physical healing, but the restoration of my spirits. The way I finally had to complete the recovery was by writing. I wrote essays about my infection and collected my own and some others in an anthology, *Personal Dispatches.* The act of putting the words into type was the final reclaiming of my self. It was done. I had faced the disease and, even if I couldn't defeat it, I wasn't going to hide from it.

When the book was published, I accepted an invitation to be interviewed by Al Diamon on Maine Public Radio. He was one of the newspeople who'd spoken to me over the years, I think—I hope—he was one of those who'd respected me. The interview was hard for both of us, we spoke openly about my infection and my own thoughts on what was ahead for me.

I knew there'd be more publicity, especially now that I was out in the open about my diagnosis, but I didn't expect an interview on public radio to reach the masses. The next morning I walked unsuspectingly into my post office branch. As soon as they saw me, all the clerks gathered at one of the desks. They were staring at me, ignoring the other customers. "Come here," one of them said. I walked up to them, not sure what was happening. "Is it true? What we heard on the radio last night?" I nodded that it was. I had flashes of the religious tracts the other postal workers had kept on their desks. I began to worry about how these men were going to react. I had visions of all the ignorance about AIDS I'd seen flashed over the television. Instead, one of the men, who I now realize was designated as their spokesperson, said to me, calmly, and clearly, "Shit, we all gotta die, John, but it must be hell to be standing on the tracks, watching the locomotive coming with your name on it." I don't think anyone else, not the most eloquent author or the most inspired political leader, has ever put it better.

And that was it, for that morning and for the past three years. Like everyone else who knows me, they ask about potential cures they read about in the newspapers and they wonder about my health, asking how I'm doing. They're happy when I seem well and they become concerned when I look haggard.

They're like Hugh and Linda, like my fellow workers at The AIDS Project, like Al Diamon, they're people who live in the same place I do, bound together not just because of geography, but because we all share a hometown.

RUNNING ON EMPTY

ON THE CHARTER FLIGHT from Paris to New York Luke sat on the aisle. Next to him, in the center seat, was a man in his mid-twenties from the French Alps, where his parents owned a small hotel for skiers. He said he cooked all winter in the hotel and then took quite a long vacation every spring. This year it was the States, since the dollar was so low.

"Not *that* low," Luke said when Sylvain mentioned he had only a hundred dollars with him for a five-week stay.

They were speaking French, since Sylvain confessed he couldn't get through even one sentence in English. Sylvain smiled and Luke envied him his looks, his health, even his youth, although that was absurd, since Luke himself was barely twenty-nine.

Next to Sylvain, by the window, sat a nun with an eager, intelligent face. Soon she had joined in the conversation. She was Sister Julia, an American, though a member of a French convent for a reason she never explained, despite their nonstop chatter for the seven and a half hours they were in the air. Her French was excellent, much better than Luke's. He noticed that Sylvain talked to her with all the grace notes kept in, whereas with Luke he simplified down to the main melody.

It turned out Luke and Sister Julia had both been in France for four years. Of course a convent was a "total immersion" undreamt of even by Berlitz. Nevertheless Luke was embarrassed to admit to his seat partners that he was a translator. From French to English, to be sure. It was pointless to explain to this handsome, confident Sylvain that a translator must be better in the "into language" than in the "out-of language," that a translator must be a stylist in his own tongue.

Sylvain was, in any event, more intrigued by Sister Julia's vows than by Luke's linguistic competence. He asked her right off how a pretty girl like her could give up sex.

"But I'm not a girl," she said. "I'm forty-six. This wimple is very handy," she said with a trace of coquetry, "for covering up gray hair."

She was not at all like the stern, bushy-eyebrowed, downy-chinned nuns who'd taught Luke all the way through high school. When Sylvain asked her if she didn't regret having never known a man—and here he even raised his muscular arms, smiled, and stretched—she said quite simply, "But I was married. I know all about men."

She told them her father had been a composer, she'd grown up an Episcopalian in Providence, Rhode Island, she'd taught music theory at Brown and built harpsichords. Her religious vocation had descended on her swiftly, but she didn't provide them with the conversion scene; she had little sense of the dramatic possibilities her life provided, or perhaps flattening out her own narrative was a penance for her. Nor was her theology orthodox. She believed in reincarnation. "Do you?" she asked them.

"I'm an atheist," Luke said. He'd never said that to a nun before, and he enjoyed saying it, even though Sister Julia wasn't the sort to be shocked or even sorrowed by someone else's lack of faith—she was blessed by the convert's egotism. There was nothing dogmatic about her clear, fresh face, her pretty gray eyes, her way of leaning into the conversation and drinking it up nor her quick nods, sometimes at variance with the crease of doubt across her forehead. When she nodded and frowned at the same time, he felt she was disagreeing with his opinions but affirming him as a person.

Sylvain appeared to be enjoying his two Americans. Luke and Sister Julia kept giving him the names and addresses of friends in the States to look up. "If you're ever in Martha's Vineyard, you must stay with Lucy. She's just lost a lot of weight and hasn't realized yet she's become very beautiful," the nun said. Luke gave him the names of two gay friends without mentioning they were gay—one in Boston, another in San Francisco. Of course Sylvain was heterosexual, that was obvious, but Luke knew his friends would get a kick out of putting up a handsome foreigner, the sort of blond who's always slightly tan, the sort of man who looks at his own crotch when he's listening and frames it with his hands when he's replying. Certainly both Luke and the nun couldn't resist overresponding even to Sylvain's most casual remarks.

When the stewardess served them lunch, Sylvain asked her in his funny English where she was from. Then he asked, "Are all zee womens in Floride as charming like you?"

The stewardess pursed her lips in smiling mock-reproach as though he were being a naughty darling and said, "It's a real nice state. France is nice, too. I'm going to learn French next. I studied Latin in high school."

Sister Julia said to Sylvain, "If you can speak English like that you won't need more than a hundred dollars."

When they all said good-bye at the airport Luke was disappointed. He'd expected something more. Well, he had Sylvain's address, and if someday Luke returned to France he'd look him up. Ill as he was, Luke couldn't bear the thought of never seeing France again, which suddenly seemed synonymous with some future rendezvous with Sylvain.

Luke changed money and planes—this time for Dallas. He was getting pretty ill. He could feel it in the heaviness of his bones, in his extreme tiredness, and he almost asked a porter to carry his bags. He had just two hundred dollars with him—he was half as optimistic as Sylvain. He'd never had enough money, and now he worried he'd end up a charity case or, even worse, dependent on his family. He was terrified of having to call on the mercy of his family.

He'd grown up as the eighth of ten children, all of them small if wiry and agile. His mother was a Chicana, but no one ever took her for Mexican—in any event she didn't appear to have much Indian blood and her mother prided herself on being "Castilian." His father was a mean little man with a tweezered mustache who'd worked his whole life as the janitor in a Lubbock, Texas, high school. He'd converted to Catholicism to please his wife and enrage his Baptist kin (Lubbock proudly called itself "The buckle of the Bible Belt"). Luke's father and brothers and sisters all shared a pleasure he'd learned how to name only years later—*Schadenfreude*, which in German means taking malicious pleasure in someone else's pain. Spite and envy were their ruling sentiments. If someone fell and hurt himself, they'd howl with glee. Their father would regale them with hissing, venomous accounts of the misfortunes of superiors at school. The one sure way to win the family's attention was to act out the humiliation that had befallen Mrs. Rodríguez after mass last Sunday or Mr. Brown, the principal, during the last PTA meeting. Luke's father grumbled at the TV, mocked the commercials, challenged the newscasters, jeered the politicians. "Look at him, he thinks he's so great, but he'll look like he's smelled a fart when he sees the final vote." Everyone would laugh except Luke's mother, who went about her work gravely, like a paid employee eager to finish up and leave.

In high school—not the public high school where his father worked, but the much smaller parochial school—Luke had emerged as the nuns' favorite. He'd been a brilliant student. Now that his brain was usually fuzzy—and had become an overcooked minestrone during the toxoplasmosis crisis, all swimming and steamy with shreds and lumps rising only to sink again—he regarded his former intelligence with respect. He'd once known the ablative absolute. He'd once read the *Symposium* in Greek without understanding the references to love between men.

Perhaps because of his miserable, mocking family, Luke had always felt unsure of himself. Nevertheless, he'd done everything expected of him, everything. He'd been a cross-country champ, he'd stayed entirely virginal, avoiding even masturbation except for rare lapses, he'd won the statewide *prix d'honneur* in French, he'd once correctly and even humorously translated on the spot an entire *Time* magazine article into Latin, though the page had been handed to him only seconds before by the judge of the Cicero Club contest.

In another era he would have grown up to be one of those priests who play basketball in a soutane and whose students complain when he beat them at arm wrestling ("Jeez, Father Luke ...").

He'd only narrowly escaped that fate. He'd found a job in a liberal, primarily Jewish private school just outside New York, and though he'd grown a beard and spouted Saint-Simonism, he hadn't been able to resist becoming the best beloved, most energetic teacher in the history of Dempster Country Day. The kids worshiped him, called him Luke, and phoned him in the middle of the night to discuss their abortions, college-entrance exams, and parents' pending divorces. Several of them had invited him to their parents' mansions where Luke, the gung-ho jock and brain—nose always burned from the soccer field and tweed-jacket pocket always misshapen from carrying around Horace's *Odes*—had had to study his own students to discover how to wield an escargot clamp, eat asparagus with fingers only, and avoid cutting the nose off the Brie.

What was harder was to keep up that ceaseless, bouncy energy that is always the hallmark of rich people who are also "social." Whereas Luke's father had beguiled his brutal brood with tales of other people's folly and chagrin, the Lords of Long Island looked at you with distrust the instant you criticized anyone—especially a superior. Envy proved your own inferiority. Since the parents of Luke's students were usually at the top of their profession or industry, they interpreted carping and quibbles as envy. They usually sided with the object of any attack. With them generosity—like stoicism and pep—had become signs of good breeding.

Luke learned generosity, too, as easily as he'd mastered snails. The ingredient he added to the package, the personal ingredient, was gratitude. He was grateful to rich people. He was grateful to almost everyone. The gratitude was the humble reverse side of the family's taste for *Schadenfreude*. And yet Luke could express his gratitude in such an earnest, simple way, in his caressing tenor voice with the baritone beginnings and endings of sentences, that no one took it for cringing—no one except Luke himself, who kept seeing his father, hat in hand, talking to the district supervisor.

Luke had left the abjection and exaltation of Dempster and found work as a translator. Working alone was less engrossing than playing Father Luke, but the thrill of wielding power or submitting to it at school had finally sickened him. As a kid he'd managed to escape from his family through studies; he'd stayed in school to consolidate that gain, but now he wanted to be alone, wanted to work alone into the night, listening to the radio, fine-tuning English sentences. Luckily he had a rent-controlled apartment on Cornelia Street in Manhattan, and luckily an older gay man, the king of the translators, had taken him under his wing. He became a translator, joining an honest if underpaid profession.

By subletting his apartment for four times what he paid, Luke had had enough money to live in Paris in a Montmartre hotel on a steep street near Picasso's old studio, a hotel of just eighteen rooms where the proprietor, a hearty woman from the Périgord, watched them as they ate the meals she prepared and urged them to pour wine into their emptied soup bowls and knock it back. "Chabrol! Chabrol!" she'd say, which was both an order and a toast. She'd point at them unsmilingly if they weren't drinking. She liked it when everyone was slightly tipsy and making conversation from table to table.

He'd never enjoyed gay life as such. At least New York clones had never struck him as sexy. In turn they hadn't liked his look—wire-rim glasses, baggy tweeds, shiny, policemen's shoes—or his looks—he was small, his eyes mocking or hostilely attentive or wet and grateful, his nose a red beak, his slim body featureless under the loose pants and outsize jackets but smooth and well-built when stripped—the pale, sweated body of a featherweight high-school wrestler, but clones had had to work to get to see it.

Luke had sought out sex with workingmen, straight men, or close approximations of that ideal. He'd haunted building sites, suburban weightlifting gyms, the bar next to the firehouse, the bowling alley across from the police station, the run-down Queens theater that specialized in kung-fu movies. He liked guys who didn't kiss, who had beer bellies, who wore T-shirts that showed through their dacron short-sleeved shirts, who watched football games, who shook their heads in frustration and muttered "Women!" He liked becoming pals with guys who, because they were too boring or too rough or not romantic or cultured enough, had lost their girlfriends.

In Paris he'd befriended a Moroccan boxer down on his luck. But very little of his time went to Ali. He spent his mornings alone in bed, surrounded by his dictionaries, and listened to the rain and translated. He ate the same Salade Auvergnate every lunch at the same neighborhood café. In the afternoons he often went to the Cluny museum. Luke liked medieval culture. He knew everything about Romanesque fortified churches and dreamed of meeting someone with a car who could take him on a tour of them.

At night he'd haunt the run-down movie palaces near Barbès-Rochechouart, the Arab quarter, or in good weather cruise the steps below Sacré-Coeur—that was where you met his type: men-without-women, chumps too broke or too dumb to get chicks, guys with girlie calendars tacked on the inner side of the closet doors, guys who practiced karate chops as they talked on the telephone to their mothers.

He didn't want to impersonate that missing girlfriend for them. No, Luke wanted to be a pal, a sidekick, and more than once he'd lain in the arms of a CRS (a French cop) who'd drawn on his Gitane *blonde* and told Luke he was *"un vrai copain,"* a real pal.

That was why he'd been surprised when he of all people had become ill. It was a gay disease and he scarcely thought of himself as gay. In fact, earlier on he'd once talked it over with an Irish teacher of English who lived in his hotel, a pedophile who couldn't get it up for anyone over sixteen. They'd agreed that neither of them counted as gay.

For him, the worst immediate effect of the disease was that it sapped his confidence. He felt he'd always lived on nerve, run on empty. He should have lived the dim life of his brothers and sisters—one a welfare mother, another a secretary in a lumber yard, two brothers in the air-conditioning business, another one an exterminator, another (the family success) an army officer who'd taken early retirement to run a sporting-goods store with an ex-football champ. He had another brother, Jeff, an iron worker who'd dropped out of the union, who lived in Milwaukee with his girl and traveled as far away as New York state to bend steel and put up the frames of buildings. Jeff was a guy who grew his hair long and partied with women executives in their early forties fed up with (or neglected by) their white-collar male contemporaries. The last thing Luke had heard, Jeff had broken up with his girl because she'd spent fifty of his bucks hiring a limo to ferry her and two of her girlfriends around Milwaukee just for the fun of it.

Luke had sprung the family trap. He'd eaten oysters with rich socialists, learned that a "gentleman" never takes seconds during the cheese course, worried over the right slang equivalents in English to French obscenities—he'd even resisted the temptation to strive to become the headmaster of Dempster Country Day. As the runt of his family, he'd always had to fight when he was a kid to get enough to eat, but even so as an adult he'd chosen freelance insecurity over a dull future with a future.

But all that had taken confidence and now he didn't have any. The translation he was working on would be his last. Translating required a hundred small dares per page in the constant trade-off between fidelity and fluency, and Luke couldn't find the necessary authority.

He never stopped worrying about money. He'd lie in bed working up imaginary budgets. When he returned to New York, Dempster Country Day might refer students to him for coaching in French, but would the parents worry that their children would be infected? He'd read of the hysteria in America. If his doctor decided he should go on AZT, how would he ever find the twelve thousand dollars a year to pay for it?

When he landed in Dallas his favorite cousin, Beth, was there. Growing up he'd called her Elizabeth. Now he was training himself to call her Beth, as she preferred. She hadn't been told he was ill and he looked for a sign that his appearance shocked her, but all she said was, "My goodness, you'll have to go to Weight-Watchers with me before long." If she'd known how hard he'd worked for every ounce on his bones, she wouldn't joke about it; his paunch, however, he knew, was bloated from the cytomegalovirus in his gut and the bottle of Pepto-Bismol he had to swallow every morning to control his diarrhea.

Beth's husband, Greg, had just died of an early heart attack. She'd mailed Luke a cassette of the funeral, but he'd never listened to it because he hadn't been able to lay his hands on a tape recorder—not a problem that would have occurred to her, she who had a ranch house stocked with self-cleaning ovens, a microwave, two Dustbusters, three TVs, dishwasher, washer and drier, and Lord knew what else. So he just patted her back and said, "It was a beautiful service. I hope you're surviving."

"I'm doing fine, Luke, just fine." There was something hard and determined about her that he admired. Beth's bright Texas smile came as a comfort. He told her he'd never seen her in such pretty dark shades of blue.

"Well, thank you, Luke. I had my colors done. It was one of the last presents Greg gave me. Have you had yours done yet?"

"No, what is it?"

"You go to this lady, she measures you in all sorts of scientific ways, skin tones and all, and then she gives you your fan. I have mine here in my purse, I always carry it, 'cause don't you know I'll see a pretty blouse and pick it up but when I get home with it it doesn't look right at *all* and when I check it out it won't be one of my hues. It will be *close* but not exact."

Beth snapped open a paper fan. Each segment was painted a different shade. "Now the dark blue is my strong color. If I wear it, I always get compliments. You complimented me, you see!"

And she laughed and let her smiling blue eyes dazzle him, as they always had. Her old-fashioned heart-shaped face made him think of Hollywood starlets of the past, as did her slight chubbiness and smile, which looked as though it were shot through gauze.

Her little speech about colors had been an act of courage, at once a pledge she was going to be cheerful as well as a subtle blend of flirting with him (as she would have flirted with any man) and giving him a beauty tip (as she might have done with another woman). She didn't know any other gay men; she wanted to be nice; she'd found this way to welcome him.

He'd been the ring-bearer in her wedding to Greg. They'd been the ideal couple, she a Texas Bluebonnet, he a football star, she small and blond, he dark and massive. Now she was just forty-five and already a widow with two sons nearly out of college, both eager to be cattlemen.

"For a while Houston was planning to be a missionary," Beth was saying, "but now he thinks he can serve the Lord just by leading a Christian life, and we know there's nothing wrong with that, don't we?" She added an emphatic "No sirree Bob," so he wouldn't have to reply.

Since Luke belonged to the disgraced Catholic side of the family, Beth was careful usually not to mention religion. Texans were brought up not to discuss religion or politics, the cause of so many gunfights just two generations ago, but Baptists were encouraged to proselytize. Beth was even about to set off on a Baptist mission to England, she said, and she asked Luke for tips about getting along with what she called "Europeans." Luke tried to picture her with her carefully streaked permanent, fan-selected colors from Nieman-Marcus, black-leather shoulder-strap Chanel bag, and diamond earrings ringing the bell of a lady in a twinset and pearls in a twee village in the Cotswolds: "Howdy, are you ready to take the Lord into your heart?" Today she was holding her urge to convert in check. She didn't want to alienate him. She loved family, and he was family, even if he was a sinner lost—damned, for he'd told her ten years ago about his vice.

The program was they were to visit relatives in East Texas and then drive over to Lubbock, where Luke would stay with his parents for a week before flying home to New York. He was so worried he might become critically ill while in Lubbock and have to remain there. He felt very uprooted, but New York—scary, expensive—was the closest thing to home. He was eager to consult a doctor awaiting him in New York.

Unlike some of his friends, who'd become resigned and either philosophical or depressed, Luke had taken his own case on and put himself in charge of finding a cure. In Paris he'd worked as a volunteer for the hot line, answering anxious questions and in return finding out the latest information and meeting the best specialists. He had a contact in Sweden who was keeping him abreast of an experiment going on there; through the French he knew the latest results in Zaire. He'd memorized the list of drugs and their side effects; he knew that the side effects of trimethoprim for the pneumonia were kidney damage, depression, loss of appetite, abdominal pain, hepatitis, diarrhea, headache, neuritis, insomnia, apathy, fever, chills, anemia, rash, light sensitivity, mouth pain, nausea, and vomiting—and those were just the results of a treatment.

The father of one of his former students at Dempster had promised to pay Luke's bills "until he got better." Luke felt getting well was a full-time job; he'd even seen all the quacks, swallowed tiny white homeopathic doses, meditated and "imaged" healthy cells engulfing foul ones, been massaged on mystic pressure points, done yoga, eaten nothing but brown rice and slimy or pickled vegetables arranged on the plate according to wind and rain principles. The one thing he couldn't bring himself to do was meet with other people who were ill.

They drove in Beth's new beige Cadillac on the beltway skirting Fort Worth and Dallas and headed the hundred miles south to Hershell, where Beth had just buried Greg and where their great-aunts Ruby and Pearl were waiting for them. Once they were out of the city and onto a two-lane road, the Texas he remembered came drifting back—the wildflowers, especially the Indian blanket and bluebells covering the grassy slopes, the men with the thick tan necks and off-white straw cowboy hats driving the pickup trucks, the smell of heat and damp lifting off the fields.

Hershell was just a flyspeck on the road. There were two churches, one Baptist and one Church of Christ, a hardware store where they still sold kerosene lamps and barbed-wire stretchers, a saddle shop where a cousin of theirs by marriage worked the leather as he sipped cold coffee and smoked Luckies, a post office, a grocery store with nearly empty shelves and the "new" grade school built of red brick in the 1950s.

Ruby's house was a yellow-brick single story with a double garage and a ceiling fan that shook the whole house when it was turned on, as though preparing for lift-off. The paintings—flowers, fruits, fields—had been done long ago by one of her aunts. Luke was given a bedroom with a double bed covered with a handsome thick white chenille bedspread—"chenille" was a word he'd always said as a child, but only now did he connect it with the French word for "caterpillar." Beth was given a room across the street with Pearl. Pearl's house had been her parents'. The house was nothing but additions. Her folks had built a one-room cabin and then added rooms on each side as they had the money and inclination to do so. She showed them pictures of their great-grandparents and their twelve children—one of the pale-eyed, square-jawed boys, named Culley, was handsome enough to step out toward them away from his plump, crazed-looking siblings. Pearl's Hershell high-school diploma was on the wall. When Luke asked her what the musical notes on it meant, she said, "Be Sharp, Be Natural but Never Be Flat."

Pearl said it right out. She was intelligent enough to recognize how funny it was, but as the local chair of the Texas Historical Society, she took pride in every detail of their heritage. The miles and miles of brand-new housing developments Luke had seen on the Dallas–Fort Worth Beltway, all with purely arbitrary names such as Mount Vernon or Versailles, had spooked him, made him grateful for these sun-bleached lean-tos, for the irises growing in the crick, for the "tabernacle," that open sided, roofed-over meeting place above the town.

He and Beth sat for hours and hours with their great-aunts, "visiting" after their supper of fried chicken and succotash. They drank their sweetened ice tea and traded stories. There were solemn moments, as when the old ladies hugged Beth and told her how courageous she was being.

"That Greg was a *fine* man," Ruby said, her eyes defiant and sharp as though someone might challenge her judgment. Her enunciation had always been clear—she'd taught elocution for years in high schools all over the state—but she hadn't weeded the country out of her voice.

Then there were the gay moments, as when Luke recounted the latest follies of folks in Paris. "Well, I declare," the ladies would exclaim, their voices dipping from pretended excitement down into real indifference. He was careful not to go on too long about a world they didn't know or care about or to shock them. He noticed they didn't ask him this time when he was going to get hitched up: perhaps he'd gone over that invisible line in their minds and become a "confirmed" bachelor. They did tease him about his "bay window," which he patted as though he hadn't noticed it before, which made them laugh.

Beth and he went on a long walk before the light died. They had a look at the folks on the corner they'd heard about who lived like pigs; the old man had gone and shot someone dead and now he was in the pokey for life, and the old woman—didn't it beat all—had a garden sale going on every day but who would want that old junk? He and Beth walked fast, with light hearts. He appreciated their shared views—they both loved and respected their aunts and they were both glad to slip away from them.

They walked down to see the old metal swing bridge; earlier Ruby had shown them a photo of Billy Andrews, in their class of 1917, swinging from the bridge as a stunt, big grin on his face, fairly popping out of his graduation suit with the celluloid collar, his strong calves squeezed into the knickers.

Oh, Luke ached for sex. He thought that if he could just lie next to a man one more time, feel once more that someone wanted him, he could die in peace. All his life he'd been on the prowl, once he'd broken his vows of virginity—in French he'd learned there were two words for boy virgins, neither comical: *un puceau* and *un rosier,* as though the boy were a rose bush, blossoms guarded by thorns. He'd lived so fast, cherished so little, but now he lingered over sexy souvenirs he'd never even summoned up before, like that time he'd followed a Cuban night watchman into a Park Avenue office building and they'd fucked in the service elevator and stopped, just for the hell of it, on every one of the forty-two floors. Or he remembered sex that hadn't happened, like that summer when he was twelve, a caddy, and he'd sat next to one of the older caddies on the bench waiting for a job in the airless, cricket-shrill heat. He'd molded his leg so perfectly to the guy's thigh that finally he'd stood up and said to Luke, real pissed-off, "What are you, some sort of fuckin' Liberace?" And he thought of the cop who'd handcuffed him to the bedstead.

As he and Beth were walking out past a field of cows standing in the fading light, he started picking a bouquet of wildflowers for Ruby—he got up to twenty-nine flowers without repeating a single variety. Beth walked with vigor, her whole body alert with curiosity. She'd always struck him as a healthy, sexy woman. He wondered if she'd remarry. With her religion and all she couldn't just pick up a man in a bar. She'd have to marry again to get laid. But would she want to? How did she keep her appetite in check?

The next day was hot enough to make them all worry what the summer would bring. They were going to what was called the graveyard working ten miles east of Hershell. Once a year the ten or so families who had kin buried there came together to set the tombstones upright, hoe and rake, stick silk or plastic flowers in the soil—real ones burned up right away—and then eat. Ruby and Pearl had both been up since dawn cooking, since after the graveyard working everyone shared in a big potluck lunch.

They drove out in Beth's "fine automobile," as the ladies called the Cadillac. Ruby was wearing a bonnet, one she'd made herself for gardening. The cemetery, which was also named after Hershell since he'd donated the land, was on top of a hill looking over green, rolling farmland. There were ten or eleven cars and pickup trucks already parked outside the metal palings that guarded the front but not the sides of the cemetery. Big women with lots of kids were already setting up for the lunch, unfolding card tables and stacking them with coolers of iced tea and plates of chicken fried in broken-potato-chip batter, potato salad, pickled watermelon rind, whole hams, black-eyed peas, loaves of Wonder Bread, baked beans served right out of the can, and pecan pies and apple pies. There weren't more than a hundred graves altogether and all of them had already been decently looked after, thanks to the contributions solicited every year by Ruby, who hired a part-time caretaker.

Luke felt a strange contentment hoeing his grandfather's grave. Pearl had to show him how to hoe and how to rake, but she didn't tease him about being a city slicker. He realized he could do no wrong in her eyes, since he was kin. Everyone here was kin. Several of the men had Luke's beaky red nose. He kept seeing his own small, well-knit body on other men—the same narrow shoulders and short legs, hairless forearms, the thinning, shiny hair gone to baldness here and there. Because of the rift in the family he'd met few of these people before and he had little enough in common with them, except he did share the same body type, possibly the same temperament.

His grandfather had been a Woodsman of the World, whatever that was, and his tomb marker was a stone tree trunk. His wife was buried under a tablet that read, "She Did The Best She Could."

Beth was standing in front of Greg's grave, which was still fresh. Luke worried that her mission to England might shake her faith. Wouldn't she see how flimsy, how recent and, well, how corny her religion was once she was in that gray and unpleasant land? They were planning, the Southern Baptists, to fan out over the English countryside. Wouldn't Beth be awed, or at least dismayed, by Gloucester Cathedral, by the polished intricacy of its cloisters? Wouldn't she see how raw, raw as this fresh grave, her beliefs were beside the civilized ironies of the Church or England? It was as though she were trying to introduce Pop Tarts into the land of scones.

During the picnic Beth told Luke that her one worry about her son Houston was that he always seemed so serious and distracted these days, as though dipped and twirled in darkness. "I tell him, Son, you must be *happy* in the Lord. The Bible tells us to be happy in our faith."

Luke couldn't resist tweaking Beth for a moment. He asked her what she thought about the scandals—adultery, group-sex parties, absconded church funds—surrounding a popular television evangelist and his wife.

"I expected it."

"You did?"

"Yes, it's good. It's a good sign. It shows that Satan is establishing his rule, which means that we'll live to see the Final Days, the Rapture of the Church." She spoke faster and with more assurance than usual. Luke realized she probably saw his disease as another proof of Satan's reign or God's punishment. He knew the Texas legislature was considering imprisoning diseased homosexuals who continued having sex.

Ruby came up to them, energized by the event, and asked him if he'd marked off a plot for himself. "You can, you know. Doesn't cost a penny"—she pronounced it "pinny." "You just put stones around where you want to lie. Up here it's all filling up but out yonder we've got lots to go."

"No," Luke said. "I want to be cremated and put in the Columbarium at Père Lachaise. In Paris."

"I declare," Ruby said, "but you've got years and *years* to reconsider," and she laughed.

That night, as the ladies visited and told family stories, Luke felt trapped and isolated. Beth sat there nodding and smiling and saying, "Auntie Pearl, now you just sit and let me." But he knew she was lonely, too, and maybe a bit frightened. Other old ladies, all widows, stopped in to visit, and Luke wondered if Beth was ready to join grief's hen club. Girls started out clinging together, whispering secrets and flouncing past boys. Then there was the longish interlude of marriage, followed by the second sorority of widowhood; all these humped necks, bleared eyes, false teeth, the wide-legged sitting posture of country women sipping weak coffee and complaining about one another. "She wanted to know what I paid for this place and I said, 'Well, Jessie, it is so *good* of you to worry about my finances, but I already have Mr. Hopkins at Farmers First to look after that for me,' and don't you know but that shut her up fast?" On and on into the night, not really vicious but complaining, spontaneously good but studiously petty, often feisty, sometimes coquettish, these women talked on and on. Those who couldn't hear nodded while their eyes timidly wandered, like children dismissed from the table but forbidden to play in their Sunday best.

Luke imagined he and Beth were both longing for a man—she for Greg, he for one of his men, one of these divorced cowboys, the sort of heartbroken man Randy Travis or George Strait sings about … They'd met a man like that during their walk past the old bridge yesterday—a sunburned man whose torso sat comfortably on his hips as though in a big, roomy saddle. This sunburned rancher had known who they were; the whole town had been alerted to their visit. He didn't exactly doff his hat to Beth but he took it off slowly and stared into it as he spoke. Without his hat on he looked kinder, which for Luke, made him less sexy. When he left he swung up into his truck and pulled it into gear all in one motion. He hadn't been at the graveyard working, although Luke had looked for him.

The next morning they drove a hundred miles west to Henderson, where Beth's mother, Aunt Olna, still lived. Her husband, now dead, had been a brother of Luke's dad—estranged because Luke's dad had married a Mex and become an "old" Catholic (for some reason people hereabouts always smiled sourly, lifted one eyebrow, and said in one breath, as though it were a bound form, "old-Catholic"). Beth's mother had grown up Church of Christ but had converted to her husband's religion years after their marriage. One day she'd simply read a pamphlet about what Baptists believed and she'd said to herself, "Well, that's what I believe, too," and had crossed over on the spot.

Aunt Olna was always harsh to Beth, ordering her around: "Not that one, Elizabeth." "This one which, Mother?" Beth would wail. Beth's mother was too "nervous" to specify her demands. "Turn here," she'd say in the car. "Turn right or left, Mother? Mother? Right or left?" Olna was also too nervous to cook. She didn't tremble, as other nervous people did. Luke figured the nervousness must be a confusion hidden deep in a body made fat from medication. Because she couldn't cook she'd taken three hundred dollars out of the bank to entertain them. She named the sum over and over again. She was proud her husband had left her "well-fixed." When Beth drove to the store, Olna said, "Greg left Beth very well-fixed. House all bought and paid for. A big *in*-surance policy. She need never worry."

Aunt Olna liked Luke. She'd always told everyone Luke was about as good as a person could get. Of course she knew almost nothing about his life, but she'd clung to her enthusiasm over the years and he'd always felt comfortable with her. And she wasn't given to gushing. When he'd praised her house, she'd said, "Everything in it is from the dime store. Always was." She told him how she'd inherited a dining-room "suit" but had to sell it because it was too fine for her house.

Even so he liked the shiny maple furniture in the front parlor, the flimsy metal TV dinner trays on legs used as side tables, the knubby milk glass candy dishes filled with Hershey's kisses. He liked the reproduction of the troubadour serenading the white-wigged girl, a sort of East Texas take on Watteau. He liked the fact there was no shower, just a big womanly tub, and that the four-poster bed in his room was so tall you had to climb up to get into it. Best of all he liked leaving his door open onto the night.

The rain steamed the sweetness up out of the mown grass and the leaves of the big old shade trees kept up a frying sound; when the rain died down it sounded as though someone had lowered the flame under the skillet. He was surrounded by women and death and yet the rain dripping over an old Texas town of darkened houses made him feel like a boy in his early teens again, a boy dying to slip away to find men. These days, of course, desire entailed hopelessness—he'd learned to match every pant of longing with a sigh of regret.

The next day the heat turned the sweet smell sour, as though spring peas had been replaced with rancid collard greens. Olna took them to lunch at a barbecue place where they ate ribs and hot biscuits. In the afternoon they drove to a nursing home to visit Olna's sister. That woman remembered having baby-sat Luke once twenty-five years ago. "My, you were a cute little boy. I wish I could see you, honey. I'd give anything to see again. My little house just sits empty and I'd love to go back to it, but I can't, I can't see to mind it. I don't know why the good Lord won't gather me in. Not no use to *no*-one."

The waiting room had a Coke machine and a snack dispenser. One of the machines was making a nasty whine. The woman's hand looked as pale as if it'd been floured through a sifter.

"My husband left me," she was saying, "and after that I sold tickets at the movie thee-ay-tur for nine dollars a week, six days a week, on Saturdays from ten till midnight, and when I asked for a raise after ten years Mr. Monroe said no." She smiled. "But I had my house and cat and I could see."

In the past, when Luke had paid these calls on relatives in nursing homes he'd felt he was on a field trip to some new and strange kind of slum, but today there was no distance between him and this woman. In a month or a week he could be as blind, less cogent, whiter.

He went for a walk with Beth through the big park the town of Henderson had recently laid out, a good fifty acres of jogging paths, tennis courts, a sports arena, a playground, and just open fields gone to weeds and wildflowers. On the way they passed a swimming pool that had been here over twenty years ago, that time Luke had served as Beth's ring-bearer. Now the pool was filled, clean, sparkling, but for some reason without a single swimmer, an unheeded invitation. "Didn't they used to have a big slide that curved halfway down and that was kept slick with water always pouring down it?" Luke asked.

"Now I believe you are one hundred percent correct," Beth said with the slightly prissy agreeableness of Southern ladies. "What a wonderful memory you have!" She'd been trained to find fascinating even the most banal remarks if a man made them. Luke wasn't used to receiving all the respect due his gender and kept looking for a mote of mockery in Beth's eye, but it wasn't there. Or perhaps she had mockery as much under control as grief or desire.

They walked at the vigorous pace Beth set and went along the cindered jogging path under big mesquite trees; their tiny leaves, immobile, set lacy shadows on the ground.

That sparkling pool, painted an inviting blue-green, and the memory of the flowing water slide and the smell of chlorine kept coming to mind. He'd played for hours and hours during an endless, cloudless summer day. Play had been rare enough for him, who'd always had early-morning newspaper-delivery jobs, afternoon hardware jobs, weekend lawn-mowing jobs, summer caddying jobs as well as the chores around the house and the hours and hours of homework, those hours his family had ridiculed and tried to put a stop to. But he'd persisted and won. He'd won.

When he and Beth reached the end of the park, they turned to the left, mounted a slight hill, and saw a parked pickup truck under a tree. Two teenage boys with red caps on were sitting inside and a third was standing unsteadily on the back of the truck, shirtless, jeans down, taking a leak. "Oh, my goodness," Beth said, "just don't look at them, Luke, and let's keep on walking."

The guys were laughing at Luke and Beth, playing loud music, probably drunk, and of course Luke looked. The guy taking a leak was methodically spraying a dark-brown circle in the pale dust. He was a redhead, freckled, tall, skinny, and his long body was hairless except where tufted blond. He looked like a streak of summer lightning.

"But they're not doing any harm," Luke said with a smile.

"You think not?" Beth spat out. "Some folks here might think—" But she interrupted herself, mastered herself, smiled her big missionary smile.

Luke felt a rage alarm his tired body and tears—what sort of tears?—sting his eyes.

Tears of humiliation: he was offended that a virus had been permitted to win an argument. He'd been the one to learn, to leave home, break free. He'd cast aside all the old sins, lived freely—but soon Beth could imagine he was having to pay for his follies with his life. It offended him that he would be exposed to her self-righteousness.

Aunt Olna invited them out to a good steak dinner in a fast-food place near the new shopping mall. The girls ordered medium-size T-bones and Luke went for a big one. But then he suffered a terrifying attack of diarrhea halfway through his meal and had to spend a sweaty, bowel-scorching thirty minutes in the toilet, listening to the piped-in music and the scrapings and flushings of other men. Aunt Olna appeared offended when he finally returned to the table, his shirt drenched and his face pale, until he explained to her he'd caught a nasty bug drinking the polluted Paris water. Then she relaxed and smiled, reassured.

When they left the restaurant Olna told the young woman cashier, "My guests tonight have come here all the way from Paris, France."

He berated himself for having fallen away from his regime of healthy food, frequent naps, jogging and aerobics, no stress. He was stifling from frustration and anger. When they returned to Olna's, it was already dark, but Luke insisted he was going jogging. Olna and Beth didn't offer the slightest objection and he realized that in their eyes he was no longer a boy but a man, a lawgiver. Or maybe they were just indifferent. People could accept anything as long as they weren't directly affected.

He ran through the streets over the railroad tracks, past Olna's new Baptist church, down dark streets past houses built on GI loans just after the war for six or seven thousand dollars. Their screened-in porches were dimly lit by yellow, mosquito-repellent bulbs. He smelled something improbably rich and spicy, then remembered Olna had told him people were taking in well-behaved, industrious Vietnamese lodgers studying at the local college—their only fault, apparently, being that they cooked up smelly food at all hours.

The Vietnamese were the only change in this town during the last twenty-five years. Otherwise it was the same houses, the same lawns, the same people playing Ping-Pong in their garages, voices ricocheting off the cement, the same leashless dogs running out to inspect him, then walking dully away.

There was the big house where Beth had married Greg so many years ago in the backyard among her mother's bushes of huge yellow roses. And there—he could feel his bowels turning over, his breath tightening, his body exuding cold sweat—there was the house where, when he was fifteen, Luke had met a handsome young man, a doctor's son, five years older and five hundred times richer, a man with black hair on his pale knuckles, a thin nose, and blue eyes, a gentle man Luke would never have picked for sex but whom he'd felt he could love, someone he'd always meant to look up again: the front doorbell glowed softly, lit from within. The house was white clapboard with green shutters, which appeared nearly black in the dim streetlight.

On and on he ran, past the cow palace where he'd watched a rodeo as a kid. Now he was entering the same park where he and Beth had walked today. He could feel his energy going, his legs so weak he could imagine losing control over them and turning an ankle or falling. He knew how quickly a life could be reduced. He dreaded becoming critically ill here in Texas; he didn't want to give his family the satisfaction.

He ran past the unlit swimming pool and again he remembered that one wonderful day of fun and leisure so many years ago. On that single day he'd felt like a normal kid. He'd even struck up a friendship with another boy and they'd gone down the water slide a hundred times, one behind the other, tobogganing.

Now he was thudding heavily past the spotlit tennis court. No one was playing, it was too hot and still, but two girls in white shorts were sitting on folding
chairs at the far end, talking. Then he was on the gravel path under low, overhanging trees. The crickets chanted slower than his pulse and from time to
time seemed to skip a beat. He passed a girl walking her dog and he gasped,
"Howdy," and she smiled. The smell of honeysuckle was so strong and he
thought he'd never really gotten the guys he'd wanted, the big high-school
jocks, the blonds with loud tenor voices, beer breath, cruel smiles, lean hips,
steady, insolent eyes, the guys impossible to befriend if you weren't exactly like
them. He thought that with so many millions of people in the world the odds
should have favored the likelihood that at least one guy like that should have
gone for him, but things hadn't turned out that way. Of course, even when you
had someone, what did you have?

But then what did anyone ever have—the impermanence of sexual possession was a better school than most for the way life would flow through your
hands.

In the distance, through the mesquite trees, he could see the lights of occasional cars nosing the dark. Then he remembered that right around here the
redhead had pissed a brown circle and Luke looked for traces of that stain under the tree. He even touched the dust, feeling for moisture. He wondered if
just entertaining the outrageous thought weren't sufficient for his purposes,
but, no, he preferred the ceremony of doing something actual. He found the
spot—or thought he did—and touched the dirt to his lips. He started running
again, chewing the grit as though it might help him to recuperate his past if
not his health.

A GOOD MAN

J IM CALLS ME in the afternoon to ask if I can give him a ride to the doctor's tomorrow because this flu thing he has is hanging on and he's decided to get something for it. I tell him I'm supposed to be going down to Olympia to help Ange and Jean remodel their spare room and kitchen. He says it's no big deal, he can take the bus. But then a couple hours later he calls me back and says could I take him now because he really isn't feeling well. So I get in my car and go over and pick him up.

Jim stands inside the front door to the building. When he opens the door I start. His face is splotched. Sweat glistens in his week-old beard. He leans in the door frame breathing hard. He holds a brown paper grocery bag. The sides of the bag are crumpled down to make a handle. He looks so small, like a school boy being sent away from home.

"I'm not going to spend the night there," he mumbles, "but I'm bringing some socks and stuff in case."

He hobbles off the porch, his free hand grabbing the railing. I reach to take the paper bag, but he clutches it tight.

We drive to Swedish hospital and park near the Emergency Room. I lean over to hug him before we get out of the car. He's wearing four layers—T-shirt, long underwear, sweatshirt, his jacket. But when I touch his back I feel the sweat through all his clothes.

"I put these on just before you came." He sounds embarrassed.

I put an arm around him to help him inside. When he's standing at the check-in desk, I see the mark the sweat makes on his jacket.

Jim hands me the paper bag. I take his arm as we walk to the examination room to wait for a doctor. We walk slowly. Jim shuffles and I almost expect him to make his standard crack about the two of us growing old together in the ancient homos home for the prematurely senile, pinching all the candy stripers' butts, but he doesn't.

He sits down on the bed in the exam room. After he catches his breath he says, "Nice drapes."

There aren't any drapes. The room is sterile and white. Jim leans back in the chair and breathes out hard. The only other sound is the fluorescent light. He coughs.

"Say something, Tonto. Tell me story."

"—I … uh …"

I pick up a packet of tongue depressers. "Hey, look at all these. How many you think they go through in a week?"

He doesn't answer.

I take an instrument off a tray. "How 'bout this?" I turn to show him but his eyes are closed. I put it back down. When I close my mouth the room is so quiet.

I can't tell stories the way Jim does.

A doctor comes in. She introduces herself as Dr. Allen and asks Jim the same questions he's just answered at the front desk—his fevers, his sweats, his appetite, his breath. She speaks softly, touching his arm as she listens to his answers. Then she pats his arm and says she'll be back in a minute.

In a few seconds a nurse comes in and starts poking Jim's arm to hook him up to an IV. Jim is so dehydrated she can't find the vein. She pokes him three times before one finally takes. Jim's arm is white and red. He lies there with his eyes closed, flinching.

Then Dr. Allen comes back with another doctor who asks Jim the same questions again. The doctors ask me to wait in the private waiting room because they want to do some tests on Jim. I kiss his forehead before I leave. "I'm down the hall, Jim."

Jim waves, but doesn't say anything. They close the door.

Half an hour later, Dr. Allen comes to the waiting room. She's holding a box of Kleenex.

"Are you his sister?"

I start to answer, but she puts her hand on my arm to stop me.

"I want you to know that hospital administration does not look favorably upon our giving detailed medical information about patients out to non-family members. And they tend to look the other way if family members want to stay past regular visiting hours."

"So," I say, "I'm his sister."

"Good. Right. OK, we need to do some more tests on Jim and give him another IV, so he needs to stay the night." She pauses. "He doesn't want to. I think he needs to talk to you."

She hands me the box of Kleenex.

Jim is lying on his back, his free elbow resting over his eyes. I walk up to him and put my hand on his leg.

"Hi."

He looks up at me, then up at the IV.

"I have to have another one of these tonight so I need to stay."

I nod.

"It's not the flu. It's pneumonia."

I nod again, and keep nodding as if he were still talking. I hear the whirr of the electric clock, the squeak of nurses' shoes in the hall.

"I haven't asked what kind."

"No."

He looks at me. I take his sweaty hand in mine.

"I don't mind going," he says, "Or being gone. But I don't want to suffer long. I don't want to take a long time going."

I try to say something to him, but I can't. I want to tell him a story, but I can't say anything.

Because I've got this picture in my head of Jim's buddy Scotty, who he grew up with in Fort Worth. And I'm seeing the three of us watching "Dynasty," celebrating the new color box Jim bought for Scotty to watch at home, and I'm seeing us getting loaded on cheap champagne, and the way Scotty laughed and coughed from under the covers and had to ask me or Jim to refill his glass or light his Benson & Hedges because he was too weak to do it himself. Then I'm seeing Jim and me having a drink the day after Scotty went, and how Jim's hands shook when he opened the first pack of cigarettes we ever shared, and how a week later Jim clammed up, just clammed right up in the middle of telling me about cleaning out Scotty's room. And I think, from the way Jim isn't talking, from the way his hand is shaking in mine, that he is seeing Scotty too.

Scotty took a long time going.

Jim stays the night at Swedish. The next night. The next.

He asks me to let some people know—his office, a few friends. Not his parents. He doesn't want to worry them. He asks me to bring him stuff from his apartment—clothes, books. I ask him if he wants his watercolors. He says no.

I go to see him every day. I bring him the *Times*, the *Blade*, *Newsweek*. It's easy for me to take off work. I only work as a temporary and I hate my jobs anyway, so I just don't call in. Jim likes having people visit, and lots of people come. Chubby Bob with his pink, bald head. Dale in his banker's suit. Mike the bouncer in his bomber jacket. Cindy and Bill on their way back out to Vashon. A bunch of guys from the baseball team. Denise and her man Chaz. Ange and Jeannie call from Olympia.

We play a lot of cards. Gin rummy. Hearts when there are enough of us. Spades. Poker. We use cut-up tongue depressors for chips. I offer to bring real ones, but Jim gets a kick out of coloring them red and blue and telling us he is a very, very, very wealthy Sugar Daddy. He also gets a big kick out of cheating.

We watch a lot of tube. I sit on the big green plastic chair by the bed. Or Dale sits on the big green chair, me on his lap, and Bob on the extra folding metal chair: We watch reruns, sitcoms, *Close Encounters.* Ancient, awful Abbot and Costellos. Miniseries set between the wars. But Jim's new favorites are hospital soaps. He becomes an instant expert on everything—all the characters' affairs, the tawdry turns of plots, the long-lost illegitimate kids. He sits up on his pillows and rants about how stupid the dialogue is, how unrealistic the gore:

"Oh come on. I could do a better gun-shot wound with a paint-by-numbers set!

"Is that supposed to be a bruise?! Yo mama, pass me the hammer now. Now!

"If that's the procedure for a suture, I am Betty Grable's legs."

He narrates softly in his stage aside: "Enter tough-as-nails head nurse. Exit sensitive young intern. Enter political appointment in admin, a shady fellow not inspired by a noble urge to help his fellow human. Enter surgeon with a secret. Exit secretly addicted pharmacist."

Then during commercials he tells us gossip about the staff here at Swedish which is far juicier than anything on TV. We howl at his trashy tales until he shushes us when the show comes back on. We never ask if what he says is true. And even if we did, Jim wouldn't tell us.

But most of the time, because I'm allowed to stay after hours as his sister, it's Jim and me alone. We stare up at the big color box, and it stares down at us like the eye of God. Sometimes Jim's commentary drifts, and sometimes he is silent. Sometimes when I look over and his eyes are closed, I get up to switch off the set, but he blinks and says, "I'm not asleep. Don't turn it off. Don't go." Because he doesn't want to be alone.

Then, more and more, he sleeps and I look up alone at the plots that end in nothing, at the almost true-to-life colored shapes, at the hazy ghosts that trail behind the bodies when they move.

Jim and I met through the temporary agency. I'd lost my teaching job and he'd decided to quit bartending because he and Scotty were becoming fanatics about their baseball team and consequently living really clean. This was good for me because I was trying, well, I was thinking I really ought to try, to clean it up a bit myself. Anyway, Jim and I had lots of awful jobs together—filing, answering phones, xeroxing, taking coffee around to arrogant fat-cat lawyers, stuffing envelopes, sticking number labels on pages and pages of incredibly stupid documents, then destroying those same documents by feeding them through the shredder. The latter was the only of these jobs I liked; I liked the idea of it. I like being paid five bucks an hour to turn everything that someone else had done into pulp.

After a while, Jim got a real, permanent job, with benefits, at one of these places. But I couldn't quite stomach the thought of making that kind of commitment.

We stayed in touch though. Sometimes I'd work late xeroxing and Jim would come entertain me and play on the new color copier. He came up with some wild things—erasing bits, then painting over them, changing the color combos, double copying. All this from a machine that was my sworn enemy for eight hours a day. We'd have coffee or go out to a show or back to their place so Scotty could try out one of his experiments in international cuisine on us before he took it to the restaurant. Also, Jim helped me move out of my old apartment.

But Jim and I really started hanging out together a lot after Scotty. Jim had a bunch of friends, but I think he wanted not to be around where he and Scotty had been together so much: the dinner parties and dance bars, the clubs, the baseball team. So he chose to run around with me. To go out drinking.

We met for a drink the day after Scotty. Then a week later, we did again. Over the third round Jim started to tell me about cleaning out Scotty's room. But all the sudden he clammed up, he just clammed right up and left. He wouldn't let me walk home with him. I tried calling him but he wouldn't answer.

Then a couple weeks later he called me and said, "Wanna go for a drink?" like nothing had happened.

We met at Lucky's. I didn't say anything about what he had started to talk about the last time we'd met, and he sure didn't mention it. Well, actually, maybe he did. We always split our tab, and this round was going to be mine. But when I reached for my wallet, he stopped me.

"This one's on me, Tonto."

"Tonto?"

"The Lone Ranger." He pointed to himself. "Rides again."

He clinked his glass to mine. "So saddle up, Tonto. We're going for a ride."

We had a standing date for Friday, six o'clock, the Lucky. With the understanding that if either of us got a better offer, we just wouldn't show up and the other would know to stop waiting about 6:30 or so. However, neither of us ever got a better offer. But we had a great time talking predator. We'd park ourselves in a corner behind our drinks and eye the merchandise. Me scouting guys for him; him looking at women for me.

"He's cute. Why don't we ask him to join us."

"Not my type ... but mmm-mmm-mmm I think somebody likes you."

"Who?"

"That one."

"Jim, I've never seen her before in my life."

"I think she likes you."

"I think she looks like a donkey. But hey, he looks really sweet. Go on, go buy him a drink."

A few times I showed up at six and saw Jim already ensconced in our corner charming some innocent, unsuspecting woman he was planning to spring on me. I usually did an abrupt about-face out of Lucky's. But one time he actually dragged me to the table to meet whoever she was. Fortunately that evening was such a disaster he didn't try that tactic again.

After a while our standing joke began to wear a little thin. I cooled it on eyeballing guys for him, but he kept teasing me, making up these incredible stories about my wild times with every woman west of the Mississippi. It bugged me for a while, but I didn't say anything. For starters, Jim wasn't the kind of guy you said shut-up to. And then, after a longer while, I realized he wasn't talking just to entertain us. His talk, his ploys to find someone for me, were his attempts to make the story of a good romance come true. Jim had come to the conclusion that neither he, nor many of his brotherhood, could any longer hope to live the good romance. He told me late one bleary, double-whiskey night, "Us boys are looking at the ugly end of the Great Experiment, Tonto. I sure hope you girls don't get in a mess like us. Ya'll will be OK, won't you? Won't ya'll girls be OK?"

Because Jim still desired, despite what he'd been through with Scott, despite how his dear brotherhood was crumbling, that some of his sibling outlaws would find good love and live in that love openly, and for a good long time, a longer time than he and Scott had had. He wanted this for everyone who marched 3rd Avenue each June, for everyone that he considered family.

He's sitting up against his pillows. I toss him the new *Texas Monthly* and kiss him hello on the forehead. He slaps his hands down on the magazine and in his sing-song voice says, "I think someone likes you!"

I roll my eyes.

He gives me his bad-cat grin. "Don't you want to know who?"

"I bet you'll tell me anyway."

"Dr. Allen."

"Oh come on, Jim, she's straight."

"And how do you know, Miss Lock-Up-Your-Daughters? Just because she doesn't wear overalls and a workshirt."

"Jim, you're worse than a Republican."

"I am, I am a wicked wicked boy. I must not disparage the Sisterhood." He flings his skinny hand up in a fist. "Right On Sister!"

I try not to laugh.

"Still, what if Dr. Allen is a breeder? I'm sure she'd be very interested in having you impart to her The Love Secrets of the Ancient Amazons."

"Jim, I'm not interested ..."

"Honey, I been watching you. I seen you scratching. I know you be itchin' fer some bitchin'."

He makes it hard not to laugh.

"Jim, if you don't zip it up, I'll have to shove a bedpan down your throat."

"In that case I'm even more glad it's about time for Dr. Allen's rounds. She'll be able to extract it from me with her maaaar-velous hands."

And in sails Dr. Allen, a couple of interns in tow.

I get up to leave.

"Oh, you don't have to leave." She smiles at me. "This is just a little check-in with Jim."

Jim winks at me behind her back.

I sit down in the folding metal chair by the window and look at downtown, at Elliott Bay, the slate gray water, the thick white sky. But I also keep looking back as Dr. Allen feels Jim's pulse, his forehead, listens to his chest. She asks him to open his mouth. She asks him how it's going today.

"Terrific. My lovely sister always cheers me up. She's such a terrific woman, you know."

I stare out the window as hard as I can.

Dr. Allen says how nice it is that Jim has such nice visitors, then tells him she'll see him later.

"See you," she says to me as she leaves.

"Yeah, see you."

The second she's out the door, Jim says, more loudly than he usually talks, "That cute Dr. Allen is such a terrific woman!"

"Jim!!" I shush him.

"And so good with her hands," he grins. "Don't you think she's cute? Almost as cute as you are when you blush."

I turn away and stare out the window again. Sure I'm blushing. And sure, I'm thinking about Dr. Allen. But what I'm thinking is why, when she was looking at him, she didn't say, "You're looking good today, Jim." Or, "You're coming right along, Jim." Or "We're gonna have to let you out of here soon, Jim, you're getting too healthy for us."

Why won't she tell him something like that?

There's a wheelchair in his room. Shiny stainless steel frame, padded leather seat. Its arms look like an electric chair.

He's so excited he won't let me kiss him hello.

"That's Silver. Your dear friend Dr. Allen says I can go out for some fresh air today."

"Really?" I'm skeptical. He's hooked to an IV again.

"Gotta take advantage of the sun. Saddle up, Tonto."

He presses the buzzer. In a couple of minutes an aide comes in to transfer the IV from his bed to the pole sticking up from the back of the chair. The drip bag hangs like a toy. I help him into his jacket and cap, put a cover across his lap and slide his hospital slippers up over his woolly socks.

"Are you sure you feel up to this?"

"Sure I'm sure. And if I don't get a cup of non-hospital coffee, I am going to lynch someone."

"OK, OK, I'll be back in a minute. I gotta go to the bathroom."

I go to the nurses' station.

"Can Jim really go out today?"

The guy at the desk looks up.

"Dr. A says it's fine. You guys can go across the street to Rex's or something. A lot of patients do. They uh ... don't have the same rules as the hospital." He puckers his lips and puts two fingers up to mime smoking.

"Uh-huh. Got it."

Back in the room I take the black plastic handles of the chair and start to push.

Jim flings his hand in the air, "Hi-Yo Silver!"

I wheel him into the hall, past doctors and aides in clean white coats, past metal trays full of plastic buckets and rubber gloves and neat white stacks of linens. Past skinny guys shuffling along in housecoats and slippers.

The elevator is huge, wide enough to carry a couple of stretchers. Jim and I are the only ones in it. I feel like we're the only people in a submarine, sinking down to some dense, cold otherworld where we won't be able to breathe. Jim watches the elevator numbers. I watch the orange reflection of the lights against his eyes.

When the elevator opens to the bustling main entrance foyer, his eyes widen. It isn't as white and quiet as he's gotten used to. In his attempt to tell himself he isn't so bad off, he's made himself forget what health looks like. I see him stare, wide-eyed and silent, as a man runs across the foyer to hug a friend, as a woman bends down to pick up a kid. I push him slowly across the foyer in case he wants to change his mind.

When the electric entry doors slide open he gasps.

"Let's blow this popcorn stand, baby." He nods across the street to Rex's. "Carry me back to the ol' saloon."

I push him out to the sidewalk. It's rougher than the slick floor of the building. Jim grips the arms of the wheelchair. We wait at the crosswalk for the light to change, Jim hunching in his wheelchair in the middle of a crowd of people standing. People glance at him then glance away. I look down at the top of his cap, the back of his neck, his shoulders.

When the light changes everyone surges across Madison. I ease the chair down where the sidewalk dips then push him into the pedestrian crossing. We're the only ones left in the street when the light turns green.

"Get a move on, Silver."

The wheels tremble, the metal rattles, the IV on the pole above him shakes. The liquid shifts. Jim's hands tighten like an armchair football fan's. His veins stand up. He sticks his head forward as if he could help us move. I push us to the other side.

We clatter into Rex's. There's the cafeteria line and a bunch of chairs and tables. I steer him to an empty table, pull a chair away and slide him in.

"Jesus," he mumbles, "I feel like a kid in a high chair."

"Coffee?"

"Yeah. And a packet of Benson & Hedges."

"Jim."

"Don't argue. If God hadn't wanted us to smoke, he wouldn't have created the tobacco lobby."

"Jim."

"For god's sake Tonto, what the hell difference will a cigarette make?"

While I stand in line, I glance at him. He's looking out the long wall of windows to Madison, watching people walk by on their own two feet, all the things they carry in their hands—briefcases, backpacks, shopping bags, umbrellas. The people in Rex's look away from him. I'm glad we're only across the street from the hospital.

I put the tray on the table in front of him. He puts his hand out for his coffee, but can't quite reach it. I hand him his cup and take mine.

"Did you get matches?"

"Light up."

"It's good to be out ... So tell me, Tonto, how's the wild west been in my absence?"

"Oh, you know, same as ever ..."

"Don't take it lightly, pardner. Same as ever is a fucking miracle."

I don't know whether to apologize or not.

When we finish our cigarettes, he points. "Another."

I light him one.

"You shouldn't smoke so much," he says as I light another for myself.

"What?! You're the one who made me haul you across the street for a butt."

"And you drink too much."

"Jim, get off my case."

He pauses. "You've got something to lose, Tonto."

I look away from him.

He sighs. "We didn't use to be so bad, did we Tonto? When did we get so bad?"

I don't say, After Scotty.

He shakes his head as if he could shake away what he is thinking. "So clean it up, girl. As a favor to the Ranger? As a favor to the ladies? Take care of that luscious body-thang of yours. Yes? Yes?"

I roll my eyes.

"Promise?"

"Jim ..." I never make promises; nobody ever keeps them.

"Promise me."

I shrug a shrug he could read as a no or yes. He knows it's all he'll get from me. He exhales through his nose like a very disappointed maiden aunt. Then slowly, regretfully, pushes the cigarettes towards me.

"These are not for you to smoke. They're for you to keep for me because La Dottoressa and her dancing Kildairettes won't let anyone keep them in the hospital. So I am entrusting them to you to bring for me when we have our little outings. And I've counted them; I'll know if you steal any."

"OK."

"Girl Scouts' honor?"

"OK, OK."

The cellophane crackles when I slip them into my jacket.

"Now. Back to the homestead, Tonto."

The Riding Days:

One hung-over morning when Jim and I were swaying queasily on the very crowded number 10 bus to downtown, I bumped into, literally, Amy. She was wearing some incredible perfume.

"Hi," I tried to sound normal. I gripped the leather ceiling strap tighter. "What are you doing out at this hour? On the bus?"

"Well, the Nordie's sale is starting today and I want to be there early. But Brian's car is in the shop so he couldn't drop me off."

"Jeez. Too bad."

"Oh, it's not that bad. He'll be getting a company car today to tide us over."

"How nice."

She smiled her pretty smile at Jim but I didn't introduce them. She got off at the Nordstrom stop.

After she got off, Jim said, "She's cute, why don't you—"

"She's straight," I snapped. "She's a breeder. Now. She used to be the woman I used to live with. In the old apartment."

"The one you've never told me about," he said.

I stared into the back of the coat of the man squished in front of me. "Jim, shut up."

"I'm sorry, babe ..." He tried to put his arm around me. I wriggled away from him.

"Hey, she's not that cute," he said when I jumped off the bus at the next stop. It was several blocks from work, but I wanted to walk.

That afternoon, Jim sent me a box of chocolates. The chocolates were delivered to me in the xerox room. They were delivered with a card. "Forget the ugly bitch. Eat us instead, you luscious thang." I shared the chocolates with the office. They made the talk, the envy of the office for a week. I kept the contents of the card a secret.

Jim sweet-talked my apartment manager into letting him into my tiny little studio apartment so he could leave me six—*six*—vases of flowers around my room when I turned twenty-seven. He taught me how to iron shirts. He wore a top hat when we went to see the Fred and Ginger festival at the U. He knew that the solution for everything, for almost everything, was a peanut butter and guacamole sandwich. He placed an ad in the *Gay News* for Valentine's Day which said, "Neurotic lesbian still on rebound seeks females for short, intense, physical encounters. No breeders." And my phone number. Then let me stay at his place and laughed at me because I was afraid the phone might ring. He brought me horrible instant cinnamon and fake apple flavored oatmeal the mornings I slept on his couch, the mornings after we'd both had more than either of us could handle and didn't want to be in our apartments alone, and said, "This'll zap your brain into gear, Mrs. Frankenstein," and threw me a clean, fresh, ironed shirt to wear to work. He fed Trudy his whole-food hippie cookies to keep her quiet so he and I could sneak out to Jean and Ange's porch for a cigarette and a couple of draws on the flask.

He wore his ridiculous bright green bermuda shorts and wagged his ass like crazy, embarrassing the hell out of me, at the Gay Pride March. He raised his fist and yelled, "Ride On, Sister, Ride On!" to the Dykes on Bikes. He slapped high-heeled, mini-skirted queens on the back and said in a husky he-man voice, "Keep the faith, brother." I got afraid some guy might slap him or hit him with his purse, or some woman might slug him. When I started to say something, Jim stopped. The march kept streaming down 3rd Avenue beside us. The June sun hit me on the head and Jim glared at me. He crossed his arms across his chest like he was trying to keep from yelling.

"Tonto, what the hell are you afraid of anyway? You may like to think of us all as a bunch of unbalanced, volatile perverts, but every single screaming fairy prancing down this boulevard and every last one of you pissed-off old Amazons is my family. My kith and my kin and my kind. My siblings. Your siblings. And if you're so worried about their behavior you should just turn your chickenshit ass around and crawl back into the nearest closet because you are on the wrong fucking ride."

I didn't say anything. He stared at me several seconds. Then a couple of punky women dancing to their boom box dragged Jim along with them. I watched their asses wag off in front of me. I started to walk. But I was ashamed to march with him again. Then, when he saw the Educational Service District workers contingent in front of us, their heads covered in paper sacks because you can still be fired from your state school teaching job for being queer, Jim turned around and hollered, "At least you don't have to keep your sweet gorgeous sexy face covered like that anymore, Tonto." I stared at my pathetic, scared, courageous former colleagues. Jim pranced back to me and yanked me into a chorus line where everyone, all these brave tough pansies, these heroic, tender dykes, had their arms around each others' backs. Jim pulled me along. I felt the firmness of his chest against my shoulder.

"This is the way it's gonna be, Tonto. Someday it's all gonna be this great."

He laughed at his own stories and he clapped at his own jokes. And he never, never, despite how many times I asked, told me which stories he'd made up, which ones were true.

And sometimes, when he's holding court from his hospital bed, and he's in the middle of telling us some outrageous story, making all of us laugh, and we're all laughing, I forget. When he's telling it like there's no tomorrow— no—like there *is*—I just forget how he is in his body.

He gets over something, then gets something else. Then he gets better then he gets worse. Then he begins to look OK and says he's ready to go home. Then he gets worse. Then he gets something else.

On the days they think he's up to it, they let me take him out. A couple times both of us walk, but other times he rides. They call it his constitutional. We call it his faggot break.

I bring him a cup of Rex's coffee and throw the cigarettes across the table to him. He counts them, purses his lips and says, "You *are* a good Girl Scout." Then he leans toward me, gestures like a little old lady for me to put my ear up close to him.

"She's just trying to make you jealous," he whispers.

"What?"

"Doc-tor A-llen," he mouths silently.

He nods across Rex's to a table in the no-smoking section. Dr. Allen is having a cup of coffee with a woman.

"She knows we come here, she hopes you'll see her with another woman and be forced to take action."

"Jim ..."

I'm sure Dr. Allen has seen us, Jim and me and the cigarettes, but I'm hoping she's taking a break from being doctor long enough to not feel obliged to come over and give Jim some healthy advice.

"She likes you *very much*, you know."

"Jim, I've probably had five minutes of conversation with the woman," I whisper, "all about you."

"Doesn't matter. It's chemistry. Animal maaag-netism."

He wants me to laugh.

"Come on, Jim. Give it a rest …"

He turns around to look at Dr. Allen. Then he looks back at me. He takes a long drag on his cigarette. He tries to sound buoyant. "Hey, I'm just trying to get you a buddy, Tonto. Who you gonna ride with when the Ranger's gone?"

One time Jim told me, this is what he said, he said, "A lie is what you tell when you're a chicken shit. But a story is what you tell for good."

"Even if it isn't true?"

"It's true. If you tell a story for good, it's true."

I had had them twice and they were always great. They truly, truly may have been the best sour cream enchiladas on the planet. But that time, after two bites, Jim threw down his fork.

"These suck."

"Jim, they're fine."

"They suck."

He pushed the plate away. "I can't eat this shit."

I handed him the hot sauce and the guacamole. "Add a little of these."

"I said I cannot eat this crap." He lifted his hands like he was trying to push something away. I started to clear the table.

"Leave it. *Leave it.*"

I put the plate down. I looked away from him. Then at him. "Let's go out for Chinese."

He didn't say anything, just nodded.

I ordered everything: egg rolls, hot and sour soup, moo goo gai pan, garlic pork, veg, rice, a few beers. He asked me to tell him a story and I did. A lewd, insulting, degrading tale about a guy at the temp agency, a swishy little closet case we both despised. I told about him being caught, bare-assed, his pecker in his paw, in the 35th floor supply room by one of the directors. Jim adored the story. He laughed really loud. He laughed until he cried. He didn't ask me if it was true.

We ate everything. All the plum sauce. All the little crackers. Every speck of rice. But we didn't open our fortune cookies.

On the way home, Jim put his arm around me and said, "You're learning, Tonto."

The enchiladas were a recipe of Scotty's.

The door is half closed. I take one step in. There's a sweeping sound in the room, a smell. The curtain has been drawn around the bed. I see a silhouette moving.

"Jim?"

"Go away." His voice is little. "I made a mess."

An aide in a white coat peeks around the curtain. He's holding a mop. He's wearing plastic gloves, a white mask over his mouth and nose. I leave.

I go up to the Rose. Rosie sees me coming through the door. She's poured a schooner for me by the time I reach the bar.

"Jesus, woman." She leans over the bar to look at me as I'm climbing onto the barstool.

"Shrunken body, shrunken head … gonna be nothing left of you soon, girl."

I reach for the beer. She stops my hand.

"We don't serve alcohol alone. You have to order something to eat with it."

"Gimme a break, Rosie. I have one dollar and—" I fish into my jeans, "55 … 56 … 57 cents."

"Sorry pal. It's policy."

"Since when."

"Since now. It's a special policy for you."

"Rosie, please."

"Don't mess with the bartender."

I drop my face into my hands. "Please Rosie."

She lifts my chin and looks at me. "If you promise to clean your plate, we'll put it on your tab."

"You don't run tabs."

She points to her chest. "I'm the boss."

As I'm finishing my beer she slaps a plate in front of me—a huge bacon-cheeseburger with all the trimmings. A mound of fries. A pint glass of milk.

She writes out the bill and pockets it. "We'll talk."

"Thanks."

I take a bite. She puts her elbows on the bar.

"How's Jim?"

"The same." My mouth is full.

She cocks her head.

I swallow. "Worse."

"Jeez …" She touches my arm. "Eat, honey. Eat something."

I eat. Sesame seed bun. Bacon. Mustard. Lettuce. Pickles. Tomatoes. Cheese. Meat. Grease on my fingers. I chew and swallow. It is so easy.

Jim on the drip-feed. Jim not keeping anything down. Or shitting it out in no time. His throat and asshole sore from everything that comes up, that runs through him. His oozy mouth. His bloody gums.

A hand on my back. "Hi."

I turn and almost choke.

"You're Jim's—"

I nod. "Yeah, right." I swallow. "You're Doctor Allen. Hi."

I wipe my mouth and hands on the napkin.

She's saying to the woman she's with, "This is Jim's sister," as if her friend's already heard of Jim. Or of me. Dr. Allen extends her hand to me. "Please, my name's Patricia."

I shake her hand.

"And this is my sister Amanda. It's her first time here—I mean—here in Seattle." She does this nervous little laugh. "She's visiting from Buffalo."

It's the woman she was having coffee with at Rex's.

"Oh Buffalo," I say, "How nice."

"I've come to see if poor Pat's life is really as boring as she tells me it is. Doesn't have to be does it?" the sister says with a grin.

I don't know what to answer. I do this little laugh.

They both look around the bar. Not wide, serious check-out sweeps of their heads, but shy quick glances. They certainly aren't old hands at this. And I think I see two different varieties of nerves here. I try to read which is the tolerant, supportive sister, and which is the one who wanted to come to this particular bar in the first place.

"Mind if we join you?"

"Uh, no. Sure. Great."

I gesture to the empty barstool next to me, then I stand up and gesture to my own. "But I was just going, actually … here, have my stool." I down half the glass of milk. "Gotta be at work early in the morning," I lie.

They look at each other and at me. I feel like one of them's about to laugh, but I don't know which. Dr. Allen sits on my stool. Jim's right. She is pretty cute.

I gulp down the rest of my milk, slap my hands on the bar and shout into the kitchen, "I owe you Rosie!"

I say to the sister, "Nice to meet you. Have a nice time in Seattle." And to the Doctor, "Nice to bump into you. See you 'round."

Then I'm standing outside on the sidewalk, shaking.

Because maybe, if I had stayed there in the bar with them, and had them buy me a beer or two, or coaxed a couple more out of Rosie, maybe I would have asked, "So which of you is the supportive sister, and which of you is the dyke?" Or maybe I would have asked, "So how 'bout it ladies. Into which of your lovely beds might I more easily insinuate myself?"

Or maybe I would have asked—no—no—but maybe I would have asked, "So, Dr. Allen, you are pretty cute, how 'bout it. How long 'til Jim goes?"

I bring him magazines and newspapers. The *Times,* the *Blade,* the *Body Politic.* They all run articles. Apparent answers, possible solutions, almost cures. Experiments and wonder drugs. A new technique. But more and more the stories are of failures. False starts. The end of hope.

Bob's been coughing the last few times he's been here. He's still at it today.

Bob coughs. I look at Dale. He looks away.

One evening in the middle of "Marcus Welby," Jim announces, "I'm bored outta my tits, girls. I wanna have a party."

Mike, who's been drooping in front of the TV set, sits up.

"I say I am ready for a paaaaar-tay!"

Mike says, "Jimmy boy, you're on."

We OK it with Dr. Allen. Mike raids the stationery store on Broadway for paper hats and confetti and party favors and cards. We call everyone and it's on for the evening after next. They limit the number of people allowed in a room at a time so Mike and I take turns hanging out by the elevator to do crowd control. Jim shrieks, he calls me "Tonto the Bouncer" and flexes his arm in skinny little she-man biceps. It's great to see everybody, and everyone brings Jim these silly presents: an inflatable plastic duck, a shake-up scene of the Space Needle, a couple of incredibly ugly fuzzy animals, a bouquet of balloons. Somebody brings him a child's watercolor set; it's the only gift he doesn't gush about.

When I start to clean the wrapping paper, he says, "Oh leave it a while." He likes the shiny colors and the rustling sound the paper makes when he shifts in bed.

When anybody leaves, he blows a kiss and says, "Bye-bye cowpoke," "Happy Trails."

He knows what he's doing.

I see it when I'm coming down the hall, a laminated sign on the door of his room. I tiptoe the last few yards because I don't want him to hear me stop to read it, acting as if I believe what it says. It's a warning, like something you'd see on a pack of cigarettes or a bottle of pesticide. It warns about the contents. It tells you not to touch.

I push myself into his room before I can give myself a chance to reconsider. I push myself towards his bed, towards his forehead to give him his regular kiss hello.

"Don't touch me."

When he pushes me away, I'm relieved.

"Do you realize they're wearing plastic gloves around me all the time now? Face masks? They've put my wallet and clothes into plastic bags. As if me and my stuff is gonna jump on 'em and bleed all over 'em, as if my sweat—"

"Jim, that's bullshit. This isn't the Middle Ages, it's 1984. And they're medical people, they should know they don't need to do that. Haven't they read—"

"Why don't you go tell 'em, Tonto? Why don't you march right over to 'em with all your little newspaper articles and you just tell 'em the truth."

"I will, Jim, I'll—"

"Oh for fuck's sake, Tonto, they *are* medical people. They know what they're doing." He covers his eyes with a hand and says wearily, "And I know what my body is doing."

He holds his skinny white hand over his eyes. I can see the bones of his forearm, the bruises on his pale, filmy skin. He looks like an old man. The sheet rises and falls unevenly with his breath.

I ought to hold him but I don't want to.

"Jim?" I say, "Jim?" I don't know if he's listening.

Inside the belt-line of my jeans, down the middle of my back and on my stomach, I feel myself begin to sweat. I start to babble. A rambling, unconnected pseudo-summary of articles I haven't brought him, a doctor-ed precis of inoperative statements, edited news-speak, jargon, evasions, unmeant promises, lies.

But I'm only half thinking of what I say, and I'm not thinking of Jim at all.

I'm thinking of me. And of how my stomach clutched when he said that about the sweat. I'm thinking that I want to get out of his room immediately and wash my hands and face and take a shower and boil my clothes and get so far away from him that I won't have to breathe the air he's breathed. Then further, to where he can't see how I, like everyone I like to think I'm so different from, can desert him at the drop of a hat, before the drop of a hat, because my good-girl Right-On-Sister sympathies extend only as far as my assurance of my immunity from what is killing him. But once the thought occurs to me that I might be in danger I'll be the first bitch on the block to saddle up and leave him in the dust.

I don't know what I say to him; I know I don't touch him.

After a while he offers me a seat to watch TV, but I don't sit. I tell him I've got to go. I tell him I have a date. He knows I'm lying.

I look around for Dr. Allen. She tells me she thinks this recent hospital policy is ludicrous. "It just increases everybody's hysteria. There's no evidence of contagion through casual contact. If these people ..." But I don't listen to the rest of what she says. My mind is still repeating *no evidence of contagion through casual contact*. I'm so relieved I'm taken out of danger. I realize I'm happier than if she'd told me Jim was going to live.

I don't listen until I hear her asking me something. I don't hear the words, just the tone in her voice.

"Huh?"

She looks at me hard. Then shakes her head and turns away. She knows what I was thinking, where the line of my loyalty runs out.

The next day before I visit him, I ask Dr. Allen, "Are you sure, if I only touch him ..."

It's the only time she doesn't look cute. She practically spits. "You won't risk anything by hugging your brother."

Her eyes make a hole in my back as I walk to his room.

I hug him very carefully, how I believe I can stay safe. He holds me longer than he usually does. He doesn't say anything, when I pull away, about the fact that I don't kiss his forehead, which shines with sweat.

"Come here," he says in his lecher voice, "Daddy's got some candy for you."

He hands me a hundred dollar bill.

"What's this?"

"What I still owe you for the TV."

"What?"

"The hundred bucks I borrowed for the color TV."

Jim wanted to buy it for Scotty when all Scotty could do was watch TV. Jim wasn't going to get paid until the end of the month so I lent it to him. He wanted to pay me back immediately but he kept having all these bills.

"Dale withdrew it from the bank for me."

"I don't want it."

He glares at me. "The Ranger is a man of honor, Tonto."

"OK, OK, but I don't want it now."

He keeps glaring. "So you want it later? You gonna ride into Wells Fargo bank and tell them part of my estate is yours?"

"Dale can—" I close my eyes.

"I owe you, Tonto. Take Dr. Allen out for the time of her life."

"Jim ..."

"Goddammit, it's all I can do."

He grabs me by the belt loop of my jeans and tries to pull me toward him but he's too weak. I step toward the bed. He stuffs the bill into my pocket.

"Now go away please. I'm tired."

Was this a conversation? Was it a story?
I wish Scotty knew how I felt about him.
He knew.
I never told him. I wish I'd said the words.
He knew.
How do you know?
He told me.
Did he? What did he say?

Scotty told me, he said, Jim loves me.

Did he really?

Yes.

Did he say anything else?

Yes. He said, I love Jim.

He said he loved me?

More than anything.

Is that true?

Yes, Jim, it's true.

This is how I learn to tell a story.

We stay away for longer than we ought. I tell him it's time to go back, but he whines like a boy who doesn't want recess to end. He chatters. For the first time since I've known him, he starts retelling stories he has told to me before, stories that lose a lot in the retelling. But finally he runs out of things to say and lets me wheel him out of Rex's.

There's a traffic jam. Cars are backed up to Broadway and everybody's honking. A couple blocks away a moving van is trying to turn onto a narrow street. People at the crosswalk are getting impatient. They look around for cops and when they don't see any, start crossing Madison between the cars.

"I'm cold," says Jim.

He puts his free hand under his blanket. I lean down to tuck the cover more closely around his legs. His face is white.

"I'm cold," he grumbles again, "I wanna go back in."

"In a minute, Jim. We can't go yet."

"But I'm freezing." He looks up. "Where's the fucking sun anyway?"

I take my jacket off and wrap it around his shoulders. The cellophane of the cigarette package crinkles. I take care not to hit the drip feed tube.

People start laying on their horns. The poor stupid van ahead is moving forward then back, inch by inch, trying to squeeze around the corner.

"It's moving, Jim. The truck is going."

"About time," he says loudly, "Doesn't the driver realize what he's holding up here?"

Then the truck stalls. There's the gag of the engine, silence, the rev of the motor, the sputter when the engine floods.

"Someone go tell that goddam driver what he's holding up here."

People in their cars look out at Jim.

"I've got to get back in," he screams, "Go! Go!" He starts shooing the cars with his hands. The drip feed swings.

I grab his arm. "Jim, the IV."

"Fuck the IV!" he yells, "Fuck the traffic. I'm going back in. I have to get back in."

"We're going, Jim, the traffic's moving now," I lie. "We're going in. Settle down, OK?"

He pushes himself up a couple of inches to see the truck.

"The truck isn't moving, Tonto."

He kicks his blanket awry and tries to find the ground with his feet. "I'm walking."

"Jim, you can't."

"So what am I supposed to do. Fly?"

"You're supposed to wait. When the traffic clears—"

"I'm sick of waiting. You said it was clearing. You lied to me. I'm sick of everyone lying. I'm sick of waiting. I'm sick—" His voice cracks.

I put my hand on his arm. "When the traffic clears I'm going to push you and Silver across the street."

"It's not a horse," he screams, "it's a goddamn wheelchair!"

He starts to tremble. He grips the arms of the chair. "It's a wheelchair full of goddamn croaking faggot!" He slaps his hands over his face and whispers, "Tonto, I don't wanna. Don't let me—I don't wanna—I don't wanna—"

I put my arms around him and pull him to me. His head is against my collarbone. His cap falls off his sweaty head. I try to hold him. He lets me a couple of seconds then he tries to pull away. He isn't strong enough. But I know what he means so I pull back. He grabs my shirt, one of his.

"I don't wanna—" he cries, "I don't wanna—"

I put my hands on the back of his head and pull him to my chest.

"I don't wanna—I don't wanna—" he sobs.

His hands and face are wet. I hold his head.

He grabs me like a child wanting something good.

When we get back to his room he's still crying. I ring for Dr. Allen. Jim asks me to leave.

I pace around in the hall. When Dr. Allen comes out of his room, she says, "He's resting. He isn't good but he's not as bad as you think. He won't want to see you for a while. Now that you've seen him like this, it's harder for him to pretend he's not afraid. You can call the nurses' station tonight if you're concerned, but don't come see him till tomorrow. And call first."

I want to tell her to tell him a story, to make him not afraid.

But I don't. I say, "I'm going to call his parents."

She looks at me.

"*Our* parents," I mumble.

"He hasn't wanted his family to know?"

"Right."

"Call them."

I call his parents that night. They say they'll fly out in the morning and be able to be with him by noon. I tell them I'll book them a hotel a five minute walk from the hospital. They want to take the airport bus in themselves.

I call him in the morning.

"Hey, buddy."

"Yo Tonto."

"Listen, you want anything special today? I'm doing my Christmas shopping on the way down to see you."

"No you're not."

"Who says?"

"Santa says. I called Jean and Ange this morning and you're going down there for the week. That remodeling you were supposed to help them with way back is getting moldy. So it's the bright lights of Olympia for you, Sex-cat."

"Jim …"

"You have to go. They're going to pay you."

"What?!"

"They said they'd have to pay somebody, and they're afraid to have a common laborer around the priceless silver. So they want you. And it's not like you've been earning it hand over fist since you've been playing candy-striper with me."

"Jim, they don't have any money."

"They do now. Jeannie managed to lawyer-talk her way into some loot for her latest auto disaster and Ange is determined to spend the cash before Jeannie throws it away on another seedy lemon. So, Tonto, you got to go. It's your sororal duty."

It was impossible to talk Jim out of anything.

"Give my best to the girls and tell Trudy the Sentinal Bitch I said a bark is a bark is a bark.

"Doesn't Alice get a hello?"

"Alice is stupid. I will not waste my sparkling wit on her."

"OK …"

Were we going to get through this entire conversation without a mention of yesterday?

"So Tonto, the Ranger is much improved today. … My folks called a while ago from DFW airport. They're on their way to see me. Thanks for calling them."

"Sure."

"We'll see you next week then."

"Right."

He hangs up the phone before I can tell him goodbye.

I drive to Olympia. Ange is outside chopping wood. When I pull into the yard she slings the axe into the center of the block. She gives me a huge hug, her great soft arms around my back, her breasts and belly big and solid against me. She holds me a long time, kisses my hair.

"Hi baby."

"Ange."

She puts her arm around my back and brings me inside. The house smells sweet. They're baking. Jeannie blows me a kiss from the kitchen.

"Hello gorgeous!"

"Jeannie my darling."

I warm my hands by the wood stove. Ange yells at Gertrude, their big ugly German shepherd, to shut up. She's a very talkative dog. Jeannie brings in a plate of whole wheat cookies. I pick up Alice the cat from the couch and drop her on the floor. She is a stupid cat. She never protests anything. I sit on the place she's made warm on the couch. Jean hands me the plate. The cookies are still warm. I hesitate. It always amazes me they can, along with Jeannie's law school scholarship, support themselves by selling this horrible homemade hippie food to health food joints.

I take a cookie. "Thanks."

"How's Jim?"

"OK …"

"Bad?"

"Yeah."

"He sounded incredibly buoyant on the phone, so we figured … we told him we'd come up to see him next week when we've finished some of this." She nods at the cans and boards and drywall stacked up outside the spare room.

"Let's get to work."

"Yeah. Let's do it."

Ange puts an old Janis Joplin on the stereo. We knock the hell out of the walls.

They cook a very healthy dinner. As she's about to sit down, Jeannie says, "Hey, we got some beer in case you wanted one. Want one?" Ange and Jean haven't kept booze in their house for years.

"No thanks." There's a jar of some hippie fruit juice on the table. "This is fine."

They look at each other. We eat.

I sleep on the couch in the living room. Gertrude sleeps in front of the wood stove. I listen to her snort. She turns around in circles before she settles down to sleep, her head out on her paws.

Jim and I used to flip for who got the couch and who got the tatami mat on the floor next to the dog. I lean up on my elbow to look at Trudy the Sentinal Bitch. Only Jim could have re-named her that. In the bedroom Ange and Jean talk quietly.

All the junk has been moved from the spare room into the living room. Some of it is stacked at the end of the couch. I toss the blanket off me and sift through the pile. Rolled-up posters, curling photographs. There's a framed watercolor of Jim's, a scene of Ange and Jeannie by the pond, with Gertrude, fishing. They look so calm together. They didn't know Jim was painting them. They didn't know how he saw them.

I find one of all of us, three summers ago when we climbed Mount Si. Jim is tall and bearded, his arms around the three of us, me and Jeannie squished together under his left, Ange hugged under his right. All of us are smiling at the cameraman, Scotty.

Two nights later the phone rings late. I'm awake, light on, blanket off, before they've answered it. When Ange comes out of the bedroom I'm already dressed.

"That was Dr. Allen. His parents are with him. You should go."

They won't let me drive. We all pile into the truck; Jeannie driving, Ange in the middle, me against the door. Jeannie doesn't stop at the signs or the red lights. She keeps an even 80 on the highway. For once, Ange doesn't razz her about her driving.

I-5 is quiet. The only things on the road are some long-haul trucks, a few cars. We see the weak beige lights of the insides of these other cars, the foggy orange lights across the valley. We drive along past sleepy Tacoma, Federal Way, the airport.

"Look, would you guys mind if I had a cigarette?"

"Go ahead baby."

Ange reaches over me and rolls down the window. I root around in my jacket for Jim's cigarettes. I'm glad I didn't make that promise to him.

We pull into the hospital parking lot. My hand is on the door before we stop.

"You go up. We'll get Bob and Dale and meet you on the floor in ten minutes."

In the elevator is a couple a little older than me. Red-eyed and sniffling like kids. We look at each other a second then look at the orange lights going up.

When the elevator opens I run. But when I see the guys in white taking things from the room in plastic bags, I stop. The man at the nurses' station looks up.

"Your parents are in the waiting room."

"My what?"

"Your parents."

Then I remember how that first night, a million years ago, when Dr. Allen had told me she couldn't tell me about Jim unless I was in his family, I had told the story of being his sister.

"Oh Christ."

"They told me to send you in when you came."

"Oh Jesus."

They've left the waiting room door open a crack. I look in. His father is wearing an overcoat. His hands lay loose around the rim of the hat in his lap. His mother is touching her husband's arm. Neither of them is talking.

I knock on the door very lightly.

They look up.

"You must be Jim's friend. Come in."

I push the door open. They both stand up and put out their hands. I shake their hands.

"Mary Carlson."

"Jim Carlson."

I introduce myself.

"The young man at the desk told us that, before she went into surgery, Dr. Allen called our daughter and that she was on her way. But we don't have a daughter."

"I'm sorry, but I—the first night Jim was here I told Dr. Allen—"

Mr. Carlson is still shaking my hand. He squeezes it hard.

"You have nothing to apologize for. Jim told us what a good friend you'd been to him. Both after Scotty, and more recently."

"Jim was a good friend too. I'm sorry I didn't call you sooner."

"We know he asked you not to. We had a few good days with him. I think he wanted to get better before he saw us," says Mrs. Carlson. "He didn't want us to have to see and have to wait the way he had to wait with Scotty."

"Yes."

"Did you know Scotty?"

"Yes."

"He was a lovely young man."

"He was good to Jim," says Mr. Carlson. "There were things about Jim it took us a long time to understand, but he was a good son." He says this slowly. "He was a good man."

"Yes."

"We loved him." Mr. Carlson's mouth is open like he's going to say more, but then there's this sound in his throat and he drops his face into his hands. "Dear God," he says, "Oh dear God."

Mrs. Carlson pulls her husband's head to her breast. His hat falls to the floor.

I pick the hat up off the floor and put it on the table. I leave the room. When I close the door, I hear his father crying.

Ange and Jean and Bob and Dale are standing at the nurses' station. The boys are in pj's and overcoats and house slippers. They look at me. I look at them. We all look at each other. Nobody says anything.

Dale walks over to the wall and puts his forehead against the wall. His shoulders shake. Bob goes over and puts his hand on Dale's back. Nobody says anything.

We get in the truck and go back to Bob and Dale's. We all insist Bob sits up front with Jean and Ange. Dale and I sit in the open back. We haul the dog-smelling woolly blanket over our knees and huddle up next to each other. I can feel the cool ribbed metal of the bottom of the truck through my jeans. Jeannie pulls us away from the bright lights of the hospital onto Madison.

It's dark but there're enough breaks in the clouds that we can see a star or two. The lights are off at Rex's, the streets are empty. Jean drives so slow and cautiously, full stops at the signs and lights, and pauses at the intersections. There's not another car on the road, but I think she hopes if she does everything very carefully, things might not break apart.

Jean stops at the light on Broadway. Dale and I look into the back window of the pickup and see their three heads—Jeannie's punky hairdo sticking up, Ange's halo of wild fuzz, Bob's shiny smooth round scalp. The collar of Bob's pj's is crooked above his housecoat. He's usually so neatly groomed, but now he looks like a rumpled, sleepy child.

Dale begins to tremble. I put my hand on his knee.

"Jim was a great guy, the greatest, but now it's like he was never here. What did he ever do that's gonna last? It's like his life was nothing."

"Jim was a good man," I say.

Dale nods.

"And he loved a good man. He loved Scotty well."

"And that's enough?"

"It's good," I say, "It's true."

Dale takes my hand. He holds it hard. It's the first time I notice he wears a ring.

He takes a breath. "Bob … you know Bob … I'm afraid maybe … I think Bob …"

He can't say it. I see his eyelashes trembling, the muscles in his jaw as he tries to keep from crying. He swallows and closes his eyes.

"Bob is a good man," says Dale.

"Yeah Dale, I know. Bob is a good man, too."

So we all go back to Bob and Dale's. I call the Carlson's hotel to leave Bob and Dale's phone number. We drink tea and sit around in the living room until someone says we ought to get some sleep.

"Well, there's plenty of pj's," says Bob. "We can have a pajama paaaaaaar-tay."

He says it before he realizes it's a Jim word. Ange and Jeannie and I try to laugh. Dale closes his eyes.

Bob and Dale get pj's for us. They wash the teacups as Ange and Jean and I change. We all look really silly in the guys' flannel pj's. When the boys come out of the kitchen and see us, they laugh. It's a real laugh. It sounds good.

Ange and Jean are going to stay in the guest room. Ange says to me, "You wanna stay with us, babe?"

Dale says, "Or you can sleep on the couch in our room."

"Thanks guys." I plop down on the living room couch. "This is fine with me."

Dale goes to the linen closet to get some sheets and blankets.

If I lie next to someone I will break apart.

I wake up first. I put the water on to boil. When Jean and Ange come out of the guest room, I say "The Katzenjammer twins."

They look at my pj's. "Triplets," Jeannie says.

"Quads," says Ange when Dale comes into the kitchen.

He gives us each a scratchy, unshaven kiss on the cheek.

"Good morning lovelies."

Jeannie nods towards the guys' room. "Our fifth?"

"Bob's asleep now. He was sweaty last night. I don't think we'll go to Jim's."

He goes to phone the bank and Janet, Bob's business partner. Jean and Ange and I look at each other.

"You want me to stay with you?" asks Jean when Dale gets off the phone.

"Naaaah," he smiles like nothing's wrong. "Bob'll be alright. You guys go help the Carlsons."

We take turns in the shower while we listen for the phone. We hear Bob coughing in the bedroom.

The Carlsons call. They want to meet at Jim's about ten to clean out the apartment. We say OK, and plan to get there a half an hour early in case there's anything we need to "straighten up." Not that we expect to find anything shocking, but if we were to run across something, even a magazine or a poster, it might be nicer if the Carlsons didn't see it.

We leave Dale sitting at the kitchen table, his hands around his coffee mug. He looks lost. He looks the way he's going to look after Bob is gone.

We take the truck and stop by the grocery store to get a bunch of cartons. I've got the keys to Jim's place. When we walk up the steps I think of Jim standing there when I came by to drive him to the hospital. We climb the gray-mustard colored carpet of the stairs. The hallways smell like food. Living people still live here.

When I open the door to the apartment everything looks different. We set the empty boxes on the living room floor and begin to look in closets and drawers, intruding in a way we never would if Jim was around. There's nothing in Jim's drawers but socks and T-shirts and underwear, nothing beneath the bed but dust, stray pennies, a couple of crusty paintbrushes.

The Carlsons get there before we can go through all the rooms.

The Carlsons don't think there'll be anything they'll want from the living room, so I start packing the books and records, wrapping the TV in towels before I put it in a box.

Jeannie and Mrs. Carlson start in the kitchen. I hear Mrs. Carlson telling Jeannie about the first time Jim made scrambled eggs, about her trying to teach "my Jims," as she calls her husband and son, to cook. She laughs as she remembers the story of the eggs. It's good to hear her laugh. In Jim's room Mr. Carlson and Ange are packing shirts into cardboard cartons. I glance in. Mr. Carlson looks so small, like a schoolboy being sent away from home. He's very slow and careful as he fastens buttons and smooths collars and folds sleeves. He creases the shirts into neat, tidy rectangles. Ange says a couple of things but Mr. Carlson doesn't answer much. So after a while she leaves him to sort through his son's ties and loafers, his jackets and suits, his baseball things, alone.

"This must have been Scotty's room," says Mrs. Carlson.

I'd been in there when Scotty was around. But after Scotty the door was never open.

The handle of the door is colored silver. Mrs. Carlson puts her hand on it. It clicks. She pushes it open. The curtain is drawn, the room is dark. But we can see around Mrs. Carlson, in front of us, that the bed and dresser and the night-table are gone. The only piece of furniture is the long desk by the window. The desk is crowded with clutter. There are pale gray-white rectangles on the walls. Ange flips on the light.

And all around is Scotty. Scotty in his red-checked lumber jacket. Scotty smiling with a three-day's growth of beard. Scotty sitting cross-legged on a mat. Scotty with long hair, a tie-dyed shirt, and sandals. Scotty in his ridiculous bright orange bermuda shorts. His firm brown stomach, his compact upper arms, him holding up a Stonewall fist and grinning. His fine hands holding something blue. His profile when he was a boy. Him resting his chin in his palms and looking sleepy. His baseball hat on backwards. His pretty shoulders, his tender sex, his hands.

In every one, his skin is tan, his body is whole, his eyes are blue and bright. We recognize some poses from old photographs, and some from Scotty as we remember him. But some are of a Scotty that we never saw; Jim's Scotty. Painted alive again by Jim.

"Dear Scotty," Mrs. Carlson says, "my Jim's beloved."

We take some stuff to a center that is starting up. We leave most of it in both their names. The TV in Scotty's. The hundred dollar bill in Jim's.

A few days later everything is over. The Carlsons are flying back to Texas. They don't want a ride to the airport but they invite us all down for coffee at their hotel. They tell us if we ever get to Texas to come see them. We all thank each other for everything and say if there's ever anything we can do. The Carlsons take some paintings to share with Scotty's family. When the airporter arrives we put their suitcases in the storage place beneath the bus. Mr. Carlson carries the paintings rolled up into tubes. When the bus pulls out Mrs. Carlson waves to us for both of them. Mr. Carlson won't let go of the tubes.

We go back to Bob and Dale's and drink more coffee. We all get pretty buzzy. Then Jean says they shouldn't put it off anymore, they need to get back to Olympia. I mumble something about starting up temping again.

Jean says, uncharacteristically, "Oh, fuck temping."

Bob laughs. "Listen to that potty mouth."

Ange reminds me that I have to go back to Olympia to get my car, and I ought to help them finish the remodeling. Both of which are true, but it's also true they know what I can't say: how much I need to be with them.

So we say "See you 'round" to Bob and Dale and get in the truck to drive back down to Oly. Ange makes me sit in the middle, between the two of them.

"Wha-chew-wont, baby I got it!!" Ange howls as she shoves Aretha into the tape deck. Aretha takes a second to catch up with Ange, but then it's the two of them singing. Ange cranks the tunes up as Jean pulls the truck out onto 15th. We turn at Pine. Jean slows the truck as we pass the Rose in case anyone cute is casually lounging around outside; no one ever is. There's a moment of stillness at the red light on Broadway, a moment of stillness between the tracks, then "Chain of Fools." Ange cranks it up even more as we turn left onto Broadway, then turn right again onto Madison and right into a traffic jam.

Ange rolls down the window as if she needs the extra room to sing. She loves the chain-chain-chaaaaaain, chain-chain-chaaaaaain parts and always does this ridiculously unsexy jerk of her shoulders and hips when she sings it. She gets especially crazy at the cha-ya-ya-ya-ya-in part near the end. She squints and tries to look very mean, meaner with each ya-ya-ya. Jeannie is good at the hoo-hoo's, which she accompanies with some extremely precise nods of her chin, and some extremely cool finger points. I sit between them and laugh.

But as the song is nearing the end and we haven't moved more than ten yards, I growl, "What is this traffic shit?"

Ange pops the cassette out of the tape deck.

"What?"

"I said, what is this traffic shit."

"Quarter of four," says Jean, "I thought we'd miss it."

"The old 'burg ain't what it used to be baby. New folks movin' in all the time. And they all have six cars and they love traffic jams. Reminds me of good ol' LA."

"Where they can all go back to in a goddamn handtruck, thank you very much."

We inch along a few minutes then come to a complete stop in front of Rex's. Pedestrians on the sidewalk look around for cops then start walking in between the cars.

Someone squeezing by in front of the truck does a knock-knock on the hood and grins at us.

"Smug asshole bastard," I snarl.

Cars start honking.

"Jesus this traffic sucks," I say louder.

Ange looks at me.

The car behind us is laying on the horn.

"Fuck the traffic," I shout.

"Hey, babe, take it easy," says Ange, "We'll get outta here soon."

I ignore her. "Fuck the traffic," I cry. I put my hands over my ears. "Fuck the traffic."

Then I hear Jim screaming, "Fuck the traffic! Don't they realize they're holding up a wheelchair full of dying faggot!" Then I hear him yelling, "So what am I supposed to do, fly?" Then he looks at me, "Tonto, I don't wanna, I don't wanna die."

Then my head is against the back of the seat. I'm rigid. Ange's hand is on my arm.

"Baby?"

Jean grinds the truck into reverse, backs up a couple inches, whacks it back into first and climbs over the sidewalk into the Seattle First National Bank parking lot. She cuts the engine.

"Baby." Ange says it hard.

She yanks me away from the back of the seat and throws her arms, her whole huge body around me. Jeannie grabs me from behind. I'm stiff. I'm like a statue. My body can't bend and I can't see. They sandwich me in between them. Spit and snot are on my face.

"Let it go, baby, let it go."

I can't say anything. My jaws are tight.

"Let it go, babe."

Ange pulls away from me enough to kiss my forehead. I break. She squeezes herself around me tight. Then they're both around me, holding me.

And then, dear Jim, held close between the bodies of our friends, I see you.

I roll you and your wheelchair out to the sidewalk. I'm worried because in the few minutes it's taken us to get from your room to here, the sky has turned gray. I tell you we ought to get back inside, but you wave that idea away. I stand above you at the pedestrian crossing and look down at the top of your cap, the back of your neck, your shoulders.

There's a traffic jam. The cars are pressed so close not even pedestrians can squeeze through. A wind is picking up. People are opening umbrellas. Cars are honking, drivers are laying on their horns. I start to say again, that we really ought to go back in, but you find my hand on the wheelchair grip and cover it with your own. You sigh like a tolerant, tired parent. You shake your head. You pat my hand then squeeze it.

"The traffic'll break in a minute, Jim."

But you aren't listening to me. You slip your hand from mine, and before I can stop you, you've unhooked the tooth of the dripfeed from your arm.

"Jim, the IV."

"Ssssh." You put your finger to your lips like you are finally going to tell the truth about a story you've been telling for so long.

You slip the blanket off your knees. You stand up alone, not needing to lean on anyone. You're tall as you used to be. You stretch your arms out to your sides and take a deep breath. I see your chest expand. You stretch your neck up and look at the sky. You throw your arm around my shoulder and pull me to you. I feel the firmness of your body and smell the good clean smell of your healthy skin the way it was the summer we climbed Mt. Si. You pull my face in front of you. You hold my face between your hands and look at me. You look inside where I can't see, where I can't look away from you. Beneath the fear the covered love, you see me, Jim. Then, like a blessing that forgives me, and a healing benediction that will seal a promise true, you kiss my forehead.

You tell me, "Tonto, girl, I'm going for a ride."

You fling your Right-On-Sister Stonewall fist up in the air then open your hand in a Hi-Yo Silver wave. I watch your hand as it stretches above you high, impossibly high. Your feet lift off the sidewalk and you rise. Above the crowded street, the hospital, above us all, you fly.

The rain begins. Cold drops hit my face when I look up at you. But you fly high above it, Jim. Your firm taut body catches glints of light from a sun that no one here below can see.

I raise a Right-On fist to answer you, but then my fist is opened, just like yours, and I am waving, Jim.

Good friend, true brother Jim, goodbye.

D.O.M.

OTIS HAD OFTEN VOWED he would never let it come to this. Today, when his mind was clearer than it had been in some time, he remembered that distinctly. Visiting his two unmarried aunts as, one after another, they were confined to nursing homes, he swore he would never share their fate. Yet here he was.

As nursing homes went, he had to admit Sunset Gardens was superior. In its pleasant garden, where he now occupied a bench, one could in seasonable weather escape much of the unpleasantness inside. There was the odor of flowers instead of the smell of incontinence which the best efforts of the staff could never entirely remove from the lounges. In addition the more troubled and troublesome ladies seldom came out, those forever crying out demands that husbands perhaps long dead, or fathers, or children get them out of here. The men, very much in the minority, seemed mostly so docile as to fade into the wallpaper but so many of the women were querulous, shrewish, or noisily addled. There were even one or two from whose once-genteel mouths poured a stream of foul language from which, in their prime, they would almost certainly have been the first to recoil. Even if more of the women were in their right mind and nice, there would still have been too many of them. Otis had, after all, lived most of his life in an atmosphere that was just the reverse, largely male. He had socialized little with women and at work, well, in his day not too many women came into sporting goods stores.

Otis' mother had escaped the fate of her sisters, he was happy to remember. She had lived, he and her less fortunate sisters agreed, long enough but not too long. Otis had hoped to share her fate of a quick, easy, and timely death instead of her sisters' prolonged twilight. The passing of the last aunt to survive had, he'd hoped, meant that he'd seen the last of nursing homes. But here he was, indubitably a patient rather than a visitor, though he couldn't remember how he got here. He'd have to take the word of the social worker, who'd told him it was the only resource once the hospital was ready to discharge him and his former neighbors organized to protest his return to his apartment. They felt he had endangered their lives by falling asleep while smoking just once too often. At any rate, the social worker had said, though he was taken to the hospital initially because of smoke inhalation, he had been found in very bad physical condition generally, the result of malnutrition and neglect or overdose of various medications. Clearly he wasn't, she said, able to look after himself any longer.

Otis remembered that he had once been full of stratagems to avoid this fate. When Aunt Rose first went into the home, Otis had felt smug in the knowledge that Chester was twelve years younger than he, a vigorous athletic type who swam every day of his life at the Y, and not just to have a gander at nude young men in the locker room. Who expected a car to mount the sidewalk and strike him down? Even with Chester gone, leaving Otis as alone as the unmarried aunts, he'd felt he had resources they lacked. Used to being independent, they could never be persuaded to live together and pool their strengths, nor to take a younger person into their home who might be leaned on in case of emergency. Otis, accustomed to sharing, had figured that when the time came that he felt he couldn't manage by himself, he would let Chester's room to a student, or perhaps find another gay widower who was willing to share.

It had never seemed to Otis that that time was quite at hand. He'd had lapses of memory, of course, forgotten doctors' appointments and things like that, but on the whole he'd still felt capable. He'd hired that Korean boy, whatever his name was, to do the housecleaning after a few dizzy spells when bending over to dust chair rungs. He'd been scrupulous, he thought, about not trying to get one too many wears out of his clothes before having them laundered or dry-cleaned. He had tried to curb any tendencies to collect string, paper bags, magazines or any of the things that so many old people cluttered their homes with. He'd asked his old friend Noah to let him know if he saw any signs that he was becoming a "saver" or a "dirty old man" in the literal sense. One couldn't, alas, be as beautiful as one once had been, but at least one could be clean and neat.

Noah, of course, had moved to Florida, was it three or five years ago? For a while Otis had tried to see things through Noah's eyes. He'd pretend that Noah was still stopping by mornings for coffee and Danish and he'd imagined whole conversations with him. A cherished coffee mug had been thrown out, in fact, because the phantom Noah had told him he was slipping in keeping a mug with a chip out of the rim just because Chester's predecessor Jake had given it to him. Good old Noah. Dead now.

The Korean boy had been gone for a while, too, he guessed, gone to New York to work in a brother's fruit store. Was there a reason why he hadn't replaced him? He remembered thinking that if he kept the windows closed tight, not so much dirt and dust would come in and it wouldn't be so necessary to clean. Somebody, he couldn't remember who, had a theory that some of his lapses of memory were a result of lack of oxygen. They'd said they could always tell when he'd been outside and had some fresh air because his mind was so much clearer than when he'd been shut up in the apartment from which endless cigarettes had drained oxygen. It had seemed a lot of bosh at the time but Otis had to admit that now that the nurses limited his smoking to the lounges or the garden, his mind was much clearer than it had been in his last months in the apartment.

He had felt so much better lately that he'd asked the social worker if perhaps he might leave the nursing home now that he was well. She had smiled and said she feared he couldn't cope. Once he left Sunset Gardens, she'd warned, he was unlikely to be lucky a second time in finding a vacancy if things didn't work out. That would mean a far, far lower level of nursing home. God forbid, thought Otis.

The meals here weren't bad, though it infuriated some of the complaining women to have him say so. They were indignant when he cleaned his plate and spoiled the effect of their refusal to eat "such garbage." There was, however, so much out there in the world that Otis wanted that he wondered if it might be worth taking a chance on a worse nursing home just to see if he could cope.

Who here could understand him, or sympathize with some of the things he missed? His gay magazines with all those lovely nude centerfolds, for instance. Here one had to make do with the magazines brought by volunteers from the churches—old copies of *Reader's Digest* or family magazines with holes in the articles where a recipe had been cut from the other side. Articles on how to keep Communists out of Central America or how to make ten easy soufflés were not exactly jerk-off material. And God knows the visible men weren't either.

Some of the orderlies, strapping young blacks who continually mopped the halls and tried to keep the odors of age and incontinence at bay, would have made good centerfolds for certain tastes, but not his. He certainly wasn't above taking a look at the outline of their underpants when it showed through their white uniforms as they bent over, but he had never shared the interest of some of his departed friends in darker-skinned people. Though he could admire their looks, certainly, as he could admire the looks of women, horses, and children, he could never lust for them. Among the church volunteers, who came to entertain(!) them with hymns and such, an occasional buttoned-up good-looking youth would appear but they always seemed like people who still feared pimples and warts if they touched themselves "there," and likely to marry girls who shared thoughts of sex as necessary, perhaps, but not nice.

The beauty of males had always been a source of pleasure to him right up there with music and art. He was starved for it here in Sunset Gardens. On the soap operas which he had never watched till he came here but which were turned on in the lounge daily, doctors were unfailingly handsome. That wasn't the reality of the nursing home. The only staff doctor who was young was also short, fat, bald, and without any compensating charm. One hoped for visitors who might be easy on the eyes, an occasional son or grandson. But by the time their parents were in Sunset Gardens the sons were elderly themselves.

At least there was this garden and the occasional passer-by. What beauties one saw one saw only briefly, but it was better than nothing. There were, these days, construction workers passing from the building being erected in the next block and a coffee shop they favored south of Sunset Gardens. That construction project would end some day and then there would be no more of the tanned and muscled men in jeans and undershirts, in some cases so much less coarse than Otis had always imagined such men would be. There would always, he hoped, be the students, for there seemed to be a college of some sort nearby. Not that youth automatically equalled beauty. Otis had never believed that and since he'd been well enough to come out to the garden here, he had certainly learned that the student body contained at least as many uglies as beauties. On a scale of 1 to 10, many would get from Otis no more than $2^3/8$. But there was that one—oh, he made up for all those that parents seemed to have put together from spare parts. It was the prospect of seeing him that kept Otis in the garden on days of good health long after he was chilled or a bit dizzy from too much sun.

That young man always seemed to have a spring in his step and his face was invariably suffused with a look that bespoke enjoyment of life. Physically he looked just a bit like Otis' favorite among the many centerfolds he had torn out to add to that collection which must have so shocked his neighbors or whoever cleaned out his apartment after he was taken to the hospital. The young man was also, Otis felt sure, gay. If anyone had asked how he knew, Otis couldn't have said, but who would be asking? To whom, in this place, could he ever say a word about such matters? He hadn't even any visitors with whom he could dish. Gay friends all seemed to be dead, housebound, or moved to warmer climates such as Otis had always felt he couldn't stand. The only people who came to see him here were the two widows with whom he had played bridge in the days when he could still remember what cards had been played. One could hardly talk about beautiful men with women so misguided that each had nurtured hopes of making Otis their second husband. After all, one was still given to saying, on her increasingly infrequent visits, "I'd never have let a husband of mine end up here!" To escape Sunset Gardens by marrying Mrs. Katzenbach would be too extreme a measure. Otis suspected she was voraciously sexual. Well, look who's talking. If there are dirty old men, why not lusty old ladies, but not in his bed, thank you.

It didn't really matter to Otis whether or not the young student was gay. After all, he was never going to know him. He was just a vision that soothed Otis' old eyes in his quick passing. For the young man never dallied, walking along purposefully as though toward pleasure, whether he was going to or from the college with his armload of books. Otis had to undress him mentally much faster than he would have liked. It was more fun if you could stare at a man and slowly fantasize his removing one piece of clothing after another. In these circumstances, Otis had to speed things up if he wanted to get down to a vision of bobbing genitals or retreating nude buns.

There had not even been that pleasure so far today. Perhaps he had no classes, perhaps he was ill? He looked healthy, but who knew these days? It was going to spoil Otis' day if he didn't get even the quick glimpse of—what was his name now? Otis had been so happy to hear a friend call after him the other day. It had delayed him as he waited for the friend but it had also enabled Otis to put a name to him at last. And now he'd forgotten it. Well, if he didn't try too hard to think of it, it would pop into his mind in time.

Meantime, there were other passersby, though Otis took less interest in them since he'd first laid eyes on Ned. Ned—yes, that was it. He knew it would come to him when he least expected it. Ned. Ned. Ned. Ned. If he said it over and over to himself, surely he wouldn't forget it again. Such a suitable name for the young man for he looked like the hero of one of the boys' books Otis had read as a child, so many of whom were named Ned. Yes, he looked exactly as a Ned should look—scrubbed, cheerful and bright. Ned. Ned. Ned. Otis didn't intend to forget again.

"The name of your son?" said a voice beside Otis.

Startled, he turned to find a wizened little man he'd never seen before whose wheelchair had been rolled up close to Otis' bench.

"Son? I don't have a son," Otis said, a bit testily.

"You were saying 'Ned,' so I thought perhaps ..."

"I was saying 'Ned'?" Otis asked. He hadn't realized he'd said anything aloud. He must watch that. Mustn't start voicing what was in his head, especially in view of the way his thoughts ran.

Suppose he suddenly said aloud, "What a gorgeous ass on that hard hat!" or "I'd love to see him when something besides his hat was hard." My God, what a commotion there'd be in the nursing home. They certainly heard worse from the foul-mouthed women, but he'd like to bet that those who took the profanity and scatology in stride would go into a disapproving flurry if sexual thoughts like that slipped out of Otis' mouth. Anger and bitterness the staff was used to, but frank admiration of a young man's body and looks by an old male resident might well get him forbidden to set foot in the garden. The highlight of his tedious days would be snatched away from him.

"My name's Wally," the little man in the wheelchair said, holding out a tremorous and liver-spotted hand.

"I don't give a damn what his name is," thought Otis, and hoped he hadn't said it aloud, "and I'm not going to try to remember it. I'm going to concentrate on Ted. No, not Ted. Damn, he's rattled it out of me already. It's not Ted. I know that much."

Clearly the man expected him to introduce himself, so grudgingly he grumped "Otis" but kept his eyes fixed on the sidewalk in case the youth whose name wasn't Ted but something like that came by.

"Actually, my name is Horace—Horace Walpole Austin," the little man said chattily, "Can you imagine being named Horace in this day and age? My father was an English lit professor who admired Walpole. But I skip the Horace and call myself Wally from the Walpole."

"My god," Otis thought, "I've always wanted more men here, but not an old chatterbox like this. If he distracts me so that I miss what's-his-name, I'll shorten his days."

"You been in Sunset Gardens long?" the man persisted. Tadpole, did he say his name was?

"I'm not sure," Otis said. "The days slip by so."

Just at that moment one of the ladies screamed and quickly vacated a chair near the flowers, in flight from a bee going about its work among the blossoms. She took refuge on a bench and Otis saw his chance to get away from this ill-timed conversation.

"Excuse me. I'm going to get that chair she just left and move it over by the fence. This bench is getting too sunny."

Moving stiffly because of his arthritis and leaning on his cane, Otis took the folding aluminum chair and set it up where, if Ned, yes, that's it, Ned, should come by, he could not fail to see him. If he thought that would discourage the newcomer, he quickly learned better. In no time the wheelchair was right beside him.

"I can't take the sun either. Had lots of skin cancers removed. I used to love the beach. Herman and I practically lived there in summer."

Otis pricked up his ears. Herman? He used to go to the beach all the time with Herman? That would bear looking into, but not right now, when Ned might be passing by. Some day he might probe to find out if he had, at last, a fellow spirit in Sunset Gardens, but this was not the time.

Oh, definitely not, because there, coming along the street with even more than his usual jauntiness was—uh—Ned. There, the name had come to him in spite of the distraction provided by Tadpole.

Otis' pulse began to quicken. Ned in any garb was beautiful to behold but, as a bonus, in today's warm and sunny weather he was wearing shorts. Not the baggy sort that the fashion world was trying to bring back, but nice short tight ones that exposed a lot of thigh. Always susceptible to nice legs, Otis could see at once that Ned's were choice.

As he came abreast of where the two old men sat, the young student turned and looked their way, which Otis had never known him to do before. On sudden impulse, Otis winked. The young man's face broke into an even broader smile than he customarily wore and, wonder of wonders, he winked back. Otis wondered if what he felt might be a heart attack.

As Ned moved briskly on toward the college, Otis heard Tadpole chuckling beside him.

"See that?" the little man asked. "He winked at me."

Otis, who had begun to feel as light as though inflated with helium, thumped to earth. He was overcome with sudden rage.

"Winked at *you?* Why would he wink at *you?*"

"Because I winked at him," the withered man said, with something like a leer.

Otis suppressed an impulse to beat Tadpole with his cane. Questions about Herman were no longer necessary, but the nerve of the old fart, daring to presume, and on top of that, daring to claim that whosis had been winking at him.

"You know something?" the unregenerate man in the wheelchair said, "I'm a student of physiognomy and body language. Just as I could tell the minute I saw you that you were another D.O.M. like me, I can tell you that boy's in love and I can also tell he's getting well laid. Never have had any trouble telling when a person's whole being is satisfied, like after first-rate sex."

"Good God," thought Otis, and was momentarily speechless.

"Not only that, but he's also gay. He's probably on his way to meet him now, judging from the spring in his step. A fellow student, perhaps, or maybe even a professor. That's why he was so kind to two old farts like us. I was always kind when I was first in love."

Tadpole's shrewd, Otis thought, but the nerve of him calling me an old fart. Then he remembered that in his mind he had used exactly the same term for the newcomer. But he was certainly presumptuous, claiming that the wink had been aimed at him. That lad had definitely not been looking in Tadpole's direction at all, but straight at Otis. Ah, well, if the illusion comforted him in these first difficult days of adjustment to the nursing home, let him go on thinking such nonsense. Otis would be kind, for he too was now very much in love, rhapsodic over the smile and return wink from What's-His-Name.

BECKY BIRTHA

IN THE LIFE

GRACE COME TO ME in my sleep last night. I feel somebody presence, in the room with me, then I catch the scent of Posner's Bergamot Pressing Oil, and that cocoa butter grease she use on her skin. I know she standing at the bedside, right over me, and then she call my name.

"Pearl."

My Christian name Pearl Irene Jenkins, but don't nobody ever call me that no more. I been Jinx to the world for longer than I care to specify. Since my mother passed away, Grace the only one ever use my given name.

"Pearl," she say again. "I'm just gone down the garden awhile. I be back."

I'm so deep asleep I have to fight my way awake, and when I do be fully woke, Grace is gone. I ease my tired bones up and drag em down the stairs, cross the kitchen in the dark, and out the back screen door onto the porch. I guess I'm half expecting Gracie to be there waiting for me, but there ain't another soul stirring tonight. Not a sound but singing crickets, and nothing staring back at me but that old weather-beaten fence I ought to painted this summer, and still ain't made time for. I lower myself down into the porch swing, where Gracie and I have sat so many still summer nights and watched the moon rising up over Old Mister Thompson's field.

I never had time to paint that fence back then, neither. But it didn't matter none, cause Gracie had it all covered up with her flowers. She used to sit right here on this swing at night, when a little breeze be blowing, and say she could tell all the different flowers apart, just by the smell. The wind pick up a scent, and Gracie say, "Smell that jasmine, Pearl?" Then a breeze come up from another direction, and she turn her head like somebody calling her and say, "Now that's my honeysuckle, now."

It used to tickle me, cause she knowed I couldn't tell all them flowers of hers apart when I was looking square at em in broad daylight. So how I'm gonna do it by smell in the middle of the night? I just laugh and rock the swing a little, and watch her enjoying herself in the soft moonlight.

I could never get enough of watching her. I always did think that Grace Simmons was the prettiest woman north of the Mason-Dixon line. Now I've lived enough years to know it's true. There's been other women in my life besides Grace, and I guess I loved them all, one way or another, but she was something special—Gracie was something else again.

She was a dark brownskin woman—the color of fresh gingerbread hot out the oven. In fact, I used to call her that—my gingerbread girl. She had plenty enough of that pretty brownskin flesh to fill your arms up with something substantial when you hugging her, and to make a nice background for them dimples in her cheeks and other places I won't go into detail about.

Gracie could be one elegant good looker when she set her mind to it. I'll never forget the picture she made, that time the New Year's Eve party was down at the Star Harbor Ballroom. That was the first year we was in The Club, and we was going to every event they had. Dressed to kill. Gracie had on that white silk dress that set off her complexion so perfect, with her hair done up in all them little curls. A single strand of pearls that could have fooled anybody. Long gloves. And a little fur stole. We was serious about our partying back then! I didn't look too bad myself, with that black velvet jacket I used to have, and the pleats in my slacks pressed so sharp you could cut yourself on em. I weighed quite a bit less than I do now, too. Right when you come in the door of the ballroom, they have a great big floor to ceiling gold frame mirror, and if I remember rightly, we didn't get past that for quite some time.

Everybody want to dance with Gracie that night. And that's fine with me. Along about the middle of the evening, the band is playing a real hot number, and here come Louie and Max over to me, all long-face serious, wanting to know how I can let my woman be out there shaking her behind with any stranger that wander in the door. Now they know good and well ain't no strangers here. The Cinnamon & Spice Club is a private club, and all events is by invitation only.

Of course, there's some thinks friends is more dangerous than strangers. But I never could be the jealous, overprotective type. And the fact is, I just love to watch the woman. I don't care if she out there shaking it with the Virgin Mary, long as she having a good time. And that's just what I told Max and Lou. I could lean up against that bar and watch her for hours.

You wouldn't know, to look at her, she done it all herself. Made all her own dresses and hats, and even took apart a old ratty fur coat that used to belong to my great aunt Malinda to make that cute little stole. She always did her own hair—every week or two. She used to do mine, too. Always be teasing me about let her make me some curls this time. I'd get right aggravated. Cause you can't have a proper argument with somebody when they standing over your head with a hot comb in they hand. You kinda at they mercy. I'm sitting fuming and cursing under them towels and stuff, with the sweat dripping all in my eyes in the steamy kitchen—and she just laughing. "Girl," I'm telling her, "you know won't no curls fit under my uniform cap. Less you want me to stay home this week and you gonna go work my job and your job too."

Both of us had to work, always, and we still ain't had much. Everybody always think Jinx and Grace doing all right, but we was scrimping and saving all along. Making stuff over and making do. Half of what we had to eat grew right here in this garden. Still and all, I guess we *was* doing all right. We had each other.

Now I finally got the damn house paid off, and she ain't even here to appreciate it with me. And Gracie's poor bedraggled garden is just struggling along on its last legs—kinda like me. I ain't the kind to complain about my lot, but truth to tell, I can't be down crawling around on my hands and knees no more—this body I got put up such a fuss and holler. Can't enjoy the garden at night proper nowadays, nohow. Since Mister Thompson's land was took over by the city and they built them housing projects where the field used to be, you can't even see the moon from here, till it get up past the fourteenth floor. Don't no moonlight come in my yard no more. And I guess I might as well pick my old self up and go on back to bed.

Sometimes I still ain't used to the fact that Grace is passed on. Not even after these thirteen years without her. She the only woman I ever lived with—and I lived with her more than half my life. This house her house, too, and she oughta be here in it with me.

I rise up by six o'clock most every day, same as I done all them years I worked driving for the C.T.C. If the weather ain't too bad, I take me a walk— and if I ain't careful, I'm liable to end up down at the Twelfth Street Depot, waiting to see what trolley they gonna give me this morning. There ain't a soul working in that office still remember me. And they don't even run a trolley on the Broadway line no more. They been running a bus for the past five years.

I forgets a lot of things these days. Last week, I had just took in the clean laundry off the line, and I'm up in the spare room fixing to iron my shirts, when I hear somebody pass through that squeaky side gate and go on around to the back yard. I ain't paid it no mind at all, cause that's the way Gracie most often do when she come home. Go see about her garden fore she even come in the house. I always be teasing her she care more about them collards and string beans than she do about me. I hear her moving around out there while I'm sprinkling the last shirt and plugging in the iron—hear leaves rustling, and a crate scraping along the walk.

While I'm waiting for the iron to heat up, I take a look out the window, and come to see it ain't Gracie at all, but two a them sassy little scoundrels from over the projects—one of em standing on a apple crate and holding up the other one, who is picking my ripe peaches off my tree, just as brazen as you please. Don't even blink a eyelash when I holler out the window. I have to go running down all them stairs and out on the back porch, waving the cord I done jerked out the iron—when Doctor Matthews has told me a hundred times I ain't supposed to be running or getting excited about nothing, with my pressure like it is. And I ain't even supposed to be *walking* up and down no stairs.

When they seen the ironing cord in my hand, them two little sneaks had a reaction all right. The one on the bottom drop the other one right on his padded quarters and lit out for the gate, hollering, "Look out, Timmy! Here come Old Lady Jenkins!"

When I think about it now, it was right funny, but at the time I was so mad it musta took me a whole half hour to cool off. I sat there on that apple crate just boiling.

Eventually, I begun to see how it wasn't even them two kids I was so mad at. I was mad at time. For playing tricks on me the way it done. So I don't even remember that Grace Simmons has been dead now for the past thirteen years. And mad at time just for passing—so fast. If I had my life to live over, I wouldn't trade in none of them years for nothing. I'd just slow em down.

The church sisters around here is always trying to get me to be thinking about dying, myself. They must figure, when you my age, that's the only excitement you got left to look forward to. Gladys Hawkins stopped out front this morning, while I was mending a patch in the top screen of the front door. She was grinning from ear to ear like she just spent the night with Jesus himself.

"Morning, Sister Jenkins. Right pretty day the good Lord seen fit to send us, ain't it?"

I ain't never known how to answer nobody who manages to bring the good Lord into every conversation. If I nod and say yes, she'll think I finally got religion. But if I disagree, she'll think I'm crazy, cause it truly is one pretty August morning. Fortunately, it don't matter to her whether I agree or not, cause she gone right on talking according to her own agenda anyway.

"You know, this Sunday is Women's Day over at Blessed Endurance. Reverend Solomon Moody is gonna be visiting, speaking on 'A Woman's Place In The Church.' Why don't you come and join us for worship? You'd be most welcome."

I'm tempted to tell her exactly what come to my mind—that I ain't never heard of no woman name Solomon. However, I'm polite enough to hold my tongue, which is more than I can say for Gladys.

She ain't waiting for no answer from me, just going right on. "I don't spose you need me to point it out to you, Sister Jenkins, but you know you ain't as young as you used to be." As if both of our ages wasn't common knowledge to each other, seeing as we been knowing one another since we was girls. "You reaching that time of life when you might wanna be giving a little more attention to the spiritual side of things than you been doing. ..."

She referring, politely as she capable of, to the fact that I ain't been seen inside a church for thirty-five years.

"...And you know what the good Lord say. 'Watch therefore, for ye know neither the day nor the hour ...' But, 'He that believeth on the Son hath everlasting life ...'"

It ain't no use to argue with her kind. The Lord is on they side in every little disagreement, and he don't never give up. So when she finally wind down and ask me again will she see me in church this Sunday, I just say I'll think about it.

Funny thing, I been thinking about it all day. But not the kinda thoughts she want me to think, I'm sure. Last time I went to church was on a Easter Sunday. We decided to go on accounta Gracie's old meddling cousin, who was always nagging us about how we unnatural and sinful and a disgrace to her family. Seem like she seen it as her one mission in life to get us two sinners inside a church. I guess she figure, once she get us in there, God gonna take over the job. So Grace and me finally conspires that the way to get her off our backs is to give her what she think she want.

Course, I ain't had on a skirt since before the war, and I ain't aiming to change my lifelong habits just to please cousin Hattie. But I did take a lotta pains over my appearance that day. I'd had my best tailor-made suit pressed fresh, and slept in my stocking cap the night before so I'd have every hair in place. Even had one a Gracie's flowers stuck in my buttonhole. And a brand new narrow-brim dove gray Stetson hat. Gracie take one look at me when I'm ready and shake her head. "The good sisters is gonna have a hard time concentrating on the preacher today!"

We arrive at her cousin's church nice and early, but of course it's a big crowd inside already on accounta it being Easter Sunday. The organ music is wailing away, and the congregation is dazzling—decked out in nothing but the finest and doused with enough perfume to outsmell even the flowers up on the altar.

But as soon as we get in the door, this kinda sedate commotion break out— all them good Christian folks whispering and nudging each other and trying to turn around and get a good look. Well, Grace and me, we used to that. We just find us a nice seat in one of the empty pews near the back. But this busy buzzing keep up, even after we seated and more blended in with the crowd. And finally it come out that the point of contention ain't even the bottom half of my suit, but my new dove gray Stetson.

This old gentleman with a grizzled head, wearing glasses about a inch thick is turning around and leaning way over the back of the seat, whispering to Grace in a voice plenty loud enough for me to hear, "You better tell you beau to remove that hat, entering in Jesus' Holy Chapel."

Soon as I get my hat off, some old lady behind me is grumbling. "I declare, some of these children haven't got no respect at all. Oughta know you sposed to keep your head covered, setting in the house of the Lord."

Seem like the congregation just can't make up its mind whether I'm supposed to wear my hat or I ain't.

I couldn't hardly keep a straight face all through the service. Every time I catch Gracie eye, or one or the other of us catch a sight of my hat, we off again. I couldn't wait to get outa that place. But it was worth it. Gracie and me was entertaining the gang with that story for weeks to come. And we ain't had no more problems with Cousin Hattie.

Far as life everlasting is concerned, I imagine I'll cross that bridge when I reach it. I don't see no reason to rush into things. Sure, I know Old Man Death is gonna be coming after me one of these days, same as he come for my mother and dad, and Gracie and, just last year, my old buddy Louie. But I ain't about to start nothing that might make him feel welcome. It might be different for Gladys Hawkins and the rest of them church sisters, but I got a whole lot left to live for. Including a mind fulla good time memories. When you in the life, one thing your days don't never be, and that's dull. Your nights neither. All these years I been in the life, I love it. And you know Jinx ain't about to go off with no Old *Man* without no struggle, nohow.

To tell the truth, though, sometime I do get a funny feeling bout Old Death. Sometime I feel like he here already—been here. Waiting on me and watching me and biding his time. Paying attention when I have to stop on the landing of the stairs to catch my breath. Paying attention if I don't wake up till half past seven some morning, and my back is hurting me so bad it take me another half hour to pull myself together and get out of the bed.

The same night after I been talking to Gladys in the morning, it take me a long time to fall asleep. I'm lying up in bed waiting for the aching in my back and my joints to ease off some, and I can swear I hear somebody else in the house. Seem like I hear em downstairs, maybe opening and shutting the icebox door, or switching off a light. Just when I finally manage to doze off, I hear somebody footsteps right here in the bedroom with me. Somebody tippy-toe-ing real quiet, creaking the floor boards between the bed and the dresser … over to the closet … back to the dresser again.

I'm almost scared to open my eyes. But it's only Gracie—in her old raggedy bathrobe and a silk handkerchief wrapped up around all them little braids in her head—putting her finger up to her lips to try and shush me so I won't wake up.

I can't help chuckling. "Hey Gingerbread Girl. Where you think you going in your house coat and bandana and it ain't even light out yet. Come on get back in this bed."

"You go on to sleep," she say. "I'm just going out back a spell."

It ain't no use me trying to make my voice sound angry, cause she so contrary when it come to that little piece of ground down there I can't help laughing. "What you think you gonna complish down there in the middle of the night? It ain't even no moon to watch tonight. The sky been filling up with clouds all evening, and the weather forecast say rain tomorrow."

"Just don't pay me no mind and go on back to sleep. It ain't the middle of the night. It's almost daybreak." She grinning like she up to something, and sure enough, she say, "This the best time to pick off them black and yellow beetles been making mildew outa my cucumber vines. So I'm just fixing to turn the tables around a little bit. You gonna read in the papers tomorrow morning bout how the entire black and yellow beetle population of number Twenty-seven Bank Street been wiped off the face of the earth—while you was up here sleeping."

Both of us is laughing like we partners in a crime, and then she off down the hall, calling out, "I be back before you even know I'm gone."

But the full light of day is coming in the window, and she ain't back yet.

I'm over to the window with a mind to holler down to Grace to get her behind back in this house, when the sight of them housing projects hits me right in the face; stacks of dirt-colored bricks and little caged-in porches, heaped up into the sky blocking out what poor skimpy light this cloudy morning brung.

It's a awful funny feeling start to come over me. I mean to get my housecoat, and go down there anyway, just see what's what. But in the closet I can see it ain't but my own clothes hanging on the pole. All the shoes on the floor is mine. And I know I better go ahead and get washed, cause it's whole lot I want to get done fore it rain, and that storm is coming in for sure. Better pick the rest of them ripe peaches and tomatoes. Maybe put in some peas for fall picking, if my knees'll allow me to get that close to the ground.

The rain finally catch up around noon time and slow me down a bit. I never could stand to be cooped up in no house in the rain. Always make me itchy. That's one reason I used to like driving a trolley for the C.T.C. Cause you get to be out every day, no matter what kinda weather coming down—get to see people and watch the world go by. And it ain't as if you exactly out in the weather, neither. You get to watch it all from behind that big picture window.

Not that I woulda minded being out in it. I used to want to get me a job with the post office, delivering mail. Black folks could make good money with the post office, even way back then. But they wouldn't out you on no mail route. Always stick em off in a back room someplace, where nobody can't see em and get upset cause some little colored girl making as much money as the white boy working next to her. So I stuck with the C.T.C. all them years, and got my pension to prove it.

The rain still coming down steady along about three o'clock, when Max call me up say do I want to come over to her and Yvonne's for dinner. Say they fried more chicken that they can eat, and anyway Yvonne all involved in some new project she want to talk to me about. And I'm glad for the chance to get out the house. Max and Yvonne got the place all picked up for company. I can smell that fried chicken soon as I get in the door.

Yvonne don't never miss a opportunity to dress up a bit. She got the front of her hair braided up, with beads hanging all in her eyes, and a kinda loose robe-like thing, in colors look like the fruit salad at a Independence Day picnic. Max her same old self in her slacks and loafers. She ain't changed in all the years I known her—cept we both got more wrinkles and gray hairs. Yvonne a whole lot younger than us two, but she hanging in there. Her and Max been together going on three years now.

Right away, Yvonne start to explain about this project she doing with her women's club. When I first heard about this club she in, I was kinda interested. But I come to find out it ain't no social club, like the Cinnamon & Spice Club used to be. It's more like a organization. Yvonne call it a collective. They never has no outings or parties or picnics or nothing—just meetings. And projects.

The project they working on right now, they all got tape recorders. And they going around tape-recording people story. Talking to people who been in the life for years and years, and asking em what it was like, back in the old days. I been in the life since before Yvonne was born. But the second she stick that microphone in my face, I can't think of a blessed thing to say.

"Come on, Jinx, you always telling us all them funny old time stories."

Then little wheels is rolling round and round, and all that smooth, shiny brown tape is slipping off one reel and sliding onto the other, and I can't think of not one thing I remember.

"Tell how the Cinnamon & Spice Club got started," she say.

"I already told you about that before."

"Well, tell how it ended, then. You never told me that."

"Ain't nothing to tell. Skip and Peaches broke up." Yvonne waiting, and the reels is rolling, but for the life of me I can't think of another word to say about it. And Max is sitting there grinning, like I'm the only one over thirty in the room and she don't remember a thing.

Yvonne finally give up and turn the thing off, and we go on and stuff ourselves on the chicken they fried and the greens I brung over from the garden. By the time we start in on the sweet potato pie, I have finally got to remembering. Telling Yvonne about when Skip and Peaches had they last big falling out, and they was both determine they was gonna stay in The Club—and couldn't be in the same room with one another for fifteen minutes. Both of em keep waiting on the other one to drop out, and both of em keep showing up, every time the gang get together. And none of the rest of us couldn't be in the same room with the two a them for even as long as they could stand each other. We'd be sneaking around, trying to hold a meeting without them finding out. But Peaches was the president and Skip was the treasurer, so you might say our hands was tied. Wouldn't neither one of em resign. They was both convince The Club couldn't go on without em, and by the time they was finished carrying on, they had done made sure it wouldn't.

Max is chiming in correcting all the details, every other breath come outa my mouth. And then when we all get up to go sit in the parlor again, it come out that Yvonne has sneaked that tape recording machine in here under that African poncho she got on, and has got down every word I said.

When time come to say good night, I'm thankful, for once, that Yvonne insist on driving me home—though it ain't even a whole mile. The rain ain't let up all evening, and is coming down in bucketfuls while we in the car. I'm half soaked just running from the car to the front door.

Yvonne is drove off down the street, and I'm halfway through the front door, when it hit me all of a sudden that the door ain't been locked. Now my mind may be getting a little threadbare in spots, but it ain't wore out yet. I know it's easy for me to slip back into doing things the way I done em twenty or thirty years ago, but I could swear I distinctly remember locking this door and hooking the key ring back on my belt loop, just fore Yvonne drove up in front. And now here's the door been open all the time.

Not a sign a nobody been here. Everything in its place, just like I left it. The slipcovers on the couch is smooth and neat. The candy dishes and ash trays and photographs is sitting just where they belong, on the end tables. Not even so much as a throw rug been moved a inch. I can feel my heart start to thumping like a blowout tire.

Must be, whoever come in here ain't left yet.

The idea of somebody got a nerve like that make me more mad than scared, and I know I'm gonna find out who it is broke in my house, even if it don't turn out to be nobody but them little peach-thieving rascals from round the block. Which I wouldn't be surprised if it ain't. I'm scooting from room to room, snatching open closet doors and whipping back curtains—tiptoeing down the hall and then flicking on the lights real sudden.

When I been in every room, I go back through everywhere I been, real slow, looking in all the drawers, and under the old glass doorstop in the hall, and in the back of the recipe box in the kitchen—and other places where I keep things. But it ain't nothing missing. No money—nothing.

In the end, ain't nothing left for me to do but go to bed. But I'm still feeling real uneasy. I know somebody or something done got in here while I was gone.

And ain't left yet. I lay wake in the bed a long time, cause I ain't too particular about falling asleep tonight. Anyway, all this rain just make my joints swell up worse, and the pains in my knees just don't let up.

The next thing I know Gracie waking me up. She lying next to me and kissing me all over my face. I wake up laughing, and she say, "I never could see no use in shaking somebody I rather be kissing." I can feel the laughing running all through her body and mine, holding her up against my chest in the dark— knowing there must be a reason why she woke me up in the middle of the night, and pretty sure I can guess what it is. She kissing under my chin now, and starting to undo my buttons.

It seem like so long since we done this. My whole body is all a shimmer with this sweet, sweet craving. My blood is racing, singing, and her fingers is sliding inside my nightshirt. "Take it easy," I say in her ear. Cause I want this to take us a long, long time.

Outside, the sky is still wide open—the storm is throbbing and beating down on the roof over our heads, and pressing its wet self up against the window. I catch ahold of her fingers and bring em to my lips. Then I roll us both over so I can see her face. She smiling up at me through the dark, and her eyes is wide and shiny. And I run my fingers down along her breast, underneath her own nightgown. ...

I wake up in the bed alone. It's still night. Like a flash I'm across the room, knowing I'm going after her, this time. The carpet treads is nubby and rough, flying past underneath my bare feet, and the kitchen linoleum cold and smooth. The back door standing wide open, and I push through the screen.

The storm is moved on. That fresh air feel good on my skin through the cotton nightshirt. Smell good, too, rising up outa the wet earth, and I can see the water sparkling on the leaves of the collards and kale, twinkling in the vines on the bean poles. The moon is riding high up over Thompson's field, spilling moonlight all over the yard, and setting all them blossoms on the fence to shining pure white.

There ain't a leaf twitching and there ain't a sound. I ain't moving either. I'm just gonna stay right here on this back porch. And hold still. And listen close. Cause I know Gracie somewhere in this garden. And she waiting for me.

About the Book and Editor

GEORGE STAMBOLIAN, Terri de la Peña, Audre Lorde, Paul Monette, Edmund White, and Jaime Manrique are just six of the writers represented in this collection of forty contemporary lesbian and gay short stories. Gathered together for the first time in one volume are writings by both lesbians and gay men who represent a multiplicity of ethnic and racial backgrounds. Irene Zahava has compiled a unique and necessary collection, selecting stories for their artistic power and for their treatment of topics that are significant in lesbian and gay life and politics today.

An alternative thematic table of contents allows the reader to understand lesbian and gay life according to its most culturally and politically significant themes: childhood/growing up; coming out/finding community; families; oppression/resistance; bisexuality; relationships/friendships; AIDS; and aging/dying.

IRENE ZAHAVA owns Smedley's Bookshop, a feminist bookstore in Ithaca, New York. She has edited seventeen collections of short stories by women, including *Word of Mouth* (two volumes), *Lesbian Love Stories* (two volumes), *My Father's Daughter,* and *My Mother's Daughter.*

Notes on Contributors

DONNA ALLEGRA has published poetry, fiction, and cultural journalism in *Azalea, Conditions, Common Lives/Lesbian Lives, Sinister Wisdom*, and other journals. Her work has frequently been anthologized, and appears in *Home Girls, The Original Coming Out Stories, Lesbian Love Stories 2*, and other collections.

DOROTHY ALLISON is the author of the short-story collection *Trash* and the novel *Bastard Out of Carolina*. Her work has appeared in numerous journals and anthologies.

BECKY BIRTHA is the author of two short-story collections, *For Nights Like This One* and *Lovers' Choice*. Her poems are collected in a volume entitled *The Forbidden Poems*.

SANDY BOUCHER has published a number of volumes of fiction and nonfiction, including *The Notebooks of Leni Clare, Heartwomen*, and *Turning the Wheel: American Women Creating the New Buddhism*.

CHRISTOPHER BRAM is the author of *Almost History, In Memory of Angel Clare*, and *Hold Tight*.

REBECCA BROWN has published two short-story collections, *Annie Oakley's Girl* and *The Terrible Girls*, as well as two novels, *The Children's Crusade* and *The Haunted House*.

LOUIE CREW is the author of numerous poems, stories, and essays. One of his stories, reprinted in this collection, originally appeared in *The Gay Nineties: An Anthology of Contemporary Gay Fiction*.

TERRI DE LA PEÑA is the author of *Margins, Latin Satins*, and *Territories*. Her stories have appeared in numerous anthologies, including *Chicana Lesbians: The Girls Our Mothers Warned Us About* and *Finding Courage*.

DAVID B. FEINBERG is the author of *Eighty-Sixed*, a novel, and *Spontaneous Combustion*, a collection of short stories.

PHILIP GAMBONE is the author of *The Language We Use Up Here*. His short stories have appeared in a number of periodicals, as well as in the *Men on Men* anthology series.

JEWELLE L. GOMEZ is the author of *The Gilda Stories*, a novel, and *Forty-Three Septembers*, a collection of essays. Her work has been widely anthologized.

RICHARD HALL is the author of *Family Fictions*, a novel, and *Fidelities: A Book of Stories*.

ESSEX HEMPHILL combines prose and poetry in his collection *Ceremonies*. He is the author of two volumes of poetry and the editor of *Brother to Brother: New Writings by Black Gay Men*. His poetry, stories, and essays have been widely published and anthologized.

WILLIAM HAYWOOD HENDERSON has published fiction and nonfiction in a number of journals and anthologies, including *The Crescent Review, Men on Men 3*, and the *Faber Book of Gay Short Fiction*. His novel, *Native*, was published in 1993.

DAVID LEAVITT is the author of *Family Dancing, The Lost Language of Cranes, Equal Affections, A Place I've Never Been*, and *While England Sleeps*. He is the co-editor of the *Penguin Book of Gay Short Fiction*.

AUDRE LORDE was the author of many volumes of poetry, including *The Marvelous Arithmetics of Distance*, which was published posthumously in 1993. Her essays appeared in *A Burst of Light* and *Sister/Outsider. Zami: A New Spelling of My Name* is Lorde's "biomythography."

LEE LYNCH has published a number of novels, short story collections, and a volume of nonfiction, including *Old Dyke Tales, The Swashbuckler, That Old Studebaker*, and *Dusty's Queen of Hearts Diner*.

JAIME MANRIQUE is a Colombian-born writer whose work has been widely published in both Spanish and English. His most recent novel is *Latin Moon in Manhattan*. He has a young adult biography of Federico Garcia Lorca forthcoming in 1994.

ARMISTEAD MAUPIN is the author of six volumes of the "tales of the city" novels, beginning with *Tales of the City* and concluding with *Sure of You*. His most recent novel is *Maybe the Moon*.

RICHARD McCANN has had fiction and poetry published in numerous periodicals and anthologies, including *The Atlantic Monthly, Esquire, Men on Men 2*, and *The Penguin Book of Gay Short Stories*. He is the author of the novel *Our Mother of Sorrows*.

JUDITH McDANIEL is the author of *Sanctuary: A Journey, Metamorphosis and Other Poems of Recovery*, and *Just Say Yes*, a novel.

VALERIE MINER has published six novels, including *All Good Women, Murder in the English Department*, and *A Walking Fire*. Her short stories are gathered in the collection *Trespassing and Other Stories*, and her nonfiction pieces are collected in *Rumors from the Cauldron: Selected Essays, Reviews and Reportage*.

PAUL MONETTE is the author of *Afterlife, Becoming a Man: Half a Life Story, Borrowed Time: An AIDS Memoir, Halfway Home, The Long Shot, Love Alone: Eighteen Elegies for Rog*, and *Taking Care of Mrs. Carroll*.

LESLÉA NEWMAN has sixteen books to her credit, including novels, short-story collections, poetry, nonfiction, and children's books. Among her recent publications are *In Every Laugh a Tear, Heather Has Two Mommies*, and *Writing from the Heart*.

JOHN PRESTON was the author of numerous books, including *Franny, The Queen of Provincetown* and the Alex Kane adventure series. He edited *Personal Dispatches: Writers Confront AIDS, Hometowns: Gay Men Write About Where They Belong*, and *Flesh and the Word: An Anthology of Erotic Writing* (2 volumes).

LEV RAPHAEL is the author of *Winter Eyes*, a novel, and the short-story collection *Dancing on Tisha B'Av*. His stories and prose have been published in many periodicals and anthologies, including *Men on Men 2*, *Certain Voices*, the *Faber Book of Gay Short Fiction*, and *Hometowns*.

RUTHANN ROBSON has published two short-story collections, *Cecile* and *Eye of the Storm*, as well as the nonfiction book *Lesbian (Out)Law: Surviving Under the Rule of Law*.

DOUGLAS SADOWNICK has published fiction, essays, and reviews in the *Los Angeles Times*, the *Advocate*, the *Village Voice*, and *American Film*. His work has appeared in *Blood Whispers: L.A. Writers on AIDS*, *Positively Gay*, and *Men on Men 4*.

MICHAEL SCHWARTZ published his first short story in the anthology *Certain Voices: Short Stories About Gay Men*.

LORRIE SPRECHER is the author of *Anxiety Attack*, a collection of humorous short fiction. Her first novel, *Sister Safety Pin*, will be published in 1994. Earlier work has appeared in *Sinister Wisdom*, *The North American Review*, *Word of Mouth 2*, and *Lesbian Love Stories 2*.

GEORGE STAMBOLIAN was the editor of the *Men on Men* anthologies (4 volumes) as well as the author of *Marcel Proust and the Creative Encounter* and *Homosexualities and French Literature* (with Elaine Marks). He edited *Twentieth Century French Fiction* and *Male Fantasies/Gay Realities: Interviews with Ten Men*.

SUSANNA J. STURGIS is the editor of three anthologies of women's fantasy and science fiction. She has published fiction, nonfiction, and poetry in *Calyx*, *Trivia*, *Sinister Wisdom*, *Sojourner*, and other journals.

ROEY THORPE has published stories in *Quickies: Lesbian Short-Shorts* and *How To: Short-Short Stories by Women*.

DONALD VINING is a playwright, diarist, essayist, and fiction and nonfiction writer. His published work includes the five-volume *A Gay Diarist* (covering 1933–1982) and a book of essays entitled *How Can You Come Out If You've Never Been In?*

JESS WELLS is the author of two volumes of short stories, *Two Willow Chairs* and *The Dress/The Sharda Stories*. Her first novel is entitled *Aftershocks*.

EDMUND WHITE is a novelist, essayist, biographer, and editor. His published work includes *A Boy's Own Story*, *The Beautiful Room Is Empty*, *States of Desire: Travels in Gay America*, and *Genet: A Biography*. He is the editor of the *Faber Book of Gay Short Fiction*.

BARBARA WILSON has published numerous novels, collections of short stories, and mysteries, including *Ambitious Women*, *Miss Venezuela*, *Murder in the Collective*, and *Gaudi Afternoon*.

VIRGINIA WITT is the author of several short stories and has just completed her first novel.

NORMAN WONG is the author of the novel *Cultural Revolution*. His fiction has appeared in the *Kenyon Review, The Threepenny Review,* and *Men on Men 4.*

SHAY YOUNGBLOOD is the author of *The Big Mama Stories*. Her work has appeared in periodicals and anthologies, including *Essence, Conditions, Common Lives/Lesbian Lives,* and *Lesbian Love Stories 2.*